Essentials
of Managerial
Finance

J. Fred Weston
University of California, Los Angeles

Eugene F. Brigham
University of Florida

Essentials of Managerial Finance

fourth edition

THE DRYDEN PRESS
Hinsdale, Illinois

Preface

Financial management continues to reflect important new developments. Strong inflationary pressures have pushed interest rates to unprecedented heights, and the resulting high cost of capital has led to profound changes in corporate financial policies and practices. Academic researchers have made significant advances, especially in the areas of capital budgeting and the cost of capital. At the same time, business practitioners are making increasing use of financial theory, and feedback from the "real world" has led to revisions in financial theory. To a large extent, these trends dictated the revisions made in this Fourth Edition of *Essentials of Managerial Finance*.

In addition to containing new materials, the revision reflects our experience, and that of others, in teaching business finance. Organizational changes have been made to provide for smoother flow and greater continuity; points that proved troublesome to students have been clarified; a few outright errors have been corrected; and, of course, descriptive materials have been updated. Moreover, the end-of-chapter questions, problems, and references have been clarified and strengthened.

Much of the specific content of the book is the result of our experience in executive development programs over a number of years. This experience, in addition to our consulting with business firms on financial problems and policies, has helped us to identify the most significant responsibilities of financial managers, the most fundamental problems facing firms, and the most feasible approaches to practical decision-making. Some topics are conceptually difficult, but so are the issues faced by financial managers. Business managers must be prepared to handle complex problems, and finding solutions to these problems necessarily involves the use of advanced tools and techniques.

v

We have not sought to avoid the many unresolved areas of business financial theory and practice. Although we could have simplified the text in many places by avoiding the difficult issues, we preferred to provide a basic framework based on the "received doctrine," then to go on to present materials on a number of important but controversial issues. It is hoped that our presentation will stimulate the reader to further inquiry.

We acknowledge that the level and difficulty of the material is somewhat uneven. Certain sections are simply descriptions of the institutional features of the financial environment and, as such, are not difficult to understand. Other parts—notably the material on capital budgeting, uncertainty, and the cost of capital—are by nature rather abstract, and, as such, are difficult for those not used to thinking in abstract terms. In some of the more complex sections, we simply outline procedures in the text, then refer the interested reader to more advanced works.

CHANGES IN THE FOURTH EDITION

The Fourth Edition of *Essentials* differs from the Third in several key respects. Some of the more significant alterations are itemized below.

1. *Updating.* Finance is a highly dynamic subject, and many changes have occurred since the Third Edition came out in 1973. Important theoretical advances have been made; and important shifts have occurred in the level and structure of interest rates, stock prices, and money and capital markets in general. These changes have been reflected in this edition.
2. *Risk analysis.* We have continued to emphasize the importance of risk analysis in financial decision-making. Although some new materials on risk are introduced, our major thrust in this revision has been to clarify and better illustrate the more analytical sections.
3. *Modifications in cost of capital presentation.* Students generally have more difficulty understanding valuation and cost of capital concepts than any other aspects of finance. We have made a major effort to clarify these concepts, as well as their relationship to the capital budgeting process. Based on class testing of the prepublication manuscript, we achieved larger gains in the students' benefits-received/time-spent ratio here than in any other section of the book.
4. *Modifications in capital budgeting presentation.* The chapters on capital budgeting under certainty and uncertainty have both been clarified significantly.
5. *End-of-chapter questions and problems.* The questions and problems have been thoroughly revised to emphasize and illustrate the major points raised in the text chapters, and to remove ambiguities. At the urging of our students, we have also provided suggested numerical answers to se-

lected problems. After working a problem, students were sometimes not sure if they had the correct answer. The suggested answers will help resolve such uncertainty.

6. Particular attention was given to the *glossary* and *index*. The completeness of these two items will ease problems that might otherwise be encountered if an instructor assigns chapters out of sequence.

Ancillary Materials

Several items are available to supplement *Essentials*. First, there are two casebooks, *Cases in Managerial Finance, 3rd Edition* and *Decisions in Financial Management: Cases,* by Eugene F. Brigham et al., designed specifically to accompany *Essentials*. Second, there are a number of readings books which can be used to supplement the text. One book in particular, *Issues in Managerial Finance,* edited by E. F. Brigham and R. E. Johnson, was prepared specifically to supplement *Essentials*. Finally, many students will find the *Study Guide* useful. The *Study Guide* highlights the key points in the text and presents a comprehensive set of problems similar to those at the end of each chapter. Each problem is solved in detail, so a student who has difficulty working the end-of-chapter problems can be aided by reviewing the *Study Guide.*

Acknowledgments

In its several revisions, the book has been worked on and critically reviewed by numerous individuals, and we have received many detailed comments and suggestions from instructors (and students) using the book in our own schools and elsewhere. All this help has improved the quality of the book, and we are deeply indebted to the following individuals, and others, for their help: M. Adler, E. Altman, J. Andrews, R. Aubey, P. Bacon, W. Beranek, V. Brewer, W. Brueggeman, R. Carleson, S. Choudhury, P. Cooley, C. Cox, D. Fischer, R. Gray, J. Griggs, R. Haugen, S. Hawk, R. Hehre, J. Henry, A. Herrmann, G. Hettenhouse, R. Himes, C. Johnson, R. Jones, D. Kaplan, M. Kaufman, D. Knight, H. Krogh, R. LeClair, W. Lee, D. Longmore, J. Longstreet, H. Magee, P. Malone, R. Moore, T. Morton, T. Nantell, R. Nelson, R. Norgaard, J. Pappas, R. Pettit, R. Pettway, J. Pinkerton, G. Pogue, W. Regan, F. Reilly, R. Rentz, R. Richards, C. Rini, R. Roenfeldt, W. Sharpe, K. Smith, P. Smith, D. Sorenson, M. Tysseland, P. Vanderheiden, D. Woods, J. Yeakel, and D. Ziegenbein for their careful reviews of this and previous editions.

We owe special thanks to Roger Bey, Keith Johnson, and Ramon Johnson for providing us with a set of problems they had developed for their classes, and also for providing us with detailed reviews of the manuscript of this book. We would like to thank C. Barngrover, S. Mansinghka, W. Eckardt, H. Rollins, H. Alwan, D. Wort, and J. Zumwalt for their assistance in helping us develop the acetate program. We would also like to express our appreciation to Bob LeClair and to The American College for their help in preparing transparencies and masters. (Note to instructors: a set of supplementary problems developed by Professors Bey, Johnson, and Johnson will be available to adoptors from The Dryden Press in the very near future. Transparencies and masters are also available from The Dryden Press.)

The Universities of California and Florida, and our colleagues on these campuses, provided us with intellectual support in bringing the book to completion. Finally, we are indebted to the Dryden Press staff—principally Mary Ellen Stocker and Martha Cobb—for their special efforts in getting the manuscript into production and for following through to the bound book.

The field of finance will continue to experience significant changes. It is stimulating to participate in these exciting developments, and we sincerely hope that *Essentials* will contribute to a better understanding of the theory and practice of finance.

Los Angeles, California   J. Fred Weston
Gainesville, Florida   Eugene F. Brigham
September 1976

Contents

Overview of Finance: Analysis, Planning, and Control

Part One

Part One consists of six chapters. The first describes the scope and nature of managerial finance and serves as an introduction to the book. Next, in Chapter 2, we examine the tax system; since a high percentage of business income is paid to the government, taxes are an important consideration in finance. In Chapter 3 we examine the construction and use of the basic ratios of financial analysis; through ratio analysis, the firm's strengths and weaknesses can be pinpointed. Chapter 4 explains two key tools used in financial planning: break-even analysis and the sources and uses of funds statement. In Chapter 5 we take up financial forecasting: given a projected increase in sales, how much money must the financial manager raise to support this level of sales? Finally, in Chapter 6, we consider the budget system through which management controls and coordinates the firm.

Finance deals, in the main, with very specific questions: Should we lease or buy the new machine? Should we expand capacity at the Hartford plant? Should we raise capital this year by long-term or short-term debt or by selling stock? Should we go along with the marketing department, which wants to expand inventories, or with the production department, which wants to reduce them? Specific questions such as these, which are typical of the types of decisions facing the financial manager, are considered in the remainder of the book. But here in Part One we take an *overview* of the firm. Because all specific decisions are made within the context of the firm's overall position, this overview is critical to an understanding of any specific proposal.

Scope and Nature of Managerial Finance

What is managerial finance? What is finance's function in the firm? What specific tasks are assigned to the financial manager? What tools and techniques are available to him, and how does one go about measuring his performance? On a broader scale, what is the role of finance in the American economy, and how can managerial finance be used to further national goals? Providing at least tentative answers to these questions is the principal purpose of this book.

CHANGING ROLE OF FINANCIAL MANAGEMENT

As with many things in the contemporary world, financial management has undergone significant changes over the years. When finance first emerged as a separate field of study in the early 1900s, the emphasis was on legalistic matters such as mergers, consolidations, the formation of new firms, and the various types of securities issued by corporations. Industrialization was sweeping the country, and the critical problem firms faced was obtaining capital for expansion. The capital markets were relatively primitive, and transfers of funds from individual savers to businesses were quite difficult. Accounting statements of earnings and asset values were unreliable, and stock trading by insiders and manipulators caused prices to fluctuate wildly; consequently, investors were reluctant to purchase stocks and bonds. In this environment, it is easy to see why finance concentrated so heavily on legal issues relating to the issuance of securities.

The emphasis remained on securities through the 1920s; however, radical changes occurred during the depression of the 1930s. Business failures during that period caused finance to focus on bankruptcy and reorganization, on corporate liquidity, and on governmental regulation of securities markets. Finance was still a descriptive, legalistic subject, but the emphasis shifted to survival rather than expansion.

During the 1940s and early 1950s, finance continued to be taught as a descriptive, institutional subject, viewed from the outside rather than from within the firm's management. However, some time was devoted to budgeting and other internal control procedures, and, stimulated by the work of Joel Dean, capital budgeting was beginning to receive attention.[1]

The evolutionary pace quickened during the late 1950s. Whereas the right-hand side of the balance sheet (liabilities and capital) had received more attention in the earlier era, increasing emphasis was being placed on asset analysis during the last half of that decade. Mathematical models were developed and applied to inventories, cash, accounts receivable, and fixed assets. Increasingly, the focus of finance shifted from the outsider's to the insider's point of view, as financial decisions within the firm were recognized to be the critical issues in corporate finance. Descriptive, institutional materials on capital markets and financing instruments were still studied, but these topics were considered within the context of corporate financial decisions.

The emphasis on decision-making has continued in recent years, with the increasing belief that sound capital budgeting procedures require accurate measurements of the cost of capital. Accordingly, ways of quantifying the cost of capital now play a key role in finance. Second, capital has been in short supply, rekindling the old interest in ways of raising funds. Third, there has been a great deal of merger activity, especially acquisitions by conglomerates, which has led to renewed interest in take-overs. Fourth, accelerated progress in transportation and communications has brought the countries of the world closer together; this, in turn, has stimulated interest in international finance. Fifth, inflation is now recognized as a critical problem, as so much of the financial manager's time is presently devoted to coping with high wages, prices, and interest rates at a time when stock prices are relatively low. Finally, there is an increasing awareness of such social ills as air and water pollution, urban blight, and unemployment among minorities. Finding his firm's realistic role in efforts to solve these problems demands much of the financial manager's attention.

The Impact of Inflation on Financial Management

During the 1950s and 1960s, prices rose at an average rate of about 1½ to 2 percent per year, but in the 1970s the rate of inflation has been as high as 12 percent per year. This "double digit inflation" has had a tremendous impact on business firms, especially on their financial operations. As a result, many

[1] Joel Dean, *Capital Budgeting* (New York: Columbia University Press, 1951).

established financial policies and practices are undergoing dramatic changes, some of which are outlined below.

1. *Interest rates.* The rate of interest on U.S. government securities (called the default-free rate) consists of a "real rate of interest" of about 4 percent plus an "inflation premium" that reflects the expected long-run rate of inflation. Accordingly, an increase in the rate of inflation is quickly translated into higher default-free interest rates. And since the cost of money to firms is the default-free rate plus a risk premium, inflation-induced increases in the default-free rate are quickly passed on to business borrowers.

2. *Planning difficulties.* Businesses operate on the basis of long-run plans. For example, a firm builds a plant only after making a thorough analysis of expected costs and revenues over the life of the plant. Reaching such estimates is not easy under the best of conditions, but during rapid inflation, when labor and materials costs are changing dramatically, accurate forecasts are especially important yet exceedingly hard to make. Efforts are, of course, being made to improve forecasting techniques, and financial planning must include more flexibility to reflect the increased level of uncertainty in the economy. Incidentally, the increased uncertainty in many industries tends to raise the risk premiums for firms in those industries, driving their costs of capital still higher.

3. *Demand for capital.* Inflation increases the amount of capital required to conduct a given volume of business. When inventories are sold, they must be replaced with more expensive goods. The costs of expanding or replacing plants are also greater, while workers demand higher wages. All of these things put pressure on financial managers to raise additional capital. At the same time, in an effort to hold down the rate of inflation, the Federal Reserve System tends to restrict the supply of loanable funds. The ensuing scramble for limited funds drives interest rates still higher.

4. *Bond price declines.* Long-term bond prices fall as interest rates rise, so, in an effort to protect themselves against such capital losses, lenders are beginning (a) to put more funds into short-term than into long-term debt, and (b) to insist upon bonds whose interest rates vary with "the general level of interest rates" as measured by an index of interest rates. Brazil and other inflation-plagued South American countries have used such index bonds for years. Unless inflation in the United States is controlled, their use is likely to increase in this country.

5. *Investment planning.* High interest rates, as well as a general shortage of capital, are causing firms to be especially wary in planning long-term investment outlays. Indeed, headlines such as "ITT Cuts Spending Plan $106 Million Because of Difficulties in Raising Funds" or "Detroit Edison to Fight Cash Shortage by Sale-Leaseback of Coal, Equipment" have become commonplace.

6. *Accounting problems.* With high rates of inflation, reported profits are distorted. The sale of low-cost inventories results in higher reported profits, but cash flows are held down as firms restock with higher-cost inventories. Similarly, depreciation charges are inadequate, as they do not reflect the new costs of replacing plant and equipment. If a firm is unaware of the "shakiness" of profits that reflect inventory valuation and inadequate depreciation charges, and if it plans dividends and capital expenditures on the basis of such figures, then it could develop serious financial problems.

Double digit inflation is a disturbing and challenging new experience for U.S. financial managers. Although no one knows what the full impact of continued inflation will be, one thing is clear—if double digit inflation does continue, many financial policies and practices will have to be modified to meet this new situation.

Increased Importance of Financial Management

Those evolutionary changes have greatly increased the importance of financial management. In earlier times, the marketing manager would project sales; the engineering and production staffs would determine the assets necessary to meet these demands; and the financial manager would simply raise the money necessary to purchase the plant, equipment, and inventories. This mode of operation is no longer prevalent—today decisions are made in a much more coordinated manner, with the financial manager directly responsible for the control process. The direction in which business is moving, as well as the increasing importance of finance, is well illustrated by the following statement:

> General Motors Corporation named Richard C. Gerstenberg, a tough-minded financial man, as its chairman and chief executive officer. The main reason Mr. Gerstenberg got the job, it's believed, is his strong financial background, making him the man of the hour when GM is increasingly worried about its profit margins and its ability to finance its growth internally.
>
> The biggest surprise in the executive reorganization was the naming of T. A. Murphy [another finance man] to the powerful post of vice chairman. Observers expressed some surprise that none of the top assignments given out was to an executive whose career had been in sales or manufacturing.

Similar events are occurring throughout the business world; as the emphasis continues to shift toward closer internal controls, financial managers will play larger and larger roles in business firms.

Organization of a Firm's Finance Department

In the typical firm, the chief financial officer, who has the title of vice-president –finance, reports to the chief executive officer and has accountable to him two key officers, the treasurer and the controller. The treasurer and his staff are responsible for raising capital and dealing with suppliers of capital, as well as for the firm's credit policy. The controller and his staff are responsible for the accounting and budgeting systems, including capital budgeting. In a sense, the treasurer handles the outside finance functions and the controller the inside functions, while the vice-president–finance has the overall responsibility for both.

GOALS OF THE FIRM

Throughout the book we operate on the assumption that management's primary goal is to maximize the wealth of its stockholders. Just how good is this assumption—does management really try to maximize stockholder wealth, or is it equally interested in profits, in sales, in survival, in the personal satisfaction of the managers themselves, in employees' welfare, or in the good of the community and society at large? Further, does management really try to *maximize,* or does it "satisfice"? That is, does it seek satisfactory rather than optimal results?

Profits versus Wealth

Let us consider the question of profits versus wealth. Suppose management is interested primarily in stockholders, making its decisions so as to maximize their welfare. Will profit maximization be best for stockholders? In answering this question, we must consider first the matter of total corporate profits versus earnings per share. Suppose a firm raises capital by selling stock and then invests the proceeds in government bonds. Total profits will rise, but more shares will be outstanding. Earnings per share would probably decline, pulling down the value of each share of stock and, hence, the existing stockholders' wealth. Thus, to the extent that profits are important, management should concentrate on earnings per share rather than on total corporate profits.

Earnings per Share Will maximization of earnings per share maximize stockholder welfare, or should other factors be considered? Consider the timing of the earnings. Suppose one project will cause earnings per share to rise by $.20 per year for five years, or $1.00 in total, while another project has no effect on earnings for four years but increases earnings by $1.25 in the fifth year. Which project is better? The answer depends upon which project adds the most to the value of the stock, and this in turn depends upon the time value of money to investors. In any event, timing is an important reason to concentrate upon wealth as measured by the price of the stock rather than upon earnings alone.

Risk Still another issue relates to risk. Suppose one project is expected to increase earnings per share by $1.00, while another is expected to raise earnings by $1.20 per share. The first project is not very risky; if it is under-taken, earnings will almost certainly rise by about $1.00 per share. The other project is quite risky, so while our best guess is that earnings will rise by $1.20 per share, we must recognize the possibility that there may be no increase whatever. Depending upon how averse stockholders are to risk, the first pro-ject may be preferable to the second.

Recognizing all those factors, managers interested in maximizing stock-holder welfare seek to maximize the value of the firm's common stock. The price of the stock reflects the market's evaluation of the firm's prospective earnings stream over time, the riskiness of this stream, and a host of other factors. The higher the price of the stock, the better is management's per-formance from the standpoint of the stockholders; thus, market price provides a performance index by which management can be judged.[2]

Maximizing Stockholder Wealth versus Other Goals

In theory, stockholders own the firm and elect the management team; man-agement, in turn, is supposed to operate in the best interests of the stock-holders. We know, however, that the stock of most large firms is widely held, so the managers of such firms have a great deal of autonomy. This being the case, might not managements pursue goals other than maximizing stock-holder wealth? Some alternative goals are examined in this section.

Maximizing versus "Satisficing" First, consider the question of *maximiz-ing*, which involves seeking the best possible outcome, versus "satisficing," which involves a willingness to settle for something less. A firm that is on the brink of bankruptcy may be forced to operate as efficiently as possible. But some argue that the management of a large, well-entrenched corporation could work to keep stockholder returns at a fair or "reasonable" level and then devote part of its efforts and resources to public service activities, to employee benefits, to higher management salaries, or to golf.

Similarly, an entrenched management could avoid risky ventures, even when the possible gains to stockholders are high enough to warrant taking the gamble. The theory behind this argument is that stockholders are gen-erally well-diversified, holding portfolios of many different stocks, so if one company takes a chance and loses, the stockholders lose only a small part of their wealth. Managers, on the other hand, are not diversified, so setbacks affect them more seriously. Accordingly, some argue that the managers of widely held firms tend to play it safe rather than aggressively seek to maximize the prices of their firms' stocks.

---

[2] A firm's stock price might, of course, decline because of factors beyond management's control. Accordingly, it is useful to look at comparative statistics; even though a firm's stock declines by 10 percent, management will have performed well if other firms in the industry decline by 20 percent.

It is extremely difficult to determine whether a particular management team is trying to maximize shareholder wealth or is merely attempting to satisfice on this factor while pursuing other goals. For example, how can we tell whether or not voluntary employee or community benefit programs are in the long-run best interests of the stockholders? Are relatively high management salaries really necessary to attract and retain excellent managers who, in turn, will keep the firm ahead of its competition? When a risky venture is turned down, does this reflect management conservatism or a correct judgment that the risks of the venture outweigh the potential rewards?

It is impossible to give definitive answers to these questions—several studies have suggested that managers are not completely stockholder-oriented, but the evidence is cloudy. It is true that more and more firms are tying management's compensation to the company's performance, and research suggests that this motivates management to operate in a manner consistent with stock price maximization. Additionally, in recent years tender offers and proxy fights have removed a number of supposedly entrenched managements; the recognition that such actions can take place has doubtless stimulated many other firms to attempt to maximize share prices.[3] Finally, a firm operating in a competitive market, or almost any firm during an economic downturn, will be forced to undertake actions that are reasonably consistent with shareholder wealth maximization. Thus, while managers may have other goals in addition to stockholder wealth maximization, there are reasons to view this as a dominant goal for most firms. And even though a management group may pursue other goals, stockholder wealth is bound to be of considerable importance. Often the same types of actions that could maximize wealth are also necessary to keep it at a satisfactory level; it may therefore be difficult, in practice, to determine which goal is dominant.

Social Responsibility   One final point that deserves consideration is *social responsibility:* Should businesses operate strictly in stockholders' best interests, or are they also partly responsible for the welfare of society at large? In tackling this question, consider first the firms whose rates of return on investment are close to normal, that is, close to the average for all firms. If such companies attempt to be socially responsible, thereby increasing their costs over what they otherwise would have been, and if the other businesses in the industry do not follow suit, then the socially oriented firms will probably be forced to abandon their efforts. Thus, any socially responsible acts that raise costs will be difficult, if not impossible, in industries subject to keen competition.

What about firms with profits above normal levels—can they not devote

[3] A tender offer is a bid by one company to buy the stock of another, while a proxy fight involves an attempt to gain control by getting stockholders to vote a new management group into office. Both actions are facilitated by low stock prices, so self-preservation can lead management to try to keep the stock value as high as possible.

resources to social projects? Undoubtedly they can; many large, successful firms do engage in community projects, employee benefit programs, and the like to a greater degree than would appear to be called for by pure profit or wealth maximization.[4] Still, publicly owned firms are constrained in such actions by capital market factors. Suppose a saver who has funds to invest is considering two alternative firms. One firm devotes a substantial part of its resources to social actions, while the other concentrates on profits and stock prices. Most investors are likely to shun the socially oriented firm, which will put it at a disadvantage in the capital market. After all, why should the stockholders of one corporation subsidize society to a greater extent than stockholders of other businesses? Thus, even highly profitable firms (unless they are closely held as opposed to publicly owned) are generally constrained against taking unilateral cost-increasing social actions.

Does all this mean that firms should not exercise social responsibility? Not at all—it simply means that most cost-increasing actions may have to be put on a mandatory rather than voluntary basis, at least initially, to insure that the burden of such action falls uniformly across all businesses. Thus, fair hiring practices, minority training programs, product safety, pollution abatement, antitrust actions, and the like are more likely to be effective if realistic rules are established initially and enforced by government agencies. It is critical that industry and government cooperate in establishing the rules of corporate behavior and that firms follow the spirit as well as the letter of the law in their actions. Thus, the rules of the game become constraints, and firms should strive to maximize shareholder wealth subject to these constraints. Throughout the book, we shall assume that managements operate in this manner.

FINANCIAL DECISIONS: RISK-RETURN TRADE-OFF

Financial decisions affect the value of a firm's stock by influencing both the size of the earnings stream, or profitability, and the riskiness of the firm. These relationships are diagrammed in Figure 1-1. Policy decisions, which are made subject to government constraints, affect both profitability and risk; these two factors jointly determine the value of the firm.

FIGURE 1-1   Valuation As the Central Focus of the Finance Function

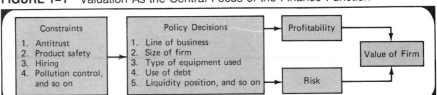

[4] Even firms such as these often find it necessary to justify such programs at stockholder meetings by appeals to long-run wealth maximization.

The primary policy decision is that of choosing the industry in which to operate—the product-market mix of the firm. When this choice has been made, both profitability and risk are determined by decisions relating to the size of the firm, the types of equipment used, the extent to which debt is employed, the firm's liquidity position, and so on. Such decisions generally affect both risk and profitability. An increase in the cash position, for instance, reduces risk; however, since cash is not an earning asset, converting other assets to cash also reduces profitability. Similarly, the use of additional debt raises the rate of return, or the profitability, on the stockholders' net worth; at the same time, more debt means more risk. The financial manager seeks to strike the particular balance between risk and profitability that will maximize the wealth of the firm's stockholders. That is called a *risk-return tradeoff,* and most financial decisions involve such tradeoffs between risk and return.

ORGANIZATION AND STRUCTURE OF THIS BOOK

The optimal structure for a finance text, if one exists, is most illusive. On the one hand, it is desirable to set out a theoretical structure first, then use the theory in later sections to explain behavior and to attack real-world decision problems. On the other hand, it is easier to understand the theoretical concepts of finance if one has a working knowledge of certain institutional details. Given this conflict, what should come first, theory or institutional background? We have wrestled with this problem, experimenting with both approaches in our own classes, and the following outline of the six parts of the book reflects our own experience and that of others who shared their ideas and preferences with us.

Part One: Overview of finance: taxes, financial analysis, planning, and control
Part Two: Working capital management
Part Three: Decisions involving long-term assets
Part Four: Sources and forms of long-term financing
Part Five: Financial structure, the cost of capital, and dividend policy
Part Six: Integrated topics in financial management

The contents of each part are next discussed briefly to provide an overview of both the book and the field of managerial finance.

Part One: Overview of Finance: Financial Analysis, Planning, and Control

Part One, which consists of Chapters 1–6, develops certain key concepts and commonly used tools of financial analysis. Included are such topics as ratio analysis, operating leverage, sources and uses of funds analysis, financial forecasting, and financial control techniques. The material provides a useful overview of finance, and the ideas and terminology developed facilitate an understanding of all the other parts of the book.

Part Two: Working Capital Management

Financial management involves the acquisition and use of assets, and to a large extent these actions are reflected in the firm's balance sheet. Accordingly, to a degree, the book is organized in a balance sheet sequence, with Part Two focusing on the top part of the balance sheet, or the "working capital" section. Working capital refers to the firm's short-term, or current, assets and liabilities, and the emphasis is placed on determining optimal levels for these items. Chapter 7 is on the theory of working capital, Chapter 8 concerns current assets, and Chapter 9 discusses current liabilities. The theory chapter sets forth a rational framework within which to consider decisions affecting the specific balance sheet items that make up working capital. Firms make two kinds of working capital decisions: (1) *strategic* decisions relating to target working capital levels, and (2) *tactical* decisions that relate to day-to-day operations. The strategic decisions are fundamentally related to the tradeoff between risk and return we discussed earlier, to alternative sources of capital, to management's view of the term structure of interest rates, to the effectiveness of internal control procedures (that is, inventory control), to credit policy decisions, and so forth. The tactical operating decisions involve short-run adjustments in current assets and current liabilities to meet temporary conditions. The most obvious short-run adjustment relates to changing sales levels—fixed assets and long-term liabilities are inflexible in the short run, so changes in market demand must be met by working capital adjustments. Working capital is also adjusted from the target levels to reflect changes in long- and short-run interest rates and other changes in the availability of, and the need for, funds.

In Chapter 8 we discuss some factors bearing on (1) target levels of each kind of current asset and (2) methods for economizing on the investment in each kind of current asset. For example, the target inventory level is determined jointly by costs of stock-outs, costs of carrying and ordering inventories, order lead times and usage rates, and the probability distributions of each of those factors. With this in mind, we base our discussion of inventories on the standard EOQ-plus-safety-stock inventory model. Then, in Chapter 9, we examine the sources and forms of short-term credit.

Part Three: Decisions Involving Long-Term Assets

In Part Three we move into the lower part of the balance sheet, examining the decisions involved in fixed-asset acquisitions. After a discussion of compound interest in Chapter 10, we take up capital budgeting techniques, explaining in some detail the mechanics of capital budgeting in Chapter 11. Next, in Chapter 12, we expand the discussion to include uncertainty, covering the basic concepts of probability distributions, the tradeoff between risk and rate of return, decision trees, and simulation.

Part Four: Sources and Forms of Long-Term Financing

In Part Four we move to the lower right-hand side of the balance sheet, examining the various kinds of long-term capital available to finance long-term investments. Chapter 13 presents an overview of the capital markets, explaining briefly certain institutional material without which no basic finance course is complete. Chapter 14 analyzes the financial characteristics of common stock, Chapter 15 examines bonds and preferred stock, Chapter 16 analyzes term loans and leases, and Chapter 17 discusses the nature and use of warrants and convertibles.

Part Five: Financial Structure, the Cost of Capital, and Dividend Policy

In Part Five we pull together the threads developed in earlier chapters. We show how (1) financial structure affects both risk and expected returns; (2) risk and return interact to determine the optimal capital structure; (3) the cost of capital, which is required when making fixed-asset decisions, is calculated; and (4) investment opportunities and cost of capital considerations interact to determine the way the firm should distribute its profits between dividends and retained earnings.

Part Six: Integrated Topics in Financial Management

In the final four chapters we take up important but somewhat specialized topics that draw upon the concepts developed in the earlier sections. In Chapter 22 we introduce dynamics into the decision process, showing how financial managers react to changing conditions in the capital markets. We next discuss the external growth of firms through mergers and holding companies, as well as the factors affecting this development, in Chapter 23. Throughout most of the text we deal with growing and successful firms; however, many firms face financial difficulties, so the causes and possible remedies to these difficulties are discussed in Chapter 24. Finally, in Chapter 25, we discuss the financial situation facing the small business firm and show how the tools of financial analysis may be applied to such a company. Chapter 25 also serves as a summary of the book.

QUESTIONS

1-1. The field of finance may be thought of as having gone through five developmental periods: (1) the time up through 1929; (2) the 1930s and early 1940s; (3) the late 1940s and early 1950s; (4) the middle and late 1950s; and (5) the 1960s and 1970s. What was the major emphasis in each period, and what economic circumstances led to this emphasis?

1-2. Why is stockholder wealth maximization thought to be a better operating goal than profit maximization?

1-3. The steel industry is dominated by eight large domestic firms, plus European and Japanese firms. How effective would a voluntary pollution control effort be in such an industry? How might the steel firms participate in setting mandatory pollution control standards? How might United States standards affect our balance of payments?

The Tax
Environment

2

The federal government is often called the most important stockholder in the American economy. This is not literally true, as the government does not "own" corporate shares in the strict sense of the word; it is, however, by far the largest recipient of business profits. Income of unincorporated businesses is subject to tax rates ranging up to 70 percent, while income of corporations is taxed at a 48 percent rate. State, and sometimes city or county taxes, must be added to these federal taxes, and dividends received by stockholders are subject to personal income taxes at the stockholders' individual tax rates.

With such a large percentage of business income going to the government, it is not surprising that taxes play an important role in financial decisions. To lease or to buy, to use common stock or debt, to make or not to make a particular investment, to merge or not to merge—all these decisions are influenced by tax factors. This chapter summarizes some basic elements of the tax structure relating to financial decisions.[1]

FISCAL POLICY

The federal government uses both monetary policy and fiscal policy to influence the level of economic activity. *Monetary policy*, which is considered in Chapter 22, deals with actions to influence the availability and cost of credit. *Fiscal policy* deals with altering the level and composition of government

[1] This chapter has benefited from the assistance of Mr. R. Wendell Buttrey, tax attorney and lecturer on taxation at the University of California, Los Angeles, and Mr. J. Bruce Sefert, lecturer on taxation at the University of Wisconsin.

receipts and expenditures to influence the level of economic activity. Since taxes constitute the primary receipt, they are an important element of fiscal policy.

Three principal methods have been employed to change tax receipts: (1) changing tax rates, (2) changing methods permitted for calculating tax-deductible depreciation (accelerated depreciation), and (3) providing for an investment tax credit for expenditures on new industrial equipment. Each of these points is discussed briefly in this section.

Changing Tax Rates

During periods of rapid and unsustainable economic expansion, especially when such expansion has inflationary consequences, the federal government may attempt to dampen the level of economic activity by increasing income tax rates. When tax rates are raised, both personal disposable incomes and corporate profits after taxes are reduced. The reduction in personal disposable incomes reduces individuals' purchasing power and thereby decreases their demand for goods and services. The reduction in corporate after-tax profits reduces the profitability of new investments and, at the same time, reduces corporate funds available for investment. On the other hand, if the economy is depressed and requires some form of stimulation, tax rates can be reduced, providing both consumers and businesses with greater purchasing power and increasing the incentive of businesses to make investments in plant and equipment.

In the past, tax rates have been changed infrequently. Such changes must be made by the Congress, and Congressional action on a decision with such a pervasive influence is not easy to obtain. Although economists and politicians have debated the idea of authorizing the President to change tax rates within certain prescribed limits, it appears unlikely that Congress will be willing to give up this power. We therefore expect that, in the foreseeable future, tax rates will be changed infrequently.

Accelerated Depreciation

Depreciation represents the cost of using productive equipment, hence depreciation charges are deductible in computing federal income taxes; the larger the depreciation charge, the lower the actual tax liability. The tax laws specify the allowed methods for calculating depreciation for purposes of computing federal income taxes. If the tax laws are changed to permit more rapid, or *accelerated*, depreciation, this will reduce tax payments and have a stimulating effect on business investments.[2]

---

[2]Federal tax statutes also consider the time over which assets must be depreciated. A reduction in the period over which an asset must be depreciated will have the same stimulating effect on the economy as would a change in permitted depreciation *methods* that increased depreciation expenses for tax purposes.

A number of different depreciation methods are authorized for tax purposes: (1) straight line, (2) units of production, (3) sum-of-years'-digits, and (4) double declining balance. These methods are explained in Appendix 2A. The last two methods listed are generally referred to as *accelerated depreciation methods;* ordinarily, they are more favorable from a tax standpoint than is straight line depreciation.

The fiscal policy implications of depreciation methods stem from two factors: (1) using accelerated depreciation reduces taxes in the early years of an asset's life, thus increasing corporate cash flows and making more funds available for investment; and (2) faster cash flows increase the profitability, or rate of return, on an investment. This second point is made clear in Chapter 11, where capital budgeting is discussed.

Depreciation methods, like tax rates, are determined by the Congress and are occasionally altered to influence the level of investment and thereby to stimulate or retard the economy. The most sweeping changes were made in 1954, when the accelerated depreciation methods listed above were first permitted, and in 1962 and 1970, when the depreciable lives of assets for tax purposes were reduced.

Investment Tax Credit

The concept of an investment tax credit was first incorporated into the federal income tax laws in 1962. Under the investment tax credit program, business firms could deduct as a *credit* against their income tax a specified percentage of the dollar amount of new investment in each of certain categories of assets. Under the rules existing in 1975, the tax credit amounted to 10 percent of the amount of new investment in assets having useful lives of eight years or more; two-thirds of 10 percent for assets having lives of six or seven years; one-third of 10 percent for assets having lives of four or five years; and no tax credit for assets having useful lives of less than four years. Thus, if a firm that otherwise would have had a $200,000 tax bill purchased an asset costing $500,000 and having a twenty-year life, it would receive a tax credit of $50,000 (equal to 10 percent of $500,000), and its adjusted tax bill would be $150,000.

The investment tax credit, like tax rates and depreciation methods, is subject to Congressional changes. During the boom in the early part of 1966, the investment tax credit was suspended in an effort to reduce investment, but it was reinstated later in the year; then it was removed again in 1969 and reinstated in 1971.

CORPORATE INCOME TAXES

Rate Structure

The first $25,000 of corporate taxable income is taxed at a 20 percent rate; the next $25,000 at a 22 percent rate; and all income over $50,000 is taxed at a 48 percent rate. If a firm's taxable income was $100,000, for example, the tax would be computed as follows:

$$
\begin{aligned}
20\% \times \$25,000 &= \$\ 5,000 \\
22\% \times\ \ 25,000 &= \ \ \ 5,500 \\
48\% \times\ \ 50,000 &= \ \underline{24,000} \\
&\ \ \ \ \underline{\$34,500}
\end{aligned}
$$

This relatively simple tax structure has wide implications for business planning. Because the tax rate more than doubles when corporate income rises above $50,000, it clearly would pay to break moderately sized companies into two or more separate corporations in order to hold the income of each unit under $50,000 and thus keep the tax rate at 22 percent. This was, in fact, done for many years by a number of firms, with some groups (retail chains, small loan companies) having literally thousands of separate corporations. However, the Tax Reform Act of 1969 eliminated the advantages of multiple corporations. If a group of firms having common ownership files separate returns for each company, then only one firm will be taxed at the low initial rates.

Corporate Capital Gains and Losses[3]

Corporate taxable income consists of two components: (1) profits from the sale of capital assets and (2) all other income, defined as *ordinary income.*

Capital assets—for example, security investments—are defined as assets not bought and sold in the ordinary course of a firm's business. Gains and losses on the sale of capital assets are defined as capital gains and losses, and under certain circumstances they receive special tax treatment. Real and depreciable property used in the business is not defined as a capital asset (Section 1221 of the Internal Revenue Code). However, Section 1231 of the code specifies that such property will be treated as a capital asset in the event of a net gain. In the event of a net loss on real and depreciable property used in the business, the full amount may be deducted from ordinary income without any of the limitations described below for capital loss treatments.[4]

The sale of a capital asset held for six months or less gives rise to a *short-term* capital gain or loss; its disposal, when held for more than six months, produces a *long-term* gain or loss. Short-term capital gains less short-term capital losses equal *net short-term gains.* Net short-term gains are added to

---

[3] Corporate capital gains and losses (as well as most other tax matters) are subject to many technical provisions. This section and the others dealing with tax matters include only the most general provisions. For special cases the student is referred to *Federal Tax Course* (Englewood Cliffs, N.J.: Prentice-Hall, 1976).

[4] This special treatment of depreciable properties should be kept in mind in connection with the material in Chapter 11 on capital budgeting. The difference between the book value of an asset and its salvage value or abandonment value, if lower than book value, can be deducted from ordinary income, and thus the full amount of this difference represents a deductible expense.

the firm's ordinary income and taxed at regular corporate income tax rates. For *net long-term capital gains* (long-term gains less long-term losses), the tax is limited to 30 percent. For example, if a corporation holds the common stock of another corporation as an investment for more than six months and then sells it at a profit, the gain is subject to a maximum tax of 30 percent. Of course, if income is below $50,000, regular tax rates of 20 or 22 percent apply.

Depreciable Assets

If an asset—for example, a machine tool—is subject to depreciation, its tax cost is defined as the original purchase price less accumulated depreciation. To illustrate, suppose a machine cost $10,000, and $5,000 of depreciation has been taken on it. Its book value, by definition, is $10,000 − $5,000 = $5,000.

If the company sells the machine for more than its book value, it may incur *either* a capital gain *or* ordinary income for tax purposes. If the gain is a recapture of depreciation, indicating that the firm had been depreciating the asset too rapidly (and charging off this depreciation as an expense to reduce ordinary income), the gain is ordinary income and is taxed accordingly. For example, if the firm sells the machine for $7,000, it incurs a $2,000 gain ($7,000 − $5,000). *However, this gain is not classified as a capital gain but, rather, as the recapture of depreciation. Therefore it is taxed as ordinary income.*

The sale of a depreciable asset is subject to the capital gains tax when the gain exceeds the amount of depreciation taken. To continue with the preceding example, if our machine had been sold for $12,000, then a total profit of $7,000 ($12,000 − $5,000) would have been incurred. Of this amount, $5,000 would represent the recapture of depreciation (since this amount of depreciation had been charged off) and would be taxed as ordinary income; the remaining $2,000 would be classified as a capital gain for tax purposes and would be taxed at a rate of 30 percent.

Finally, if the firm sells the machine for $3,000, it incurs a $2,000 loss ($5,000 book value minus $3,000 received). This net loss can be deducted in full from ordinary income without any limitations.

Deductibility of Capital Losses

A net capital loss is not deductible from ordinary income. For example, if in 1977 a corporation had ordinary income of $100,000 and a net capital loss of $25,000 (that is, capital losses for the year exceeded capital gains for the year by $25,000), it still paid a tax on the ordinary income at the normal rate of 20 percent on the first $25,000, 22 percent on the next $25,000, and 48 percent on the remaining $50,000, a total tax of $34,500. The net capital loss may, however, be carried back for three years and then forward for five years and may be used to offset capital gains during that period. For example, if this corporation has a net capital gain of $75,000 in 1978, its *taxable net capital gain* in that year is $75,000 less the carry-over of $25,000, or $50,000. The tax on the net gain is 30 percent, or $15,000, which is added to the tax on its ordinary income.

Dividend Income

Another important rule is that 85 percent of dividends received by one corporation from another is exempt from taxation.[5] For example, if corporation H owns stock in corporation S and receives $100,000 in dividends from corporation S, it must pay taxes on only $15,000 of the $100,000. Assuming H is in the 48 percent tax bracket, the tax is $7,200, or 7.2 percent of the dividends received. The reason for this reduced tax is that to subject intercorporate dividends to the full corporate tax rate would eventually lead to triple taxation. First, firm S would pay its regular taxes. Then firm H would pay a second tax. Finally, H's own stockholders would be subject to taxes on their dividends. The 85 percent dividend exclusion thus reduces the multiple taxation of corporate income.

Deductibility of Interest and Dividends

Interest payments made by a corporation are a deductible expense to the firm, but dividends paid on its own stock are not deductible. Thus, if a firm raises $100,000 and contracts to pay the suppliers of this money 7 percent, or $7,000 a year, the $7,000 is deductible if the $100,000 is debt. It is not deductible if the $100,000 is raised as stock and the $7,000 is paid as dividends.[6] This differential treatment of dividends and interest payments has an important effect on the manner in which firms raise capital, as we show in Chapter 20.

Payment of Tax in Installments

Firms must estimate their taxable income for the current year and pay one-fourth of the estimated tax on April 15, June 15, September 15, and December 15 of the current year. The *estimated* taxes paid must be at least 80 percent of actual taxes or the firm will be subjected to penalties. Any dif-

---

[5] If the corporation receiving the dividends owns 80 percent or more of the stock of a dividend-paying firm, it may file a consolidated tax return. In this case, there have been no dividends as far as the Internal Revenue Service is concerned, so there is obviously no tax on dividends received. On the internal books of the related corporations there may be an accounting entry entitled "dividends" used to transfer funds from the subsidiary to the parent, but this is of no concern to the IRS.

[6] There are limits on the deductibility of interest payments on some forms of securities issued in connection with mergers. See Chapter 23.

ferences between estimated and actual taxes are payable by March 15 of the following year. For example, if a firm expects to earn $100,000 in 1977 and to owe a tax of $34,500 on this income, then it must file an *estimated income statement* and pay $8,625 on the 15th of April, June, September, and December of 1977. By March 15, 1978 it must file a final income statement and pay any short-fall (or receive a refund for overages) between estimated and actual taxes.

Net Operating Carry-Back and Carry-Forward

Any ordinary corporate operating loss can be carried back three years and forward five years. The law states that the loss must first be carried back to the earliest year, the remainder applied to the second earliest year, and so on. For example, an operating loss in 1977 may be used to reduce taxable income in 1974, 1975, 1976, 1978, 1979, 1980, 1981, and 1982; this sequence *must* be followed.

The purpose of permitting this loss averaging is to avoid penalizing corporations whose incomes fluctuate widely. To illustrate, suppose the Ritz Hotel made $100,000 before taxes in all years except 1977, when it suffered a $600,000 operating loss. The Ritz would use the *carry-back* feature to recompute its taxes for 1974, using $100,000 of the operating losses to reduce the 1974 profit to zero, and would recover the amount of taxes paid in that year; that is, in 1978 Ritz would receive a refund of its 1974 taxes because of the loss experienced in 1977. Since $500,000 of unrecovered losses would still be available, Ritz would do the same thing for 1975 and 1976. Then, in 1978, 1979, and 1980, it would apply the *carry-forward* loss to reduce its profits to zero in each of these years.

The right to carry losses forward and backward has made some corporations attractive buys. For example, Atlas Corporation and Howard Hughes bought RKO Pictures because of a $30 million tax-loss credit. A corporation may acquire another firm that has had a tax loss, operate it as a subsidiary, and then present consolidated returns for tax purposes. In the RKO Pictures case, the $30 million loss would be worth $15 million to Atlas, assuming Atlas pays state and federal income taxes at a 50 percent rate. A loss corporation may be a doubly attractive buy if the purchaser is able to operate the business effectively and turn it into a profitable corporation at the same time that he benefits from the tax-loss carry-forward.

The tax law places severe restrictions on this privilege. First, if more than 50 percent of the stock changes hands within two years after the purchase, then no loss carry-over is provided. The same is true if any aspect of the old business is essentially abandoned. The objective of these limitations is to prevent a firm from merging for the sole purpose of taking advantage of the tax law. If it merges primarily to avoid taxes, the loss privilege may be disallowed.

Improper Accumulation

A special surtax on improperly accumulated income is provided for by Section 531 of the Internal Revenue Code, which states that earnings accumulated by a corporation are subject to penalty rates *if the purpose of the accumulation is to enable the stockholders to avoid the personal income tax.* The penalty rate is 27.5 percent on the first $100,000 of improperly accumulated taxable income for the current year and 38.5 percent on all amounts over $100,000. Of income not paid out in dividends, a cumulative total of $100,000 (the balance sheet item Retained Earnings) is prima facie retainable for the reasonable needs of the business. This is a benefit for small corporations. Although there is a penalty rate on all amounts over $100,000 shown to be unnecessary to meet the reasonable needs of the business, many companies do indeed have legitimate reasons for retaining earnings over $100,000 and are not subject to the penalty rate.

Retained earnings are used to pay off debt, to finance growth, and to provide the corporation with a cushion against possible cash drains caused by losses. How much a firm should properly accumulate for uncertain contingencies is a matter of judgment. Fear of the penalty taxes that may be imposed under Section 531 may cause a firm to pay out a higher rate of dividends than it otherwise would.

Sometimes Section 531 may stimulate mergers. A clear illustration is provided by the purchase of the Toni Company (home permanents) by the Gillette Safety Razor Company. The sale was made at a time when Toni's sales volume had begun to level off. Since earnings retention might have been difficult to justify, the owners of Toni, the Harris brothers, were faced with the alternatives of paying penalty rates for improper accumulation of earnings or of paying out the income as dividends. Toni's income after corporate taxes was $4 million a year; with the Harris brothers' average personal income tax of 75 percent, only $1 million a year would have been left after they paid personal taxes on dividends. By selling Toni for $13 million, they realized a $12 million capital gain (their book value was $1 million). After paying the 25 percent capital gains tax on the $12 million, or $3 million, the Harrises realized $10 million after taxes ($13 million sale price less $3 million tax). Thus, Gillette paid the equivalent of three and one-quarter years' after-corporate-tax earnings for Toni, while the Harris brothers received ten years' after-personal-income-tax net income for it. The tax factor made the transaction advantageous to both parties.

Election of Legal Form for Tax Purposes

The broad aspects of the federal corporate income tax have now been covered. Because the federal income tax on individuals is equally important for many business decisions, the main outlines of this part of the tax system must be discussed. In the next section, the individual tax structure is examined and compared with the corporate tax structure, thus providing a basis for making an intelligent choice as to which form of organization a firm should elect for tax purposes.

PERSONAL INCOME TAX

Of some five million firms in the United States, over four million are organized as individual proprietorships or as partnerships. The income of firms organized as individual proprietorships or as partnerships is taxed as personal income to the owners or the partners. The net income of a proprietorship or a partnership is reported to provide a basis for determining the individual's income tax liability. Thus, as a business tax, the individual income tax may be as important as the corporate income tax.

Individual Income Tax Structure[7]

The tax rates applicable to the single individual are outlined in Table 2–1; rates applicable to married couples filing joint returns are shown in Table 2–2. Because joint returns are permitted whether or not one spouse earns the entire income, this privilege has the effect of lowering applicable tax rates. Other rate schedules (not shown here) apply to married couples filing separate returns and to unmarried individuals who qualify for head-of-household status.

When the taxpayer's income will be derived mainly from the enterprise he contemplates forming, he should compare the average rates of taxation when deciding whether to be taxed as a corporation or as an individual. For single returns, the personal rate rises above the corporate rate at about $12,000, while for joint returns the point at which the personal tax rate begins to exceed the corporate rate is $20,000. Thus, for a firm with a net income of $1 million, there is no question but that the corporate form of business should be used. The tax advantage helps to explain why our largest businesses utilize the corporate form of organization. At incomes in the region of the $20,000 dividing line, whether the corporate or the noncorporate form will be most advantageous depends upon the facts of the case. If a firm finds it necessary to pay out a substantial part of its earnings in dividends, the non-corporate form is likely to be advantageous, because the "double taxation" is avoided. However, the corporate form is satisfactory if most of the earnings are to be retained.

---

[7] See instructions to IRS Form 1040 for details on personal income tax matters.

TABLE 2–1   Tax Rates for Single Individuals (1975 Rates)

Taxable Income Over:	but Not Over:	Tax Equals	of Excess Over:	Average Tax Rate at Upper Limit of Each Class Interval
$ 0	$ 500	$ 0 + 14%	$ 0	14.0%
500	1,000	70 + 15	500	14.5
1,000	1,500	145 + 16	1,000	15.0
1,500	2,000	225 + 17	1,500	15.5
2,000	4,000	310 + 19	2,000	17.3
4,000	6,000	690 + 21	4,000	18.5
6,000	8,000	1,110 + 24	6,000	19.9
8,000	10,000	1,590 + 25	8,000	20.9
10,000	12,000	2,090 + 27	10,000	21.9
12,000	14,000	2,630 + 29	12,000	22.9
14,000	16,000	3,210 + 31	14,000	23.9
16,000	18,000	3,830 + 34	16,000	25.1
18,000	20,000	4,510 + 36	18,000	26.1
20,000	22,000	5,230 + 38	20,000	27.2
22,000	26,000	5,990 + 40	22,000	29.2
26,000	32,000	7,590 + 45	26,000	32.1
32,000	38,000	10,290 + 50	32,000	34.9
38,000	44,000	13,290 + 55	38,000	37.7
44,000	50,000	16,590 + 60	44,000	40.3
50,000	60,000	20,190 + 62	50,000	43.9
60,000	70,000	26,390 + 64	60,000	46.8
70,000	80,000	32,790 + 66	70,000	49.2
80,000	90,000	39,390 + 68	80,000	51.3
90,000	100,000	46,190 + 69	90,000	53.1
100,000	. . . .	53,090 + 70	100,000	—

Example: Taxable income is $7,000; tax is $1,110 + $240 = $1,350. *Note:* The 1969 Tax Reform Act limits the personal income tax rate for both single and joint returns to 50 percent if the income is in the form of salary or income from personal services. The income from a business organized as a partnership or a proprietorship is taxed at rates up to 70 percent, unless the income of the business is primarily attributed to the personal services of the owner (as in the case of a partnership of doctors).

Individual Capital Gains and Losses

As with corporations, the distinction between short-term and long-term gains and losses is the six-month holding period. Net short-term gains are taxed at regular rates; the tax on long-term gains may be computed in either of two ways. First, the taxpayer may pay a flat rate of 25 percent on net long-term gains. Alternatively, he may pay the ordinary tax rate on *one-half* the amount of the net long-term gains.[8] The taxpayer should compute his tax under each of these methods and then select the one that results in the lower tax bill.

[8] The 25 percent option is not available on capital gains in excess of $50,000; thus on a $100,000 capital gain, $50,000 would be taxed at 25 percent, while one-half of the remainder would be taxed as ordinary income.

TABLE 2–2 Tax Rates for Married Individuals Filing Joint Returns (1975 Rates)

Taxable Income Over:	but Not Over:	Tax Equals	of Excess Over:	Average Tax Rate at Upper Limit of Each Class Interval
$ 0	$ 1,000	$ 0 + 14%	$ 0	14.0
1,000	2,000	140 + 15	1,000	14.5
2,000	3,000	290 + 16	2,000	15.0
3,000	4,000	450 + 17	3,000	15.5
4,000	8,000	620 + 19	4,000	17.4
8,000	12,000	1,380 + 22	8,000	18.8
12,000	16,000	2,260 + 25	12,000	20.4
16,000	20,000	3,260 + 28	16,000	21.9
20,000	24,000	4,380 + 32	20,000	23.6
24,000	28,000	5,660 + 36	24,000	25.4
28,000	32,000	7,100 + 39	28,000	27.1
32,000	36,000	8,660 + 42	32,000	28.7
36,000	40,000	10,340 + 45	36,000	30.4
40,000	44,000	12,140 + 48	40,000	32.0
44,000	52,000	14,060 + 50	44,000	34.7
52,000	64,000	18,060 + 53	52,000	38.2
64,000	76,000	24,420 + 55	64,000	40.8
76,000	88,000	31,020 + 58	76,000	43.2
88,000	100,000	37,980 + 60	88,000	45.2
100,000	120,000	45,180 + 62	100,000	48.0
120,000	140,000	57,580 + 64	120,000	50.3
140,000	160,000	70,380 + 66	140,000	52.2
160,000	180,000	83,580 + 68	160,000	54.0
180,000	200,000	97,180 + 69	180,000	55.5
200,000	. . . .	110,980 + 70	200,000	—

Note: The maximum rate on earned income is 50 percent. See footnote to Table 2–1.

For example, a married couple with an income of $32,000 from non-capital sources and a $10,000 long-term capital gain would compute their tax in two ways: (1) apply the normal tax rates on $32,000 plus one-half of $10,000 = $37,000, or (2) apply the normal tax on $32,000, plus 25 percent of $10,000. The first method would produce a tax of $10,790; the second, a tax of $11,160. The taxpayer would naturally elect the first method in this case.

In general, for joint returns the 25 percent option is beneficial only if the taxable income exceeds $44,000, the point at which the marginal tax rate reaches 50 percent. Note that individual and corporate treatments differ in two ways: (1) corporations do not have the option of having only one-half their capital gains taxed at normal rates, and (2) the corporate capital gains tax rate is 30 percent versus 25 percent for individuals.

Personal capital losses, short term or long term, can be carried forward without a time limit and deducted against either short-term or long-term capital gains. In addition, if the capital losses carried forward are not exhausted in the current year, 50 percent of long-term capital losses, up to a limit of $1,000 a year, may be charged off as a deduction against ordinary income. In other words, if an individual has $2,000 of long-term capital losses, he may deduct 50 percent of this amount, or $1,000, from his ordinary income. If the net long-term capital loss is in excess of $2,000, then any amount above $2,000 may be carried forward until it is exhausted. Short-term capital losses are not cut in half; that is, short-term losses can be deducted from ordinary income up to the $1,000 limit. Capital losses may not be carried back by individuals.

Moreover, Section 1244 of the Revenue Act of 1958 provides that individuals who invest in the stock of small corporations and suffer a loss on that stock may, for tax purposes, treat such a loss up to $25,000 a year ($50,000 on a joint return) as an ordinary loss rather than as a capital loss. A corporation is defined for this purpose as a small corporation, and the loss on its stock can be treated as an ordinary loss, if its common stock does not exceed $500,000 and if its total net worth—common stock plus retained earnings—does not exceed $1 million. This provision also encourages the formation of, and investment in, small corporations.

Dividend Income

The first $100 of dividend income received by an individual stockholder is excluded from taxable income. If stock is owned jointly by a husband and a wife, the exclusion is $200. If only one spouse owns stock, however, the total exclusion is generally only $100, the exception being in community property states, where $200 may be excluded regardless of which spouse is the registered owner.

To illustrate, if a family's gross income consists of $12,000 of salary plus $500 of dividends on stock owned by the husband, the gross taxable income (before deductions) is $12,400. However, if the stock is jointly owned, the taxable gross income would be $12,300, because $200 of the dividend income would be excluded.

Personal Deductions

A $750 deduction is allowed for the taxpayer and each of his dependents. The deduction is doubled on any taxpayer who is over sixty-five years old or is blind. A family of four—husband, wife, and two dependent children, none blind or over sixty-five—would thus have personal deductions of four times $750, or $3,000.[9]

Other Deductions

Certain other items are also deductible from income before computing taxes —medical expenses (subject to limitations), interest payments, state and

---

[9] The personal deduction has been changed frequently in recent years, so check current regulations rather than rely on the data given here.

local taxes, and contributions, among others. A taxpayer has the choice of either itemizing these deductions or taking the standard deduction, which is computed (in 1975) as the *lower* of $2,600 for joint returns or $2,300 for single individuals, or 16 percent of gross taxable income. In addition, in 1975 a *tax credit* of $30 per exemption was allowed; thus, for a family of four, the tax credit would amount to $30 $\times$ 4 = $120.

Example: In 1975 a family of four filing a joint return has an income consisting of $11,000 salary and $500 dividends on stock owned jointly by the husband and the wife. They take the standard deduction. Their gross income is $11,500, but $200 dividends are excluded, leaving a gross taxable income of $11,300. Personal deductions are $3,000 and the standard deduction is $1,808, the lesser of $2,600 or 16 percent of $11,300; their taxable income is therefore $6,492. From Table 2–2 we find that the tax is $1,093.48, calculated as $620 plus 19 percent of $2,492. However, they receive a tax credit of $120, so their net tax payment will be $973.48.

Partnership, or Proprietorship, or Corporation?

Subchapter S of the Internal Revenue Code provides that some incorporated businesses may elect to be taxed as proprietorships or as partnerships. The main regulations governing permission to make this election include:

1. The firm must be a domestic corporation and must not be affiliated with a group eligible to file consolidated tax returns. (Ordinarily, 80 percent ownership of a subsidiary is required for filing consolidated returns.)
2. The firm may not have more than ten stockholders, all of whom must be individuals.
3. The firm may not derive over 20 percent of its gross receipts from royalties, rents, dividends, interest, annuities, and gains on sales of securities.

   Although the foregoing tax factors make it difficult to generalize on whether the corporate or the noncorporate form is more advantageous from a tax standpoint, the essential variables for making an analysis are provided. In general, the advantage now seems to be on the side of the corporation, particularly since a firm may obtain the many benefits of its corporate status and yet elect to be taxed as a proprietorship or a partnership.

SUMMARY

This chapter provides some basic background on the tax environment within which business firms operate.

Corporate Taxes

The *corporate tax rate* structure is simple. The tax rate is 20 percent on income up to $25,000, 22 percent on the next $25,000, and 48 percent on all income over $50,000. Estimated taxes are paid in quarterly installments during the year in which the income is earned; when the returns are filed, the actual tax liability will result either in additional payments or in a refund due. *Operating losses* may be carried back for three years and forward for five years. *Capital losses* may not be treated as a deduction from operating income, but they may be used to offset capital gains. Corporate capital losses may be carried back for three years and forward for five years. Net long-term capital gains are taxed at a 30 percent rate (as compared with 25 percent for individuals).

Eighty-five percent of the *dividends received* by a corporation owning stock in another firm is excluded from the receiving firm's taxable income, and the receiving firm must pay full taxes on the remaining 15 percent of the dividends. *Dividends paid* are not treated as a tax-deductible expense. Regardless of the size of its earnings, a corporation does not have to pay dividends if it needs funds for expansion. If, however, the funds are not used for a legitimate purpose and if earnings are retained merely to enable stockholders to avoid paying personal income taxes on dividends received, the firm will be subject to an *improper-accumulations tax. Interest received* is taxable as ordinary income; *interest paid* is a deductible expense.

Personal Income Tax

Unincorporated business income is taxed at the personal tax rates of the owners. Personal income tax rates for both individuals and married persons filing jointly are *progressive*—the higher one's income, the higher his tax rate. Personal income tax rates start at 14 percent of taxable income and rise to either 50 percent or 70 percent of taxable income, depending upon the source of that income. Corporate income tax rates range from 20 to 48 percent. Thus, at lower incomes the personal income tax rate is lower if a business is organized as a proprietorship or a partnership; at higher incomes the corporate tax rate is lower. This fact has a significant bearing on whether a business chooses to be taxed as a corporation or as a proprietorship or a partnership.

Short-term *capital gains* are taxed at ordinary rates; long-term gains, at 25 percent or one-half the normal tax rate, whichever is lower, for individuals (but at 30 percent for corporations). Capital losses can be used to offset capital gains. One-half of an individual's net capital losses in any year can be deducted from ordinary income up to a limit of $1,000 a year. Capital losses in excess of $2,000 can be carried forward indefinitely until used up.

The foregoing material on the United States tax system is not designed to make a tax expert of the reader. It merely provides a few essentials for recognizing the tax aspects of business financial problems and for developing an awareness of the kinds of situations that should be taken to tax specialists for further guidance. These basics are, however, referred to frequently throughout the text, because income taxes are often an important factor in business financial decisions.

QUESTIONS

2-1. Compare the marginal and the average tax rates of corporations with taxable incomes of $5,000, $30,000, $50,000, $500,000, $5,000,000, and $50,000,000. Can you make such a comparison for sole proprietorships or for partnerships?

2-2. Which is the more relevant tax rate, the marginal or the average, in determining the form of organization for a new firm? Have recent changes in the tax laws made the form of organization more or less important than formerly?

2-3. For tax purposes, how does the treatment of interest expense compare with the treatment of common stock dividends from each of the following standpoints: a firm paying the interest or the dividends, an individual recipient, and a corporate recipient?

2-4. Compare the treatment of capital gains and losses with ordinary gains and losses in corporate income tax returns.

2-5. What is the present corporate carry-back and carry-forward tax provision for ordinary income? What is the purpose of this provision?

2-6. What is the purpose of the Internal Revenue Code provision dealing with improper accumulation of corporate surplus revenue?

2-7. Why is personal income tax information important for a study of business finance?

2-8. How do the tax rates for capital gains and losses affect an individual's investment policies and opportunities for financing a small business?

PROBLEMS

2-1. A corporation has a net income of $59,800 before interest charges. Assuming interest charges amount to $4,500,

    a. How much income tax must the corporation pay?

    b. What is the marginal tax rate?

2-2. John Sayles is a married man with two children. His gross income for 1975 is $20,000, which includes $1,600 of corporate dividends received by his wife. He files a joint return and takes the standard deduction. What is his personal income tax liability for 1975?

2-3. The taxable income (losses are shown in parenthesis) of the Johnson Corporation, formed in 1973, is shown below:

1973	$(250,000)
1974	125,000
1975	175,000
1976	325,000
1977	(125,000)

What is the corporate tax liability for each year?

2-4. The Davidson Corporation's projected income statement for 1975 is shown here:

Gross taxable income	$150,000
Tax payable	58,500
Net income after taxes	$91,500

Bond Manufacturing Corporation projects a $50,000 loss in 1975. Davidson feels that managerial talent can turn Bond into a profitable operation. If the two companies merged prior to January 1, 1976, what would be the merged corporation's income for 1975? What is the difference in tax liability for Davidson before and after the merger?

2-5. In 1975 Grey Manufacturing earned $400,000 before taxes on sales of $8 million. In 1973 it acquired working control of Reaction Products, Inc., for $250,000, and it disposed of the stock in 1975 for $500,000. (Grey controlled less than 80 percent of Reaction.) Dividends paid by Reaction to Grey during 1975 amounted to $25,000.
   a. What is Grey's tax for 1975?
   b. What would Grey's tax have been if Reaction had declared a further dividend of $50,000 in 1975 and if Grey had sold the stock, purchased in 1973, for $450,000?

2-6. Dalton Company purchased for $500,000 a new kiln with a useful life of ten years and no salvage value. Dalton uses only double declining balance and straight line depreciation methods. What is the maximum depreciation allowance on the kiln for each year?

2-7. The following information applies to Kaiser, Inc., a firm which was formed in 1974:

	1974	1975	1976	1977
Net operating income (loss)	$30,000	($50,000)	$50,000	$60,000
Net long-term capital gains (loss)	(3,000)	1,000	1,000	1,500
Dividend income	1,000	1,000	1,000	1,000
Interest paid	2,000	3,000	3,000	4,000
Dividends paid	0	0	500	75

Also in 1977 Kaiser sold a computer operated lathe for $20,000. Its original cost was $15,000 and its book value in 1977 was $10,000. For each year determine the tax liability of Kaiser, Inc.

Depreciation Methods

2A Appendix

The four principal methods of depreciation—straight line, sum-of-years'-digits, double declining balance, and units of production—and their effects on a firm's taxes are illustrated in this appendix. We will begin by assuming that a machine is purchased for $1,100 and has an estimated useful life of ten years or ten thousand hours. It will have a scrap value of $100 after ten years of use or after ten thousand hours, whichever comes first. Table 2A-1 illustrates each of the four depreciation methods and compares the depreciation charges of each method over the ten-year period.

STRAIGHT LINE

With the straight line method, a uniform annual depreciation charge of $100 a year is provided. This figure is arrived at by simply dividing the economic life into the total cost of the machine minus the estimated salvage value:

$$\frac{(\$1,100 \text{ cost} - \$100 \text{ salvage value})}{10 \text{ years}} = \frac{\$100 \text{ a year}}{\text{depreciation charge.}}$$

If the estimated salvage value is not in excess of 10 percent of the original cost, it can be ignored, but we are leaving it for illustrative purposes.

31

TABLE 2A–1 Comparison of Depreciation Methods for a 10-year, $1,100 Asset with a $100 Salvage Value

Year	Straight Line	Depreciation Methods Double Declining Balance	Sum-of-Years-Digits	Units of Production[a]
1	$ 100	$220	$ 182	$ 200
2	100	176	164	180
3	100	141	145	150
4	100	113	127	130
5	100	90	109	100
6	100	72	91	80
7	100	58	73	60
8	100	46	55	50
9	100	37	36	30
10	100	29	18	20
Total	$1,000	$982	$1,000	$1,000

[a] The assumption is made that the machine is used the following number of hours: first year, 2,000; second year, 1,800; third year, 1,500; fourth year, 1,300; fifth year, 1,000; sixth year, 800; seventh year, 600; eighth year, 500; ninth year, 300; tenth year, 200.

DOUBLE DECLINING BALANCE

The double declining balance (DDB) method of accelerated depreciation requires the application of a constant rate of depreciation each year to the undepreciated value of the asset at the close of the previous year. In this case, since the annual straight line rate is 10 percent a year ($100 ÷ $1,000), the double declining rate would be 20 percent (2 × 10 percent). This rate is applied to the full purchase price of the machine, not to the cost less salvage value. Therefore, depreciation under the DDB method is $220 during the first year (20 percent × $1,100). Depreciation amounts to $176 in the second year and is calculated by applying the 20 percent rate to the undepreciated value of the asset,

$$20\% \times (1,100 - \$220) = \$176,$$

and so on, as the undepreciated balance declines. Notice that under DDB the asset is not fully depreciated at the end of the tenth year. In our example the remaining depreciation would be taken in the tenth year.[1]

---

[1] Actually, the company would switch from DDB to straight line whenever straight line depreciation on the remaining book value of the asset exceeds the DDB amount. Thus, in the ninth year the book value is $184, leaving $84 to be depreciated, so straight line depreciation would be $42 versus $37 if the change were not made.

SUM-OF-YEARS'-DIGITS

Under the sum-of-years'-digits method, the yearly depreciation allowance is determined as follows:

1. Calculate the sum of the years' digits; in our example, there is a total of 55 digits: $1 + 2 + 3 + 4 + 5 + 6 + 7 + 8 + 9 + 10 = 55$. This figure can also be arrived at by means of the sum of an algebraic progression equation where N is the life of the asset:

$$\text{Sum} = N \left(\frac{N + 1}{2} \right)$$

$$= 10 \left(\frac{10 + 1}{2} \right) = 55.$$

2. Divide the number of remaining years by the sum of years' digits and multiply this fraction by the depreciable cost (total cost minus salvage value) of the asset:

Year 1: $\dfrac{10}{55}$ ($1,000) = $182 depreciation.

Year 2: $\dfrac{9}{55}$ ($1,000) = $164 depreciation.

$\vdots$

Year 10: $\dfrac{1}{55}$ ($1,000) = $18 depreciation.

UNITS OF PRODUCTION

Under the units of production method, the expected useful life of ten thousand hours is divided into the depreciable cost (purchase price minus salvage value) to arrive at an hourly depreciation rate of 10 cents. Since, in our example, the machine is run for two thousand hours in the first year, the depreciation in that year is $200; in the second year, $180; and so on. With this method, depreciation charges cannot be estimated precisely ahead of time; the firm must wait until the end of the year to determine what usage has been made of the machine and hence its depreciation.

EFFECT OF DEPRECIATION ON TAXES PAID

The effect of the accelerated methods on a firm's income tax payment is easily demonstrated. In the first year, should the firm choose to use the straight line method, only $100 may be deducted from its earnings to arrive at earnings before taxes (the amount of earnings to which the tax rate applies). However, using any one of the other three methods, the firm would have a much greater deduction and, therefore, a lower tax liability.

CHANGING THE DEPRECIABLE LIFE OF AN ASSET

Depreciation charges may actually be accelerated without resorting to changing the depreciation method simply by shortening the estimated life of an asset. The federal government establishes certain guidelines that set legal limits on the minimum life of classes of assets; by lowering these limits, the government can accomplish ends similar to permitting accelerated methods. Halving the minimum depreciable life of an asset, for example, would effectively double the annual rate of depreciation.

Ratio Analysis

3

Planning is the key to the financial manager's success. Financial plans may take many forms, but any good plan must be related to the firm's existing strengths and weaknesses. The strengths must be understood if they are to be used to proper advantage, and the weaknesses must be recognized if corrective action is to be taken. For example, are inventories adequate to support the projected level of sales? Does the firm have too heavy an investment in accounts receivable, and does this condition reflect a lax collection policy? The financial manager can plan his future financial requirements in accordance with the forecasting and budgeting procedures we will present in succeeding chapters, but his plan must begin with the type of financial analysis developed in this chapter.

BASIC FINANCIAL STATEMENTS

Because ratio analysis employs financial data taken from the firm's balance sheet and income statement, it is useful to begin this chapter with a review of these accounting reports. For illustrative purposes, we shall use data taken from the Walker-Wilson Manufacturing Company, a producer of specialized machinery used in the automobile repair business. Formed in 1965, when Charles Walker and Ben Wilson set up a small plant to produce certain tools they had developed while in the army, Walker-Wilson grew steadily and earned the reputation of being one of the best small firms in its line of business. In December 1975, both Walker and Wilson were killed in a crash of their private plane, and for the next two years the firm was managed by Walker-Wilson's accountant.

35

TABLE 3-1 Walker-Wilson Company
Illustrative balance sheet (thousands of dollars)

Assets	Dec. 31, 1976	Dec. 31, 1977	Claims on Assets	Dec. 31, 1976	Dec. 31, 1977
Cash	$ 52	$ 50	Accounts payable	$ 87	$ 60
Marketable securities	175	150	Notes payable, 8%	110	100
Receivables	250	200	Accruals	10	10
Inventories	355	300	Provision for federal income taxes	135	130
Total current assets	$ 832	$ 700	Total current liabilities	$ 342	$ 300
Gross plant and equipment	$1,610 $1,800		First mortgage bonds, 5% *	520	500
Less depreciation	400 500		Debentures, 6%	200	200
Net plant and equipment	1,210	1,300	Common stock (600,000 shares)	$600	$600
			Retained earnings	380	400
			Total net worth	980	1,000
Total assets	$2,042	$2,000	Total claims on assets	$2,042	$2,000

*The sinking fund requirement for the mortgage bonds is $20,000 a year.

In 1978, the widows, who are the principal stockholders in Walker-Wilson, acting on the advice of the firm's bankers and attorneys, engaged David Thompson as president and general manager. Although Thompson is experienced in the machinery business, especially in production and sales, he does not have a detailed knowledge of his new company, so he has decided to conduct a careful appraisal of the firm's position and, on the basis of this position, to draw up a plan for future operations.

Balance Sheet

Walker-Wilson's balance sheet, given in Table 3–1, shows the value of the firm's assets, and of the claims on these assets, at two particular points in time, December 31, 1976, and December 31, 1977. The assets are arranged from top to bottom in order of decreasing liquidity; that is, assets toward the top of the column will be converted to cash sooner than those toward the bottom of the column. The top group of assets—cash, marketable securities, accounts receivable, and inventories, which are expected to be converted into cash within one year—is defined as *current assets.* Assets in the lower part of the statement—plant and equipment—are not expected to be converted to cash within one year; these are defined as *fixed assets.*

The right side of the balance sheet is arranged similarly. Those items toward the top of the Claims column mature, and must be paid off, relatively soon; those further down the column are due in the more distant future. Current liabilities must be paid within one year; because the firm never has to "pay off" common stockholders, common stock and retained earnings represent "permanent" capital.

Income Statement

Walker-Wilson's income statement is shown in Table 3–2. Sales are shown at the top of the statement; various costs, including income taxes, are deducted to arrive at the net income available to common stockholders. The figure on the last line represents earnings per share (*EPS*), calculated as net income divided by number of shares outstanding.

Statement of Retained Earnings

Earnings may be paid out to stockholders as dividends or retained and reinvested in the business. Stockholders like to receive dividends, of course, but if earnings are plowed back into the business, the value of the stockholders' position in the company increases. Later in the book we shall consider the pros and cons of retaining earnings versus paying them out in dividends, but for now we are simply interested in the effects of dividends and retained earnings on the balance sheet. For this purpose, accountants use the statement of retained earnings, illustrated for Walker-Wilson in Table 3–3. Walker-Wilson earned $120,000 during the year, paid $100,000 in dividends to stockholders, and plowed $20,000 back into the business. Thus the retained earnings at the end of 1977, as shown both on the balance sheet and on the statement of retained earnings, is $400,000, which is $20,000 larger than the year-end 1976 figure.

TABLE 3–2 Walker-Wilson Company
Illustrative income statement
For year ended December 31, 1977

Net sales		$3,000,000
Cost of goods sold		2,580,000
Gross profit		$ 420,000
Less: Operating expenses		
Selling	$22,000	
General and administrative	40,000	
Lease payment on office building	28,000	90,000
Gross operating income		$ 330,000
Depreciation		100,000
Net operating income		$ 230,000
Add: Other income		
Royalties		15,000
Gross income		$ 245,000
Less: Other expenses		
Interest on notes payable	$ 8,000	
Interest on first mortgage	25,000	
Interest on debentures	12,000	45,000
Net income before income tax		$200,000
Federal income tax (at 40%)		80,000
Net income, after income tax, available to common stockholders		$ 120,000
Earnings per share (*EPS*)		$ .20

TABLE 3–3 Walker-Wilson Company
Statement of retained earnings
For year ended December 31, 1977 (thousands of dollars)

Balance of retained earnings, December 31, 1976	$380
Add: Net income, 1977	120
	$500
Less: Dividends to stockholders	100
Balance of retained earnings, December 31, 1977	$400

Relationship among the Three Statements

It is important to recognize that the balance sheet is a statement of the firm's financial position *at a point in time*, whereas the income statement shows the results of operations *during an interval of time.* Thus, the balance sheet represents a snapshot of the firm's position on a given date, while the income statement is based on a flow concept, showing what occurred between two points in time.

The statement of retained earnings indicates how the retained earnings account on the balance sheet is adjusted between balance sheet dates. Since its inception, Walker-Wilson had retained a total of $380,000 by December 31, 1976. In 1977 it earned $120,000, and $20,000 of this amount was retained. Thus, the retained earnings shown on the balance sheet for December 31, 1977, is $400,000.

When a firm retains earnings, it generally does so to expand the business —that is, to finance the purchase of assets such as plant, equipment, and inventories. As a result of operations in 1977, Walker-Wilson has $20,000 available for that purpose. Sometimes retained earnings will be used to build up the cash account, but retained earnings as shown on the balance sheet are *not* cash. Through the years they have been invested in bricks and mortar and other assets, so retained earnings as shown on the balance sheet are not "available" for anything. The earnings *for the current year* may be available for investment, but the *past retained earnings* have already been employed.

Stated another way, the balance sheet item "retained earnings" simply shows how much of their earnings the stockholders, through the years, have elected to reinvest in the business. Thus, the retained earnings account shows the additional investment the stockholders as a group have made in the business, over and above their initial investment at the inception of the company and through any subsequent issues of stock.

BASIC TYPES OF FINANCIAL RATIOS

Each type of analysis has a purpose or use that determines the different relationships emphasized in the analysis. The analyst may, for example, be a banker considering whether or not to grant a short-term loan to a firm. He is primarily interested in the firm's near-term, or liquidity, position, so he stresses ratios that measure liquidity. In contrast, long-term creditors place far more emphasis on earning power and on operating efficiency. They know that unprofitable operations will erode asset values and that a strong current position is no guarantee that funds will be available to repay a 20-year bond issue. Equity investors are similarly interested in long-term profitability and efficiency. Management is, of course, concerned with all those aspects of financial analysis—it must be able to repay its debts to long- and short-term creditors as well as earn profits for stockholders.

It is useful to classify ratios into four fundamental types:

1. *Liquidity ratios*, which measure the firm's ability to meet its maturing short-term obligations.
2. *Leverage ratios*, which measure the extent to which the firm has been financed by debt.
3. *Activity ratios*, which measure how effectively the firm is using its resources.
4. *Profitability ratios*, which measure management's overall effectiveness as shown by the returns generated on sales and investment.

Specific examples of each ratio are given in the following sections, where the Walker-Wilson case history is used to illustrate their calculation and use.

Liquidity Ratios

Generally, the first concern of the financial analyst is liquidity: Is the firm able to meet its maturing obligations? Walker-Wilson has debts totaling $300,000 that must be paid within the coming year. Can these obligations be satisfied? Although a full liquidity analysis requires the use of cash budgets (described in Chapter 6), ratio analysis, by relating the amount of cash and other current assets to the current obligations, provides a quick and easy-to-use measure of liquidity. Two commonly used liquidity ratios are presented below.

Current Ratio   The current ratio is computed by dividing current assets by current liabilities. Current assets normally include cash, marketable securities, accounts receivable, and inventories; current liabilities consist of accounts payable, short-term notes payable, current maturities of long-term debt, accrued income taxes, and other accrued expenses (principally wages). The current ratio is the most commonly used measure of short-term solvency, since it indicates the extent to which the claims of short-term creditors are covered by assets that are expected to be converted to cash in a period roughly corresponding to the maturity of the claims.

The calculation of the current ratio for Walker-Wilson at year-end 1977 is shown below.

$$\text{Current ratio} = \frac{\text{current assets}}{\text{current liabilities}} = \frac{\$700,000}{\$300,000} = 2.3 \text{ times.}$$

$$\text{Industry average} = 2.5 \text{ times.}$$

The current ratio is slightly below the average for the industry, 2.5, but not low enough to cause concern. It appears that Walker-Wilson is about in line with most other firms in this particular line of business. Since current assets are near maturing, it is highly probable that they could be liquidated at close to book value. With a current ratio of 2.3, Walker-Wilson could liquidate current assets at only 43 percent of book value and still pay off current creditors in full.[1]

Although industry average figures are discussed later in the chapter, it should be stated at this point that the industry average is not a magic number that all firms should strive to maintain. In fact, some very well managed firms will be above it, and other good firms will be below it. However, if a firm's ratios are very far removed from the average for its industry, the analyst must be concerned about why this variance occurs; that is, a deviation from the industry average should signal the analyst to check further.

Quick Ratio or Acid Test The quick ratio is calculated by deducting inventories from current assets and dividing the remainder by current liabilities. Inventories are typically the least liquid of a firm's current assets and the assets on which losses are most likely to occur in the event of liquidation. Therefore, this measure of the firm's ability to pay off short-term obligations without relying on the sale of inventories is important.

$$\text{Quick, or acid test, ratio} = \frac{\text{current assets} - \text{inventory}}{\text{current liabilities}} = \frac{\$400,000}{\$300,000}$$

$$= 1.3 \text{ times.}$$

$$\text{Industry average} = 1.0 \text{ times.}$$

The industry average quick ratio is 1, so Walker-Wilson's 1.3 ratio compares favorably with other firms in the industry. Thompson knows that if the marketable securities can be sold at par and if he can collect the accounts receivable, he can pay off his current liabilities without selling any inventory.

Leverage Ratios

Leverage ratios, which measure the funds supplied by owners as compared with the financing provided by the firm's creditors, have a number of implications. First, creditors look to the equity, or owner-supplied funds, to provide a margin of safety. If owners have provided only a small proportion of total financing, the risks of the enterprise are borne mainly by the creditors. Second, by raising funds through debt, the owners gain the benefits of maintaining control of the firm with a limited investment. Third, if the firm earns more on the borrowed funds than it pays in interest, the return to the owners is magnified. For example, if assets earn 6 percent and debt costs only 4 percent, there is a 2 percent differential accruing to the stockholders. Leverage cuts

---

[1] $(1/2.3) = .43$, or 43 percent. Note that $(.43)$ $(\$700,000) \approx \$300,000$, the amount of current liabilities.

both ways, however; if the return on assets falls to 3 percent, the differential between that figure and the cost of debt must be made up from equity's share of total profits. In the first instance, where assets earn more than the cost of debt, leverage is favorable; in the second, it is unfavorable.

Firms with low leverage ratios have less risk of loss when the economy is in a recession, but they also have lower expected returns when the economy booms. Conversely, firms with higher leverage ratios run the risk of large losses but also have a chance of gaining high profits. The prospects of high returns are desirable, but investors are averse to risk. Decisions about the use of leverage, then, must balance higher expected returns against increased risk.[2]

In practice, leverage is approached in two ways. One approach examines balance sheet ratios and determines the extent to which borrowed funds have been used to finance the firm. The other approach measures the risks of debt by income statement ratios designed to determine the number of times fixed charges are covered by operating profits. These sets of ratios are complementary, and most analysts examine both leverage ratios.

Total Debt to Total Assets The ratio of total debt to total assets, generally called the *debt ratio*, measures the percentage of total funds provided by creditors. Debt includes current liabilities and all bonds. Creditors prefer moderate debt ratios, since the lower the ratio, the greater the cushion against creditors' losses in the event of liquidation. In contrast to the creditors' preference for a low debt ratio, the owners may seek high leverage either (1) to magnify earnings or (2) because raising new equity means giving up some degree of control. If the debt ratio is too high, there is a danger of encouraging irresponsibility on the part of the owners. The stake of the owners can become so small that speculative activity, if it is successful, will yield a substantial percentage return to the owners. If the venture is unsuccessful, however, only a moderate loss is incurred by the owners because their investment is small.

$$\text{Debt ratio} = \frac{\text{total debt}}{\text{total assets}} = \frac{\$1,000,000}{\$2,000,000} = 50\%.$$

$$\text{Industry average} = 33\%.$$

Walker-Wilson's debt ratio is 50 percent; this means that creditors have supplied half the firm's total financing. Since the average debt ratio for this industry—and for manufacturing generally—is about 33 percent, Walker-Wilson would find it difficult to borrow additional funds without first raising more equity capital. Creditors would be reluctant to lend the firm more money,

---

[2] The problem of determining optimum leverage for a firm with given risk characteristics is examined extensively in Chapters 19 and 20.

and Thompson would probably be subjecting the stockholders to undue dangers if he sought to increase the debt ratio still more by borrowing.[3]

Times Interest Earned   The times-interest-earned ratio is determined by dividing earnings before interest and taxes (gross income in Table 3–2) by the interest charges. The times-interest-earned ratio measures the extent to which earnings can decline without resultant financial embarrassment to the firm because of inability to meet annual interest costs. Failure to meet this obligation can bring legal action by the creditors, possibly resulting in bankruptcy. Note that the before-tax profit figure is used in the numerator. Because income taxes are computed after interest expense is deducted, the ability to pay current interest is not affected by income taxes.

$$\text{Times interest earned} = \frac{\text{gross income}}{\text{interest charges}}$$

$$= \frac{\text{profit before taxes} + \text{interest charges}}{\text{interest charges}}$$

$$= \frac{\$245,000}{\$45,000} = 5.4 \text{ times.}$$

$$\text{Industry average} = 8.0 \text{ times.}$$

Walker-Wilson's interest charges consist of three payments totaling $45,000 (see Table 3–2). The firm's gross income available for servicing these charges is $245,000, so the interest is covered 5.4 times. Since the industry average is 8 times, the company is covering its interest charges by a minimum margin of safety and deserves only a fair rating. This ratio reinforces the conclusion based on the debt ratio that the company is likely to face some difficulties if it attempts to borrow additional funds.

Fixed Charge Coverage   This ratio is similar to the times-interest-earned ratio, but it is somewhat more inclusive in that it recognizes that many firms lease assets and incur long-term obligations under lease contracts.[4] As we show in Chapter 16, leasing has become quite widespread in recent years, making this ratio preferable to the times-interest-earned ratio for most financial analyses. "Fixed charges" are defined as interest plus annual long-term lease obligations, and the fixed charge coverage ratio is defined as follows:

---

[3]The ratio of debt to equity is also used in financial analysis. The debt to assets (D/A) and debt to equity (D/E) ratios are simply transformations of one another:

$$D/E = \frac{D/A}{1 - D/A} \quad \text{and} \quad D/A = \frac{D/E}{1 + D/E}.$$

Both ratios increase as a firm of a given size (total assets) uses a greater proportion of debt, but D/A rises linearly and approaches a limit of 100 percent while D/E rises exponentially and approaches infinity.

[4]Generally, a long-term lease is defined as one extending at least 3 years into the future. Thus, rent incurred under a 1-year lease would not be included in the fixed charge coverage ratio, but rental payments under a 3-year or longer lease would be defined as fixed charges.

$$\text{Fixed charge coverage} = \frac{\begin{matrix}\text{profit} & \text{interest} & \text{lease}\\ \text{before taxes} + \text{charges} + \text{obligations}\end{matrix}}{\text{interest charges} + \text{lease obligations}}$$

$$= \frac{\$200,000 + \$45,000 + \$28,000}{\$45,000 + \$28,000}$$

$$= 3.74 \text{ times.}$$

$$\text{Industry average} = 5.5 \text{ times.}$$

Walker-Wilson's fixed charges are covered 3.7 times, as opposed to an industry average of 5.5 times. Again, this indicates that the firm is somewhat weaker than creditors would prefer it to be, and it further points up the difficulties Thompson would likely encounter if he should attempt additional borrowing.[5]

Activity Ratios

Activity ratios measure how effectively the firm employs the resources at its command. These ratios all involve comparisons between the level of sales and the investment in various asset accounts. The activity ratios presume that a "proper" balance should exist between sales and the various asset accounts—inventories, accounts receivable, fixed assets, and others. As we shall see in the following chapters, this is generally a good assumption.

Inventory Turnover The inventory turnover is defined as sales divided by inventories.

$$\text{Inventory turnover} = \frac{\text{sales}}{\text{inventory}} = \frac{\$3,000,000}{\$300,000} = 10 \text{ times.}$$

$$\text{Industry average} = 9 \text{ times.}$$

Walker-Wilson's turnover of 10 compares favorably with an industry average of 9 times. This suggests that the company does not hold excessive stocks of inventory; excess stocks are, of course, unproductive and represent an investment with a low or zero rate of return. This high inventory turnover also reinforces Thompson's faith in the current ratio. If the turnover was low—say 3 or 4 times—Thompson would wonder whether the firm was holding damaged or obsolete materials not actually worth their stated value.

Two problems arise in calculating and analyzing the inventory turnover ratio. First, sales are at market prices; if inventories are carried at cost, as they

---

[5] A still more complete coverage ratio is the *debt service coverage ratio*, defined similarly to the fixed charge coverage except that mandatory annual payments to retire long-term debt (amortization payments, discussed in Chapter 16) are also included in the denominator. The ratio is not widely used, primarily because sinking fund obligations are not generally known to outside analysts. Moreover, it is difficult to develop industry averages for this ratio because of the absence of data. The information on lease obligations, in contrast, is almost always available in footnotes to financial statements.

generally are, it would be more appropriate to use cost of goods sold in place of sales in the numerator of the formula. Established compilers of financial ratio statistics such as Dun & Bradstreet, however, use the ratio of sales to inventories carried at cost. To develop a figure that can be compared with those developed by Dun & Bradstreet, it is therefore necessary to measure inventory turnover with sales in the numerator, as we do here.

The second problem lies in the fact that sales occur over the entire year, whereas the inventory figure is for one point in time. This makes it better to use an average inventory for the year, computed by adding the 12 end-of-month inventory figures and dividing by 12. If it is determined that the firm's business is highly seasonal, or if there has been a strong upward or downward sales trend during the year, it becomes essential to make some such adjustment. Neither of these conditions holds for Walker-Wilson; to maintain comparability with industry averages, Thompson did not use the average inventory figure.

Average Collection Period The average collection period, which is a measure of the accounts receivable turnover, is computed in two steps: (1) annual sales are divided by 360 to get the average daily sales;[6] (2) daily sales are divided into accounts receivable to find the number of days' sales tied up in receivables. This is defined as the average collection period, because it represents the average length of time that the firm must wait after making a sale before receiving cash. The calculations for Walker-Wilson show an average collection period of 24 days, slightly above the 20-day industry average.

Step 1: $\qquad$ Sales per day $= \dfrac{\$3,000,000}{360} = \$8,333.$

Step 2: Average collection period $= \dfrac{\text{receivables}}{\text{sales per day}} = \dfrac{\$200,000}{\$8,333} = 24 \text{ days.}$

$$\text{Industry average} = 20 \text{ days.}$$

This ratio can also be evaluated by comparison with the terms on which the firm sells its goods. For example, Walker-Wilson's sales terms call for payment within 20 days, so the 24-day collection period indicates that customers, on the average, are not paying their bills on time. If the trend in the collection period over the past few years had been rising while the credit policy

---

[6] Because information on credit sales is generally unavailable, total sales must be used. Since all firms do not have the same percentage of credit sales, there is a good chance that the average collection period will be somewhat in error. Also, note that for convenience, the financial community generally uses 360 rather than 365 as the number of days in the year for purposes such as these.

has not changed, this would be even stronger evidence that steps should be taken to expedite the collection of accounts receivable.

One nonratio financial tool should be mentioned in connection with accounts receivable analysis—the *aging schedule*, which breaks down accounts receivable according to how long they have been outstanding. The aging schedule for Walker-Wilson is given below.

Age of Account (Days)	Percent of Total Value of Accounts Receivable
0–20	50
21–30	20
31–45	15
46–60	3
over 60	12
Total	100

The 24-day collection period looked bad by comparison with the 20-day terms, and the aging schedule shows that the firm is having especially serious collection problems with some of its accounts. Fifty percent are overdue, many for over a month. Others pay quite promptly, bringing the average down to only 24 days, but the aging schedule shows this average to be somewhat misleading.

Fixed Asset Turnover   The ratio of sales to fixed assets measures the turnover of plant and equipment.

$$\text{Fixed assets turnover} = \frac{\text{sales}}{\text{net fixed assets}} = \frac{\$3,000,000}{\$1,300,000} = 2.3 \text{ times.}$$

$$\text{Industry average} = 5.0 \text{ times.}$$

Walker-Wilson's turnover of 2.3 times compares poorly with the industry average of 5 times, indicating that the firm is not using its fixed assets to as high a percentage of capacity as are the other firms in the industry. Thompson should bear this fact in mind when his production people request funds for new capital investments.

Total Assets Turnover   The final activity ratio measures the turnover of all the firm's assets—it is calculated by dividing sales by total assets.

$$\text{Total assets turnover} = \frac{\text{sales}}{\text{total assets}} = \frac{\$3,000,000}{\$2,000,000} = 1.5 \text{ times.}$$

$$\text{Industry average} = 2.0 \text{ times.}$$

Walker-Wilson's turnover of total assets is well below the industry average. The company is simply not generating a sufficient volume of business for the size of its asset investment. Sales should be increased, or some assets should be disposed of, or both steps should be taken.

Profitability Ratios

Profitability is the net result of a large number of policies and decisions. The ratios examined thus far reveal some interesting things about the way the firm is operating, but the profitability ratios give final answers about how effectively the firm is being managed.

Profit Margin on Sales   The profit margin on sales, computed by dividing net income after taxes by sales, gives the profit per dollar of sales.

$$\text{Profit margin} = \frac{\text{net profit after taxes}}{\text{sales}} = \frac{\$120,000}{\$3,000,000} = 4\%.$$

$$\text{Industry average} = 5\%.$$

Walker-Wilson's profit margin is somewhat below the industry average of 5 percent, indicating that the firm's sales prices are relatively low or that its costs are relatively high, or both.

Return on Total Assets   The ratio of net profit to total assets measures the return on total investment in the firm, or the ROI, as it is frequently called.[7]

$$\text{Return on total assets} = \frac{\text{net profit after taxes}}{\text{total assets}} = \frac{\$120,000}{\$2,000,000} = 6\%.$$

$$\text{Industry average} = 10\%.$$

Walker-Wilson's 6 percent return is well below the 10 percent average for the industry. This low rate results from the low profit margin on sales and from the low turnover of total assets.

Return on Net Worth   The ratio of net profit after taxes to net worth measures the rate of return on the stockholders' investment.

$$\text{Return on net worth} = \frac{\text{net profit after taxes}}{\text{net worth}} = \frac{\$120,000}{\$1,000,000} = 12\%.$$

$$\text{Industry average} = 15\%.$$

Walker-Wilson's 12 percent return is below the 15 percent industry average but not as far below as the return on total assets. In a later section of this chapter, where the du Pont method of analysis is applied to the Walker-Wilson case, we will see why this is so.

---

[7] In calculating the return on total assets, it is sometimes desirable to add interest to net profits after taxes to form the numerator of the ratio. The theory here is that since assets are financed by both stockholders and creditors, the ratio should measure the productivity of assets in providing returns to both classes of investors. We have not done so at this point because the published averages we use for comparative purposes exclude interest. Later in this book, however, when we deal with public utilities, we do add back interest. This addition has a material bearing on the value of the ratio for utilities (which have large amounts of fixed assets financed by debt), and the revised ratio is the one normally used for them.

Summary of the Ratios

The individual ratios, which are summarized in Table 3–4, give Thompson a reasonably good idea of Walker-Wilson's main strengths and weaknesses. First, the company's liquidity position is reasonably good—its current and quick ratios appear to be satisfactory by comparison to the industry averages. Second, the leverage ratios suggest that the company is rather heavily indebted. With a debt ratio substantially higher than the industry average, and with coverage ratios well below the industry averages, it is doubtful that Walker-Wilson could do much additional debt financing except on relatively unfavorable terms. Even if Thompson could borrow more, to do so would be subjecting the company to the danger of default and bankruptcy in the event of a business downturn.

Turning to the activity ratios, the inventory turnover and average collection period both indicate that the company's current assets are pretty well in balance, but the low fixed asset turnover suggests that there has been too heavy an investment in fixed assets. This low fixed asset turnover means, in effect, that the company probably could have operated with a smaller investment in fixed assets. Had the excessive fixed asset investment not been made, the company could have avoided some of its debt financing and would now have lower interest payments. This, in turn, would have led to improved leverage and coverage ratios.

The profit margin on sales is low, indicating that costs are too high or that prices are too low, or both. In this particular case, the sales prices are in line with other firms; high costs are, in fact, the cause of the low margin. Further, the high costs can be traced to (1) high depreciation charges and (2) high interest expenses. Both these costs are, in turn, attributable to the excessive investment in fixed assets.

Returns on both total investment and net worth are also below the industry averages. These relatively poor results are directly attributable to the low profit margin on sales, which lowers the numerators of the ratios, and to the excessive investment, which raises the denominators.

Trend Analysis

While the preceding ratio analysis gives a reasonably good picture of Walker-Wilson's operation, it is incomplete in one important respect—it ignores the time dimension. The ratios are snapshots of the picture at one point in time, but there may be trends in motion that are in the process of rapidly eroding a relatively good present position. Conversely, an analysis of the ratios over the past few years may suggest that a relatively weak position is being improved at a rapid rate.

TABLE 3–4 Summary of Financial Ratio Analysis

Ratio	Formula for Calculation	Calculation	Industry Average	Evaluation
Liquidity				
Current	$\dfrac{\text{current assets}}{\text{current liabilities}}$	$\dfrac{\$\ 700,000}{\$\ 300,000} = 2.3 \text{ times}$	2.5 times	Satisfactory
Quick, or acid test	$\dfrac{\text{current assets} - \text{inventory}}{\text{current liabilities}}$	$\dfrac{\$\ 400,000}{\$\ 300,000} = 1.3 \text{ times}$	1.0 times	Good
Leverage				
Debt to total assets	$\dfrac{\text{total debt}}{\text{total assets}}$	$\dfrac{\$1,000,000}{\$2,000,000} = 50 \text{ percent}$	33 percent	Poor
Times interest earned	$\dfrac{\text{profit before taxes plus interest charges}}{\text{interest charges}}$	$\dfrac{\$\ 245,000}{\$\ 45,000} = 5.4 \text{ times}$	8.0 times	Fair
Fixed charge coverage	$\dfrac{\text{income available for meeting fixed charges}}{\text{fixed charges}}$	$\dfrac{\$\ 273,000}{\$\ 73,000} = 3.7 \text{ times}$	5.5 times	Poor
Activity				
Inventory turnover	$\dfrac{\text{sales}}{\text{inventory}}$	$\dfrac{\$3,000,000}{\$\ 300,000} = 10 \text{ times}$	9 times	Satisfactory
Average collection period	$\dfrac{\text{receivables}}{\text{sales per day}}$	$\dfrac{\$\ 200,000}{\$\ 8,333} = 24 \text{ days}$	20 days	Satisfactory
Fixed assets turnover	$\dfrac{\text{sales}}{\text{fixed assets}}$	$\dfrac{\$3,000,000}{\$1,300,000} = 2.3 \text{ times}$	5.0 times	Poor
Total assets turnover	$\dfrac{\text{sales}}{\text{total assets}}$	$\dfrac{\$3,000,000}{\$2,000,000} = 1.5 \text{ times}$	2 times	Poor
Profitability				
Profit margin on sales	$\dfrac{\text{net profit after taxes}}{\text{sales}}$	$\dfrac{\$\ 120,000}{\$3,000,000} = 4 \text{ percent}$	5 percent	Poor
Return on total assets	$\dfrac{\text{net profit after taxes}}{\text{total assets}}$	$\dfrac{\$\ 120,000}{\$2,000,000} = 6.0 \text{ percent}$	10 percent	Poor
Return on net worth	$\dfrac{\text{net profit after taxes}}{\text{net worth}}$	$\dfrac{\$\ 120,000}{\$1,000,000} = 12.0 \text{ percent}$	15 percent	Poor

FIGURE 3–1   Illustration of Trend Analysis

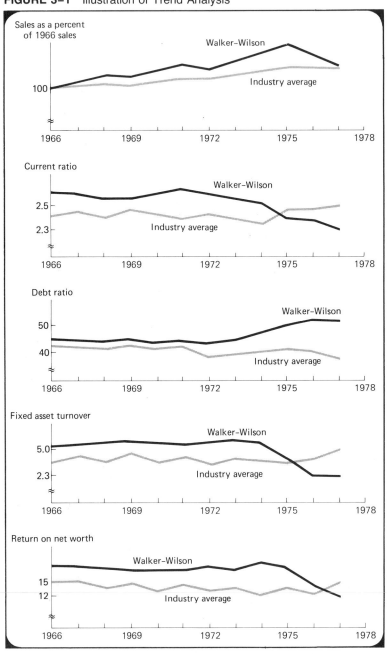

The method of trend analysis is illustrated in Figure 3–1, which shows graphs of Walker-Wilson's sales, current ratio, debt ratio, fixed assets turnover, and return on net worth. The figures are compared with industry averages; industry sales have been rising steadily over the entire period, and the industry average ratios have been relatively stable throughout. Thus, any trends in the company's ratios are due to its own internal conditions, not to national influences affecting all firms. In addition, Walker-Wilson's deterioration since the death of the two principal officers is quite apparent. Prior to 1975, Walker-Wilson was growing more rapidly than the average firm in the industry; during the following two years, however, sales actually declined.

Walker-Wilson's liquidity position as measured by its current ratio has also gone downhill in the past two years. Although the ratio is only slightly below the industry average at the present time, the trend suggests that a real liquidity crisis may develop during the next year or two unless corrective action is taken immediately.

The debt ratio trend line shows that Walker-Wilson followed industry practices closely until 1974, when the ratio jumped to a full 10 percentage points above the industry average. Similarly, the fixed assets turnover declined during 1974, even though sales were still rising. The records reveal that the company borrowed heavily during 1974 to finance a major expansion of plant and equipment. Walker and Wilson had intended to use this additional capacity to generate a still higher volume of sales and to retire the debt out of expected high profits. Their untimely death, however, led to a decrease in sales rather than an increase, and the expected high profits that were to be used to retire the debt did not materialize. The analysis suggests that the bankers were correct when they advised Mrs. Walker and Mrs. Wilson of the need for a change in management.

DU PONT SYSTEM OF FINANCIAL ANALYSIS

The du Pont system of financial analysis has achieved wide recognition in American industry, and properly so. It brings together the activity ratios and profit margin on sales and shows how these ratios interact to determine the profitability of assets. The nature of the system, modified somewhat, is set forth in Figure 3–2.

The right side of the figure develops the turnover ratio. That section shows how current assets (cash, marketable securities, accounts receivable, and inventories), when added to fixed assets, gives total investment. Total investment divided into sales gives the turnover of investment.

The left side of the figure develops the profit margin on sales. The individual expense items, plus income taxes, are subtracted from sales to produce net profits after taxes. Net profits divided by sales gives the profit

FIGURE 3-2 Modified du Pont System of Financial Control Applied to Walker-Wilson

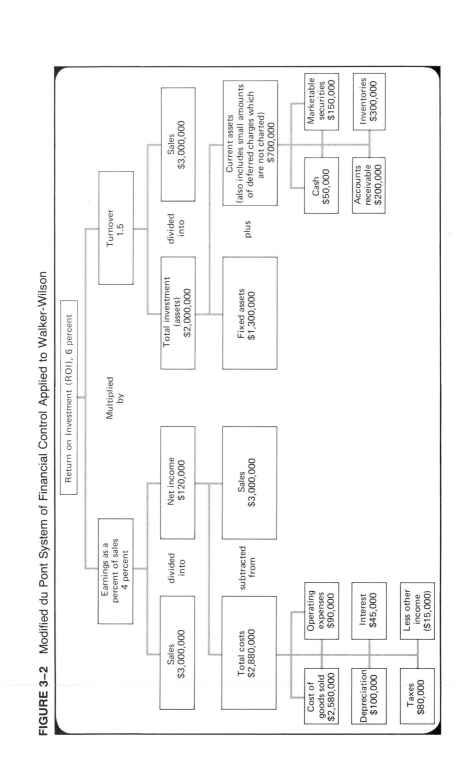

margin on sales. When the asset turnover ratio on the right side of Figure 3–2 is multiplied by the profit margin on sales developed on the left side of the figure, the product is the return on total investment (ROI) in the firm. This can be seen from the following formula:

$$\frac{\text{sales}}{\text{investment}} \times \frac{\text{profit}}{\text{sales}} = \text{ROI.}$$

Walker-Wilson's turnover was seen to be 1.5 times, as compared to an industry average of 2 times; its margin on sales was 4 percent, as compared to 5 percent for the industry. Multiplied together, turnover and profit margin produced a return on assets equal to 6 percent, a rate well below the 10 percent industry average. If Thompson is to bring Walker-Wilson back to the level of the rest of the industry, he should strive to boost both his profit margin and his total asset turnover. Tracing back through the du Pont system should help him in this task.

Extending the du Pont System to Include Leverage

Although Walker-Wilson's return on total assets is well below the 10 percent industry average, the firm's 12 percent return on net worth is only slightly below the 15 percent industry average. How can the return on net worth end up so close to the industry average when the return on total assets is so far below the average? The answer is that Walker-Wilson uses more debt than the average firm in the industry.

Only half of Walker-Wilson's assets is financed with net worth; the other half is financed with debt. This means that the entire 6 percent return on assets (which is computed after interest charges on debt) goes to the common stockholders, so their return is boosted substantially. The precise formula for measuring the effect of financial leverage on stockholder returns is shown below.

$$\text{Rate of return on net worth} = \frac{\text{return on assets (ROI)}}{\text{percent of assets financed by net worth}}$$

$$= \frac{\text{return on assets (ROI)}}{1.0 - \text{debt ratio}}.$$

Calculation for Walker-Wilson:

$$\text{Return on net worth} = \frac{6\%}{1.0 - 0.50} = \frac{6\%}{0.5} = 12\%.$$

Calculation for the industry average:

$$\text{Return on net worth} = \frac{10\%}{1.0 - 0.33} = \frac{10\%}{0.67} = 15\%.$$

This formula is useful for showing how financial leverage can be used to increase the rate of return on net worth.[8] But increasing returns on net worth by using more and more leverage causes the leverage ratios to rise higher and higher above the industry norms. Creditors resist this tendency, so there are limitations to the practice. Moreover, greater leverage increases the risk of bankruptcy and thus endangers the firm's stockholders. Since widows Walker and Wilson are entirely dependent on income from the firm for their support, they would be in a particularly bad position if the firm goes into default. Consequently, Thompson would be ill-advised to attempt to use leverage to boost the return on net worth much further.

RATES OF RETURN IN DIFFERENT INDUSTRIES

Would it be better to have a 5 percent margin on sales and a total asset turnover of 2 times, or a 2 percent sales margin and a turnover of 5 times? It makes no difference—in either case the firm has a 10 percent return on investment. Actually, most firms are not free to make the kind of choice posed in the above question. Depending on the nature of its industry, the firm *must* operate with more or fewer assets, and it will experience a turnover that depends on the characteristics of its particular line of business. In the case of a dealer in fresh fruits and vegetables, fish, or other perishable items, the turnover should be high—every day or two would be most desirable. In contrast, some lines of business require very heavy fixed investment or long production periods. A hydroelectric utility company, with its heavy investment in dams and transmission lines, requires heavy fixed investment; a shipbuilder or an aircraft producer needs a long production period. Such companies necessarily have a low asset turnover rate but a correspondingly higher profit margin on sales.

If a grocery chain has a high turnover, and a chemical producer, with its heavy investment in fixed assets, a low turnover, would you expect to find differences in their profit margins on sales? In general, you would—the chemical producer should have a considerably higher profit margin to offset its lower turnover. Otherwise, the grocery business would be much more profitable than the chemical, investment would flow into the grocery industry, and profits in this industry would be eroded to the point where the rate of return was about equal to that in the chemical industry.

We know, however, that leverage must be taken into account when considering the rate of return on net worth. If the firms in one industry have a somewhat lower return on total assets but use slightly more financial leverage

---

[8] There are limitations on this statement—specifically, the return on net worth increases with leverage only if the return on assets exceeds the rate of interest on debt, after considering the tax deductibility of interest payments. This whole concept is explored in detail in Chapter 19, which is devoted entirely to financial leverage.

than do those in another industry, both sets of firms may end up with approximately the same rate of return on net worth.[9]

These points, which are all necessary for a complete understanding of ratio analysis, are illustrated in Table 3–5. There we see how turnover and profit margins interact with each other to produce varying returns on assets, and also how financial leverage affects the returns on net worth. Hercules, Inc., Safeway Stores, and the average of all manufacturing firms are compared. Hercules, with its very heavy fixed asset investment, is seen to have a relatively low turnover; Safeway, a typical chain food store, has a very high sales-to-assets ratio. Hercules, however, ends up with about the same rate of return on assets because its high profit margin on sales compensates for its low turnover. Both Safeway and Hercules use financial leverage to increase their return on net worth.

TABLE 3–5 Turnover, Profit Margins, and Returns on Net Worth

	Sales to Total × Assets (Times)	Profit to Sales (Percent)	= Profit to Total Assets (Percent)	Debt to Total Assets (Percent)	Profit to Net Worth[a] (Percent)
All manufacturing firms	1.60	5.6	8.9	41	15.1
Hercules Incorporated (chemical producer)	1.15	8.5	9.8	32	14.4
Safeway Stores (food retailer)	5.23	1.8	9.4	40	15.7

[a] The figures in this column may be found as

$$\text{Profit to net worth} = \frac{\text{profit to total assets}}{1 - \text{debt to total assets}}.$$

Reprinted by permission of Safeway Stores, Incorporated, and Hercules Incorporated.

SOURCES OF COMPARATIVE RATIOS

In our analysis of the Walker-Wilson Company, industry average ratios were frequently used. Where may such averages be obtained? Some important sources are listed below.

Dun & Bradstreet

Probably the most widely known and used of the industry average ratios are those compiled by Dun & Bradstreet, Inc. D&B provides fourteen ratios

[9] The factors that make it possible for firms to use more leverage are taken up in Chapters 15 and 19. It may be stated now, however, that the primary factor favoring leverage is sales stability.

calculated for a large number of industries. Sample ratios and explanations are shown in Table 3–6. The complete data give the fourteen ratios, with the interquartile ranges,[10] for 125 lines of business activity based on their financial statements. The 125 types of business activity consist of 71 manufacturing and construction categories, 30 categories of wholesalers, and 24 categories of retailers.

Robert Morris Associates

Another group of useful ratios can be found in the annual *Statement Studies* compiled and published by the Robert Morris Associates, which is the national association of bank loan officers. These are representative averages based on financial statements received by banks in connection with loans made. Eleven ratios are computed for 125 lines of business.

Quarterly Financial Report for Manufacturing Corporations

The Federal Trade Commission (FTC) and the Securities and Exchange Commission (SEC) jointly publish quarterly data on manufacturing companies. Both balance sheet and income statement data are developed from a systematic sample of corporations. The reports are published perhaps six months after the financial data have been made available by the companies. They include an analysis by industry groups and by asset size and financial statements in ratio form (or common-size analysis) as well. The FTC-SEC reports are a rich source of information and are frequently used for comparative purposes.

Individual Firms

Credit departments of individual firms compile financial ratios and averages on their (1) customers in order to judge their ability to meet obligations and (2) suppliers in order to evaluate their financial ability to fulfill contracts. The First National Bank of Chicago, for instance, compiles semiannual reports on the financial data for finance companies. The National Cash Register Company gathers data for a large number of business lines.

---

[10] The median and the quartile ratios can be illustrated by an example. The median ratio of current assets to current debt of manufacturers of airplane parts and accessories, as shown in Table 3–6, is 1.81. To obtain this figure, the ratios of current assets to current debt for each of the 59 concerns were arranged in a graduated series, with the largest ratio at the top and the smallest at the bottom. The median ratio of 1.81 is the ratio halfway between the top and the bottom. The ratio of 2.40, representing the upper quartile, is one quarter of the way down the series from the top (or halfway between the top and the median). The ratio 1.42, representing the lower quartile, is one quarter of the way up from the bottom (or halfway between the median and the bottom).

TABLE 3-6 Dun & Bradstreet Ratios for Selected Industries

Line of Business (and Number of Concerns Reporting)	Current Assets to Current Debt (Times)	Net Profits on Net Sales (Per-cent)	Net Profits on Tangible Net Worth (Per-cent)	Net Profits on Net Working Capital (Per-cent)	Net Sales to Tangible Net Worth (Times)	Net Sales to Net Working Capital (Times)	Collection Period (Days)	Net Sales to Inventory (Times)	Fixed Assets to Tangible Net Worth (Per-cent)	Current Debt to Tangible Net Worth (Per-cent)	Total Debt to Tangible Net Worth (Per-cent)	Inventory to Net Working Capital (Per-cent)	Current Debt to Inventory (Per-cent)	Funded Debts to Net Working Capital (Per-cent)
3522[a] Agricultural Implements and Machinery (74)	3.78	7.15	21.44	36.82	5.27	8.13	25	6.1	21.5	22.5	47.5	71.3	44.6	17.8
	2.27	4.12	14.59	20.68	3.21	4.60	39	3.9	33.5	49.3	80.0	104.9	72.0	37.0
	1.52	3.23	8.30	14.95	2.34	2.98	52	3.1	63.6	115.3	149.6	161.4	98.4	50.9
3722-23-29 Airplane Parts & Accessories (59)	2.40	8.12	27.78	44.96	4.46	8.27	34	8.6	27.9	43.2	58.0	73.8	87.9	14.1
	1.81	5.25	18.11	32.21	3.43	5.29	46	5.9	48.4	61.5	103.5	103.4	100.0	47.5
	1.42	3.10	11.90	17.76	2.72	4.20	61	3.9	75.5	112.5	179.1	154.7	141.9	65.8
3714 Automobile Parts and Accessories (84)	3.77	6.75	18.89	32.11	3.89	6.54	35	8.0	25.7	23.5	47.3	60.5	56.5	14.6
	2.58	4.59	14.60	20.32	2.99	4.63	42	5.3	39.6	38.0	77.8	86.2	79.7	41.6
	2.03	3.22	8.65	14.09	2.19	3.23	51	4.2	55.5	63.4	116.9	100.5	113.7	59.9
2515 Bedsprings and Mattresses (49)	3.60	2.69	11.53	15.03	5.85	8.52	30	11.7	15.6	22.9	48.7	54.8	55.6	3.6
	2.33	2.06	6.46	10.95	3.48	5.79	42	8.2	28.1	45.9	72.8	76.8	93.6	26.6
	1.87	0.80	2.71	5.11	2.61	4.34	55	5.5	49.3	76.3	133.9	114.5	154.8	52.1
2082 Breweries (27)	3.34	6.48	15.15	63.72	3.23	11.34	8	21.6	53.7	13.1	20.4	33.3	108.2	9.6
	2.59	4.75	10.38	34.27	2.49	8.51	16	16.4	59.4	21.3	38.6	46.5	137.8	118.6
	1.88	1.28	2.55	8.23	1.72	5.13	24	11.4	81.9	34.1	97.5	87.7	194.9	176.2
287 Chemicals, Agricultural (33)	2.98	3.87	11.78	44.91	5.11	13.41	32	10.4	29.5	33.6	58.4	62.1	89.5	24.1
	1.73	2.02	7.58	17.73	3.46	6.72	55	6.6	53.6	73.1	111.0	106.6	122.9	47.9
	1.33	0.95	1.56	2.80	1.98	4.15	87	5.0	71.2	123.0	165.9	160.5	237.3	75.2
281 Chemicals, Industrial (60)	2.77	8.15	16.07	50.01	3.09	7.05	39	10.1	42.6	20.1	31.8	65.2	76.1	44.0
	2.28	5.53	12.45	30.32	1.95	5.03	50	6.9	68.8	30.0	58.9	84.7	98.5	94.2
	1.51	3.93	9.03	17.95	1.52	3.39	59	5.5	88.9	50.0	106.0	100.1	128.7	152.4
1511 Contractors, Building Construction (188)	2.06	3.14	19.04	33.04	12.51	20.41	b	b	9.5	61.7	119.4	b	b	11.9
	1.49	1.38	12.39	16.38	8.09	11.52	b	b	22.2	138.0	188.4	b	b	27.4
	1.27	0.74	6.20	9.14	4.32	5.79	b	b	42.1	239.8	318.0	b	b	83.4

[a] Standard Industrial Classification (SIC) categories.

[b] Building trades contractors have no inventories in the credit sense of the term. As a general rule, they have no customary selling terms, such contracts being a special job for which individual terms are arranged.

Source: Key Business Ratios 1966, 1972, and 1976 by the Business Economics Division of Dun & Bradstreet, Inc. Reprinted by permission of Dun & Bradstreet.

Trade Associations and Public Accountants

Financial ratios for many industries are compiled by trade associations and constitute an important source to be checked by a financial manager seeking comparative data. These averages are usually the best obtainable. In addition to balance sheet data, they provide detailed information on operating expenses, which makes possible an informed analysis of the efficiency of the firms.

USE OF FINANCIAL RATIOS IN CREDIT ANALYSIS

In this chapter we have discussed a rather long list of ratios and have learned what each ratio is designed to measure. Sometimes it will be unnecessary to go beyond a few calculations to determine that a firm is in very good or very bad condition, but often the analysis is equivalent to a detective-story investigation—what one ratio will not indicate, another may. Also, a relation vaguely suggested by one ratio may be corroborated by another. For these reasons, it is often useful to calculate a number of different ratios.

In numerous situations, however, a few ratios will tell the story. For example, a credit manager who has a great many invoices flowing across his desk each day may limit himself to three ratios as evidence of whether the prospective buyer of his goods will pay promptly: (1) He may use either the current or the quick ratio to determine how burdened the prospective buyer is with current liabilities; (2) he may use the debt to total assets ratio to determine how much of the prospective buyer's own funds are invested in the business; (3) he may use any one of the profitability ratios to determine whether or not the firm has favorable prospects. If the profit margin is high enough, it may justify the risk of dealing with a slow-paying customer—profitable companies are likely to grow and thus to become better customers in the future. However, if the profit margin is low in relation to other firms in the industry, if the current ratio is low, and if the debt ratio is high, a credit manager probably will not approve a sale involving an extension of credit.[11]

Of necessity, the credit manager is more than a calculator and a reader of financial ratios. Qualitative factors may override quantitative analysis. For instance, oil companies, in selling to truckers, often find that the financial ratios are poor, and if they based their decisions solely on financial ratios, they would not make sales. Or, to take another example, profits may have been low for a period, but if the customer understands why profits have been

---

[11] Statistical techniques have been developed to improve the use of ratios in credit analysis. One such development is the discriminant analysis model reported by Edward I. Altman ["Financial Ratios, Discriminant Analysis, and the Prediction of Corporate Bankruptcy," *Journal of Finance* 23 (September 1968)]. In his model, Altman combines a number of liquidity, leverage, activity, and profitability ratios to form an index of a firm's probability of going bankrupt. His model has predicted bankruptcy quite well one or two years in the future.

low and can remove the cause of the difficulty, a credit man may be willing to approve a sale to him. The credit man's decision is also influenced by his own firm's profit margin. If the selling firm is making a large profit on sales, it is in a better position to take credit risks than if its own margin is low. Ultimately, the credit manager must judge a customer with regard to his character and management ability, and intelligent credit decisions must be based on careful consideration of conditions in the selling firm as well as in the buying firm.

USE OF FINANCIAL RATIOS IN SECURITY ANALYSIS

We have emphasized the use of financial analysis by the financial manager and by outside credit analysts. However, this type of analysis is also useful in security analysis, that is, in the analysis of the investment merits of stocks and bonds. When the emphasis is on security analysis, the principal focus is on judging the long-run profit potential of the firm. Profitability is dependent in large part on the efficiency with which the firm is run; because financial analysis provides insights into this factor, it is useful to the security analyst.

SOME LIMITATIONS OF RATIO ANALYSIS

Although ratios are exceptionally useful tools, they do have limitations and must be used with caution. Ratios are constructed from accounting data, and accounting data are subject to different interpretations and even to manipulation. For example, two firms may use different depreciation methods or inventory valuation methods; depending on the procedures followed, reported profits can be raised or lowered. Similar differences can be encountered in the treatment of research and development expenditures, pension plan costs, mergers, product warranties, and bad-debt reserves. Further, if firms use different fiscal years, and if seasonal factors are important, this can influence the comparative ratios. Thus, if the ratios of two firms are to be compared, it is important to analyze the basic accounting data upon which the ratios were based and to reconcile any major differences.

A financial manager must also be cautious when judging whether a particular ratio is "good" or "bad" and in forming a composite judgment about a firm on the basis of a set of ratios. For example, a high inventory turnover ratio could indicate efficient inventory management, but it could also indicate a serious shortage of inventories and suggest the likelihood of stock-outs. Further, there is nothing sacred about the industry average figures—after all, any management worth its salt will try to be better than average.

Ratios, then, are extremely useful tools. But as with other analytical methods, they must be used with judgment and caution, not in an unthinking, mechanical manner.

SUMMARY

Ratio analysis, which relates balance sheet and income statement items to one another, permits the charting of a firm's history and the evaluation of its present position. Such analysis also allows the financial manager to anticipate reactions of investors and creditors and thus gives him a good insight into how his attempts to acquire funds are likely to be received.

Basic Types of Ratios   Ratios are classified into four basic types: (1) liquidity, (2) leverage, (3) activity, and (4) profitability. Data from the Walker-Wilson Manufacturing Company were used to compute each type of ratio and to show how a financial analysis is made in practice. An almost unlimited number of ratios may be calculated, but in practice a limited number of each type is sufficient. We have discussed in this chapter what are probably the twelve most common ratios.

Use of Ratios   A ratio is not a meaningful number in and of itself—it must be compared with something before it becomes useful. The two basic kinds of comparative analysis are (1) trend analysis, which involves computing the ratios of a particular firm for several years and comparing the ratios over time to see if the firm is improving or deteriorating, and (2) comparisons with other firms in the same industry. These two comparisons are often combined in the graphic analysis illustrated in Figure 3–1.

du Pont System   The du Pont system shows how the return on investment is dependent upon asset turnover and the profit margin. The system is generally expressed in the form of the following equation:

$$\frac{sales}{investment} \times \frac{profit}{sales} = ROI.$$

The first term, investment turnover, times the profit margin equals the rate of return on investment. The kinds of actions we discussed in this chapter can be used to effect needed changes in turnover and the profit margin and thus improve the return on investment.

The du Pont system can be extended to encompass financial leverage and to examine the manner in which turnover, sales margins, and leverage all combine to determine the rate of return on net worth. The following equation is used to show this relationship:

$$\text{Rate of return on net worth} = \frac{\text{return on assets (ROI)}}{1.0 - \text{debt ratio}}.$$

Rates of Return in Different Industries   The extended du Pont system shows why firms in different industries—even though they have widely different turnovers, profit margins, and debt ratios—may end up with very similar rates of return on net worth. In general, firms dealing with relatively perishable commodities are expected to have high turnovers but low profit margins; firms whose production processes require heavy investments in fixed assets are expected to have low turnover ratios but high profit margins.

QUESTIONS

3-1. "A uniform system of accounts, including identical forms for balance sheets and income statements, would be a most reasonable requirement for the SEC to impose on all publicly owned firms." Discuss.

3-2. We have divided financial ratios into four groups: liquidity, leverage, activity, and profitability. We could also consider financial analysis as being conducted by four groups of analysts: management, equity investors, long-term creditors, and short-term creditors.

    a. Explain the nature of each type of ratio.

    b. Explain the emphasis of each type of analyst.

3-3. Why can norms with relatively well-defined limits be stated in advance for some financial ratios but not for others?

3-4. How does trend analysis supplement the basic financial ratio calculations and their interpretation?

3-5. Why would you expect the inventory turnover figure to be more important to a grocery store than to a shoe repair store?

3-6. How can a firm have a high current ratio and still be unable to pay its bills?

3-7. "The higher the rate of return on investment (ROI), the better the firm's management." Is this statement true for all firms? Explain. If you disagree with the statement, give examples of instances in which it might not be true.

3-8. What factors would you, as a financial manager, want to examine if a firm's rate of return (a) on assets or (b) on net worth is too low?

3-9. Profit margins and turnover rates vary from industry to industry. What industry characteristics account for these variations? Give some contrasting examples to illustrate your answer.

3-10. Which relation would you, as a financial manager, prefer: (a) a profit margin of 10 percent and a capital turnover of 2, or (b) a profit margin of 20 percent and a capital turnover of 1? Can you think of any firm with a relation similar to b?

PROBLEMS

3-1. The following data were taken from the financial statements of the Coit Corporation for the calendar year 1977. The norms given below are industry averages for the furniture industry.

    a. Fill in the ratios for Coit.

    b. Indicate by comparison with the industry norms the possible errors in management policies reflected in these financial statements.

Coit Corporation
Income statement
For year ended December 31, 1977

Sales		$690,000
Cost of goods sold		
Materials	$260,000	
Labor	165,000	
Heat, light, and power	25,000	
Indirect labor	40,000	
Depreciation	15,000	505,000
Gross profit		$185,000
Selling expenses	$ 70,000	
General and administrative expenses	80,000	150,000
Operating profit		$ 35,000
Less: interest expense		6,050
Net profit before taxes		$ 28,950
Less: federal income taxes (assumed		
50% rate)		14,475
Net profit		$14,475

	Ratios	
Ratio	Coit	Norm
current assets / current liabilities	_____	2.5 times
debt / total assets	_____	35%
times interest earned	_____	7 times
sales / inventories	_____	9.9 times
average collection period	_____	33 days
sales / total assets	_____	2.2 times
net profit / sales	_____	3.2%
net profit / total assets	_____	7.0%
net profit / net worth	_____	10.7%

Coit Corporation
Balance sheet
December 31, 1977

Cash	$ 55,000	Accounts payable	$ 40,000
Receivables	70,000	Notes payable (5%)	55,000
Inventory	200,000	Other current liabilities	25,000
Total current assets	$325,000	Total current liabilities	$120,000
Net fixed assets	150,000	Long-term debt (6%)	55,000
		Net worth	300,000
Total assets	$475,000	Total claims on assets	$475,000

3-2. General Steel Company has $800,000 in current assets and $200,000 in current liabilities. How much can its short-term debt (notes payable) increase without violating a current ratio of 3 to 1? The funds from the additional notes payable will be used to increase inventory.

3-3. Griffin Supply Company, a small manufacturer of surgical supplies and equipment, has been plagued with relatively low profitability in recent years. As a result, the board of directors replaced the president of the firm. The new president, Pat Roffman, asks you to make an analysis of the firm's financial position using the du Pont system. The most recent financial statements are reproduced below.

a. Calculate some ratios which you feel would be useful in this case.

b. Construct a du Pont chart of analysis for Griffin similar to the one in Figure 3–2.

c. Do the balance sheet accounts or the income statement figures seem to be primarily responsible for the low profits?

d. Which specific accounts seem to be most out of line in relation to other firms in the industry?

	Industry Average Ratios
Current ratio	2/1
Quick ratio	1/1
Debt to total assets	30%
Times interest earned	7 times
Fixed charge coverage	5 times
Inventory turnover	10 times
Average collection period	15 days
Fixed assets turnover	6 times
Total assets turnover	3 times
Net profit on sales	3%
Return on total assets	9%
Return on net worth	12.8%

Griffin Supply Company
Balance sheet
December 31, 1977
(thousands of dollars)

Cash	$ 450	Accounts payable	$ 450
Marketable securities	330	Notes payable (6%)	450
Net receivables	660	Other current liabilities	210
Inventories	1,590	Total current liabilities	$1,110
Total current assets	$3,030	Long-term debt (5%)	240
Gross fixed assets	$2,250	Total liabilities	$1,350
Less: depreciation	780	Common stock	$1,140
Net fixed assets	1,470	Retained earnings	2,010
		Total stockholders' equity	3,150
Total assets	$4,500	Total claims on assets	$4,500

Griffin Supply Company
Income statement
For year ended December 31, 1977
(thousands of dollars)

Net sales	$7,950	
Cost of goods sold	6,600	
Gross profit		$1,350
Operating expenses	$ 735	
Depreciation expense	120	
Interest expense	45	
Total expenses		900
Net income before tax		$ 450
Taxes 50%		225
Net income		$ 225

3-4. Indicate the effects of the transactions listed below on each of the following: total current assets, working capital, current ratio, and net profit. Use + to indicate an increase, − to indicate a decrease, and 0 to indicate no effect. State necessary assumptions and assume an initial current ratio of more than 1 to 1.

	Total Current Assets	Net Working Capital*	Current Ratio	Net Profit
1. Cash is acquired through issuance of additional common stock.	___	___	___	___
2. Merchandise is sold for cash.	___	___	___	___
3. Federal income tax due for the previous year is paid.	___	___	___	___
4. A fixed asset is sold for less than book value.	___	___	___	___

	Total Current Assets	Net Working Capital*	Current Ratio	Net Profit
5. A fixed asset is sold for more than book value.	___	___	___	___
6. Merchandise is sold on credit.	___	___	___	___
7. Payment is made to trade creditors for previous purchases.	___	___	___	___
8. A cash dividend is declared and paid.	___	___	___	___
9. Cash is obtained through bank loans.	___	___	___	___
10. Short-term notes receivable are sold at a discount.	___	___	___	___
11. Previously issued stock rights are exercised by company stockholders.	___	___	___	___
12. A profitable firm increases its fixed assets depreciation allowance account.	___	___	___	___
13. Marketable securities are sold below cost.	___	___	___	___
14. Uncollectible accounts are written off against the allowance account.	___	___	___	___
15. Advances are made to employees.	___	___	___	___
16. Current operating expenses are paid.	___	___	___	___
17. Short-term promissory notes are issued to trade creditors for prior purchases.	___	___	___	___
18. Ten-year notes are issued to pay off accounts payable.	___	___	___	___
19. A wholly depreciated asset is retired.	___	___	___	___
20. A *cash* sinking fund for the retirement of bonds is created; a reserve for bond sinking fund is also created.	___	___	___	___
21. Bonds are retired by use of the cash sinking fund.	___	___	___	___
22. Accounts receivable are collected.	___	___	___	___
23. A stock dividend is declared and paid.	___	___	___	___
24. Equipment is purchased with short-term notes.	___	___	___	___
25. The allowance for doubtful accounts is increased.	___	___	___	___
26. Merchandise is purchased on credit.	___	___	___	___
27. Controlling interest in another firm is acquired by the issuance of additional common stock.	___	___	___	___
28. Earnings are added to the reserve for bond sinking fund.	___	___	___	___
29. An unconsolidated subsidiary pays the firm a cash dividend from current earnings.	___	___	___	___
30. The estimated taxes payable are increased.	___	___	___	___

*Net working capital is defined as current assets minus current liabilities.

Profit Planning

4

The preceding chapter described how ratios are used in financial analysis and showed how the basic ratios are related to one another. A major area of financial management involves a continuous review of these ratios to insure that no aspects of the firm's existing operations are getting out of control—this key element of the system of financial controls designed to maximize operating efficiency is discussed in Chapter 5. Still other tools are available to aid the financial manager in the planning and control process. Two of these—(1) break-even analysis, which is especially useful when considering plant expansion and new product decisions, and (2) the sources and uses of funds statement, which is an important aid in seeing how the firm has obtained funds and how these funds have been used—are discussed in this chapter.

BREAK-EVEN ANALYSIS

Break-even analysis is an analytical technique for studying the relations among fixed costs, variable costs, and profits. If a firm's costs were all variable, the problem of break-even volume would seldom arise; by having some variable and some fixed costs, the firm must suffer losses until a given volume has been reached.

Break-even analysis is a formal profit-planning approach based on established relations between costs and revenues. It is a device for determining the point at which sales will just cover total costs. If the firm is to avoid losses, its sales must cover all costs—those that vary directly with production and those that do not change as production levels change. Costs that fall into each of those categories are outlined in Table 4–1.

TABLE 4–1   Fixed and Variable Costs

Fixed Costs[a]	Direct or Variable Costs
Depreciation on plant and equipment Rentals Interest charges on debt Salaries of research staff Salaries of executive staff General office expenses	Factory labor Materials Sales commissions

[a]Some of these costs—for example, salaries and office expenses—could be varied to some degree; however, firms are reluctant to reduce these expenditures in response to temporary fluctuations in sales. Such costs are often called *semivariable* costs.

FIGURE 4–1   Break-even Chart

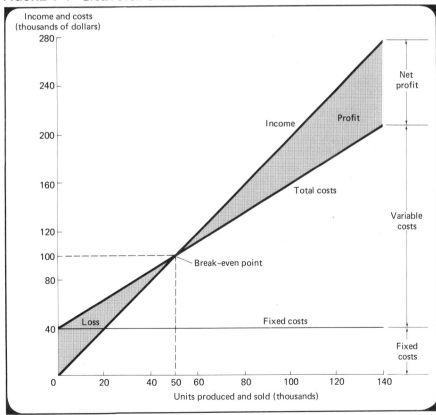

The nature of break-even analysis is depicted in Figure 4–1, the basic break-even chart. The chart is on a unit basis, with volume produced shown on the horizontal axis and costs and income measured on the vertical axis. Fixed costs of $40,000 are represented by a horizontal line; they are the same (fixed) regardless of the number of units produced. Variable costs are assumed to be $1.20 a unit. Total costs rise by $1.20, the amount of the variable costs, for each additional unit produced. Production is assumed to be sold at $2 a unit, so the total income is pictured as a straight line, which must also increase with production. The slope (or the rate of ascent) of the total-income line is steeper than that of the total-cost line. This must be true, because the firm is gaining $2.00 of revenue for every $1.20 paid out for labor and materials, the variable costs.

Up to the break-even point, found at the intersection of the total-income and total-cost lines, the firm suffers losses. After that point, the firm begins

TABLE 4–2 Relations among Units Sold, Total Variable Costs, Fixed Costs, Total Costs, and Total Income

A. Trial-and-error Calculations

Units Sold	Total Variable Costs	Fixed Costs	Total Costs	Sales	Net Profit (Loss)
20,000	$ 24,000	$40,000	$ 64,000	$ 40,000	$(24,000)
40,000	48,000	40,000	88,000	80,000	(8,000)
50,000	60,000	40,000	100,000	100,000	—
60,000	72,000	40,000	112,000	120,000	8,000
80,000	96,000	40,000	136,000	160,000	24,000
100,000	120,000	40,000	160,000	200,000	40,000
120,000	144,000	40,000	184,000	240,000	56,000
140,000	168,000	40,000	208,000	280,000	72,000

B. Algebraic Solution to Break-even Point

1. The break-even quantity is defined as that volume of output at which revenue is just equal to total costs (fixed costs plus variable costs).

2. Let:

   P = sales price per unit
   Q = quantity produced and sold
   F = fixed costs
   V = variable costs per unit.

3. Then:

   $P \cdot Q = F + V \cdot Q$
   $P \cdot Q - V \cdot Q = F$
   $Q(P - V) = F$

   $Q = \dfrac{F}{P - V}$ at break-even Q.

4. Illustration:

   $Q = \dfrac{\$40,000}{\$2.00 - \$1.20}$
   $= 50,000$ units.

to make profits. Figure 4–1 indicates a break-even point at a sales and cost level of $100,000 and a production level of 50,000 units.

More exact calculations of the break-even point can be derived algebraically or by trial and error. In section A of Table 4–2, profit and loss relations are shown for various levels of sales; in section B the algebraic calculations are carried out.

Nonlinear Break-even Analysis

In break-even analysis, linear (straight-line) relationships are generally assumed. Although introducing nonlinear relationships complicates matters slightly, it is easy enough to extend the analysis in this manner. For example, it is reasonable to think that increased sales can be obtained only if sales prices are reduced. Similarly, empirical studies suggest that the average variable cost per unit falls over some range of output and then begins to rise. These assumptions are illustrated in Figure 4–2. There we see a loss region when sales are low, then a profit region (and a maximum profit), and finally another loss region at very high output levels.

FIGURE 4–2 Nonlinear Break-even Chart

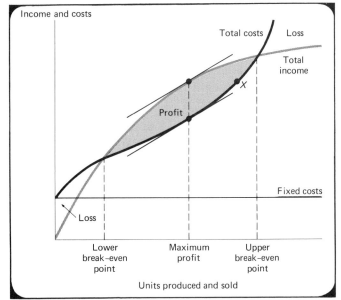

Note: The angle of a line from the origin to a point on the total-income line measures price (that is, total income/units sold = price), and a line from the origin to the total-costs curve measures cost per unit. It can be seen that the angle of the line to the income curve declines as we move toward higher sales, which means that price reductions are necessary to obtain higher unit sales volume. Unit costs (total costs/units produced) declines to point X, the tangency point of a line from the origin to the total-costs curve, then begins to rise.

The slopes of the total-costs and total-income lines measure marginal cost (MC) and marginal revenue (MR), respectively. At the point where the slopes of the two total curves are equal, MR = MC, and profits are at a maximum.

Although nonlinear break-even analysis is intellectually appealing, linear analysis is probably more appropriate for the uses to which it is put. Break-even charts allow focus to be placed on the key elements: sales, fixed costs, and variable costs. Even though linear break-even charts are drawn extending from *zero* output to very high output levels, no one who uses them would ordinarily be interested in or even consider the high and low extremes. In other words, users of break-even charts are really interested only in a "relevant range"; within this range linear functions are for the most part reasonably accurate.

An Example of Break-even Analysis: New Product Decision

Break-even analysis can be used in three separate but related ways:

1. To analyze a program to modernize and automate, where the firm would be operating in a more mechanized, automated manner and substituting fixed costs for variable costs. This topic is covered later in this chapter under the section on operating leverage.
2. To study the effects of a general expansion in the level of operations. This topic is covered in the section entitled "Break-even Point Based on Dollar Sales."
3. In new product decisions: How large must the sales volume on a new product be if the firm is to break even on the proposed project? This topic is illustrated in this section.

The textbook publishing business provides a good example of the effective use of break-even analysis for new product decisions. To illustrate, consider the hypothetical example of the analysis of the production costs of a college textbook as described in Table 4–3. The costs and revenues are graphed in Figure 4–3.

TABLE 4–3 Hypothetical Cost and Revenue Figures for a Textbook

Fixed costs	
Copy editing	$ 3,000
Art work	1,000
Type setting	36,000
Total fixed costs	$40,000

Variable costs per copy	
Printing and binding	$ 1.10
Bookstore discounts	2.00
Salesmen's commissions	.25
Author's royalties	1.00
General and administrative costs	.50
Total variable costs per copy	$ 4.85
Sales price per copy	$10.00

FIGURE 4–3   Break-even Chart for a Hypothetical Textbook

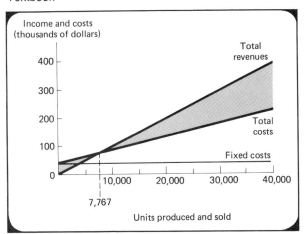

The fixed costs can be estimated quite accurately; the variable costs, most of which are set by contracts, can also be estimated precisely (and they are linear). The sales price is variable, but competition keeps prices within a sufficiently narrow range to make a linear total-revenue curve reasonable. Applying the formula, we find the break-even sales volume to be 7,767 copies.

Publishers know the size of the total market for a given book, the competition, and so forth. With these data as a base, they can estimate the possibility that sales of a given book will reach or exceed the break-even point. If the estimate is that they will not, the publisher may consider cutting production costs by spending less on art work and editing, using a lower grade of paper, negotiating with the author on royalty rates, and so on. In this particular business—and for new product decisions in many others—linear break-even analysis has proved itself to be a useful tool.

Break-even Point Based on Dollar Sales

Calculating break-even points on the basis of dollar sales instead of on units of output is frequently useful. The main advantage of this method, which is illustrated in Table 4–4, is that it enables one to determine a general break-even point for a firm that sells many products at varying prices. Furthermore, the procedure requires a minimum of data. Only three values are needed: sales, fixed costs, and variable costs. Sales and total-cost data are readily available from annual reports of corporations and from investment manuals. Total costs must then be segregated into fixed and variable components. The major fixed charges (rent, interest, depreciation, and general and administrative expenses) may be taken from the income statement. Finally, variable costs are calculated by deducting fixed costs from total costs.

TABLE 4–4 Calculation of Break-even Point Based on Dollar Sales

$$\text{Break-even point} \atop \text{(sales volume)} = \frac{\text{total fixed costs}}{1 - \dfrac{\text{total variable costs}}{\text{total sales volume}}} = \frac{FC}{1 - \dfrac{VC}{S}}$$

Procedure

Take any sales level and use the related data to determine the break-even point. For example, assume that 20,000 units were actually produced and sold, and use the data related to that output in Table 4–2:

$$\text{Break-even point} = \frac{\$40,000}{1 - \dfrac{\$24,000}{\$40,000}} = \frac{\$40,000}{0.4} = \$100,000.$$

Rationale

1. At the break-even point, sales (S_B) are equal to fixed cost (FC) plus variable cost (VC):

$$S_B = FC + VC. \tag{4-1}$$

2. Because both the sales price and the variable cost per unit are assumed to be constant in break-even analysis, the ratio VC/S for *any* level of sales is also constant and may be found from the annual income statement.
3. Since variable cost is a constant percentage of sales, equation 4–1 can be rewritten as follows:

$$S_B = FC + \frac{VC}{S}(S_B)$$

$$S_B\left(1 - \frac{VC}{S}\right) = FC$$

$$S_B = \frac{FC}{1 - \dfrac{VC}{S}} \quad \text{at break-even } S.$$

Operating Leverage

To a physicist, leverage implies the use of a lever to raise a heavy object with a small force. To a layman, if a person has leverage, his smallest word or action can accomplish a lot. In business terminology, a high degree of leverage implies that a relatively small change in sales results in a large change in profits. We can divide leverage into two categories: (1) *financial leverage,* discussed briefly in Chapter 3 (and much more extensively in Chapter 19), and (2) *operating leverage,* the subject of this section.

The significance of the degree of operating leverage is clearly illustrated by Figure 4–4. Three firms, A, B, and C, with differing degrees of leverage, are contrasted. Firm A has a relatively small amount of fixed charges—it does not have much automated equipment, so its depreciation cost is low. Note, however, that A's variable-cost line has a relatively steep slope, denoting that its variable costs per unit are higher than those of the other firms.

FIGURE 4–4 Operating Leverage

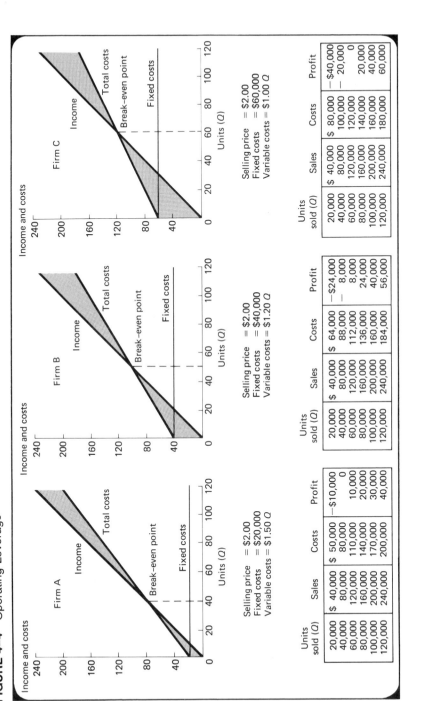

Firm A

Units sold (Q)	Sales	Costs	Profit
20,000	$ 40,000	$ 50,000	–$10,000
40,000	80,000	80,000	0
60,000	120,000	110,000	10,000
80,000	160,000	140,000	20,000
100,000	200,000	170,000	30,000
120,000	240,000	200,000	40,000

Selling price = $2.00
Fixed costs   = $20,000
Variable costs = $1.50 Q

Firm B

Units sold (Q)	Sales	Costs	Profit
20,000	$ 40,000	$ 64,000	–$24,000
40,000	80,000	88,000	— 8,000
60,000	120,000	112,000	8,000
80,000	160,000	136,000	24,000
100,000	200,000	160,000	40,000
120,000	240,000	184,000	56,000

Selling price = $2.00
Fixed costs   = $40,000
Variable costs = $1.20 Q

Firm C

Units sold (Q)	Sales	Costs	Profit
20,000	$ 40,000	$ 80,000	–$40,000
40,000	80,000	100,000	— 20,000
60,000	120,000	120,000	0
80,000	160,000	140,000	20,000
100,000	200,000	160,000	40,000
120,000	240,000	180,000	60,000

Selling price = $2.00
Fixed costs   = $60,000
Variable costs = $1.00 Q

Firm B is considered to have a normal amount of fixed costs in its operations. It uses automated equipment (with which one operator can turn out a few or many units at the same labor cost) to about the same extent as the average firm in the industry. Firm B breaks even at a higher level of operations than does firm A. At a production level of 40,000 units, B is losing $8,000 but A breaks even.

On the other hand, firm C has the highest fixed costs. It is highly automated, using expensive, high-speed machines that require very little labor per unit produced. With such an operation, its variable costs rise slowly. Because of the high overhead resulting from charges associated with the expensive machinery, firm C's break-even point is higher than that for either firm A or firm B. Once firm C reaches its break-even point, however, its profits rise faster than do those of the other firms.

Degree of Operating Leverage

Operating leverage can be defined more precisely in terms of the way a given change in volume affects profits. For this purpose we use the following definition: *The degree of operating leverage is defined as the percentage change in operating income that results from a percentage change in units sold.* Algebraically,

$$\text{Degree of operating leverage} = \frac{\text{percentage change in operating income}}{\text{percentage change in sales}}.$$

For firm B in Figure 4–4, the degree of operating leverage (OL_B) at 100,000 units of output is

$$\text{Degree of } OL_B = \frac{\dfrac{\Delta\text{profit}}{\text{profit}}}{\dfrac{\Delta Q}{Q}}$$

$$= \frac{\dfrac{\$56,000 - \$40,000}{\$40,000}}{\dfrac{120,000 - 100,000}{100,000}} = \frac{\dfrac{\$16,000}{\$40,000}}{\dfrac{20,000}{100,000}}$$

$$= \frac{40\%}{20\%} = \boxed{2.0}.$$

Here Δprofit is the increase in profit, Q is the quantity of output in units, and ΔQ is the increase in output. For this calculation, we assume an increase in volume from 100,000 to 120,000 units, but the calculated degree of OL would have been the same for any other increase from 100,000 units.

For linear break-even, a formula has been developed to aid in calculating the degree of operating leverage at any level of output, Q:[1]

$$\text{Degree of operating leverage at point } Q = \frac{Q(P - V)}{Q(P - V) - F} \quad (4\text{--}2)$$

$$= \frac{S - VC}{S - VC - F}. \quad (4\text{--}2a)$$

Here P is the price per unit, V is the variable cost per unit, F is fixed costs, S is total sales, and VC is total variable costs. Equation 4–2 expresses the relationship in terms of units, while equation 4–2a expresses it in terms of total dollar figures. Using the equations, we find firm B's degree of operating leverage at 100,000 units of output to be

$$OL_B \text{ at } 100,000 \text{ units} = \frac{100,000(\$2.00 - \$1.20)}{100,000(\$2.00 - \$1.20) - \$40,000}$$

$$= \frac{\$200,000 - \$120,000}{\$200,000 - \$120,000 - \$40,000}$$

$$= \frac{\$80,000}{\$40,000} = \boxed{2.0}.$$

The two methods must, of course, give consistent answers.

Equation 4–2 can also be applied to firms A and C. When this is done, we find A's degree of operating leverage at 100,000 units to be 1.67 and that of C to be 2.5. Thus, for a 100 percent increase in volume, firm C, the company with the most operating leverage, will experience a profit increase of 250 percent; for the same 100 percent volume gain, firm A, the one with the least leverage, will have only a 167 percent profit gain.

In summary, the calculation of the degree of operating leverage shows algebraically the same pattern that Figure 4–4 shows graphically—that the profits of firm C, the company with the most operating leverage, are most sensitive to changes in sales volume, while those of firm A, which has only

---

[1]Equation 4–2 is developed as follows:
The change in output is defined as ΔQ. Fixed costs are constant, so the change in profits is $\Delta Q(P - V)$, where P = price per unit and V = variable cost per unit. The initial profit is $Q(P - V) - F$, so the percentage change in profit is:

$$\frac{\Delta Q(P - V)}{Q(P - V) - F}.$$

The percentage change in output is $\Delta Q/Q$, so the ratio of the change in profits to the change in output is:

$$\frac{\frac{\Delta Q(P - V)}{Q(P - V) - F}}{\frac{\Delta Q}{Q}} = \frac{\Delta Q(P - V)}{Q(P - V) - F} \cdot \frac{Q}{\Delta Q} = \frac{Q(P - V)}{Q(P - V) - F}.$$

a small amount of operating leverage, are relatively insensitive to volume changes. Firm B, with an intermediate degree of leverage, lies between the two extremes.[2]

Cash Break-even Analysis

Some of the firm's fixed costs are noncash outlays, and for a period some of its revenues may be in receivables. The cash break-even chart for firm B, constructed on the assumption that $30,000 of the fixed costs from the previous illustration are depreciation charges and, therefore, a noncash outlay, is shown in Figure 4–5.[3] Because fixed cash outlays are only $10,000, the cash break-even point is at 12,500 units rather than 50,000 units, which is the profit break-even point.

FIGURE 4–5   Cash Break-even Analysis

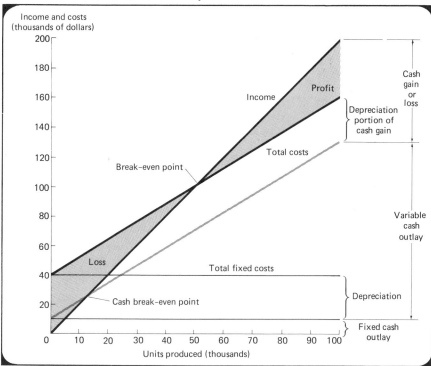

²The degree of operating leverage is a form of *elasticity concept* and, thus, is akin to the familiar price elasticity developed in economics. Since operating leverage is an elasticity, it varies depending upon the particular part of the break-even graph that is being considered. For example, in terms of our illustrative firms the degree of operating leverage is greatest close to the break-even point, where a very small change in volume can produce a very large percentage increase in profits simply because the base profits are close to zero near the break-even point.

³The nature of depreciation as a noncash charge is explained later in this chapter.

Cash break-even analysis does not fully represent cash flows—for this a cash budget is required. But cash break-even analysis is useful because it provides a picture of the flow of funds from operations. A firm could incur a level of fixed costs that would result in losses during periods of poor business but large profits during upswings. If cash outlays are small, even during periods of losses the firm might still be operating above the cash break-even point. Thus, the risks of insolvency, in the sense of inability to meet cash obligations, would be small. This allows a firm to reach out for higher profits through automation and operating leverage.

Limitations of Break-even Analysis

Break-even analysis is useful in studying the relations among volume, prices, and costs; it is thus helpful in pricing, cost control, and decisions about alternative expansion programs. It has limitations, however, as a guide to managerial actions.

Linear break-even analysis is especially weak in what it implies about the sales possibilities for the firm. Any linear break-even chart is based on a constant sales price. Therefore, in order to study profit possibilities under different prices, a whole series of charts is necessary, one chart for each price. Alternatively, nonlinear break-even analysis can be used.

With regard to costs, break-even analysis is also deficient—the relations indicated by the chart do not hold at all outputs. As sales increase, existing plant and equipment are worked to capacity; both this situation and the use of additional workers and overtime pay cause variable costs to rise sharply. Additional equipment and plant are required, thus increasing fixed costs. Finally, over a period the products sold by the firm change in quality and quantity. Such changes in product mix influence the level and slope of the cost function. Linear break-even analysis is useful as a first step in developing the basic data required for pricing and for financial decisions. But more detailed analysis, perhaps including nonlinear analysis, is required before final judgments can be made.

SOURCES AND USES OF FUNDS STATEMENT

When a firm requests a loan, the bank's loan officer will doubtless pose these three questions: What has the firm done with the money it had? What will it do with the new funds? How will it repay the loan? The sources and uses statement helps provide answers to these questions, as well as to questions that other interested parties may have about the firm. This information may indicate that the firm is making progress or that problems are arising.

Depreciation as a Source of Funds

Before going on to construct a sources and uses of funds statement, it is useful to pause and consider why, in financial analysis, we consider depreciation to be a source of funds. First, what is depreciation? In effect, it is an annual charge against income which reflects the cost of the capital equipment used in the production process. For example, suppose a machine with an expected useful life of 10 years and a 0 expected salvage value was purchased in 1975 for $100,000. This $100,000 cost must be charged against production during those 10 years; otherwise, profits will be overstated. If the machine is depreciated by the straight-line method, the annual charge is $10,000. This amount is deducted from sales revenues, along with such other costs as labor and raw materials, to determine income. *However, depreciation is not a cash outlay—funds were expended back in 1975, so the depreciation charged against income in 1977 is not a cash outlay, as are labor or charges for raw materials.*

To illustrate the significance of depreciation in cash flow analysis, let us consider the Dallas Fertilizer and Chemical Company, which has the following income statement for 1977:

Sales	$300,000,000
Costs excluding depreciation	$270,000,000
Depreciation	10,000,000
Profit before tax	$ 20,000,000
Taxes	8,000,000
Profit after tax	$ 12,000,000

Assuming that sales are for cash and that all costs except depreciation are paid during 1977, how much cash was available from operations to pay dividends, retire debt, or make investments in fixed or current assets or both? The answer is $22 million, the sum of profit after tax plus depreciation. The sales are all for cash, so the firm took in $300 million in cash money. Its costs other than depreciation were $270 million, and these were paid in cash, leaving $30 million. Depreciation *is not* a cash charge—the firm does not pay out the $10 million of depreciation expenses—so $30 million of cash money is still left after depreciation. Taxes, on the other hand, are paid in cash, so $8 million for taxes must be deducted from the $30 million gross operating cash flow, leaving a net cash flow from operations of $22 million. This $22 million is, of course, exactly equal to profit after tax plus depreciation: $12 million plus $10 million equals $22 million.

This example shows the rationale behind the statement that depreciation is a source of funds. However, we should note that without sales revenues, depreciation would *not* be a source of funds. If a strike idles the plant, the $300 million of sales revenues would vanish; cash flows from depreciation would evaporate.[4] Nevertheless, most firms do not suffer shutdowns for long periods, so normally a firm's depreciation does indeed constitute a source of funds as we use the term.

Sources and Uses Analysis

Several steps are involved in constructing a sources and uses statement. First, the changes in balance sheet items from one year to the next must be tabulated and then classified as either a source or a use of funds, according to the following pattern:

- *Source of funds:* (1) decrease in asset item or (2) increase in liability item
- *Use of funds:* (1) increase in asset item or (2) decrease in liability item.

Table 4–5 gives Dallas Chemical's comparative balance sheets for 1976 and 1977, and also net changes in each item classified as to source or use.

TABLE 4–5 Dallas Fertilizer and Chemical Company
Comparative Balance Sheets and Sources and Uses of Funds
(millions of dollars)

	Dec. 31, 1976	Dec. 31, 1977	Sources	Uses
Cash	$ 10	$ 5	$ 5	
Marketable securities	25	15	10	
Net receivables	15	20		$ 5
Inventories	25	30		5
Gross fixed assets	150	180		30
Less: Accumulated depreciation[a]	(40)	(50)	10	
Net fixed assets	110	130		
Total assets	$185	$200		
Accounts payable	$ 10	$ 6		4
Notes payable	15	10		5
Other current liabilities	10	14	4	
Long-term debt	60	70	10	
Preferred stock	10	10	—	—
Common stock	50	50	—	—
Retained earnings	30	40	10	
Total claims on assets	$185	$200		

[a]The accumulated depreciation is actually a contra-asset that appears on the left side of the balance sheet. Note that it is deducted, not added, when totaling the column.

[4]This potential problem was brought to the authors' attention in connection with a project involving a financial plan for Communications Satellite Corporation. Comsat has very healthy projected cash flows that would seem able to support a substantial amount of debt. However, Comsat's revenues are derived almost entirely from three satellites (over the North Atlantic, Pacific, and Indian Oceans), and if these satellites failed it would take months to replace them. Thus, when we recognized the degree of uncertainty about these cash flows, we adjusted downward our estimates of how much debt Comsat could safely carry.

The next step in constructing a sources and uses statement involves (1) making adjustments to reflect net income and dividends and (2) isolating changes in working capital (current assets and current liabilities). These changes are reflected in the sources and uses statement shown in Table 4–6. Net income in 1977 amounted to $12 million, and dividends of $2 million were paid. The $12 million is treated as a source, the $2 million as a use. The $10 million retained earnings shown in Table 4–5 is deleted from Table 4–6 to avoid double counting. Notice that Dallas Chemical had no net change in working capital—the increases were exactly equal to the decreases. This was merely a coincidence; ordinarily there will be some change in net working capital.

What does this statement of sources and uses of funds tell the financial manager? It tells him that plant size was expanded and that fixed assets amounting to $30 million were acquired. Inventories and net receivables also increased as sales increased. The firm needed funds to meet working capital and fixed assets demands.

TABLE 4–6 Dallas Fertilizer and Chemical Company
Statement of Sources and Uses of Funds, 1977
(millions of dollars)

	Amount		Percent	
Sources				
Net income		$12	23.5	
Depreciation		10	19.6	
Decreases in working capital				43.1
Reduction in cash	$ 5		9.8	
Sales of marketable securites	10		19.6	
Increase in other liabilities	4		7.9	
Total decrease in working capital		19		37.3
Increase in long-term debt		10		19.6
Total sources of funds		$51		100.0
Uses				
Increases in working capital:				
Inventory investment	$ 5		9.8	
Increase in receivables	5		9.8	
Reduction in notes payable	5		9.8	
Reduction in accounts payable	4		7.9	
Total increases in working capital		$19		37.3
Gross fixed assets expansion		30	58.8	
Dividends to stockholders		2	3.9	62.7
Total uses of funds		$51		100.0

Previously, Dallas had been financing its growth through bank credit (notes payable). In the present period of growth, management decided to obtain some financing from permanent sources (long-term debt). It obtained enough long-term debt not only to finance some of the asset growth but also to pay back some of its bank credit and to reduce accounts payable. In addition to the long-term debt, funds were obtained from earnings and from depreciation charges. Moreover, the firm had been accumulating marketable securities in anticipation of this expansion program, and some were sold to pay for new buildings and equipment. Finally, cash had been accumulated in excess of the firm's needs and was also worked down. In summary, this example illustrates how the sources and uses of funds statement can provide both a fairly complete picture of recent operations and a good perspective on the flow of funds within the company.

Pro Forma Sources and Uses of Funds

A *pro forma*, or projected, sources and uses of funds statement can also be constructed to show how a firm plans to acquire and employ funds during some future period. In the next chapter we will discuss financial forecasting, which involves the determination of future sales, the level of assets necessary to generate these sales (the left side of the projected balance sheet), and the manner in which these assets will be financed (the right side of the projected balance sheet). Given the projected balance sheet and supplementary projected data on earnings, dividends, and depreciation, the financial manager can construct a pro forma sources and uses of funds statement to summarize his firm's projected operations over the planning horizon. Such a statement is obviously of much interest to lenders as well as to the firm's own management.

SUMMARY

This chapter analyzes two important financial tools, *break-even analysis* and the *sources and uses of funds statement*, and the key concept of *operating leverage*.

Break-even Analysis   Break-even analysis is a method of relating fixed costs, variable costs, and total revenues to show the level of sales that must be attained if the firm is to operate at a profit. The analysis can be based on the number of units produced or on total dollar sales. It can also be used for the entire company or for a particular product or division. Further, with minor modifications, break-even analysis can be put on a cash basis instead of a profit basis. Ordinarily, break-even analysis is conducted on a linear, or straight-line, basis. However, this is not necessary—nonlinear break-even analysis is feasible and at times desirable.

Operating Leverage   Operating leverage is defined as the extent to which fixed costs are used in operations. The *degree of operating leverage*, defined as the percentage change in operating income that results from a specific percentage change in units sold, provides a precise measure of how much operating leverage a particular firm is employing. Break-even analysis provides a graphic view of the effects of changes in sales on profits; the degree of operating leverage presents the same picture in algebraic terms.

Sources and Uses of Funds Statement   The sources and uses of funds statement indicates where cash came from and how it was used. When a firm wishes to borrow funds, one of the first questions posed by the bank's loan officer is "What has the firm done with the money it had?" This question is answered by the sources and uses of funds statement. The information it provides may indicate that the firm is making progress or that problems are arising. Sources and uses data may also be analyzed on a *pro forma*, or projected, basis to show how a firm plans to acquire and employ funds during some future period.

Break-even analysis, operating leverage, and sources and uses statements are all fundamental concepts for the financial manager, and they are encountered time and time again throughout the remainder of this book.

QUESTIONS

4-1. What benefits can be derived from break-even analysis?

4-2. What is operating leverage? Explain how profits or losses can be magnified in a firm with a great deal of operating leverage as opposed to a firm without this characteristic.

4-3. What data are necessary to construct a break-even chart?

4-4. What is the general effect of each of the following changes on a firm's break-even point?

a. An increase in selling price with no change in units sold.

b. A change from the leasing of a machine for $5,000 a year to the purchase of the machine for $100,000. The useful life of this machine will be twenty years, with no salvage value. Assume straight-line depreciation.

c. A reduction in variable labor costs.

4-5. Why is depreciation considered to be a source of funds?

PROBLEMS

4-1. For Mathis Industries the following relations exist: each unit of output is sold for $75; for output up to 25,000 units the fixed costs are $240,000; variable costs are $35 a unit.

a. What is the firm's gain or loss at sales of 5,000 units? of 8,000 units?

b. What is the break-even point? Illustrate by means of a chart.

c. What is Mathis' degree of operating leverage at sales of 5,000 and 8,000 units?

d. What happens to the break-even point if the selling price rises to $85? What is the significance of the change to financial management? Illustrate by means of a chart.

e. What occurs to the break-even point if the selling price rises to $85 but variable costs rise to $45 a unit? Illustrate by means of a chart.

4-2. Win Corporation's only product is an oil additive for automobile engines. Win's 1976 after tax profit was $60,000 on sales of $750,000. Its average tax rate is 40 percent. The oil additive sells for $5 per unit and has a variable cost of $4 per unit.

a. What is Win's annual total fixed cost?

b. What is its break-even point in units? in dollars?

c. If Win's after tax profits increase by $30,000 to $90,000, when sales increase to 200,000 units, what is Win's degree of operating leverage at 150,000 units?

4-3. Use the data in 4-2 to answer the following.

What would be the effect on the break-even point of Win Corporation if:

a. Fixed costs increase by $20,000.

b. The average tax rate was 50 percent instead of 40 percent; after tax profits remain at $60,000. Sales and variable costs remain at $750,000 and $600,000, respectively, but fixed costs decline to $30,000.

c. Unit variable costs increased $0.50 and fixed costs decreased by $5,000 to $45,000.

4-4. Digital Electronics is considering developing a new miniature calculator. The quantity (Q) sold is a function of the price (P) where

$$Q = 2,000 - 50P.$$

Per unit variable costs are $10 and fixed costs are $10,000. Graphically determine the break-even point for the calculator in units and dollars.

4-5. The Toledo Tire Company is currently considering two possible mutually exclusive plant modernizations. Under the first, newer and more efficient machinery would be added; this would tend to reduce labor costs and, because of much less waste, raw material usage. The other alternative would involve a more extensive changeover in the plant to an entirely new process for forming and curing rubber. The second procedure would involve a more extensive investment in both plant and equipment, but it would result in larger savings in labor and materials costs.

The current sales level is about 76,500 units a year at a price of $40 each, but volume has fluctuated from year to year with changes in general economic conditions. The firm's management is primarily concerned with the extent to which profitability will be affected by each alternative project in relation to risk. (For current purposes, riskiness may be considered to be a function of the probability of not reaching the break-even point.) A break-down of costs for the current sales volume is given below, together with estimates of what each item would be after each of the modernization proposals.

Estimated Costs	Currently	Modernization I	Modernization II
Depreciation on plant and equipment	$513,000	$630,000	$787,500
Depreciation on building	288,000	360,000	468,000
Property taxes	36,000	45,000	63,000
Salary expense	639,000	693,000	778,500
Other fixed expenses	54,000	72,000	99,000
Factory labor	625,500	468,000	270,000
Raw materials	450,000	378,000	270,000
Variable selling expenses	72,000	72,000	72,000

a. Determine the break-even point in units for the firm, assuming (1) no moderni-zation is undertaken, (2) the first program is undertaken, and (3) the second pro-gram is undertaken.

b. Compute the degree of operating leverage at the current volume (76,500 units) for each of the three possibilities.

c. Compute profits for each alternative, assuming future sales of 76,500 units. Profits for each alternative at other sales levels have been calculated (to save you work) and are given below:

Unit Sales	Profits
No Modernization	
65,000	$ 95,000
90,000	720,000
100,000	970,000
Modernization I	
65,000	$ 20,000
90,000	720,000
100,000	1,000,000
Modernization II	
65,000	$ (116,000)
90,000	684,000
100,000	1,004,000

d. Rank the alternatives in terms of potential riskiness.

e. How would the decision if and how to modernize be affected by the expectation of large fluctuations in future sales?

f. (To be worked at the option of the instructor.) Suppose we have estimated the following probability distribution for sales:

Probability	Sales (in Units)
.1	65,000
.3	76,500
.3	90,000
.3	100,000

Use this information to determine the expected values of the three alternative courses of action.

g. Which project is best? What factors would influence your decision?

4-6. The consolidated balance sheets for the Ashe Corporation at the beginning and end of 1978 are shown below.

Ashe Corporation
Balance Sheet
Beginning and end 1978
(millions of dollars)

	Jan. 1	Dec. 31	Source	Use
Cash	$ 45	$ 21	_____	_____
Marketable securities	33	0	_____	_____
Net receivables	66	90	_____	_____
Inventories	159	225	_____	_____
Total current assets	$303	$336	_____	_____
Gross fixed assets	225	450	_____	_____
Less: reserve for depreciation	(78)	(123)	_____	_____
Net fixed assets	147	327	_____	_____
Total assets	$450	$663	_____	_____
	Jan. 1	Dec. 31	Source	Use
Accounts payable	$ 45	$ 54	_____	_____
Notes payable	45	9	_____	_____
Other current liabilities	21	45	_____	_____
Long-term debt	24	78	_____	_____
Common stock	114	192	_____	_____
Retained earnings	201	285	_____	_____
Total claims on assets	$450	$663	_____	_____

The company bought $225 million worth of fixed assets. The charge for current depreciation was $45 million. Earnings after taxes were $114 million, and the company paid out $30 million in dividends.

    a. Fill in the amount of source or use in the appropriate column.

    b. Prepare a percentage statement of sources and uses of funds.

    c. Briefly summarize your findings.

Financial Forecasting

5

The planning process is an integral part of the financial manager's job. As we will see in subsequent chapters, long-term debt and equity funds are raised infrequently and in large amounts, primarily because the cost per dollar raised by selling such securities decreases as the size of the issue increases. Because of these considerations, it is important that the firm have a working estimate of its total needs for funds for the next few years. It is therefore useful to examine methods of forecasting the firm's overall needs for funds, and this is the subject of the present chapter.

CASH FLOW CYCLE

We must recognize that firms need assets to make sales; if sales are to be increased, assets must also be expanded. Growing firms require new investments—immediate investment in current assets and, as full capacity is reached, investment in fixed assets as well. New investments must be financed, and new financing carries with it commitments and obligations to service the capital obtained.[1] A growing, profitable firm is likely to require additional cash for investments in receivables, inventories, and fixed assets. Such a firm can, therefore, have a cash flow problem. The nature of this problem, as well as the cause and effect relationship between assets and sales, is illustrated in the following discussion, in which we trace the consequences of a series of transactions.

[1]"Servicing" capital refers to the payment of interest and principal on debt and to dividends and retained earnings (the cost of equity capital) on common stocks.

Effects on the Balance Sheet

1. Two partners invest a total of $50,000 to create the Glamour Galore Dress Company. The firm rents a plant; equipment and other fixed assets cost $30,000. The resulting financial situation is shown by Balance Sheet 1.

2. Glamour Galore receives an order to manufacture 10,000 dresses. The receipt of an order in itself has no effect on the balance sheet, but in preparation for the manufacturing activity, the firm buys $20,000 worth of cotton cloth on terms of net 30 days. Without additional investment by the owners, total assets increase by $20,000, financed by the trade accounts payable to the supplier of the cotton cloth.

BALANCE SHEET 1

Assets		Liabilities	
Current Assets		Capital stock	$50,000
Cash	$20,000		
Fixed Assets			
Plant and equipment	30,000		
Total assets	$50,000	Total liabilities and net worth	$50,000

After the purchase, the firm spends $20,000 on labor for cutting the cloth to the required pattern. Of the $20,000 total labor cost, $10,000 is paid in cash and $10,000 is owed in the form of accrued wages. These two transactions are reflected in Balance Sheet 2, which shows that total assets increase to $80,000. Current assets are increased; net working capital—total current assets minus total current liabilities—remains constant. The current ratio declines to 1.67, and the debt ratio rises to 38 percent. The financial position of the firm is weakening. If it should seek to borrow at this point, Glamour Galore could not use the work in process inventories as collateral, because a lender could find little use for partially manufactured dresses.

BALANCE SHEET 2

Assets		Liabilities	
Current Assets		Accounts payable	$20,000
Cash	$10,000	Accrued wages payable	10,000
Inventories		Total current liabilities	$30,000
Work in process		Capital stock	50,000
Materials	20,000		
Labor	20,000		
Total current assets	$50,000		
Fixed Assets			
Plant and equipment	30,000	Total liabilities and	
Total assets	$80,000	net worth	$80,000

3. In order to complete the dresses, the firm incurs additional labor costs of $20,000 and pays in cash. It is assumed that the firm desires to maintain a minimum cash balance of $5,000. Since the initial cash balance is $10,000, Glamour Galore must borrow an additional $15,000 from its bank to meet the wage bill. The borrowing is reflected in notes payable in Balance Sheet 3. Total assets rise to $95,000, with a finished goods inventory of $60,000. The current ratio drops to 1.4, and the debt ratio rises to 47 percent. These ratios show a further weakening of the financial position.

BALANCE SHEET 3

Assets		Liabilities	
Current Assets		Accounts payable	$20,000
Cash	$ 5,000	Notes payable	15,000
Inventory		Accrued wages payable	10,000
Finished goods	60,000		
Total current assets	$65,000	Total current liabilities	$45,000
Fixed Assets		Capital stock	50,000
Plant and equipment	30,000	Total liabilities and	
Total assets	$95,000	net worth	$95,000

4. Glamour Galore ships the dresses on the basis of the original order, invoicing the purchaser for $100,000 within 30 days. Accrued wages and accounts payable have to be paid now, so Glamour Galore must borrow an additional $30,000 in order to maintain the $5,000 minimum cash balance. These transactions are shown in Balance Sheet 4.

BALANCE SHEET 4

Assets		Liabilities	
Current Assets		Notes payable	$ 45,000
Cash	$ 5,000	Total current liabilities	$ 45,000
Accounts receivable	100,000	Capital stock	$ 50,000
Total current assets	$105,000	Retained earnings	40,000
Fixed Assets		Total net worth	$ 90,000
Plant and equipment	30,000	Total liabilities and	
Total assets	$135,000	net worth	$135,000

Note that in Balance Sheet 4, finished goods inventory is replaced by receivables, with the markup reflected as retained earnings. This causes the debt ratio to drop to 33 percent. Since the receivables are carried at the sales price, current assets increase to $105,000 and the current ratio rises to 2.3. Compared with the conditions reflected in Balance Sheet 3, most of the financial ratios show improvement. However, the absolute amount of debt is large.

Whether the firm's financial position is really improved depends upon the credit worthiness of the purchaser of the dresses. If the purchaser is a good credit risk, Glamour Galore may be able to borrow further on the basis of the accounts receivable.

5. The firm receives payment for the accounts receivable, pays off the bank loan, and is in the highly liquid position shown by Balance Sheet 5. If a new order for 10,000 dresses is received, it will have no effect on the balance sheet, but a cycle similar to the one we have been describing will begin.

BALANCE SHEET 5

Assets		Liabilities	
Current Assets		Capital stock	$50,000
Cash	$60,000	Retained earnings	40,000
Fixed Assets			
Plant and equipment	$30,000	Total liabilities and	
Total assets	$90,000	net worth	$90,000

6. The idea of the cash flow cycle can now be generalized. An order that requires the purchase of raw materials is placed with the firm. The purchase in turn generates an account payable. As labor is applied, work-in-process inventories build up. To the extent that wages are not fully paid at the time labor is used, accrued wages will appear on the liability side of the balance sheet. As goods are completed, they move into finished goods inventories. The cash needed to pay for the labor to complete the goods may make it necessary for the firm to borrow.

Finished goods inventories are sold, usually on credit, which gives rise to accounts receivable. As the firm has not received cash, this point in the cycle represents the peak in financing requirements. If the firm did not borrow at the time finished goods inventories were at their maximum, it may do so as inventories are converted into receivables by credit sales. Income taxes, which were not considered in the example, can add to the problem. As accounts receivable become cash, short-term obligations can be paid off.

FINANCING PATTERNS

The influence of sales on current asset levels has just been illustrated. Over the course of several cycles, the fluctuations in sales will be accompanied in

most industries by a rising long-term trend. Figure 5–1 shows the consequences of such a pattern. Total permanent assets increase steadily in the
form of current and fixed assets. Increases of this nature should be financed
by long-term debt; by equity; or by "spontaneous" increases in liabilities, such
as accrued taxes and wages and accounts payable, which naturally accompany increasing sales. However, temporary increases in assets can be
covered by short-term liabilities. The distinction between temporary and
permanent asset levels may be difficult to make in practice, but it is neither
illusory nor unimportant. Short-term financing for the financing of long-term
needs is dangerous. A profitable firm may become unable to meet its cash
obligations if funds borrowed on a short-term basis have become tied up in
permanent asset needs.

FIGURE 5–1 Fluctuating versus Permanent Assets

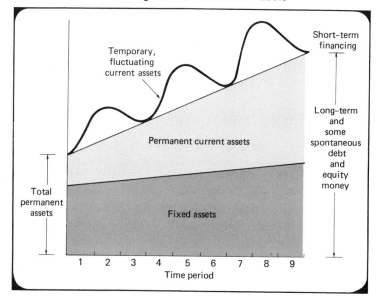

PERCENT-OF-SALES METHOD

It is apparent from the preceding discussion that *the most important variable
that influences a firm's financing requirements is its projected dollar volume
of sales. A good sales forecast is an essential foundation for forecasting
financial requirements.* In spite of its importance, we shall not go into sales
forecasting here; rather, we simply assume that a sales forecast has been
made, then estimate financial requirements on the basis of this forecast.[2]

[2]For a discussion of demand forecasting, see E. F. Brigham and J. L. Pappas, *Managerial Economics*
(Hinsdale, Ill.: Dryden Press, 1976).

The principal methods of forecasting financial requirements are described in this and the following sections.

The simplest approach to forecasting financial requirements expresses the firm's needs in terms of the percentage of annual sales invested in each individual balance sheet item. As an example, consider the Moore Company, whose balance sheet as of December 31, 1977, is shown in Table 5–1. The company's sales are running at about $500,000 a year, which is its capacity limit; the profit margin after tax on sales is 4 percent. During 1977, the company earned $20,000 after taxes and paid out $10,000 in dividends, and it plans to continue paying out half of net profits as dividends. How much additional financing will be needed if sales expand to $800,000 during 1978? The calculating procedure, using the percent-of-sales method, is explained below.[3]

TABLE 5–1 The Moore Company
Balance sheet
December 31, 1977

Assets		Liabilities	
Cash	$ 10,000	Accounts payable	$ 50,000
Receivables	85,000	Accrued taxes and wages	25,000
Inventories	100,000	Mortgage bonds	70,000
Fixed assets (net)	150,000	Common stocks	100,000
		Retained earnings	100,000
		Total liabilities and	
Total assets	$345,000	net worth	$345,000

First, isolate those balance sheet items that can be expected to vary directly with sales. In the case of the Moore Company, this step applies to each category of assets—a higher level of sales necessitates more cash for transactions, more receivables, higher inventory levels, and additional fixed plant capacity. On the liability side, accounts payable as well as accruals may be expected to increase with increases in sales. Retained earnings will go up as long as the company is profitable and does not pay out 100 percent of earnings, but the percentage increase is not constant. However, neither common stock nor mortgage bonds would increase spontaneously with an increase in sales.

The items that can be expected to vary directly with sales are tabulated as a percentage of sales in Table 5–2. For every $1.00 increase in sales,

[3]We recognize, of course, that as a practical matter, business firms plan their needs in terms of specific items of equipment, square feet of floor space, and other factors, and not as a percentage of sales. However, the outside analyst does not have access to this information; the manager, even though he has the information on specific items, needs to check his forecasts in aggregate terms. The percent-of-sales method serves both these needs surprisingly well.

assets must increase by $.69; this $.69 must be financed in some manner. Accounts payable will increase spontaneously with sales, as will accruals; these two items will supply $.15 of new funds for each $1.00 increase in sales. Subtracting the 15 percent for spontaneously generated funds from the 69 percent funds requirement leaves 54 percent. Thus, for each $1.00 increase in sales, the Moore Company must obtain $.54 of financing either from retained earnings or from external sources.

TABLE 5–2 The Moore Company
Balance sheet items expressed as a percent of sales
December 31, 1977
(percent)

Assets		Liabilities	
Cash	2.0	Accounts payable	10.0
Receivables	17.0	Accrued taxes and wages	5.0
Inventories	20.0	Mortgage bonds	na[a]
Fixed assets (net)	30.0	Common stock	na[a]
		Retained earnings	na[a]
Total assets	69.0	Total liabilities and net worth	15.0

Assets as percent of sales	69.0
Less: Spontaneous increase in liabilities	15.0
Percent of each additional dollar of sales that must be financed	54.0

[a]Not applicable.

In the case at hand, sales are scheduled to increase from $500,000 to $800,000, or by $300,000. Applying the 54 percent developed in the table to the expected increase in sales leads to the conclusion that $162,000 will be needed.

Some of that need will be met by retained earnings. Total sales during 1978 will be $800,000; if the company earns 4 percent after taxes on this volume, profits will amount to $32,000. Assuming that the 50 percent dividend payout ratio is maintained, dividends will be $16,000 and $16,000 will be retained. Subtracting the retained earnings from the $162,000 that was needed leaves a figure of $146,000—this is the amount of funds that must be obtained through borrowing or by selling new common stock.

This process may be expressed in equation form:[4]

----

[4]If the forecast is for more than one year, then the retained earnings part of the equation, $MS_2(1-d)$, must be modified to $MS_T(1-d)$, where S_T is total sales during the forecast period.

$$\text{External funds needed} = \frac{A}{S}(\Delta S) - \frac{L}{S}(\Delta S) - MS_2(1-d).$$

Here

$\dfrac{A}{S}$ = assets that increase spontaneously with sales as a percent of sales

$\dfrac{L}{S}$ = those liabilities that increase spontaneously with sales as a percent of sales

ΔS = change in sales

M = profit margin

S_2 = *total sales projected for the year*

d = the dividend payout percentage.

For the Moore Company, then,

$$\text{External funds needed} = .69\,(300{,}000) - .15\,(300{,}000)$$
$$- .04\,(800{,}000)\,(.5)$$

$$= 54\,(300{,}000) - .02\,(800{,}000)$$

$$= \$146{,}000.$$

The $146,000 found by the formula method must, of course, equal the amount derived previously.

Notice what would have occurred if the Moore Company's sales forecast for 1978 had been only $515,000, or a 3 percent increase. Applying the formula, we find the external funds requirements as follows:

$$\text{External funds needed} = .54\,(15{,}000) - .02\,(515{,}000)$$

$$= \$8{,}100 - \$10{,}300$$

$$= (\$2{,}200).$$

In this case, no external funds are required. In fact, the company will have $2,200 in excess of its requirements; it should therefore plan to increase dividends, retire debt, or seek additional investment opportunities. The example shows not only that higher levels of sales bring about a need for funds but also that while small percentage increases can be financed through retained earnings, larger increases cause the firm to go into the market for outside capital. In other words, a certain level of growth can be financed from internal sources, but higher levels of growth require external financing.[5]

---

[5] At this point, one might ask two questions: "Shouldn't depreciation be considered as a source of funds, and won't this reduce the amount of external funds needed?" The answer to both questions is no. In the percent-of-sales method, we are implicitly assuming that funds generated through depreciation (in the sources and uses of funds sense) must be used to replace the assets to which the depreciation is applicable. Accordingly, depreciation does not enter the calculations in this forecasting technique; it is netted out.

The percent-of-sales method of forecasting financial requirements is neither simple nor mechanical, although an explanation of the ideas requires simple illustrations. Experience in applying the technique in practice suggests the importance of understanding (1) the basic technology of the firm and (2) the logic of the relation between sales and assets for the particular firm in question. A great deal of experience and judgement is required to apply the technique in actual practice.

The percent-of-sales method is most appropriately used for forecasting relatively short-term changes in financing needs. It is less useful for longer term forecasting for reasons that are best described in connection with the analysis of the regression method of financial forecasting discussed in the next sections.

SCATTER DIAGRAM, OR SIMPLE REGRESSION, METHOD

An alternative method used for forecasting financial requirements is the scatter diagram, or simple regression, method. A scatter diagram is a graphic portrayal of joint relations. Proper use of the scatter diagram method requires practical but not necessarily statistical sophistication.

Table 5–3 and Figure 5–2 illustrate the use of the scatter diagram method and also demonstrate its superiority over the percent-of-sales method for long range forecasting. As in all financial forecasting, the sales forecast is the starting point. The financial manager is given the sales forecast, or he may participate in formulating it. Suppose he has data through 1977 and is making a forecast of inventories for 1982, as indicated in Table 5–3. If he is using the simple regression method, he draws a line through the points for 1972 through 1977, as shown in Figure 5–2. The line that fits the scatter of points in this example is a straight line. It is called the line of best fit, or the regression line. Of course, all points seldom fall exactly on the regression line, and the line itself may be curved as well as linear.[6]

If the percent-of-sales method had been used, some difficulties would have arisen immediately. Table 5–3 gives inventory as a percent of sales for 1972 through 1977. What relation should be used? The 44 percent for 1972? The 11 percent for 1977? Or some average of the relations? If the relation for 1977 had been used, a forecast of $55,000 for inventories in 1982 would have been made, compared with $42,000 by the scatter diagram method. That forecast represents a large error.

The regression method is thus seen to be superior for forecasting financial requirements, particularly for longer term forecasts. When a firm is likely

---

[6]In these illustrations, inventories are used as the item to be forecast. Much theory suggests that inventories increase as a square root of sales. This characteristic would tend to turn the regression line between inventories and sales slightly downward. Also, improvements in inventory control techniques would curve the line downward. However, the increased diversity of types, models, and styles tends to increase inventories. Applications by the authors' students of the regression method to hundreds of companies indicate that the linear straight-line relations frequently represent the line of best fit or, at worst, involve only a small error. If the line were in fact curved over, a curved line could be fitted to the data and used for forecasting purposes.

TABLE 5–3   Relationship between Inventory and Sales

Year	Sales	Inventory	Inventory as a Percent of Sales
1972	$ 50,000	$22,000	44
1973	100,000	24,000	24
1974	150,000	26,000	17
1975	200,000	28,000	14
1976	250,000	30,000	12
1977	300,000	32,000	11
.	.	.	.
.	.	.	.
.	.	.	.
1982 (estimated)	500,000	40,000	8

to have a base stock of inventory or fixed assets, the ratio of the item to sales declines as sales increase. In such cases, the percent-of-sales method results in large errors.[7]

FIGURE 5–2   Illustrative Relation between Sales and Inventory

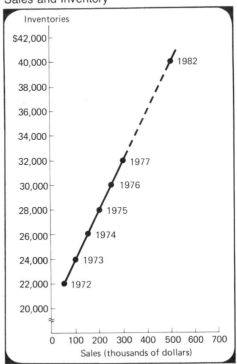

Sales (thousands of dollars)

[7]The widespread use of the percentage method makes for lax control. It would be easy to reduce inventories below the $55,000 percent-of-sales forecast level and still be inefficient because the correct target amount is closer to $40,000.

MULTIPLE REGRESSION METHOD

A more sophisticated approach to forecasting a firm's assets calls for the use of *multiple regression analysis.* In simple regression, sales are assumed to be a function of only one variable; in multiple regression, sales are recognized to depend upon a number of variables. For example, in simple regression we might state that sales are strictly a function of GNP. With multiple regression, we might say that sales are dependent upon both GNP and a set of additional variables. For example, sales of ski equipment depend upon (1) the general level of prosperity as measured by GNP, personal disposable income, or other indicators of aggregate economic activity; (2) population increases; (3) number of lifts operating; (4) weather conditions; (5) advertising, and so forth.

We shall not go into detail on the use of multiple regression analysis at this time. However, most computer installations have "canned" regression programs incorporated into their systems, making it extremely easy to use multiple regression techniques; multiple regression is widely used by at least the larger corporations.

COMPARISON OF FORECASTING METHODS

Thus far we have considered four methods used in financial forecasting: (1) percent of sales, (2) scatter diagram, or simple linear regression, (3) curvilinear simple regression, and (4) multiple regression. In this section we will summarize and compare those methods.

Percent of Sales

The percent-of-sales method of financial forecasting assumes that certain balance sheet items vary directly with sales; that is, that the ratio of a given balance sheet item to sales remains constant. The postulated relationship is shown in Figure 5–3. *Notice that the percent-of-sales method implicitly assumes a linear relationship that passes through the origin.* The slope of the line representing the relationship may vary, but the line always passes through the origin. Implicitly, the relationship is established by finding one point, or ratio, such as that designated as X in Figure 5–3, and then connecting this point with the origin. Then, for any projected level of sales, the forecasted level of the particular balance sheet item can be determined.

Scatter Diagram, or Simple Linear Regression

The scatter diagram method differs from the percent-of-sales method principally in that it does not assume that the line of relationship passes through the origin. In its simplest form, the scatter diagram method calls for calculating the ratio between sales and the relevant balance sheet item at two points in time, extending a line through these two points, and using the line to describe the relationship between sales and the balance sheet item. The accuracy of the regression is improved if more points are plotted, and the regression line can be fitted mathematically (by a technique known as the method of least squares) as well as drawn in by eye.

FIGURE 5–3   Percent-of-sales

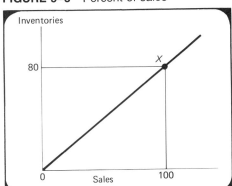

The scatter diagram method is illustrated in Figure 5–4, where the percent-of-sales relationship is also shown for comparison. The error induced by the use of the percent-of-sales method is represented by the gap between the two lines. At a sales level of 125, the percent-of-sales method would call for an inventory of 100 versus an inventory of only 90 using a scatter diagram forecast. *Notice that the error is very small if sales continue to run at approximately the current level, but the gap widens and the error increases as sales deviate in either direction from current levels, as they probably would if a long-run forecast was being made.*

FIGURE 5–4   Scatter Diagram, or Simple Linear Regression

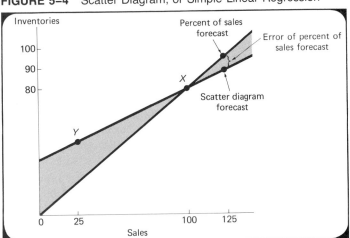

Curvilinear Simple Regression

Linear scatter diagrams, or linear regressions, assume that the slope of the regression line is constant. Although this condition does frequently exist, it is not a universal rule. Figure 5-5 illustrates the application of curvilinear simple regression to forecasting financial relationships. We have drawn this hypothetical illustration to show a flattening curve, which implies a decreasing relationship between sales and inventory beyond point X, the current level of operations. In this case, the forecast of inventory requirements at a sales level of 125 would be too high if the linear regression method was used (but too low if sales declined from 100 to 50).

FIGURE 5-5 Curvilinear Simple Regression

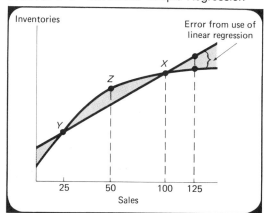

Multiple Regression

In our illustrations to this point, we have been assuming that the observations fell exactly on the relationship line. This implies perfect correlation, something that, in fact, seldom occurs. In practice, the actual observations would be scattered about the regression line as shown in Figure 5-6. What causes the deviations from the regression line? One answer, if linear regression is used, is that the actual line of relationship might be curvilinear. But if curvilinear regression is used and deviations still occur, we must seek other explanations for the scatter around the regression line. The most obvious answer is that inventories are determined by other factors in addition to sales. Inventory levels are certainly influenced by work stoppages at the plants of suppliers. If a steel fabricator anticipates a strike in the steel industry, he will stock up on steel products. Such hedge buying would cause actual inventories to be above the level forecast on the basis of sales projections. Then, assuming a strike does occur and continues for many months, inventories will be drawn down and may end up well below the predicted level. Multiple regression techniques, which introduce additional variables (such as work stoppages) into the analysis, are employed to further improve financial forecasting.

FIGURE 5–6   Multiple Regression: Deviations in the Forecast

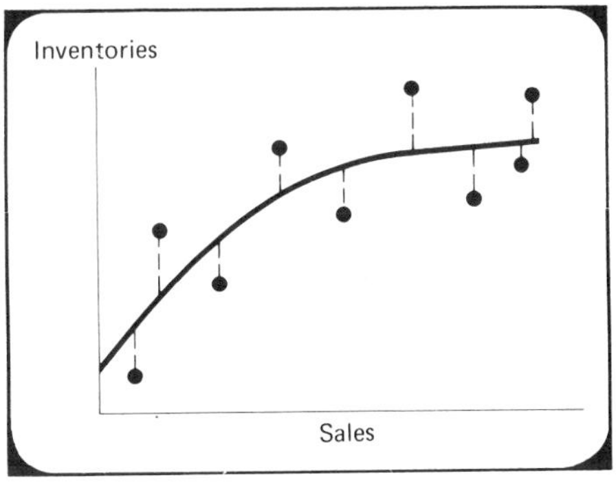

The need to employ more complicated forecasting techniques varies from situation to situation. For example, the percent-of-sales method may be perfectly adequate for making short-run forecasts where conditions are relatively stable, while curvilinear multiple regression may be deemed essential for longer run forecasts in more dynamic industries. As in all other applications of financial analysis, the cost of using more refined techniques must be balanced against the benefits of increased accuracy.

SUMMARY

Firms need assets to make sales; if sales are to be increased, assets must also be expanded. The first section of this chapter illustrates the relationship between sales and assets and shows how even a growing, profitable firm can have a cash flow problem.

The most important causal variable in determining financial requirements is a firm's projected dollar volume of sales; a good sales forecast is an essential foundation for forecasting financial requirements. The two principal methods used for making financial forecasts are (1) the percent-of-sales method and (2) the regression method. The first has the virtue of simplicity— the forecaster computes past relationships between asset and liability items and sales, assumes these same relationships will continue, and then applies the new sales forecast to get an estimate of the financial requirements.

However, since the percent-of-sales method assumes that the balance-sheet-to-sales relationships will remain constant, it is only useful for relatively short-run forecasting. When longer range forecasts are being made, the regression method is preferable because it allows for changing balance-sheet-to-sales relationships. Further, linear regression can be expanded to curvilinear regression, and simple regression to multiple regression. These more complex methods are useful in certain circumstances, but their increased accuracy must be balanced against the increased costs of using them.

The tools and techniques we have discussed in this chapter are generally used in the following manner: As a first step, one of the long-range forecasting techniques is used to make a long-run forecast of the firm's financial requirements over a three- to five-year period. This forecast is then used to make the strategic financing plans during the planning period. Long lead times are necessary when companies sell bonds or stocks; otherwise financial managers might be forced to go into the market for funds during unfavorable periods.

In addition to the long-run strategic forecasting, the financial manager must also make accurate short-run forecasts to be sure that bank funds will be available to meet seasonal and other short-run requirements. We consider this topic in the following chapter.

QUESTIONS

5-1. What should be the approximate point of intersection between the sales-to-asset regression line and the vertical axis (Y-axis intercept) for the following: inventory, accounts receivable, fixed assets? State your answer in terms of positive, zero, or negative intercept. Can you think of any accounts that might have a negative intercept?

5-2. How does forecasting financial requirements in advance of needs assist the financial manager to perform his responsibilities more effectively?

5-3. Explain how a downturn in the business cycle could cause either a cash shortage for a firm or have the opposite effect and generate excess cash.

5-4. Explain this statement: "Current assets to a considerable extent represent permanent assets."

5-5. What advantages might multiple regression techniques have over simple regression in forecasting sales? What might be some drawbacks in the actual use of this technique?

PROBLEMS

5-1. The Tobin Supply Company is a wholesale steel distributor. It purchases steel in carload lots from more than twenty producing mills and sells to several thousand steel users. The items carried include sheets, plates, wire products, bolts, windows, pipe, and tubing.

The company owns two warehouses, each housing 15,000 square feet, and contemplates the erection of another warehouse of 20,000 square feet. The nature of the steel supply business requires that the company maintain large inventories to take care of customer requirements in the event of mill strikes or other delays.

In examining patterns from 1971 through 1976, the company found a rather consistent relation between the following accounts as a percent of sales.

Current assets	50%
Net fixed assets	20%
Accounts payable	5%
Other current liabilities, including accruals and provision for income taxes but not bank loans	5%
Net profit after taxes	2%

The company's sales for 1977 were $3 million, and its balance sheet on December 31, 1977, was as follows:

Tobin Supply Company, Balance sheet, December 31, 1977

Current assets	$1,500,000	Accounts payable	$ 150,000
Fixed assets	600,000	Notes payable	300,000
		Other current liabilities	150,000
		Total current liabilities	$ 600,000
		Mortgage loan	100,000
		Common stock	250,000
		Retained earnings	1,150,000
Total assets	$2,100,000	Total liabilities and net worth	$2,100,000

The company expects its sales to increase by $200,000 each year. If this is achieved, what will its financial requirements be at the end of the five-year period? Assume that accounts not tied directly to sales (for example, notes payable) remain constant. Assume also that the company pays no dividends.

a. Construct a *pro forma* balance sheet for the end of 1982, using "additional financing needed" as the balancing item.

b. What are the crucial assumptions made in your projection method?

5-2. One useful test, or guide, for evaluating a firm's financial structure in relation to its industry is by comparison with financial ratio composites for its industry. A new firm, or one contemplating entering a new industry, may use such industry composites as a guide to what its financial position is likely to approximate after the initial settling-down period.

The following data represent the ratios for the printing industry for 1977.

Sales to net worth	4 times
Current debt to net worth	50%
Total debt to net worth	80%
Current ratio	2.2 times
Net sales to inventory	8 times
Average collection period	40 days
Fixed assets to net worth	70%

Creative Printers, Inc., Pro forma balance sheet, December 31, 1977

Cash	$_____	Current debt	$_____
Accounts receivable	_____	Long-term debt	_____
Inventory	_____	Total debt	_____
Current assets	_____	Net worth	_____
Fixed assets	_____	Total liabilities and	
Total assets	$_____	net worth	$_____

a. Complete the above *pro forma* balance sheet (round to nearest thousand) assuming Creative Printers' 1977 sales are $3,200,000.

b. What does the use of the financial ratio composites accomplish?

c. What other factors will influence the financial structure of the firm?

5-3. The 1977 sales of Minneapolis Controls, Inc., amounted to $12 million. Common stock and notes payable are constant. The dividend payout ratio is 60 percent. Retained earnings as shown on the December 31, 1976, balance sheet were $124,000. The percent of sales in each balance sheet item that varies directly with sales are expected to be as follows:

Cash	4%
Receivables	16
Inventories	18
Net fixed assets	35
Accounts payable	12
Accruals	6
Profit rate (after taxes) on sales	2

a. Complete the balance sheet given on the following page.

b. Now suppose that in 1978 sales increase by 5 percent over 1977 sales. How much additional (external) capital will be required?

c. Construct the year-end 1978 balance sheet. Assume that any required funds are borrowed as "notes payable."

d. What would happen to capital requirements under each of the following conditions? Answer in words, without calculations.

1. The profit margin went (i) from 2 percent to 6 percent? (ii) from 2 percent to 1 percent? Set up an equation to illustrate your answer.

2. The dividend payout rate (i) was raised from 60 percent to 90 percent? (ii) was lowered from 60 percent to 20 percent? Set up an equation to illustrate your answer.

3. Credit terms on sales were relaxed substantially.

e. Suppose now that the firm was started in 1975 and that data for 1975 and 1976 are available, with sales levels of $1 million and $2 million respectively. If the percent-of-sales figures for these years are as shown in the following tabulations, what does this imply about the appropriateness of the percent-of-sales forecasting method for the various balance sheet accounts? (No calculations are required; discuss verbally.)

	1975 Sales = $1 million	1976 Sales = $2 million
Cash	5.0%	3.0%
Receivables	10.0	12.0
Inventories	20.0	15.0
Net fixed assets	37.0	32.0
Accounts payable	13.0	12.5
Accruals	4.0	4.5
Profit rate (after taxes) on sales	1.0	1.5

Minneapolis Controls, Inc., Balance sheet, December 31, 1977

Cash	_____	Accounts payable	_____
Receivables	_____	Notes payable	630,000
Inventory	_____	Accruals	_____
Total current assets	_____		
Fixed assets	_____	Total current liabilities	_____
		Common stock	5,750,000
		Retained earnings	_____
Government securities	0	Total liabilities and	
Total assets	_____	net worth	_____

Financial Planning and Control: Budgeting

In the preceding chapter we first examined the relationship between assets and sales. Then we considered several procedures the financial manager can use to forecast his requirements. In addition to his long-range forecasts, the financial manager is also concerned with short-term needs for funds. It is embarrassing for a corporate treasurer to "run out of money." Even though he may be able to negotiate a bank loan on short notice, his plight may cause the banker to question the soundness of the firm's management and, accordingly, to reduce the company's line of credit or raise the interest rate. Therefore, attention must be given to short-term budgeting, with special emphasis on cash forecasting, or *cash budgeting,* as it is commonly called.

The cash budget is, however, only one part of the firm's overall budget system. The nature of the budget system, and especially the way it can be used for both planning and control purposes, is also discussed in this chapter.

BUDGETING

A budget is simply a financial plan. A household budget itemizes the family's sources of income and describes how this income will be spent: so much for food, housing, transportation, entertainment, education, savings, and so on. Similarly, the federal budget indicates the government's income sources and allocates funds to defense, welfare, agriculture, education, and the like. By the same token, a firm's budget is a plan detailing how funds will be spent on labor, raw materials, capital goods, and so on, and also how the funds for these expenditures will be obtained. Just as the federal budget can be

104

used as a device to insure that the Department of Defense, Department of Agriculture, and others limit their expenditures to specified amounts, the corporate budget can also be used as a device for formulating the firm's plans and for exercising control over the various departments.

Budgeting is, thus, a management tool used for both *planning* and *control.* Depending on the nature of the business, detailed plans may be formulated for the next few months, the next year, the next five years, or even longer. A company engaged in, say, heavy construction is constantly extending bids that may or may not be accepted; it cannot, and indeed need not, plan as far ahead as an electric utility company. The electric utility can base its projections on population growth, which is predictable for five- to ten-year periods, and it *must* plan asset acquisitions years ahead because of the long lead times involved in constructing dams, nuclear power plants, and the like.

NATURE OF THE BUDGETING PROCESS

Fundamentally, the budgeting process is a method to improve operations; it is a continuous effort to specify what should be done to get the job completed in the best possible way. Corporate budgeting should not be thought of as a device for limiting expenditures: the budgeting process is a tool for obtaining the most productive and profitable use of the company's resources. The budget requires a set of performance standards, or targets, that can be compared to actual results; this process is called "controlling to plan." It is a continuous monitoring procedure, reviewing and evaluating performance with reference to the previously established standards.

Establishing standards requires a realistic understanding of the activities carried on by the firm. Arbitrary standards, set without a basic understanding of the minimum costs as determined by the nature of the firm's operations, can do more harm than good. Budgets imposed in an arbitrary fashion may represent impossible targets at the one extreme or standards that are too lax at the other. If standards are unrealistically high, frustrations and resentment will develop. If standards are unduly lax, costs will be out of control, profits will suffer, and morale will deteriorate. However, a set of budgets based on a clear understanding and careful analysis of operations can play an important, positive role for the firm.[1]

---

[1]The authors are familiar with one case where an unrealistic budget ruined a major national corporation. Top management set impossible performance and growth goals for the various divisions. The divisions, in an effort to meet the sales and profit projections, expanded into high-risk product lines (especially real estate development ventures), employed questionable accounting practices that tended to overstate profits, and the like. Debt financing was emphasized in order to leverage earnings. Things looked good for several years, but eventually the true situation became apparent. Top management brought in a team of consultants in an attempt to correct the problems, but it was too late—the firm was beyond help. The interesting point, to us, is that the consultants traced the firm's difficulties *directly* back to the unrealistic targets that were established by top management without adequate consultation with the division managers.

Budgets can provide valuable guides to both high-level executives and middle-management personnel. Well-formulated and effectively developed budgets make subordinates aware that top management has a realistic understanding of the nature of the operations in the business firm, and such a budget can be an important communication link between top management and the divisional personnel whom they guide.

Budgets also represent planning and control devices that enable management to anticipate change and adapt to it. Business operations in today's economic environment are complex and are subject to heavy competitive pressures. In such an environment many kinds of changes take place. The rate of growth of the economy as a whole fluctuates, and these fluctuations affect different industries in a number of different ways. If a firm plans ahead, the budget and control process can provide management with a better basis for understanding the firm's operations in relation to the general environment. This increased understanding leads to faster reactions to developing events, thus increasing the firm's ability to perform effectively.

The budgeting process, in summary, improves internal coordination. Decisions for each product at every stage—at the research, engineering, production, marketing, personnel, and financial levels—all have an impact on the firm's profits. Planning and control is the essence of profit planning, and the budget system provides an integrated picture of the firm's operations as a whole. Therefore, the budget system enables the manager of each division to see the relation of his part of the enterprise to the totality of the firm. For example, a production decision to alter the level of work-in-process inventories, or a marketing decision to change the terms under which a particular product is sold, can be traced through the entire budget system to show its effects on the firm's overall profitability. The budgeting system is thus a most important financial tool.

Budget System

The overall nature of the budget process is outlined in Figure 6–1. Budgeting is a part of the total planning activity in the firm, so we must begin with a statement of corporate goals or objectives. The statement of goals (shown in the box at the top of the figure) determines the second section of the figure, the corporate long-range plan. Moving down the figure, we see that a segment of the corporate long-range plan includes a long-range sales forecast. This forecast requires a determination of the number and types of products that will be manufactured both at present and in the future years encompassed by the long-range plan: this is the product mix strategy.

Short-term forecasts and budgets are formulated within the framework of the long-range plan. For example, one might begin with a sales forecast covering six months or one year. The short-term sales forecast provides a basis for (and is dependent on) the broad range of policies indicated in the lower portion of Figure 6–1. *First,* there are manufacturing policies covering the choice of types of equipment, plant layout, and production-line arrangements. In addition, the kind of durability built into the products and their associated costs will be considered. *Second,* a broad set of marketing policies must be formulated. These relate to such items as the development of the firm's own sales organization versus the use of outside sales organizations; the number of salesmen, and the method by which they will be compensated; the forms of, types of, and amounts spent on advertising; and other factors. *Third* are the research and general management policies. Research policies relate to relative emphasis on basic versus applied research and the product areas emphasized by both types of research. *Fourth* are financial policies, the subject of this chapter. The four major policy sets must be established simultaneously, as each affects the other. We shall concentrate on financial control policies, but it is important to realize the interdependencies between financial and other policies.

FIGURE 6–1 Overall View of the Total Budgeting Process

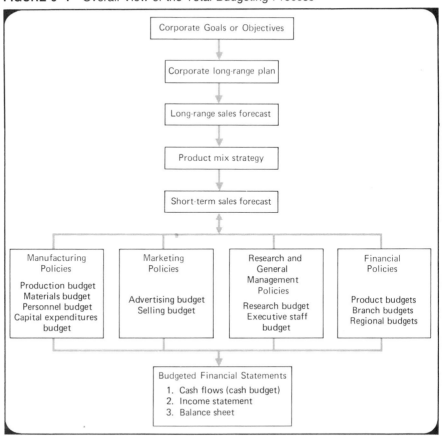

Financial Control Policies

Financial control policies include the organization and content of various kinds of financial control budgets. These include a budget for individual products and for every significant activity of the firm. In addition, budgets will be formulated to control operations at individual branch offices. Those budgets, in turn, are grouped and modified to control regional operations.

In a similar manner, policies established at the manufacturing, marketing, research, and general management levels give rise to a series of budgets. For example, the production budget will reflect the use of materials, parts, labor, and facilities; each of the major elements in a production budget is likely to have its own individual budget program. There will be a materials budget, a labor or personnel requirements budget, and a facilities or long-run capital expenditures budget. After the product is produced, the next step in the process will call for a marketing budget. Related to the overall process are the general office and executive requirements, which will be reflected in the general and administrative budget system.

The results of projecting all those elements of cost are reflected in the budgeted (also called "pro forma" or "projected") income statement. The anticipated sales give rise to the various types of investments needed to produce the products; these investments, plus the beginning balance sheet, provide the necessary data for developing the assets side of the balance sheet.

Those assets must be financed, and a cash flow analysis—the cash budget—is required. The cash budget indicates the combined effects of the budgeted operations on the firm's cash flows. A positive net cash flow indicates that the firm has ample financing. However, if an increase in the volume of operations leads to a negative cash flow, additional financing will be required. And that will lead directly to choices of financing, which is the subject of a considerable portion of the remainder of the book.

Since the structures of the income statement and the balance sheet have already been covered in Chapter 3, the rest of this section will deal with the two remaining aspects of the budgeting process—the cash budget and the concept of variable, or flexible, budgets.

CASH BUDGETING

The cash budget indicates not only the total amount of financing that is required but its timing as well. This statement shows the amount of funds needed month by month, week by week, or even on a daily basis; it is one of the financial manager's most important tools. Because a clear understanding of the nature of cash budgeting is important, the process is described by means of an example that makes the elements of the cash budget explicit.

Marvel Toy is a medium-sized toy manufacturer. Sales are highly seasonal, with the peak occurring in September when retailers stock up for the Christmas season. All sales are made on terms that allow a cash discount on payments made within 30 days; if the discount is not taken, the full amount must be paid in 60 days. However, Marvel, like most other companies, finds that some of its customers delay payment up to 90 days. Experience shows that on 20 percent of the sales, payment is made within 30 days; on 70 percent of the sales, payment is made during the second month after the sale; while on 10 percent of the sales, payment is made during the third month.

Marvel's production is geared to future sales. Purchased materials and parts, which amount to 70 percent of sales, are bought the month before the company expects to sell the finished product. Its own purchase terms permit Marvel to delay payment on its purchases for one month. In other words, if August sales are forecast at $30,000, then purchases during July will amount to $21,000, and this amount will actually be paid in August.

Wages and salaries, rent, and other cash expenses are given in Table 6–1. The company also has a tax payment of $8,000 coming due in August. Its capital budgeting plans call for the purchase in July of a new machine tool costing $10,000, payment to be made in September. Assuming the company needs to keep a $5,000 cash balance at all times and has $6,000 on July 1, what are Marvel's financial requirements for the period July through December?

The cash requirements are worked out in the cash budget shown in Table 6–1. The top half of the table provides a worksheet for calculating collections on sales and payments on purchases. The first line in the worksheet gives the sales forecast for the period May through January—May and June sales are necessary to determine collections for July and August. Next, cash collections are given. The first line of this section shows that 20 percent of the sales during any given month are collected that month. The second shows the collections on the prior month's sales—70 percent of sales in the preceding month. The third line gives collections from sales two months earlier— 10 percent of sales in that month. The collections are summed to find the total cash receipts from sales during each month under consideration.

With the worksheet completed, the cash budget itself can be considered. Receipts from collections are given on the top line. Next, payments during each month are summarized. The difference between cash receipts and cash payments is the net cash gain or loss during the month; for July, there is a net cash loss of $4,200. The initial cash on hand at the beginning of the month is added to the net cash gain or loss during the month to yield the cumulative cash that will be on hand if no financing is done; at the end of July, Marvel Toy will have cumulative cash equal to $1,800. The desired cash balance, $5,000, is subtracted from the cumulative cash balance to determine the amount of financing that the firm needs if it is to maintain the desired level of cash. At the end of July we see that Marvel will need $3,200; thus, loans outstanding will total $3,200 at the end of July.

TABLE 6–1 Marvel Toy Company Cash Budget

					Worksheet				
	May	June	July	Aug.	Sept.	Oct.	Nov.	Dec.	Jan.
Sales (net of cash discounts)	$10,000	$10,000	$20,000	$30,000	$40,000	$20,000	$20,000	$10,000	$10,000
Collections									
First month (20%)	$ 2,000	$ 2,000	$ 4,000	$ 6,000	$ 8,000	$ 4,000	$ 4,000	$ 2,000	$ 2,000
Second month (70%)		7,000	7,000	14,000	21,000	28,000	14,000	14,000	7,000
Third month (10%)			1,000	1,000	2,000	3,000	4,000	2,000	2,000
Total	$ 2,000	$ 9,000	$12,000	$21,000	$31,000	$35,000	$22,000	$18,000	$11,000
Purchases (70% of next month's sales)	$ 7,000	$14,000	$21,000	$28,000	$14,000	$14,000	$7,000	7,000	
Payments (one month lag)		7,000	14,000	21,000	28,000	14,000	14,000	7,000	7,000
				Cash Budget					
Receipts									
Collections			$12,000	$ 21,000	$ 31,000	$ 35,000	$22,000	$18,000	
Payments									
Purchases			14,000	21,000	28,000	14,000	14,000	7,000	
Wages and salaries			1,500	2,000	2,500	1,500	1,500	1,000	
Rent			500	500	500	500	500	500	
Other expenses			200	300	400	200	200	100	
Taxes			—	—	—	—	—	—	
Payment on machine			—	8,000	10,000	—	—	—	
Total payments			$16,200	$ 31,800	$ 41,400	$ 16,200	$16,200	$ 8,600	
Net cash gain (loss) during month			$ (4,200)	$(10,800)	$(10,400)	$ 18,800	$ 5,800	$ 9,400	
Cash at start of month if no borrowing is done			6,000	1,800	(9,000)	(19,400)	(600)	5,200	
Cumulative cash (= cash at start plus gains or minus losses)			$ 1,800	$ (9,000)	$(19,400)	$ (600)	$ 5,200	$14,600	
Less: Desired level of cash			(5,000)	(5,000)	(5,000)	(5,000)	(5,000)	(5,000)	
Total loans outstanding to maintain $5,000 cash balance			$ 3,200	$ 14,000	$ 24,400	$ 5,600			
Surplus cash			—	—	—	—	200	$ 9,600	

This same procedure is used in the following months. Sales will expand seasonally in August; with the increased sales will come increased payments for purchases, wages, and other items. Moreover, the $8,000 tax bill is due in August. Receipts from sales will go up too, but the firm will still be left with a $10,800 cash deficit during the month. The total financial requirements at the end of August will be $14,000—the $3,200 needed at the end of July plus the $10,800 cash deficit for August. Thus, loans outstanding will total $14,000 at the end of August.

Sales peak in September, and the cash deficit during this month will amount to another $10,400. The total need for funds through September will increase to $24,400. Sales, purchases, and payments for past purchases will fall markedly in October; collections will be the highest of any month because they reflect the high September sales. As a result, Marvel Toy will enjoy a healthy $18,800 cash surplus during October. This surplus can be used to pay off borrowings, so the need for financing will decline by $18,800, to $5,600.

Marvel will have another cash surplus in November, and this extra cash will permit the company to eliminate completely the need for financing. In fact, the company is expected to have $200 in surplus cash by the month's end, while another cash surplus in December will swell the extra cash to $9,600. With such a large amount of unneeded funds, Marvel's treasurer will doubtless want to make investments in some interest-bearing securities or put the funds to use in some other way.[2]

VARIABLE, OR FLEXIBLE, BUDGETS

Budgets are planned allocations of a firm's resources, based on forecasts for the future. Two important elements influence actual performance. One is the impact of external influences over which the firm has little or no control—developments in the economy as a whole and competitive developments in the firm's own industry. The second element, which is controllable by the firm, is its level of efficiency at a given volume of sales. It is useful to separate the impact of these two elements, as this separation is necessary for evaluating individual performances.

The essence of the variable budget system is to introduce flexibility into budgets by recognizing that certain types of expenditures will vary at different levels of output. Thus, a firm might have an alternative level of outlay budgeted for different volumes of operation—high, low, medium. One of management's responsibilities is to determine which of the alternative budgets should be in effect for the planning period under consideration.

[2]Types of investments for excess funds are discussed in Chapter 8.

The regression method, which we described in the preceding chapter in connection with financial forecasting, may also be used to establish the basis for flexible budgeting. The use of the concept can be illustrated by a specific example. Suppose that a retail store, the Hubler Department Store, has had the experience indicated by the historical data set forth in Table 6–2. It is apparent from the data that the number of employees the firm needs is dependent upon the dollar volume of sales that occurs during a month. This is seen more easily from a scatter diagram such as that in Figure 6–2. The freehand regression line is sloped positively because the number of employees increases as the volume of sales increases. The independent variable, dollar volume of sales, is called the *control variable.* Variations in the control variable cause changes in total expenses. The volume of sales

TABLE 6–2   Hubler Department Store
Relationship between sales and employees

Month	Sales (in millions of dollars)	Number of Employees
January	4	42
February	5	51
March	6	60
April	7	75
May	10	102
June	8	83
July	5	55
August	9	92

FIGURE 6–2   Scatter Diagram and Regression Line: Hubler Department Store

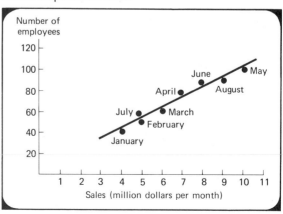

can be forecast, and the number of employees can be read from the regression chart. The relations are expressed in tabular form in Table 6–3. Given the forecast of sales, standards are provided for the expected number of employees and the weekly payroll.[3]

TABLE 6–3   Hubler Department Store
               Budget allowance

Sales (millions of dollars)	Number of Employees	Weekly Payroll Estimate (average wage, $100)
$ 6	62	$ 6,200
7	72	7,200
8	82	8,200
9	92	9,200
10	102	10,200
11	112	11,200

PROBLEMS OF BUDGETING

Four major problems are encountered when using budget systems. First, budgetary programs can grow to be so complete and so detailed that they become cumbersome, meaningless, and unduly expensive. Overbudgeting is dangerous.

Second, budgetary goals may come to supersede enterprise goals. A budget is a tool, not an end in itself. Enterprise goals by definition supersede subsidiary plans of which budgets are a part. Moreover, budgets are based on future expectations that may not be realized. There is no acceptable reason for neglecting to alter budgets as circumstances change. This reasoning is the core of the argument in favor of more flexible budgets.

Third, budgets can tend to hide inefficiencies by continuing initial expenditures in succeeding periods without proper evaluation. Budgets growing from precedent usually contain undesirable expenditures. They should not be used as umbrellas under which slovenly, inefficient management can hide. Consequently, the budgetary process must contain provision for reexamination of standards and other bases of planning by which policies are translated into numerical terms.

[3]Note that regression analysis provides even more flexibility in budgeting than do the high, medium, and low levels mentioned earlier. Also, it is possible to include *confidence levels* when using the regression method. For example, Table 6–3 shows that when volume is at $8 million, we expect to have 82 employees and a weekly payroll of $8,200. Although this relationship would probably not hold *exactly,* we might find that actual observations lie within 78 and 86 employees at this sales volume 95 percent of the time. Thus, 95 percent confidence levels would encompass the range 78–86. Similar ranges could be determined for other volumes; management might, as a matter of control policy, investigate whenever actual performances were outside this expected range.

Finally, case study evidence suggests that the use of budgets as a pressure device defeats their basic objectives. Budgets, if used as instruments of tyranny, cause resentment and frustrations, which in turn lead to inefficiency. In order to counteract this effect, it has been recommended that top management increase the participation of subordinates during the preparatory stages of the budgets.

USE OF FINANCIAL PLANS AND BUDGETS

Forecasts, or long-range plans, are necessary in all the firm's operations. The personnel department must have a good idea of the scale of future operations if it is to plan its hiring and training activities properly. The production department must be sure that the productive capacity is available to meet the projected product demand, and the finance department must be sure that funds are on hand to meet the firm's financial requirements.

The tools and techniques discussed in this and the preceding chapters are actually used in several separate, but related, ways. First, the percent-of-sales method or, preferably, the regression method is used to make a long-range forecast of financial requirements over a projected three- to five-year period. This forecast is then used to draw up the strategic financing plans during the planning period. The company might, for example, plan to meet its financial requirements with retained earnings and short-term bank debt during, say, 1979 and 1980, float a bond issue in 1981, use retained earnings in 1982, and finally sell an issue of common stock in 1983. Fairly long lead times are necessary when companies sell bonds or stocks; otherwise, they might be forced to go into the market during unfavorable periods.

In addition to the long-run strategic planning, the financial manager must also make accurate short-run forecasts to be sure that funds will be available to meet seasonal and other short-run requirements. He might, for example, have a meeting with his bank's loan officer to discuss his company's need for funds during the coming year. Prior to the meeting, he would have his accountants prepare a detailed cash budget showing the need for money during each of the coming twelve months. The cash budget would show the maximum amount that would be needed during the year, how much would be needed during each month, and how cash surpluses would be generated at some point to enable the firm to repay the bank loan.

The financial manager would also have his firm's most recent, and its pro forma, balance sheets and income statements. He would have calculated the key financial ratios to show both his actual and his projected financial positions to the banker. If the firm's financial position is sound and if its cash budget appears reasonable, the bank will commit itself to make the required funds available. Even if the bank decides that the company's request is unreasonable and denies the loan request, the financial manager will have time to seek other sources of funds. While it might not be pleasant to have to look elsewhere for money, it is much better to know ahead of time that the loan request will be refused.

DIVISIONAL CONTROL IN A DECENTRALIZED FIRM

In our discussion of the du Pont system of financial control in Chapter 3, we considered its use for the firm as a whole rather than for different divisions of a single firm. The du Pont system can, however, also be used to control the various parts of a multidivisional firm.

For organizational reasons, large firms are generally set up on a decentralized basis. For example, a firm such as General Electric establishes separate divisions for heavy appliances, light appliances, power transformers, fossil fuel generating equipment, nuclear generating equipment, and so on. Each division is defined as a *profit center,* or financial responsibility center. Each profit center has its own investments—its fixed and current assets, together with a share of such general corporate assets as research labs and headquarters buildings—and each is expected to earn an appropriate return on its investment.

The corporate headquarters, or central staff, typically controls the various divisions by a form of the du Pont system. When it is used for divisional control, the procedure is frequently referred to as ROI (return on investment) control. If a particular division's ROI falls below a target figure, then the centralized corporate staff assists the division's own financial staff trace back through the du Pont system to determine the cause of the substandard ROI. Each division manager is judged by his division's ROI, and he is rewarded or penalized accordingly. Therefore, division managers are motivated to keep their ROIs up to the target level. These individual actions, in turn, should maintain the total firm's ROI at an appropriate level.

In addition to its use in managerial control, ROI can be used to allocate funds to the various divisions. The firm as a whole has financial resources— retained earnings, cash flow from depreciation, and the ability to obtain additional debt and equity funds from capital markets. Those funds can be allocated to different divisions on the basis of divisional ROI's, with divisions having high ROI's receiving more funds than those with low ROI's.[4]

A number of problems may arise if ROI control is used without proper safeguards. Since the divisional managers are rewarded on the basis of their ROI performance, if their morale is to be maintained it is absolutely essential that the divisional managers feel that their divisional ROI does indeed provide

---

[4]The point of this procedure is to increase the total firm's ROI. To maximize the overall ROI, marginal ROI's between divisions should be equalized.

an accurate measure of relative performance. But ROI is dependent on a number of factors in addition to managerial competence. Some of them are listed below.

1. *Depreciation:* ROI is very sensitive to depreciation policy. If one division is writing off assets at a relatively rapid rate, its annual profits and, hence, its ROI will be reduced.

2. *Book value of assets:* If an older division is using assets that have been largely written off, both its current depreciation charges and its investment base will be low. This will make its ROI high in relation to newer divisions.

3. *Transfer pricing:* In most corporations some divisions sell to other divisions. In General Motors, for example, the Fisher Body Division sells to the Chevrolet Division; in such cases the price at which goods are transferred between divisions has a fundamental effect on divisional profits. If the transfer price of auto bodies is set relatively high, then Fisher Body will have a relatively high ROI and Chevrolet a relatively low ROI.

4. *Time periods:* Many projects have long gestation periods—expenditures must be made for research and development, plant construction, market development, and the like; such expenditures will add to the investment base without a commensurate increase in profits for several years. During this period, a division's ROI could be seriously reduced; without proper constraints, its division manager could be improperly penalized. Especially when we recognize the frequency of personnel transfers in larger corporations, we can see that the timing problem could possibly cause managers to refrain from making long-term investments that are in the best interests of the firm.

5. *Industry conditions:* If one division is operating in an industry where conditions are favorable and rates of return are high, whereas another is in an industry suffering from excessive competition, such environmental differences may cause the favored division to look good and the unfavored division to look bad, quite apart from any differences in their respective managers. Signal Companies' aerospace division, for example, could hardly be expected to show up as well as their truck division in a year like 1976, when the entire aerospace industry was suffering severe problems and truck sales were booming. External conditions must be taken into account when appraising ROI performance.

Because of those problems, divisions' ROI's must be supplemented with other criteria when evaluating performance. For example, a division's growth rate in sales, profits, and market share, as well as its ROI in comparison with other firms in its own industry, have all been used as a part of the overall control and evaluation procedure.

Although ROI control has been used with great success in American industry, the system cannot be used in a mechanical sense by inexperienced personnel. As with most other tools, it is a good one if used properly, but it is a destructive one if misused.

EXTERNAL USES OF FINANCIAL FORECASTS AND BUDGETS

We have stressed the use of planning and budgeting for internal purposes, that is, to increase the efficiency of a firm's operations. With relatively minor modifications, those same tools and techniques can be used in both credit analysis and security analysis. For example, outside security analysts can make a forecast of a given firm's sales and, through the income statement and balance sheet relationships, can prepare pro forma (projected) balance sheets and income statements. Credit analysts can make similar projections to aid in estimating the likely need for funds by their customers and the likelihood that borrowers can make prompt repayment.

This kind of analysis has actually been conducted on a large scale in recent years. Very complete financial data going back some twenty years on several thousand large, publicly owned corporations are now available on magnetic tapes (Standard and Poor's Compustat tapes). These tapes are being used by security analysts in highly sophisticated ways. From what we have seen, analyses conducted in such a manner offer large potential benefits. The same tapes, frequently supplemented with additional data, are being used by the major lending institutions—banks and insurance companies—to forecast their customers' needs for funds and, thus, to plan their own financial requirements.

SUMMARY

A budget is a plan stated in terms of specific expenditures for specific purposes. It is used for both planning and control, its overall purpose being to improve internal operations, thereby reducing costs and raising profitability. A budgeting system starts with a set of performance standards, or targets. The targets constitute, in effect, the firm's financial plan. The budgeted figures are compared with actual results—this is the control phase of the budget system, and it is a critical step in well-operated companies.

Although the entire budget system is of vital importance to corporate management, one aspect of the system is especially important to the financial manager—the cash budget. The cash budget is, in fact, the principal tool for making short-run financial forecasts. Cash budgets, if used properly, are highly accurate and can pinpoint the funds that will be needed, when they will be needed, and when cash flows will be sufficient to retire any loans that might be necessary.

A good budget system will recognize that some factors lie outside the firm's control. Especially important here is the state of the economy and its effects on sales, and *flexible budgets* will be set up as targets for the different departments assuming different levels of sales. Also, a good system will insure that those responsible for carrying out a plan are involved in its preparation; this procedure will help guard against the establishment of un-realistic targets and unobtainable goals.

As a firm becomes larger, it is necessary for it to decentralize operations to some extent, and decentralized operations require some centralized control over the various divisions. The principal tool used for such control is the return on investment (ROI) method. There are problems with ROI control. But if care is taken in its use, the method can be quite valuable to a decentralized firm.

QUESTIONS

6-1. What use might a confidence interval scheme have in variable budgeting?

6-2. Why is a cash budget important even when there is plenty of cash in the bank?

6-3. What is the difference between the long-range financial forecasting concept (for example, the percent-of-sales method) and the budgeting concept? How might they be used together?

6-4. Assume that a firm is making up its long-run financial budget. What period should this budget cover—one month, six months, one year, three years, five years, or some other period? Justify your answer.

6-5. Why is a detailed budget more important to a large, multidivisional firm than to a small, single-product firm?

6-6. Assume that your uncle is a major stockholder in a multidivisional firm that uses a naive ROI criterion for evaluating divisional managers and bases managers' salaries in large part on this evaluation. You can have the job of division manager in any division you choose. If you are a salary maximizer, what divisional characteristics would you seek? If, because of your "good performance," you became president of the firm, what changes would you make?

PROBLEMS

6-1. The Simms Company is planning to request a line of credit from its bank. The following sales forecasts have been made for 1976 and 1977:[5]

May 1976	$150,000
June	150,000
July	300,000
August	450,000
September	600,000
October	300,000
November	300,000
December	75,000
January 1977	150,000

[5]This problem is adapted from *Cases in Managerial Finance,* second edition, Case 5.

Collection estimates were obtained from the credit and collection department as follows: collected within the month of sale, 5 percent; collected the month following the sale, 80 percent; collected the second month following the sale, 15 percent. Payments for labor and raw materials are typically made during the month following the month in which these costs are incurred. Total labor and raw materials costs are estimated for each month as follows (payments are made the following month):

May 1976	$ 75,000
June	75,000
July	105,000
August	735,000
September	255,000
October	195,000
November	135,000
December	75,000

General and administrative salaries will amount to approximately $22,500 a month; lease payments under long-term lease contracts will be $7,500 a month; depreciation charges are $30,000 a month; miscellaneous expenses will be $2,250 a month; income tax payments of $52,500 will be due in both September and December; and a progress payment of $150,000 on a new research laboratory must be paid in October. Cash on hand on July 1 will amount to $110,000, and a minimum cash balance of $75,000 should be maintained throughout the cash budget period.

a. Prepare a monthly cash budget for the last six months of 1976.

b. Prepare an estimate of required financing (or excess funds) for each month during the period, that is, the amount of money that the Simms Company will need to borrow (or will have available to invest) each month.

c. Suppose receipts from sales come in uniformly during the month (that is, cash payments come in 1/30th each day), but all outflows are paid on the fifth of the month. Would this have an effect on the cash budget; that is, would the cash budget you have prepared be valid under these assumptions? If not, what could be done to make a valid estimation of financing requirements?

6-2. Gulf and Eastern, Inc., is a diversified multinational corporation that produces a wide variety of goods and services, including chemicals, soaps, tobacco products, toys, plastics, pollution control equipment, canned food, sugar, motion pictures, and computer software.[6] The corporation's major divisions were brought together in the early 1960s under a decentralized form of management; each division was evaluated in terms of its profitability, efficiency, and return on investments. This decentralized organization persisted through most of the decade, during which Gulf and Eastern experienced a high average growth rate in total assets, earnings, and stock prices.

Toward the end of 1975, however, those trends were reversed. The organization was faced with declining earnings, unstable stock prices, and a generally uncertain future. This situation persisted into 1976, but during that year a new president, Lynn Thompson, was appointed by the board of directors. Thompson, who had served for a time on the financial staff of I.E. du Pont, used the du Pont system to evaluate the various divisions. All showed definite weaknesses.

---

[6] This problem is taken from *Cases in Managerial Finance,* second edition.

Thompson reported to the board that a principal reason for the poor overall performance was a lack of control by central management over each division's activities. She was particularly disturbed by the consistently poor results of the corporation's budgeting procedures. Under that system, each division manager drew up a projected budget for the next quarter, along with estimated sales, revenue, and profit; funds were then allocated to the divisions, basically in proportion to their budget requests. However, actual budgets seldom matched the projections; wide discrepancies occurred and this, of course, resulted in a highly inefficient use of capital.

In an attempt to correct the situation, Thompson asked the firm's chief financial officer to draw up a plan to improve the budgeting, planning, and control processes. When the plan was submitted, its basic provisions included the following:

1. To improve the quality of the divisional budgets, the division managers should be informed that the continuance of wide variances between their projected and actual budgets would result in dismissal.

2. A system should be instituted under which funds would be allocated to divisions on the basis of their average return on investment (ROI) during the last four quarters. Since funds were short, divisions with high ROIs would get most of the available money.

3. Only about one-half of each division manager's present compensation should be received as salary; the rest should be in the form of a bonus related to the division's average ROI for the quarter.

4. Each division should submit to the central office for approval all capital expenditure requests, production schedules, and price changes. Thus, the company would be *recentralized*.

a. 1. Is it reasonable to expect the new procedures to improve the accuracy of budget forecasts?

2. Should all divisions be expected to maintain the same degree of accuracy?

3. In what other ways might the budgets be made?

b. 1. What problems would be associated with the use of the ROI criterion in allocating funds among the divisions?

2. What effect would the period used in computing ROI (that is, four quarters, one quarter, two years, and so on) have on the effectiveness of this method?

3. What problems might occur in evaluating the ROI in the crude rubber and auto tires divisions? between the sugar products and pollution control equipment divisions?

c. What problems would be associated with rewarding each manager on the basis of his division's ROI?

d. How well would Thompson's policy of recentralization work in a highly diversified corporation such as this, particularly in light of her financial officer's three other proposals?

Working Capital Management

Part Two

In Part One, we analyzed the firm's operations in an overall, aggregate manner. Now we must examine the various aspects of the firm's financial picture in more detail. In Part Two, we focus on the top half of the balance sheet, studying current assets, current liabilities, and the interrelationship between these two sets of accounts. This type of analysis is commonly called *working capital management.*

In Chapter 7, we examine some general principles of overall working capital management. Then, in Chapter 8, we consider the determinants of current assets: cash, marketable securities, accounts receivable, and inventories. Finally, in Chapter 9, we discuss current liabilities, considering in some detail the principal sources and forms of short-term funds.

Working Capital Policy

7

Working capital refers to a firm's investment in short-term assets—cash, short-term securities, accounts receivable, and inventories. *Net working capital* is defined as current assets minus current liabilities. *Working capital management* refers to all aspects of the administration of both current assets and current liabilities.

No new theories or basic principles are involved in working capital management—rather, this phase of financial management simply requires the application of valuation concepts developed throughout the text. Current asset holdings should be expanded to the point where marginal returns on increases in such assets are just equal to the cost of capital required to finance these increases, while current liabilities should be used in place of long-term debt whenever their use lowers the average cost of capital.

IMPORTANCE OF WORKING CAPITAL MANAGEMENT

Working capital management includes a number of aspects that make it an important topic for study, and we will now consider some of them.

Time Devoted to Working Capital Management

Surveys indicate that the largest portion of a financial manager's time is devoted to the day-by-day internal operations of the firm; this may be appropriately subsumed under the heading "working capital management." Since so

123

much time is spent on working capital decisions, it is appropriate that the subject be covered carefully in managerial finance courses.

Investment in Current Assets

Characteristically, current assets represent more than half the total assets of a business firm. Because they represent a large investment and because this investment tends to be relatively volatile, current assets are worthy of the financial manager's careful attention.

Importance for Small Firms

Working capital management is particularly important for small firms. A small firm may minimize its investments in fixed assets by renting or leasing plant and equipment, but there is no way it can avoid an investment in cash, receivables, and inventories. Therefore, current assets are particularly significant for the financial manager of a small firm. Further, because a small firm has relatively limited access to the long-term capital markets, it must necessarily rely heavily on trade credit and short-term bank loans, both of which affect net working capital by increasing current liabilities.

Relationship between Sales Growth and Current Assets

The relationship between sales growth and the need to finance current assets is close and direct. For example, if the firm's average collection period is forty days and if its credit sales are $1,000 a day, it will have an investment of $40,000 in accounts receivable. If sales rise to $2,000 a day, the investment in accounts receivable will rise to $80,000. Sales increases produce similar immediate needs for additional inventories and, perhaps, for cash balances. All such needs must be financed, and since they arise so quickly, it is imperative that the financial manager keep himself aware of developments in the working capital segment of the firm. Of course, continued sales increases will require additional long-term assets, which must also be financed. However, fixed asset investments, while critically important to the firm in a strategic, long-run sense, do not generally have the same urgency as do current asset investments.

ORIGINAL CONCEPT OF WORKING CAPITAL

The term "working capital" originated at a time when most industries were closely related to agriculture. Processors would buy crops in the fall, process them, sell the finished product, and end up just before the next harvest with relatively low inventories. Bank loans with maximum maturities of one year were used to finance both the purchase and the processing costs, and these loans were retired with the proceeds from the sale of the finished products.

The situation is depicted in Figure 7–1. There fixed assets are shown to be growing steadily over time, while current assets jump at harvest season, then decline during the year, ending at zero just before the next crop is harvested. Short-term credit is used to finance current assets, and fixed assets are financed with long-term funds. Thus, the top segment of the graph deals with working capital.

FIGURE 7–1 Fixed and Current Assets and Their Financing

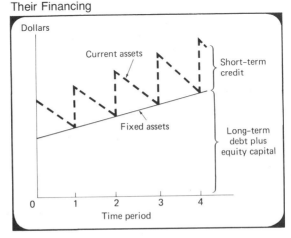

The figure represents, of course, an idealized situation—current assets build up gradually as crops are purchased and processed; inventories are drawn down less regularly; and ending inventory balances do not decline to zero. Nevertheless, the example does illustrate the general nature of the production and financing process, and working capital management consists of decisions relating to the top section of the graph—managing current assets and arranging the short-term credit used to finance them.

EXTENDING THE WORKING CAPITAL CONCEPT

As the economy became less oriented toward agriculture, the production and financing cycles of "typical" businesses changed. Although seasonal patterns still existed, and business cycles also caused asset requirements to fluctuate, it became apparent that current assets rarely, if ever, dropped to zero. This realization led to the development of the idea of "permanent current assets," diagrammed in Figure 7–2. As the figure is drawn, it maintains the traditional notion that permanent assets should be financed with long-term capital, while temporary assets should be financed with short-term credit.

FIGURE 7–2 Fluctuating versus Permanent Assets

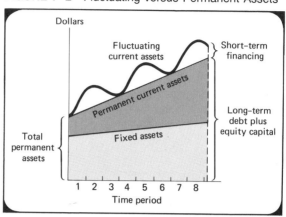

The pattern shown in Figures 7–1 and 7–2 is considered to be desirable because it minimizes the risk that the firm may be unable to pay off its maturing obligations. To illustrate, suppose a firm borrows on a one-year basis and uses the funds obtained to build and equip a plant. Cash flows from the plant (profits plus depreciation) are not sufficient to pay off the loan at the end of the year, so the loan must be renewed. If for some reason the lender refuses to renew the loan, then the firm has problems. Had the plant been financed with long-term debt, however, cash flows would have been sufficient to retire the loan, and the problem of renewal would not have arisen. Thus, if a firm finances long-term assets with permanent capital and short-term assets with temporary capital, its financial risk is lower than it would be if long-term assets were financed with short-term debt.

At the limit, a firm can attempt to match the maturity structure of its assets and liabilities exactly. A machine expected to last for five years could be financed by a five year loan; a twenty year loan building could be financed by a twenty-year mortgage bond; inventory expected to be sold in twenty days could be financed by a twenty-day bank loan; and so forth. Actually, of course, uncertainty about the lives of assets prevents this exact maturity matching. We will examine this point in the following sections.

Figure 7–2 shows the situation for a firm that attempts to match asset and liability maturities exactly. Such a policy could be followed, but firms may follow other maturity-matching policies if they desire. Figure 7–3, for example, illustrates the situation for a firm that finances all its fixed assets with long-term capital but part of its permanent current assets with short-term credit.[1]

---

[1]Firms generally have some short-term credit in the form of "spontaneous" funds—accounts payable and accruals (see Chapter 5). Used within limits, these constitute "free" capital, so virtually all firms employ at least some short-term credit at all times. We could modify the graphs to take this into account, but nothing is lost by simply abstracting from spontaneous funds, as we do.

FIGURE 7–3   Fluctuating versus Permanent Assets

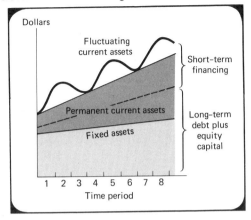

The dashed line could have even been drawn *below* the line designating fixed assets, indicating that all the current assets and part of the fixed assets are financed with short-term credit; this would be a highly aggressive, non-conservative position, and the firm would be very much subject to potential loan renewal problems.

Alternatively, as in Figure 7–4, the dashed line could be drawn *above* the line designating permanent current assets, indicating that permanent capital is being used to meet seasonal demands. In this case, the firm uses a small amount of short-term credit to meet its peak seasonal requirements, but it also meets a part of its seasonal needs by "storing liquidity" in the form of marketable securities during the off-season. The humps above the dashed line represent short-term financing; the troughs below the dashed line represent short-term security holdings.

FIGURE 7–4   Fluctuating versus Permanent Assets and Liabilities

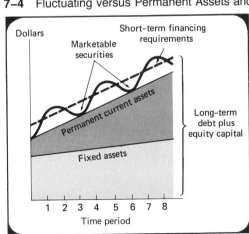

LONG-TERM VERSUS SHORT-TERM DEBT

The larger the percentage of funds obtained from long-term sources, the more conservative the firm's working capital policy. The reason for this, of course, is that during times of stress the firm may not be able to renew its short-term debt. This being so, why would firms ever use short-term credit (other than spontaneous credit)? Why not just use long-term funds? There are three primary answers to this question: flexibility, cost, and risk.

Flexibility

If the need for funds is seasonal or cyclical, the firm may not want to commit itself to long-term debt. Such debt can be refunded, provided the loan agreement includes a call or prepayment provision, but, even so, prepayment penalties can be expensive. Accordingly, if a firm expects its needs for funds to diminish in the near future, or if it thinks there is a good chance that such a reduction will occur, it may choose short-term debt for the flexibility it provides.

A cash budget is used to analyze the flexibility aspect of the maturity structure of debt. To illustrate, suppose Communications Satellite Corporation (Comsat) is planning to launch a series of satellites in 1978 with an estimated life of seven years. This generation of satellites will provide cash flows—depreciation plus profit—over its seven-year life. If Comsat uses debt to finance the series, it will schedule the debt's retirement to the expected cash flows from the project. A long-term bond issue would not be appropriate.

Cost of Long-Term versus Short-Term Debt

The cost aspect of the maturity decision involves *the term structure of interest rates,* or the relationship between the maturity of debt and the interest rate on the debt. Interest rates are frequently lower on short-term debt than on long-term debt. In March 1976, for example, discussions with investment bankers indicated that Comsat could borrow on the following terms:

Loan Maturity	Interest Rate (Percent)
90 days	6½
6 months	7
1 year	7½
3 years	8
5 years	8¼
10 years	8½
20 years	9

These points are graphed in Figure 7–5, a chart commonly called a yield curve, or the term to maturity curve.

FIGURE 7–5 The Term Structure of Interest Rates for Comsat,
March 1976

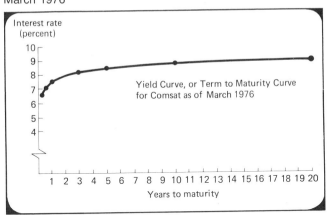

While the yield curve presented in Figure 7–5 is a fairly typical one, with short-term rates considerably lower than long-term rates, there are times when the yield curve is downward sloping.[2] At such times, which almost always occur when both long-term and short-term rates are relatively high, short-term money costs more than long-term debt. Nevertheless, since short-term rates have *generally* been lower than long-term rates, a firm's capital will probably be less costly if it borrows short term rather than long term.

Risk of Long-Term versus Short-Term Debt

Even though short-term debt is generally less expensive than long-term debt, use of short-term debt subjects the firm to more risk than does long-term debt. This risk effect occurs for two reasons: (1) If a firm borrows on a long-term basis, its interest costs will be relatively stable over time, but if it borrows on a short-term basis, its interest expenses will fluctuate widely, at times going quite high. For example, from January to June 1974, the short-term rate for large corporations almost doubled, going from 6½ percent to 12 percent, and then falling back to 7 percent in 1975. (2) If a firm borrows heavily on a short-term basis, it may find itself unable to repay this debt or it may be in such a shaky financial position that the lender will not extend the loan; thus, the firm could be forced into bankruptcy. We elaborate on these risk factors in the following sections.

Interest Rate Fluctuations Figure 7–6 shows the pattern of long-term and short-term interest rates during the 1960s and early 1970s. The long-term rate is represented by the Aaa bond rate, which is the rate on high-grade, long-

---

[2]In Chapter 22, we spell out these relationships in detail, giving data on the term structure of debt at various points in time.

term (twenty-five years or more) corporate bonds; the short-term rate is represented by the rate on prime commercial paper, which is the four-to-six month debt of top quality firms.

FIGURE 7–6   Long and Short-Term Interest Rates

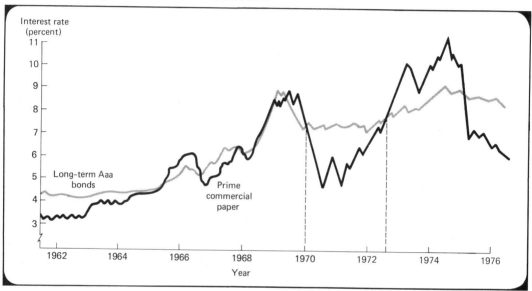

Several points should be noted about the graph. *First,* both long-term and short-term rates generally rose over the period. *Second,* short-term rates are more volatile than long-term rates. *Third,* only during 1966 and parts of 1969, 1970, 1973, and 1974 were long-term rates below short-term rates. It is worth noting that, except for a period of a few months in the mid-1950s, the long-term rate was consistently above the short-term rate in all years from 1929 to 1966. This confirms the point we made earlier about the yield curve generally sloping upward: whenever the long-term rate in Figure 7–6 is above the short-term rate, the yield curve in Figure 7–5 must be upward sloping.

Impact of a Rise in Rates on Interest Expenses   During a part of 1970 the yield curve was flat, indicating that long-term and short-term rates were the same. This can be seen in Figure 7–6, which shows that the long-term and short-term rates were both about 7 percent. Now suppose that in 1970 we were considering two firms, each with $100 million of debt. Firm S has only short-term debt; firm L only long-term debt. Both are stable, mature companies: the total assets of each remain relatively constant from year to year, and the debt of each stays at the $100 million level.

Firm S must "turn over" its debt every year, borrowing at the prevailing short-term interest rate. For simplicity, we assume that firm L's debt will not mature for twenty years, so that it's interest rate is fixed at 7 percent for the next twenty years regardless of what happens to either long-term or short-term rates in the intervening years.

Now consider the interest expense of the two firms one year later, in 1971. Firm L still has $100 million of 7 percent debt, so its interest expense is $7 million annually. Firm S, on the other hand, has $100 million of debt that now costs 5 percent, so its interest expense has fallen to $5 million. If other costs and revenues have remained constant between 1970 and 1971, firm L's profits after interest will have remained constant, but those of firm S will have risen sharply. The significant point is that while firm L *knows* what its future interest expenses will be, firm S does not, and this very absence of precise knowledge makes firm S the more risky one.

Danger of Being Unable to Refund   In addition to the risk of fluctuating interest charges, firm S faces another risk vis-à-vis firm L: S may run into temporary difficulties that prevent it from being able to refund its debt. Remember that when S's debt matures each year, the firm must negotiate new loans with its creditors. S must, of course, pay the going short-term rate, but suppose the loan comes up for renewal at a time when the firm is facing labor problems, a recession in demand for its products, extreme competitive pressures, or some other set of difficulties that has reduced its earnings.

The creditors will look at firm S's ratios, especially the times-interest-earned and current ratios, to judge its credit worthiness. S's current ratio is, of course, always lower than that of L, but in good times this will be overlooked—if earnings are high, the interest will be well covered and lenders will tolerate a low current ratio. If, however, earnings decline, pulling down the interest coverage ratio, creditors will certainly reevaluate the credit worthiness of firm S. At the very least, because of the perceived increased riskiness of the company, creditors will raise the interest rate charged; at the extreme, they will refuse to renew the loan. In the latter event, the firm will be forced to raise the funds needed to pay off the loan by selling assets at bargain basement prices, borrowing from other sources at exorbitant interest rates, or, in the extreme, going bankrupt.

Example of the Risk-Return Tradeoff

Thus far we have seen that short-term debt is typically less costly than long-term debt, but that using short-term debt entails greater risk than does using long-term debt. Thus, we are faced with a tradeoff between risk and rate of return. Although we are not prepared to resolve the conflict between risk and rate of return at this point in the book, a further example will help to clarify the issues involved.

Table 7–1 illustrates the nature of the tradeoff. Here, we assume that the firm has $100 million of assets, one-half held as fixed assets and the other half as current assets, and that it will earn 15 percent before interest and taxes on these assets. The debt ratio has been set at 50 percent, but the policy issue of whether to use short-term debt, costing 6 percent, or long-term debt, costing 8 percent, has not been determined. Working through the relationships, we see that a conservative policy of using no short-term credit results in a rate of return on equity of 11 percent, while the more aggressive policy of using only short-term credit boosts the rate of return to 12 percent.

TABLE 7–1   Effect of Maturity Structure of Debt on Return on Equity (Millions of dollars)

	Conservative	Average	Aggressive
Current assets	$ 50.00	$ 50.00	$ 50.00
Fixed assets	50.00	50.00	50.00
Total assets	$100.00	$100.00	$100.00
Short-term credit (6%)	—	25.00	50.00
Long-term debt (8%)	50.00	25.00	—
Current ratio	∞	2:1	1:1
Earnings before interest and taxes (EBIT)	15.00	15.00	15.00
Less interest	4.00	3.50	3.00
Taxable income	$ 11.00	$ 11.50	$ 12.00
Less taxes at 50%	5.50	5.75	6.00
Earnings on common stock	$ 5.50	$ 5.75	$ 6.00
Rate of return on common stock (%)	11.0	11.5	12.0

What occurs when uncertainty is introduced into this example? We noted earlier that a firm which makes extensive use of short-term credit may find its earnings fluctuating widely. Suppose, for example, that interest rates rise significantly—a rise from 6 percent to 10 percent is not at all unrealistic. This rise would not affect the firm using the conservative policy, but it would increase the interest expense under the average policy to $4.5 million and under the aggressive policy to $5 million. The rates of return on equity for the three policies would consequently be 11.0 percent, 10.5 percent, and 10.0 percent, respectively—a reversal in relative ranking by rate of return. Of course, a decline in interest rates would have the opposite effect on the rates of return, but it should be clear that the variability of the return under an aggressive policy is more than that under a conservative policy.

Fluctuations in earnings before interest and taxes (EBIT) can pose even more severe problems—if EBIT declines, lenders may simply refuse to renew short-term debt or agree to renew it only at very high rates of interest. To illustrate this, suppose the EBIT of $15 million in Table 7–1 declines to only $5 million. Since the firm's ability to repay has diminished, creditors would certainly be reluctant to lend to it. This would cause creditors to require a higher return on their investment and, thus, raise the interest expense, which would, of course, jeopardize the firm's future even more and, at the same time, compound the effects of the declining EBIT on stockholder returns.

It is possible for the general level of interest rates to rise at the same time a firm's EBIT is falling, and the compound effects could cause the situation to deteriorate so much that the aggressive firm could not renew its credit at any interest rate. The result is bankruptcy.

Notice that if the firm follows a conservative policy of using all long-term debt, it need not worry about short-term, *temporary* changes either in the term structure of interest rates or in its own EBIT. Its only concern is with its long-run performance, and its conservative financial structure may permit it to survive in the short run to enjoy better times in the long run.

Extending the Example

These concepts can be incorporated into our example.[3] A firm has assets of $100 million and is considering the three financial structures, or policies, shown in Table 7–1. Management makes estimates of the future level of riskless interest rates (the Treasury bill rate) and the level of EBIT for the coming year. Management knows that the firm's earnings for next year will be the prime determinant of the risk premium that will be added to the riskless rate.[4]

Probability distributions for riskless rates and EBIT are given in Table 7–2. Assuming that the two probability distributions are independent of each other, we can determine the expected interest rate for the next year by the technique shown in Table 7–3. Column 1 gives the possible riskless rates of return. Column 2 gives the possible risk premiums, or the premiums investors require as compensation for making risky loans. Column 3 combines the riskless rates of interest with the risk premiums to give the possible rates of interest the firm may face. Column 4 gives the joint probabilities—the probability of the simultaneous occurrence of each possible riskless rate and risk premium. Column 5 gives the products of each joint probability multiplied by its associated interest rate; the sum of column 5 is the expected interest rate or 11.74 percent.

---

[3]This illustration uses the concept of a probability distribution, a topic discussed at some length in Chapter 12. A probability is the chance of an event occurring, or the odds on the occurrence of the event. The sum of the probabilities must equal 1.0, or 100 percent. The statistical aspects of this section may be omitted without loss of continuity if the statistical concepts are totally new.

[4]As we see in detail later in the book, the higher the risk associated with a given loan, the higher the interest rate lenders require on the loan. The difference between the United States government bond rate and the rate the firm must pay is defined as the *risk premium*. Obviously, the risk premium for AT&T or General Motors is lower than that for a smaller, less seasoned borrower.

TABLE 7–2 Probability Distributions for
Riskless Rates and EBIT

Treasury Bill Rate One Year Hence	
(i)	Probability
3%	.2
5	.3
7	.3
9	.2

EBIT for Next Year and Associated Risk Premiums Expected on Next Year's Renewal of Short-Term Credit		
EBIT	Risk Premium	Probability
(5.00) million	25.0%	.15
5.00	5.0	.20
15.00	2.0	.30
25.00	1.2	.20
35.00	1.0	.15

Since the expected value of the firm's short-term rate exceeds the long-term rate, 8 percent, the firm should probably use long-term rather than short-term financing. More important, however, is the fact that there is a 15 percent probability that the interest rate will be 28 percent or higher. Because total debt is $50 million, a 28 percent rate of interest would require an EBIT of $14 million to break even. But, at the time when this high rate is applied, EBIT would be *minus* $5 million, so the firm would run a loss before taxes of $19 million. This loss would reduce equity and increase the debt ratio, making the situation even more tense the next time the loan comes up for renewal. Good times might be just around the corner, but the aggressive firm, if its EBIT is subject to wide swings, may not survive until then.

Our example is unrealistic in that few firms will be able to actually generate the data needed to construct a table like Table 7–3. However, the events described are certainly *not* unrealistic, and the example does illustrate that the maturity structure of a firm's debt affects its overall risk. The example also shows that the risk tolerance of the firm with respect to the maturity composition of its liabilities depends to a large extent on the amount of risk already present in the firm owing to industry business risk, operating leverage, and overall financial leverage. It is important to keep the overall risk level of the firm within reasonable limits. Thus, a firm with high business risk should probably not use a very aggressive policy in its financial structure and especially not in its maturity structure, but a firm in a stable industry might use such a policy to advantage. Of course, the firm's asset maturity structure has a bearing on its ability to employ short-term debt, and we cover this topic in the next section.

TABLE 7–3 Firm's Expected Interest Rate One Year Hence

i (1)	Risk Premium (2)	Interest Rate to Firm (3) = (1) + (2)	Joint Probability[a] (4)	Product (5) = (3) × (4)
3%	1.0%	4.0%	.030	.120%
	1.2	4.2	.040	.168
	2.0	5.0	.060	.300
	5.0	8.0	.040	.320
	25.0	28.0	.030	.840
5%	1.0	6.0	.045	.270
	1.2	6.2	.060	.372
	2.0	7.0	.090	.630
	5.0	10.0	.060	.600
	25.0	30.0	.045	1.350
7%	1.0	8.0	.045	.360
	1.2	8.2	.060	.492
	2.0	9.0	.090	.810
	5.0	12.0	.060	.720
	25.0	32.0	.045	1.440
9%	1.0	10.0	.030	.300
	1.2	10.2	.040	.408
	2.0	11.0	.060	.660
	5.0	14.0	.040	.560
	25.0	34.0	.030	1.020
			1.000	

Expected interest rate = 11.740%

[a] Joint probabilities are developed by multiplying the probabilities contained in Table 7–2 by each other. For example, the joint probability at the top of column 4 is the product .2 × .15 = .03; the second is the product .2 × .20 = .04; and so on. The expected value, or most likely interest rate, is found by multiplying the possible interest rates shown in column 3 by the joint probabilities given in column 4, then adding these products.

RELATIONSHIP OF CURRENT ASSETS TO SALES

In the chapters that deal with capital budgeting, we will see that capital budgeting decisions involve estimating the stream of benefits expected from a given project and then discounting these expected cash flows back to the present to find the present value of the project. Although current asset investment analysis is similar to fixed asset analysis in the sense that it also requires estimates of the effects of such investments on profits, it is different in three key respects. *First,* the time element is of vital importance in fixed asset analysis but not of much significance in current asset analysis; accordingly, compound interest and other aspects of the timing problem play a major role in capital budgeting but only a minor one in current asset analysis. *Second,* increasing the firm's current assets—especially cash and marketable securities—while holding constant expected production and sales reduces the riskiness of the firm, but it also reduces the overall return on assets. *Third,* although both fixed and current asset holdings are functions of *expected* sales, only current assets can be adjusted to *actual* sales in the short run; hence, adjustments to short-run fluctuations in demand lie in the domain of working capital management.

Some of these ideas are illustrated in Figure 7–7, which shows the short-run relationship between the firm's current assets and output. The firm's fixed assets are assumed to be $50 million, and they cannot be altered in response to short-run fluctuations in output. Three possible current asset policies are depicted. CA_1 represents a conservative policy: relatively large balances of cash and marketable securities are maintained, large "safety stocks" of inventories[5] are kept on hand, and the firm maximizes sales by adopting a "liberal" credit policy that causes a high level of accounts receivable. Policy CA_2 is somewhat less conservative than CA_1, while CA_3 represents a risky, aggressive policy.

FIGURE 7–7   Relationship between Current Assets and Output

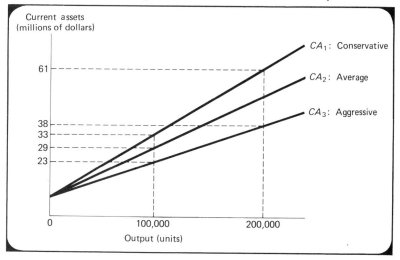

Current asset holdings are highest at any output level under policy CA_1, lowest under CA_3. For example, at an output of 100,000 units, CA_1 calls for $33 million of current assets versus only $23 million for CA_3. If demand strengthens and short-run plans call for production to increase from 100,000 to 200,000 units, current asset holdings will likewise increase. Under policy CA_1, current assets rise to $61 million; under CA_3, the increase is to only $38 million. As we shall see in the following section, the more aggressive policy will lead to a higher expected rate of return, but it also entails greater risk.

[5] The concept of inventory safety stocks is discussed in Chapter 8.

Risk-Return Tradeoff for Current Asset Holdings

If it could forecast perfectly, a firm would hold *exactly* enough cash to make disbursements as required, *exactly* enough inventories to meet production and sales requirements, *exactly* the accounts receivable called for by an optimal credit policy, and no marketable securities unless the interest returns on such assets exceeded the cost of capital, which is an unlikely occurrence. The current asset holdings under the perfect foresight case would be the theoretical minimum for a profit-maximizing firm. Any larger holdings would, in the sense of the du Pont chart we described in Chapter 3, increase the firm's assets without a proportionate increase in its returns, thus lowering its rate of return on investment. Any smaller holdings would mean the inability to pay bills on time, lost sales and production stoppages because of inventory shortages, and lost sales because of an overly restrictive credit policy.

When uncertainty is introduced into the picture, current asset management involves (1) determination of the minimum required balances of each type of asset and (2) addition of a safety stock to account for the fact that forecasters are imperfect. If a firm follows policy CA_1 in Figure 7–7, it is adding relatively large safety stocks; if it follows CA_3, its safety stocks are minimal. Policy CA_3, in general, produces the highest expected returns on investment, but it also involves the greatest risk—that is, following this policy may actually result in the *lowest* rate of return.

The effect of the three alternative policies on expected profitability is illustrated in Table 7–4. Under the conservative policy, CA_1, the rate of return on assets before interest and taxes is 13.5 percent; the return rises to 15 percent for an average policy and to 17 percent for the risky, aggressive policy, CA_3. However, we know that CA_3 is the most risky policy, since lost sales, lost customer goodwill, and bad credit ratings caused by poor liquidity ratios could combine to bring the actual realized rate of return well below the anticipated 17 percent.

TABLE 7–4   Effects of Alternative Current Asset Policies on Rates of Return and Asset Turnover

	Conservative (CA_1)	Average (CA_2)	Risky (CA_3)
Sales			
Units	200,000	200,000	200,000
Dollars	$100,000,000	$100,000,000	$100,000,000
EBIT	$ 15,000,000	$ 15,000,000	$ 15,000,000
Current assets	$ 61,000,000	$ 50,000,000	$ 38,000,000
Fixed assets	50,000,000	50,000,000	50,000,000
Total assets	$111,000,000	$100,000,000	$ 88,000,000
Rate of return on assets (EBIT/assets)	13.5%	15.0%	17.0%

In the real world, things are considerably more complex than this simple example suggests. For one thing, different types of current assets affect both risk and returns differently. Increased holdings of cash do more to improve the firm's risk posture than a similar dollar increase in marketable securities, but idle cash penalizes earnings more severely than does the same investment in marketable securities. Generalizations become even more difficult when we move on to accounts receivable and inventories, because it becomes increasingly difficult to measure either the earnings penalty or the risk reduction that results from increasing the balances of these items beyond their theoretical minimums. In subsequent chapters, we consider determining the optimal balances of each type of current asset, where *optimal* is defined to include the theoretical minimum plus an optimal safety stock. First, however, we must complete our generalized discussion of working capital policy by combining current asset and current liability management.

WORKING CAPITAL POLICY: COMBINING CURRENT ASSET AND CURRENT LIABILITY MANAGEMENT

Table 7–5 illustrates the effect of working capital policy on expected returns and on risk as measured by the current ratio. A conservative policy calling for no short-term debt and large holdings of current assets results in a 9.6 percent expected after-tax return on equity and a very high current ratio. The actual return would probably be quite close to 9.6 percent. An aggressive policy, with minimal holdings of current assets and short-term rather than long-term debt, raises the expected return to 14 percent, but the current ratio under this policy is only .86, a dangerously low level for most industries. Simultaneously, the increasing risks associated with the aggressive policy might adversely affect stock market opinion about the company; therefore, even if working capital policy pushes rates of return up, the net effect still might be to lower stock prices.

Can we resolve this risk/return tradeoff to determine *precisely* the firm's optimal working capital policy, that is, the working capital policy that will maximize the value of existing common stock? In theory, the answer is yes, but in practice it is no. Determining the optimal policy would require detailed information on a complex set of variables, information that is unobtainable today. Progress is being made in the development of computer simulation models designed to help determine the effects of alternative financial policy choices, including working capital decisions, but no one using such models would suggest that they can actually reach *optimal* solutions. We can, however, establish guidelines, or ranges of values, for each type of current asset, and we do have ways of examining the various types of short-term financing and their effects on the cost of capital. Because such information, used with good judgment, can be most helpful to the financial manager, we will consider these topics in the remaining chapters of Part Two.

TABLE 7–5 Effects of Working Capital Policy on the Rate of Return on Common Equity

	Conservative Long-Term Debt Large Investment in Current Assets (CA_1)	*Average* Average Use of Short-Term Debt; Average Investment in Current Assets (CA_2)	*Aggressive* All Short-Term Debt; Minimal Investment in Current Assets (CA_3)
Current assets	$ 61,000,000	$ 50,000,000	$ 38,000,000
Fixed assets	50,000,000	50,000,000	50,000,000
Total assets	$111,000,000	$100,000,000	$ 88,000,000
Current liabilities (6%)	—	$ 25,000,000	$ 44,000,000
Long-term debt (8%)	$ 55,500,000	$ 25,000,000	—
Total debt (debt/assets = 50%)	$ 55,500,000	$ 50,000,000	$ 44,000,000
Equity	55,500,000	50,000,000	44,000,000
Total liabilities and net worth	$111,000,000	$100,000,000	$ 88,000,000
Sales in dollars	$100,000,000	$100,000,000	$100,000,000
EBIT	$ 15,000,000	$ 15,000,000	$ 15,000,000
Less: interest	4,400,000	3,500,000	2,640,000
Taxable income	$ 10,600,000	$ 11,500,000	$ 12,360,000
Taxes (50%)	5,300,000	5,750,000	6,180,000
Earnings on equity	$ 5,300,000	$ 5,750,000	$ 6,180,000
Rate of return on equity	9.6%	11.5%	14.0%
Current ratio	a	2:1	.86

[a] Under policy CA_1, the current ratio is shown to be infinitely high. Actually, the firm would doubtless have some spontaneous credit, but the current ratio would still be quite high.

SUMMARY

Working capital refers to a firm's investment in short-term assets—cash, short-term securities, accounts receivable, and inventories. *Gross working capital* is defined as the firm's total current assets; *net working capital* is current assets minus current liabilities. *Working capital management* involves all aspects of the administration of both current assets and current liabilities.

Working capital policy is concerned with two sets of relationships among balance sheet items. First is the policy question of the level of total current assets to be held. Current assets vary with sales, but the ratio of current assets to sales is a policy matter. If the firm elects to operate aggressively, it will hold relatively small stocks of current assets. This will reduce the required level of investment and increase the expected rate of return on investment. However, an aggressive policy also increases the likelihood of running out of cash or inventories or of losing sales because of an excessively tough credit policy.

The second policy question concerns the relationship between types of assets and the way these assets are financed. One policy calls for matching asset and liability maturities, financing short-term assets with short-term debt, and long-term assets with long-term debt or equity. If this policy is followed, the maturity structure of the debt is determined by the level of fixed versus current assets. However, short-term debt is frequently less expensive than long-term debt, so the expected rate of return may be higher if short-term debt is used. Offsetting this return advantage is the fact that large amounts of short-term credit increase the risks (1) of having to renew this debt at higher interest rates and (2) of not being able to renew the debt at all if the firm experiences difficulties.

Both aspects of working capital policy involve risk/return tradeoffs. In the following chapter, we examine methods used to determine the optimal levels of each type of current assets. Then, in Chapter 9, we examine alternative sources and forms of short-term credit.

QUESTIONS

7-1. How does the seasonal nature of a firm's sales influence the decision about the amount of short-term credit in the financial structure?

7-2. "Merely increasing the level of current asset holdings does not necessarily reduce the riskiness of the firm. Rather, the composition of the current assets, whether highly liquid or highly illiquid, is the important factor to consider." What is your reaction to this statement?

7-3. What is the advantage of matching the maturities of assets and liabilities?

7-4. There have been times when the term structure of interest rates has been such that short-term rates were higher than long-term rates. Does this necessarily imply that the best financial policy for a firm would be to use all long-term debt and no short-term debt? Explain your answer.

7-5. Assuming a firm's volume of business remained constant, would you expect it to have higher cash balances (demand deposits) during a tight-money period or an easy-money period? Does this situation have any ramifications for federal monetary policy?

PROBLEMS

7-1. Freund Corp. maintains a current ratio of 2.5 and current assets are a constant 30 percent of sales. Freund has $500,000 of long-term debt. Short-term loans are maintained at 75 percent of current liabilities. Sales forecasts for the next three years are as follows:

Year	Sales
1	$3,000,000
2	4,000,000
3	4,500,000

If all short-term notes can be obtained at an 8 percent interest rate, how much interest must Freund pay on its short-term notes in each of the next three years?

7-2. The Morton Paper Corporation is attempting to determine an optimal level of current assets for the coming year. Management expects sales to increase to approximately $1.8 million as a result of asset expansion presently being undertaken. Fixed assets total $900,000, and the firm wishes to maintain a 50 percent debt ratio. Morton's interest cost is currently 6 percent on both short-term debt and the longer term debt which the firm uses in its permanent structure. Three alternatives regarding the projected current asset level are available to the firm: (1) an aggressive policy requiring current assets of only 45 percent of projected sales; (2) an average policy of 50 percent of sales as current assets; and (3) a conservative policy under which the current asset level would be 60 percent of sales. The firm expects to generate earnings before interest and taxes at a rate of 15 percent on total sales.

   a. What is the expected return on equity under each alternative current asset level? (Assume a 50 percent tax rate.)

   b. In this problem, we have assumed that (1) the level of expected sales is independent of current asset policy and (2) interest rates are independent of this policy. Are these valid assumptions?

   c. How would the overall riskiness of the firm vary under each policy? Discuss specifically such questions as the effect of current asset management on demand, expenses, fixed charge coverage, risk of insolvency, and so on.

7-3. The Cane Card Company is attempting to project its financial requirements for the next ten-year period. The firm is a relative newcomer to the industry, having been in business only three years. Initially, the firm was totally unknown and found financing, particularly of a permanent nature, quite difficult to obtain. As a result, Cane was literally "forced" to structure the right-hand side of its balance sheet as follows:

Trade credit payable	$200,000
Short-term bank borrowing	240,000
Common equity	440,000
Total claims	$880,000

   In the three years the firm has been very successful, increasing its total capitalization by $120,000 of retained earnings. It is now in a position where it could obtain a long-term loan for ten years from an insurance company at a rate of 11 percent in place of all or any of its present short-term borrowings. Alternatively, it could renew its existing $240,000 loan, or any part thereof, on a one-year loan from the bank at a rate of 9 percent.

   George Groves, the financial vice-president, is considering three possible financing plans: (1) to renew the 1-year loan with the bank; (2) to borrow $240,000 from the insurance company; and (3) to borrow $120,000 from each. Groves has estimated short-term riskless rates, the premiums that Cane might have to pay over the riskless rate for three possible "states of the economy," and the probability of each possibility. The *average* rates that the firm would likely pay over the next ten years on its short-term borrowings are shown below.

State of Economy	Cane EBIT*	Riskless Rate	Cane Risk Premium	Joint Probability
Good	$300,000	4%	2%	.125
Good	300,000	6	2	.125
Average	160,000	6	4	.250
Average	160,000	8	4	.250
Bad	20,000	8	10	.125
Bad	20,000	10	10	.125

*Earnings before interest and taxes.

a. Assuming a 50 percent tax rate, compute expected profits under each of Groves' three alternative financing plans. (Ignore possible growth effects. The expected EBIT is $160,000 under each plan.)

b. On the basis of Groves' estimates, what is the worst profit that could result under each alternative? the best? (Assume no loss carry-back provision in the tax law.) Interpret your results and recommend a financing plan for Cane.

c. Is there anything to prevent Cane from refinancing its short-term debt with the insurance company, thus converting it to long-term debt, at some future date if and when the short-term rate to the firm becomes unreasonably high?

d. In both this problem and the example in the chapter, some very high interest rates were averaged into the computation of an expected short-term interest rate. If such rates would "ruin" a firm, can you see any problem with using them in this computation?

7-4. Research Project. Determine a yield curve for high-grade corporate debt, and explain how a financial manager may use a yield curve in determining the best method of financing his working capital requirements.

Current Asset Management

8

In the preceding chapter we viewed working capital management in a general, overall sense. Now we focus our attention on the firm's investment in specific current assets, examining cash, marketable securities, accounts receivable, and inventories. According to the Federal Trade Commission, current assets represent approximately 59 percent of manufacturing companies' assets, so current asset management is clearly an important subject.

CASH MANAGEMENT

Controlling the investment in current assets begins with cash management. Cash consists of the firm's holdings of currency and demand deposits, with demand deposits being by far the more important for most firms.

Why Hold Cash?

Businesses or individuals have three primary motives for holding cash: (1) the *transactions motive,* (2) the *precautionary motive,* and (3) the *speculative motive.*

Transactions Motive The transactions motive for holding cash is to enable the firm to conduct its ordinary business—making purchases and sales. In some lines of business, such as the utilities, where billings can be cycled throughout the month, cash inflows can be scheduled and synchronized closely with the need for the outflow of cash. Hence, we expect the cash-to-

143

revenues ratio and cash-to-total-assets ratio for utility firms to be relatively low. In retail trade, by contrast, sales are more random, and a number of transactions may actually be conducted by physical currency. As a consequence, retail trade requires higher ratios of cash to sales and to total assets.

The seasonality of a business may give rise to a need for cash for the purchase of inventories. For example, raw materials may be available only during a harvest season, as in the food-canning business. Or sales may be seasonal, as are department store sales around the Christmas and the Easter holidays, giving rise to an increase in needs for cash.

Precautionary Motive   The precautionary motive relates primarily to the predictability of cash inflows and outflows. If predictability is high, less cash must be held against an emergency or any other contingency. Another factor that strongly influences the precautionary motive for holding cash is the ability to borrow additional cash on short notice when circumstances necessitate. Borrowing flexibility is primarily a matter of the strength of the firm's relations with banking institutions and other credit sources.

The precautionary motive for holding cash is actually satisfied in large part by holding near-money assets—short-term government securities and the like.

Speculative Motive   The speculative motive for holding cash is to be ready for profit-making opportunities that may arise. By and large, business accumulations of cash for speculative purposes are not widely found. Holding cash is more common among individual investors. However, the cash and marketable securities account may rise to rather sizable levels on a temporary basis as funds are accumulated to meet specific future needs. An example of this was Comsat's 1976 position, when the company held about $100 million of cash and marketable securities. Comsat was planning to establish a domestic communications satellite system, and a substantial amount of funds was necessary for the project.

Advantages of Adequate Cash: Specific Points

In addition to these general motives, sound working capital management requires maintenance of an ample amount of cash for several specific reasons. First, it is essential that the firm have sufficient cash to take trade discounts. A commonly encountered billing procedure, or term of trade, allows a 2 percent discount if the bill is paid within ten days, with full payment required in thirty days in any event. (This is usually stated as 2/10, net 30.) Since the net amount is due in thirty days, failure to take the discount means paying this extra 2 percent for using the money an additional twenty days. If one were to pay 2 percent for every twenty-day period over the year, there would be eighteen such periods:

$$18 = \frac{360 \text{ days}}{20 \text{ days}}.$$

This represents an annual interest rate of 36 percent.[1] Most firms have a cost of capital that is substantially lower than 36 percent.

Second, since the current and acid test ratios are key items in credit analysis, it is essential that the firm, in order to maintain its credit standing, meet the standards of the line of business in which it is engaged. A strong credit standing enables the firm to purchase goods from trade suppliers on favorable terms and to maintain its line of credit with banks and other sources of credit.

Using the knowledge about the general nature of cash flows presented in Chapter 5, the financial manager may be able to improve the inflow-outflow pattern of cash. He can do so by better synchronization of flows and by reduction of float, as will be explained in the following sections.

Synchronization of Cash Flows

An example of synchronization demonstrates how cash flows may be improved by more frequent requisitioning of funds by divisional offices from the firm's main or central office. Some Gulf Oil Corporation divisional field offices, for instance, formerly requisitioned funds once or twice a week; now the treasurer's office insists on daily requisitions, thus keeping cash on tap as much as four days longer. On the basis of 20 offices, each requiring $1 million a week, these staggered requisitions free the equivalent of $10 million for one day each week. At 6 percent interest, this earns better than $84,000 a year.

Moreover, effective forecasting can reduce the investment in cash. The cash flow forecasting at CIT Credit Corporation illustrates this idea. An assistant treasurer forecasts planned purchases of automobiles by the dealers. He estimates daily the number of cars shipped to the 10,000 dealers who finance their purchases through CIT. He then estimates how much money

---

[1]The following equation may be used for calculating the cost, on an annual basis, of not taking discounts:

$$\text{Cost} = \frac{\text{discount percent}}{(100 - \text{discount percent})} \times \frac{360}{(\text{final due date} - \text{discount period})}.$$

The denominator in the first term, $(100 - \text{discount percent})$, equals the funds made available by not taking the discount. To illustrate, the cost of not taking a discount when the terms are 2/10, net 30 is computed.

$$\text{Cost} = \frac{2}{98} \times \frac{360}{20} = 0.0204 \times 18 = 36.72\%.$$

Notice that the calculated cost can be reduced by paying late. Thus if the illustrative firm pays in 60 days rather than the specified 30, the credit period becomes $60 - 10 = 50$, and the calculated cost becomes

$$\text{Cost} = \frac{2}{98} \times \frac{360}{50} = 0.0204 \times 7.2 = 14.7\%.$$

In periods of excess capacity, some firms may be able to get away with late payments, but such firms may suffer a variety of problems associated with being a "slow-payer" account.

should be deposited in Detroit banks that day to pay automobile manufacturers. On one day he estimated a required deposit of $6.4 million; the actual bill for the day was $6.397 million, a difference of one-tenth of 1 percent. Although such close forecasting cannot be achieved by every firm, the system enables CIT to economize on the amount of money it must borrow and thereby keeps interest expense to a minimum.

Expediting Collections and Check Clearing

Another important method of economizing on the amount of cash required is to hasten the process of clearing checks. Checks sent from customers in distant cities are subject to delays because of the time required for the check to travel in the mail and the time required for clearing through the banking system.

Even after a check has been received by a firm and deposited in its account, the funds cannot be spent until the check has cleared. The bank in which the check was deposited presents the check to the bank on which it was drawn. Only when this latter bank transfers funds to the bank of deposit are they available for use by the depositor. Checks are generally cleared through the Federal Reserve System or through a clearinghouse set up by the banks in a particular city. Of course, if the check is drawn on the bank of deposit, that bank merely transfers funds by bookkeeping entries from one depositor to another. The length of time required for checks to clear is a function of the distance between the payer's and the payee's banks; in the case of clearinghouses, it can range from one day to three or four days. The maximum time for checks cleared through the Federal Reserve System is two days.

To reduce this delay, a *lock-box plan* can be used. If a firm makes sales in large amounts at far distances, it can establish a lock box in a post office located in the customer's area. It can arrange to have customers send payments to the postal box in their city and then have a bank pick up the checks and deposit them in a special checking account. The bank then has the checks cleared in the local area and remits by wire to the firm's bank of deposit. If the distant customers are scattered, the firm can establish the lock box in its local city and have the checks picked up by its own bank. The bank begins the clearing process, notifying the firm that a check has been received. In this way the clearing process starts before the firm processes the check. By these methods, collection time can be reduced by one to five days. Examples of freeing funds in the amount of $5 million or more by these methods have been cited by firms.

Slowing Disbursements

Just as expediting the collection process conserves cash, slowing down disbursements accomplishes the same thing by keeping cash on hand for longer periods. One obviously could simply delay payments, but this involves equally obvious difficulties. Firms have, in the past, devised rather ingenious methods for "legitimately" lengthening the collection period on their own checks, ranging from maintaining deposits in distant banks to using slow, awkward payment procedures. Since such practices are usually recognized for what they are, there are severe limits to their use.

The most widely publicized of these procedures in recent years is the use of drafts. While a check is payable upon demand, a draft must be transmitted to the issuer, who approves it and deposits funds to cover it, after which it can be collected. AT&T has used drafts: "In handling its payrolls, for instance, AT&T can pay an employee by draft on Friday. The employee cashes the draft at his local bank, which sends it on to AT&T's New York bank. It may be Wednesday or Thursday before the draft arrives. The bank then sends it to the company's accounting department, which has until 3 P.M. that day to inspect and approve it. Not until then does AT&T deposit funds in its bank to pay the draft."[2] Insurance companies also use drafts to pay claims.

Both banks and those who receive drafts dislike them—they represent an awkward, clumsy, costly anachronism in an age when computer transfer mechanisms are reducing the time and expense involved in transfers of funds.

Using Float

Float is defined as the difference between the balance shown in a firm's (or individual's) checkbook balance and the balance on the bank's books. Suppose a firm writes, on the average, checks in the amount of $5,000 each day. It takes about six days for these checks to clear and be deducted from the firm's bank account. Thus, the firm's own checking records show a balance $30,000 less than the bank's records. If the firm receives checks in the amount of $5,000 daily but loses only four days while these checks are being deposited and cleared, its own books have a balance that is, because of this factor, $20,000 larger than the bank's balance. Thus the firm's float—the difference between the $30,000 and the $20,000—is $10,000.

If a firm's own collection and clearing process is more efficient than that of the recipients of its checks—and this is generally true of larger, more efficient firms—then the firm could show a negative balance on its own records and a positive balance on the books of its bank. Some firms indicate that they *never* have true positive cash balances. One large manufacturer of construction equipment stated that, while its account according to its bank's records shows an average cash balance of about $2 million, its *actual* cash balance is *minus* $2 million; it has $4 million of float. Obviously, the firm must be able to forecast its positive and negative clearings accurately in order to make such heavy use of float.

---

[2]"More Firms Substitute Drafts for Checks to Pay, Collect Bills," *The Wall Street Journal* (August 29, 1971).

Cost of Cash Management[3]

We have just described a number of procedures that may be used to hold down cash balance requirements. Implementing these procedures, however, is not a costless operation. How far should a firm go in making its cash operations more efficient? As a general rule, the firm should incur these expenses so long as their marginal returns exceed their marginal expenses.

For example, suppose that by establishing a lock-box system and increasing the accuracy of cash inflow and outflow forecasts, a firm can reduce its investment in cash by $1 million. Further, suppose that the firm borrows at a rate of 12 percent. The steps taken have released $1 million, and the cost of capital required to carry this $1 million investment in cash is $120,000. If the costs of the procedures necessary to release the $1 million are less than $120,000, the move is a good one; if the costs exceed $120,000, the greater efficiency is not worth the cost. It is clear that larger firms, with larger cash balances, can better afford to hire the personnel necessary to maintain tight control over their cash positions. Cash management is one element of business operations in which economies of scale are clearly present.

Very clearly, the value of careful cash management depends upon the costs of funds invested in cash, which in turn depend upon the current rate of interest. In the 1970s, with interest rates at high levels, firms are devoting more care than ever to cash management.

DETERMINING THE MINIMUM CASH BALANCE

Thus far we have seen that cash is held primarily for transactions purposes; the other traditional motives for holding cash, the speculative and precautionary motives, are today met largely by reserve borrowing power and by holdings of short-term marketable securities. Some minimum cash balance— which may actually be negative if float is used effectively—is required for transactions, and an additional amount over and above this figure may be held as a safety stock. For many firms the total of transactions balances plus safety stock constitutes the minimum cash balance, the point at which the firm either borrows additional cash or sells part of its portfolio of marketable securities. For many other firms, however, banking relationships require still larger balances.

Compensating Balances

We have seen that banks provide services to firms—they clear checks, operate lock-box plans, supply credit information, and the like. These services cost the bank money, so the bank must be compensated for rendering them.

---

[3]We are abstracting from the security aspects of cash management, that is, the prevention of fraud and embezzlement. These topics are better covered in accounting than in finance courses.

Banks earn most of their income by lending money at interest, and most of the funds they lend are obtained in the form of deposits. If a firm maintains a deposit account with an average balance of $100,000, and if the bank can lend these funds at a return of $8,000, then the account is, in a sense, worth $8,000 to the bank. Thus, it is to the bank's advantage to provide services worth up to $8,000 to attract and hold the account.

Banks determine first the costs of the services rendered to their larger customers and then the average account balances necessary to provide enough income to compensate for these costs. These balances are defined as *compensating balances* and are often maintained by firms instead of paying cash service charges to the bank.[4]

Compensating balances are also required by some bank loan agreements. During periods when the supply of credit is restricted and interest rates are high, banks frequently insist that borrowers maintain accounts that average some percentage of the loan amount—15 percent is a typical figure—as a condition for granting the loan. If the balance is larger than the firm would otherwise maintain, then the effective cost of the loan is increased; the excess balance presumably "compensates" the bank for making a loan at a rate below what it could earn on the funds if they were invested elsewhere.[5]

Compensating balances can be established (1) as *an absolute minimum,* say $100,000, below which the actual balance must never fall, or (2) as *a minimum average balance,* perhaps $100,000, over some period, generally a month. The absolute minimum is a much more restrictive requirement, because the average amount of cash held during the month will be above $100,000 by the amount of transactions balances. The $100,000 in this case is "dead money" from the firm's standpoint. Under the minimum average, however, the balance could fall to zero one day provided it was $200,000 some other day, with the average working out to $100,000. Thus, the $100,000 in this case is available for transactions.

Statistics on compensating balance requirements are not available, but average balances are typical and absolute minimums rare for business accounts. Discussions with bankers, however, indicate that absolute balance requirements are less rare during times of extremely tight money such as prevailed during the late 1960s and early 1970s.

Minimum Cash Balance

The firm's minimum cash balance is set as the larger of (1) its transactions balances plus precautionary balances (that is, safety stocks) or (2) its required compensating balances. Statistics are not available on which factor is gen-

---

[4]Banks are compensated for services rendered either by compensating balances or by direct fees.
[5]The interest rate effect of compensating balances is discussed further in Chapter 9.

erally controlling, but in our experience compensating balance requirements generally dominate, except for firms subject to absolute minimum balances.[6]

Overdraft System

Most countries outside the United States use *overdraft systems.* In such a system a depositor writes checks in excess of his balance, and his bank automatically extends a loan to cover the shortage. The maximum amount of such loans must, of course, be established ahead of time. Statistics are not available on the usage of overdrafts in the United States, but a number of firms have worked out informal, and in some cases formal, overdraft arrangements. Further, the use of overdrafts has been increasing in recent years.

MARKETABLE SECURITIES

Firms sometimes report sizable amounts of such short-term marketable securities as Treasury bills or bank certificates of deposit among their current assets. Why might marketable securities be held? The two primary reasons —as a substitute for cash and as a temporary investment—are considered in this section.

Substitute for Cash

Some firms hold portfolios of marketable securities in lieu of larger cash balances, liquidating part of the portfolio to increase the cash account when cash outflows exceed inflows. Data are not available to indicate the extent of this practice, but our impression is that it is not common. Most firms prefer to let their banks maintain such liquid reserves, with the firms themselves borrowing to meet temporary cash shortages.

Temporary Investment

In addition to using marketable securities as a buffer against cash shortages, firms also hold them on a strictly temporary basis. Firms engaged in seasonal operations, for example, frequently have surplus cash flows during part of

---

[6]This point is underscored by an incident that occurred at a professional finance meeting. A professor presented a scholarly paper that used operations research techniques to determine "optimal cash balances" for a sample of firms. He then reported that actual cash balances of the firms greatly exceeded their "optimal" balances, suggesting inefficiency and the need for more refined techniques. The discussant of the paper made her comments short and sweet. She reported that she wrote and asked the sample firms why they had so much cash; they uniformly replied that their cash holdings were set by compensating balance requirements. The model was useful to determine the optimal cash balance in the absence of compensating balance requirements, but it was precisely those requirements that determined actual balances. Since the model did not include compensating balances as a determinant of cash balances, its usefulness is questionable,

the year, deficit cash flows during other months. (See Table 6–1 for an example.) Such firms may purchase marketable securities during their surplus periods, then liquidate them when cash deficits occur. Other firms, particularly in capital goods industries, where fluctuations are violent, attempt to accumulate cash or near-cash securities during a downturn in order to be ready to finance an upturn in business volume.

Firms also accumulate liquid assets to meet predictable financial requirements. For example, if a major modernization program is planned for the near future, or if a bond issue is about to mature, the marketable securities portfolio may be increased to provide the required funds. Furthermore, marketable securities holdings are frequently large immediately preceding quarterly corporate tax payment dates.

Firms may also accumulate resources as a protection against a number of contingencies. When they make uninsurable product warranties, companies must be ready to meet any claims that may arise. Firms in highly competitive industries must have resources to carry them through substantial shifts in the market structure. A firm in an industry in which new markets are emerging—for example, foreign markets—needs to have resources to meet developments; these funds may be on hand for fairly long periods.

Criteria Used in Selecting Security Portfolios

Different types of securities, varying in risk of default, marketability, and length of maturity, are available. We will discuss some of the characteristics of these securities, and the criteria that are applied in choosing among them, here.

Risk of Default   The firm's liquidity portfolio is generally held for a specific, known need; if it should depreciate in value, the firm would be financially embarrassed. Further, most nonfinancial corporations do not have investment departments specializing in appraising securities and determining the probability of their going into default. Accordingly, the marketable securities portfolio is generally confined to securities with a minimal risk of default. However, the lowest risk securities also provide the lowest returns, so safety is bought at the expense of yield.

Marketability   The security portfolio is usually held to provide liquid reserves or to meet known needs at a specific time. In either case, the firm must be able to sell its holdings and realize cash on short notice. Accordingly, the securities held in the portfolio must be readily marketable.

Maturity   We shall see in Chapter 18 that the price of a long-term bond fluctuates much more with changes in interest rates than does the price of a similar short-term security. Further, as we saw in the last chapter, interest rates fluctuate widely over time. These two factors combine to make long-term bonds riskier than short-term securities for a firm's marketable security portfolio. However, partly because of this risk differential, higher yields are more frequently available on long-term than on short-term securities, so again risk-return tradeoffs must be recognized.

Given the motives most firms have for holding marketable security portfolios, it is generally not feasible for them to be exposed to a high degree of risk from interest rate fluctuations. Accordingly, firms generally confine their marketable securities portfolios to the shorter maturities. Only if the securities are expected to be held for a long period, and not be subject to forced liquidation on short notice, will long-term securities be held.

Investment Alternatives

The main investment alternatives open to business firms are given in Table 8–1. Rates available on U.S. Treasury securities range from 5.5 percent for those with short maturities to 8 percent for long-term bonds. High-quality, nongovernment debt securities offer yields ranging from 6 to 8.6 percent. Yields on common stocks (discussed in Chapter 18) are too uncertain to warrant inclusion in the table.

TABLE 8–1   Alternative Marketable Securities for Investment

	Approximate Maturities[a]	Approximate Yields[b] July 12, 1976
U.S. Treasury bills	91–182 days	5.5%
U.S. Treasury certificates	9–12 months	6.1
U.S. Treasury notes	1–5 years	7.2
U.S. Treasury bonds	Over 5 years	8.0
Negotiable certificates of deposit with U.S. banks	Varies, up to 3 years	6.7
Prime commercial paper	Varies, up to 270 days	6.0
Eurodollar bank time deposits	Varies, up to 1 year	6.5
Bonds of other corporations (AAA)	Varies, up to 30 years	8.6
Stocks of other corporations		?
Stocks of the firm in question (treasury stock)		?

[a]The maturities are those at issue date. For outstanding securities, maturities varying almost by day or week are available.
[b]Estimated yields for median maturities in the class.

Depending on how long he anticipates holding the funds, the financial manager decides upon a suitable maturity pattern for his holdings. The numerous alternatives can be selected and balanced in such a way that he obtains the maturities and risks appropriate to the financial situation of his firm. Commercial bankers, investment bankers, and brokers provide the financial manager with detailed information on each of the forms of investments in the list. Because their characteristics change with shifts in financial market conditions, it would be misleading to attempt to give detailed descriptions of these investment outlets here. The financial manager must keep up to date on these characteristics. He should follow the principle of making investment selections that offer maturities, yields, and risks appropriate to his firm.

MANAGEMENT OF ACCOUNTS RECEIVABLE: CREDIT POLICY

The level of accounts receivable is determined by (1) the volume of credit sales and (2) the average period between sales and collections. The average collection period is partially dependent upon economic conditions—during a recession or a period of extremely tight money, customers may be forced to delay payment—but it is also dependent upon a set of controllable factors, or *credit policy variables.* The major policy variables include (1) *credit standards,* or the maximum riskiness of acceptable credit accounts; (2) *credit period,* or the length of time for which credit is granted; (3) *discounts* given for early payment; and (4) the firm's *collection policy.* We first discuss each policy variable separately and in qualitative rather than quantitative terms; then we illustrate the interaction of these elements and discuss the actual establishment of a firm's credit policy.

Credit Standards

If a firm makes credit sales to only the strongest of customers, it will never have bad debt losses, and it will not incur much in the way of expenses for a credit department. On the other hand, it will probably be losing sales, and the profit foregone on these lost sales could be far larger than the costs it has avoided. Determining the optimal credit standard involves equating the marginal costs of credit to the marginal profits on the increased sales.

Marginal costs include production and selling costs, but we may abstract from these at this point and consider only those costs associated with the "quality" of the marginal accounts, or *credit quality costs.* These costs include (1) default, or bad debt losses; (2) higher investigation and collection costs; and (3) if less credit-worthy customers delay payment longer than stronger customers, higher costs of capital tied up in receivables.

Since credit costs and credit quality are correlated, it is important to be able to judge the quality of an account. First, how should we define "quality"? Perhaps the best way is in terms of the probability of default. These probability estimates are, for the most part, subjective estimates, but credit rating is a well-established practice, and a good credit manager can make reasonably accurate judgments of the probability of default by different classes of customers.

To evaluate the credit risk, credit managers consider the five C's of credit: character, capacity, capital, collateral, conditions. *Character* refers to the probability that a customer will *try* to honor his obligations. This factor is of considerable importance, because every credit transaction implies a *promise* to pay. Will the creditor make an honest effort to pay his debts, or is he likely to try to get away with something? Experienced credit men frequently insist that the moral factor is the most important issue in a credit evaluation.

Capacity is a subjective judgment of the ability of the customer. This is gauged by his past record, supplemented by physical observation of the customer's plant or store and business methods. *Capital* is measured by the general financial position of the firm as indicated by a financial ratio analysis, with special emphasis on the tangible net worth of the enterprise. *Collateral* is represented by assets that the customer may offer as a pledge for security of the credit extended to him. Finally, *conditions* refer to the impact of general economic trends on the firm or to special developments in certain areas of the economy that may affect the customer's ability to meet his obligations.

The five C's of credit represent the factors by which the credit risk is judged. Information on these items is obtained from the firm's previous experience with the customer, supplemented by a well-developed system of information-gathering groups. Two major sources of external information are available. The first is the work of the credit associations. By periodic meetings of local groups and by correspondence, information on experience with debtors is exchanged. More formally, Credit Interchange, a system developed by the National Association of Credit Management for assembling and distributing information of debtors' past performance, is provided. The interchange reports show the paying record of the debtor, the industries from which he is buying, and the trading areas in which his purchases are being made.

The second source of external information is the work of the credit-reporting agencies, the best known of which is Dun & Bradstreet. Agencies that specialize in coverage of a limited number of industries also provide information. Representative of these are the National Credit Office and the Lyon Furniture Mercantile Agency. These agencies provide factual data that can be used by the credit manager in his credit analysis; they also provide ratings similar to those available on corporate bonds.

An individual firm can translate its credit information into risk classes, grouped according to the probability of loss associated with sales to a customer. The combination of rating and supplementary information might lead to the following groupings of loss experience.

Risk Class Number	Loss Ratio (in percentages)
1	None
2	0–½
3	½–1
4	1–2
5	2–5
6	5–10
7	10–20
8	over 20

If the selling firm has a 20 percent margin over the sum of direct operating costs and all delivery and selling costs, and if it is producing at less than full capacity, it may adopt the following credit policies. It may sell on customary credit terms to groups 1 to 5; sell to groups 6 and 7 under more stringent credit terms, such as cash on delivery; and require advance payments from group 8. As long as the bad debt loss ratios are less than 20 percent, the additional sales are contributing something to overhead.

Statistical techniques, especially regression analysis and discriminant analysis,[7] have been used with some success in judging credit worthiness. These methods work best when individual credits are relatively small and a large number of borrowers are involved. Thus, they have worked best in retail credit, consumer loans, mortgage lending, and the like. As the increase in credit cards and similar procedures builds up, as computers are used more frequently, and as credit records on individuals and small firms are developed, statistical techniques promise to become much more important than they are today.[8]

Terms of Credit

The terms of credit specify the period for which credit is extended and the discount, if any, given for early payment. For example, as we saw earlier, if a firm's credit terms to all approved customers are stated as "2/10, net 30," then a 2 percent discount from the stated sales price is granted if payment is made within ten days, and the entire amount is due thirty days from the invoice date if the discount is not taken. If the terms are stated "net 60," this indicates

[7]Discriminant analysis is similar to multiple regression analysis, except that it partitions a sample into two components on the basis of a set of characteristics. The sample, for example, might be loan applicants at a consumer loan company. The components into which they are classified might be those likely to make prompt repayment and those likely to default. The characteristics might be such factors as whether the applicant owns his home, how long he has been with his employer, and so forth.

[8]It has been said that the biggest single deterrent to the increased automation of credit processes is George Orwell's classic book, *1984*, in which he described the social dangers of centralized files of information on individuals. Orwell's omnipresent watcher, Big Brother, is mentioned frequently in Congressional sessions discussing mass storage of information relevant to credit analysis.

that no discount is offered and that the bill is due and payable sixty days after the invoice date.

If sales are seasonal, a firm may use seasonal datings. Jensen, Inc., a bathing suit manufacturer, sells on terms of "2/10, net 30, May 1 dating." This means that the effective invoice date is May 1, so the discount may be taken until May 10, or the full amount must be paid on May 30, regardless of when the sale was made. Jensen produces output throughout the year, but retail sales of bathing suits are concentrated in the spring and early summer. Because of its practice of offering seasonal datings, Jensen induces some customers to stock up early, saving Jensen storage costs and also "nailing down sales."

Credit Period   Lengthening the credit period stimulates sales, but there is a cost to tying up funds in receivables. For example, if a firm changes its terms from net 30 to net 60, the average receivables for the year might rise from $100,000 to $300,000, with the increase caused partly by the longer credit terms and partly by the larger volume of sales. If the cost of capital needed to finance the investment in receivables is 8 percent, then the marginal cost of lengthening the credit period is $16,000 ($= $200,000 \times 8$ percent). If the incremental profit (sales price minus all direct production, selling, and credit costs associated with the additional sales) exceeds $16,000, then the change in credit policy is profitable. Determining the optimal credit period involves locating that period where marginal profits on increased sales are exactly offset by the costs of carrying the higher amount of accounts receivable.

Cash Discounts   The effect of granting cash discounts may be analyzed similarly to the credit period. For example, if a firm changes its terms from "net 30" to "2/10, net 30," it may well attract customers who want to take discounts, thereby increasing gross sales. Also, the average collection period will be shortened, as some old customers will pay more promptly to take advantage of the discount. Offsetting these benefits is the cost of the discounts taken. The optimal discount is established at the point where costs and benefits are exactly offsetting.

Collection Policy

Collection policy refers to the procedures the firm follows to obtain payment of past-due accounts. For example, a letter may be sent to such accounts when the account is ten days past due; a more severe letter, followed by a telephone call, may be used if payment is not received within thirty days; and the account may be turned over to a collection agency after ninety days.

The collection process can be expensive in terms of both out-of-pocket expenditures and lost goodwill, but at least some firmness is needed to prevent an undue lengthening in the collection period and to minimize outright losses. Again, a balance must be struck between the costs and benefits of different collection policies.

Accounts Receivable versus Accounts Payable

Whenever goods are sold on credit, two accounts are created—an asset item entitled an *account receivable* appears on the books of the selling firm, and a liability item called an *account payable* appears on the books of the purchaser. At this point, we are analyzing the transaction from the viewpoint of the seller, so we have concentrated on the type of variables under his control. In Chapter 9, we will examine the transaction from the viewpoint of the purchaser. There we will discuss accounts payable as a source of funds and consider the cost of these funds vis-à-vis funds obtained from other sources.

Establishing a Credit Policy: An Illustration[9]

Rexford Drug and Chemical Company manufactures and distributes drugs and related items to retail drugstores throughout the United States and Canada. At a recent board meeting, several directors voiced concern over the firm's rising bad debt losses and increasing investment in accounts receivable. This group suggested to the financial vice-president that he instruct his credit manager to tighten up the credit policy. Several other directors, including the marketing vice-president, took exception to this suggestion, stating that a tougher credit policy would cause Rexford to lose profitable sales. This group emphasized that the gross profit margin on sales is 50 percent, and stated that, if anything, credit terms should be relaxed. After a heated discussion, the meeting broke up; but before adjournment, the board instructed Jim Nantell, the financial vice-president, to conduct a study of the firm's credit policy. Nantell directed his credit manager, Bob Carleton, to study the firm's policy and to report on the desirability of instituting changes.

Carleton decided to draw up two new credit policies as alternatives to the one currently in use. One could be described as an easy credit policy, the other a tough credit policy. The current policy is an "average" policy in the sense that it closely corresponds to the practices of other drug supply firms.

The new plans require changes in all four credit policy variables. The "easy" credit policy involves (1) extending credit to a more risky class of customers, (2) extending the allowable payment period, (3) raising the cash discount allowed for prompt payments, and (4) reducing the "pressure" of the collection procedure on overdue accounts. The new terms will be 3/15, net 45, instead of the current 2/10, net 30. Those changes are expected to increase sales, but they will also increase the losses on bad debts and the investment in accounts receivable.

---

[9]In part of this example we employ statistical concepts that may be unfamiliar to the reader. However, the "words" are more important than the "numbers," so if the statistics are confusing, just concentrate on the verbal sections.

The "tough" credit policy involves tightening credit standards; reducing credit terms to 1/10, net 20; and increasing the collection efforts on overdue accounts. It will result in lower sales but also in lower bad debt losses and a smaller investment in accounts receivable. Working with the sales manager, Carleton developed probability estimates of the *changes* in sales and in costs that could result from the two new policies. This information is represented in Table 8–2, where the expected change in profits under each plan is also computed.

TABLE 8–2 Incremental Profits from Credit Policy Changes (Dollars in millions)

Increase in Sales (1)	Profit Margin (2)	Increase in Gross Profit (3) = (1) × (2)	Probability of Sales Change (4)	Increase (or Decrease) in Cost (5)	Conditional Probability (6)	Increase (or Decrease) in Net Profit (7) = (3) − (5)	Joint Probability (8) = (4) × (6)	Product (9) = (7) × (8)
				Easy credit policy				
$ 100	.50	$ 50	.20	$ 50	.30	—	.06	—
				60	.40	$(10)	.08	$(.80)
				70	.30	(20)	.06	(1.20)
200	.50	100	.60	80	.30	20	.18	3.60
				90	.40	10	.24	2.40
				100	.30	—	.18	—
300	.50	150	.20	120	.30	30	.06	1.80
				130	.40	20	.08	1.60
				140	.30	10	.06	.60
			1.00				1.00	

Expected increase in profit = $ 8.00

Increase in Sales (1)	Profit Margin (2)	Increase in Gross Profit (3) = (1) × (2)	Probability of Sales Change (4)	Increase (or Decrease) in Cost (5)	Conditional Probability (6)	Increase (or Decrease) in Net Profit (7) = (3) − (5)	Joint Probability (8) = (4) × (6)	Product (9) = (7) × (8)
				Tough credit policy				
$(50)	.50	$(25)	.25	$(20)	.20	$(5)	.05	$(.25)
				(30)	.60	5	.15	.75
				(40)	.20	15	.05	.75
(150)	.50	(75)	.50	$(50)	.20	(25)	.10	(2.50)
				(60)	.60	(15)	.30	(4.50)
				(70)	.20	(5)	.10	(.50)
(250)	.50	(125)	.25	(90)	.20	(1.75)	.05	(1.75)
				(100)	.60	(3.75)	.15	(3.75)
				(110)	.20	(.75)	.05	(.75)
			1.00				1.00	

Expected increase in profit = $(12.5)

Columns 1, 2, and 3 give alternative sales levels, profit margins, and profits. Column 4 gives the estimated probability of each gross profit outcome;

column 5 gives an estimate of the incremental costs, including production, general and administrative, and credit costs, associated with each sales change. Notice that these cost estimates are themselves subject to probability distributions. For example, if sales increase by $100 million, costs may increase by $50, $60, or $70 million; the conditional probability estimate of each cost outcome is given in column 6.

Depending on which sales and cost increases actually occur, net profit will increase or decrease by the amount given in column 7. The joint probabilities, which represent the products of the probabilities in columns 4 and 6, give the probability of each net profit increase, and these joint probabilities are used to derive the expected profits under each proposed credit policy change. Since the easier credit policy produces positive incremental profits, this policy is superior to the present policy and much superior to that of tightening credit.

Two points should be noted. First, this kind of analysis requires that some very difficult judgments be made—estimating the changes in sales and costs associated with changes in credit policies is, to say the least, a highly uncertain business. Second, even if the sales and cost estimates are reasonably accurate, there is no assurance that some other credit policy would not be even better. For instance, an easy credit policy that involved a different mix of the four policy variables might be superior to the one examined in Table 8–2.

For both these reasons, firms usually "iterate" slowly toward optimal credit policies. One or two credit variables are changed slightly, the effect of the changes is observed, and a decision is made to change these variables even more or to retract the changes. Further, different credit policies are appropriate at different times, depending on economic conditions. We see, then, that credit policy is not a static, once-for-all-time decision. Rather, it should be fluid, dynamic, and ever changing in an effort to reach a continually moving optimal target.

INVENTORY

Manufacturing firms generally have three kinds of inventories: (1) raw materials, (2) work in process, and (3) finished goods. The levels of *raw material inventories* are influenced by anticipated production, seasonality of production, reliability of sources of supply, and efficiency of scheduling purchases and production operations.

Work-in-process inventory is strongly influenced by the length of the production period, which is the time between placing raw material in production and completing the finished product. Inventory turnover can be increased by decreasing the production period. One means of accomplishing this is perfecting engineering techniques to speed up the manufacturing process.

Another means of reducing work in process is to buy items rather than make them.

The level of *finished goods inventories* is a matter of coordinating production and sales. The financial manager can stimulate sales by changing credit terms or by allowing credit to marginal risks. Whether the goods remain on the books as inventories or as receivables, the financial manager has to finance them. Many times, firms find it desirable to make the sale and thus take one step nearer to realizing cash. The potential profits can outweigh the additional collection risk.

Our primary focus in this section is control of investment in inventories. *Inventory models* have been developed as an aid in this task and have proved extremely useful in minimizing inventory requirements. As our examination of the du Pont system in Chapter 3 showed, any procedure that can reduce the investment required to generate a given sales volume may have a beneficial effect on the firm's rate of return and hence on the value of the firm.

DETERMINANTS OF THE SIZE OF INVENTORIES

Although wide variations occur, inventory-to-sales ratios are generally concentrated in the 12-to-20 percent range, and inventory-to-total assets ratios are concentrated in the 16-to-30 percent range.

The major determinants of investment in inventory are the following: (1) level of sales, (2) length and technical nature of the production processes, and (3) durability versus perishability, or style factor, in the end product. Inventories in the tobacco industry, for example, are high because of the long curing process. Similarly, in the machinery-manufacturing industries, inventories are large because of the long work-in-process period. However, inventory ratios are low in coal mining and in oil and gas production because no raw materials are used and the goods in process are small in relation to sales. Because of the seasonality of the raw materials, average inventories are large in the canning industry.

With respect to durability and style factors, large inventories are found in the hardware and the precious-metals industries because durability is great and the style factor is small. Inventory ratios are low in baking because of the perishability of the final product. Inventories are low in printing because the items are manufactured to order and require negligible finished inventories.

Within limits set by the economics of a firm's industry, there exists a potential for improvement in inventory control from the use of computers and operations research. Although the techniques are far too diverse and complicated for a complete treatment in this text, the financial manager should be prepared to make use of the contributions of specialists who have developed effective procedures for minimizing the investment in inventory.

Illustrative of the techniques at the practical level is Harris Electronic's inventory system, which works like this: Tabulator cards are inserted in each package of five electronic tubes leaving Harris's warehouse. As the merchandise is sold, the distributor collects the cards and files his replacement order without doing paper work. He simply sends in the cards, which are identified by account number, type of merchandise, and price of the units he orders.

Western Union Telegraph Co. equipment accepts the punched cards and transmits information on them to the warehouse, where it is duplicated on other punched cards. A typical order of 5,000 tubes of varying types can be received in about 17 minutes, assembled in about 90 minutes, and delivered to Boston's Logan Airport in an additional 45 minutes. Orders from 3,000 miles away can be delivered within 24 hours, a saving of 13 days in some cases.

Information on the order also goes into a computer which keeps on file stock-on-hand data for each item. When an order draws the stock down below the *order point,* this triggers action in the production department—additional units of the item are then manufactured for stock. In the next section, we examine both the optimal order point and the number of units that should be manufactured, which is called the *economic ordering quantity* (EOQ).

GENERALITY OF INVENTORY ANALYSIS

Managing assets of all kinds is basically an inventory problem—the same method of analysis applies to cash and fixed assets as applies to inventories themselves. First, a basic stock must be on hand to balance inflows and outflows of the items, with the size of the stock depending upon the patterns of flows, whether regular or irregular. Second, because the unexpected may always occur, it is necessary to have safety stocks on hand. They represent the little extra to avoid the costs of not having enough to meet current needs. Third, additional amounts may be required to meet future growth needs. These are anticipation stocks. Related to anticipation stocks is the recognition that there are optimum purchase sizes, defined as *economic ordering quantities.* In borrowing money, in buying raw materials for production, or in purchasing plants and equipment, it is cheaper to buy more than just enough to meet immediate needs.

With the foregoing as a basic foundation, we can develop the theoretical basis for determining the optimal investment in inventory, which is illustrated in Figure 8–1. Some costs rise with larger inventories—among these are warehousing costs, interest on funds tied up in inventories, insurance, obsolescence, and so forth. Other costs decline with larger inventories—these include the loss of profits resulting from sales lost because of running out of stock, costs of production interruptions caused by inadequate inventories, possible purchase discounts, and so on.

FIGURE 8–1 Determination of Optimum Investment in Inventory

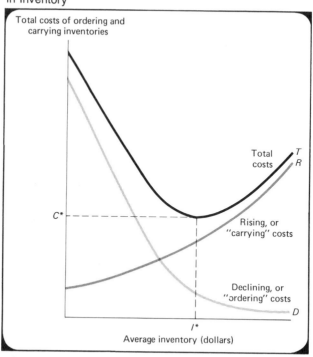

The costs that decline with higher inventories are designated by curve *D* in Figure 8–1; those that rise with larger inventories are designated by curve *R*. Curve *T* is the total of the *R* and *D* curves, and it represents the total cost of ordering and holding inventories. At the point where the absolute value of the slope of the *R* curve is equal to the absolute value of the slope of the *D* curve (that is, where *marginal* rising costs are equal to *marginal* declining costs), the *T* curve is at a minimum. This represents the optimum size of investment in inventory.

INVENTORY DECISION MODELS

The generalized statements in the preceding section can be made much more specific. In fact, it is usually possible to specify the curves shown in Figure 8–1, at least to a reasonable approximation, and actually to find the minimum point on the total cost curve. Since entire courses (in operations research programs) are devoted to inventory control techniques, and since a number of books have been written on the subject, we obviously cannot deal with inventory decision models in a very complete fashion. The model we illustrate, however, is probably more widely used—even by quite sophisticated firms—than any other, and it can be readily expanded to encompass any refinements one cares to make.

The costs of holding inventories—the cost of capital tied up, storage costs, insurance, depreciation, and so on—rise as the size of inventory holdings increases. Conversely, the cost of ordering inventories—the cost of placing orders, shipping and handling, quantity discounts lost, and so on— falls as the average inventory increases. The total cost of inventories is the summation of these rising and declining costs, or the *T* curve in Figure 8–1. It has been shown that, under reasonable assumptions, the minimum point on the *T* curve can be found by an equation called the EOQ formula:

$$EOQ = \sqrt{\frac{2FS}{CP}}.$$

Here

EOQ = the economic ordering quantity, or the optimum quantity to be ordered each time an order is placed.

F = fixed costs of placing and receiving an order.

S = annual sales in units.

C = carrying cost expressed as a percentage of inventory value.

P = purchase price per unit of inventory.

For any level of sales, dividing S by EOQ indicates the number of orders that must be placed each year. The average inventory on hand—the average balance sheet inventory figure—will be

$$\text{Average inventory} = \frac{EOQ}{2}.$$

The derivation of the EOQ model assumes (1) that usage is at a constant rate and (2) that delivery lead times are constant. In fact, usage is likely to vary considerably for most firms—demand may be unexpectedly strong for any number of reasons; if it is, the firm will run out of stock and will suffer sales losses or production stoppages. Similarly, delivery lead times will vary depending on weather, strikes, demand in the suppliers' industries, and so on. Because of these factors, firms add *safety stocks* to their inventory holdings, and the average inventory becomes

$$\text{Average inventory} = \frac{EOQ}{2} + \text{safety stock}.$$

The size of the safety stock will be relatively high if uncertainties about usage rates and delivery times are great, low if these factors do not vary greatly. Similarly, the safety stock will be larger if the costs of running out of stock are great. For example, if customer ill will would cause a permanent loss of business or if an elaborate production process would have to stop if an item were out of stock, then large safety stocks will be carried.[10]

USE OF EOQ MODEL: AN ILLUSTRATION

Let us assume that the following values are determined to be appropriate for a particular firm:

S = sales = 100 units.
C = carrying cost = 20 percent of inventory value.
P = purchase price = $1 per unit.
F = fixed cost of ordering = $10.

Substituting these values into the formula, we obtain

$$EOQ = \sqrt{\frac{2FS}{CP}}$$

$$= \sqrt{\frac{2 \times 10 \times 100}{0.2 \times 1}} = \sqrt{\frac{2000}{0.2}} = \sqrt{10,000}$$

$$= 100 \text{ units.}$$

If the desired safety stock is 10 units, then the average inventory (A) will be

$$A = \frac{EOQ}{2} + \text{safety stock}$$

$$= \frac{100}{2} + 10$$

$$= 60 \text{ units.}$$

Since the cost of purchasing or manufacturing inventory is $1 a unit, the average inventory in dollars will be $60 for this item.

SUMMARY

In this chapter we focused attention on four types of current assets—cash, marketable securities, accounts receivable, and inventories. First, we examined the motives for holding cash and ways of minimizing the investment in cash. With this background, we considered the minimum cash balances a firm is likely to hold. This minimum will be the higher (1) of compensating balance requirements or (2) of transactions balances plus a safety stock.

[10]Formal methods have been developed to assist in striking a balance between the costs of carrying larger safety stocks and the cost of stock-outs (inventory shortages). A discussion of these models, which go beyond the scope of this book, can be found in most production textbooks.

Marketable securities are held as a substitute for "cash safety stocks" and as temporary investments while the firm is awaiting permanent investment of funds. "Safety stocks" are almost always held in low-risk, short-maturity securities; temporary investments are held in securities whose maturity depends upon the length of time before the funds are permanently employed.

The investment in accounts receivable is dependent (1) upon sales and (2) upon the firm's credit policy. The credit policy, in turn, involves four controllable variables: credit standards, the length of the credit period, cash discounts, and the collection policy. The significant aspect of credit policy is its effect on sales: an easy credit policy will stimulate sales but involves costs of capital tied up in receivables, bad debts, discounts, and higher collection costs. The optimal credit policy is one in which these costs are just offset by the profits on sales generated by the credit policy change.

Inventories—raw materials, work in process, and finished goods—are necessary in most businesses. Rather elaborate systems for controlling the level of inventories have been designed. These systems frequently use computers for keeping records of all the items in stock; an inventory control model that considers anticipated sales, ordering costs, and carrying costs can be used to determine EOQ's for each item.

The basic inventory model recognizes that certain costs (carrying costs) rise as average inventory holdings increase but that certain other costs (ordering costs and stock-out costs) fall as average inventory holdings rise. These two sets of costs make up the total cost of ordering and carrying inventories, and the EOQ model is designed to locate an optimal order size that will minimize total inventory costs.

QUESTIONS

8-1. How can better methods of communication reduce the necessity for firms to hold large cash balances?

8-2. "The highly developed financial system of the United States, with its myriad of different near-cash assets, has greatly reduced cash balance requirements by reducing the need for transactions balances." Discuss this statement.

8-3. Would you expect a firm with a high growth rate to hold more or less precautionary and speculative cash balances than a firm with a low growth rate? Explain.

8-4. Many firms that find themselves with temporary surplus cash invest these funds in Treasury bills. Since Treasury bills frequently have the lowest yield of any investment security, why are they chosen as investments?

8-5. Assume that a firm sells on terms of net 30 and that its accounts are, on the average, thirty days overdue. What will its investment in receivables be if its annual credit sales are approximately $720,000?

8-6. "It is difficult to judge the performance of many of our employees but not that of the credit manager. If he's performing perfectly, credit losses are zero; and the higher our losses (as a percent of sales), the worse his performance." Evaluate this statement.

8-7. Explain how a firm may reduce its investment in inventory by having its supplier hold raw materials inventories and its customers hold finished goods inventories. What are the limitations of such a policy?

8-8. What factors are likely to reduce the holdings of inventory in relation to sales in the future? What factors will tend to increase the ratio? What, in your judgment, is the net effect?

8-9. What are the probable effects of the following on inventory holdings?

    a. Manufacture of a part formerly purchased from an outside supplier.

    b. Greater use of air freight.

    c. Increase, from seven to seventeen, in the number of styles produced.

    d. Your firm receives large price reductions from a manufacturer of bathing suits if they are purchased in December and January.

8-10. Inventory decision models are designed to facilitate the minimization of the cost of obtaining and carrying inventory. Describe the basic nature of the fundamental inventory control model, discussing specifically the nature of increasing costs, decreasing costs, and total costs. Illustrate your discussion with a graph.

PROBLEMS

8-1. Hayes Associates is short on cash and is attempting to determine if it would be advantageous for them to forego the discount on this month's purchases or to borrow funds to take advantage of the discount. The discount terms are 2/10, net 45. What is the maximum annual interest rate that Hayes Associates should pay on borrowed funds? Why? What are some of the intangible disadvantages associated with foregoing discount?

8-2. Scott, Inc. currently has a centralized billing system located in New York City. However, over the years their customers have gradually become less concentrated on the East Coast and now cover the entire United States. On average, it requires five days from the time customers mail payments until Scott is able to receive, process, and deposit their payments. To shorten this time lag, Scott is considering installing a lock-box collection system. They estimate that they will be able to reduce the time lag from customer mailing to deposit by three and one-half days. Scott has a daily average collection of $700,000.

    a. What is the reduction in cash balances that Scott could achieve by initiating the lock-box system?

    b. If Scott has an opportunity cost of 8 percent, how much is the lock-box system worth on an annual basis?

    c. What is the maximum monthly charge that Scott could pay for the lock-box system?

8-3. Standard Distributors, whose sales are on a credit basis, makes a routine credit evaluation of all its customers at least once each year. It finds that this procedure allows it to rank its customers in categories from 1 to 5, in order of increasing risk. On the basis of past experience, the firm has found the following bad debt loss percentage and average collection period on the accounts in each category:

Category	Percentage Bad Debts	Average Collection Period
1	None	10 days
2	0.5	12
3	2.0	20
4	5.0	30
5	10.0	60

The firm's current credit policy is to extend unlimited credit to firms in categories 1 to 3, limited credit to firms in category 4, and no more credit to firms in category 5.

The result of this policy is that orders totaling $250,000 from category 4 firms and $750,000 from category 5 firms are turned down each year. If the firm makes a 9 percent gross profit margin on sales (gross profit on sales = sales less cost of goods sold) and has an opportunity cost on investments in receivables of 9 percent, what would be the net effect on profits of extending full credit to category 4? to category 5?

8-4. A firm issues checks in the amount of $1 million each day and deducts them from its own records at the close of business on the day they are written. On average, the bank receives and clears (that is, deducts from the firm's bank balance) the checks the evening of the fourth day after they are written; for example, a check written on Monday will be cleared on Friday afternoon. The firm's loan agreement with the bank requires it to maintain a $750,000 minimum average compensating balance; this is $250,000 greater than the cash safety stock the firm would otherwise have on deposit.

a. Assuming that the firm makes deposits in the late afternoon (and the bank includes the deposit in the day's transactions), how much must the firm deposit each day to maintain a sufficient balance once it reaches a steady state?

b. How many days of float does the firm carry?

c. What ending daily balance should the firm try to maintain at the bank and on its own records?

d. Explain how float can help increase the value of the firm's common stock. Use a partial balance sheet, and the du Pont system concept, in your answer.

8-5. Callaway Electronics Company is considering changing its credit terms from 2/15, net 30, to 3/10, net 45. All its sales are "credit sales," but 75 percent of the customers presently take the 2 percent cash discount; under the new terms this percentage is expected to decline to 65 percent. The average collection period is also expected to change under the new policy, from 17 days at present to 20 days under the new plan. (Note that these averages are heavily weighted with customers who pay within ten days.) Expected sales, before discounts are deducted, are $600,000 with the present terms, but $675,000 if the new terms are used. Assume that (1) Callaway earns a 12 percent profit margin after all costs, including credit costs, on present sales after a change in credit policy, (2) sales will have a 12 percent margin *before* incremental credit-associated costs, and (3) a 5 percent opportunity cost applies to the investment in receivables. Calculate

a. the increase in gross profits

b. the increase in discount costs

c. the increased cost of carrying receivables

d. the net change in pretax profits.

8-6. The following relations for inventory purchase and storage costs have been established for the Lomer Fabricating Corporation.

1. Orders must be placed in multiples of 100 units.
2. Requirements for the year are 300,000 units. (Use 50 weeks in a year for calculations.)
3. The purchase price per unit is $3.
4. Carrying cost is 25 percent of the purchase price of goods.
5. Cost per order placed is $20.00.
6. Desired safety stock is 10,000 units (on hand initially).
7. Two weeks are required for delivery.

a. What is the economical order quantity?

b. What is the optimal number of orders to be placed?

c. At what inventory level should a reorder be made?

(Hint: the inventory level should be sufficient to cover the amount used during delivery, plus the safety stock.)

Major Sources and Forms of Short-Term Financing

9

In Chapter 7 we discussed the maturity structure of the firm's debt and showed how this structure can affect both risk and expected returns. However, a variety of short-term credits are available to the firm, and the financial manager must know the advantages and disadvantages of each. Accordingly, in the present chapter we take up the main forms of short-term credit, considering both the characteristics and the sources of this credit.

Short-term credit is defined as *debt originally scheduled for repayment within one year.* We discuss the three major sources of funds with short maturities in this chapter. Ranked in descending order by volume of credit supplied to business, the main sources of short-term financing are (1) trade credit between firms, (2) loans from commercial banks, and (3) commercial paper.

TRADE CREDIT[1]

In the ordinary course of events, a firm buys its supplies and materials on credit from other firms, recording the debt as an *account payable*. Accounts payable, or *trade credit*, as it is commonly called, is the largest single category of short-term credit, and it represents about 40 percent of the current liabilities of nonfinancial corporations. This percentage is somewhat larger for smaller

---

[1] In Chapter 8 we discussed trade credit from the point of view of minimizing investment in current assets. In the present chapter we look at "the other side of the coin," viewing trade credit as a *source* of financing rather than as a *use* of financing. In Chapter 8, the use of trade credit by our customers resulted in an asset investment called *accounts receivable*. In the present chapter, the use of trade credit gives rise to short-term obligations, generally called *accounts payable*.

169

firms; because small companies may not qualify for financing from other sources, they rely rather heavily on trade credit.

Trade credit is a *spontaneous* source of financing in that it arises from ordinary business transactions. For example, suppose a firm makes average purchases of $2,000 a day on terms of net 30. On the average it will owe 30 times $2,000, or $60,000, to its suppliers. If its sales, and consequently its purchases, double, accounts payable will also double to $120,000. The firm will have spontaneously generated an additional $60,000 of financing. Similarly, if the terms of credit are extended from thirty to forty days, accounts payable will expand from $60,000 to $80,000; thus, lengthening the credit period, as well as expanding sales and purchases, generates additional financing.

Credit Terms

The terms of sale, or *credit terms*, describe the payment obligation of the buyer. In the following discussion we outline the four main factors that influence the length of credit terms.

Economic Nature of Product   Commodities with high sales turnover are sold on relatively short credit terms; the buyer resells the product rapidly, generating cash that enables him to pay the supplier. Groceries have a high turnover, but perishability also plays a role. The credit extended for fresh fruits and vegetables might run from five to ten days, whereas the credit extended on canned fruits and vegetables would more likely be fifteen to thirty days. Terms for items that have a slow retail turnover, such as jewelry, may run six months or longer.

Seller Circumstances   Financially weak sellers must require cash or exceptionally short credit terms. For example, farmers sell livestock to meat-packing companies on a cash basis. In many industries, variations in credit terms can be used as a sales promotion device. Although the use of credit as a selling device could endanger sound credit management, the practice does occur, especially when the seller's industry has excess capacity. Also, a large seller could use his position to impose relatively short credit terms. However, the reverse appears more often in practice; that is, financially strong sellers are suppliers of funds to small firms.

Buyer Circumstances   In general, financially sound retailers who sell on credit may, in turn, receive slightly longer terms. Some classes of retailers regarded as selling in particularly risky areas (such as clothing) receive extended credit terms, but they are offered large discounts to encourage early payment.

Cash Discounts   A cash discount is a reduction in price based on payment within a specified period. The costs of not taking cash discounts often exceed the rate of interest at which the buyer can borrow, so it is important that a firm be cautious in its use of trade credit as a source of financing—it could be quite expensive. If the firm borrows and takes the cash discount, the period during which accounts payable remain on the book is reduced. The effective length of credit is thus influenced by the size of discounts offered.

Illustrative Credit Terms   Credit terms typically express the amount of the cash discount and the date of its expiration, as well as the final due date. Earlier, we noticed that one of the most frequently encountered terms is 2/10, net 30. (If payment is made within ten days of the invoice date, a 2 percent cash discount is allowed. If the cash discount is not taken, payment is due thirty days after the date of invoice.) The cost of not taking cash discounts can be substantial, as shown here.[2]

Credit Terms	Costs of Credit if Cash Discount Not Taken (Percent)
1/10, net 20	36.36
1/10, net 30	18.18
2/10, net 20	73.44
2/10, net 30	36.72

CONCEPT OF "NET CREDIT"

Trade credit has double-edged significance for the firm. It is a source of credit for financing purchases, and it is a use of funds to the extent that the firm finances credit sales to customers. For example, if, on the average, a firm sells $3,000 of goods a day with an average collection period of forty days, at any balance sheet date it will have accounts receivable of approximately $120,000.

If the same firm buys $2,000 worth of materials a day and the balance is outstanding for twenty days, accounts payable will average $40,000. *The firm is extending net credit for $80,000, the difference between accounts receivable and accounts payable.*

Large firms and well-financed firms of all sizes tend to be net suppliers of trade credit; small firms and undercapitalized firms of all sizes tend to be net users of trade credit. It is impossible to generalize about whether it is better to be a net supplier or a net user of trade credit—the choice depends upon the firm's own circumstances and conditions, and the various costs and benefits of receiving and using trade credit must be analyzed as described here and in Chapter 8.

[2] The method of calculating the effective interest rate on accounts payable was described in Chapter 8.

Advantages of Trade Credit as a Source of Financing

Trade credit, a customary part of doing business in most industries, is convenient and informal. A firm that does not qualify for credit from a financial institution may receive trade credit because previous experience has familiarized the seller with the credit-worthiness of his customer. As the seller knows the merchandising practices of the industry, he is usually in a good position to judge the capacity of his customer and the risk of selling to him on credit. The amount of trade credit fluctuates with the buyer's purchases, subject to any credit limits that may be operative.

Whether trade credit costs more or less than other forms of financing is a moot question. Sometimes trade credit can be surprisingly expensive to the buyer. The user often does not have any alternative forms of financing available, and the costs to the buyer may be commensurate with the risks to the seller. But in some instances trade credit is used simply because the user does not realize how expensive it is. In such circumstances, careful financial analysis may lead to the substitution of alternative forms of financing for trade credit.

At the other extreme, trade credit may represent a virtual subsidy or sales promotion device offered by the seller. The authors know, for example, of cases where manufacturers quite literally supplied *all* the financing for new firms by selling on credit terms substantially longer than those of the new company. In one instance a manufacturer, eager to obtain a dealership in a particular area, made a loan to the new company to cover operating expenses during the initial phases and geared the payment of accounts payable to cash receipts. Even in such instances, however, the buying firm must be careful that it is not really paying a hidden financing cost in the form of higher product prices than could be obtained elsewhere. Extending credit involves a cost to the selling firm, and this firm may well be raising its own prices to offset the "free" credit it extends.

SHORT-TERM FINANCING BY COMMERCIAL BANKS

Commercial bank lending appears on the balance sheet as *notes payable* and is second in importance to trade credit as a source of short-term financing. Banks occupy a pivotal position in the short-term and intermediate-term money markets. Their influence is greater than appears from the dollar amounts they lend because the banks provide nonspontaneous funds. As the financing needs of the firm increase, it requests the banks to provide the additional funds. If the request is denied, often the alternative is to slow down the rate of growth or to cut back operations.

Characteristics of Loans from Commercial Banks

In the following sections, the main characteristics of lending patterns of commercial banks are briefly described.

Forms of Loans   A single loan obtained from a bank by a business firm is not different in principle from a loan obtained by an individual. In fact, it is often difficult to distinguish a bank loan to a small business from a personal loan. A loan is obtained by signing a conventional promissory note. Repayment is made in a lump sum at maturity (when the note is due) or in installments throughout the life of the loan.

A *line of credit* is a formal or an informal understanding between the bank and the borrower concerning the maximum loan balance the bank will allow the borrower. For example, a bank loan officer may indicate to a financial manager that the bank regards his firm as "good" for up to $80,000 for the forthcoming year. Subsequently, the manager signs a promissory note for $15,000 for ninety days—he is said to be "taking down" $15,000 of his total line of credit. This amount is credited to the firm's checking account at the bank. At maturity, the checking account will be charged for the amount of the loan. Interest may be deducted in advance or may be paid at the maturity of the loan. Before repayment of the $15,000, the firm may borrow additional amounts up to a total of $80,000.

A more formal procedure may be followed if the firm is quite large. To illustrate, Chrysler Corporation arranged a line of credit for over $100 million with a group of banks. The banks were formally committed to lend Chrysler the funds if they were needed. Chrysler, in turn, paid a commitment fee of approximately one-quarter of 1 percent of the unused balance of the commitment to compensate the banks for making the funds available.

Maturity   Commercial banks concentrate on the short-term lending market. Short-term loans make up about two-thirds of bank loans by dollar amount, whereas "term loans" (loans with maturities longer than one year) make up only one-third.

Security   If a potential borrower is a questionable credit risk, or if his financing needs exceed the amount that the loan officer of the bank considers to be prudent on an unsecured basis, some form of security is required. More than one-half the dollar value of bank loans is secured; the forms of security are described later in this chapter. In terms of the number of bank loans, two-thirds are secured or endorsed by a third party who guarantees payment of the loan in the event the borrower defaults.

Compensating Balances   Banks typically require that a regular borrower maintain an average checking account balance equal to 15 or 20 percent of the outstanding loan. These balances, which are commonly called *compensating balances*, are a method of raising the effective interest rate. For example, if a firm needs $80,000 to pay off outstanding obligations, but must maintain a 20 percent compensating balance, it must borrow $100,000 to be able to obtain the required $80,000. If the stated interest is 5 percent, the effective cost is actually 6¼ percent—$5,000 divided by $80,000 equals 6.25 percent.[3] These *loan* compensating balances are, of course, added to any *service* compensating balances (discussed in Chapter 8) that the firm's bank may require.

Repayment of Bank Loans   Because most bank deposits are subject to withdrawal on demand, commercial banks seek to prevent firms from using bank credit for permanent financing. A bank may therefore require its borrowers to "clean up" their short-term bank loans for at least one month each year. If a firm is unable to become free of bank debt at least part of each year, it is using bank financing for permanent needs and should develop additional sources of long-term or permanent financing.

Cost of Commercial Bank Loans   Most loans from commercial banks have recently cost from 5 to 12 percent, with the effective rate depending upon the characteristics of the firm and the level of interest rates in the economy. If the firm can qualify as a "prime risk" because of its size and financial strength, the rate of interest will be one-half to three-quarters of 1 percent above the rediscount rate charged by federal reserve banks to commercial banks. On the other hand, a small firm with below-average financial ratios may be required to provide collateral security and to pay an effective rate of interest of more than 12 percent.

"Regular" Interest   Determination of the effective, or true, rate of interest on a loan depends on the stated rate of interest and the method of charging interest used by the lender. If the interest is paid at the maturity of the loan, the stated rate of interest is the effective rate of interest. For example, on a $10,000 loan for one year at 5 percent, the interest is $500:

$$\text{"Regular" loan, interest paid at maturity:} \quad \frac{\text{interest}}{\text{borrowed amount}} = \frac{\$500}{\$10,000} = 5\%.$$

Discounted Interest   If the bank deducts the interest in advance (*discounts* the loan), the effective rate of interest is increased. On the $10,000 loan for one year at 5 percent, the discount is $500, and the borrower obtains the use of only $9,500. The effective rate of interest is 5.3 percent versus 5 percent on a "regular" loan:

$$\text{Discounted loan:} \quad \frac{\text{interest}}{\text{borrowed amount} - \text{interest}} = \frac{\$500}{\$9,500} = 5.3\%.$$

---

[3]Note, however, that the compensating balance is generally set as a minimum monthly *average;* if the firm would maintain this average anyway, the compensating balance requirement does not entail higher effective rates.

Installment Loan   If the loan is repaid in 12 monthly installments but the interest is calculated on the original balance, then the effective rate of interest is even higher. The borrower has the full amount of the money only during the first month, and by the last month he has already paid eleven-twelfths of the loan. Thus our hypothetical borrower pays $500 for the use of about half the amount he receives. The amount received is $10,000 or $9,500, depending upon the method of charging interest, but the *average* amount outstanding during the year is only $5,000 or $4,750. If interest is paid at maturity, the approximate effective rate on an installment loan is calculated as follows:

$$\text{Interest rate on original amount of installment loan} = \frac{\$500}{\$5,000} = 10\%.$$

Under the discounting method, the effective cost of the installment loan would be approximately 10.5 percent:

$$\text{Interest rate on discounted installment loan} = \frac{\$500}{\$4,750} = 10.53\%.$$

The point to note here is that interest is paid on the *original* amount of the loan, not on the amount actually outstanding (the declining balance), and this causes the effective interest rate to be approximately double the stated rate. Interest is calculated by the installment method on most consumer loans (for example, automobile loans), but it is not often used for business loans larger than about $5,000.

Choice of Bank or Banks

Banks have close relations with their borrowers. There is much personal association over the years, and the business problems of the borrower are frequently discussed. Thus, the bank often provides informal management counseling services. A potential borrower seeking bank relations should recognize the important differences among banks, which are considered in the following discussion.

1. Banks have different basic policies toward risk. Some banks are inclined to follow relatively conservative lending practices; others engage in what are properly termed "creative banking practices." The policies reflect partly the personalities of officers of the bank and partly the characteristics of the bank's deposit liabilities. Thus a bank with fluctuating deposit liabilities in a static community will tend to be a conservative lender. A bank whose deposits are growing with little interruption may follow "liberal" credit policies. A large bank with broad diversification over geographical regions or among industries served can obtain the benefit of combining and averaging risks. Thus, marginal credit risks that might be unacceptable to a small bank or to a specialized unit bank can be pooled by a branch banking system to reduce the overall risks of a group of marginal accounts.

2. Some bank loan officers are active in providing counsel and in stimulating development loans with firms in their early and formative years. Certain banks have specialized departments to make loans to firms expected to become growth firms. The personnel of these departments can provide much counseling to customers.

3. Banks differ in the extent to which they will support the activities of the borrower in bad times. This characteristic is referred to as the degree of *loyalty* of the banks. Some banks may put great pressure on a business to liquidate its loans when the firm's outlook becomes clouded, whereas others will stand by the firm and work diligently to help it attain a more favorable condition.

4. Banks differ greatly in the degree of loan specialization. Larger banks have separate departments specializing in different kinds of loans, such as real estate, installment loans, and commercial loans, among others. Within these broad categories there may be a specialization by line of business, such as steel, machinery, or textiles. The strengths of smaller banks are likely to reflect the nature of the business and the economic environment in which the banks operate. They tend to become specialists in specific lines, such as oil, construction, and agriculture, to name a few. The borrower can obtain more creative cooperation and more active support if he goes to the bank that has the greatest experience and familiarity with his particular type of business. The financial manager should therefore choose his bank with care. A bank that is excellent for one firm may be unsatisfactory for another.

5. The size of a bank can be an important characteristic. Since the maximum loan a bank can make to any one customer is generally limited to 10 percent of capital accounts (capital stock plus retained earnings), it will generally not be appropriate for large firms to develop borrowing relationships with small banks.

6. With the heightened competition between commercial banks and other financial institutions, the aggressiveness of banks has increased. Modern commercial banks now offer a wide range of financial and business services. Most large banks have business development departments that provide counseling to firms and serve as intermediaries on a wide variety of their requirements.

COMMERCIAL PAPER

Commercial paper consists of promissory notes of *large* firms and is sold primarily to other business firms, insurance companies, pension funds, and banks. Although the amounts of commercial paper outstanding are much smaller than bank loans outstanding, this form of financing has grown rapidly in recent years.

Maturity and Cost

Maturities of commercial paper generally vary from two to six months, with an average of about five months. The rates on prime commercial paper vary, but they are generally about one-half of 1 percent below those on prime business loans. And, since compensating balances are not required for commercial paper, the *effective* cost differential is still wider.[4]

Use

The use of the open market for commercial paper is restricted to a comparatively small number of concerns that are exceptionally good credit risks. Dealers prefer to handle the paper of concerns whose net worth is $10 million or more and whose annual borrowing exceeds $1 million.

Appraisal of Use

The commercial paper market has some significant advantages. (1) It permits the broadest and the most advantageous distribution of paper. (2) It provides more funds at lower rates than do other methods. (3) The borrower avoids the inconvenience and expense of financing arrangements with a number of institutions, each of which requires a compensating balance. (4) Publicity and prestige accrue to the borrower as his product and his paper become more widely known. (5) Finally, the commercial paper dealer frequently offers valuable advice to his clients.

A basic limitation of the commercial paper market is that the size of the funds available is limited to the excess liquidity that corporations, the main suppliers of funds, may have at any particular time. Another disadvantage is that a debtor who is in temporary financial difficulty receives little consideration because commercial paper dealings are impersonal. Bank relations, on the other hand, are much more personal; a bank is much more likely to help a good customer weather a temporary storm than is a commercial paper dealer.[5]

---

[4]However, this factor is offset to some extent by the fact that firms issuing commercial paper are sometimes required by commercial paper dealers to have unused bank lines of credit to back up their outstanding commercial paper, and fees must be paid on these lines.

[5]This point was emphasized dramatically in the aftermath of the Penn-Central bankruptcy. Penn-Central had a large amount of commercial paper which went into default and embarrassed corporate treasurers who had been holding the paper as part of their liquidity reserves. Immediately after the bankruptcy, the commercial paper market dried up to a large extent, and some companies that had relied heavily on this market found themselves under severe liquidity pressure as their commercial paper matured and could not be refunded. Chrysler, for example, had to seek bank loans of over $500 million because it could not sell commercial paper for a time. Without adequate bank lines, Chrysler might well have been forced into bankruptcy itself, even though it was basically sound, because of the "Penn-Central panic." Incidentally, the Federal Reserve Board recognized that many other firms would be in the same position as Chrysler, so the Fed expanded bank reserves in order to enable the banking system to take up the slack caused by the withdrawal of funds from the commercial paper market.

USE OF SECURITY IN SHORT-TERM FINANCING

Given a choice, it is ordinarily better to borrow on an unsecured basis, as the bookkeeping costs of secured loans are often high. However, it frequently happens that a potential borrower's credit rating is not sufficiently strong to justify the loan. If the loan can be secured by the borrower's putting up some form of collateral to be claimed by the lender in the event of default, then the lender may extend credit to an otherwise unacceptable firm. Similarly, a firm that could borrow on an unsecured basis may elect to use security if it finds that this will induce lenders to quote a lower interest rate.

Several different kinds of collateral can be employed—marketable stocks or bonds, land or buildings, equipment, inventory, and accounts receivable. Marketable securities make excellent collateral, but few firms hold portfolios of stocks and bonds. Similarly real property (land and buildings) and equipment are good forms of collateral, but they are generally used as security for long-term loans. The bulk of secured short-term business borrowing involves the pledge of short-term assets—accounts receivable or inventories.

In the past, state laws varied greatly with regard to the use of security in financing. In the late 1960s, however, all states passed a *Uniform Commercial Code,* which standardized and simplified the procedure for establishing loan security.

The heart of the Uniform Commercial Code is the *Security Agreement,* a standardized document, or form, on which the specific assets that are pledged are stated. The assets can be items of equipment, accounts receivable, or inventories. Procedures for financing under the Uniform Commercial Code are described in the following sections.

FINANCING ACCOUNTS RECEIVABLE

Accounts receivable financing involves either the *pledging of receivables* or the *selling of receivables (factoring).* The *pledging of accounts receivable* is characterized by the fact that the lender not only has a lien on the receivables but also has recourse to the borrower (seller); if the person or the firm that bought the goods does not pay, the selling firm must take the loss. In other words, the risk of default on the accounts receivable pledged remains with the borrower. Also, the buyer of the goods is not ordinarily notified about the pledging of the receivables. The financial institution that lends on the security of accounts receivable is generally either a commercial bank or one of the large industrial finance companies.

Factoring, or selling accounts receivable, involves the purchase of accounts receivable by the lender without recourse to the borrower (seller). The buyer of the goods is notified of the transfer and makes payment directly to the lender. Since the factoring firm assumes the risk of default on bad accounts, it must do the credit checking. Accordingly, factors provide not only money but also a credit department for the borrower. Incidentally, the same financial institutions that make loans against pledged receivables also serve as factors. Thus, depending on the circumstances and the wishes of the borrower, a financial institution will provide either form of receivables financing.

Procedure for Pledging Accounts Receivable

The financing of accounts receivable is initiated by a legally binding agreement between the seller of the goods and the financing institution. The agreement sets forth in detail the procedures to be followed and the legal obligations of both parties. Once the working relation has been established, the seller periodically takes a batch of invoices to the financing institution. The lender reviews the invoices and makes an appraisal of the buyers. Invoices of companies that do not meet the lender's credit standards are not accepted for pledging. The financial institution seeks to protect itself at every phase of the operation. Selection of sound invoices is the essential first step in safeguarding the financial institution. If the buyer of the goods does not pay the invoice, the lender still has recourse against the seller of the goods. However, if many buyers default, the seller may be unable to meet his obligation to the financial institution.

Additional protection is afforded the lender in that the loan will generally be for less than 100 percent of the pledged receivables; for example, the lender may advance the selling firm 75 percent of the amount of the pledged receivables.

Procedure for Factoring Accounts Receivable

The procedure for factoring is somewhat different from that for pledging. Again, an agreement between the seller and the factor is made to specify legal obligations and procedural arrangements. When the seller receives an order from a buyer, a credit approval slip is written and immediately sent to the factoring company for a credit check. If the factor does not approve the sale, the seller generally refuses to fill the order. This procedure informs the seller, prior to the sale, about the buyer's credit-worthiness and acceptability to the factor. If the sale is approved, shipment is made and the invoice is stamped to notify the buyer to make payment directly to the factoring company.

The factor performs three functions in carrying out the normal procedure as outlined above: (1) credit checking, (2) lending, and (3) risk bearing. The seller can select various combinations of these functions by changing provisions in the factoring agreement. For example, a small or a medium-sized firm can avoid establishing a credit department. The factor's service might well be less costly than a department that may have excess capacity for the firm's credit volume. At the same time, if the firm uses part of the time of a non-credit specialist to perform credit checking, lack of education, training, and experience may result in excessive losses.

The seller may utilize the factor to perform the credit-checking and risk-taking functions but not the lending function. The following procedure is carried out on receipt of a $10,000 order. The factor checks and approves the invoices. The goods are shipped on terms of net 30. Payment is made to the factor, who remits to the seller. But assume that the factor has received only $5,000 by the end of the credit period. He must still remit $10,000 to the seller (less his fee, of course). If the remaining $5,000 is never paid, the factor sustains a $5,000 loss.

Now consider the more typical situation in which the factor performs a lending function by making payment in advance of collection. The goods are shipped and, even though payment is not due for 30 days, the factor immediately makes funds available to the seller. Suppose $10,000 of goods is shipped; the factoring commission for credit checking is 2½ percent of the invoice price, or $250; and the interest expense is computed at a 9 percent annual rate on the invoice balance, or $75.[6] The seller's accounting entry is as follows:

Cash	$9,175	
Interest expense	75	
Factoring commission	250	
Reserve: due from factor on collection of account	500	
Accounts receivable		$10,000

The $500 "due from factor on collection of account" in the entry is a reserve established by the factor to cover disputes between sellers and buyers on damaged goods, goods returned by the buyers to the seller, and failure to make outright sale of goods. The amount is paid to the seller firm when the factor collects on the account.

Factoring is normally a continuous process instead of the single cycle described above. The seller of the goods receives orders; he transmits the purchase orders to the factor for approval; on approval, the goods are shipped; the factor advances the money to the seller; the buyers pay the factor when payment is due; and the factor periodically remits any excess reserve to the seller of the goods. Once a routine is established, a continuous circular flow of goods and funds takes place between the seller, the buyers of the goods,

---

[6]Since the interest is only for one month, we take one-twelfth of the stated rate, 9 percent, and multiply this by the $10,000 invoice price:

$$\frac{1}{12} \times 0.09 \times \$10,000 = \$75.$$

Note that the effective rate of interest is really above 9 percent, because a discounting procedure is used and the borrower does not get the full $10,000. In many instances, however, the factoring contract calls for interest to be computed on the invoice price *less* the factoring commission and the reserve account.

and the factor. Thus, once the factoring agreement is in force, funds from this source are *spontaneous.*

Cost of Receivables Financing

Accounts receivable pledging and factoring services are convenient and advantageous, but they can be costly. The credit-checking commission is 1 to 3 percent of the amount of invoices accepted by the factor. The cost of money is reflected in the interest rate of 8 to 12 percent charged on the unpaid balance of the funds advanced by the factor. Where the risk to the factor is excessive, he purchases the invoices (with or without recourse) at discounts from face value.

Evaluation of Receivables Financing

It cannot be said categorically that accounts receivable financing is always either a good or a poor method of raising funds for an individual business. Among the advantages is, first, the flexibility of this source of financing. As the firm's sales expand and more financing is needed, a larger volume of invoices is generated automatically. Because the dollar amounts of invoices vary directly with sales, the amount of readily available financing increases. Second, receivables or invoices provide security for a loan that a firm might otherwise be unable to obtain. Third, factoring provides the services of a credit department that might otherwise be available to the firm only under much more expensive conditions.

Accounts receivable financing also has disadvantages. First, when invoices are numerous and relatively small in dollar amount, the administrative costs involved may render this method of financing inconvenient and expensive. Second, the firm is using a highly liquid asset as security. For a long time, accounts receivable financing was frowned upon by most trade creditors. In fact, such financing was regarded as confession of a firm's unsound financial position. It is no longer regarded in this light, and many sound firms engage in receivables pledging or factoring. However, the traditional attitude causes some trade creditors to refuse to sell on credit to a firm that is factoring or pledging its receivables, on the grounds that this practice removes one of the most liquid of the firm's assets and, accordingly, weakens the position of other creditors.

Future Use of Receivables Financing

We might make a prediction at this point—in the future, accounts receivable financing will increase in relative importance. Computer technology is rapidly advancing toward the point where credit records of individuals and firms can be kept in computer memory units. Systems have been devised so that a retailer can have a unit on hand that, when an individual's magnetic credit card is inserted into a box, gives a signal that his credit is "good" and that a bank is willing to "buy" the receivable created when the store completes the sale. The cost of handling invoices will be greatly reduced over present-day costs because the new systems will be so highly automated. This will make it possible to use accounts receivable financing for very small sales, and it will reduce the cost of all receivables financing. The net result will be a marked expansion of accounts receivable financing.

INVENTORY FINANCING

A rather large volume of credit is secured by business inventories. If a firm is a relatively good credit risk, the mere existence of the inventory may be a sufficient basis for receiving an unsecured loan. If the firm is a relatively poor risk, the lending institution may insist upon security, which often takes the form of a blanket lien against the inventory. Alternatively, *trust receipts* or *field warehouse receipts* can be used to secure the loan. These methods of using inventories as security are discussed below.

Blanket Inventory Lien

The blanket inventory lien gives the lending institution a lien against all inventories of the borrower. However, the borrower is free to sell inventories; thus the value of the collateral can be reduced.

Trust Receipts

Because of the weaknesses of the blanket lien for inventory financing, another kind of security is used—the trust receipt. A trust receipt is an instrument acknowledging that the borrower holds the goods in trust for the lender. When trust receipts are used, the borrowing firm, on receiving funds from the lender, conveys a trust receipt for the goods. The goods can be stored in a public warehouse or held on the premises of the borrower. The trust receipt provides that the goods are held in trust for the lender or are segregated in the borrower's premises on behalf of the lender, and proceeds from the sale of goods held under trust receipts are transmitted to the lender at the end of each day. Automobile dealer financing is the best example of trust receipt financing.

One defect of trust receipt financing is the requirement that a trust receipt must be issued for specific goods. For example, if the security is bags of coffee beans, the trust receipts must indicate the bags by number. In order to validate its trust receipts, the lending institution would have to send a man to the premises of the borrower to see that the bag numbers are correctly listed. Furthermore, complex legal requirements of trust receipts require the attention of a bank officer. Problems are compounded if borrowers are widely separated geographically from the lender. To offset these inconveniences, *warehousing* is coming into wide use as a method of securing loans with inventory.

Warehouse Financing

Like trust receipts, warehouse financing uses inventory as security. A *public warehouse* represents an independent third party engaged in the business of storing goods. Sometimes a public warehouse is not practical because of the bulkiness of goods and the expense of transporting them to and from the borrower's premises. *Field warehouse* financing represents an economical method of inventory financing in which the warehouse is established at the place of the borrower. To provide inventory supervision, the lending institution employs a third party in the arrangement, the field warehousing company. This company acts as the control (or supervisory) agent for the lending institution.

Field warehousing is illustrated by a simple example. Suppose a potential borrower has stacked iron in an open yard on his premises. A field warehouse can be established if a field warehousing concern places a temporary fence around the iron and erects a sign stating: "This is a field warehouse supervised and conducted by the Lawrence Warehousing Corporation." These are minimal conditions, of course.

The example illustrates the two elements in the establishment of a warehouse: (1) public notification of the field warehouse arrangement and (2) supervision of the field warehouse by a custodian of the field warehouse concern. When the field warehousing operation is relatively small, the second condition is sometimes violated by hiring an employee of the borrower to supervise the inventory. This practice is viewed as undesirable by the lending institution, because there is no control over the collateral by a person independent of the borrowing concern.[7]

The field warehouse financing operation is described best by a specific illustration. Assume that a tomato canner is interested in financing his operations by bank borrowing. The canner has sufficient funds to finance 15 to 20 percent of his operations during the canning season. These funds are adequate to purchase and process an initial batch of tomatoes. As the cans are put into boxes and rolled into the storerooms, the canner needs additional funds for both raw materials and labor.

---

[7]This absence of independent control was the main cause of the breakdown that resulted in the huge losses connected with the loans to the Allied Crude Vegetable Oil Company headed by Anthony (Tino) DeAngelis. American Express Field Warehousing Company hired men from Allied's staff as custodians. Their dishonesty was not discovered because of another breakdown—the fact that the American Express touring inspector did not actually take a physical inventory of the warehouses. As a consequence, the swindle was not discovered until losses running into the hundreds of millions of dollars had been suffered. See Norman C. Miller, *The Great Salad Oil Swindle* (Baltimore, Md.: Penguin Books, 1965), pp. 72–77.

Because of the canner's poor credit rating, the bank decides that a field warehousing operation is necessary to secure its loans. The field warehouse is established, and the custodian notifies the lending institution of the description, by number, of the boxes of canned tomatoes in storage and under his control. Thereupon the lending institution establishes for the canner a deposit on which he can draw. From this point on, the bank finances operations. The canner needs only enough cash to initiate the cycle. The farmers bring more tomatoes; the canner processes them; the cans are boxed, and the boxes are put into the field warehouse; field warehouse receipts are drawn up and sent to the bank; the bank establishes further deposits for the canner on the basis of the receipts; the canner can draw on the deposits to continue the cycle.

Of course, the canner's ultimate objective is to sell the canned tomatoes. As the canner receives purchase orders, he transmits them to the bank, and the bank directs the custodian to release the inventories. It is agreed that, as remittances are received by the canner, they will be turned over to the bank. These remittances by the canner pay off the loans made by the bank.

Typically, a seasonal pattern exists. At the beginning of the tomato harvesting and canning season, the canner's cash needs and loan requirements begin to rise and reach a maximum by the end of the canning season. It is hoped that, just before the new canning season begins, the canner has sold a sufficient volume to have paid off the loan completely. If for some reason the canner has had a bad year, the bank may carry him over another year to enable him to work off his inventory.

Acceptable Products   In addition to canned foods, which account for about 17 percent of all field warehouse loans, many other product inventories provide a basis for field warehouse financing. Some of these are miscellaneous groceries, which represent about 13 percent; lumber products, about 10 percent; and coal and coke, about 6 percent.

These products are relatively nonperishable and are sold in well-developed, organized markets. Nonperishability protects the lender if he should have to take over the security. For this reason a bank would not make a field warehousing loan on perishables such as fresh fish. However, frozen fish, which can be stored for a long time, can be field warehoused. An organized market aids the lender in disposing of an inventory that it takes over. Banks are not interested in going into the canning or the fish business. They want to be able to dispose of an inventory within a matter of hours and with the expenditure of a minimum amount of time.

Cost of Financing   The fixed costs of a field warehousing arrangement are relatively high; such financing is therefore not suitable for a very small firm. If a field warehouse company sets up the field warehouse itself, it will typically set a minimum charge of about $1,000 a year, plus about 1 or 2 percent of the amount of credit extended to the borrower. Furthermore, the financing institution will charge from 8 to 12 percent interest. The minimum size of an efficient field warehousing operation requires an inventory of about $100,000.

Appraisal   The use of field warehouse financing as a source of funds for business firms has many advantages. First, the amount of funds available is flexible because the financing is tied to the growth of inventories, which in turn is related directly to financing needs. Second, the field warehousing arrangement increases the acceptability of inventories as loan collateral. Some inventories would not be accepted by a bank as security without a field warehousing arrangement. Third, the necessity for inventory control, safekeeping, and the use of specialists in warehousing has resulted in improved warehouse practices. The services of the field warehouse companies have often saved money for the firm in spite of the costs of financing mentioned above. The field warehouse company may suggest inventory practices which reduce the labor that the firm has to employ, and reduce inventory damage and loss as well.

The major disadvantage of a field warehousing operation is the fixed cost element, which reduces the feasibility of this form of financing for small firms.

SUMMARY

Short-term credit is defined as debt originally scheduled for repayment within one year. This chapter has discussed the three major sources of short-term credit—trade credit between firms, loans from commercial banks, and commercial paper—as well as methods of securing this credit.

Trade Credit   Trade credit, represented by accounts payable, is the largest single category of short-term credit and is especially important for smaller firms. Trade credit is a *spontaneous source of financing* in that it arises from ordinary business transactions; as sales increase, so does the supply of financing from accounts payable.

Bank Credit   Bank credit occupies a pivotal position in the short-term money market. Banks provide the marginal credit that allows firms to expand more rapidly than is possible through retained earnings and trade credit; to be denied bank credit often means that a firm must slow its rate of growth.

Bank interest rates are quoted in three ways—regular compound interest, discount interest, and installment interest. Regular interest needs no adjustment—it is "correct" as stated. Discount interest requires a small upward adjustment to make it comparable to regular compound interest rates. Installment interest rates require a large adjustment, and frequently the true interest rate is double the quoted rate for an installment loan.

Commercial Paper   Bank loans are personal in the sense that the financial manager meets with the banker, discusses the terms of the loan with him, and reaches an agreement that requires direct and personal negotiation. Commercial paper, however, although it is physically quite similar to a bank loan, is sold in a broad, impersonal market. A California firm might, for example, sell commercial paper to a manufacturer in the Midwest.

Only the very strongest firms are able to use the commercial paper markets—the nature of these markets is such that the firm selling the paper must have a reputation so good that buyers of the paper are willing to buy it without any sort of credit check. Interest rates in the commercial paper market are the lowest available to business borrowers.

Use of Security in Short-Term Financing   The most common forms of collateral used for short-term credit are inventories and accounts receivable. Accounts receivable financing can be done either by *pledging the receivables* or by selling them outright, frequently called *factoring.* When the receivables are pledged, the borrower retains the risk that the person or firm who owes the receivable will not pay; in factoring, this risk is typically passed on to the lender. Because the factor takes the risk of default, he will typically investigate the purchaser's credit; therefore, the factor can perform three services—a lending function, a risk-bearing function, and a credit-checking function. When receivables are pledged, the lender typically performs only the first of these three functions. Consequently, factoring is generally quite a bit more expensive than is pledging accounts receivable.

Loans secured by inventories are not satisfactory under many circumstances. For certain kinds of inventory, however, the technique known as *field warehousing* is used to provide adequate security to the lender. Under a field warehousing arrangement, the inventory is under the physical control of a warehouse company, which releases the inventory only on order from the lending institution. Canned goods, lumber, steel, coal, and other standardized products are goods usually covered in field warehouse arrangements.

QUESTIONS

9-1. It is inevitable that firms will obtain a certain amount of their financing in the form of trade credit, which is, to some extent, a free source of funds. What are some other factors that lead firms to use trade credit?

9-2. "Commercial paper interest rates are always lower than bank loan rates to a given borrower. Nevertheless, many firms perfectly capable of selling commercial paper employ higher cost bank credit." Discuss the statement, indicating (a) why commercial paper rates are lower than bank rates and (b) why firms might use bank credit in spite of its higher cost.

9-3. "Trade credit has an explicit interest rate cost if discounts are available but not taken. There are also some intangible costs associated with the failure to take discounts." Discuss.

9-4. A large manufacturing firm that had been selling its products on a 3/10, net 30 basis changed its credit terms to 1/20, net 90. What changes might be anticipated on the balance sheets of the manufacturer and of its customers?

9-5. The availability of bank credit is more important to small firms than to large ones. Why is this so?

9-6. What factors should a firm consider in selecting its primary bank? Would it be feasible for a firm to have a primary deposit bank (the bank where most of its funds are deposited) and a different primary loan bank (the bank where it does most of its borrowing)?

9-7. Indicate whether each of the following changes would raise or lower the cost of a firm's accounts receivable financing, and why this occurs:

a. The firm eases up on its credit standards in order to increase sales.

b. The firm institutes a policy of refusing to make credit sales if the amount of the purchase (invoice) is below $100. Previously, about 40 percent of all invoices were below $100.

c. The firm agrees to give recourse to the finance company for all defaults.

d. The firm, which already has a recourse arrangement, is merged into a larger, stronger company.

e. A firm without a recourse arrangement changes its terms of trade from net 30 to net 90.

9-8. Would a firm that manufactures specialized machinery for a few large customers be more likely to use some form of inventory financing or some form of accounts receivable financing? Why?

9-9. "A firm that factors its accounts receivable will look better in a ratio analysis than one that discounts its receivables." Discuss.

9-10. Why would it not be practical for a typical retailer to use field warehousing?

9-11. List an industry, together with your reasons for including it, that might be expected to use each of the following forms of credit:

a. field warehousing

b. factoring

c. accounts receivable discounting

d. trust receipts

e. none of these.

PROBLEMS

9-1. What is the equivalent annual interest rate that would be lost if a firm failed to take the cash discount under each of the following terms?

a. 1/15, net 30

b. 2/10, net 60

c. 3/10, net 60

d. 2/10, net 40

e. 1/10, net 40.

9-2. Dixon Associates is negotiating with Commerce Bank for a $100,000, one-year loan. Commerce Bank has offered Dixon the following three alternatives:

a. A 12 percent interest rate, no compensating balance, and interest due at the end of the year.

b. A 10 percent interest rate, a 20 percent compensating balance, and interest due at the end of the year.

c. A 9 percent interest rate, a 15 percent compensating balance, and the loan is discounted.

If Dixon wishes to minimize the effective interest rate, which alternative would they choose?

9-3. Wagner Industries is having difficulty paying its bills and is considering foregoing its trade discounts on $100,000 of accounts payable. As an alternative, Wagner can obtain a sixty-day note with a 12 percent annual interest rate. The note is discounted. Trade credit terms are 2/10, net 70.

a. Which alternative has the lower effective cost?

b. If trade discounts are not taken, what conclusions may outsiders draw?

9-4. Supreme Catsup Company is considering the following two alternatives for financing next year's canning operations:

a. Establishing a $1,000,000 line of credit with a 12 percent annual interest rate on the used portion and a 1 percent commitment fee rate on the unused portion. A $150,000 compensating balance is required at all times on the entire $1 million line.

b. Use field warehousing to finance $850,000 of inventory. Financing charges are a flat fee of $500, plus 2 percent of the maximum amount of credit extended, plus a 10 percent annual interest rate on all outstanding credit. Supreme has $150,000 of funds available for inventory financing, so financing requirements will be equal to the expected inventory level minus $150,000.

All financing is done on the first of the month and is sufficient to cover the value of the inventory at the end of the month. Expected inventory levels are as follows:

Month	Amount	Month	Amount
July	$ 150,000	January	$600,000
August	400,000	February	450,000
September	600,000	March	350,000
October	800,000	April	225,000
November	1,000,000	May	100,000
December	750,000	June	0

Which financing plan has the lowest cost? (Hints: Borrowing under bank loan in July equals $150,000 and in December $750,000; under the field warehouse plan, July borrowings are zero and December borrowings are $600,000.)

9-5. Collins Manufacturing needs an additional $100,000. The financial manager is considering two methods of obtaining this money: a loan from a commercial bank or through a factoring arrangement.

The bank charges 8 percent per annum interest, discount basis. A 12 percent compensating balance is also required.

The factor is willing to purchase Collins' accounts receivable and to advance the amount purchased, less a 3 percent factoring commission on the invoices purchased each month. (All sales are on 30 day terms). An 8 percent annual interest rate will be charged on the total invoice price and deducted in advance. Also, with the factoring agreement, Collins can eliminate its Credit Department and reduce credit expenses by $2,000 per month. Bad debt losses of 1 percent on the factored amount can also be avoided.

    a. How much should the bank loan be for in order to net $100,000? How much accounts receivable should be factored to net $100,000?

    b. What are the effective interest rates, and the annual total dollar costs, including credit department expenses and bad debt losses, associated with each financing arrangement?

    c. Discuss some considerations other than cost that may influence management's decision between factoring and a commercial bank loan.

9-6. Fair Deal Co. estimates that due to the seasonal nature of their business they will require an additional $200,000 of cash for the month of November. Fair Deal has three options available to provide the needed funds.

    a. Establish a one year line of credit for $200,000 with a commercial bank. The commitment fee would be .5 percent and the interest charge on the used funds would be 10 percent per annum. The minimum time that the funds may be used is thirty days.

    b. Forego the November trade discount of 2/10, net 40 on $200,000 of accounts payable.

    c. Issue $200,000 of sixty-day commercial paper at an 8 percent per annum interest rate. Since the funds only are required for thirty days, the excess funds ($200,000) are invested in 7 percent per annum marketable securities for the month of December. The total transaction fee on purchasing and selling the marketable securities is 1/2 of 1 percent of the fair value.

Which financing arrangement results in the lowest cost?

Decisions Involving Long-Term Assets

Part Three

In Part Two, we dealt with the top portion of the firm's balance sheet—the current assets and liabilities. Now, in Part Three, we move down to the lower left side of the statement, focusing on the decisions involved in fixed asset acquisitions.

In Chapter 10 we discuss the concepts of compound interest and the time value of money, important subjects in all long-term financial decisions. Capital budgeting—the planning of expenditures whose returns will extend beyond one year—is covered in Chapter 11. Uncertainty about both the costs and the returns associated with a project is introduced in Chapter 12; since projects differ in riskiness, that chapter develops methods of analysis which can be used to incorporate risk into the decision-making process.

The Interest Factor
in Financial Decisions

Investing in fixed assets should, logically, be taken up at this point. However, the long-term nature of fixed investments makes it necessary to consider first the theory of compound interest—the "math of finance." Compound interest is essential to an understanding of capital budgeting, the topic of the following chapter, and interest rate theory is also an integral part of several other topics taken up later in the text. Financial structure decisions, lease versus purchase decisions, bond refunding operations, security valuation techniques, and the whole question of the cost of capital are some other subjects that cannot be understood without a knowledge of compound interest.

Many people are afraid of the subject of compound interest and simply avoid it. It is certainly true that many successful businessmen—even some bankers—know essentially nothing of the subject. However, as technology advances, as more and more engineers become involved in general management, and as modern business administration programs turn out more and more highly qualified graduates, this "success in spite of yourself" pattern will become more and more difficult to achieve. Furthermore, a fear of compound interest relationships is quite unfounded—the subject matter is simply not that difficult. Almost all problems involving compound interest can be handled satisfactorily with only a few basic formulas.

COMPOUND VALUE

A person deposits $1,000 in a savings and loan association that pays 4 percent interest compounded annually. How much will he have at the end of one year? To treat the matter systematically, let us define the following terms:

$$P_0 = \text{principal, or beginning amount at time 0.}$$

$$i = \text{interest rate.}$$

$$I = \text{total dollar amount of interest earned.}$$

$$P_n = \text{principal value at the end of } n \text{ periods.}$$

When n equals 1, P_n may be calculated as follows:

$$P_1 = P_0 + I$$
$$= P_0 + P_0 i \qquad\qquad (10\text{--}1)$$
$$= P_0 (1 + i).$$

Equation 10–1 shows that the ending amount (P_1) is equal to the beginning amount (P_0) times the factor $(1 + i)$. In the example, where $P_0 = \$1,000$, $i = 4$ percent, and n is one year, P_n is determined as follows:

$$P_1 = \$1,000(1.0 + .04) = \$1,000(1.04) = \$1,040.$$

Multiple Periods

If the person leaves the $1,000 on deposit for five years, to what amount will it have grown at the end of that period? Equation 10–1 can be used to construct Table 10–1, which indicates the answer. Note that P_2, the balance at the end of the second year, is found as follows:

$$P_2 = P_1 (1 + i) = P_0 (1 + i)(1 + i) = P_0 (1 + i)^2.$$

Similarly, P_3, the balance after three years, is found as

$$P_3 = P_2 (1 + i) = P_0 (1 + i)^3.$$

TABLE 10–1 Compound Interest Calculations

Period	Beginning Amount	$\times$	$(1 + i)$	$=$	Ending Amount (P_n)
1	$1,000		1.04		$1,040
2	1,040		1.04		1,082
3	1,082		1.04		1,125
4	1,125		1.04		1,170
5	1,170		1.04		1,217

In general, P_n, the compound amount at the end of any year n, is found as

$$P_n = P_0 (1 + i)^n. \qquad\qquad (10\text{--}2)$$

Equation 10-2 is the fundamental equation of compound interest. Note that Equation 10-1 is simply a special case of Equation 10-2, where $n = 1$.

While it is necessary to understand the derivation of Equation 10-2 in order to understand much of the material in the remainder of this chapter (as well as material to be covered in subsequent chapters), the concept can be applied quite readily in a mechanical sense. Tables have been constructed for values of $(1 + i)^n$ for wide ranges of i and n. Table 10-2 is illustrative, while Table A-1, in Appendix A at the end of the book, is a more complete table.

TABLE 10-2 Compound Value of $1 (*CVIF*): $CVIF = (1 + i)^n$

Period	1%	2%	3%	4%	5%	6%	7%	8%	9%	10%
1	1.010	1.020	1.030	1.040	1.050	1.060	1.070	1.080	1.090	1.100
2	1.020	1.040	1.061	1.082	1.102	1.124	1.145	1.166	1.188	1.210
3	1.030	1.061	1.093	1.125	1.158	1.191	1.225	1.260	1.295	1.331
4	1.041	1.082	1.126	1.170	1.216	1.262	1.311	1.360	1.412	1.464
5	1.051	1.104	1.159	1.217	1.276	1.338	1.403	1.469	1.539	1.611
6	1.062	1.126	1.194	1.265	1.340	1.419	1.501	1.587	1.677	1.772
7	1.072	1.149	1.230	1.316	1.407	1.504	1.606	1.714	1.828	1.949
8	1.083	1.172	1.267	1.369	1.477	1.594	1.718	1.851	1.993	2.144
9	1.094	1.195	1.305	1.423	1.551	1.689	1.838	1.999	2.172	2.358
10	1.105	1.219	1.344	1.480	1.629	1.791	1.967	2.159	2.367	2.594
11	1.116	1.243	1.384	1.539	1.710	1.898	2.105	2.332	2.580	2.853
12	1.127	1.268	1.426	1.601	1.796	2.012	2.252	2.518	2.813	3.138
13	1.138	1.294	1.469	1.665	1.886	2.133	2.410	2.720	3.066	3.452
14	1.149	1.319	1.513	1.732	1.980	2.261	2.579	2.937	3.342	3.797
15	1.161	1.346	1.558	1.801	2.079	2.397	2.759	3.172	3.642	4.177

Letting *CVIF* ($\equiv$ compound value interest factor) $= (1 + i)^n$, Equation 10-2 may be written as $P_n = P_0 (CVIF)$. It is necessary only to go to an appropriate interest table to find the proper interest factor. For example, the correct interest factor for the illustration given in Table 10-1 can be found in Table 10-2. Look down the Period column to 5, then across this row to the appropriate number in the 4 percent column to find the interest factor, 1.217. Then, using this interest factor, we find the compound value of the $1,000 after five years as

$$P_n = P_0 (CVIF) = \$1,000(1.217) = \$1,217.$$

Notice that this is precisely the same figure that was obtained by the long method in Table 10-1.

Graphic View of the Compounding Process: Growth

Figure 10–1 shows how the interest factors for compounding increase, or grow, as the compounding period increases. Curves could be drawn for any interest rate, including fractional rates; we have plotted curves for 0 percent, 5 percent, and 10 percent. The curves in the graph were plotted from data taken from Table 10–2.

FIGURE 10–1 Relationship between Compound Value Interest Factors, Interest Rates, and Time

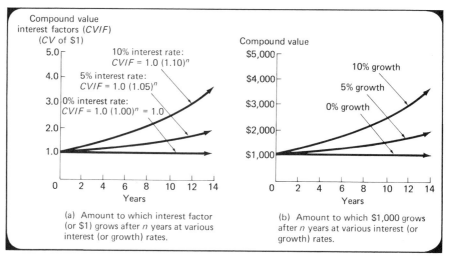

(a) Amount to which interest factor (or $1) grows after n years at various interest (or growth) rates.

(b) Amount to which $1,000 grows after n years at various interest (or growth) rates.

Figure 10–1 shows how $1 (or any other sum) grows over time at various rates of interest. The higher the rate of interest, the faster the rate of growth. The interest rate is, in fact, the growth rate: If a sum is deposited and earns 5 percent, then the funds on deposit grow at the rate of 5 percent per year.

PRESENT VALUE

Suppose you are offered the alternative of either $1,217 at the end of five years or X dollars today. There is no question but that the $1,217 will be paid in full (perhaps the payer is the United States government); having no current need for the money, you would deposit it in a savings association paying 4 percent interest. (Four percent is defined to be your "opportunity cost.") How small must X be to induce you to accept the promise of $1,217 five years hence?

Table 10–1 shows that the initial amount of $1,000 growing at 4 percent a year yields $1,217 at the end of five years. Thus, you should be indifferent in your choice between $1,000 today and $1,217 at the end of five years. *The $1000 is defined as the present value of $1,217 due in five years when the applicable interest rate is 4 percent.* It should be noted that the subscript zero in the term P_0 indicates the present. Hence present value quantities may be identified by either P_0 or PV.

Finding present values (or *discounting,* as it is commonly called) is simply the reverse of compounding, and Equation 10-2 can readily be transformed into a present value formula.

$$\text{Present value} = P_0 = \frac{P_n}{(1+i)^n} = P_n\left[\frac{1}{(1+i)^n}\right]. \tag{10-3}$$

Tables have been constructed for the term in brackets for various values of i and n; Table 10-3 is an example. A more complete table, Table A-2, is found in Appendix A at the end of the book. For the illustrative case being considered, look down the 4 percent column in Table 10-3 to the fifth row. The figure shown there, 0.822, is the present value interest factor (*PVIF*) used to determine the present value of $1,217 payable in five years, discounted at 4 percent.

$$P_0 = P_5\,(PVIF)$$

$$= \$1,217(0.822)$$

$$= \$1,000.$$

TABLE 10-3 Present Values of $1 (*PVIF*): $PVIF = \dfrac{1}{(1+i)^n} = \dfrac{1}{CVIF}$

Period	1%	2%	3%	4%	5%	6%	7%	8%	9%	10%	12%	14%	15%
1	.990	.980	.971	.962	.952	.943	.935	.926	.917	.909	.893	.877	.870
2	.980	.961	.943	.925	.907	.890	.873	.857	.842	.826	.797	.769	.756
3	.971	.942	.915	.889	.864	.840	.816	.794	.772	.751	.712	.675	.658
4	.961	.924	.889	.855	.823	.792	.763	.835	.708	.683	.636	.592	.572
5	.951	.906	.863	.822	.784	.747	.713	.681	.650	.621	.567	.519	.497
6	.942	.888	.838	.790	.746	.705	.666	.630	.596	.564	.507	.456	.432
7	.933	.871	.813	.760	.711	.665	.623	.583	.547	.513	.452	.400	.376
8	.923	.853	.789	.731	.677	.627	.582	.540	.502	.467	.404	.351	.327
9	.914	.837	.766	.703	.645	.592	.544	.500	.460	.424	.361	.308	.284
10	.905	.820	.744	.676	.614	.558	.508	.463	.422	.386	.322	.270	.247

Graphic View of the Discounting Process

Figure 10-2 shows how the interest factors for discounting decrease as the discounting period increases. The curves in the figure were plotted from data taken from Table 10-3; they show that the present value of a sum to be received at some future date decreases (1) as the payment date is extended further into the future and (2) as the discount rate increases. If relatively high discount rates apply, funds due in the future are worth very little today; even at relatively low discount rates, funds due in the distant future are not worth much today. For example, $1,000 due in ten years is worth $247 today if the discount rate is 15 percent, but it is worth $614 today at a 5 percent discount rate. Similarly, $1,000 due in ten years at 10 percent is worth $386 today, but at the same discount rate $1,000 due in five years is worth $621 today.[1]

FIGURE 10–2 Relationship between Present Value Interest Factors, Interest Rates, and Time

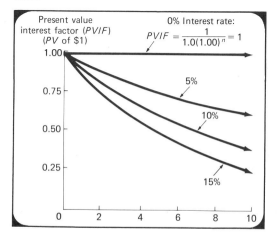

COMPOUND VALUE VERSUS PRESENT VALUE

Because a thorough understanding of compound value concepts is vital in order to understand the remainder of both this chapter and the book, and because compound interest gives many students trouble, it will be useful to examine in more detail the relationship between compounding and discounting.

Notice that Equation 10–2, the basic equation for compounding, was developed from the logical sequence set forth in Table 10–1: the equation merely presents in mathematical form the steps outlined in the table. The present value interest factor ($PVIF_{i,n}$) in Equation 10–3, the basic equation for discounting or finding present values, was found as the *reciprocal* of the

---

[1]Notice that Figure 10–2 is *not* a mirror image of Figure 10–1. The curves in Figure 10–1 approach ∞ as n increases; in Figure 10–2, the curves approach zero, not − ∞, as n increases.

compound value interest factor $(CVIF_{i,n})$ for the same i, n combination:

$$PVIF_{i,n} = \frac{1}{CVIF_{i,n}}.$$

For example, the *compound value* interest factor for 4 percent over five years is seen in Table 10–2 to be 1.217. The *present value* interest factor for 4 percent over five years must be the reciprocal of 1.217:

$$PVIF_{4\%, 5 \text{ years}} = \frac{1}{1.217} = .822.$$

The *PVIF* found in this manner must, of course, correspond with the *PVIF* shown in Table 10–3.

The reciprocal nature of the relationship between present value and compound value permits us to find present values in two ways—by multiplying or by dividing. Thus, the present value of $1,000 due in five years and discounted at 4 percent may be found as

$$P_0 = PV = P_n(PVIF_{i,n}) = P_n \left[\frac{1}{1+i}\right]^n = \$1,000(.822) = \$822,$$

or

$$P_0 = PV = \frac{P_n}{CVIF_{i,n}} = \frac{P_5}{(1+i)^n} = \frac{\$1,000}{1.217} = \$822.$$

In the second form, it is easy to see why the present value of a given future amount (P_n) declines as the discount rate increases.

To conclude this comparison of present and compound values, compare Figures 10–1 and 10–2. Notice that the vertical intercept is at 1.0 in each case, but compound value interest factors rise while present value interest factors decline. The reason for this divergence is, of course, that present value factors are reciprocals of compound factors.

COMPOUND VALUE OF AN ANNUITY

An annuity is defined as a series of payments of a fixed amount for a specified number of years. Each payment occurs at the end of the year.[2] For example, a promise to pay $1,000 a year for three years is a three-year annuity. If you were to receive such an annuity and were to deposit each annual payment in a savings account paying 4 percent interest, how much would you have at the end of three years? The answer is shown graphically

---

[2] Had the payment been made at the beginning of the period, each receipt would simply have been shifted back one year. The annuity would have been called an *annuity due;* the one in the present discussion, where payments are made at the end of each period, is called a *regular annuity* or, sometimes, a *deferred annuity.*

in Figure 10–3. The first payment is made at the end of year 1, the second at the end of year 2, and the third at the end of year 3. The last payment is not compounded at all; the next to the last is compounded for one year; the second from the last for two years; and so on back to the first, which is compounded for $(n - 1)$ years. When the compound values of each of the payments are added, their total is the sum of the annuity. In the example, this total is $3,122.

FIGURE 10–3 Graphic Illustration of an Annuity: Compound Sum

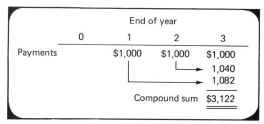

Expressed algebraically, with S_n defined as the compound sum, R as the periodic receipt, n as the length of the annuity, and $CVIF_a$ as the compound value interest factor for an annuity, the formula for S_n is

$$S_n = R(1 + i)^{n-1} + R(1 + i)^{n-2} + \cdots + R(1 + i)^1 + R(1 + i)^0$$
$$= R[(1 + i)^{n-1} + (1 + i)^{n-2} + \cdots + (1 + i)^1 + (1 + i)^0]$$
$$= R[CVIF_a].$$

The expression in brackets, $CVIF_a$, has been given values for various combinations of n and i. An illustrative set of these annuity interest factors is given in Table 10–4; a more complete set may be found in Table A–3 in Appendix A. To find the answer to the three-year, $1,000 annuity problem, simply refer

TABLE 10–4 Sum of an Annuity of $1 for n Years $(CVIF_a)$: $CVIF_a = \dfrac{(1 + i)^n - 1}{i}$

Period	1%	2%	3%	4%	5%	6%	7%	8%
1	1.000	1.000	1.000	1.000	1.000	1.000	1.000	1.000
2	2.010	2.020	2.030	2.040	2.050	2.060	2.070	2.080
3	3.030	3.060	3.091	3.122	3.152	3.184	3.215	3.246
4	4.060	4.122	4.184	4.246	4.310	4.375	4.440	4.506
5	5.101	5.204	5.309	5.416	5.526	5.637	5.751	5.867
6	6.152	6.308	6.468	6.633	6.802	6.975	7.153	7.336
7	7.214	7.434	7.662	7.898	8.142	8.394	8.654	8.923
8	8.286	8.583	8.892	9.214	9.549	9.897	10.260	10.637
9	9.369	9.755	10.159	10.583	11.027	11.491	11.978	12.488
10	10.462	10.950	11.464	12.006	12.578	13.181	13.816	14.487

to Table 10–4, look down the 4 percent column to the row for the third year, and multiply the factor 3.122 by $1,000. The answer is the same as the one derived by the long method illustrated in Figure 10–3:

$$S_n = R \times CVIF_a \qquad (10-4)$$

$$S_3 = \$1,000 \times 3.122 = \$3,122.$$

Notice that $CVIF_a$ for the sum of an annuity is always *larger* than the number of years the annuity runs.

PRESENT VALUE OF AN ANNUITY

Suppose you were offered the following alternatives: a three-year annuity of $1,000 a year or a lump-sum payment today. You have no need for the money during the next three years, so if you accept the annuity you would simply deposit the receipts in a savings account paying 4 percent interest. How large must the lump-sum payment be to make it equivalent to the annuity? The graphic illustration shown in Figure 10–4 will help explain the problem.

FIGURE 10–4   Graphic Illustration of an Annuity: Present Value

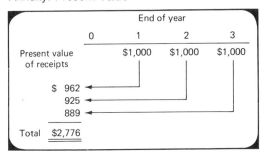

The present value of the first receipt is $R[1/(1 + i)]$; the second is $R[1/(1 + i)]^2$; and so on. Defining the present value of an annuity of n years as A_n, and with $PVIF_a$ defined as the present value interest factor for an annuity, we may write the following equation:

$$A_n = R\left[\frac{1}{1+i}\right]^1 + R\left[\frac{1}{1+i}\right]^2 + \cdots + R\left[\frac{1}{1+i}\right]^n$$

$$= R\left[\frac{1}{(1+i)} + \frac{1}{(1+i)^2} + \cdots + \frac{1}{(1+i)^n}\right] \qquad (10-5)$$

$$= R[PVIF_a].$$

Again, tables have been worked out for the $PVIF_a$, the term in the brackets. Table 10–5 is illustrative; a more complete table is found in Table A–4 in Appendix A. From Table 10–5, the $PVIF_a$ for a three-year, 4 percent annuity is found to be 2.775. Multiplying this factor by the $1,000 annual receipt gives $2,775, the present value of the annuity. This figure departs from the long-method answer shown in Figure 10–4 only by a rounding difference:

$$A_n = R \times PVIF_a \qquad (10\text{--}6)$$

$$A_3 = \$1,000 \times 2.775$$

$$= \$2,775.$$

Notice that $PVIF_a$ for the *present value* of an annuity is always *less* than the number of years the annuity runs, whereas $CVIF_a$ for the *sum* of an annuity is *larger* than the number of years. Also, notice that the $PVIF_a$ factor for any year n can be obtained by summing the $PVIF$ factors from 1 to n, that is,

$$PVIF_a = \sum_{t=0}^{n} PVIF.$$

To illustrate, if $n = 3$ and $i = 10\%$, then, from Table 10–3, we obtain $PVIF$ values, sum them, and find they differ from the $PVIF_a$ factor in Table 10–5 only by a rounding error: $PVIF_a = .909 + .826 + .751 = 2.486$.

TABLE 10–5 Present Value of an Annuity of $1: $PVIF_a = \dfrac{1 - \dfrac{1}{(1 + i)^n}}{i}$

Period	1%	2%	3%	4%	5%	6%	7%	8%	9%	10%
1	0.990	0.980	0.971	0.962	0.952	0.943	0.935	0.926	0.917	0.909
2	1.970	1.942	1.913	1.886	1.859	1.833	1.808	1.783	1.759	1.736
3	2.941	2.884	2.829	2.775	2.723	2.673	2.624	2.577	2.531	2.487
4	3.902	3.808	3.717	3.630	3.546	3.465	3.387	3.312	3.240	3.170
5	4.853	4.713	4.580	4.452	4.329	4.212	4.100	3.993	3.890	3.791
6	5.795	5.601	5.417	5.242	5.076	4.917	4.766	4.623	4.486	4.355
7	6.728	6.472	6.230	6.002	5.786	5.582	5.389	5.206	5.033	4.868
8	7.652	7.325	7.020	6.733	6.463	6.210	6.971	5.747	5.535	5.335
9	8.566	8.162	7.786	7.435	7.108	6.802	6.515	6.247	5.985	5.759
10	9.471	8.983	8.530	8.111	7.722	7.360	7.024	6.710	6.418	6.145

ANNUAL PAYMENTS TO ACCUMULATE A FUTURE SUM

Thus far in the chapter all the equations have been based on Equation 10–2. The present value equation merely involves a transposition of Equation 10–2, and the annuity equations merely take the sum of the basic compound interest equation for different values of n. We now examine some additional modifications of the equations.

Suppose we want to know the amount of money that must be deposited at 5 percent for each of the next five years in order to have $10,000 available to pay off a debt at the end of the fifth year. Dividing both sides of Equation 10–4 by $CVIF_a$, we obtain

$$R = \frac{S_n}{CVIF_a}.$$

Looking up the sum of an annuity interest factor for five years at 5 percent in Table 10–4 and dividing that figure into $10,000, we find

$$R = \frac{\$10,000}{5.526} = \$1,810.$$

Thus, if $1,810 is deposited each year in an account paying 5 percent interest, at the end of five years the account will have accumulated $10,000. We will employ this procedure in later chapters when we discuss sinking funds set up to provide for bond retirements.

ANNUAL RECEIPTS FROM AN ANNUITY

Suppose that on September 1, 1977, you receive an inheritance of $7,000. The money is to be used for your education and is to be spent during the academic years beginning September 1978, 1979, and 1980. If you place the money in a bank account paying 4 percent annual interest and make three equal withdrawals at each of the specified dates, how large can each withdrawal be to leave you with exactly a zero balance after the last one has been made?

The solution requires application of the present value of an annuity formula, Equation 10–6. Here, however, we know that the present value of the annuity is $7,000, and the problem is to find the three equal annual payments when the interest rate is 4 percent. This calls for dividing both sides of Equation 10–6 by $PVIF_a$ to make Equation 10–7.

$$A_n = R \times PVIF_a \qquad (10\text{–}6)$$

$$R = \frac{A_n}{PVIF_a}. \qquad (10\text{–}7)$$

The interest factor ($PVIF_a$) is found in Table 10–5 to be 2.775; substituting this value into Equation 10–7, we find the three equal annual withdrawals to be $2,523 a year:

$$R = \frac{\$7,000}{2.775} = \$2,523.$$

This particular kind of calculation is used frequently in setting up insurance and pension plan benefit schedules; it is also used to find the periodic payments necessary to retire a loan within a specified period. For example, if you want to retire a $7,000 bank loan, bearing interest at 4 percent on the unpaid balance, in three equal annual installments, the amount of each payment is $2,523. In this case, you are the borrower, and the bank is "buying" an annuity with a present value of $7,000.

DETERMINING INTEREST RATES

In many instances the present values and cash flows associated with a payment stream are known, but the interest rate involved is not known. Suppose a bank offers to lend you $1,000 today if you sign a note agreeing to pay the bank $1,217 at the end of five years. What rate of interest would you be paying on the loan? To answer the question we must use Equation 10–2:

$$P_n = P_0 (1 + i)^n = P_0 (CVIF). \tag{10-2}$$

Simply solve for CVIF, then look up this value of CVIF in Table 10–2 (or A–1) under the row for the fifth year:

$$CVIF = \frac{P_5}{P_0} = \frac{\$1,217}{\$1,000} = 1.217.$$

Looking across the row for the fifth year, we find the value 1.217 in the 4 percent column; therefore, the interest rate on the loan is 4 percent.

Precisely the same approach is taken to determine the interest rate implicit in an annuity. For example, suppose a bank will lend you $2,775 if you sign a note in which you agree to pay the bank $1,000 at the end of each of the next three years. What interest rate is the bank charging you? To answer the question, solve Equation 10–6 for $PVIF_a$, then look up $PVIF_a$ in Table 10–5 or (A–4):

$$A_n = R \times PVIF_a \tag{10-6}$$

$$PVIF_a = \frac{A_3}{R} = \frac{\$2,775}{\$1,000} = 2.775.$$

Looking across the third-year row, we find the factor 2.775 under the 4 percent column; therefore the bank is lending you money at 4 percent.

PRESENT VALUE OF AN UNEVEN SERIES OF RECEIPTS

Recall that the definition of an annuity includes the words *fixed amount*—in other words, annuities deal with constant, or level, payments or receipts. Although many financial decisions do involve constant payments, many important decisions are concerned with uneven flows of cash. In particular, the

kinds of fixed asset investments dealt with in the following chapter very frequently involve uneven flows. Consequently, it is necessary to expand our
analysis to deal with varying payment streams. Since most of the applications
call for present values, not compound sums or other figures, this section is
restricted to the present value *(PV)*.

To illustrate the calculating procedure, suppose someone offers to sell
you a series of payments consisting of $300 after one year, $100 after two
years, and $200 after three years. How much would you be willing to pay for
the series, assuming the appropriate discount rate (interest rate) is 4 percent?
To determine the purchase price, simply compute the present value of the
series; the calculations are worked out in Table 10–6. The receipts for each
year are shown in the second column; the discount factors (from Table 10–3)
are given in the third column; and the product of these two columns, the
present value of each individual receipt, is given in the last column. When the
individual present values in the last column are added, the sum is the present
value of the investment, $558.90. Under the assumptions of the example, you
should be willing to pay this amount for the investment.

Table 10–6 Calculating the Present Value of an Uneven Series of Payments

Period	Receipt	×	Interest Factor (PVIF)	=	Present Value (PV or P_0)
1	$300		.962		$288.60
2	100		.925		92.50
3	200		.889		177.80
				PV of investment	$558.90

Had the series of payments been somewhat different—say $300 at the
end of the first year, $200 at the end of the second year, then eight annual pay-
ments of $100 each—we would probably want to use a different procedure for
finding the investment's present value. We could, of course, set up a calculating table such as Table 10–6, but because most of the payments are part of
an annuity we can use a short cut. The calculating procedure is shown in Table
10–7, and the logic of the table is diagrammed in Figure 10–5.

FIGURE 10–5 Graphic Illustration of Present Value Calculations for an Uneven
Series of Payments That Includes an Annuity

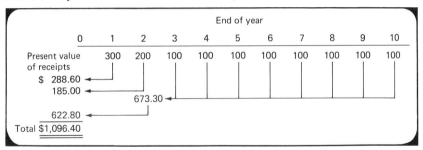

Section 1 of Table 10–7 deals with the $300 and the $200 received at the end of the first and second years respectively; their present values are found to be $288.60 and $185. Section 2 deals with the eight $100 payments. In part (a), the value of a $100, 8-year, 4 percent annuity is found to be $673.30. However, the first receipt under the annuity comes at the end of the third year, so it is worth less than $673.30 today. Specifically, it is worth the present value of $673.30, discounted back two years at 4 percent, or $622.80; this calculation is shown in part (b) of section 2.[3] When the present values of the first two payments are added to the present value of the annuity component, the sum is the present value of the entire investment, or $1,096.40.

Table 10–7 Calculating Procedure for an Uneven Series of Payments That Includes an Annuity

1. *PV* of $300 due in 1 year = $300(0.962) =	$ 288.60
PV of $200 due in 2 years = $200(0.925) =	185.00
2. *PV* of eight-year annuity with $100 receipts	
(a) *PV* at beginning of year 3: $100(6.733) = $673.30	
(b) *PV* of $673.30 = $673.30(0.925) =	622.80
3. *PV* of total series =	$1,096.40

SEMIANNUAL AND OTHER COMPOUNDING PERIODS[4]

In all the examples used thus far, it has been assumed that returns were received once a year, or annually. For example, in the first section of the chapter, dealing with compound values, it was assumed that funds were placed on deposit in a savings and loan association and grew by 4 percent a year. However, suppose the advertised rate had been 4 percent compounded *semiannually.* What would this have meant? Consider the following example.

You deposit $1,000 in a bank savings account and receive a return of 4 percent compounded semiannually. How much will you have at the end of one year? Semiannual compounding means that interest is actually paid each six months, a fact taken into account in the tabular calculations in Table 10–8. Here, the annual interest rate is divided by 2, but twice as many compounding periods are used because interest is paid twice a year. Comparing the amount on hand at the end of the second six-month period, $1,040.40, with what would have been on hand under annual compounding, $1,040, shows that semiannual compounding is better from the standpoint of the saver. *This result occurs, of course, because he earns interest on interest more frequently.*

---

[3]The present value of the annuity portion, $622.80, could also have been found by subtracting *PVIF*$_a$ for a two-year annuity from the *PVIF*$_a$ for a ten-year annuity, then multiplying the result by $100.
[4]This section can be omitted without loss of continuity.

Table 10-8   Compound Interest Calculations with Semiannual Compounding

Period	Beginning amount (P_0)	×	($1 + i$)	=	Ending amount (P_n)
1	$1,000.00		(1.02)		$1,020.00
2	1,020.00		(1.02)		1,040.40

General formulas can be developed for use when compounding periods are more frequent than once a year. To demonstrate this, Equation 10-2 is modified as follows:

$$P_n = P_0(1 + i)^n. \tag{10-2}$$

$$P_n = P_0\left(1 + \frac{i}{m}\right)^{mn} \tag{10-8}$$

Here, m is the number of times per year compounding occurs. When banks compute daily interest, the value of m is set at 365, and Equation 10-8 is applied.

The interest tables can be used when compounding occurs more than once a year. Simply divide the nominal, or stated, interest rate by the number of times compounding occurs, and multiply the years by the number of compounding periods per year. For example, to find the amount to which $1,000 will grow after five years if semiannual compounding is applied to a stated 4 percent interest rate, divide 4 percent by 2 and multiply the five years by 2. Then look in Table 10-2 (or Table A-1) under the 2 percent column and in the row for the tenth period. You find an interest factor of 1.219. Multiplying this by the initial $1,000 gives a value of $1,219, the amount to which $1,000 will grow in five years at 4 percent compounded semiannually. This compares with $1,217 for annual compounding.

The same procedure is applied in all the cases covered—compounding, discounting, single payments, and annuities. To illustrate semiannual compounding in finding the present value of an annuity, for example, consider the case described in the above section, Present Value of an Annuity: $1,000 a year for three years, discounted at 4 percent. With annual compounding (or discounting) the interest factor is 2.775, and the present value of the annuity is $2,775. For semiannual compounding look under the 2 percent column and in the year-6 row of Table 10-5, to find an interest factor of 5.601. This is now multiplied by half of $1,000, or the $500 received each six months, to get the present value of the annuity, $2,800. The payments come a little more rapidly —the first $500 is paid after only six months (similarly with other payments), so the annuity is a little more valuable if payments are received semiannually rather than annually.

By letting m approach infinity, Equation 10-8 can be modified to the special case of *continuous compounding*. Continuous compounding is extremely useful in theoretical finance, and it also has practical applications. For example, some banks and savings associations pay interest on a continuous basis.

A SPECIAL CASE OF SEMIANNUAL COMPOUNDING: BOND VALUES[5]

Most bonds pay interest semiannually, so semiannual compounding procedures are appropriate for determining bond values. To illustrate, suppose a particular bond pays interest in the amount of $30 each six months, or $60 a year. The bond will mature in ten years, paying $1,000 (the "principal") at that time. Thus, if you buy the bond you will receive an annuity of $30 each six months, or twenty payments in total, plus $1,000 at the end of ten years (or twenty six-month periods). What is the bond worth, assuming that the appropriate market discount (or interest) rate is (A) 6 percent; (B) higher than 6 percent, say 8 percent; and (C) lower than 6 percent, say 4 percent?

PART A: 6% discount rate.
   Step 1. You are buying an annuity plus a lump sum of $1,000.
            Find the PV of the interest payments:
   1. Use $i/m = 6\%/2 = 3\%$ as the "interest rate."
   2. Look up the $PVIF_a$ in Table A–4 for 20 periods at 3 percent, which is 14.877.
   3. Find the PV of the stream of interest payments:
      PV of the interest = $30 $(PVIF_a)$
                         = $30(14.877) = $446.

   Step 2. Find the PV of the $1,000 maturity value:
   1. Use $i/m = 6\%/2 = 3\%$ as the "interest rate."[6]
   2. Look up the PVIF in Table A–2 for twenty periods at 3 percent, which is .554.
   3. Find the PV of that value at maturity:
      PV of the maturity value = $1,000$(PVIF)$
                              = $1,000(.554) = $554.

   Step 3. Combine the two component PV's to determine the value of the bond:
            Bond value = $446 + $554 = $1,000.

PART B: 8% discount rate. Repeating the process, we have
   Step 1. 8%/2 = 4% = the "interest rate."
            $PVIF_a$ from Table A–4 = 13.59.
            PVIF from Table A–2 = .456.

   Step 2. Bond value = $30(13.59) + $1,000(.456)
                       = $408 + $456
                       = $864.

---

[5]This section may be omitted without loss of continuity.
   [6]This question is sometimes raised: "Why not discount the $1,000 at 6% over 10 years rather than at 3 percent for 20 six-month periods?" The answer is that the same compounding rate should be used for different elements in a cash flow stream. Six percent compounded semiannually (3 percent each six months) is different from 6 percent annually, so for consistency the $1,000 must be discounted at 3 percent over twenty periods. Also, bonds are actually priced in the market as we have calculated, so for consistency with the "real world" our procedure must be followed.

Notice that the bond is worth less when the going rate of interest for investments of similar risk is 8 percent than when it is 6 percent. At a price of $864, this bond provides an annual rate of return of 8 percent; at a price of $1,000, it provides an annual return of 6 percent. If 6 percent is the "going rate of return" on a bond of a given degree of risk, then whenever interest rates in the economy rise to the point where bonds of this degree of risk have an 8 percent return, the price of our bond will decline to $864, at which price it will yield the competitive rate of return, 8 percent.

PART C: 4% discount rate. Using the same process produces the following results:

Step 1. 4 percent/2 = 2 percent = the "interest rate."
  $PVIF_a$ from Table A–4 = 16.351.
  $PVIF$ from Table A–2 = .673.

Step 2. Bond value = $30(16.351) + $1,000(.673)
  = $491 + $673 = $1,164.

The bond is worth *more* than $1,000 when the going rate of interest is less than 6 percent, because then it offers a yield higher than the going rate. Its price rises to $1,164, where it provides a 4 percent annual rate of return. This calculation illustrates the fact that when interest rates in the economy decline, the prices of outstanding bonds rise.

APPROPRIATE COMPOUNDING OR DISCOUNTING RATES

Throughout the chapter, assumed compounding or discounting rates have been used in the examples. Although we will cover the subject in depth later in the book, it is useful at this point to give some idea of what the appropriate interest rate for a particular investment might be.[7]

The starting point is, of course, the general level of interest rates in the economy as a whole. This level is set by the interaction of supply-and-demand forces, with demand for funds coming largely from businesses, individual borrowers, and the federal government when it is running a deficit. Funds are supplied by individual and corporate savers and, under the control of the Federal Reserve System, by the creation of money by banks. Depending on the relative levels of supply and demand, the basic pattern of interest rates is determined.

There is no one rate of interest in the economy—rather, there is, at any given time, an array of different rates. The lowest rates are found on the safest investments, the highest rates on the most risky ones. Usually, there is less risk on investments that mature in the near future than on longer term investments, so higher rates are usually associated with long-term investments.

---

[7]For convenience, in this chapter we speak of "interest rates," which implies that only debt is involved. In later chapters this concept is broadened considerably, and the term "rate of return" is used in lieu of "interest rate."

There are other factors that affect interest rate differentials (also called "yield" differentials), but a discussion of these factors is best deferred until later in the book.

A person faced with the kinds of decisions considered in this chapter must accept the existing set of interest rates found in the economy. If he has money to invest, he can invest in short-term United States government securities and incur no risk whatever. However, he will generally have to accept a relatively low yield on his investment. If he is willing to assume a little more risk, he can invest in high-grade corporate bonds and get a higher fixed rate of return. If he is willing to accept still more risk, he can move into common stocks to obtain variable (and hopefully higher) returns (dividends plus capital gains) on his investment. Other alternatives include bank and savings and loan deposits, long-term governments, mortgages, apartment houses, land held for speculation, and so on.

Risk Premiums

With only a limited amount of money to invest, one must pick and choose among investments; the final selection involves a tradeoff between risk and returns. Suppose, for example, that you are indifferent between a five-year government bond yielding 4 percent a year, a five-year corporate bond yielding 5 percent, and a share of stock on which you can expect a 6 percent return. Given this situation, you can take the government bond as a riskless security, and you attach a 1 percent risk premium to the corporate bond and a 2 percent risk premium to the share of stock. Risk premiums, then, are the added returns that risky investments must command over less risky ones if there is to be a demand for risky assets. The concept of the risk premium is discussed in detail in Chapter 18.

Opportunity Costs

Although there are many potential investments available in the economy at any given time, a particular individual actively considers only a limited number of them. After making adjustments for risk differentials, he ranks the various alternatives from the most attractive to the least. Then, presumably, our investor puts his available funds in the most attractive investment. If he is offered a new investment, he must compare it with the best of the existing alternatives. If he takes the new investment, he must give up the opportunity of investing in the best of his old alternatives. *The yield on the best of the alternatives is defined as the opportunity cost of investing in the new alternative.* For example, suppose you have funds invested in a bank time deposit that pays 6 percent. Now suppose that someone offers you another investment of equal risk. To make the new investment, you must withdraw funds from the bank deposit; therefore *6 percent is defined as the opportunity cost of the new investment.* You could determine the interest rate on the new investment (using Equation 10–2); if the new investment yields more than 6 percent, make the switch. The interest rates used in the examples throughout this chapter were all determined as opportunity costs available to the person in the example. This concept is also used in the following chapter, where we consider business decisions on investments in fixed assets, or the *capital budgeting decision.*

SUMMARY

A knowledge of compound interest and present value techniques is essential to an understanding of many important aspects of finance: capital budgeting, financial structure, security valuation, and many other topics. The basic principles of compound interest, together with the most important formulas used in practice, were described in this chapter:

Compound Value:

$$P_n = P_0(1 + i)^n.$$

Present Value (*PV*):

$$P_0 = P_n\left[\frac{1}{(1 + i)^n}\right].$$

Compound Value of an Annuity:

Compound value = $CVIF_a$ × annual receipt.

Present Value of an Annuity:

PV of annuity = $PVIF_a$ × annual receipt.

Other Uses of the Basic Equations   The four basic interest formulas can be used in combination to find such things as the present value of an uneven series of receipts. The formulas can also be transformed to find (1) the annual payments necessary to accumulate a future sum, (2) the annual receipts from a specified annuity, (3) the periodic payments necessary to amortize a loan, and (4) the interest rate implicit in a loan contract.

Appropriate Interest Rate   The appropriate interest rate to be used is critical when working with compound interest problems. The true nature of the interest rates to be used when working with business problems can be understood only after the chapters dealing with the cost of capital have been examined; this chapter concluded with a brief discussion of some of the factors that determine the appropriate rate of interest for a particular problem—the risk of the investment and the investor's opportunity cost of money.

QUESTIONS

10-1. What kinds of financial decisions require explicit consideration of the interest factor?

10-2. Compound interest relations are important for decisions other than financial ones. Why are they important to marketing managers?

10-3. Would you rather have an account in a savings and loan association that pays 5 percent interest compounded semiannually or 5 percent interest compounded daily? Why?

10-4. For a given interest rate and a given number of years, is the interest factor for the sum of an annuity larger or smaller than the interest factor for the present value of the annuity?

10-5. Suppose you are examining two investments, A and B. Both have the same maturity, but A pays a 6 percent return and B yields 5 percent. Which investment is probably riskier? How do you know it is riskier?

PROBLEMS

10-1. Which amount is worth more at 7 percent: $1,000 today or $2,000 after ten years?

10-2. At a growth rate of 8 percent, how long does it take a sum to double?

10-3. a. What amount would be paid for a $1,000, fifteen-year bond that pays $30 interest semiannually ($60 a year) and is sold to yield 10 percent, compounded semiannually?

    b. What would be paid if the bond is sold to yield 6 percent?

    c. What would be paid if semiannual interest payments are $45 and the bond is sold to yield 8 percent?

10-4. On December 31, Craig Fields buys a building for $60,000, payable 15 percent down and the balance in 20 equal annual installments that are to include principal plus 10 percent compound interest on the declining balance. What are the equal installments?

10-5. The Scott Company is establishing a sinking fund to retire an $800,000 mortgage that matures on December 31, 1989. The company plans to put a fixed amount into the fund each year for fifteen years. The first payment will be made on December 31, 1975, the last on December 31, 1989. The company anticipates that the fund will earn 8 percent a year. What annual contributions must be made to accumulate the $800,000 as of December 31, 1989?

10-6. You have just purchased a newly issued $1,000, five-year Dot Company bond for $1,000. This bond pays $40 in interest payments semiannually ($80 a year); call this bond A. You are also negotiating the purchase of a $1,000, five-year Dot Company bond which returns $25 in semiannual interest payments and has five years remaining before it matures; call this bond B.

    a. What is the "going rate of return" on bonds of the risk and maturity of Dot Company's bonds?

    b. What should you be willing to pay for bond B?

    c. How would your answer for the value of bond B change if bond A had paid $20 in semiannual interest instead of $40, but still sold for $1,000? The second bond still pays $25 semiannually and $1,000 at the end of five years.

10-7. You need $66,132 at the end of twenty years. You know that the best you can do is to make equal payments into a bank account on which you can earn 5 percent interest compounded annually.

    a. What amount must you plan to pay annually to achieve your objective? The first payment is to be made at the end of the first year.

    b. Instead of making annual payments, you decide to make one lump-sum payment today. To achieve your objective of $66,132 at the end of the twenty-year period, what should this sum be? You can still earn 5 percent interest compounded annually on your account.

10-8. You can buy a note at a price of $10,250. If you buy the note, you will receive five annual payments of $2,500, the first payment to be made one year from today. What rate of return, or yield, does the note offer?

10-9. You can buy a bond for $1,000 that will pay no interest during its 5-year life but will have a value of $1,276 when it matures. What rate of interest will you earn if you buy the bond and hold it to maturity?

10-10. A bank agrees to lend you $1,000 today in return for your promise to pay the bank $1,419 six years from today. What rate of interest is the bank charging you?

10-11. If earnings in 1976 are $2.16 a share, while ten years earlier, in 1966, they were $1, what has been the rate of growth in earnings?

10-12. The Hudson Company's sales last year were $1 million.

    a. Assuming that sales grow 15 percent a year, calculate sales for each of the next five years.

    b. Plot the sales projections.

    c. If your graph is correct, your projected sales curve is nonlinear. If it had been linear, would this have indicated a constant, increasing, or decreasing percentage growth rate?

10-13. You are considering two investment opportunities, A and B. A is expected to pay $300 a year for the first ten years, $500 a year for the next fifteen years, and nothing thereafter. B is expected to pay $1,000 a year for ten years, and nothing thereafter. You find that alternative investments of similar risk yield 7 percent and 16 percent for A and B respectively.

    a. Find the present value of each investment. Show calculations.

    b. Which is the more risky investment? Why?

    c. Assume that your rich uncle will give you your choice of investments without cost to you, and that (1) you must hold the investment for its entire life (cannot sell it) or (2) you are free to sell it at its going market price. Which investment would you prefer under each of the two conditions?

10-14. The Hudson Company's common stock paid a dividend of $1 last year. Dividends are expected to grow at a rate of 15 percent for each of the next five years.

    a. Calculate the expected dividend for each of the next five years.

    b. Assuming that the first of these five dividends will be paid one year from now, what is the present value of the five dividends? Given the riskiness of the dividend stream, 15 percent is the appropriate discount rate.

    c. Assume that the price of the stock will be $20 five years from now. What is the present value of this "terminal value?" Use a 15 percent discount rate.

    d. Assume that you will buy the stock, receive the five dividends, then sell the share; how much should you be willing to pay for it?

e. Do not do any calculations for this question, but explain in words what would happen to the price of this stock (1) if the discount rate declined because the riskiness of the stock declined or (2) if the growth rate of the dividend stream increased.

10-15. The Pettway Printing Company is considering the purchase of a new press that will provide the following net cash flow (or profit) stream:

Year	
1	$10,000
2	20,000
3	30,000
4	40,000
5	50,000
6	60,000

a. What is the present value of the profit stream, using a 10 percent discount rate?

b. If the press costs $100,000, should Pettway Printing purchase it?

Capital Budgeting Techniques

Capital budgeting involves the entire process of planning expenditures whose returns are expected to extend beyond one year. The choice of one year is arbitrary, of course, but it is a convenient cutoff point for distinguishing between kinds of expenditures. Obvious examples of capital outlays are expenditures for land, buildings, and equipment, and for permanent additions to working capital associated with plant expansion. An advertising or promotion campaign, or a program of research and development, is also likely to have an impact beyond one year, so they too can be classified as capital budgeting expenditures.

Capital budgeting is important for the future well-being of the firm: it is also a complex, conceptually difficult topic. As we shall see later in this chapter, the optimum capital budget—the level of investment that maximizes the present value of the firm—is simultaneously determined by the interaction of supply and demand forces under conditions of uncertainty. Supply forces refer to the supply of capital to the firm, or its *cost of capital schedule.* Demand forces relate to the investment opportunities open to the firm, as measured by the *stream of revenues* that will result from an investment decision. *Uncertainty* enters the decision because it is impossible to know exactly either the cost of capital or the stream of revenues that will be derived from a project.

To facilitate an exposition of the investment decision process, we have broken the topic down into its major components. In this chapter, we consider the capital budgeting process and the techniques generally employed by reasonably sophisticated business firms. Here our focus is on the time factor, and the compound interest concepts covered in the preceding chapter are used extensively. Uncertainty is explicitly and formally considered in Chapter 12, and the cost of capital concept is developed and related to capital budgeting in Chapters 18 through 20, after a discussion of the sources and forms of long-term capital in Chapters 13 through 17.

SIGNIFICANCE OF CAPITAL BUDGETING

A number of factors combine to make capital budgeting perhaps the most important decision with which financial management is involved. Further, all departments of a firm—production, marketing, and so on—are vitally affected by the capital budgeting decisions, so all executives, no matter what their primary responsibility, must be aware of how capital budgeting decisions are made. These points are discussed in this section.

Long-Term Effects

First and foremost, the fact that the results continue over an extended period means that the decision maker loses some of his flexibility. He must make a commitment into the future. For example, the purchase of an asset with an economic life of ten years requires a long period of waiting before the final results of the action can be known.

Asset expansion is fundamentally related to expected future sales. A decision to buy or to construct a fixed asset that is expected to last five years involves an implicit five-year sales forecast. Indeed, the economic life of a purchased asset represents an implicit forecast for the duration of the economic life of the asset. Hence, failure to forecast accurately will result in overinvestment or underinvestment in fixed assets.

An erroneous forecast of asset requirements can result in serious consequences. If the firm has invested too much in assets, it will incur unnecessarily heavy expenses. If it has not spent enough on fixed assets, two serious problems may arise. First, the firm's equipment may not be sufficiently modern to enable it to produce competitively. Second, if it has inadequate capacity, it may lose a portion of its share of the market to rival firms. To regain lost customers typically requires heavy selling expenses, price reductions, or both.

Raising Funds

Another reason for the importance of capital budgeting is that asset expansion typically involves substantial expenditures. Before a firm spends a large amount of money, it must make the proper plans—large amounts of funds are not available automatically. A firm contemplating a major capital expenditure program may need to arrange its financing several years in advance to be sure of having the funds required for the expansion.

A SIMPLIFIED VIEW OF CAPITAL BUDGETING

Capital budgeting is, in essence, an application of a classic proposition from the economic theory of the firm: namely, a firm should operate at the point where its marginal revenue is just equal to its marginal cost. When this rule is applied to the capital budgeting decision, marginal revenue is taken to be the percentage rate of return on investments, while marginal cost is the firm's marginal cost of capital.

A simplified version of the concept is depicted in Figure 11–1(a). Here the horizontal axis measures the dollars of investment during a year, while the vertical axis shows both the percentage cost of capital and the rate of return on projects. The projects are denoted by boxes—project A, for example, calls for an outlay of $3 million and promises a 17 percent rate of return; project B requires $1 million and yields about 16 percent; and so on. The last investment, project G, simply involves buying 4 percent government bonds, which may be purchased in unlimited quantities. In Figure 11–1(b) the concept is generalized to show smoothed investment opportunity schedules (*IRR*), and three alternative schedules are presented.[1]

FIGURE 11–1   Illustrative Capital Budgeting Decision Process

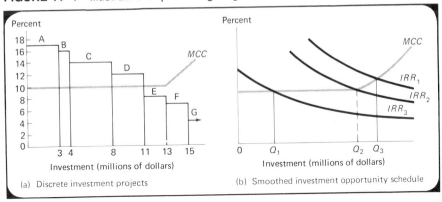

(a) Discrete investment projects

(b) Smoothed investment opportunity schedule

The curve *MCC* designates the marginal cost of capital, or the cost of each additional dollar acquired for purposes of making capital expenditures. As it is drawn in 11–1(a), the marginal cost of capital is constant at 10 percent until the firm has raised $13 million, after which the marginal cost of capital curve turns up.[2] To maximize profits, the firm should accept projects A through D, obtaining and investing $11 million, and reject E, F, and G.

---

[1]The investment opportunity schedules measure the rate of return on each project. The rate of return on a project is generally called the *internal rate of return* (*IRR*). This is why we label the investment opportunity schedules *IRR*. The process of calculating the *IRR* is explained later in this chapter.

[2]The reasons for assuming this particular shape for the marginal cost of capital curve are explained in Chapter 20.

Notice that three alternative investment opportunity schedules are shown in 11–1(b). IRR_1 designates relatively many good investment opportunities, while IRR_3 designates relatively few good projects. The three different curves could be interpreted as applying either to three different firms or to one firm at three different times. As long as the IRR curve cuts the MCC curve to the left of Q_2—for example, at Q_1—the marginal cost of capital is constant. To the right of Q_2—for example, at Q_3—the cost of capital is rising. Therefore, if investment opportunities are such that the IRR curve cuts the MCC curve to the right of Q_2, the *actual* marginal cost of capital (a single point) varies depending on the IRR curve. In this chapter we generally *assume* that the IRR curve cuts the MCC curve to the left of Q_2, thus permitting us to assume that the cost of capital is constant. This assumption is relaxed in Chapter 20, where we show how the MCC varies with the amount of funds raised during a given year.

APPLICATION OF THE CONCEPT

At the applied level, the capital budgeting process is much more complex than the preceding example suggests. Projects do not just appear; a continuing stream of good investment opportunities results from hard thinking, careful planning, and, often, large outlays for research and development. Moreover, some very difficult measurement problems are involved: the sales and costs associated with particular projects must be estimated, frequently for many years into the future, in the face of great uncertainty. Finally, some difficult conceptual and empirical problems arise over the methods of calculating rates of return and the cost of capital.

Businessmen are required to take action, however, even in the face of the kinds of problems described; this requirement has led to the development of procedures that assist in making optimal investment decisions. One of these procedures, forecasting, was discussed in Chapter 5; uncertainty is discussed in formal terms in the next chapter; and the important subject of the cost of capital is deferred to Chapter 20. The essentials of the other elements of capital budgeting are taken up in the remainder of this chapter.

Investment Proposals

Aside from the actual generation of ideas, the first step in the capital budgeting process is to assemble a list of the proposed new investments, together with the data necessary to appraise them. Although practices vary from firm to firm, proposals dealing with asset acquisitions are frequently grouped according to the following four categories:

1. Replacements.
2. Expansion: additional capacity in existing product lines.
3. Expansion: new product lines.
4. Other (for example, pollution control equipment).

These groupings are somewhat arbitrary, and it is frequently difficult to decide the appropriate category for a particular investment. In spite of such problems, the scheme is used quite widely and, as we shall see, with good reason.

Ordinarily, replacement decisions are the simplest to make. Assets wear out or become obsolete, and they must be replaced if production efficiency is to be maintained. The firm has a very good idea of the cost savings to be obtained by replacing an old asset, and it knows the consequences of non-replacement. All in all, the outcomes of most replacement decisions can be predicted with a high degree of confidence.

An example of the second investment classification is a proposal for adding more machines of the type already in use, or the opening of another branch in a city-wide chain of food stores. Expansion investments are frequently incorporated in replacement decisions. To illustrate, an old, inefficient machine may be replaced by a larger and more efficient one.

A degree of uncertainty—sometimes extremely high—is clearly involved in expansion, but the firm at least has the advantage of examining past production and sales experience with similar machines or stores. When it considers an investment of the third kind, expansion into new product lines, little if any experience data are available on which to base decisions. To illustrate, when Union Carbide decided to develop the laser for commercial application, it had very little idea of either the development costs or the specific applications to which lasers could be put. Under such circumstances, any estimates must at best be treated as very crude approximations.

The "other" category is a catchall and includes intangibles; an example is a proposal to boost employee morale and productivity by installing a music system. Mandatory pollution control devices, which must be undertaken even though they produce no revenues, are another example of the "other" category. Major strategic decisions such as plans for overseas expansion, or mergers, might also be included here, but more frequently they are treated separately from the regular capital budget.

ADMINISTRATIVE DETAILS

The remaining aspects of capital budgeting involve administrative matters. Approvals are typically required at higher levels within the organization as we move away from replacement decisions and as the sums involved increase. One of the most important functions of the board of directors is to approve the major outlays in a capital budgeting program. Such decisions are crucial for the future well-being of the firm.

The planning horizon for capital budgeting programs varies with the nature of the industry. When sales can be forecast with a high degree of reliability for ten to twenty years, the planning period is likely to be correspondingly long; electric utilities are an example of such an industry. Also, when the product-technology developments in the industry require an eight-to-ten-year cycle to develop a new major product, as in certain segments of the aerospace industry, a correspondingly long planning period is necessary.

After a capital budget has been adopted, payments must be scheduled. Characteristically, the finance department is responsible for scheduling payments and for acquiring funds to meet payment schedule requirements. The finance department is also primarily responsible for cooperating with the members of operating divisions to compile systematic records on the uses of funds and the uses of equipment purchased in capital budgeting programs. Effective capital budgeting programs require such information as the basis for periodic review and evaluation of capital expenditure decisions—the feedback and control phase of capital budgeting, often called the "post audit."

The foregoing represents a brief overview of the administrative aspects of capital budgeting; the analytical problems involved are considered next.

CAPITAL BUDGETING ANALYSIS: CHOOSING AMONG ALTERNATIVE PROPOSALS

In most firms there are more proposals for projects than the firm is able or willing to finance. Some proposals are good, others are poor, and methods must be developed for distinguishing between the good and the poor. Essentially, the end product is a ranking of the proposals and a cutoff point for determining how far down the ranked list to go.

In part, proposals are eliminated because they are *mutually exclusive*. Mutually exclusive proposals are alternative methods of doing the same job. If one piece of equipment is chosen to do the job, the others will not be required. Thus, if there is a need to improve the materials handling system in a chemical plant, the job may be done either by conveyer belts or by fork trucks. The selection of one method of doing the job makes it unnecessary to use the others. They are mutually exclusive items.

Independent items are pieces of capital equipment that are being considered for different kinds of projects or tasks that need to be accomplished. For example, in addition to the materials handling system, the chemical firm may need equipment to package the end product. The work would require a packaging machine, and the purchase of equipment for this purpose would be independent of the equipment purchased for materials handling.

To distinguish among the many items that compete for the allocation of the firm's capital funds, a ranking procedure must be developed. This procedure requires, first, calculating the estimated benefits from the use of equipment and, second, translating the estimated benefits into a measure of the advantage of the purchase of the equipment. Thus, an estimate of benefits is required, and a method for converting the benefits into a ranking measure must be developed.

IMPORTANCE OF GOOD DATA

Most discussions of measuring the cash flows associated with capital projects are relatively brief, but it is important to emphasize *that in the entire capital budgeting procedure, probably nothing is of greater importance than a reliable estimate of the cost savings or revenue increases that will be achieved from the prospective outlay of capital funds.* The increased output and sales revenue resulting from expansion programs are obvious benefits. Cost reduction benefits include changes in quality and quantity of direct labor; in amount and cost of scrap and rework time; in fuel costs; and in maintenance expenses, down time, safety, flexibility, and so on. So many variables are involved that it is obviously impossible to make neat generalizations. However, this should not minimize the crucial importance of the required analysis of the benefits derived from capital expenditures. Each capital equipment expenditure must be examined in detail for possible additional costs and savings.

All the subsequent procedures for ranking projects are no better than the data input—the old saying, "garbage in, garbage out," is certainly applicable to capital budgeting analysis. Thus, the data assembly process is not a routine clerical task to be performed on a mechanical basis. It requires continuous monitoring and evaluation of estimates by those competent to make such evaluations—engineers, accountants, economists, cost analysts, and other qualified persons.

After costs and benefits have been estimated, they are utilized for ranking alternative investment proposals. How this ranking is accomplished is our next topic.

RANKING INVESTMENT PROPOSALS

The point of capital budgeting—indeed, the point of all financial analysis—is to make decisions that will maximize the value of the firm's common stock. The capital budgeting process is designed to answer two questions: (1) Which of several mutually exclusive investments should be selected? (2) How many projects, in total, should be accepted?

Among the many methods used for ranking investment proposals, three are discussed here:[3]

1. *Payback method (or payback period):* number of years required to return the original investment.

---

[3] A number of "average rate of return" methods have been discussed in the literature and used in practice. These methods are generally unsound and, with the widespread use of computers, completely unnecessary. We discussed them in earlier editions, but they are deleted from this edition.

2. *Net present value (NPV) method:* present value of future returns discounted at the appropriate cost of capital, minus the cost of the investment.
3. *Internal rate of return (IRR) method:* interest rate which equates the present value of future returns to the investment outlay.

Future returns are, in all cases, defined as the net profits after taxes, plus depreciation, that result from a project. In other words, returns are synonymous with cash flows from investments. Next, the nature and characteristics of the three methods are illustrated and explained. To make the explanations more meaningful, the same data are used to illustrate each procedure.

Payback Method

Assume that two projects are being considered by a firm. Each requires an investment of $1,000. The firm's marginal cost of capital is 10 percent.[4] The net cash flows from investments A and B are shown in Table 11–1.

TABLE 11–1 Net Cash Flows: Profit after Taxes Plus Depreciation

Year	A	B
1	$500	$100
2	400	200
3	300	300
4	100	400
5		500
6		600

The *payback period* is the number of years it takes a firm to recover its original investment from net cash flows. Since the cost is $1,000, the payback period is two and one-third years for project A and four years for project B. If the firm were employing a three-year payback period, project A would be accepted, but project B would be rejected.

Although the payback period is very easy to calculate, it can lead to the wrong decisions. As the illustration demonstrates, it ignores income beyond the payback period. If the project is one maturing in later years, the use of the payback period can lead to the selection of less desirable investments. Projects with longer payback periods are characteristically those involved in long-range planning—developing a new product or tapping a new market. These are just the strategic decisions which do not yield their highest returns

---

[4] A discussion of how the cost of capital is calculated is presented in Chapter 20. For now, the cost of capital should be considered as the firm's opportunity cost of making a particular investment. That is, if the firm does not make a particular investment, it "saves" the cost of this investment, and if it can invest these funds in another project that provides a return of 10 percent, then its "opportunity cost" of making the first investment is 10 percent.

for a number of years. This means that the payback method may be biased against the very investments that are most important to a firm's long-run success.

Recognition of the longer period over which an investment is likely to yield savings points up another weakness in the use of the payback method for ranking investment proposals: its failure to take into account the time value of money. To illustrate, consider two assets, X and Y, each costing $300 and each having the following cash flows:

Year	X	Y
1	200	100
2	100	200
3	100	100

Each project has a two-year payback; hence, each would appear equally desirable. However, we know that a dollar today is worth more than a dollar next year, so project X, with its faster cash flow, is certainly more desirable.

The use of the payback period is sometimes defended on the grounds that returns beyond three or four years are fraught with such great uncertainty that it is best to disregard them altogether in a planning decision. However, that is clearly an unsound procedure. Some investments with the highest returns are those which may not come to fruition for eight to ten years. The new product cycle in industries involving advanced technologies may not have a payoff for eight or nine years. Furthermore, even though returns that occur after three, four, or five years may be highly uncertain, it is important to make a judgment about the likelihood of their occurring. To ignore them is to assign a zero probability to these distant receipts. This can hardly produce the best results.

Another defense of the payback method is that a firm which is short of cash must necessarily give great emphasis to a quick return of its funds so that they may be put to use in other places or in meeting other needs. However, this does not relieve the payback method of its many shortcomings, and there are better methods for handling the cash shortage situation.[5]

A third reason for using payback is that, typically, projects with faster paybacks have more favorable short-run effects on earnings per share. Firms that use payback for this reason are sacrificing future growth for current accounting income, and in general such a practice will not maximize the value of the firm. The discounted cash flow techniques discussed in the next section, if used properly, automatically give consideration to the present earnings versus future growth tradeoff and strike the balance that will maximize the firm's value.

---

[5]We interpret a cash shortage to mean that the firm has a high opportunity cost for its funds and a high cost of capital. We would consider this high cost of capital in the internal rate of return method or the net present value method, thus taking account of the cash shortage.

Also, the payback method is sometimes used simply because it is so easy to apply. If a firm is making many small capital expenditure decisions, the costs of using more complex methods may outweigh the benefits of possibly "better" choices among competing projects. Thus, many electric utility companies with very sophisticated capital budgeting procedures use discounted cash flow techniques for larger projects, but they use payback on certain small, routine replacement decisions. When these sophisticated companies do use the payback method, however, they generally do so only after special studies have indicated that the payback method will provide sufficiently accurate answers for the decisions at hand.

Finally, many firms use payback in combination with one of the discounted cash flow procedures described below. The *NPV* or *IRR* method is used to appraise a project's profitability, while the payback is used to show how long the initial investment will be at risk; that is, payback is used as a risk indicator. Recent surveys have shown that when larger firms use payback in connection with major projects, it is almost always used in this manner.

Net Present Value Method

As the flaws in the payback method were recognized, people began to search for methods of evaluating projects that would recognize that a dollar received immediately is preferable to a dollar received at some future date. This recognition led to the development of *discounted cash flow (DCF) techniques* to take account of the time value of money. One such discounted cash flow technique is called the "net present value method," or sometimes simply the "present value method." *To implement this approach, find the present value of the expected net cash flows of an investment, discounted at the cost of capital, and subtract from it the initial cost outlay of the project.*[6] If the net present value is positive, the project should be accepted; if negative, it should be rejected. If the two projects are mutually exclusive, the one with the higher net present value should be chosen.

The equation for the net present value (*NPV*) is[7]

$$NPV = \left[\frac{R_1}{(1+k)^1} + \frac{R_2}{(1+k)^2} + \cdots + \frac{R_N}{(1+k)^N} \right] - C$$

$$= \sum_{t=1}^{N} \frac{R_t}{(1+k)^t} - C. \tag{11-1}$$

---

[6] If costs are spread over several years, this must be taken into account. Suppose, for example, that a firm bought land in 1974, erected a building in 1975, installed equipment in 1976, and started production in 1977. One could treat 1974 as the base year, comparing the present value of the costs as of 1974 to the present value of the benefit stream as of that same date.

[7] The second equation is simply a shorthand expression in which sigma (Σ) signifies "sum up" or add the present values of *N* profit terms. If $t = 1$, then $R_t = R_1$ and $1/(1+k)^t = 1/(1+k)^1$; if $t = 2$, then $R_t = R_2$ and $1/(1+k)^t = 1/(1+k)^2$; and so on, until $t = N$, the last year the project provides any profits. The symbol

Here R_1, R_2, and so forth, represent the net cash flows; k is the marginal cost of capital; C is the initial cost of the project; and N is the project's expected life.

The net present values of projects A and B are calculated in Table 11–2. Project A has an *NPV* of $80, while B's *NPV* is $400. On this basis, both should be accepted if they are independent, but B should be the one chosen if they are mutually exclusive.

TABLE 11–2 Calculating the Net Present Value *(NPV)* of Projects with $1,000 Cost

	Project A			Project B		
Year	Net Cash Flow	PVIF (10%)	PV of Cash Flow	Net Cash Flow	PVIF (10%)	PV of Cash Flow
1	$500	.91	$ 455	$100	.91	$ 91
2	400	.83	332	200	.83	166
3	300	.75	225	300	.75	225
4	100	.68	68	400	.68	272
5				500	.62	310
6				600	.56	336
	PV of inflows		$1,080			$1,400
	Less: cost		– 1,000			– 1,000
	NPV		$ 80			$ 400

When a firm takes on a project with a positive *NPV,* the value of the firm increases by the amount of the *NPV.* In our example, the value of the firm increases by $400 if it takes on project B, but by only $80 if it takes on project A. Viewing the alternatives in this manner, it is easy to see why B is preferred to A, and it is also easy to see the logic of the *NPV* approach.

Internal Rate of Return Method

The internal rate of return *(IRR)* is defined as the *interest rate that equates the present value of the expected future cash flows, or receipts, to the initial cost outlay.* The equation for calculating the internal rate of return is

$$\frac{R_1}{(1 + r)^1} + \frac{R_2}{(1 + r)^2} + \cdots + \frac{R_N}{(1 + r)^N} - C = 0$$

$$\sum_{t=1}^{N} \frac{R_t}{(1 + r)^t} - C = 0. \qquad (11\text{–}2)$$

$\sum_{t=1}^{N}$ simply says "go through the following process: Let $t = 1$ and find the PV of R_1; then let $t = 2$ and find the PV of R_2. Continue until the PV of each individual profit has been found; then add the PVs of these individual profits to find the PV of the asset."

Here we know the value of C and also the values of $R_1, R_2, \ldots, R_N$, but we do not know the value of r. Thus, we have an equation with one unknown, and we can solve for the value of r. Some value of r will cause the sum of the discounted receipts to equal the initial cost of the project, making the equation equal to zero, and that value of r is defined as the internal rate of return; that is, the solution value of r is the *IRR*.

Notice that the internal rate of return formula, Equation 11–2, is simply the *NPV* formula, Equation 11–1, solved for that particular value of k that causes the *NPV* to equal zero. In other words, the same basic equation is used for both methods, but in the *NPV* method the discount rate *(k)* is specified and the *NPV* is found, while in the *IRR* method the *NPV* is specified to equal zero and the value of r that forces the *NPV* to equal zero is found.

The internal rate of return may be found by trial and error. First, compute the present value of the cash flows from an investment, using an arbitrarily selected interest rate. (Since the cost of capital for most firms is in the range of 10–15 percent, projects will hopefully promise a return of at least 10 percent. Therefore, 10 percent is a good starting point for most problems.) Then compare the present value so obtained with the investment's cost. If the present value is higher than the cost figure, try a higher interest rate and go through the procedure again. Conversely, if the present value is lower than the cost, lower the interest rate and repeat the process. Continue until the present value of the flows from the investment is approximately equal to its cost. *The interest rate that brings about this equality is defined as the internal rate of return.*[8]

This calculation process is illustrated in Table 11–3 for projects A and B. First, the 10 percent interest factors are obtained from Table A–2 at the end of the book. These factors are then multiplied by the cash flows for the corresponding years, and the present values of the annual cash flows are placed in the appropriate columns. For example, the *PVIF* of .91 is multiplied by $500, and the product, $455, is placed in the first row of column A.

The present values of the yearly cash flows are then summed to get the investment's total present value. Subtracting the cost of the project from this figure gives the net present value. As the net present values of both investments are positive at the 10 percent rate, increase the rate to 15 percent and try again. *At this point the net present value of investment A is approximately zero, which indicates that its internal rate of return is approximately 15 percent. Continuing, B is found to have an internal rate of return of approximately 20 percent.*[9]

[8] In order to reduce the number of trials required to find the internal rate of return, it is important to minimize the error at each iteration. One reasonable approach is to make as good a first approximation as possible, then to "straddle" the internal rate of return by making fairly large changes in the interest rate early in the iterative process. In practice, if many projects are to be evaluated or if many years are involved, one would not work out the calculations by hand but would use a computer. Computational techniques have been developed to enable us to find the *IRR* in three or four trials.

[9] The *IRR* can also be estimated graphically. First, calculate the *NPV* at two or three discount rates as in Table 11–3. Next, plot these *NPV*s against the discount rates—see Figure 11–2 in the next section for an example. The horizontal axis intercept is the *IRR;* with graph paper and a sharp pencil, the *IRR* can be estimated to three decimal places.

TABLE 11–3 Finding the Internal Rate of Return

		Cash Flows (R_t Values)	
	Year	R_A	R_B
C = Investment = $1,000	1:R_1 = $500	$100
	2:R_2 = 400	200
	3:R_3 = 300	300
	4:R_4 = 100	400
	5:R_5 =	500
	6:R_6 =	600

	10 Percent			15 Percent			20 Percent		
		Present Value			Present Value			Present Value	
Year	PVIF	A	B	PVIF	A	B	PVIF	A	B
1	0.91	455	91	0.87	435	87	0.83	415	83
2	0.83	332	166	0.76	304	152	0.69	276	138
3	0.75	225	225	0.66	198	198	0.58	174	174
4	0.68	68	272	0.57	57	228	0.48	48	192
5	0.62		310	0.50		250	0.40		200
6	0.56		336	0.43		258	0.33		198
Present value		1,080	1,400		994	1,173		913	985
Net present value = $PV - C$		80	400		(6)	173		(87)	(15)

What is so special about the particular interest rate that equates the cost of a project with the present value of its receipts? Suppose a firm obtains all its capital by borrowing from a bank, and the interest cost of this debt is 6 percent. If the internal rate of return on a particular project is calculated to be 6 percent, the same as the cost of capital, then the firm would be able to invest in the project, use the cash flow generated by the investment to pay off the principal and interest on the bank loan, and come out exactly even on the transaction. If the internal rate of return exceeds 6 percent, the project would be profitable; if the internal rate of return is less than 6 percent, taking on the project would result in losses. It is this "break-even" characteristic that makes us interested in the internal rate of return.

Assuming that the firm uses a cost of capital of 10 percent, the internal rate of return criterion states that, if projects A and B are independent, both should be accepted—they both do better than "break even." If they are mutually exclusive, B ranks higher and should be accepted, while A should be rejected.

A more complete illustration of how the internal rate of return would be used in practice is given in Table 11–4. Assuming a 10 percent cost of capital, the firm should accept projects 1 through 7, reject projects 8 through 10, and have a total capital budget of $10 million.

TABLE 11-4   The Prospective-Projects Schedule

Nature of Proposal	Amount of Funds Required	Cumulative Total	IRR
1. Purchase of leased space	$2,000,000	$ 2,000,000	23%
2. Mechanization of accounting system	1,200,000	3,200,000	19
3. Modernization of office building	1,500,000	4,700,000	17
4. Addition of power facilities	900,000	5,600,000	16
5. Purchase of affiliate	3,600,000	9,200,000	13
6. Purchase of loading docks	300,000	9,500,000	12
7. Purchase of tank trucks	500,000	10,000,000	11
			10% cutoff
8. Installation of conveyor system	200,000	10,200,000	9
9. Construction of new plant	2,300,000	12,500,000	8
10. Purchase of executive aircraft	200,000	12,700,000	7

IRR for Level Cash Flows

If the cash flows from a project are level, or equal in each year, then the project's internal rate of return can be found by a relatively simple process. In essence, such a project is an annuity: the firm makes an outlay, *C,* and receives a stream of cash flow benefits, *R,* for a given number of years. The *IRR* for the project is found by applying Equation 10–6, discussed in Chapter 10.

To illustrate, suppose a project has a cost of $10,000 and is expected to produce cash flows of $1,627 a year for ten years. The cost of the project, $10,000, is the present value of an annuity of $1,627 a year for ten years, so applying Equation 10–6 we obtain

$$\frac{\text{Cost}}{R} = \frac{\$10,000}{\$1,627} = 6.146 = PVIF_a.$$

Looking up $PVIF_a$ in Table A–4, across the ten-year row, we find it (approximately) under the 10 percent column. Accordingly, 10 percent is the *IRR* on the project. In other words, 10 percent is the value of *r* that would satisfy Equation 11–2 when *R* is constant at $1,627 for ten years and *C* is $10,000. This procedure works only if the project has constant annual cash flows; if it does not, the *IRR* must be found by trial and error or by using a computer.

BASIC DIFFERENCES BETWEEN THE *NPV* AND *IRR* METHODS[10]

As noted above, the *NPV* method (1) accepts all independent projects whose *NPV* is greater than zero and (2) ranks mutually exclusive projects

---

[10]This section is relatively technical and may be omitted on a first reading without loss of continuity.

by their *NPV*'s, selecting the project with the higher *NPV* according to Equation 11–3:

$$NPV = \sum_{t=1}^{N} \frac{R_t}{(1+k)^t} - C. \qquad (11\text{–}3)$$

The *IRR* method, on the other hand, finds the value of *r* that forces the *NPV* of Equation 11–4 to equal zero:

$$NPV = \sum_{t=1}^{N} \frac{R_t}{(1+r)^t} - C = 0. \qquad (11\text{–}4)$$

The *IRR* method calls for accepting independent projects where *r,* the internal rate of return, is greater than *k,* the cost of capital, and for selecting among mutually exclusive projects depending on which has the higher *IRR.*

It is apparent that the only structural difference between the *NPV* and *IRR* methods lies in the discount rates used in the two equations—all the values in the equations are identical except for *r* and *k.* Further, we can see that if *r* > *k,* then *NPV* > 0.[11] *Accordingly, the two methods give the same accept-reject decisions for specific projects—if project J is acceptable under the* NPV *criterion, it is also acceptable if the* IRR *method is used.*

However, under certain conditions the *NPV* and *IRR* methods can *rank* projects differently, and if mutually exclusive projects are involved or if capital is limited, then rankings can be important. The conditions under which different rankings can occur are as follows:

1. The cost of one project is larger than that of the other.
2. The timing of the projects' cash flows differ. For example, the cash flows of one project may increase over time, while those of the other decrease, or the projects may have different expected lives.

The first point can be seen by considering two mutually exclusive projects, L and S, of greatly differing sizes. Project S calls for the investment of $1.00 and yields $1.50 at the end of one year. Its *IRR* is 50 percent, and at a 10 percent cost of capital its *NPV* is $0.36. Project L costs $1 million and yields $1.25 million at the end of the year. Its *IRR* is only 25 percent, but its *NPV* at 10 percent is $113,625. The two methods rank the projects differently: *IRR_S* > *IRR_L*, but *NPV_L* > *NPV_S*. This is, of course, an extreme case, but whenever projects differ in size, the *NPV* and the *IRR* can give different rankings.[12]

[11] This can be seen by noting that *NPV* = 0 if and only if *r* = *k:*

$$NPV = \sum_{t=1}^{N} \frac{R_t}{(1+k)^t} - C = \sum_{t=1}^{n} \frac{R_t}{(1+r)^t} - C = 0,$$

If *r* > *k,* then *NPV* > 0, and if *r* < *k,* then *NPV* < 0. We should also note that, under certain conditions, there may be more than one root to Equation 11–4, hence multiple *IRRs* are found. See Appendix 10A of *Managerial Finance* for a more detailed discussion of the multiple root problem.

[12] Projects of different size *could* be ranked the same by the *NPV* and *IRR* methods; that is, different sizes do not necessarily mean different rankings.

The effect of differential cash flows is somewhat more difficult to understand, but it can be illustrated by an example. Consider two projects, A and B, whose cash flows over their three-year lives are given below:

	Cash Flow from Project	
Year	A	B
1	$1,000	$ 100
2	500	600
3	100	1,100

Project A's cash flows are higher in the early years, but B's cash flows increase over time and exceed those of A in later years. Each project costs $1,200, and their NPVs, discounted at the specified rates, are shown below:

	NPV	
Discount Rate	A	B
0%	$ 400	$ 600
5	300	400
10	200	200
15	100	50
20	50	(85)
25	(25)	(175)
30	(100)	(250)

At a zero discount rate, the NPV of each project is simply the sum of its receipts less its cost. Thus, the NPV of project A at 0 percent is $1,000 + $500 + $100 − $1,200 = $400; that of project B is $100 + $600 + $1,100 − $1,200 = $600. As the discount rate rises from zero, the NPVs of the two projects fall from these values.

The NPVs are plotted against the appropriate discount rates in Figure 11–2, a graph defined as a *present value profile*. Notice that the vertical axis intercept is the NPV when the discount rate is zero, while the horizontal axis intercept shows each project's IRR. The internal rate of return is defined as that point where NPV is zero; therefore, A's IRR is 22 percent, while B's is 17 percent. Because its largest cash flows come late in the project's life, when the discounting effects of time are most significant, B's NPV falls rapidly as the discount rate rises. However, since A's cash flows come early, when the impact of higher discount rates is not so severe, its NPV falls less rapidly as interest rates increase.

Notice that if the cost of capital is below 10 percent, B has the higher NPV but the lower IRR, while at a cost of capital above 10 percent A has both the higher NPV and the higher IRR. We can generalize these results: *Whenever the NPV profiles of two projects cross one another, a conflict will exist if the cost of capital is below the cross-over rate.* For our illustrative projects, no conflict would exist if the firm's cost of capital exceeded 10 percent, but the two methods would rank A and B differently if k is less than 10 percent.

FIGURE 11–2 Present Value Profile

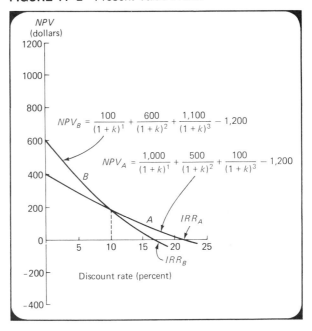

WHICH RANKING TECHNIQUE, *NPV* OR *IRR*, SHOULD BE USED?

How should conflicts between the *NPV* and *IRR* methods be resolved; for example, when the *NPV* and *IRR* methods yield conflicting rankings, which of two mutually exclusive projects should be selected? Assuming that management is seeking to maximize the value of the firm, the correct decision is to select the project with the higher *NPV*. After all, the *NPV*s measure the projects' contributions to the value of the firm, so the one with the higher *NPV* must be contributing more to the firm's value. *This line of reasoning leads to the conclusion that firms should, in general, use the NPV method for evaluating capital investment proposals.*[13] Recognizing this point, sophisticated

[13]The question of *why* the conflict arises is an interesting one. Basically, it has to do with the reinvestment of cash flows—the *NPV* method implicitly assumes reinvestment at the marginal cost of capital *(MCC)*, while the *IRR* method implicitly assumes reinvestment at the internal rate of return. For a value-maximizing firm, reinvestment at the *MCC* is the better assumption. The rationale is as follows: A value-maximizing firm will expand to the point where it accepts all projects yielding more than the *MCC* (these projects will have *NPV* > 0). How these projects are financed is irrelevant—the point is, they will be financed and accepted. Now consider the question of the cash flows from a particular project; if these cash flows are reinvested, at what rate will reinvestment occur? All projects that yield more than the cost of capital have already been accepted; thus, these cash flows can only be invested in physical assets yielding *less than* the *MCC*, or else be used in lieu of other capital with a cost of *MCC*. A rational firm will take the second alternative, so reinvested cash flows will save the firm the cost of capital. This means, in effect, that cash flows are reinvested to yield the cost of capital, which is the assumption implicit in the *NPV* method. For a detailed discussion see Appendix 10A in *Managerial Finance*.

firms generally rely on the *NPV* method. These firms often calculate (by computer) both the *NPV* and the *IRR,* but they rely on the *NPV* when conflicts arise among mutually exclusive projects.

CAPITAL BUDGETING PROJECT EVALUATION

Thus far the problem of measuring cash flows—the benefits used in the present value calculations above—has not been dealt with directly. This matter will now be discussed, and a few simple examples given. The procedures developed here can be used both for expansion and for replacement decisions.

Simplified Model for Determining Cash Flows[14]

One way of considering the cash flows attributable to a particular investment is to think of them in terms of comparative income statements. This is illustrated in the following example.

The Widget Division of the Culver Company, a profitable, diversified manufacturing firm, purchased a machine five years ago at a cost of $7,500. The machine had an expected life of fifteen years at time of purchase and a zero estimated salvage value at the end of the fifteen years. It is being depreciated on a straight-line basis and has a book value of $5,000 at present. The division manager reports that he can buy a new machine for $12,000 (including installation) which, over its ten-year life, will expand sales from $10,000 to $11,000 a year. Further, it will reduce labor and raw materials usage sufficiently to cut operating costs from $7,000 to $5,000. The new machine has an estimated salvage value of $2,000 at the end of ten years. The old machine's current market value is $1,000. Taxes are at a 40 percent rate and are paid quarterly, and the firm's cost of capital is 10 percent. Should Culver buy the new machine?

The decision calls for five steps: (1) estimate the actual cash outlay attributable to the new investment, (2) determine the incremental cash flows, (3) find the present value of the incremental cash flows, (4) add the present value of the expected salvage value to the present value of the total cash flows, and (5) see whether the *NPV* is positive or whether the *IRR* exceeds the cost of capital. These steps are explained further in the following sections.

Estimated Cash Outlay   The net initial cash outlay consists of these items: (1) payment to the manufacturer, (2) tax effects, and (3) proceeds from the sale of the old machine. Culver must make a $12,000 payment to the manufacturer of the machine, but its next quarterly tax bill will be reduced because

---

[14]The procedure described in this section facilitates an understanding of the capital investment analysis process, but for repeated calculations, the alternative worksheet illustrated in the next section is preferred.

of the loss it will incur when it sells the old machine: tax saving = (loss) (tax rate) = ($4,000) (.4) = $1,600. The tax reduction will occur because the old machine, which is carried at $5,000, will be written down by $4,000 ($5,000 less $1,000 salvage value) immediately if the new one is purchased.

To illustrate, suppose the Culver Company's taxable income in the quarter in which the new machine is to be purchased would have been $100,000 without the purchase of the new machine and the consequent write-off of the old machine. With a 40 percent tax rate, Culver would have had to write a check for $40,000 to pay its tax bill. However, if it buys the new machine and sells the old one, it will take an operating loss of $4,000—the $5,000 book value on the old machine less the salvage value. (The loss is an operating loss, not a capital loss, because it is in reality simply recognizing that depreciation charges, an operating cost, were too low during the old machine's five-year life.)[15] With this $4,000 additional operating cost, next quarter's taxable income will be reduced from $100,000 to $96,000, and the tax bill from $40,000 to $38,400. This means, of course, that the firm's cash outflow for taxes will be $1,600 less *because* it has purchased the new machine.

In addition, there is to be a cash inflow of $1,000 from the sale of the old machine.

The net result is that the purchase of the new machine involves an immediate net cash outlay of $9,400; this is its cost for capital budgeting purposes:

Invoice price of new machine	$12,000
Less: Tax savings	−1,600
Salvage of old machine	−1,000
Net cash outflow (cost)	$ 9,400

If additional working capital is required as a result of a capital budgeting decision, as would generally be true for expansion-type investments (as opposed to cost-reducing replacement investments), this factor must be taken into account. The amount of *net* working capital (additional current assets required as a result of the expansion minus any spontaneous funds generated by the expansion) is estimated and added to the initial cash outlay. We assume that Culver will not need any additional working capital, hence this factor is ignored in this example.

Annual Benefits   Column 1 in Table 11–5 shows the Widget Division's estimated income statement as it would be without the new machine; column 2 shows the statement as it will look if the new investment is made. (It is assumed that these figures are applicable for each of the next ten years; if this is not the case, then cash flow estimates must be made for each year.) Column 3 shows the differences between the first two columns, and the sum of

---

[15] If Culver traded in the old machine as partial payment for the new one, the loss would be added to the depreciable cost of the new machine, and there would be no immediate tax savings.

column 3 gives the difference between the new and the old cash flows, $2,000. This is the incremental cash flow produced by the new machine; it is the benefit stream to be discounted at the cost of capital.

TABLE 11–5 Comparative Income Statement Framework for Considering Cash Flows

	(1) Without new Investment	(2) With new Investment	(3) (2) – (1) Difference (Δ)
Sales	$10,000	$11,000	$1,000
Operating costs (C)	$7,000	$5,000	– $2,000
Depreciation (D)	500	1,000	500
Deductible costs (C + D)	7,500	6,000	– 1,500
Taxable income (I)	$ 2,500	$ 5,000	$2,500
Less: Income taxes (t = 40%)	1,000	2,000	1,000
Profit after taxes (P)	$ 1,500	$ 3,000	$1,500
Cash flow (P + D)	$ 2,000	$ 4,000	$2,000

Note: The possible cash inflows from the sale of the old machine are not reflected on the above income statements. These effects are accounted for in the estimate of the cash outlay for the new machine. Also, note that when the *minus* $1,500 difference in deductible costs is subtracted from the increase in sales, the result is an increase in taxable income.

Finding the PV of the Benefits   The next step is to determine the present value of the benefit stream. The interest factor for a ten-year, 10 percent annuity is found to be 6.145 from Appendix Table A–4. This factor, when multiplied by the $2,000 incremental cash flow, results in a present value of $12,290.

Salvage Value   The new machine has an estimated salvage value of $2,000; that is, Culver expects to be able to sell the machine for $2,000 when it is retired ten years from now. The present value of an inflow of $2,000 due in ten years is $772, found as $2,000 × .386. If additional working capital had been required and included in the initial cash outlay, this amount would be added to the salvage value of the machine because the working capital will be recovered if and when the project is abandoned.

Notice that the salvage value is a return of capital, not taxable income, so it is *not* subject to income taxes. Of course, when the new machine is actually retired ten years hence, it may be sold for more or less than the expected $2,000, so either taxable income or a deductible operating loss may arise, but $2,000 is the best present estimate of the new machine's eventual salvage value.

Determining the Net Present Value The project's net present value is found as the sum of the present values of the inflows, or benefits, less the outflows, or costs:

Inflows: *PV* of annual benefits	$12,290
PV of salvage value, new machine	772
Less: Net cash outflow, or cost	(9,400)
Net present value *(NPV)*	$ 3,662

Since the *NPV* is positive, the project should be accepted.

Summary of Cash Flows

Table 11–6 summarizes the five-step budgeting decision process described above. Using the Culver Company investment problem as an example, we first calculate the total outflows for the proposed project by subtracting from the cost of the new machine the sum of the funds received from the sale of the old machine plus the tax savings resulting from that sale. Recall that a $4,000 operating loss will occur if the old machine with a book value of $5,000 is sold for $1,000. Since the old machine is sold at a loss, the $1,000 received from the sale is not taxed. Only the *gain* on the sale of any asset is taxed. Further, the $4,000 loss is a tax deduction for next quarter's tax payment, and it results in a tax saving of $1,600.

Next, we calculate the net annual benefits, then find the present value of this benefit stream, which is $12,290.

We now find the present value of the expected salvage value of the new machine, $772. Since salvage value is a *return of capital,* not taxable income, no taxes are deducted from the salvage value.

Finally, we sum up the *PV* of the inflows and then deduct the project cost to determine the *NPV,* $3,662 in this example. Since the *NPV* is positive, the project should be accepted.[16]

---

[16]The internal rate of return on the project could have been computed and found to be 18 percent. Because this is substantially in excess of the 10 percent cost of capital, the internal rate of return method also indicates that the investment should be undertaken. In this case, the *IRR* is found as follows:

$$PV \text{ of benefit stream} + PV \text{ of salvage} - \text{cost} = 0.$$

$$\sum_{t=1}^{10} \frac{\$2,000}{(1 + IRR)^t} + \frac{\$2,000}{(1 + IRR)^{10}} - \$9,400 = 0.$$

$2,000 (*IF* for *PV* of 10-year annuity) + $2,000 (*PV* of $1 in 10 years) − $9,400 = 0.

Try *PVIF*s for 18%:

$2,000 (4.494) + $2,000 (.191) − $9,400 = $8,988 + $382 − $9,400 = $ − 30,

which is very close to zero, indicating that the internal rate of return is approximately equal to 18 percent.

TABLE 11–6 Worksheet for Capital Budgeting Project Evaluation

1. *Project Cost, or Initial Outflows Required to Undertake the Project*[a]
Investment in new equipment	$12,000
Receipt from sale of old machine	(1,000)
Add (or subtract) the taxes (or tax savings) resulting from the gain (or loss) on the old machine: tax rate (*t*) times gain or loss	(1,600)
Total project cost	$ 9,400

2. *Calculation of Annual Benefits*
Change in sales	$ 1,000
Less: Change in costs	(2,000)
Change in depreciation	500
Change in taxable income	$ 2,500
Less: taxes at 40%	1,000
Change in after-tax profits	$ 1,500
Plus: Change in depreciation	500
Change in cash flow	$ 2,000

3. *Present Value of Benefits*
Change in cash flow × interest factor $2,000 × 6.145 =	$12,290

4. *Present Value of Expected Salvage*
Expected salvage value × interest factor $2,000 × .386 =	$ 772

5. *Net Present Value*
PV of inflows: Annual benefits	$12,290
Salvage	772
	$13,062
Less: Project cost	9,400
NPV	$ 3,662

[a]If project costs are incurred over a number of years, then the present value of project costs must be calculated.

ALTERNATIVE CAPITAL BUDGETING WORKSHEET[17]

Table 11–7 presents an alternative worksheet for evaluating capital projects. The top section shows net cash flows at the time of investment; since all these flows occur immediately, no discounting is required and the interest factor is 1.0. The lower section of the table shows future cash flows—benefits from increased sales and/or reduced costs, depreciation, and salvage value. These flows do occur over time, so it is necessary to convert them to present values. The *NPV* as determined in the alternative format, $3,662, agrees with the figure as calculated in Table 11–6.

[17]This section may be omitted without loss of continuity.

TABLE 11–7 Alternative Worksheet for Capital Budgeting Project Evaluation

	Amount before Tax	Amount after Tax[a]	Year Event Occurs	PV Factor at 10%	PV
Outflows at time investment is made					
Investment in new equipment	$12,000	$12,000	0	1.0	$12,000
Salvage value of old	(1,000)	(1,000)	0	1.0	(1,000)
Tax effect of the sale[d]	(4,000)	(1,600)	0	1.0	(1,600)
Increased working capital (if necessary)	[b]	—	0	1.0	—
Total initial outflows (PV of costs)					$ 9,400
Inflows, or annual returns					
Benefits[c]	$ 3,000	$ 1,800	1–10	6.145	$11,061
Depreciation on new (annual)[d]	1,000	400	1–10	6.145	2,458
Depreciation on old (annual)[d]	(500)	(200)	1–10	6.145	(1,229)
Salvage value on new	2,000	2,000	10	.386	772
Return of working capital (if necessary)	[b]	—	10	.386	—
Total periodic inflows (PV of benefits)					$13,062

$NPV = PV$ of benefits less PV of cost $= \$13,062 - \$9,400 = \$3,662.$

[a] Amount after tax equals amount before tax times t or $(1 - t)$, where t = tax rate.
[b] Not applicable.
[c] Benefits are multiplied by $(1 - t)$.
[d] Deductions (tax loss and depreciation) are multiplied by t.

CAPITAL RATIONING

Ordinarily, firms operate as illustrated in Figure 11–1 above; that is, they take on investments to the point where the marginal returns from investment are just equal to their estimated marginal cost of capital. For firms operating in this way, the decision process is as described above—they make those investments having positive net present values, reject those whose net present values are negative, and choose between mutually exclusive investments on the basis of the higher net present value. However, a firm will occasionally set an absolute limit on the size of its capital budget for any one year that is less than the level of investment it would undertake on the basis of the criteria described above.

The principal reason for such action is that some firms are reluctant to engage in external financing (borrowing, or selling stock). One management, recalling the plight of firms with substantial amounts of debt in the 1930s, may simply refuse to use debt. Another management, which has no objection to selling debt, may not want to sell equity capital for fear of losing some measure of voting control. Still others may refuse to use any form of outside financing, considering both safety and control to be more important than additional profits. These are all cases of capital rationing, and they result in limiting the rate of expansion to a slower pace than would be dictated by "purely rational profit-maximizing behavior."[18]

Project Selection under Capital Rationing

How should projects be selected under conditions of capital rationing? First, note that under conditions of true capital rationing, the firm's value is not being maximized—if management was maximizing, then it would move to the point where the marginal project's *NPV* was zero, and capital rationing as defined would not exist. So, if a firm uses capital rationing, it has ruled out value maximization. The firm may, however, want to maximize value *subject to the constraint that the capital ceiling is not exceeded.* Following constrained maximization behavior will, in general, result in a lower value than following unconstrained maximization, but some type of constrained maximization may produce reasonably satisfactory results. Linear programming is one method of constrained maximization that has been applied to capital rationing. To our knowledge, this method has not been widely applied, but much work is going on in the area, and linear programming may, in the future, prove useful in capital budgeting.[19]

If a financial manager does face capital rationing, and if he cannot get the constraint lifted, what should he do? His objective should be to select projects, subject to the capital rationing constraint, such that the sum of the projects' *NPV*s is maximized. Linear programming can be used, but there is really no practical alternative that will approximate the true maximum. Reasonably satisfactory results may be obtained by ranking projects by their internal rates of return and then, starting at the top of this list of projects, by taking investments of successively lower rank until the available funds have been exhausted. However, no investment with a negative *NPV* (or an internal rate of return below the cost of capital) should be undertaken.

---

[18]We should make three points here. First we *do not* necessarily consider a decision to hold back on expansion irrational. If the owner of a firm has what *he* considers to be plenty of income and wealth, then it might be quite rational for him to "trim his sails," relax, and concentrate on enjoying what he has already earned rather than on earning still more. Such behavior would not, however, be appropriate for a publicly owned firm.

The second point is that it is not correct to interpret as capital rationing a situation where the firm is willing to sell additional securities at the going market price but finds that it cannot because the market will simply not absorb more of its issues. Rather, such a situation indicates that the cost-of-capital curve is rising. If more acceptable investments are indicated than can be financed, then the cost of capital being used is too low and should be raised.

Third, firms sometimes set a limit on capital expenditures, not because of a shortage of funds, but because of limitations on other resources, especially managerial talent. A firm might, for example, feel that its personnel development program is sufficient to handle an expansion of no more than 10 percent a year, then set a limit on the capital budget to insure that expansion is held to that rate. This is not *capital* rationing—rather, it involves a downward reevaluation of project returns if growth exceeds some limit; that is, expected rates of return are, after some point, a decreasing function of the level of expenditures.

[19]For a further discussion of programming approaches to capital budgeting, see Appendix 10A in *Managerial Finance.*

A firm might, for example, have the investment opportunities shown in Table 11–8 and only $6 million available for investment. In this situation, the firm would probably accept projects 1 through 4 and project 6, ending with a capital budget of $5.9 million, and a cumulative *NPV* of $2.6 million. Under no circumstances should it accept project 8, 9, or 10, as they all have internal rates of return of less than 10 percent (and also net present values less than zero).

TABLE 11–8   The Prospective-Projects Schedule

Nature of Proposal	Project's Cost	Cumulative Total of Costs	Internal Rate of Return	PV of Benefits	Project's NPV
1. Purchase of leased space	$2,000,000	$ 2,000,000	23%	$3,200,000	$1,200,000
2. Mechanization of accounting system	1,200,000	3,200,000	19	1,740,000	540,000
3. Modernization of office building	1,500,000	4,700,000	17	2,070,000	570,000
4. Addition of power facilities	900,000	5,600,000	16	1,125,000	225,000
5. Purchase of affiliate	3,600,000	9,200,000	13	4,248,000	648,000
6. Purchase of loading docks	300,000	9,500,000	12	342,000	42,000
7. Purchase of tank trucks	500,000	10,000,000	11	540,000	40,000
			——— cutoff ———		
8. Installation of conveyor system	200,000	10,200,000	9	186,000	(14,000)
9. Construction of new plant	2,300,000	12,500,000	8	2,093,000	(207,000)
10. Purchase of executive aircraft	200,000	12,700,000	7	128,000	(72,000)

SUMMARY

Capital budgeting, which involves commitments for large outlays whose benefits (or drawbacks) extend well into the future, is of the greatest significance to a firm. Decisions in these areas will, therefore, have a major impact on the future well-being of the firm. This chapter focused on how capital budgeting decisions can be made more effective in contributing to the health and growth of a firm. The discussion stressed the development of systematic procedures and rules for preparing a list of investment proposals, for evaluating them, and for selecting a cutoff point.

The chapter emphasized that one of the most crucial phases in the process of evaluating capital budget proposals is obtaining a dependable estimate of the benefits that will be obtained from undertaking the project. It cannot be overemphasized that the firm must allocate to competent and experienced personnel the making of these judgments.

Determining Cash Flows   The cash inflows from an investment consist of the incremental profit after taxes plus the incremental depreciation; the cash outflow is the cost of the investment less the salvage value received on an old machine plus any tax loss (or less any tax savings) when the machine is sold.

Ranking Investment Proposals   Three commonly used procedures for ranking investment proposals were discussed in the chapter:

Payback is defined as the number of years required to return the original investment. Although the payback method is used frequently, it has serious conceptual weaknesses, because it ignores the facts (1) that some receipts come in beyond the payback period and (2) that a dollar received today is more valuable than a dollar received in the future.

Net present value (NPV) is defined as the present value of future returns, discounted at the cost of capital, minus the cost of the investment. The *NPV* method overcomes the conceptual flaws noted in the use of the payback method.

Internal rate of return (IRR) is defined as the interest rate that equates the present value of future returns to the investment outlay. The IRR method, like the *NPV* method, meets the objections to the payback approach.

In most cases, the two discounted cash flow methods give identical answers to these questions: Which of two mutually exclusive projects should be selected? How large should the total capital budget be? However, under certain circumstances conflicts may arise. Such conflicts are caused by the fact that the *NPV* and *IRR* methods make different assumptions about the rate at which cash flows may be reinvested, or the opportunity cost of cash flows. In general, the assumption of the *NPV* method (that the opportunity cost is the cost of capital) is the correct one. Accordingly, our preference is for using the *NPV* method to make capital budgeting decisions.

QUESTIONS

11-1. A firm has $100 million available for capital expenditures. Suppose project A involves the purchase of $100 million of grain, shipping it overseas, and selling it within a year at a profit of $20 million. The project has an *IRR* of 20 percent, an *NPV* of $20 million, *and it will cause earnings per share (EPS) to rise within one year.* Project B calls for the use of the $100 million to develop a new process, acquire land, build a plant, and begin processing. Project B, which is not postponable, has an *NPV* of $50 million and an *IRR* of 30 percent, but the fact that some of the plant costs will be written off immediately, combined with the fact that no revenues will be generated for several years, means that accepting project B will *reduce* short-run *EPS*.

    a. Should the short-run effects on *EPS* influence the choice between the two projects?

    b. How might situations such as the one described here influence a firm's decision to use payback as a screening criterion?

11-2. Are there conditions under which a firm might be better off if it chooses a machine with a rapid payback rather than one with the largest rate of return?

11-3. Company X uses the payback method in evaluating investment proposals and is considering new equipment whose additional net after-tax earnings will be $150 a year. The equipment costs $500 and its expected life is ten years (straight line depreciation). The company uses a three-year payback as its criterion. Should the equipment be purchased under the above assumptions?

11-4. What are the most critical problems that arise in calculating a rate of return for a prospective investment?

11-5. What other factors in addition to rate of return analysis should be considered in determining capital expenditures?

11-6. Would it be beneficial for a firm to review its past capital expenditures and capital budgeting procedures? Why?

11-7. Fiscal and monetary policies are tools used by the government to stimulate the economy. Explain, using the analytical devices developed in this chapter, how each of the following might be expected to stimulate the economy by encouraging investment.

    a. A speed-up of tax-allowable depreciation.

    b. An easing of interest rates.

    c. Passage of a new federal program giving more aid to the poor.

    d. An investment tax credit.

PROBLEMS

11-1. Two projects, Red and Blue, are being considered in this year's capital budget. Calculate the IRR and NPV on each project and indicate the correct adopt-reject decision for each. The projects are not mutually exclusive. Your firm's cost of capital is 12 percent. The outlay for Red is $9869, and it is $17,845 for Blue. Cash flows are shown below:

	Cash Flows	
Year	Red	Blue
1	$3,300	$6,500
2	3,300	6,500
3	3,300	6,500
4	3,300	6,500
5	3,300	6,500

11-2. Two pieces of equipment are available, High Quality (HQ) and Low Quality (LQ). Seeing that they perform the same function, you will choose HQ or LQ, but not both. HQ is more expensive to purchase, but is more productive than LQ because it requires less labor. Calculate NPV and IRR on both projects and decide which project to adopt. The cost of capital is 10 percent. LQ has a cost of $13,302, while HQ costs $16,628.

| | Cash Flows | |
Year	LQ	HQ
1	$4,000	$5,000
2	4,000	5,000
3	4,000	5,000
4	4,000	5,000
5	4,000	5,000
6	4,000	5,000

11-3. Low Calorie Cola is contemplating replacing one of its bottling machines with a newer and more efficient machine. The old machine has a book value of $500,000 and a remaining useful life of five years. The firm does not expect to realize any return from scrapping the old machine in five years, but if it is sold now to another firm in the industry, Low Calorie would receive $300,000 for it.

The new machine has a purchase price of $1.1 million, an estimated useful life of five years, and an estimated salvage value of $100,000. The new machine is expected to economize on electric power usage, labor, and repair costs, and also to reduce defective bottles; in total, an annual saving of $200,000 will be realized if the new machine is installed. (Note: To calculate depreciation, assume that the salvage value *is* deducted from cost to get the depreciable cost.) The company is in the 40 percent tax bracket, has a 10 percent cost of capital, and uses straight line depreciation.

    a. What is the initial cash outlay required for the new machine?
    b. What are the cash flows in years 1–5?
    c. What is the cash flow from the salvage value in year 5?
    d. Should Low Calorie purchase the new machine? Support your answer.
    e. In general, how would each of the following factors affect the investment decision, and how should each be treated?
        1. The expected life of the existing machine decreases.
        2. Capital rationing is imposed on the firm.
        3. The cost of capital is not constant but is rising.
        4. Improvements in the equipment to be purchased are expected to occur each year, and the result will be to increase the returns or expected savings from new machines over the savings expected with this year's model for every year in the foreseeable future.

11-4. The Winfield Company is using a machine whose original cost was $72,000. The machine is two years old and has a current market value of $16,000. The asset is being depreciated over a twelve-year original life toward a zero estimated final salvage value. Depreciation is on a straight line basis, and the tax rate is 50 percent.

Management is contemplating the purchase of a replacement which costs $75,000 and has an estimated salvage value of $10,000. The new machine will have a greater capacity, and annual sales are expected to increase from $1 million to $1.01 million, or by $10,000. Operating efficiencies with the new machine will also produce expected savings of $10,000 a year. Depreciation is on a straight line basis over a ten-year life, the cost of capital is 8 percent, and a 50 percent tax rate is applicable. The company's total depreciation costs are currently $120,000 and total annual operating costs are $800,000.

a. Should the firm replace the asset? Use the method shown in Table 11–7 to solve the problem.

b. How would your decision be affected if a second new machine is available that costs $140,000, has a $20,000 estimated salvage value, and is expected to provide $25,000 in annual savings over its ten-year life? It also increases sales by $10,000 a year. (There are now three alternatives: (1) keep the old machine, (2) replace it with a $75,000 machine, or (3) replace it with a $140,000 machine.) Depreciation is still on a straight line basis. For purposes of answering this question use both the *NPV,* which you must calculate, and the *IRR,* which you may assume to be 25 percent for the $75,000 project and 17 percent for the $140,000 project.

c. Disregarding the changes in part b—that is, under the original assumption that one $75,000 replacement machine is available—how would your decision be affected if a new generation of equipment is expected to be on the market in about two years that will provide increased annual savings and have the same cost, asset life, and salvage value?

d. What factors in addition to the quantitative factors listed above are likely to require consideration in a practical situation?

e. How would your decision be affected if the asset lives of the various alternatives were not the same?

11-5. The Elmwood Company is considering the purchase of a new machine tool to replace an obsolete one. The machine being used for the operation has both a tax book value and a market value of zero; it is in good working order and will last, physically, for at least an additional fifteen years. The proposed machine will perform the operation so much more efficiently that Elmwood engineers estimate that labor, material, and other direct costs of the operation will be reduced $4,500 a year if it is installed. The proposed machine costs $24,000 delivered and installed, and its economic life is estimated to be fifteen years with zero salvage value. The company expects to earn 12 percent on its investment after taxes (12 percent is the firm's cost of capital). The tax rate is 50 percent, and the firm uses straight line depreciation.

a. Should Elmwood buy the new machine?

b. Assume that the tax book value of the old machine had been $6,000, that the annual depreciation charge would have been $400, and that it had no sale value. How do these assumptions affect your answer?

c. Change part b to give the old machine a market value of $4,000.

d. Change part b to assume that the annual saving would be $6,000. (The change in part c is not made; the machine is *not* sold for $4,000.)

e. Rework part a assuming the relevant cost of capital is now 6 percent. What is the significance of this? What can be said about parts b, c, and d under this assumption?

f. In general, how would each of the following factors affect the investment decision, and how should each be treated?

1. The expected life of the existing machine decreases.

2. Capital rationing is imposed on the firm.

3. The cost of capital is not constant but is rising.

4. Improvements in the equipment to be purchased are expected to occur each year, and the result will be to increase the returns or expected savings from new machines over the saving expected with this year's model for every year in the foreseeable future.

11-6. Each of two mutually exclusive projects involves an investment of $6,000. Cash flows (after-tax profits plus depreciation) are $4,000 a year for two years for project S and $1,600 a year for six years for project L.

a. Compute the present value of each project if the firm's cost of capital is 0 percent, 6 percent, 10 percent, 20 percent.

b. Compute the internal rate of return for each project.

c. Graph the present values of the two projects, putting *NPV* on the *Y*-axis and the cost of capital on the *X*-axis.

d. Could you have determined the *IRR* of the projects from your graph? Explain.

e. Which project would you select, assuming no capital rationing and a constant cost of capital of (1) 8 percent, (2) 10 percent, (3) 12 percent? Explain.

f. If capital was severely rationed, which project would you select?

Invertment Decisions
under Uncertainty

12 In order to develop the theory and methodology of capital budgeting in a systematic manner, the "riskiness" of alternative projects was not treated explicitly in the preceding chapter. However, since investors and financial managers are risk averters, they should take into account whether one project is more risky than another when choosing between projects. Several approaches to risk analysis are discussed in this chapter.

We should point out that in the literature of finance, risk analysis is frequently treated in one of two distinctly different ways—either it is ignored, as was done for the most part in the preceding chapter; or it is treated in a highly formalistic, mathematical manner. The first approach, ignoring risk, is dangerous at best and downright misleading at worst. The second, the mathematical approach, is frequently not feasible in business situations because (1) vital statistical information is unavailable and (2) all the theoretical concepts have not yet been completely worked out. We are unwilling to ignore risk, but we are reluctant to take a formal, mathematical approach to the subject in an introductory textbook. Accordingly, we attempt to chart a middle course by presenting the essential elements of risk analysis at an intuitive level.

RISK IN FINANCIAL ANALYSIS

The riskiness of an asset is defined in terms of the likely variability of future returns from the asset. For example, if one buys a $1 million short-term government bond expected to yield 5 percent, then the return on the investment, 5 percent, can be estimated quite precisely, and the investment is defined as

245

relatively risk free. However, if the $1 million is invested in the stock of a company just being organized to prospect for uranium in Central Africa, then the probable return cannot be estimated precisely. The rate of return on the $1 million investment could range from minus 100 percent to some extremely large figure, and because of this high variability, the project is defined as relatively risky. Similarly, sales forecasts for different products of a single firm might exhibit differing degrees of riskiness. For example, Union Carbide might be quite sure that sales of its Eveready batteries will range between 50 and 60 million for the coming year, but be highly uncertain about how many units of a new laser measuring device will be sold during the year.

Risk, then, is associated with project variability—the more variable the expected future returns, the riskier the investment. However, we can define risk more precisely, and it is useful to do so. This more precise definition requires a step-by-step development, which constitutes the remainder of this section.

Probability Distributions

Any investment decision—or, for that matter, almost *any* kind of business decision—implies a forecast of future events that is either explicit or implicit. Ordinarily, the forecast of annual cash flow is a single figure, or *point estimate,* frequently called the "most likely" or "best" estimate. For example, one might forecast that the cash flows from a particular project will be $500 a year for three years.

How good is this point estimate; that is, how confident is the forecaster of his predicted return? Is he very certain, very uncertain, or somewhere in between? This degree of uncertainty can be defined and measured in terms of the forecaster's *probability distribution*—the probability estimates associated with each possible outcome. In its simplest form, a probability distribution could consist of just a few potential outcomes. For example, in forecasting cash flows, we could make an optimistic estimate, a pessimistic estimate, and a most likely estimate; or, alternatively, we could make high, low, and "best guess" estimates. We might expect our high, or optimistic, estimate to be realized if the national economy booms, our pessimistic estimate to hold if the economy is depressed, and our best guess to occur if the economy runs at a normal level. These ranges are illustrated in Table 12–1. The figures in the table represent some improvement over our earlier best-guess estimate of $500, as additional information has been provided. However, some critical information is still missing: How likely is it that we will have a boom, a recession, or normal economic conditions? If we have estimates of the probabilities of these events, we can develop a weighted average cash flow estimate and a measure of our degree of confidence in this estimate. This point is explored in the next section.

TABLE 12–1 Expected Cash Flows under Different Economic Conditions

State of the Economy	Cash Flows
Recession	$400
Normal	500
Boom	600

Risk Comparisons

To illustrate how the probability distribution concept can be used to compare the riskiness of alternative investment projects, suppose we are considering two investment decisions each calling for an outlay of $1,000 and each expected to produce a cash flow of $500 a year for three years. (The best-estimate cash flow is $500 a year for each project.) If the discount rate is 10 percent, we can use the methods developed in the preceding chapter to estimate each project's net present value:

$$NPV = \$500 \times 2.487 - \$1,000$$

$$= \$1,243.50 - \$1,000$$

$$= \$243.50 \text{ for each project.}$$

The projects have the same expected returns; does this mean that they are equally desirable? To answer this question, we need to know whether the projects are also equally risky, since "desirability" depends upon both returns and risk.

Let us suppose that project A calls for the replacement of an old machine used in normal operations by a more efficient one, and the benefits are labor and raw material savings that will result. Project B, on the other hand, calls for the purchase of an entirely new machine to produce a new product, the demand for which is highly uncertain. The replacement machine (project A) will be used more, hence savings will be greater, if demand for the product is high. Expected demand for the new product (project B) is also greatest when the economy is booming.

We stated above that the expected annual returns from each project are $500. Let us assume that these figures were developed in the following manner:

1. First, we estimate project returns under different states of the economy as in Table 12–2. Tables of this kind are typically referred to as *payoff matrices*.

TABLE 12–2 Payoff Matrix for Projects A and B

State of the Economy	Annual Cash Flows	
	Project A	Project B
Recession	$400	$ 0
Normal	500	500
Boom	600	1,000

2. Next, we estimate the likelihood of different states of the economy. Assume our economic forecasts indicate that, given current trends in economic indicators, the chances are 2 out of 10 that a recession will occur, 6 out of 10 that the economy will be normal, and 2 out of 10 that there will be a boom.

3. Redefining the word "chance" as *probability,* we find that the probability of a recession is $2/10 = .2$, or 20 percent; the probability of normal times is $6/10 = .6$, or 60 percent; and the probability of a boom is $2/10 = .2$, or 20 percent. Notice that the probabilities add up to 1.0, or 100 percent: $.2 + .6 + .2 = 1.0$, or 100 percent.

4. Finally, in Table 12–3 we calculate weighted averages of the possible returns by multiplying each dollar return by its probability of occurrence. When column 4 of the table is summed, we obtain a weighted average of the outcomes for each alternative under various states of the economy; this weighted average is defined as the *expected value* of the cash flows from the project. It need not, of course, be equal to the project's outcome for a normal state of the economy, although it is in this case.

TABLE 12–3 Calculation of Expected Values

State of the Economy (1)	Probability of This State's Occurring (2)	Outcome if This State Occurs (3)	(2) × (3) (4)
Project A			
Recession	0.2	$ 400	$ 80
Normal	0.6	500	300
Boom	0.2	600	120
	1.0	Expected value =	$500
Project B			
Recession	0.2	$ 0	$ 0
Normal	0.6	500	300
Boom	0.2	1,000	200
	1.0	Expected value =	$500

We can graph the results shown in Table 12–3 to obtain a picture of the variability of actual outcomes; this is shown in the bar charts in Figure 12–1. The height of each bar signifies the probability that a given outcome will occur. The range of probable outcomes for project A is from $400 to $600, with an average or *expected value* of $500. The expected value for project B is also $500, but the range of possible outcomes is from $0 to $1,000.

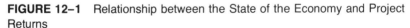

FIGURE 12–1   Relationship between the State of the Economy and Project Returns

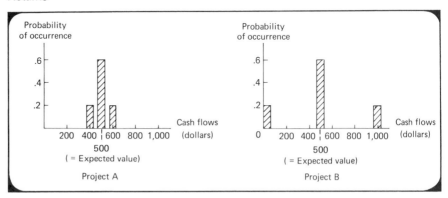

Continuous Distributions   Thus far we have assumed that only three states of the economy can exist: recession, normal, and boom. Actually, of course, the state of the economy could range from a deep depression, as in the early 1930s, to a fantastic boom; and there are an unlimited number of possibilities in between. Suppose we had the time and patience to assign a probability to each possible state of the economy (with the sum of the probabilities still equaling 1.0) and to assign a monetary outcome to each project for each state of the economy. We would have a table similar to Table 12–3 except that it would have many more entries for "Probability" and "Outcome if this state occurs." These tables could be used to calculate expected values as shown above, and the probabilities and outcomes could be graphed as the continuous curves presented in Figure 12–2. Here we have changed the assumptions so that there is zero probability that project A will yield less than $400 or more than $600, and so that there is zero probability that project B will yield less than $0 or more than $1,000.

Figure 12–2 is a graph of the *probability distributions* of returns on projects A and B. In general, the tighter the probability distribution, or, alternatively stated, the more peaked the distribution, the lower the risk on a project. The tighter the probability distribution, of course, the more likely it is that the actual outcome will be close to the expected value. Since project A has a relatively tight probability distribution, its *actual* profits are likely to be closer to the *expected* $500 than are those of project B.

FIGURE 12-2 Probability Distribution Showing Relationship between the State of the Economy and Project Returns

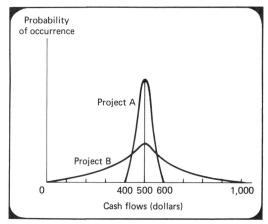

Note: The assumptions regarding the probabilities of various outcomes have been changed from those in Figure 12-1. The probability of obtaining *exactly* $500 was 60 percent in Figure 12-1; in Figure 12-2 it is *much smaller*, because here there are many possible outcomes instead of just three. With continuous distributions as in Figure 12-2, it is more appropriate to ask, "What is the probability of obtaining *at least* some specified value?" than to ask what the probability is of obtaining exactly that value. This cumulative probability is equal to the area under the probability distribution curve up to the point of interest.

Risk versus Uncertainty

Sometimes a distinction is made between *risk* and *uncertainty.* When this distinction is made, risk is associated with those situations in which a probability distribution of the returns on a given project can be estimated; uncertainty is associated with those situations in which insufficient evidence is available even to estimate a probability distribution. We do not make this distinction; risk and uncertainty are used synonymously in this chapter.

We do, however, recognize that probability distributions of expected returns can themselves be estimated with greater or lesser precision. In some instances, the probability distribution can be estimated *objectively* with statistical techniques. For example, a large oil company may be able to estimate from past recovery data the probability distribution of recoverable oil reserves in a given field. When statistical procedures can be used, risk is said to be measured by *objective probability distributions.* There are, however, many situations in which statistical data cannot be used. For example, a company considering the introduction of a totally new product will have some idea about the required investment outlay, the demand for the product, the production costs, and so forth. These estimates will not, however, be determined by statistics; they will be determined subjectively and are defined as *subjective probability distributions.*

Measuring Risk: The Standard Deviation

Risk is a difficult concept to grasp, and a great deal of controversy has surrounded attempts to define and measure it. However, a common definition of risk, and one that is satisfactory for our purposes, is stated in terms of probability distributions such as those presented in Figure 12–2: *The tighter the probability distribution of expected future returns, the smaller the risk of a given project.* According to this definition, project A is less risky than project B because the actual return for A should be closer to the expected return than is true for B.

To be most useful, our measure of risk should have some definite value —we need a *measure* of the tightness of the probability distribution of project returns. One such measure, and the one we shall use, is the *standard deviation,* the symbol for which is σ, read "sigma." The smaller the standard deviation, the tighter the probability distribution and, accordingly, the lower the riskiness of the project.[1] Project A's standard deviation is found to be $63.25; that of project B is $316.20. Other projects available to the firm could be evaluated for riskiness in similar fashion, thus providing the financial manager with information on both the risk (σ) and the expected profitability *(NPV or IRR)* of capital projects.

---

[1] The standard deviation of a distribution is found as follows:

1. Calculate the expected value of the distribution:

$$\text{Expected value} = \bar{R} = \sum_{i=1}^{n} (R_i P_i). \tag{12–1}$$

Here R_i is the return associated with the ith outcome; P_i is the probability of occurrence of that ith outcome; and $\bar{R}$, the expected value, is a weighted average of the various possible outcomes, each weighted by the probability of its occurrence. (See Table 12–3.)

2. Subtract the expected value from each possible outcome to obtain a set of deviations about the expected value:

$$\text{Deviation}_i = R_i - \bar{R}.$$

3. Square each deviation, multiply the squared deviation by the probability of occurrence for its related outcome, and sum these products to obtain the *variance* of the probability distribution:

$$\text{Variance} = \sigma^2 = \sum_{i=1}^{n} (R_i - \bar{R})^2 P_i. \tag{12–2}$$

4. The standard deviation is found by obtaining the square root of the variance:

$$\text{Standard deviation} = \sigma = \sqrt{\sum_{i=1}^{n} (R_i - \bar{R})^2 P_i}. \tag{12–3}$$

5. Calculation of the standard deviation for project A:

Measuring Risk: The Coefficient of Variation

Certain problems can arise when the standard deviation is used as a measure of risk. To illustrate, consider Figure 12–3, which shows the probability distributions for investments C and D. Investment C has an expected return of $1,000 and a standard deviation of $300. Investment D also has a standard deviation of $300, but its expected return is $4,000. The likely percentage deviation from the mean of investment C is considerably higher than that from the mean of investment D, or, put another way, C has more risk *per dollar of return* than D. On this basis, it is reasonable to assign a higher degree of risk to investment C than to investment D even though they have identical standard deviations.

FIGURE 12–3 Probability Distributions of Two Investments with Different Expected Returns

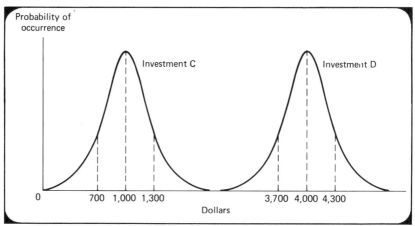

a. The expected value, or the mean, was found in Table 12–3 to be $500.

b.

$R_i - \bar{R}$	$= (R_i - \bar{R})$	$(R_i - \bar{R})^2$	$(R_i - \bar{R})^2 P_i$
400 − 500	− 100	10,000	(10,000)(.2) = 2,000
500 − 500	0	0	(0)(.6) = 0
600 − 500	+ 100	10,000	(10,000)(.2) = 2,000
			σ_A^2 = 4,000

$$\sigma_A = \sqrt{\sigma_A^2} = \sqrt{4,000} = \$63.25.$$

c. By the same procedure, we find project B's standard deviation to be $316.20. Since B's standard deviation is larger, it is the riskier project.

If a probability distribution is normal (symmetrically bell shaped), the *actual outcome* will lie within ± 1 standard deviation of the *expected value* 68 percent of the time.

The best procedure for eliminating this problem is to divide the standard deviation (σ) by the mean expectation ($\overline{R}$) to obtain the *coefficient of variation* (v):

$$v = \frac{\sigma}{\overline{R}}.$$

For investment C, we divide the $300 standard deviation by the $1,000 mean expectation, obtaining .30 as the coefficient of variation; investment D's coefficient of variation is calculated to be .075. Henceforth, we shall use the coefficient of variation to compare the riskiness of alternative investments whenever the standard deviation might be misleading. In general, the coefficient of variation should be used when appraising returns stated in dollars, while the standard deviation is used to appraise the riskiness of returns stated as percentage rates of return.

Riskiness over Time

We can also use Figure 12–2 above to consider the riskiness of a stream of receipts over time. Visualize, for example, investment A as being the expected cash flow from a particular project during year 1, and investment B as being the expected cash flow from the *same* project in the tenth year. The expected return is the same for each of the two years, but the subjectively estimated standard deviation (hence the coefficient of variation) is larger for the more distant return. In this case, riskiness is *increasing over time.*

Figure 12–4 may help to clarify the concept of increasing riskiness over time. Figure 12–4(a) simply shows the probability distribution of expected cash flows in two years—years 1 and 10. The distribution is flatter in year 10, indicating that there is more uncertainty about expected cash flows in distant years. Figure 12–4(b) represents a three-dimensional plot of the expected cash flows over time and their probability distributions. The probability distributions should be visualized as extending out from the page. The dashed lines show the standard deviations attached to the cash flows of each year; the fact that these lines diverge from the expected cash flow line indicates that riskiness is increasing over time. If risk was thought of as being constant over time—that is, if the cash flow in a distant year could be estimated equally as well as the cash flow of a close year—then the standard deviation would be constant and the boundary lines would not diverge from the expected cash flow line. The fact that the standard deviation is increasing over time, while the expected return is constant, would, of course, cause the coefficient of variation to increase similarly.

FIGURE 12–4 Risk as a Function of Time

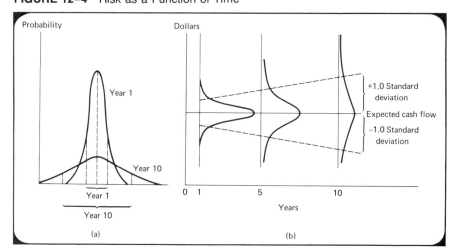

PORTFOLIO RISK

When considering the riskiness of a particular investment, it is frequently use-ful to consider the relationship between the investment in question and other existing assets or potential investment opportunities. To illustrate, a steel company may decide to diversify into residential construction materials. It knows that when the economy is booming, the demand for steel is high and the returns from the steel mill are large. Residential construction, on the other hand, tends to be countercyclical: when the economy as a whole is in a re-cession, the demand for construction materials is high.[2] Because of these divergent cyclical patterns, a diversified firm with investments in both steel and construction could expect to have a more stable pattern of revenues than would a firm engaged exclusively in either steel or residential construction. In other words, the deviations of the returns on the *portfolio of assets,* σ, may be less than the sum of the deviations of the returns from the individual assets.[3]

---

[2]The reason for the countercyclical behavior of the residential construction industry has to do with the availability of credit. When the economy is booming, interest rates are high. High interest rates seem to dis-courage potential home buyers more than they do other demanders of credit. As a result, the residential con-struction industry shows marked countercyclical tendencies.

[3]These conclusions obviously hold also for portfolios of financial assets—stocks and bonds. In fact, the basic concepts of portfolio theory were developed specifically for common stocks by Harry Markowitz and were first presented in his article, "Portfolio Selection," *Journal of Finance,* 7, no. 1 (March 1952), 77–91. The logical extension of portfolio theory to capital budgeting calls for considering firms as having "port-folios of tangible assets."

This point is illustrated in Figure 12–5: 12–5(a) shows the rate of return variations for the steel plant, 12–5(b) shows the fluctuations for the residential construction material division, and 12–5(c) shows the rate of return for the combined company. When the returns from steel are large, those from residential construction are small, and vice versa. As a consequence, the combined rate of return is relatively stable.

FIGURE 12–5 Relationship of Returns on Two Hypothetical Investments

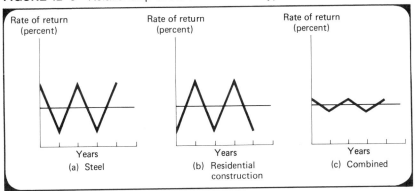

If two sets of data tend to move together, they are said to be *positively correlated*, while if they tend to move in opposite directions, they are *negatively correlated.* If we calculate the correlation between rates of return on the steel and construction divisions, we find the correlation coefficient to be negative—whenever rates of return on the steel plant are high, those on the construction material plants are low. If any two projects, A and B, have a high degree of *negative correlation,* then taking on the two investments reduces the firm's overall risk. This risk reduction is defined as a *portfolio effect.*

On the other hand, if there had been a high *positive correlation* between projects A and B—that is, if returns on A were high at the same time those on B were high—overall risk could not have been reduced significantly by diversification. If the correlation between A and B had been +1.0, the risk reduction would have been zero, so no portfolio effects would have been obtained.

If the returns from the two projects were completely uncorrelated—that is, if the correlation coefficient between them was zero—then diversification would benefit the firm to at least some extent. The larger the number of uncorrelated, or independent, projects the firm takes on, the smaller will be the variation in its overall rate of return.[4] Uncorrelated projects are not as useful for

---

[4]The principle involved here is the so-called law of large numbers. As the number of independent projects is increased, the standard deviation of the returns on the portfolio of projects will decrease with the square root of the number of projects taken on. This statement assumes, of course, that the means and standard deviations of the individual projects are approximately equal.

reducing risk as are negatively correlated ones, but they are better than positively correlated projects.

Correlation coefficients range from +1.0, indicating perfect positive correlations, to −1.0, indicating perfect negative correlation. If the correlation coefficient is zero, then the projects are independent, or uncorrelated.

We can summarize the arguments on portfolio risk that have been presented thus far:

1. If *perfectly negatively correlated* projects are available in sufficient number, then diversification can completely eliminate risk. Perfect negative correlation is, however, almost never found in the real world.
2. If *uncorrelated* projects are available in sufficient number, then diversification can reduce risk significantly—to zero at the limit.
3. If all alternative projects are *perfectly positively correlated,* then diversification does not reduce risk at all.

In fact, most projects are *positively* correlated but not *perfectly* correlated. The degree of intercorrelation among projects depends upon economic factors, and these factors are usually amenable to analysis. Returns on investments in projects closely related to the firm's basic products and markets will ordinarily be highly correlated with returns on the remainder of the firm's assets, and such investments will not generally reduce the firm's risk. However, investments in other product lines and in other geographic markets may have a low degree of correlation with other components of the firm and may, therefore, reduce overall risk. Accordingly, if an asset's returns are not too closely related to the firm's other major assets (or, better still, are negatively correlated with other investments), this asset is more valuable to a risk-averting firm than is a similar asset whose returns are positively correlated with the bulk of the assets. The recognition of this fact was one of the driving forces behind the trend toward conglomerate mergers during the 1950s and 1960s.[5]

ALTERNATIVE METHODS OF TREATING RISK

Investors are, in general, risk averters, so if a firm takes an action that increases its risk level, this action will lower its value, all other things being the

[5]We should, however, make three points. First, if a relatively safe business such as a bank acquires a relatively risky business such as an oil wildcatter, then even though returns on the two businesses are not perfectly correlated, the bank will probably be more risky after the merger than before. Second, when one company acquires another in a different business, there is always a danger that the acquiring firm simply will not know how to run the acquired firm, and that the end result will be low and unstable returns; after all, one major element in risk is degree of expertise, and corporate diversification may lead a management group outside its area of competence. Finally, in this section we have disregarded the possibility of stockholder diversification. Thus a stockholder might buy the stock of steel and construction firms and diversify himself, making diversification at the corporate level unnecessary from the stockholder's viewpoint. More will be said on this point later in the chapter, and also in Chapter 20.

same. To compensate for this, a firm should require a higher expected return on more risky investments than it does on less risky investments. The definition of risk should, of course, include the coefficient of variation of returns on a project; it should also contain the correlation between the returns on a particular project and on the firm's other existing or potential assets (the portfolio effect of the project). For simplification, in this section we shall assume that all projects are perfectly correlated with one another, permitting us to disregard portfolio effects and to define a project's risk simply in terms of its variability.

Several different approaches to risk analysis may be taken. The four most common of these—the *purely informal method,* the *risk-adjusted discount rate method, sensitivity analysis,* and *simulation*—are examined in the following discussion.

Informal Method

The most common method of dealing with risk is on a strictly informal basis. For example, the net present values based on single-valued estimates of annual returns (using the firm's cost of capital) might be calculated. The decision maker would recognize that some projects are riskier than others. If the net present values of two mutually exclusive projects are reasonably close to each other, the less risky one is chosen. The extent by which the *NPV* of the riskier project must exceed that of the less risky project before the riskier project will be selected is not specified—the decision rules are strictly internal to the decision maker.

This approach may be formalized slightly by presenting the decision maker with both the mean expectation and the coefficient of variation of the *NPV*s. These provide him with an objective estimate of risk, but he still chooses among risky projects in an unspecified manner, using judgment factors that have not been reduced to a formal basis.

Risk-Adjusted Discount Rates

An alternative procedure for taking risk into account calls for making adjustments to the discount rate, *k.* Risk-adjusted discount rates are based on investors' tradeoff functions between risk and return. For example, suppose a firm determines that its stockholders are willing to trade between risk and return as shown in Figure 12–6. The upward-sloping line is defined as a *market indifference curve,* or a *risk-return tradeoff function.*[6] The average investor is indifferent to a riskless asset with a sure 5 percent rate of return, a

---

[6]A modified version of the risk-return tradeoff function known as the "capital market line" is defined in Chapter 18.

moderately risky asset with a 7 percent expected return, and a very risky asset with a 15 percent expected return. As risk increases, higher and higher returns on investment are required to compensate investors for the additional risk.

FIGURE 12–6   Hypothetical Relationship between Risk and Rate of Return

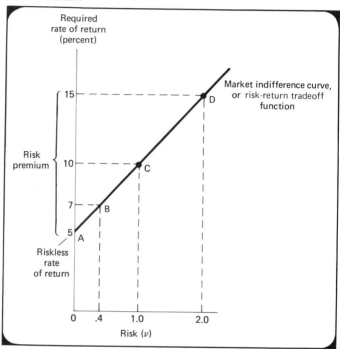

The difference between the required rate of return on a particular risky asset and the rate of return on a riskless asset is defined as the *risk premium* on the risky asset. In the hypothetical situation depicted in Figure 12–6, the riskless rate is assumed to be 5 percent; a 2 percent risk premium is required to compensate for a coefficient of variation of .4, and a 10 percent risk premium is attached to an investment with a coefficient of variation as high as 2.0. The average investor is indifferent between risky investments B, C, and D, and the riskless asset A.

If a particular firm's stock is located at point C on the risk indifference curve—that is, investors expect the rate of return on the stock to be 10 percent, but the coefficient of variation of returns is 1.0—then it should use a 10 percent cost of capital for average projects, higher rates for more risky projects (15 percent at point D, where v = 2.0), and lower rates for less risky projects (7 percent for point B, where v = .4).[7] Obviously, if a firm with a given average

---

[7] For simplification, we assume at this point that the firm is financed with only equity capital. This assumption is relaxed when the cost of capital is considered in detail in Chapter 20.

risk takes on a disproportionately large number of high-risk projects, then the firm's average cost of capital will increase—it will move into a higher risk class.

Using Risk-Adjusted Discount Rates: An Illustration   We can illustrate the use of risk-adjusted discount rates with an example. The Walter Watch Company is considering the manufacture of two mutually exclusive types of watchbands. One band is specifically designed for Walter watches and cannot be used with those of other manufacturers; the other is adaptable to a wide variety of watches, both Walter's and those of competitive watch companies. The expected investment outlay for design, engineering, production setup, and so on, is $100,000 for each alternative. Expected cash inflows are $20,000 a year for eight years if the bands are usable only with Walter watches (project A), and $22,000 a year for eight years if the bands can be used with a wide variety of watches (project B). However, because of its captive market, the standard deviation of expected annual returns from project A is only $3,000, while that of project B is $20,000. In view of this risk differential, Walter Watch's management decides that project A should be evaluated with a 10 percent cost of capital and project B with a 14 percent cost of capital. Which project should be selected?

We can calculate the risk-adjusted *NPV* for each project as follows:

$$NPV_A = \$20,000 \ (IF \text{ for eight-year, 10\% annuity}) - \$100,000$$
$$= \$20,000 \ (5.335) - \$100,000$$
$$= \$6,700.$$
$$NPV_B = \$22,000 \ (IF \text{ for eight-year, 14\% annuity}) - \$100,000$$
$$= \$22,000 \ (4.639) - \$100,000$$
$$= \$2,058.$$

Project B would have had the higher *NPV* if both projects had been evaluated at the same cost of capital, but when different discount rates are used to account for risk differentials, the analysis indicates that Walter Watch should choose the less risky alternative of manufacturing bands for its own watches.

Sensitivity Analysis

The *NPV* of a project will, in the final analysis, depend upon such factors as quantity of sales, sales prices, input costs, and the like. If these values turn out to be favorable—that is, if output and sales prices are high, and costs are low—then profits, the realized rate of return, and the actual *NPV* will be high, and conversely if poor results are experienced. Recognizing these causal relationships, businessmen often calculate projects' *NPV*s under alternative assumptions, then see just how sensitive *NPV* is to changing conditions. One example that recently came to the authors' attention involves a fertilizer company that was comparing two alternative types of phosphate plants. Fuel represents a major cost, and one plant uses coal, which may be obtained under a long-term, fixed-cost contract, while the other uses oil, which must be purchased at current market prices. Considering present and projected future prices, the oil-fired plant looks better—it has a considerably higher *NPV*. However, oil prices are volatile, and if prices rise by more than the expected rate, this plant will be unprofitable. The coal-fired plant, on the other hand, has a lower *NPV* under the expected conditions, but this *NPV* is not sensitive to changing conditions in the energy market. The company finally selected the coal plant because the sensitivity analysis indicated it to be less risky.

Monte Carlo Simulation Analysis

Sensitivity analysis as practiced by the fertilizer company described above is informal in the sense that no probabilities are attached to the likelihood of various outcomes. Monte Carlo *simulation analysis* represents a refinement which does employ probability estimates. In this section we first describe how *decision trees* can be used to attach probabilities to different outcomes, and then we illustrate how full-scale computer simulation can be employed to analyze major projects.

Decision Trees   Most important decisions are not made once-and-for-all at one point in time. Rather, decisions are made in stages. For example, a petroleum firm considering the possibility of expanding into agricultural chemicals might take the following steps: (1) spend $100,000 for a survey of supply-demand conditions in the agricultural chemical industry; (2) if the survey results are favorable, spend $500,000 on a pilot plant to investigate production methods; and (3) depending on the costs estimated from the pilot study and the demand potential from the market study, either abandon the project, build a large plant, or build a small one. Thus, the final decision actually is made in stages, with subsequent decisions depending on the results of previous decisions.

The sequence of events can be mapped out like the branches of a tree, hence the name *decision tree*. As an example, consider Figure 12–7. There it is assumed that the petroleum company has completed its industry supply-demand analysis and pilot plant study, and has determined that it should proceed to develop a full-scale production facility. The firm must decide whether to build a large plant or a small one. Demand expectations for the plant's products are 50 percent for high demand, 30 percent for medium demand, and 20 percent for low demand. Depending upon demand, net cash flows (sales revenues minus operating costs, all discounted to the present) will range from $8.8 million to $1.4 million if a large plant is built, and from $2.6 million to $1.4 million if a small plant is built.

FIGURE 12–7   Illustrative Decision Tree

Action (1)	Demand conditions (2)	Probability (3)	Present value of cash flows (4)	Less Initial Cost (5)	Possible *NPV* [(4) - (5)] (6)	Column (6) times Column (3) (7)
	high	.5	$8,800,000	$5,000,000	$3,800,000	$1,900,000
	medium	.3	$3,500,000	$5,000,000	($1,500,000)	($450,000)
Build big plant: invest $5 million	low	.2	$1,400,000	$5,000,000	($3,600,000)	($720,000)
Decision point					Expected *NPV*	$730,000
Build small plant: invest $2 million	high	.5	$2,600,000	$2,000,000	$600,000	$300,000
	medium	.3	$2,400,000	$2,000,000	$400,000	$120,000
	low	.2	$1,400,000	$2,000,000	($600,000)	($120,000)
					Expected *NPV*	$300,000

Note: The figures in column 4 are the annual cash flows from operations—sales revenues minus cash operating costs—discounted at an appropriate rate.

The initial costs of the large and small plants are shown in column 5; when these investment outlays are subtracted from the *PV* of cash flows, the result is the set of possible *NPV*s shown in column 6. One, but only one, of these *NPV*s will actually occur. Finally, we multiply column 6 by column 3 to obtain column 7, and the sums in column 7 give the expected *NPV*s of the large and small plants.

Because the expected *NPV* of the larger plant ($730,000) is larger than that of the small plant ($300,000), should the decision be to build the large plant? Perhaps, but not necessarily. Notice that the range of outcomes is greater if the large plant is built, with the possible *NPV*s (column 4 in Figure 12–7 minus the investment cost) varying from $3.8 million to *minus* $3.6 million. However, a range of only $600,000 to minus $600,000 exists for the small plant. Since the required investments for the two plants are not the same, we must examine the coefficients of variation of the net present value possibilities in order to determine which alternative actually entails the greater risk. The coefficient of variation for the large plant's present value is 4.3, while that for the small plant is only 1.5.[8] Thus, risk is greater if the decision is to build the large plant.

[8] Using Equation 12–3 and the data on possible returns in Figure 12–7, the standard deviation of returns for the larger plant is found to be $3.155 million, and that for the smaller one is $458,260. Dividing each of these standard deviations by the expected returns for their respective plant size gives the coefficients of variation.

Computer Simulation

The concepts embodied in decision tree analysis can be extended to computer simulation. To illustrate the technique, let us consider a proposal to build a new textile plant. The cost of the plant is not known for certain, although it is expected to run about $150 million. If no problems are encountered, the cost can be as low as $125 million, while an unfortunate series of events— strikes, unprojected increases in materials costs, technical problems, and the like—could result in the investment outlay running as high as $225 million.

Revenues from the new facility, which will operate for many years, will depend on population growth and income in the region, competition, developments in synthetic fabrics research, and textile import quotas. Operating costs will depend on production efficiency, materials and labor cost trends and the like. Since both sales revenues and operating costs are uncertain, annual profits are also uncertain.

Assuming that probability distributions can be assigned to each of the major cost and revenue determinants, a computer program can be constructed to simulate what is likely to happen. In effect, the computer selects one value at random from each of the relevant distributions, combines it with other values selected from the other distributions, and produces an estimated profit and net present value or rate of return on investment.[9] This particular profit and rate of return occur, of course, only for the particular combination of values selected during this trial. The computer goes on to select other sets of values and to compute other profits and rates of return repeatedly, for perhaps several hundred trials. A count is kept of the number of times each rate of return is computed, and when the computer runs are completed, the frequency with which the various rates of return occurred can be plotted as a frequency distribution.

The procedure is illustrated in Figures 12–8 and 12–9.[10] Figure 12–8 is a flow chart outlining the simulation procedure described above while Figure 12–9 illustrates the frequency distribution of rates of return generated by such a simulation for two alternative projects, X and Y, each with an expected cost of $20 million. The expected rate of return on investment X is 15 percent, and that of investment Y is 20 percent. However, these are only the *average* rates of return generated by the computer; simulated rates range from −10 percent to +45 percent for investment Y and from 5 to 25 percent for investment X. The standard deviation generated for X is only 4 percentage points—68 percent of the computer runs had rates of return between 11 and 19 percent— while that for Y is 12 percentage points. Clearly, then, investment Y is riskier than investment X.

---

[9] If the variables are not independent, then conditional probabilities must be employed. For example, if demand is weak, then both sales in units and sales prices are likely to be low, and these interrelationships must be taken into account in the simulation.

[10] The methodology illustrated in Figure 12–8 was developed in an article by David B. Hertz, "Risk Analysis in Capital Investment," *Harvard Business Review* (January–February 1964), 95–106.

FIGURE 12–8   Simulation for Investment Planning

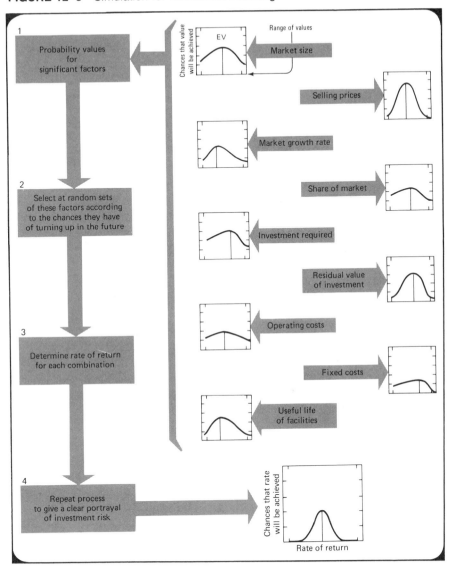

The computer simulation has provided us with both an estimate of the expected returns on the two projects and an estimate of their relative risks. A decision about which alternative should be chosen can now be made, perhaps by using the risk-adjusted discount rate method or perhaps in a judgmental, informal manner by the decision-maker.

FIGURE 12–9 Expected Rates of Return on Investments X and Y

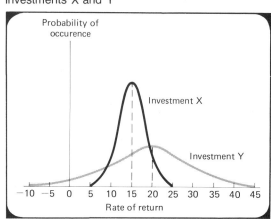

However, computer simulation is not always feasible for risk analysis. The technique involves obtaining probability distributions about a number of variables—investment outlays, unit sales, product prices, input prices, asset lives, and so on—and a fair amount of programming and machine-time costs. Therefore, full-scale simulation is not generally worthwhile except for large and expensive projects, such as major plant expansions or new-product decisions. In those cases, however, when a firm is deciding whether to accept a major undertaking involving millions of dollars, computer simulation can provide valuable insights into the relative merits of alternative strategies.

PUBLIC EXPENDITURE DECISIONS

Before concluding this chapter, we should point out that capital budgeting under uncertainty is a problem facing government agencies as well as firms. A series of hearings before Congress on methods and procedures of capital budgeting at the federal level revealed (1) that congressional leaders and the heads of the major governmental agencies agreed that governmental capital budgeting should be conducted under a method equivalent to our risk-adjusted discount rate procedure, but (2) that federal agencies are having a difficult time determining appropriate discount rates.[11] In other words, the federal government tends to follow the same capital budgeting procedures as do the more sophisticated business firms, and the procedures described in this chapter and the preceding one are applicable to both.

[11] U.S. Congress, Subcommittee on Economy in Government of the Joint Economic Committee, *Economic Analysis of Public Investment Decisions: Interest Rate Policy and Discounting Analysis* (Washington, D.C.: U.S. Government Printing Office, 1968).

SUMMARY

Two facts of life in finance are (1) that investors are averse to risk and (2) that at least some risk is inherent in most business decisions. Given investor aversion to risk and differing degrees of risk in different financial alternatives, it is necessary to consider risk in financial analysis.

Our first task is to define what we mean by risk; our second task is to measure it. The concept of *probability* is a fundamental element in both the definition and the measurement of risk. A *probability distribution* shows the probability of occurrence of each possible outcome, assuming a given investment is undertaken. The mean, or weighted average, of the distribution is defined as the *expected value* of the investment. The *coefficient of variation* of the distribution or, sometimes, the *standard deviation,* both of which measure the extent to which actual outcomes are likely to vary from the expected value, are used as measures of risk.

Under most circumstances, more distant returns are considered to be more risky than near-term returns. Thus, the standard deviation and coefficient of variation for distant cash flows are likely to be higher than those for cash flows expected relatively soon, even when the cash flows are from the same project.

In appraising the riskiness of an individual capital investment, not only the variability of the expected returns of the project itself but also the correlation between expected returns on this project and the remainder of the firm's assets must be taken into account. This relationship is called the *portfolio effect* of the particular project. Favorable portfolio effects are strongest when a project is negatively correlated with the firm's other assets, weakest when positive correlation exists. Portfolio effects lie at the heart of the firm's efforts to diversify into product lines not closely related to the firm's main line of business.

Risk differentials are frequently dealt with in a strictly informal manner. However, as firms become increasingly sophisticated, greater and greater efforts are being expended to deal with risk in a formal manner. When risk is treated formally, the most common technique is the *risk-adjusted discount rate method,* which increases the cost of capital used to discount more risky projects' returns. To use this method, the firm must first estimate investors' *risk-return tradeoff function,* then use this estimate to develop *risk premiums* for the riskier projects. A great deal of judgment is necessary when implementing this concept, but more and more firms are deciding that even inexact attempts to account for risk are better than no attempts at all.

Decision-making under uncertainty, especially for large projects, is facilitated by two other analytical techniques: *decision trees* and *simulation analysis.* Decision trees map out the sequence of events in a decision problem, helping a firm to trace events through time and to examine the complex set of probabilities. Computer simulation is used to generate frequency distributions of possible outcomes *(stochastic simulation)* or to determine the effects of changes in various operating conditions *(sensitivity analysis)*.

QUESTIONS

12-1. Define the following terms, using graphs to illustrate your answers wherever feasible:
   a. risk
   b. uncertainty
   c. probability distribution
   d. expected value
   e. standard deviation
   f. coefficient of variation
   g. portfolio effects
   h. risk-adjusted discount rate

12-2. The probability distribution of a less risky expected return is more peaked than that of a risky return. What shape would the probability distribution have (1) for completely certain returns and (2) for completely uncertain returns?

12-3. Project A has an expected return of $500 and a standard deviation of $100. Project B also has a standard deviation of $100 but an expected return of $300. Which project is the more risky? Why?

12-4. Assume that residential construction and industries related to it are countercyclical to the economy in general and to steel in particular. Does this negative correlation between steel and construction-related industries necessarily mean that a savings and loan association, whose profitability tends to vary with construction levels, would be less risky if it diversified by acquiring a steel distributor?

12-5. "The use of the market indifference curve concept illustrated in Figure 12–6 as a basis for determining risk-adjusted discount rates is all right in theory, but it cannot be applied in practice. Investors' reactions to risk cannot be measured precisely, so it is actually impossible to construct a set of risk-adjusted discount rates for different classes of investment." Comment on this statement.

12-6. What is the value of decision trees in managerial decision making?

12-7. In computer simulation, the computer makes a large number of "trials" to show what the various outcomes of a particular decision might be if the decision could be made many times under the same conditions. In practice, the decision will be made only once, so how can simulation results be useful to the decision-maker?

PROBLEMS

12-1. An investment proposal has been analyzed and the following information has been established.

	Cash Flow
Probability	Amount
.3	$15,000
.5	20,000
.2	25,000

The outlay is $100,000, the expected life is ten years, and your cost of capital is 12 percent. Assume zero salvage.

  a. Calculate the expected NPV and expected IRR.

  b. Calculate the probability that the investment will be a good one, i.e., have NPV > O.

12-2. The Rowan Company is faced with two mutually exclusive investment projects. Each project costs $4,500 and each has an expected life of three years. Annual net cash flows from each project begin one year after the initial investment is made and have the following probability distributions.

	Probability	Cash Flow
Project A:	2	$ 4,000
	.6	4,500
	.2	5,000
Project B:	.2	0
	.6	4,500
	.2	12,000

Rowan has decided to evaluate the riskier project at a 12 percent rate and the less risky project at a 10 percent rate.

  a. What is the expected value of the annual net cash flows from each project?

  b. What is the risk-adjusted *NPV* of each project?

  c. If it were known that project B was negatively correlated with other cash flows of the firm, while project A was positively correlated, how would this knowledge affect your decision?

12-3. Your firm is considering the purchase of a tractor. It has been established that this tractor will cost $32,000, will produce revenues in the neighborhood of $10,000 (before tax), and will be depreciated via straight line to zero in eight years. The board of directors, however, had a heated debate as to whether the tractor could be expected to last eight years. Specifically, Wayne Brown insisted that he knew of some which had lasted five years only. Tom Miller agreed with Wayne but argued that it was more likely that the tractor would give eight years of service. Wayne agreed. Finally, Ralph Evans said he had seen some last as long as ten years. Given this discussion, the board asked you to prepare a sensitivity analysis to ascertain how important the uncertainty about the life of the tractor is. Assume a 40 percent tax rate on both income and capital loss, zero salvage value, and a cost of capital of 10 percent.

12-4. You have an investment opportunity for which the outlay as well as cash flows are uncertain. Careful analysis has produced the following subjective probability assessments.

Outlay		Annual Cash Flow	
Probability	Amount	Probability	Amount
.4	$80,000	.2	$14,000
.3	100,000	.5	16,000
.2	120,000	.3	18,000
.1	140,000		

Let your cost of capital be 12 percent, life expectancy ten years, and zero salvage.

a. Construct a decision tree for this investment to show probabilities, payoffs, and expected NPV.

b. Calculate the expected NPV, again using expected cash flow and expected outlay.

c. What is the probability of and the NPV of the worst possible outcome?

d. What is the probability of and the NPV of the best possible outcome?

e. Compute the probability that this will be a good investment.

12–5. Suppose that the life of the investment in problem 12–4 is also uncertain, and that you have secured the following subjective probability assessment for the life of the investment.

Investment Life	
Probability	Years
.2	8
.6	10
.2	12

a. Calculate the expected NPV incorporating this new information. Explain why this is the same as before.

b. Show how to draw an expanded decision tree with this information, but do not fill in all the numbers.

Sources and Forms of Long-Term Financing

Part Four

In the introductory section, we analyzed the firm in an overall, aggregate sense. Next, in Part Two, we considered the top half of the balance sheet, analyzing current assets, current liabilities, and the interactions between the two. Then, in Part Three, we moved to the lower left side of the balance sheet, examining the process by which firms decide on investments in fixed assets. Now, in Part Four, we move to the lower right side of the balance sheet, to consider the various types of long-term funds available to the firm when it seeks long-term external capital.

Chapter 13 presents an overview of the capital markets, explaining briefly certain institutional material without which no basic finance course is complete. Chapter 14 analyzes the financial characteristics of common stock; Chapter 15 examines bonds and preferred stock; Chapter 16 analyzes term loans and leases; and Chapter 17 discusses the nature and use of warrants and convertibles. This institutional background is essential for an understanding of Part Five, Financial Structure and the Cost of Capital, where we take up the question of the optimal mix of long-term funds.

The Market for Long-Term Securities

SECURITY MARKETS

There are two basic types of security markets—the *organized exchanges,* typified by the New York Stock Exchange, and the less formal *over-the-counter markets.*[1] Since the organized exchanges have actual physical market locations and are easier to describe and understand, we shall consider them first. With this foundation it will be easier to comprehend the nature of the over-the-counter market.

Organized Security Exchanges

The organized security exchanges are tangible, physical entities. Each of the larger ones occupies its own building, has specifically designated members, and has an elected governing body—its board of governors. Members are said to have "seats" on the exchange, although everybody stands up. These seats, which are bought and sold, represent the right to trade on the exchange. In 1968, seats on the New York Stock Exchange (NYSE) sold at a record high of $515,000; in 1975 they sold for about $65,000.

Most of the larger stock brokerage firms own seats on the exchanges and designate one or more of the officers of the firm as members of the exchange. The exchanges are open daily, and the members meet in a large room equipped with telephones, telegraphs, and other electronic equipment that

[1]There is also a "private" market in which the borrowing firm goes directly to the lending institutions; this is the market for *private placements,* or *direct placements,* as it is frequently called. The primary instrument used in this market is the *term* loan, described in Chapter 16.

enables each brokerage house member to communicate with the offices of his firm throughout the country.

Like other markets, a security exchange facilitates communication between buyers and sellers. For example, Merrill Lynch, Pierce, Fenner and Smith, Inc., (the largest brokerage firm) might receive an order in its Atlanta office from a customer who wants to buy 100 shares of General Motors stock. Simultaneously, a brokerage house in Denver might receive an order from a customer wishing to sell 100 shares of GM. Each broker would communicate by wire with his firm's representative on the NYSE. Other brokers throughout the country are also communicating with their own exchange members. The exchange members with *sell orders* offer the shares for sale and they are bid for by the members with *buy orders.* Thus, the exchanges operate as *auction markets.*[2]

Special procedures are available for handling large blocks of securities. For example, if General Motors, whose stock is already listed on the NYSE, plans to sell a new issue of stock, the exchange has facilities that make it easier for the market to absorb the new issue. Similarly, if a large mutual fund or pension fund wants to sell a large block of a listed stock, procedures are available that facilitate the sale without putting undue pressures on the stock price.

Stock Market Reporting

Securities that are traded on the organized security exchanges are called *listed securities,* and are distinguished from other securities, known as *unlisted securities.* (Unlisted securities are traded in the over-the-counter market, which is discussed below.)

Quite a lot of information is available dealing with transactions among listed securities, and the very existence of this information reduces the uncertainty inherent in security investments. This reduction of uncertainty, of course, makes listed securities relatively attractive to investors, and it lowers the cost of capital to firms.[3] We cannot delve deeply into the matter of financial reporting—this is more properly the field of investment analysis—but it is useful to explain the most widely used service, the New York Stock Exchange reporting system.

Figure 13–1 is a section of "the stock market page" taken from the *Wall Street Journal* of April 28, 1976. Stocks are listed alphabetically, the first being Abbott Labs, a drug company. The two columns on the left show the highest and the lowest prices at which the stocks have sold during the year; Abbott has traded in the range from $47½ to $37¾. The figure just to the right of the

---

[2]This discussion is highly simplified. The exchanges have members known as "specialists," who facilitate the trading process by keeping an inventory of shares of the stocks in which they specialize. If a buy order comes in at a time when no sell order arrives, the specialist may sell off some of his inventory. Similarly, if a sell order comes in, the specialist will buy and add to his inventory.

[3]If you think the stock markets today are risky, just imagine what it was like in the era *before* the existence of the SEC, routine reporting, and the like!

company's abbreviated name is the dividend expected for the year; Abbott Labs is expected to pay $0.88 a share in 1976. Next comes the *P/E* ratio, or the current price of the stock divided by its earnings per share during the last year. (Price/earnings ratios are discussed at some length in Chapter 18.)

FIGURE 13–1 Stock Market Transactions

| –1976– | | | P.E. | Sales | | | | Net |
High	Low	Stocks Div.	Ratio	100s	High	Low	Close	Chg.
		–A–A–A–						
47½	37¾	AbbtLab .88	16	172	46	44¼	44⅞–	1⅛
51⅞	38	ACF In 2.60	9	140	49½	48⅞	48⅞–	½
10¼	8⅛	AcmeClv .50	7	11	9⅜	9⅛	9⅛+	⅛
4½	2¾	AdmDg .04e	7	19	3¾	3½	3⅜	. . .
12⅜	9⅞	AdmEx .91e	. . .	30	11⅜	11¼	11⅜+	¼
5¾	4	Adms Millis	8	37	5⅛	4⅞	5	. . .
13½	7¾	Addressog	15	92	9⅞	9⅜	9½	. . .
9¾	7¼	AdvInv .18e	. . .	10	9	8⅞	9 +	⅛
28	22½	AetnaLf 1.08	14	625	26⅝	26⅛	26⅛–	⅜
9¼	4⅜	Aguirre Co	90	3	8⅛	8⅛	8⅛–	⅛
14⅜	9⅝	Ahmans .20	7	42	13⅞	13½	13½–	¼
6⅞	2⅞	Aileen Inc	18	33	4¼	4	4⅛	. . .
82⅝	68⅝	AirPrd .20b	20	24	80¾	80⅜	80⅜–	⅜
20⅜	13	AirbnFrt .60	16	109	20⅞	20⅝	20⅝+	¼
26½	17¼	AircoInc 1	7	202	26⅜	26	26¼+	¾
4	1⅞	AJ Industris	8	20	3⅛	3	3	. . .
25¾	18⅜	Akzona 1.20	14	33	23⅜	23⅛	23⅜–	⅛
15⅞	13⅛	Ala Gas 1.28	8	5	14⅜	14¼	14⅜+	⅛

After the *P/E* ratio comes the volume of trading for the day; 17,200 shares of Abbott Labs stock were traded on April 27, 1976. Following the volume come the high and the low prices for the day and the closing price. On April 27 Abbott traded as high as $46 and as low as $44¼, while the last trade was at $44⅞ (or $44.875). The last column gives the change from the closing price on the previous day. Abbott Labs was down 1⅛, or $1.125, so the previous close must have been $46 (since $46 – 1⅛ = $44⅞, the indicated closing price on April 27.)

A set of footnotes always accompanies the stock market quotes, giving additional information about specific issues. Most of these notes refer to dividends, and they can best be understood after our discussion of this topic in Chapter 21, so we defer further comment on Figure 13–1 until that chapter.

Benefits Provided by Security Exchanges

Organized security exchanges are said to provide important benefits to businesses in at least four ways.

1. Security exchanges facilitate the investment process by providing a marketplace in which to conduct transactions efficiently and relatively inexpensively. Investors are thus assured that they will have a place in which to sell their securities, if they decide to do so. The increased liquidity thus provided by the exchanges makes investors willing to accept a lower rate of return on securities than they would otherwise require. This means that exchanges lower the cost of capital to businesses.

2. By providing a market, exchanges create an institution in which continuous transactions test the values of securities. The purchases and sales of securities record judgments on the values and prospects of companies and their securities. Companies whose prospects are judged favorably by the investment community will have higher values, thus facilitating new financing and growth.
3. Security prices are relatively more stable because of the operation of the security exchanges. Organized markets improve liquidity by providing continuous markets which make for more frequent, but smaller, price changes. In the absence of organized markets, price changes would be less frequent but more violent.
4. The securities markets aid in the digestion of new security issues and facilitate their successful flotation.

These benefits are important, but not all firms are in a position to utilize the exchanges. Such firms can, however, get many of the same benefits by having their securities traded in the over-the-counter market.

OVER-THE-COUNTER SECURITY MARKETS

In contrast to the formal security exchanges, the over-the-counter market is a nebulous, intangible organization. Perhaps an explanation of the name "over the counter" will help clarify exactly what this market is. The exchanges operate as auction markets—buy and sell orders come in more-or-less simultaneously, and the exchanges are used to match these orders. But if a stock is traded less frequently, perhaps because it is the stock of a new or a small firm, few buy and sell orders come in, and matching them within a reasonable length of time would be difficult. To avoid this problem, brokerage firms maintain an inventory of the stocks. They buy when individual investors wish to sell, and sell when investors want to buy. At one time the inventory of securities was kept in a safe, and when bought and sold, the stocks were literally passed "over the counter."

Today, over-the-counter markets are defined as all facilities that provide for security transactions not conducted on the organized exchanges. These facilities consist primarily (1) of the relatively few brokers who hold inventories of over-the-counter securities and who are said to "make a market" in these securities and (2) of the thousands of brokers who act as agents in bringing these dealers together with investors. The dealers who make a market in a particular stock will, upon request, quote a price at which they are willing to buy the stock (the "bid" price) and a price at which they will sell shares (the "asked" price). The spread between bid and asked prices represents the dealer's mark-up, or profit.

In terms of numbers of issues, the majority of stocks are traded over the counter. However, because the stocks of larger companies are listed on the exchanges, it is estimated that two-thirds of the dollar volume of stock trading takes place on the exchanges. The situation is reversed in the bond market. Although the bonds of a number of the larger companies are listed on the NYSE bond list, over 95 percent of bond transactions take place in the over-the-counter market. The reason for this is that bonds typically are traded among the large financial institutions, for example, life insurance companies and pension funds, which deal in very large blocks of securities. It is relatively easy for the over-the-counter bond dealers to arrange the transfer of large blocks of bonds among the relatively few holders of the bonds. It would be impossible to conduct similar operations in the stock market among the literally millions of large and small stockholders.[4]

DECISION TO LIST STOCK

The exchanges have certain requirements that firms must meet before their stock can be listed—these requirements relate to size of company, number of years in business, earnings record, number of shares outstanding and their market value, and the like. In general, requirements become more stringent as we move from the regional exchanges toward the NYSE.

The firm itself makes the decision to seek to list or not to list its securities on an exchange. Typically, the stocks of new and small companies are traded over the counter—there is simply not enough activity to justify the use of an auction market for such stocks. As the company grows, establishes an earnings record, expands the number of shares outstanding, and increases its list of stockholders, it may decide to apply for listing on one of the regional exchanges. For example, a Chicago company might list on the Midwest Stock Exchange, or a West Coast company might list its stock on the Pacific Coast Exchange. As the company grows still more, and as its stock becomes distributed throughout the country, it may seek a listing on the American Stock Exchange, the smaller of the two national exchanges. Finally, if it becomes one of the nation's leading firms, it could switch to the Big Board, the New York Stock Exchange.

[4]During the 1960s and 1970s two new kinds of market were developed—the so-called "third market" and "fourth market." The third market refers to trades of large blocks of listed stocks off the floor of the exchange, with a brokerage house acting as an intermediary between two institutional investors. The fourth market refers to direct transfers of blocks of stock among institutional investors without an intermediary broker. These trends are leading to a drastic restructuring of the security markets, but the materials in this chapter are valid under any likely developments.

Also, in the 1970s yet another market was developed—the *options* market, wherein investors (or speculators) trade in options to buy stocks. To illustrate options trading, on April 27, 1976 Union Carbide stock closed on the NYSE at $72¼. One could buy on the Chicago Board Options Exchange (CBOE), the largest options exchange, an option (called a "call") to buy 100 shares of Union Carbide at a price of $70 anytime within the next 180 days. The price of the option was $662.50, or $6.625 per share. Thus, a premium of $4.38 per share ($6.625 − ($72.25 − $70) = $4.38) is paid for the option. If Carbide goes up by more than $4.38 during the next six months, the options purchaser will make a profit. Otherwise, he loses.

Assuming a company qualifies, many people believe that listing is beneficial both to it and to its stockholders. Listed companies receive a certain amount of free advertising and publicity, and their status as a listed company enhances their prestige and reputation. This probably has a beneficial effect on the sales of the products of the firm, and it probably is advantageous in terms of lowering the required rate of return on the common stock. Investors respond favorably to increased information, increased liquidity, and increased prestige; by providing investors with these services in the form of listing their companies' stocks, financial managers lower their firms' costs of capital.

INVESTMENT BANKING

In the American economy, saving is done by one group of persons, while investing is done by another. ("Investing" is used here in the sense of actually putting money into plant, equipment, and inventory, not in the sense of buying securities.) Thus, savings are placed with financial intermediaries who, in turn, make the funds available to firms wishing to acquire plant and equipment and to hold inventories.

One of the major institutions performing this channeling role is the *investment banking* institution. The term "investment banker" is somewhat misleading in that investment bankers are neither investors nor bankers. That is, they do not invest their own funds permanently nor are they repositories for individuals' funds, as are commercial banks or savings banks. What, then, is the nature of investment banking?

The many activities of investment bankers may be described first in general terms and then with respect to specific functions. The historical and traditional function of the investment banker has been to act as the middleman in channeling driblets of savings and funds of individuals into the purchase of business securities, primarily bonds. The investment banker does this by purchasing and distributing the new securities of individual companies. Specifically, the investment banker performs the functions of underwriting, distribution of securities, and advice and counsel.

Underwriting

Underwriting is the insurance function of bearing the risks of adverse price fluctuations during the period in which a new issue of securities is being distributed. The nature of the underwriting function of the investment banker can best be conveyed by an example. A business firm needs $10 million. It selects an investment banker, conferences are held, and the decision is made to issue $10 million of bonds. An underwriting agreement is drawn up; on a specific day, the investment banker presents the company with a check for $10 million (less commission). In return, the investment banker receives bonds in denominations of $1,000 each, which he sells to the public.

The company receives the $10 million about eight days after the offering. Often the banker has sold the issue by this time. However, it can take the investment banker ten, twenty, thirty days, six months, or longer to sell bonds. If in the interim the bond market collapses, the investment banker will be carrying the risk of loss on the sale of the bonds.

There have been dramatic instances of bond market collapses within one week after an investment banker has bought $50 million or $100 million of bonds. For example, in the spring of 1974 an issue of New Jersey Sporting Arena bonds dropped $140 per $1,000 bond during the underwriting period, costing the underwriters an estimated $8 million loss. However, the issuing firm does not need to be concerned about the risk of market price fluctuations while the investment banker is selling the bonds. The firm has received its money. *One fundamental economic function of the investment banker, then, is to underwrite the risk of a decline in the market price between the time the investment banker transmits the money to the firm and the time the bonds are placed in the hands of their ultimate buyers.* For this reason, the investment banker is often called an *underwriter:* he is an underwriter of risk during the distribution period.

Distribution

The second function of the investment banker is marketing new issues of securities. The investment banker is a specialist who has a staff and dealer organization to distribute securities. He can, therefore, perform the physical distribution function more efficiently and more economically than could an individual corporation. Sporadically, whenever it wished to sell an issue of securities, each corporation would find it necessary to establish a marketing or selling organization. This would be a very expensive and ineffective method of selling securities. The investment banker has a permanent, trained staff and dealer organization continually available to distribute the securities. In addition, the investment banker's reputation for selecting good companies and pricing securities fairly builds up a broad clientele over a period, further increasing the ease with which he can sell securities.

Advice and Counsel

Since the investment banker is engaged in the origination and sale of securities, through experience he becomes an expert in advising about terms and characteristics of securities that will appeal to investors. The advice and guidance of the investment banker in determining the characteristics and provisions of securities so that they will be successfully marketed is valuable. Furthermore, the reputation of the investment banker, as a seller of the securities, depends upon the subsequent performance of the securities. Therefore, he will often sit on the boards of directors of firms whose securities he has sold. In this way he is able to provide continuing financial counsel and to increase the firm's probability of success.

INVESTMENT BANKING OPERATION

Probably the best way to gain a clear understanding of the investment banking function is to trace the history of a new issue of securities.[5] Accordingly, in this section we describe the steps necessary to issue new securities.

Preunderwriting Conferences

First, the members of the issuing firm and the investment banker hold preunderwriting conferences, at which they discuss the amount of capital to be raised, the type of security to be issued, and the terms of the agreement.

Memorandums will be written by the treasurer of the issuing company to the firm's directors and other officers, describing alternative proposals suggested at the conferences. Meetings of the board of directors of the issuing company will be held to discuss the alternatives and to attempt to reach a decision.

At some point, the issuer enters an agreement with the investment banker that a flotation will take place. The investment banker will then begin to conduct an underwriting investigation. If the company is proposing to purchase additional assets, the underwriter's engineering staff may make an analysis of the proposed acquisition. A public accounting firm will be called upon to make an audit of the issuing firm's financial situation and they will also aid in the preparation of the registration statements for the Securities and Exchange Commission (SEC) in connection with these issues.

A firm of lawyers will be called in to interpret and judge the legal aspects of the flotation. In addition, the originating underwriter, who will be the manager of the subsequent underwriting syndicate, will make an exhaustive investigation of the prospects of the company.

When the investigations are completed but before registration with the SEC, an underwriting agreement will be drawn up by the investment banker. Terms of the tentative underwriting agreement may be modified through discussions between the underwriter and the issuing company, but finally an agreement will be reached on all underwriting terms except the actual price of the securities.

Registration Statement

A registration statement will then be filed with the SEC. The statutes set a twenty-day waiting period (which in practice may be shortened or lengthened

---

[5]The process described here relates primarily to situations where the firm doing the financing picks an investment banker, then negotiates with him over the terms of the issue. An alternative procedure, used extensively only in the public utility industry, is for the selling firm to specify the terms of the new issue, then to have investment bankers bid for the entire new issue by use of *sealed bids*. The very high fixed costs that an investment banker must incur to investigate thoroughly the company and its new issue rule out sealed bids except for the very largest issues. The operation described in this section is called *negotiated underwriting;* competition is keen among underwriters, of course, to develop and maintain working relations with business firms.

by the SEC) during which time its staff analyzes the registration statement to determine whether there are any omissions or misrepresentations of fact. The SEC may file exceptions to the registration statement or may ask for additional information from the issuing company or the underwriters during the examination period. During this period, the investment bankers are not permitted to offer the securities for sale, although they may print preliminary prospectuses with all the customary information except the offering price.

Pricing the Securities

The actual price the underwriter pays the issuer is not generally determined until the close of the registration period. There is no universally followed practice, but one common arrangement for a new issue of stock calls for the investment banker to buy the securities at a prescribed number of points below the closing price on the last day of registration. For example, in April 1976 the stock of Wilcox Chemical Company had a current price of $38, and had traded between $35 and $40 a share during the previous three months. The firm and the underwriter agreed that the investment banker would buy 200,000 new shares at $2.50 below the closing price on the last day of registration. The stock closed at $36 on the day the SEC released the issue, so the firm received $33.50 a share. Typically, such agreements have an escape clause that provides for the contract to be voided if the price of the securities ends below some predetermined figure. In the illustrative case, this "upset" price was set at $34 a share. Thus, if the closing price of the shares on the last day of registration had been $33.50, Wilcox would have had the option of withdrawing from the agreement.

The preceding arrangement holds, of course, only for additional offerings of the stock of firms whose old stock was previously traded. When a company "goes public" for the first time, the investment banker and the firm will negotiate a price in accordance with the valuation principles described in Chapter 18.

The investment banker will have an easier job if the issue is priced relatively low. The issuer of the securities naturally wants as high a price as possible. Some conflict of interest on price therefore arises between the investment banker and the issuer. If the issuer is financially sophisticated and makes comparisons with similar security issues, the investment banker is forced to price close to the market.

Underwriting Syndicate

The investment banker with whom the issuing firm has conducted its discussions will not typically handle the purchase and distribution of the issue alone, unless the issue is a very small one. If the sums of money involved are large and the risk of price fluctuation is substantial, the investment banker forms a syndicate in an effort to minimize the amount of risk he carries. A syndicate is a temporary association for the purpose of carrying out a specific objective. The nature of the arrangements for a syndicate in the underwriting and sale of a security through an investment banker may best be understood with the aid of Figure 13–2.

FIGURE 13–2   Diagram of Sales of $100 Million of Bonds through Investment Bankers

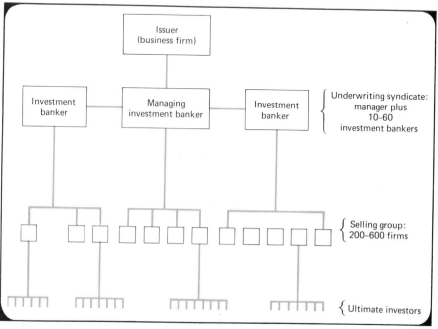

The managing underwriter invites other investment bankers to participate in the transaction on the basis of their knowledge of the particular kind of offering to be made and on the basis of their strength and dealer contacts in selling securities of this type. Each investment banker has business relations with other investment bankers and dealers; thus, each investment banker has a selling group consisting of himself and other investment bankers and dealers.

Some firms combine all these characteristics. For example, Merrill Lynch, Pierce, Fenner and Smith underwrites some issues and manages the underwriting of others. On still other flotations, it will be invited by the manager to join in the distribution of the issue. It also purchases securities as a dealer and carries an inventory of those securities. It publishes lists of securities it has for sale. In addition to being a dealer, Merrill Lynch, of course, carries on substantial activity as a broker. An individual investment firm may carry on all these functions, just as a department store sells many varieties of merchandise.

There are also firms with a narrower range of functions—specialty dealers, specialty brokers, and specialty investment counselors. Thus, in the financial field there is specialization of financial functions, as well as department store types of operations. A *dealer* purchases securities outright, holds them in inventory as a grocery store would hold its inventory, and sells them at whatever price he can get. He may benefit from price appreciation or he may suffer a loss on declines, as any merchandiser does. A *broker,* on the other hand, takes orders for purchases and transmits them to the proper exchange; his gain is the commission he charges for the service.

Syndicates are used in the distribution of securities for three reasons: (1) A single investment banker may be financially unable to handle a large issue alone. (2) The originating house may desire to spread the risk even if it is financially able to handle the issue alone. (3) The utilization of several selling organizations, as well as other underwriters, permits an economy of selling effort and expense and encourages broader, nationwide distribution.

Participating underwriters and dealers are provided with full information on all phases of these financing transactions, and they share in the underwriting commission. Suppose that an investment banker buys $10 million worth of bonds to be sold at par, or $1,000 each. If the investment banker receives a two-point spread, he will buy the bonds from the issuer at 98; thus, he must pay the issuer $9.8 million for the issue of $10 million. Typically, on a two-point spread, the managing underwriter will receive the first one-quarter of 1 percent for originating and managing the syndicate. Next the entire underwriting group will receive about three-quarters of 1 percent. Members of the selling group receive about 1 percent as a sales commission.

If the manager of the underwriting group makes a sale to an ultimate purchaser of the securities, he will receive the ¼ percent as manager, ¾ percent as underwriter, and 1 percent as seller—the full 2 percent. If he wholesales some of the securities to members of the selling group who make the ultimate sale, the latter will receive the 1 percent selling commission and the manager will receive the other 1 percent for managing and underwriting the issue. If the issue is managed by one firm, underwritten by a second, and sold by a third, the 2 percent commission is divided, with 1 percent going to the selling firm, ¾ percent to the underwriter, and ¼ percent to the manager of the underwriting group.

Ordinarily, each underwriter's liability is limited to his agreed-upon commitment. For example, if an investment banker participates in a $20 million offering and agrees to see to it that $5 million of the securities are sold, his responsibility ends when he sells his $5 million.

Selling Group

The selling group is formed primarily for the purpose of distributing securities; it consists of dealers, who take relatively small participations from the members of the underwriting group. The underwriters act as wholesalers; members of the selling group act as retailers. The number of houses in a selling group depends partly upon the size of the issue. A selling group may have as many as 300 to 400 dealers; for example, the one for Communications Satellite Corporation consisted of 385 members.

The operation of the selling group is controlled by the *selling group agreement,* which usually covers the following major points.

Description of the Issue   The description is set forth in a report on the issue, the prospectus, which fully describes the issue and the issuer.

Concession   Members of the selling group subscribe to the new issue at a public offering price less the *concession* given to them as a commission for their selling service. In the preceding example, this was 1 percent.

Handling Purchased Securities   The selling group agreement provides that no member of the selling group be permitted to sell the securities below the public offering price. The syndicate manager invariably "pegs" the quotation in the market by placing continuous orders to buy at the public offering price. A careful record is kept of bond or stock certificate numbers so that repurchased bonds may be identified with the member of the selling group who sold them. The general practice is to cancel the commission on such securities and add brokerage costs incurred in the repurchase. Repurchased securities are then placed with other dealers for sale.[6]

Duration of Selling Group   The most common provision in selling group agreements is that the group has an existence of thirty days, subject to earlier termination by the manager. The agreement may be extended, however, for an additional eighty days by members representing 75 percent of the selling group.

Offering and Sale

After the selling group has been formed, the actual offering takes place. Publicity for the sale is given in advance of the offering date. Advertising material is prepared for release as soon as permissible. The actual day of the offering is chosen with a view to avoiding temporary congestion in the security market and other unfavorable events or circumstances.

The formal public offering is called "opening the books," an archaic term reflecting ancient customs of the investment banking trade. When the books

---

[6]Without these repurchase arrangements, a member of the selling group could sell his share of the securities on the open market instead of to new purchasers. Since the pegging operation is going on, there would be a ready market for the securities; consequently, a penalty is necessary to avoid thwarting of the syndicate operation.

are opened, the manager accepts subscriptions to the issue from both selling group participants and outsiders who may wish to buy. If the demand is great, the books may be closed immediately and an announcement made that the issue is oversubscribed; the issue is said to "fly out the window." If the reception is weak, the books may remain open for an extended period.

Market Stabilization

During the period of the offering and distribution of securities, the manager of the underwriting group typically stabilizes the price of the issue. The duration of the price-pegging operation is usually thirty days. The price is pegged by placing orders to buy at a specified price in the market. The pegging operation is designed to prevent a cumulative downward movement in the price, which would result in losses for all members of the underwriting group. As the manager of the underwriting group has the major responsibility, he assumes the task of pegging the price.

If the market deteriorates during the offering period, the investment banker carries a rather substantial risk. For this reason, the pegging operation may not be sufficient to protect the underwriters. In one Pure Oil Company issue of $44 million convertible preferred stock, only $1 million of shares were sold at the $100 offering price. At the conclusion of the underwriting agreement, initial trading took place at $74, incurring for the investment bankers a loss of over $11 million ($43 million × 26 percent). In a recent Textron issue, the offering was reduced from $100 million to $50 million because of market congestion, and still 5 percent of the bonds were unsold after the initial offering. Other such cases can be cited.

It has been charged that pegging the price during the offering period constitutes a monopolistic price-fixing arrangement. Investment bankers reply, however, that not to peg the price would increase the risk and therefore the underwriting cost to the issuer. On balance, it appears that the pegging operation has a socially useful function. The danger of monopolistic pricing is avoided, or at least mitigated substantially, by competitive factors. If an underwriter attempts to set a monopolistic price on a particular issue of securities, the investor can turn to thousands of other securities that are not price pegged. The degree of control over the market by the underwriter in a price-pegging operation seems negligible.

COSTS OF FLOTATION

The cost of selling new issues of securities is put into perspective in Table 13–1. The table summarizes the data on cost of flotation in the last available report on the subject by the SEC. Although these data are somewhat old, the figures are still appropriate, and two important generalizations can be drawn from them:

1. The cost of flotation for common stock is greater than for preferred stocks, and the costs of both are greater than the cost of flotation for bonds.
2. The cost of flotation as a percentage of the gross proceeds is greater for small issues than for large ones.

TABLE 13–1 Costs of Flotation 1961–1965
(Costs expressed as percentage of gross proceeds)

Size of Issue (Millions of Dollars)	Debt			Preferred Stock			Common Stock		
	Under-writing Com-mission	Other Expenses	Total Costs	Under-writing Com-mission	Other Expenses	Total Costs	Under-writing Com-mission	Other Expenses	Total Costs
Under 0.5	7.4	8.0	15.4	7.9	8.0	16.0	11.3	7.3	18.5
0.5–0.9	7.2	3.1	10.3	8.0	3.1	11.1	9.7	4.9	14.6
1.0–1.9	7.0	3.4	10.4	8.0	3.4	11.4	8.6	3.0	11.6
2.0–4.9	4.2	1.2	5.4	4.8	1.2	6.1	7.4	1.7	9.1
5.0–9.9	1.5	0.6	2.1	1.0	0.6	1.6	6.7	1.0	7.6
10.0–19.9	1.0	0.4	1.4	1.4	0.4	1.8	6.2	0.6	6.9
20.0–49.9	1.0	0.4	1.4	2.7	0.4	3.1	4.9	0.8	5.6
50.0 and over	0.8	0.3	1.1	1.4	0.3	1.7	2.3	0.3	2.6

Sources: For common and preferred stocks: Securities and Exchange Commission, *Cost of Flotation of Registered Equity Issues, 1963–1965* (Washington, D.C.: U.S. Government Printing Office, March 1970), Tables 3 and 10. For debt: Underwriting costs estimated on basis of Irwin Friend, et al., *Investment Banking and the New Issues Market* (Cleveland: World Publishing Company, 1967), Table 7–1, pp. 408, 409: Reprinted by Permission of the author. Because of rounding errors, totals may not equal the sum of the parts. Preferred stocks were used infrequently, and because of the small sample size the figures for this group are suspect.

What are the reasons for these relationships? The explanations are found in the amount of risk involved and in the job of physical distribution. Bonds are generally bought in large blocks by a relatively few institutional investors, whereas stocks are bought by millions of individuals. For this reason the distribution job is harder for common stock, and the expenses of marketing it are greater. Similarly, stocks are more volatile than bonds, so underwriting risks are larger for stock than for bond flotations.

The explanation for the variation in cost with the size of issue is also easily found. In the first place, certain fixed expenses are associated with any distribution of securities: the underwriting investigation, the preparation of the registration statement, legal fees, and so forth. Since these expenses are relatively large and fixed, their percentage of the total cost of flotation runs high on small issues. Second, small issues are typically those of relatively less well known firms, so underwriting expenses may be larger than usual because the danger of omitting vital information is greater. Furthermore, the selling job is more difficult: salesmen must exert greater effort to sell the securities of a less well known firm. For these reasons the underwriting commission, as a percentage of the gross proceeds, is relatively high for small issues.

Flotation costs are also influenced by whether or not the issue is a "rights offering," and if it is, by the extent of the underpricing.[7] If rights are used and if the underpricing is substantial, then the investment banker bears little risk of inability to sell the shares. Further, very little selling effort will be required in such a situation. These two factors combine to enable a company to float new securities to its own stockholders at a relatively low cost.

REGULATION OF SECURITY TRADING

The operations of investment bankers, exchanges, and over-the-counter markets described in the previous sections of this chapter are significantly influenced by a series of federal statutes enacted during and after 1933. The financial manager is affected by these laws for several reasons: (1) Corporate officers are subjected to personal liabilities. (2) The laws affect the ease and costs of financing, and they also affect the behavior of the money and capital markets in which the corporations' securities are sold and traded. (3) Investors' willingness to buy securities is influenced by the existence of safeguards provided by these laws.

Securities Act of 1933

The first of the securities acts, the Securities Act of 1933, followed Congressional investigations of the stock market collapse of 1929–1932. The reasons motivating the act were (1) the large losses to investors, (2) the failures of many corporations on which little information had been provided, and (3) the misrepresentations that had been made to investors.

The basic objective of the Securities Act of 1933 was to provide for both *full disclosure* of relevant information and a *record of representations.* It seeks to achieve these objectives by the following means:

1. It applies to all interstate offerings to the public (some exemptions are government bonds and bank stocks) in amounts of $500,000 or more.
2. Securities must be registered at least twenty days before they are publicly offered. The registration statement provides financial, legal, and technical information about the company. A prospectus summarizes this information for use in selling the securities. If information is inadequate or misleading, the SEC will delay or stop the public offering. Obtaining the information required to review the registration statement may result in a waiting period that exceeds twenty days.
3. After the registration has become effective, the securities may be offered if accompanied by the prospectus. Preliminary or "red herring" prospectuses may be distributed to potential buyers during the waiting period.

---

[7] "Rights offerings" involve the sale of stock to existing stockholders. This topic is discussed extensively in Chapter 14.

4. If the registration statement or prospectus contains misrepresentations or omissions of material facts, any purchaser who suffers a loss may sue for damages. Liabilities and severe penalties may be imposed on the issuer, its officers, directors, accountants, engineers, appraisers, underwriters, and all others who participated in the preparation of the registration statement.

The act provides for full disclosure. It also has resulted in a procedure for obtaining a record of representations.

Securities Exchange Act of 1934

The Securities Exchange Act of 1934 extends the disclosure principle, as applied to new issues by the act of 1933, to trading in already issued securities (the "secondhand" securities market). It seeks to accomplish this by the following measures:

1. It establishes a Securities and Exchange Commission (the Federal Trade Commission had been administering the act of 1933).
2. It provides for registration and regulation of national securities exchanges. Companies whose securities are listed on an exchange must file reports similar to registration statements with both the SEC and the stock exchange and must provide periodic reports as well.
3. It provides control over corporate "insiders." Officers, directors, and major stockholders of a corporation must file monthly reports of changes in holdings of the stock of the corporation. Any short-term profits from such transactions are payable to the corporation.
4. The act gives the SEC the power to prohibit manipulation by such devices as pools (aggregations of funds used to affect prices artificially), wash sales (sales between members of the same group to record artificial transaction prices), and pegging the market other than during stock flotations.
5. The SEC is given control over the proxy machinery and practices.
6. Control over the flow of credit into security transactions is established by giving the board of governors of the Federal Reserve System the power to control margin requirements.

APPRAISAL OF REGULATION OF SECURITY TRADING

Why should security transactions be regulated? It may be argued that a great body of relevant knowledge is necessary to make an informed judgment of the value of a security. Moreover, security values are subject to great gyrations, which influence stability and business conditions generally. Hence, social well-being requires that orderly markets be promoted.

The objectives of the regulation may be summarized into three points:

1. To protect the amateur investor from fraud and to provide him with a basis for more informed judgments.
2. To control the volume of bank credit to finance security speculation.
3. To provide orderly markets in securities.

Progress has been made on all three counts. There has been some cost in the increased time and expense involved in new flotations by companies, although the benefits seem worth their costs. The regulations are powerless to prevent investors from investing in unsound ventures or to prevent stock prices from skyrocketing during booms and falling greatly during periods of pessimism. Still, requirements for increased information have been of great value in easing gyrations and preventing fraud and gross misrepresentations.

From the standpoint of the financial manager, regulation has a twofold significance: (1) It affects the cost of issuing securities. (2) It affects the riskiness of securities, hence the rate of return investors require when they purchase stocks and bonds. As we will see in subsequent chapters, these two factors have an important bearing on the firm's cost of capital, and through the capital budgeting process, on its investment decisions. Further, since business investment is a key determinant of employment and production in the economy, we will see that efficient capital markets have an important impact on all of society.

SUMMARY

Securities are traded both on *exchanges* and in the *over-the-counter market.* The stocks of larger industrial and utility companies are generally listed on an exchange; stocks of financial institutions, small industrial firms, and practically all bonds are traded over the counter. From the standpoint of the financial manager, listing on an exchange seems advantageous for seasoned issues. The over-the-counter market may aid in the seasoning process until the security can meet the requirements for listing.

The investment banker provides middleman services to both the seller and the buyer of new securities. He helps plan the issue, underwrites it, and handles the job of selling the issue to the ultimate investor. The cost of this service to the issuer is related to the magnitude of the total job the banker must perform to place the issue. The investment banker must also look to the interests of his brokerage customers; if these investors are not satisfied with the banker's products, they will deal elsewhere.

Flotation costs are lower for bonds, higher for preferred stocks, and highest for common stock. Larger companies have lower flotation costs than smaller ones for each type of security, and most companies can cut their stock flotation costs by issuing the new securities to stockholders through rights offerings. (Rights offerings are discussed in Chapter 14.)

The financial manager should be familiar with the federal laws regulating the issuance and trading of securities, because they influence his liabilities and affect financing methods and costs. Regulation of securities trading seeks (1) to provide information that investors can utilize as a basis for judging the merits of securities, (2) to control the volume of credit used in securities trading, and (3) to provide orderly securities markets. The laws do not, however, prevent either purchase of unsound issues or wide price fluctuations. They raise somewhat the costs of flotation but have probably decreased the cost of capital by increasing public confidence in the securities markets.

QUESTIONS

13-1. State several advantages to a firm that lists its stock on a major stock exchange.

13-2. Would you expect the cost of capital of a firm to be affected if it changed its status from one traded over the counter to one traded on the New York Stock Exchange? Explain.

13-3. Evaluate the following statement: The fundamental purpose of the federal security laws dealing with new issues is to prevent investors, principally small ones, from sustaining losses on the purchase of stocks.

13-4. Suppose two firms were each selling $10 million of common stock. The firms are similar—that is, they are of the same size, are in the same industry, have the same leverage, and have other similarities—except that one is publicly owned and the other is closely held. Would their costs of flotation be the same? If different, state the probable relationships. If the issue were $10 million of bonds, would your answer be the same?

13-5. Define these terms: brokerage firm, underwriting group, selling group, and investment banker.

13-6. Each month the Securities and Exchange Commission publishes a report of the transactions made by the officers and directors of listed firms in their own companies' equity securities. Why do you suppose the SEC makes this report?

13-7. Prior to 1933, investment banking and commercial banking were both carried on by the same firm. In that year, however, the Banking Act required that these functions be separated. On the basis of your knowledge of investment banking and commercial banking, discuss the pros and cons of this forced separation.

13-8. Before entering a formal agreement, investment bankers investigate quite carefully the companies whose securities they underwrite; this is especially true of the issues of firms going public for the first time. Since the bankers do not themselves plan to hold the securities but plan to sell them to others as soon as possible, why are they so concerned about making careful investigations? Does your answer to the question have any bearing on the fact that investment banking is a very difficult field to "break into"?

13-9. If competitive bidding was required on all security offerings, would flotation costs be higher or lower? Would the size of the issuing firm be material in determining the effects of required competitive bidding?

13-10. Since investment bankers price new issues in relation to outstanding issues, should a spread exist between the yields on the new and the outstanding issues? Discuss this matter separately for stock issues and bond issues.

13-11. What problems are raised by the increasing purchase of equities by institutional investors?

PROBLEMS

13-1. Your firm is planning to sell $1.5 million of bonds with a fifteen-year maturity. The going rate on debt of this quality and maturity will be 10 percent. However, total costs of the underwriting have been estimated to be 10.5 percent of gross proceeds. Calculate the cost of this debt to your firm. (Hint: Let the coupon rate be 10 percent so the bonds will sell at face value, then solve for the IRR which will make the future payments on the bond equal to face value less 10.5 percent, i.e., to $895 per bond.)

13-2. If your firm were to sell preferred stock in the amount of $1.5 million, the total flotation expense would be about 11.5 percent of gross proceeds. If the going rate on preferred stock of the same quality as your firm's is 12 percent, what will be the effective cost of the preferred stock issue? Assume the stock will remain outstanding in perpetuity.

13-3[8]**.** In March 1975, three executives of the Hughes Aircraft Company, one of the largest privately owned corporations in the world, decided to break away from Hughes and to set up a company of their own. The principal reason for this decision was capital gains; Hughes Aircraft stock is all privately owned, and the corporate structure makes it impossible for executives to be granted stock purchase options. Hughes' executives receive substantial salaries and bonuses, but this income is all taxable at normal tax rates, and no capital gains opportunities are available.

The three men, Jim Adcock, Robert Goddard, and Rick Aiken, have located a medium-size electronics manufacturing company available for purchase. The stock of this firm, Baynard Industries, is all owned by the founder, Joseph Baynard. Although the company is in excellent shape, Baynard wants to sell it because of his failing health. A price of $5.7 million has been established, based on a price/earnings ratio of 12 and annual earnings of $475,000. Baynard has given the three prospective purchasers an option to purchase the company for the agreed price; the option is to run for six months, during which time the three men are to arrange financing with which to buy the firm.

Adcock has consulted with Jules Scott, a partner in the New York investment banking firm of Williams Brothers and an acquaintance of some years' standing, to seek his assistance in obtaining the funds necessary to complete the purchase. Adcock, Goddard, and Aiken each have some money available to put into the new enterprise, but they need a substantial amount of outside capital. There is some possibility of borrowing part of the money, but Scott has discouraged this idea. His reasoning is, first, that Baynard Industries is already highly leveraged, and if the purchasers were to borrow additional funds, there would be a very severe risk that they would be unable to service this debt in the event of a recession in the electronics industry. Although the firm is currently earning $475,000 a year, this figure could quickly turn into a loss in the event of a few canceled defense contracts or cost miscalculations.

Scott's second reason for discouraging a loan is that Adcock, Goddard, and Aiken plan not only to operate Baynard Industries and seek internal growth but also to use the corporation as a vehicle for making further acquisitions of electronics companies. This being the case, Scott believes that it would be wise for the company to keep any borrowing potential in reserve for use in later acquisitions.

Scott proposes that the three partners obtain funds to purchase Baynard Industries in accordance with the figures shown in Table P13–1.

[8]This case study is taken from E. F. Brigham, Timothy J. Nantell, Robert T. Aubey, and Richard H. Pettway, *Cases in Managerial Finance*, 2d ed. (New York: Holt, Rinehart and Winston, Inc., 1974).

TABLE P13–1 Baynard Industries

Price paid to Joseph Baynard			$5,700,000
(12 × $475,000 earnings)			
Authorized shares		5,000,000	
Initially issued shares		1,125,000	
Initial distribution of shares:			
Adcock	100,000 shares at $1.00		$ 100,000
Goddard	100,000 shares at $1.00		100,000
Aiken	100,000 shares at $1.00		100,000
Williams Brothers	125,000 shares at $7.00		875,000
Public stockholders	700,000 shares at $7.00		4,900,000
	1,125,000		$6,075,000
Underwriting costs: 5% of $4,900,000		$245,000	
Legal fees, and so on, associated with issue		45,000	$ 290,000
			$5,785,000
Payment to Joseph Baynard			5,700,000
Net funds to Baynard Industries			$ 85,000

Baynard Industries would be reorganized with an authorized 5,000,000 shares, with 1,125,000 to be issued at the time the transfer takes place and the other 3,875,000 to be held in reserve for possible issuance in connection with acquisitions. Adcock, Goddard, and Aiken would each purchase 100,000 shares at a price of $1 a share, the par value. Williams Brothers would purchase 125,000 shares at a price of $7. The remaining 700,000 shares would be sold to the public at a price of $7 a share.

Williams Brothers' underwriting fee would be 5 percent of the shares sold to the public, or $245,000. Legal fees, accounting fees, and other charges associated with the issue would amount to $45,000, for a total underwriting cost of $290,000. After deducting the underwriting charges and the payment to Baynard from the gross proceeds of the stock sale, the reorganized Baynard Industries would receive funds in the amount of $85,000 which would be used for internal expansion purposes.

As a part of the initial agreement, Adcock, Goddard, and Aiken each would be given options to purchase an additional 80,000 shares at a price of $7 a share one year from now. Williams Brothers would be given an option to purchase an additional 100,000 shares at $7 a share in one year.

a. What is the total underwriting charge, expressed as a percentage of the funds raised by the underwriter? Does this charge seem reasonable in the light of published statistics on the cost of floating new issues of common stock?

b. Suppose that the three men estimate the following probabilities for the firm's stock price one year from now:

Price	Probability
$ 1	.05
$ 5	.10
$ 9	.35
13	.35
17	.10
21	.05

Assuming Williams Brothers exercises its options, calculate the following ratio (ignore time-discount effects):

$$\frac{\text{Total proceeds to Williams Brothers}}{\text{Funds raised by underwriter}}$$

Disregard Williams Brothers' profit on the 125,000 shares it bought outright at the initial offering. Comment on the ratio.

c. Are Adcock, Goddard, and Aiken purchasing their stock at a "fair" price? Should the prospectus disclose the fact that they would buy their stock at $1 a share, whereas public stockholders would buy their stock at $7 a share?

d. Would it be reasonable for Williams Brothers to purchase its initial 125,000 shares at a price of $1.

e. Do you foresee any problems of control for Adcock, Goddard, and Aiken?

f. Would the expectation of an exceptionally large need for investment funds next year be a relevant consideration in deciding on the amount of funds to be raised now?

Common Stock

14 Common equity, or if unincorporated firms are being considered, partnership or proprietorship interests, constitutes the first source of funds to a new business and the base of support for borrowing by existing firms. Accordingly, our discussion of specific forms of long-term financing will begin with an analysis of common stock.

APPORTIONMENT OF INCOME, CONTROL, AND RISK

The nature of equity ownership depends upon the form of the business or organization. The central problem revolves around an apportionment of certain rights and responsibilities among those who have provided the funds necessary for the operation of the business.

The rights and responsibilities attaching to equity consist of positive considerations—income potential and control of the firm—and negative considerations—loss potential, legal responsibility, and personal liability.

General Rights of Holders of Common Stock

The rights of holders of common stock in a business corporation are established by the laws of the state in which the corporation is chartered and by the terms of the charter granted by the state. The characteristics of charters are relatively uniform on many matters, including the following two:

Collective Rights Certain collective rights are usually given to the holders of common stock. Some of the more important rights allow stockholders (1) to

292

amend the charter with the approval of the appropriate officials in the state of incorporation; (2) to adopt and amend bylaws; (3) to elect the directors of the corporation; (4) to authorize the sale of fixed assets; (5) to enter into mergers; (6) to change the amount of authorized common stock; and (7) to issue preferred stock, debentures, bonds, and other securities.

Specific Rights Holders of common stock also have specific rights as individual owners. (1) They have the right to vote in the manner prescribed by the corporate charter. (2) They may sell their stock certificates, their evidence of ownership, and in this way transfer their ownership interest to other persons. (3) They have the right to inspect the corporate books.[1] (4) They have the right to share residual assets of the corporation on dissolution; however, the holders of common stock are last among the claimants to the assets of the corporation.

Apportionment of Income

Two important positive considerations are involved in equity ownership: income and control. The right to income carries risks of loss. Control also involves responsibility and liability. In an individual proprietorship, using only funds supplied by the owner, the owner has a 100 percent right to income and control and to loss and responsibility. As soon as the proprietor incurs debt, however, he has entered into contracts that place limitations on his complete freedom to control the firm and to apportion the firm's income.

In a partnership, these rights are apportioned among the partners in an agreed manner. In the absence of a formal agreement, a division is made by state law. In a corporation more significant issues arise concerning the rights of the owners.

Apportionment of Control

Through the right to vote, holders of common stock have legal control of the corporation. As a practical matter, however, in many corporations the principal officers constitute all, or a majority of, the members of the board of directors. In such circumstances the board of directors may be controlled by the management, rather than vice versa. Management control, or control of a business by other than its owners, results. However, numerous examples demonstrate that stockholders can reassert their control if they are dissatisfied with the policies of the corporation. In recent years, proxy battles with the aim of altering corporate policies have occurred fairly often, and firms whose managers are unresponsive to stockholders' desires are subject to takeover bids by other firms.

---

[1]Obviously, a corporation cannot have its business affairs disturbed by allowing every stockholder to go through any record that he would like to inspect. A corporation could not wisely permit a competitor who happened to buy shares of its common stock to look at all the corporation records. There must be, and there are, practical limitations to this right.

As receivers of residual income, holders of common stock are frequently referred to as the ultimate entrepreneurs in the firm. They are the ultimate owners, and they have the ultimate control. Presumably the firm is managed on behalf of its owners, the holders of common stock, but there has been much dispute about the actual situation. The point of view has been expressed that the corporation is an institution with an existence separate from the owners', and that the corporation exists to fulfill certain functions for stockholders as only one among other important groups, such as workers, consumers, and the economy as a whole. This view may have some validity, but it should also be noted that ordinarily the officers of a firm are also large stockholders. In addition, more and more firms are relating officers' compensation to the firm's profit performance, either by granting executives stock purchase options or by giving bonuses. These actions are, of course, designed to make managers' personal goals more consistent with those of the stockholders—to increase the firm's earnings and stock price.

Apportionment of Risk

Another consideration involved in equity ownership is risk. Because, on liquidation, holders of common stock are last in the priority of claims, the portion of capital they contribute provides a cushion for creditors if losses occur on dissolution. The equity-to-total-assets ratio indicates the percentage by which assets may shrink in value on liquidation before creditors will incur losses.

For example, compare two corporations, A and B, whose balance sheets are shown in Table 14–1. The ratio of equity to total assets in corporation A is 80 percent. Total assets would therefore have to shrink by 80 percent before creditors would lose money. By contrast, in corporation B the extent by which assets may shrink in value on liquidation before creditors lose money is only 40 percent.

TABLE 14–1 Balance Sheets for Corporations A and B

	Corporation A			*Corporation B*	
	Debt	$ 20		Debt	$ 60
	Equity	80		Equity	40
Total assets $100	Total claims $100		Total assets $100	Total claims $100	

COMMON STOCK FINANCING

Before undertaking an evaluation of common stock financing, it is desirable to describe some of its additional important characteristics. These topics include

(1) the nature of voting rights, (2) the nature of the preemptive right, and (3) variations in the forms of common stock.

Nature of Voting Rights

For each share of common stock owned, the holder has the right to cast one vote at the annual meeting of stockholders of the corporation or at such special meetings as may be called.

Proxy   Provision is made for the temporary transfer of the right to vote by an instrument known as a *proxy*. The transfer is limited in its duration, typically for a specific occasion such as the annual meeting of stockholders.

The SEC supervises the use of the proxy machinery and issues frequent rules and regulations seeking to improve its administration. SEC supervision is justified for several reasons. First, if the proxy machinery is left wholly in the hands of management, there is a danger that the incumbent management will be self-perpetuated. Second, if it is made easy for minority groups of stockholders and opposition stockholders to oust management, there is danger that they may gain control of the corporation for temporary advantages or to place their friends in management positions.

Cumulative Voting   A method of voting that has come into increased prominence is cumulative voting. Cumulative voting for directors is required in twenty-two states, including California, Illinois, Pennsylvania, Ohio, and Michigan. It is permissible in eighteen, including Delaware, New York, and New Jersey. Ten states make no provision for cumulative voting.

Cumulative voting permits multiple votes for a single director. For example, suppose six directors are to be elected. The owner of 100 shares can cast 100 votes for each of the six openings. Cumulatively, then, he has 600 votes. When cumulative voting is permitted, the stockholder may accumulate his votes and cast 600 votes for *one* director, instead of 100 each for *six* directors. Cumulative voting is designed to enable a minority group of stockholders to obtain some voice in the control of the company by electing at least one director to the board.

The nature of cumulative voting is illustrated by use of the following formula:

$$r = \frac{d \times S}{D + 1} + 1. \tag{14-1}$$

Here,

r = number of shares required to elect a desired number of directors,

d = number of directors stockholder desires to elect,

S = total number of shares of common stock outstanding and entitled to vote,[2] and

D = total number of directors to be elected.

The formula may be made more meaningful by an example. The ABC company will elect six directors. There are fifteen candidates and 100,000 shares entitled to vote. If a group desires to elect two directors, how many shares must it have?

$$r = \frac{2 \times 100,000}{6 + 1} + 1 = 28,572. \tag{14-2}$$

Observe the significance of the formula. Here, a minority group wishes to elect one-third of the board of directors. They can achieve their goal by owning less than one-third the number of shares of stock.[3]

Alternatively, assuming that a group holds 40,000 shares of stock in this company, how many directors would it be possible for the group to elect, following the rigid assumptions of the formula? The formula can be used in its present form or can be solved for d and expressed as

$$d = \frac{(r-1)(D+1)}{S}. \tag{14-3}$$

Inserting the figures, the calculation would be

$$d = \frac{39,999 \times 7}{100,000} = 2.8. \tag{14-4}$$

The 40,000 shares could elect two and eight-tenths directors. Since directors cannot exist as fractions, the group can elect only two directors.

As a practical matter, suppose that in the above situation the total number of shares is 100,000. Hence 60,000 shares remain in other hands. The voting of all the 60,000 shares may not be concentrated. Suppose the 60,000 shares (cumulatively, 360,000 votes) not held by our group are distributed equally among ten candidates, 36,000 shares held by each candidate. If our group's 240,000 votes are distributed equally for each of six candidates, we could elect all six directors even though we do not have a majority of the stock.

Actually, it is difficult to make assumptions about how the opposition votes will be distributed. What is shown here is a good example of game theory. One rule in the theory of games is to assume that your opponents will do the worst they can do to you and to counter with actions to minimize the

[2]An alternative that may be agreed to by the contesting parties is to define S as the number of shares *voted,* not *authorized to vote.* This procedure, which in effect gives each group seeking to elect directors the same percentage of directors as their percentage of the voted stock, is frequently followed. When it is used a group that seeks to gain control with a minimum investment must estimate the percentage of shares that will be voted and then obtain control of more than 50 percent of that number.

[3]Note also that at least 14,287 shares must be controlled to elect one director. As far as electing a director goes, any number less than 14,287 constitutes a useless minority.

maximum loss. This is the kind of assumption followed in the formula. If your opposition concentrates its votes in the optimum manner, what is the best you can do to work in the direction of your goal? Other plausible assumptions can be substituted if there are sufficient facts to support alternative hypotheses about the behavior of the opponents.

Preemptive Right

The preemptive right gives holders of common stock the first option to purchase additional issues of common stock. In some states the preemptive right is made a part of every corporate charter; in others, it is necessary to insert the preemptive right specifically in the charter.

The purpose of this right is twofold. First, it protects the power of control of present stockholders. If it were not for this safeguard, the management of a corporation under criticism from stockholders could prevent stockholders from removing it from office by issuing a large number of additional shares at a very low price and purchasing these shares itself. Management would thereby secure control of the corporation to frustrate the will of the current stockholders.

The second, and by far the more important, protection that the preemptive right affords stockholders regards dilution of value. For example, assume that 1,000 shares of common stock, each with a price of $100, are outstanding, making the total market value of the firm $100,000. An additional 1,000 shares are sold at $50 a share, or for $50,000, thus raising the total market value of the firm to $150,000. When the total market value is divided by the new total shares outstanding, a value of $75 a share is obtained. Thus, selling common stock at below market value will dilute the price of the stock and will be detrimental to present stockholders and beneficial to those who purchased the new shares. The preemptive right prevents such occurrences. This point is discussed at length later in this chapter.

Forms of Common Stock[4]

Classified   Classified common stock was used extensively in the late 1920s, sometimes in ways that misled investors. During that period, class A common stock was usually nonvoting, and class B was typically voting. Thus promoters

---

[4]Accountants also use the term "par value" to designate an arbitrary value assigned when stock is sold. When a firm sells newly issued stock, it must record the transaction on its balance sheet. For example, suppose a newly created firm commences operations by selling 100,000 shares at $10 a share, raising a total of $1 million. This $1 million must appear on the balance sheet, but what will it be called? One choice would be to assign the stock a "par value" of $10 and label the $1 million "common stock." Another choice would be to assign a $1 par value and show $100,000 ($1 par value times 100,000 shares) as "common stock" and $900,000 as "paid-in surplus." Still another choice would be to disregard the term "par value" entirely—that is, use no-par stock—and record the $1 million as "common stock." Since the choice is quite arbitrary for all practical purposes, more and more firms are adopting the last procedure and abolishing the term "par value." Because there are quite enough useful concepts and terms in accounting and finance, we heartily applaud the demise of useless ones such as this.

could control companies by selling large amounts of class A stock while retaining class B stock.

In more recent years there has been a revival of class B common for sound purposes. It is used by small, new companies seeking to acquire funds from outside sources. Common stock A is sold to the public and typically pays dividends; it has full voting rights. Common stock B, however, is retained by the organizers of the company, but dividends are not paid on it until the company has established its earning power. By the use of the classified stock, the public can take a position in a conservatively financed growth company without sacrificing income.

Founders' Shares   Founders' shares are somewhat like class B stock except that they carry *sole* voting rights and typically do not have the right to dividends for a number of years. Thus the organizers of the firm are able to maintain complete control of the operations in the crucial initial development of the firm. At the same time, other investors are protected against excessive withdrawals of funds by owners.

EVALUATION OF COMMON STOCK AS A SOURCE OF FUNDS

Thus far, the chapter has covered the main characteristics of common stock, frequently referred to as equity shares. By way of a summary of the important aspects of common stock, we now appraise this type of financing from the standpoint of the issuer.

From Viewpoint of Issuer

Advantages   First, common stock does not entail fixed charges. If the company generates the earnings, it can pay common stock dividends. In contrast to bond interest, however, there is no legal obligation to pay dividends. Second, common stock carries no fixed maturity date. Third, since common stock provides a cushion against losses for creditors, the sale of common stock increases the credit-worthiness of the firm. Fourth, common stock may at times be sold more easily than debt. Common stock appeals to certain investor groups for two reasons: (1) it typically carries a higher expected return than does preferred stock or debt, and (2) it provides the investor with a better hedge against inflation than does straight preferred stock or bonds because it represents the ownership of the firm. Ordinarily, common stock increases in value when the value of real assets rises during an inflationary period.

Disadvantages   First, the sale of common stock extends voting rights or control to the additional stockowners who are brought into the company. For this reason, among others, additional equity financing is often avoided by small and new firms. The owner-managers may be unwilling to share control of their companies with outsiders.

Second, common stock gives more owners the right to share in income. The use of debt may enable the firm to utilize funds at a fixed low cost, whereas common stock gives equal rights to new stockholders to share in the net profits of the firm.

Third, as we saw in Chapter 13, the costs of underwriting and distributing common stock are usually higher than those for underwriting and distributing preferred stock or debt. Flotation costs for selling common stock are characteristically higher because (1) costs of investigating an equity security investment are higher than investigating the feasibility of a comparable debt security, and (2) stocks are more risky, which means equity holdings must be diversified, which in turn means that a given dollar amount of new stock must be sold to a greater number of purchasers than the same amount of debt.

Fourth, as we shall see in Chapter 20, if the firm has less debt than is called for in the optimum capital structure, the average cost of capital will be higher than necessary.

Fifth, common stock dividends are not deductible as an expense for calculating the corporation's income subject to the federal income tax, but bond interest is deductible. The impact of this factor is reflected in the relative cost of equity capital vis-a-vis debt capital.

From a Social Viewpoint

Common stock should also be considered from a social standpoint. Common stock is a desirable form of financing because it renders business firms, hence a major segment of the economy, less vulnerable to the consequences of declines in sales and earnings. If sales and earnings decline, common stock financing involves no fixed charges, the payment of which might force the firm into reorganization or bankruptcy.

However, another aspect of common stock financing may have less desirable social consequences. Common stock prices fall in recessions, and this causes a rise in the cost of equity capital.[5] The rising cost of equity raises the overall cost of capital, which in turn reduces investment. This reduction further aggravates the recession. However, an expanding economy is accompanied by rising stock prices, and with rising stock prices comes a drop in the cost of capital. This, in turn, stimulates investment, which may add to a developing inflationary boom. In summary, a consideration of its effect on the cost of capital suggests that stock financing may tend to amplify cyclical fluctuations.

[5]See Chapter 18.

Just how these opposing forces combine to produce a net effect is unknown, but the authors believe that the first is the stronger; that is, stock financing tends to stabilize the economy.

USE OF RIGHTS IN FINANCING

If the preemptive right is contained in a particular firm's charter, then it must offer any new common stock to existing stockholders. If the charter does not prescribe a preemptive right, the firm has a choice of making the sale to its existing stockholders or to an entirely new set of investors. If the sale is to the existing stockholders, the stock flotation is called a *rights offering.* Each stockholder is issued an option to buy a certain number of the new shares, and the terms of the option are contained on a piece of paper called a *right.* Each stockholder receives one right for each share of stock he owns. The advantages and disadvantages of rights offerings are described in this section.

THEORETICAL RELATIONSHIPS

Several issues confront the financial manager who is deciding on the details of a rights offering. The various considerations can be made clear by the use of illustrative data on the Southeast Company, whose balance sheet and income statement are given in Table 14–2.

TABLE 14–2 Southeast Company Financial statements before rights offering

Partial balance sheet		
	Total debt, 5%	$ 40,000,000
	Common stock	10,000,000
	Retained earnings	50,000,000
Total assets $100,000,000	Total liabilities and capital	$100,000,000

Partial income statement	
Total earnings	$10,000,000
Interest on debt	2,000,000
Income before taxes	8,000,000
Taxes (50% assumed)	4,000,000
Earnings after taxes	4,000,000
Earnings per share (1,000,000 shares)	$4
Market price of stock (price/earnings ratio of 25 assumed)	$100

Southeast earns $4 million after taxes and has 1 million shares outstanding, so earnings per share are $4. The stock sells at 25 times earnings, or for

$100 a share. The company plans to raise $10 million of new equity funds through a rights offering and decides to sell the new stock to shareholders for $80 a share. The questions now facing the financial manager are

1. How many rights will be required to purchase a share of the newly issued stock?
2. What is the value of each right?
3. What effect will the rights offering have on the price of the existing stock?

We will now analyze each of these questions.

Number of Rights Needed to Purchase a New Share

Southeast plans to raise $10 million in new equity funds and to sell the new stock at a price of $80 a share. Dividing the subscription price into the total funds to be raised gives the number of shares to be issued:

$$\text{Number of new shares} = \frac{\text{funds to be raised}}{\text{subscription price}} = \frac{\$10,000,000}{\$80}$$

$$= 125,000 \text{ shares.}$$

The next step is to divide the number of new shares into the number of previously outstanding shares to get the number of rights required to subscribe to one share of the new stock. Note that stockholders always get one right for each share of stock they own:

$$\begin{array}{l}\text{Number of rights needed to} \\ \text{buy a share of the stock}\end{array} = \frac{\text{old shares}}{\text{new shares}} = \frac{1,000,000}{125,000} = 8 \text{ rights.}$$

Therefore, a stockholder will have to surrender eight rights plus $80 to receive one of the newly issued shares. Had the subscription price been set at $95 a share, 9.5 rights would have been required to subscribe to each new share; if the price had been set at $10 a share, only one right would have been needed.

Value of a Right

It is clearly worth something to be able to buy, for less than $100, a share of stock selling for $100. The right provides this privilege, so the right must have a value. To see how the theoretical value of a right is established, we continue with the example of the Southeast Company, assuming that it will raise $10 million by selling 125,000 new shares at $80 a share.

First, notice that the *market value* of the old stock was $100 million: $100 a share times 1 million shares. (The book value is irrelevant.) When the firm sells the new stock, it brings in an additional $10 million. As a first approximation, we assume that the market value of the common stock increases by exactly this $10 million. Actually, the market value of all the common stock will go up by more than $10 million if investors think the company will be able to invest these funds at a yield substantially in excess of the cost of equity capital, but it will go up by less than $10 million if investors are doubtful of the company's ability to put the new funds to work profitably in the near future.

Under the assumption that market value exactly reflects the new funds brought in, the total market value of the common stock after the new issue will be $110 million. Dividing this new value by the new total number of shares outstanding, 1.125 million, we obtain a new market value of $97.78 a share. Therefore, we see that after the financing has been completed, the price of the common stock will have fallen from $100 to $97.78.

Since the rights give the stockholders the privilege of buying for only $80 a share of stock that will end up being worth $97.78, thus saving $17.78, is $17.78 the value of each right? The answer is "no," because eight rights are required to buy one new share; we must divide $17.78 by 8 to get the value of each right. In the example each one is worth $2.22.

Ex Rights

The Southeast Company's rights have a very definite value, and this value accrues to the holders of the common stock. But what happens if stock is traded during the offering period? Who will receive the rights, the old owners or the new? The standard procedure calls for the company to set a "holder-of-record date," then for stock to go *ex rights* four trading days prior to the holder-of-record date. If the stock is sold prior to the ex rights date, the new owner will receive the rights; if it is sold on or after the ex rights date, the old owner will receive them. For example, on October 15, Southeast Company might announce the terms of the new financing, stating that rights will be mailed out on December 1 to stockholders of record as of the close of business on November 15. Anyone buying the old stock on or before November 11 will receive the rights; anyone buying the stock on or after November 12 will *not* receive the rights. Thus, November 12 is the *ex rights date;* before November 12 the stock sells *rights on.* In the case of Southeast Company, the *rights-on price* is $100, the *ex rights price* is $97.78.

Formula Value of a Right

Rights On   Equations have been developed for determining the value of rights without going through all the procedures described above. While the stock is still selling rights on, the value at which the rights will sell when they are issued can be found by use of the following formula:

$$\text{Value of one right} = \frac{\text{market value of stock, rights on} - \text{subscription price}}{\text{number of rights required to purchase one share plus 1}}.$$

$$R = \frac{M_0 - S}{N + 1}. \tag{14-5}$$

Here

M_0 = the rights-on price of the stock

S = the subscription price

N = the number of rights required to purchase a new share of stock

R = the value of one right.

Substituting the appropriate values for the Southeast Company, we obtain

$$R = \frac{\$100 - \$80}{8 + 1} = \frac{\$20}{9} = \$2.22.$$

This agrees with the value of the rights we found by the long procedure.

Ex Rights Suppose you are a stockholder in the Southeast Company. When you return to the United States from a trip to Europe, you read about the rights offering in the newspaper. The stock is now selling ex rights for $97.78 a share. How can you calculate the theoretical value of a right? Simply using the following formula, which follows the logic described in preceding sections, you can determine the value of each right to be $2.22:

$$\text{Value of one right} = \frac{\text{market value of stock, ex rights} - \text{subscription price}}{\text{number of rights required to purchase one share}}.$$

$$R = \frac{M_e - S}{N}. \tag{14-6}$$

$$R = \frac{\$97.78 - \$80}{8} = \frac{\$17.78}{8} = \$2.22.$$

Here M_e is the ex rights price of the stock.[6]

---

[6]We developed Equation 14–6 directly from the verbal explanation given in the above section, "Value of a Right." Equation 14–5 can then be derived from Equation 14–6 as follows:

1. Note that

$$M_e = M_0 - R. \tag{14-7}$$

EFFECTS ON POSITION OF STOCKHOLDERS

A stockholder has the choice of exercising his rights or selling them. If he has sufficient funds, and if he wants to buy more shares of the company's stock, the stockholder will exercise the rights. If he does not have the money or does not want to buy more stock, he will sell his rights. In either case, provided the formula value of the rights holds true, the stockholder will neither benefit nor lose by the rights offering. This statement can be made clear by considering the position of an individual stockholder in the Southeast Company.

The stockholder had eight shares of stock before the rights offering. The eight shares each had a market value of $100 a share, so the stockholder had a total market value of $800 in the company's stock. If he exercises his rights, he will be able to purchase one additional share at $80 a share, a new investment of $80; his total investment is now $880. He now owns nine shares of his company's stock, which, after the rights offering, has a value of $97.78 a share. The value of his stock is $880, exactly what he has invested in it.

Alternatively, if he sold his eight rights, which have a value of $2.22 a right, he would receive $17.78 in cash. But his original eight shares now have a market price of $97.78 a share. The $782.22 market value of his stock plus the $17.78 in cash is the same as the original $800 market value of stock with which he began. From a purely mechanical or arithmetical standpoint, the stockholder neither benefits nor gains from the sale of additional shares of stock through rights. Of course, if he forgets to exercise or sell his rights, or if brokerage costs of selling the rights are excessive, then a stockholder can suffer a loss. But, in general, the issuing firm makes special efforts to minimize brokerage costs, and adequate time is given to enable the stockholder to take some action, so losses are minimal.

Oversubscription Privilege

Even though the rights are very valuable and *should* be exercised, some stockholders will doubtless neglect to do so. Still, all the stock *will* be sold because of the *oversubscription privilege* contained in most rights offerings.

---

2. Substitute Equation 14–7 into Equation 14–6, obtaining

$$R = \frac{M_0 - R - S}{N}. \tag{14-8}$$

3. Simplify Equation 14–8 as follows, ending with Equation 14–5. This completes the derivation.

$$RN = M_0 - R - S$$
$$RN + R = M_0 - S$$
$$R(N + 1) = M_0 - S \tag{14-5}$$
$$R = \frac{M_0 - S}{N + 1}.$$

The oversubscription privilege gives subscribing stockholders the right to buy, on a pro rata basis, all shares not taken in the initial offering. To illustrate, if John Doe owns 10 percent of the stock in Southeast Company and if 20 percent of the rights offered by the company are not exercised (or sold) by the stockholders to whom they were originally given, then John Doe could buy an additional 2.5 percent of the new stock.[7] Since this stock is a bargain—$80 for stock worth $97.78—John Doe and other stockholders would use the oversubscription privilege, thus assuring the full sale of the new stock issue.

Relation between Market Price and Subscription Price

We can now investigate the factors influencing the use of rights and, if the rights are used, the level at which the subscription price will be set. The articles of incorporation of the Southeast Company permit it to use rights or not, depending on whether it judges their use to be advantageous to the company and its stockholders. The financial vice-president of the company is considering three alternative methods of raising the additional sum of $10 million.

Alternative 1   Southeast Company could sell to the public through investment bankers additional shares at approximately $100 a share, the company netting approximately $96 a share; thus, it would need to sell 105,000 shares in order to cover the underwriting commission.

Alternative 2   The company could sell additional shares through rights, using investment bankers and paying a commission of 1 percent on the total dollar amount of the stock sold plus an additional ¾ percent on all shares unsubscribed and taken over by the investment bankers. Allowing for the usual market pressure when common stock is sold, the new shares would be sold at a 20 percent discount, or at $80. Thus, 125,000 additional shares would be offered through rights. With eight rights, an additional share could be purchased at $80.

We noted above that stockholders are given the right to subscribe to any unexercised rights on a pro rata basis. Only shares not subscribed to on either the original or secondary basis are sold to the underwriters and subjected to the ¾ percent additional commission.

Alternative 3   The company could sell additional shares through rights at $10 a share. Investment bankers would not be employed at all. The number of additional shares of common stock to be sold would be one million. For each right held, existing stockholders would be permitted to buy one share of the new common stock.

[7]Eighty percent of the stock was subscribed. Doe subscribed to 10/80, or 12.5 percent of the stock that was taken; he can obtain 12.5 percent of the unsubscribed stock. Therefore, his oversubscription allocation is 12.5 percent × 20 = 2.5 percent of the new stock.

Under alternative 1, investment bankers are used and rights would not be utilized at all. In this circumstance the underwriting commission, or flotation cost, is approximately 4 percent. In alternative 2, where rights are used with a small discount, the underwriting commission is reduced, because the discount removes much of the risk of not being able to sell the issue. The underwriting commission consists of two parts—1 percent on the original issue and an additional ¾ of 1 percent commission on all unsubscribed shares the investment bankers are required to take over and sell. Thus, the actual commission will range somewhere between 1 percent and 1¾ percent. Under alternative 3, the subscription price is $10 a share. With such a large concession, the company does not need to use investment bankers at all, because the rights are certain to have value and to be either exercised or sold. Which of the three alternatives is superior?

Alternative 1 will provide a wider distribution of the securities sold, thus lessening any possible control problems. Also, it provides assurance from the investment bankers that the company will receive the $10 million involved in the new issue. The company pays for these services in the form of underwriting charges. The stock price, after the issue, should be approximately $100.

Under alternative 2, by utilizing rights, the company reduces its underwriting expenses. There is also a small reduction in the unit price per share, from $100 to $97.78 a share. Moreover, some stockholders may neither exercise nor sell their rights, thus suffering a loss. Existing stockholders will buy some of the new shares, so the distribution is likely to be less wide. Because of the underwriting contract, the firm, under alternative 2, is also assured of receiving the funds sought. Finally, it is often argued that investors like the opportunity of purchasing additional shares through rights offerings and that the use of rights offerings increases "stockholder loyalty."

Alternative 3 involves no underwriting expense, and it results in a substantial decrease in the unit price of shares. Initially, however, the shares will be less widely distributed. Note that alternative 3 has a large stock-split effect, which results in a much lower final stock price per share.[8] Many people feel that there is an optimal stock price—one that will produce a maximum total market value of the shares—and that this price is generally in the range of $30 to $60 a share. If this is the feeling of Southeast's directors, they may believe that alternative 3 permits them to reach this more desirable price range, while at the same time reducing flotation costs on the new issue. However, since the rights have a substantial value, any stockholder who fails either to exercise or to sell them would suffer a serious loss.

The three alternatives are summarized in Table 14–3. The alternative that is most advantageous depends upon the company's needs. If the company is strongly interested in a wider distribution of its securities, alternative 1

---

[8]Stock splits are discussed in Chapter 21. Basically, a stock split is simply the issuance of additional shares to existing stockholders for *no* additional funds. Stock splits "divide the pie into more pieces."

is preferable. If it is most interested in reducing the unit price of its shares and is confident that the lower unit price will induce wider distribution of its shares, alternative 3 will be chosen. If the company's needs are moderate in both directions, alternative 2 may offer a satisfactory compromise. Whether rights will be used and the level of the subscription price both depend upon the needs of the company at a particular time.

TABLE 14–3 Summary of Three Methods of Raising Additional Money

	Advantages	*Disadvantages*
Alternative 1	1. Wider distribution 2. Certainty of receiving funds	1. High underwriting costs
Alternative 2	1. Smaller underwriting costs 2. Lower unit price of shares 3. Certainty of receiving funds 4. Increase stockholder loyalty	1. More narrow distribution 2. Losses to forgetful stockholders
Alternative 3	1. No underwriting costs 2. Substantial decrease in unit price of shares 3. Increase stockholder loyalty	1. More narrow distribution 2. Severe losses to forgetful stockholders

Exercise of Rights

Interestingly enough, it is expected that in most cases a small percentage of stockholders may neglect to exercise their rights or to sell them. In a recent offering, the holders of 1½ percent of the shares of General Motors common stock did not exercise their rights. The loss involved to these stockholders was $1.5 million. In a recent AT&T issue, the loss to shareholders who neglected to exercise their rights was $960,000.

Market Price and Subscription Price

Measured from the registration date for the new issue of the security, the average percentage by which the subscription prices of new issues were below their market prices has been about 15 percent in recent years. Examples of price concessions of 40 percent or more are observed in a small percentage of issues, but the most frequently encountered discounts are from 10 to 20 percent.

Effect on Subsequent Behavior of Market Price of Stock

It is often stated that new issues of stock through rights will depress the price of the existing common stock of the company. To the extent that a subscription price in connection with the rights offering is lower than the market price, there will be a "stock-split effect" on the market price of the common stock. With the prevailing market price of Southeast Company's stock at $100 and a $10 subscription price, the new market price will probably drop to about $55.

But the second question is whether, because of the rights offering, the actual new market price will be $55 or lower or higher. Again, empirical analysis of the movement in stock prices during rights offerings indicates that generalization is not practical. What happens to the market price of the stock ex rights and after the rights trading period depends upon the prospects of the issuing company.

ADVANTAGES OF USE OF RIGHTS IN NEW FINANCING

We have seen that the preemptive right gives the shareholders the protection of preserving their pro rata share in the earnings and control of the company. The firm also benefits. By offering new issues of securities to the existing stockholders, it increases the likelihood of a favorable reception for the stock. By their ownership of common stock in the company, these investors have already indicated a favorable evaluation of the company. They may be receptive to the purchase of additional shares, particularly when the additional reasons indicated below are taken into account.

The shares purchased with rights are also subject to lower margin requirements. For example, margin requirements since January 1974 have been 50 percent; in other words, a person buying listed stocks must have at least $50 of his own funds for every $100 of securities purchased. However, if shares of new issues of stocks are purchased with rights, only $25 per $100 of common stock purchased must be furnished by the investor himself; he is permitted by law to borrow up to 75 percent of the purchase price. Furthermore, the absence of a clear pattern in the price behavior of the adjusted market price of the stocks and rights before, during, and after the trading period may enhance interest in the investment possibilities of the instruments.

These factors may offset the tendency toward a downward pressure on the price of the common stock occurring at the time of a new issue.[9] With the increased interest in, and advantages afforded by, the rights offering, the "true" or "adjusted" downward price pressure may actually be avoided.

A related advantage is that the flotation costs to an issuer associated with a rights offering will be lower than the costs of a public flotation. Costs referred to here are cash costs. For example, the flotation costs of industrial

---

[9]The downward pressure develops because of an increase in the supply of securities without a necessarily equivalent increase in the demand. Generally it is a temporary phenomenon, and the stock tends to return to the theoretical price after a few months. Obviously, if the acquired funds are invested at a very high rate of return, the stock price benefits; if the investment does not turn out well, the stock price suffers.

issues of common stock in 1955 were 9 percent on public issues compared with 3.8 percent of the proceeds to the company on rights offerings.[10] The financial manager may obtain positive benefits from underpricing. Since a rights offering is a stock split to a certain degree, it will cause the market price of the stock to fall to a level lower than it otherwise would have been. But stock splits may increase the number of shareholders in a company by bringing the price of a stock into a more attractive trading level. Furthermore, because a rights offering is an indirect stock split, it may result in additional dividends for the stockholders.

Finally, the total effect of the rights offering may be to stimulate an enthusiastic response from stockholders and the investment market as a whole, with the result that opportunities for financing become more attractive to the firm. Thus, the financial manager may be able to engage in common stock financing at lower costs and under more favorable terms.

SUMMARY

In this chapter, a number of characteristics of common stock financing have been presented. The advantages and disadvantages of external equity financing, compared with the use of preferred stock and debt, have been described. The purpose of the descriptive background material has been to provide a basis for making sound decisions when financing by common stock is being considered as a possible alternative.

The chapter also discussed the key decisions confronting the financial manager when he considers a rights offering, and indicated the major features bearing on such decisions. Rights offerings may be used effectively by financial managers to increase the goodwill of shareholders. If the new financing associated with the rights represents a sound decision—one likely to result in improved earnings for the firm—a rise in stock values will probably result. The use of rights will permit shareholders to preserve their positions or to improve them. However, if investors feel that the new financing is not well advised, the rights offering may cause the price of the stock to decline by more than the value of the rights.

Because the rights offering is directed to existing shareholders, it may be possible to reduce the costs of floating the new issue.

A major decision for financial managers in a rights offering is to set the subscription price, or the amount of the concession, from the existing market price of the stock. Formulas reflecting the static effects of a rights offering indicate that neither the stockholders nor the company benefits or loses from the price changes. The rights offering has the effect of a stock split. The level set for the subscription price will, to a great degree, reflect the objectives and effects of a stock split.

[10]H. W. Stevenson, *Common Stock Financing* (Ann Arbor: University of Michigan, 1957), p. 61.

The subsequent price behavior of the rights and the common stock in the associated new offering will reflect the earnings and dividends prospects of the company, as well as the underlying developments in the securities markets. The new financing associated with the rights offering may be an indicator of prospective growth in the sales and earnings of the company. The stock-split effects of the rights offering may be used to alter the company's dividend payments. The effects of these developments on the market behavior of the rights and the securities before, during, and after the rights trading period will reflect the expectations of investors toward the outlook for earnings and dividends per share.

QUESTIONS

14-1. What percentage could total assets shrink in value on liquidation before creditors incur losses in each of the following cases:
  a. Equity to total asset ratio, 50 percent?
  b. Debt to equity ratio, 50 percent?
  c. Debt to total asset ratio, 40 percent?

14-2. How many shares must a minority group own in order to assure election of two directors if nine new directors will be elected and 200,000 shares are outstanding? Assume cumulative voting exists.

14-3. Should the preemptive right entitle stockholders to purchase convertible bonds before they are offered to outsiders?

14-4. It is frequently stated that the primary purpose of the preemptive right is to allow individuals to maintain their proportionate share of the ownership and control of a corporation. Just how important do you suppose this consideration is for the average stockholder of a firm whose shares are traded on the New York or the American stock exchanges? Is the preemptive right likely to be of more importance to stockholders of closely held firms?

14-5. How would the success of a rights offering be affected by a declining stock market?

14-6. What are some of the advantages and disadvantages of setting the subscription price on a rights offering substantially below the current market price of the stock?

14-7. Is a firm likely to get wider distribution of shares if it sells new stock through a rights offering or directly to underwriters? Why would a company be interested in getting a wider distribution of shares?

PROBLEMS

14-1. The Rolley Company needs to raise $10 million in common stock. The price per share is now $50 for Rolley. Underwriters have informed you that they will price the new issue at $48 per share to make sure it moves out. Further, total expenses of 7.2 percent of gross proceeds will be required in the flotation of this stock. How many shares of Rolley should be sold to net the firm $10 million after underpricing and flotation expenses?

14-2. The common stock of Irving Development Company is selling for $55 on the market. The stockholders are offered one new share at a subscription price of $25 for every five shares held. What is the value of each right?

14-3. American Appliance Company common stock is priced at $72 a share on the market. Notice is given that stockholders may purchase one new share at a price of $40 for every seven shares held. You hold 120 shares at the time of notice.

a. At approximately what price will each right sell on the market?

b. Why will this be the approximate price?

c. What effect will the issuance of rights have on the original market price? Why?

14-4. Shawn has 300 shares of Piper Industries. The market price per share is $75. The company now offers stockholders one new share to be purchased at $60 for every four shares held.

a. Determine the value of each right.

b. Assume that Shawn (1) uses 80 rights and sells the other 220, or (2) sells 300 rights at the market price you have calculated. Prepare a statement showing the changes in her position under the above assumptions.

14-5. The Eastman Company has the following balance sheet and income statement:

The Eastman Company

Balance Sheet before Rights Offering	Total debt (6%)	$ 7,000,000
	Common stock (100,000 shares)	3,000,000
	Retained earnings	4,000,000
Total assets $14,000,000	Total liabilities and capital	$14,000,000

Income Statement before Rights Offering	
Earning rate: 12% on total assets	
Total earnings	$ 1,680,000
Interest on debt	420,000
Income before taxes	$ 1,260,000
Taxes (50% rate assumed)	630,000
Earnings after taxes	$ 630,000
Earnings per share	$ 6.30
Dividends per share (56% of earnings)	$ 3.53
Price/earnings ratio	15 times
Market price per share	$94.50

The Eastman Company plans to raise an additional $5 million through a rights offering. The additional funds will continue to earn 12 percent. The price/earnings ratio is assumed to remain at 15 times, dividend payout will continue to be 56 percent, and the 50 percent tax rate will remain in effect. (Do not attempt to use the formulas given in the chapter for this problem. Additional information is given here which violates the "other things constant" assumption inherent in the formula.)

a. Assuming subscription prices of $25, $50, and $80 a share:

1. How many additional shares of stock will have to be sold?

2. How many rights will be required to purchase one new share?

3. What will be the new earnings per share?

4. What will be the new market price per share?

5. What will be the new dividend per share if the dividend payout ratio is maintained?

b. What is the significance of your results?

14-6. The Freezer-Mate Food Company is principally engaged in the business of growing, processing, and marketing a variety of frozen vegetables and is a major company in this field. High-quality products are produced and marketed at premium prices.

During each of the past several years the company's sales have increased and the needed inventories have been financed from short-term sources. The officers have discussed the idea of refinancing their bank loans with long-term debt or common stock. A common stock issue of 310,000 shares sold at this time (present market price $72 a share) would yield $21 million after expenses. This same sum could be raised by selling twelve-year bonds with an interest rate of 8 percent and a sinking fund to retire the bonds over their twelve-year life. (See statements below.)

a. Should Freezer-Mate Food refinance the short-term loans? Why?

b. If the bank loans should be refinanced, what factors should be considered in determining which form of financing to use? (This question should not be an--swered in terms of precise cost of capital calculations. Rather, a more qualitative and subjective analysis is appropriate. The only calculations necessary are some simple ratios. Careful interpretation of these ratios is necessary, however, to understand and discuss the often complex, subjective judgment issues involved.)

Food Processing Industry Financial Ratios

Current ratio	2.2 times
Sales to total assets	2.0 times
Sales to inventory	5.6 times
Average collection period	22.0 days
Current debt/total assets	25–30%
Long-term debt/total assets	10–15%
Preferred/total assets	0.5%
Net worth/total assets	60–65%
Profits to sales	2.3%
Net profits to total assets	4.0%
Profits to net worth	8.4%
Expected growth rate of earnings and dividends	6.5%

Freezer-Mate Food Company
Consolidated balance sheet
March 31, 1975* (in millions of dollars)

Current assets	$141	Accounts payable	$12	
Fixed plant and equipment	57	Notes payable	36	
Other assets	12	Accruals	15	
		Total current liabilities		$ 63
		Long-term debt, 5%		63
		Preferred stock		9
		Common stock (par $6)	$12	
		Retained earnings	63	
		Net worth		75
Total assets	$210	Total claims on assets		$210

*The majority of harvesting activities do not begin until late April or May.

Freezer-Mate Food Company
Consolidated statement of income
Year ended March 31 (in millions of dollars)

	1972	1973	1974	1975
Net sales	225.0	234.6	292.8	347.1
Cost of goods sold	146.1	156.6	195.3	230.4
Gross profit	78.9	78.0	97.5	116.7
Other expenses	61.8	66.0	81.0	88.5
Operating income	17.1	12.0	16.5	28.2
Other income (net)	(3.3)	(4.2)	(5.7)	(9.3)
Earnings before tax	13.8	7.8	10.8	18.9
Taxes	7.2	3.3	5.4	9.6
Net profit	6.6	4.5	5.4	9.3
Preferred dividend	0.3	0.3	0.3	0.3
Earnings available to common stock	$ 6.3	$ 4.2	$ 5.1	$ 9.0
Earnings per share	$ 3.15	$ 2.10	$ 2.55	$ 4.50
Cash dividends per share	1.29	1.44	1.59	1.80
Price range for common stock				
High	$ 66.00	$ 69.00	$ 66.00	$ 81.00
Low	30.00	42.00	51.00	63.00

Fixed Income Securities: Debt and Preferred Stock

15 There are many classes of fixed income securities: long term and short term, secured and unsecured, marketable and nonmarketable, participating and nonparticipating, senior and junior, and so on.

Different classes of investors favor different classes of securities, and tastes change over time. An astute financial manager knows how to "package" his securities at a given point in time to make them most attractive to the most potential investors, thereby keeping his cost of capital to a minimum. This chapter deals with the two most important types of long-term, fixed income securities—bonds and preferred stocks.

INSTRUMENTS OF LONG-TERM DEBT FINANCING

For an understanding of long-term forms of financing, we need some familiarity with technical terminology. The discussion of long-term debt therefore begins with an explanation of several important instruments and terms.

Bond

Most people have had some experience with short-term promissory notes. A *bond* is simply a long-term promissory note.

Mortgage

A *mortgage* represents a pledge of designated property for a loan. Under a *mortgage bond,* the corporation pledges certain real assets as security for

314

the bond. A mortgage bond is therefore secured by real property.[1] The pledge is a condition of the loan.

Debenture

A *debenture* is a long-term bond that is *not* secured by a pledge of any specific property. However, like other general creditor claims, it is secured by any property not otherwise pledged.

Indenture

Since a bond is a long-term promissory note, a long-term relation between borrower and lender is established in a document called an *indenture.* When it is a matter of an ordinary sixty- or ninety-day promissory note, few new developments are likely to occur in the life or affairs of the borrower to endanger repayment. The lender looks closely at the borrower's current position, because current assets are the main source of repayment. A bond, however, is a long-term contractual relationship between the issuer of the bond and the bondholders; over such an extended period the bondholder has cause to worry that the firm's position might change materially.

In the ordinary common stock or preferred stock certificate or agreement, the details of the contractual relation can be summarized in a few paragraphs. The bond indenture, however, may be a document of several hundred pages covering a large number of factors that will be important to the contractual parties. It discusses the form of the bond and the instrument. It provides a complete description of property pledged. It specifies the authorized amount of the bond issue. It contains protective clauses, or *covenants,* which are detailed and which usually include limits on indebtedness, restrictions on dividends, and a sinking fund provision. Generally a minimum current ratio requirement, as well as provisions for redemption or call privileges, are also added.

Trustee

Not only is a bond of long duration, but the issue is also likely to be of substantial size. Before the rise of the large aggregations of savings through insurance companies or pension funds, no single buyer was able to buy an issue of such size. Bonds were therefore issued in denominations of $1,000 each and were sold to a large number of purchasers. To facilitate communication between the issuer and the numerous bondholders, another device was instituted, the trustee, who is the representative of the bondholders. The

---

[1] There is also the *chattel mortgage,* which is secured by personal property, but this is generally an intermediate-term instrument. *Real property* is defined as real estate—land and building. *Personal property* is defined as anything else, including equipment, inventories, furniture, and so on.

trustee is presumed to act at all times for the protection of the bondholders and on their behalf.

Any legal person, including a corporation, is considered competent to act as a trustee. Typically, however, the duties of the trustee are handled by a department of a commercial bank.

The trustee has three main responsibilities. (1) The trustee certifies the issue of bonds. This duty involves making certain that all the legal requirements for drawing up the bond contract and the indenture have been carried out. (2) The trustee polices the behavior of the corporation in its performance of the responsibilities set forth in the indenture provisions. (3) The trustee is responsible for taking appropriate action on behalf of the bondholders if the corporation defaults on payment of interest or principal.

It is said that in many corporate bond defaults in the early 1930s, trustees did not act in the best interests of the bondholders. The trustees did not conserve the assets of the corporation effectively. Often they did not take early action, so that corporation executives continued their salaries and disposed of assets under conditions favorable to themselves but detrimental to the bondholders. Assets pledged as security for the bonds were sold; specific security was, thus, no longer available. The result in many instances was that holders of mortgage bonds found themselves more in the position of general creditors than in that of secured bondholders.

As a consequence of such practices, the Trust Indenture Act of 1939 was passed in order to give more protection to bondholders. It provides that trustees must be given sufficient power to act on behalf of bondholders. The indenture must fully disclose rights and responsibilities and must not be deceptive. There is provision for changes in the indenture at the option of the bondholders. It is specifically required that prompt, protective action be taken by the trustees for bondholders if default occurs. Provision is made for making certain that an arm's-length relation exists between the issuing corporation and the trustee, and the corporation must make periodic reports to its trustee to enable him to carry out his protective responsibilities.

Call Provision

A *call provision* gives the issuing corporation the right to call in the bond for redemption. If it is used, the call provision generally states that the company must pay an amount greater than the par value of the bond, with this additional sum being defined as the *call premium.* The call premium is typically set equal to one year's interest if the bond is called during the first year, with the premium declining at a constant rate each year thereafter. For example, the call premium on a $1,000 par value, twenty-year, 6 percent bond would generally be $60 if called during the first year, $57 if called during the second year (calculated by reducing the $60, or 6 percent, premium by one-twentieth), and so on.

As pointed out later in this chapter, the call privilege is valuable to the firm but potentially detrimental to the investor, especially if the bond is issued in a period when interest rates are thought to be cyclically high. Accordingly, the interest rate on a new issue of callable bonds will exceed that on a new issue of noncallable bonds. For example, on May 24, 1976, Great Falls Power Company sold an issue of A-rated bonds to yield 9.375 percent. These bonds were callable immediately. On the same day, Midwest Electric sold an issue of A-rated bonds to yield 9.20 percent. Midwest's bonds were noncallable for ten years. Investors were apparently willing to accept a 0.175 percent lower interest rate on Midwest's bonds for the assurance that the relatively high (by historic standards) rate of interest would be earned for at least ten years. Great Falls, on the other hand, had to incur a 0.175 percent higher annual interest rate for the privilege of calling the bonds in the event of a subsequent decline in interest rates. We will discuss the analysis for determining when to call an issue later in this chapter.

Sinking Fund

A *sinking fund* is a provision that facilitates the orderly retirement of a bond issue. Typically, the sinking fund provision requires the firm to buy and retire a portion of the bond issue each year. Sometimes the stipulated sinking fund payment is tied to sales or earnings of the current year, but usually it is a mandatory fixed amount. If it is mandatory, a failure to meet the sinking fund payment causes the bond issue to be thrown into default and could lead the company into bankruptcy. Obviously, then, a sinking fund can constitute a dangerous cash drain on the firm.

In most cases the firm is given the right to handle the sinking fund in either of two ways. (1) It may call a certain percentage of the bonds at a stipulated price each year—for example, 2 percent of the original amount at a price of $1,050; the actual bonds to be called, which are numbered serially, are determined by a lottery. (2) It may spend the funds provided by the sinking fund payment to buy the bonds on the open market. The firm will do whichever results in the greatest reduction of outstanding bonds for a given expenditure. Therefore, if interest rates have risen (and the price of the bonds has fallen), the firm will choose the open market alternative. If interest rates have fallen and bond prices have risen, the company will elect to use the option of calling bonds.

It must be recognized that the call provision of the sinking fund may at times work to the detriment of bondholders. If, for example, the bond carries a 7 percent interest rate, and if yields on similar securities are 4 percent, the bond will sell for well above par. A sinking fund call at par would thus greatly disadvantage some bondholders. On balance, securities that provide for a sinking fund and continuing redemption are likely to be offered initially on a lower yield basis than are securities without such a fund. Since sinking funds provide additional protection to investors, sinking fund bonds are likely to sell initially at higher prices; hence, they have a lower cost of capital to the issuer.

Funded Debt

Funded debt is simply long-term debt. When a firm is said to be planning to "fund" its floating debt, it will replace short-term securities by long-term securities. Funding does not imply placing money with a trustee or other repository; it is simply part of the jargon of finance and means "long term."[2]

SECURED BONDS

Secured long-term debt may be classified according to (1) the priority of claims, (2) the right to issue additional securities, and (3) the scope of the lien.

Priority of Claims

A senior mortgage has prior claims on assets and earnings. Senior railroad mortgages, for example, have been called the "mortgages next to the rail," implying that they have the first claim on the land and assets of the railroad corporations.

A junior mortgage is a subordinate lien, such as a second or a third mortgage. It is a lien or claim junior to others.

Right to Issue Additional Securities

Mortgage bonds may also be classified with respect to the right to issue additional obligations pledging already encumbered property.

In the case of a *closed-end mortgage,* a company may not sell additional bonds, beyond those already issued, secured by the property specified in the mortgage. For example, assume that a corporation with plant and land worth $5 million has a $2 million mortgage on these properties. If the mortgage is closed end, no more bonds having first liens on this property may be issued. Thus a closed-end mortgage provides greater security to the bond buyer. The ratio of the amount of the senior bonds to the value of the property will not be increased by subsequent issues.

If the bond indenture is silent on this point, it is called an *open-end mortgage.* Its nature may be illustrated by referring to the example cited above. Against property worth $5 million, bonds of $2 million are sold. If an additional first mortgage bond of $1 million is subsequently sold, the property has been pledged for a total of $3 million of bonds. If, on liquidation, the property sold for $2 million, the original bondholders would receive 67 cents on the dollar. If the mortgage had been closed end, they would have been fully paid.

---

[2]Tampa Electric Company provides a good example of funding. This company has a continuous construction program. Typically, it uses short-term debt to finance construction expenditures. However, once short-term debt has built up to about $75 million, the company sells a stock or bond issue, uses the proceeds to pay off its bank loans, and starts the cycle again. The high flotation costs of small security issues make this process desirable.

Most characteristic is the *limited open-end mortgage.* Its nature may be indicated by continuing the example. A first mortgage bond issue of $2 million, secured by the property worth $5 million, is sold. The indenture provides that an additional $1 million worth of bonds—or an additional amount of bonds up to 60 percent of the original cost of the property—may be sold. Thus, the mortgage is open only up to a certain point.

Scope of the Lien

Bonds may also be classified with respect to the scope of their lien. When a *specific lien* exists, the security for a first mortgage or a second mortgage is a specifically designated property. A lien is granted on certain specified property. On the other hand, a *blanket mortgage* pledges all real property currently owned by the company. Real property includes only land and those things affixed thereto, so a blanket mortgage would not be a mortgage on cash, accounts receivables, or inventories because these items are personal property. A blanket mortgage gives more protection to the bondholder than does a specific mortgage because it provides a claim on all real property owned by the company.

UNSECURED BONDS

Debentures

A *debenture* is an unsecured bond and, as such, provides no lien on specific property as security for the obligation. Debenture holders are therefore general creditors whose claim is protected by property not otherwise pledged. The advantage of debentures from the standpoint of the issuer is that he leaves his property unencumbered for subsequent financing. However, in practice the use of debentures depends on the nature of the firm's assets and its general credit strength.

If the credit position of a firm is exceptionally strong, it can issue debentures—it simply does not need specific security. However, the credit position of a company may be so weak that it has no alternative to the use of debentures—all its property may already be encumbered. American Telephone & Telegraph's vast financing program since the end of World War II has been mainly through debentures, both convertible and straight debentures. AT&T is such a strong institution that it does not have to provide security for its debt issues.

Debentures are also issued by companies in industries where it would not be practical to provide a lien through a mortgage on fixed assets. Examples of such an industry would be the large mail order houses and the finance companies, which characteristically do not have large fixed assets in relation to their total assets. The bulk of their assets is in the form of inventory or receivables, neither of which is satisfactory security for a mortgage lien.

Subordinated Debentures

The term "subordinate" means below or inferior. Thus, *subordinated debt* has claims on assets after unsubordinated debt in the event of liquidation. Debentures may be subordinated to designated notes payable—usually bank loans—or to any or all other debt. In the event of liquidation or reorganization, the debentures cannot be paid until senior debt *as named in the indenture* has been paid. Senior debt typically does not include trade accounts payable. How the subordination provision strengthens the position of senior-debt holders is shown in Table 15–1.

TABLE 15–1 Illustration of Bankruptcy Payments to Senior Debt, Other Debt, and Subordinated Debt

Financial Structure	Book Value (1)	Percent of Total Debt (2)	Initial Allocation (3)	Actual Payment (4)	Percent of Original Claim Satisfied (5)
	I. $200 available for claims on liquidation				
Bank debt	$200	50%	$100	$150	75%
Other debt	100	25	50	50	50
Subordinated debt	100	25	50	0	0
Total debt	$400	100%	$200	$200	50%
Net worth	300				0
Total	$700				29%
	II. $300 available for claims on liquidation				
Bank debt	$200	50%	$150	$200	100%
Other debt	100	25	75	75	75
Subordinated debt	100	25	75	25	25
Total debt	$400	100%	$300	$300	75%
Net worth	300				0
Total	$700				43%

Steps: 1. Express each type of debt as a percentage of total debt (column 2).
2. Multiply the debt percentages (column 2) by the amount available, obtaining the initial allocations shown in column 3.
3. The subordinated debt is subordinate to bank debt. Therefore, the initial allocation to subordinate debt is added to the bank debt allocation until it has been exhausted or until the bank debt is finally paid off. This is given in column 4.

Where $200 is available for distribution, the subordinated debt has a claim on 25 percent of $200, or $50. However, this claim is subordinated only to the bank debt (the only senior debt) and is added to the $100 claim of the bank. As a consequence, 75 percent of the bank's original claim is satisfied.

Where $300 is available for distribution, the $75 allocated to the subordinated debt is divided into two parts: $50 goes to the bank and the other $25 remains for the subordinated debt holders. In this situation, the senior bank debt holders are fully paid off, 75 percent of other debt is paid, and the subordinated debt receives only 25 percent of its claim.

Subordination is frequently required. Alert credit managers of firms supplying trade credit, or commercial bank loan officers, typically will insist upon subordination, particularly where debt is owed to the principal stockholders or officers of a company. Also, convertible bonds are virtually always subordinated; in this case, they are subordinated to all the firm's other debt.

Preferred stock, in comparison to subordinated debt, suffers from the disadvantage that preferred stock dividends are not deductible as an expense for tax purposes. The interest on subordinated debentures is an expense for tax purposes. Some people have referred to subordinated debentures as being much like a special kind of preferred stock, the dividends of which are deductible as an expense for tax purposes. Subordinated debt has therefore become an increasingly important source of corporate capital.

The reasons for the use of subordinated debentures are clear. They offer a great tax advantage over preferred stock, yet they do not restrict the ability of the borrower to obtain senior debt, as would be the case if all debt sources were on an equal basis.

Subordinated debentures are further stimulated by periods of tight money when commercial banks may require a greater equity base for short-term financing. Subordinated debentures provide a greater equity cushion for loans from commercial banks or other forms of senior debt. The use of subordinated debentures also illustrates the development of hybrid securities that emerge to meet changing situations that develop in the capital market.

Income Bonds

Income bonds typically arise from corporate reorganizations, and these bonds pay interest only if income is actually earned by the company. Because the company, having gone through reorganization, has been in difficult financial circumstances, interest is not a fixed charge; the principal, however, must be paid when due.

Income bonds are like preferred stock in that management is not required to pay interest if it is not earned. However, they differ from preferred stock in that if interest has been earned, management is required to pay it, and also in that interest paid on income bonds is deductible for income tax purposes while preferred dividends are not.

The main characteristic and distinct advantage of the income bond is that interest is payable only if the company achieves some earnings. Since earnings calculations are subject to differing interpretations, the indenture of the income bond carefully defines income and expenses. If it did not, long, drawn-out litigation might result.

Some income bonds are cumulative indefinitely (if interest is not paid, it "accumulates" and must be paid at some future date); others are cumulative for the first three to five years, after which time they become noncumulative.

Income bonds usually contain sinking fund provisions to provide for their retirement. The payments to the sinking funds range between ½ and 1 percent of the face amount of the original issue. Because the sinking fund payments are typically dependent on earnings, a fixed-cash drain on the company is avoided.

Sometimes income bonds are convertible. There are sound reasons for their being convertible if they arise out of a reorganization. Creditors who receive income bonds in exchange for defaulted obligations have a less desirable position than they had previously. Since they have received something based on an adverse and problematical forecast of the future of the company, it is appropriate that if the company should prosper, income bondholders should be entitled to participate. When income bonds are issued in situations other than reorganization, the convertibility feature is a "sweetener" likely to make the issue more attractive to prospective bond buyers.

Typically, income bonds do not have voting rights when they are issued. Sometimes bondholders are given the right to elect one, two, or some specified number of directors if interest is not paid for a certain number of years.

CHARACTERISTICS OF LONG-TERM DEBT

From Viewpoint of Holder

Risk   Debt is favorable to the holder because it gives him priority both in earnings and in liquidation. Debt also has a definite maturity and is protected by the covenants of the indenture.

Income   The bondholder has a fixed return; except in the case of income bonds, interest payments are not contingent on the level of earnings of the company. However, debt does not participate in any superior earnings of the company, and gains are limited in magnitude. Note particularly that bondholders suffer during inflationary periods. A twenty-year, 6 percent bond pays $60 of interest each year. Under inflation, the purchasing power of this $60 is eroded, causing a loss in real value to the bondholder.[3] Frequently, long-term

---

[3]Recognizing this fact, investors demand higher interest rates during inflationary periods. This point is discussed at length in Chapters 18 and 22.

debt is callable. If bonds are called, the investor receives funds that must be reinvested to be kept active.

Control   The bondholder usually does not have the right to vote. However, if the bonds go into default, then bondholders will, in effect, take control of the company.

An overall appraisal of the characteristics of long-term debt indicates that for the investor it is good from the standpoint of risk, has limited advantages with regard to income, and is weak with respect to control.

From Viewpoint of Issuer

Advantages   The issuer of a bond has the following advantages.

1. The cost of debt is definitely limited. Bondholders do not participate in superior profits if earned.
2. Not only is the cost limited, but typically the expected yield is lower than the cost of common stock.
3. The owners of the corporation do not share their control when debt financing is used.
4. The interest payment on debt is deductible as a tax expense.
5. Flexibility in the financial structure of the corporation may be achieved by inserting a call provision in the bond indenture.

Disadvantages   Following are the disadvantages to the bond issuer.

1. Debt is a fixed charge; there is greater risk if the earnings of the company fluctuate because the corporation may be unable to meet these fixed charges.
2. As we will see in Chapter 18, higher risk brings higher capitalization rates on equity earnings. Thus, even though leverage is favorable and raises earnings per share, the higher capitalization rates attributable to leverage may drive the common stock value down.
3. Debt usually has a definite maturity date. Because of the fixed maturity date, the financial officer must make provision for repayment of the debt.
4. Since long-term debt is a commitment for a long period, it involves risk; the expectations and plans on which the debt was issued may change. The debt may prove to be a burden, or it may prove to have been advantageous. For example, if income, employment, the price level, and interest rates all fall greatly, the assumption of a large amount of long-term debt may prove to have been an unwise financial policy. The railroads are always given as an example in this regard. They were able to meet their ordinary operating expenses during the 1930s but were unable to meet the heavy financial charges they had undertaken earlier, when the prospects for the railroads looked more favorable than they turned out to be.
5. In a long-term contractual relationship, the indenture provisions are likely to be much more stringent than they are in a short-term credit agreement.

Hence the firm may be subject to much more disturbing and crippling restrictions in the indenture of a long-term debt arrangement than would be the case if it had borrowed on a short-term basis or had issued common stock.

6. There is a limit on the extent to which funds can be raised through long-term debt. Generally accepted standards of financial policy dictate that the debt ratio shall not exceed certain limits. These standards of financial prudence set limits or controls on the extent to which funds may be raised through long-term debt. When debt gets beyond these limits, its cost rises rapidly.

DECISIONS ON USE OF LONG-TERM DEBT

When a number of alternative methods of long-term financing are under consideration, the following conditions favor the use of long-term debt:

1. Sales and earnings are relatively stable, or a substantial increase in future sales and earnings is expected to provide a significant benefit from the use of leverage.
2. A substantial rise in the price level is expected in the future, making it advantageous for the firm to incur debt that will be repaid with cheaper dollars.
3. The existing debt ratio is relatively low for the line of business.
4. Management thinks the price of the common stock in relation to that of bonds is temporarily depressed.
5. Sale of common stock would involve problems of maintaining the existing control pattern in the company.

Decisions about the use of debt may also be considered in terms of the average cost of capital curve as developed in Chapter 20. There we will see that firms have optimal capital structures, or perhaps optimal ranges, and that the average cost of capital is higher than it need be if the firm uses a nonoptimal amount of debt. The factors listed above all relate to the optimal debt ratio: Some cause the optimal ratio to increase; others cause it to decrease.

Whenever the firm is contemplating raising new outside capital and is choosing between debt and equity, it is implicitly making a judgment about its actual debt ratio in relation to the optimal ratio. For example, consider Figure 15–1, which shows the assumed shape of the Longstreet Company's average cost of capital schedule. If Longstreet is planning to raise outside capital, it must make a judgment about whether it is presently at point A or point B. If it decides that it is at A, it should issue debt; if it believes that it is at B, the decision should be to sell new common stock. This, of course, is a judgment decision, but all the factors discussed in this chapter must be considered when the decision is being made. This subject is discussed further in Chapter 20.

FIGURE 15–1 The Longstreet Company's Average Cost of Capital Schedule

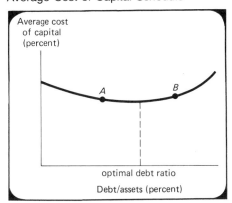

NATURE OF PREFERRED STOCK

Preferred stock has claims and rights ahead of common stock, but behind all bonds. The preference may be a prior claim on earnings, a prior claim on assets in the event of liquidation, or a preferential position with regard to both earnings and assets.

Hybrid Form

The hybrid nature of preferred stock becomes apparent when we try to classify it in relation to bonds and common stock. The priority feature and the (generally) fixed dividend indicate that preferred stock is similar to bonds. Payments to the preferred stockholders are limited in amount so that the common stockholders receive the advantages (or disadvantages) of leverage. However, if the preferred dividends are not earned, the company can forgo paying them without danger of bankruptcy. In this characteristic, preferred stock is similar to common stock. Moreover, failure to pay the stipulated dividend does not cause default of the obligation, as does failure to pay bond interest.

Debt and Equity   In some types of analysis, preferred stock is treated similarly to debt. For example, if the analysis is being made by a *common stockholder* considering the earnings fluctuations induced by fixed-charge securities, preferred stock would be treated like debt. Suppose, however, that the analysis is by a *bondholder* studying the firm's vulnerability to *failure* brought on by declines in sales or in income. Since the dividends on preferred stock are not a fixed charge in the sense that failure to pay them would represent a default of an obligation, preferred stock represents a cushion; it provides an additional equity base. From the point of view of *stockholders,* it is a leverage-inducing instrument much like debt. From the point of view of *creditors,* it constitutes additional net worth. Preferred stock may therefore be treated either as debt or as equity, depending on the nature of the problem under consideration.[4]

MAJOR PROVISIONS OF PREFERRED STOCK ISSUES

Because the possible characteristics, rights, and obligations of any specific security vary so widely, a point of diminishing returns is quickly reached in a descriptive discussion of different kinds of securities. As economic circumstances change, new kinds of securities are manufactured. The possibilities are numerous. The kinds and varieties of securities are limited chiefly by the imagination and ingenuity of the managers formulating the terms of the security issues. It is not surprising, then, that preferred stock can be found in a variety of forms. We will now look at the main terms and characteristics in each case and examine the possible variations in relation to the kinds of situations or circumstances in which they could occur.[5]

Priority in Assets and Earnings

Many provisions in a preferred stock certificate are designed to reduce risk to the purchaser in relation to the risk carried by the holder of common stock. Preferred stock usually has priority with regard to earnings and assets. Two provisions designed to prevent undermining these preferred stock priorities are often found. The first states that, without the consent of the holders of the preferred stock, there can be no subsequent sale of securities having a prior or equal claim on earnings. The second provision seeks to hold earnings in the firm. It requires a minimum level of retained earnings before common stock dividends are permitted. In order to assure the availability of liquid assets that may be converted into cash for the payment of dividends, the maintenance of a minimum current ratio may also be required.

Par Value

Unlike common stock, preferred stock usually has a par value, and this value is a meaningful quantity. First, it establishes the amount due to the preferred stockholders in the event of liquidation. Second, the preferred dividend is frequently stated as a percentage of the par value. For example, J. I. Case has preferred stock outstanding that has a par value of $100, and the dividend is

---

[4]Accountants generally include preferred stock in the equity portion of the capital structure. But preferred is *very different* from common equity.

[5]Much of the data in this section is taken from a study by Donald E. Fischer and Glenn A. Wilt, Jr., "Non-Convertible Preferred Stocks as a Financing Instrument," *Journal of Finance,* 23 (September 1968), pp. 611–624.

stated to be 7 percent of par. It would, of course, be just as appropriate for the Case preferred stock to state simply that the annual dividend is $7; on many preferred stocks the dividends are stated in this manner rather than as a percentage of par value.

Cumulative Dividends

A high percentage of dividends on preferred stocks is cumulative—all past preferred dividends must be paid before common dividends may be paid. The cumulative feature is therefore a protective device. If the preferred stock was not cumulative, preferred and common stock dividends could be passed by for a number of years. The company could then vote a large common stock dividend, but only the stipulated payment to preferred stock. Suppose the preferred stock with a par value of $100 carried a 7 percent dividend. Suppose the company did not pay dividends for several years so that it accumulated funds that would enable it to pay in total about $50 in dividends. It could pay one $7 dividend to the preferred stock and a $43 dividend to the common stock. Obviously, this device could be used to evade the preferred position that the holders of preferred stock have tried to obtain. The cumulative feature prevents such evasion.[6]

Large arrearages on preferred stock would make it difficult to resume dividend payments on common stock. To avoid delays in beginning common stock dividend payments again, a compromise arrangement with the holders of common stock is likely to be worked out. A package offer is one possibility; for example, a recapitalization plan may provide for an exchange of shares. The arrearage will be wiped out by the donation of common stock with a value equal to the amount of the preferred dividend arrearage, and the holders of preferred stock are thus given an ownership share in the corporation. In addition, resumption of current dividends on the preferred may be promised. Whether these provisions are worth anything depends on the future earnings prospects of the company.

The advantage to the company of substituting common stock for dividends in arrears is that it can start again with a clean balance sheet. If earnings recover, dividends can be paid to the holders of common stock without making up arrearages to the holders of preferred stock. The original common stockholders, of course, will have given up a portion of their ownership of the corporation.

Convertibility

Approximately 40 percent of the preferred stock that has been issued in recent years is convertible into common stock. For example, one share of a particular

---

[6]Note, however, that compounding is absent in most cumulative plans. In other words, the arrearages themselves earn no return.

preferred stock could be convertible into 2.5 shares of the firm's common stock at the option of the preferred stockholder. The nature of convertibility is discussed in Chapter 17.

Some Infrequent Provisions

Some of the other provisions occasionally encountered in preferred stocks include the following.

Voting Rights   Sometimes a preferred stock is given the right to vote for directors. When this feature is present, it generally permits the preferred stock to elect a *minority* of the board, say three out of nine directors. The voting privilege becomes operative only if the company has not paid the preferred dividend for a specified period, for example, six, eight, or ten quarters.

Sinking Fund   Some preferred issues have a sinking fund requirement. When they do, the sinking fund ordinarily calls for the purchase and retirement of a given percentage of the preferred stock each year.

Maturity   Preferred stocks almost never have maturity dates on which they must be retired. However, if the issue has a sinking fund, this effectively creates a maturity date.

Call Provision   A call provision gives the issuing corporation the right to call in the preferred stock for redemption, the same as for bonds. If it is used, the call provision generally states that the company must pay an amount greater than the par value of the preferred stock, with this additional sum being defined as the *call premium.* For example, a $100 par value preferred stock might be callable at the option of the corporation at $108 a share.

EVALUATION OF PREFERRED STOCK

From Viewpoint of Issuer

An important advantage of preferred stock from the viewpoint of the issuer is that, in contrast to bonds, the obligation to make fixed interest payments is avoided. Also, a firm wishing to expand because its earning power is high may obtain higher earnings for the original owners by selling preferred stock with a limited return rather than by selling common stock.

Advantages   By selling preferred stock the financial manager avoids the provision of equal participation in earnings that the sale of additional common stock would require. Preferred stock also permits a company to avoid sharing control through participation in voting. In contrast to bonds, it enables the firm to conserve mortgagable assets. Since preferred stock typically has no maturity and no sinking fund, it is more flexible than bonds.

Disadvantages   Characteristically, preferred stock must be sold on a higher yield basis than that for bonds. Preferred stock dividends are not deductible as a tax expense, a characteristic that makes their cost differential very great in comparison with that of bonds.[7] As we shall see in Chapter 20, the after tax cost of debt is approximately half the stated coupon rate for profitable firms. The cost of preferred, however, is the full percentage amount of the preferred dividend. This fact has greatly reduced the use of preferred stocks in recent years.

From Viewpoint of Investor

In fashioning securities, the financial manager needs to consider the investor's point of view. Frequently it is asserted that preferred stocks have so many disadvantages both to the issuer and to the investor that they should never be issued. Nevertheless, preferred stock is issued in substantial amounts.

Advantages   Preferred stock provides the following advantages to the investor. (1) Preferred stocks provide reasonably steady income. (2) Preferred stockholders have a preference over common stockholders in liquidation; numerous examples can be cited where the prior-preference position of holders of preferred stock saved them from losses incurred by holders of common stock. (3) Many corporations (for example, insurance companies) like to hold preferred stock as investments because 85 percent of the dividends received on these shares is not taxable.

Disadvantages   Preferred stock also has some disadvantages to investors. (1) Although the holders of preferred stock bear a substantial portion of ownership risk, their returns are limited. (2) Price fluctuations in preferred stock are far greater than those in bonds, yet yields on bonds are frequently higher than those on preferred stock. (3) The stock has no legally enforceable right to dividends. (4) Accrued dividend arrearages are seldom settled in cash comparable to the amount of the obligation that has been incurred.

---

[7] Historically, a given firm's preferred stock generally carried higher rates than its bonds because of the greater risk inherent in preferred stocks from the holder's viewpoint. However, as is noted below, the fact that preferred dividends are largely exempt from the corporate income tax has made preferred stock attractive to corporate investors. In recent years, high-grade preferreds, on average, have sold on a lower yield basis than high-grade bonds. In 1965, Fischer and Wilt ("Non-Convertible Preferred Stocks as a Financing Instrument") found that bonds had a yield 0.39 percentage points *above* preferred stocks. Thus, a very strong firm could sell preferreds to yield about 0.3 percent less than bonds. As an example, on March 27, 1973, AT&T sold a preferred issue that yielded 7.28 percent to an investor. On that same date, AT&T bonds yielded 7.55 percent, or 0.27 percent more than the preferred. The tax treatment accounted for this differential; the *after-tax* yield was greater on the preferred stock than on the bonds.

Recent Trends

Because of the nondeductibility of preferred stock dividends as a tax expense, many companies have retired their preferred stock. Often debentures or subordinated debentures will be offered to preferred stockholders in exchange. The interest on the debentures is deductible as a tax expense, whereas preferred stock dividends are not deductible.

When the preferred stock is not callable, the company must offer terms of exchange that are sufficiently attractive to induce the preferred stockholders to agree to the exchange. Characteristically, bonds or other securities in an amount somewhat above the recent value of the preferred stock will be issued in exchange. Sometimes bonds equal in market value to the preferred stock will be issued, along with additional cash or common stock, to provide an extra inducement to the preferred stockholders. Sometimes the offer will be bonds equal to only a portion of the current market value of the preferred with an additional amount, represented by cash or common stock, that will bring the total amount offered to the preferred stockholders to something over its market value as of a recent date.

U.S. Steel's replacement of its 7 percent preferred stock in 1965 illustrates one of these exchange patterns. U.S. Steel proposed that its 7 percent preferred stock be changed into 4⅝ percent thirty-year bonds at a rate of $175 principal amount of bonds for each preferred share. On August 17, 1965, when the plan was announced, the preferred stock was selling at $150. U.S. Steel also announced that the conversion would increase earnings available to common stock by $10 million yearly, or 18 cents a share at 1965 federal income tax rates; this was sufficient inducement to persuade the company to give the preferred stockholders the added $25 a share.

Tax considerations have reduced the use of straight preferred stock, but a countertrend has been the use of convertible preferred stock in mergers.[8] The reasoning here also involves taxes. The owners of the acquired firm frequently are willing to sell out because they are seeking to escape the worries associated with ownership and management. Consequently, they can be more easily induced to sell out if they are offered a fixed-income security. However, if bonds (or cash) are offered for the shares of the acquired firm, the selling stockholders must pay a capital gains tax on any proceeds received in excess of their cost basis. Frequently, this would involve a heavy capital gains tax liability. If the exchange is convertible preferred stock of the acquiring company for common stock of the acquired firm, the exchange can qualify for exemption on the capital gains liability. In this manner the stockholders of the acquired firm can receive a fixed income security, avoid an immediate capital gains liability, and receive additional benefits from the conversion feature if the price of the acquiring firm's common stock rises.

---

[8]Convertibles are discussed in detail in Chapter 17 and financial aspects of mergers are discussed in Chapter 23.

The use of convertible preferreds has been most noticeable among merger-minded conglomerate corporations. Such conglomerates are frequently "growth" companies with low dividend payout policies, and they frequently buy out firms that have been paying substantial dividends. If the merger was accomplished by an exchange of stock, the stockholders of the acquired company would suffer a reduction in their dividend receipts. The use of a convertible preferred can avoid this dividend dilution and thus enhance the chances that the acquired firm's stockholders will approve the merger.

DECISION MAKING ON USE OF PREFERRED STOCK

We can now distill the circumstances favoring the use of preferred stock from the foregoing analysis. As a hybrid security, the use of preferred stock is favored by conditions that fall between those favoring the use of common stock and those favoring the use of debt.

When a firm's profit margin is high enough to more than cover preferred stock dividends, it will be advantageous to employ leverage. However, if the firm's sales and profits are subject to considerable fluctuations, the use of debt with fixed interest charges may be unduly risky. Preferred stock may offer a happy compromise. The use of preferred stock will be strongly favored if the firm already has a debt ratio that is high in relation to the reference level maximum for the line of business.

Relative costs of alternative sources of financing are always important considerations. When the market prices of common stocks are relatively low, the costs of common stock financing are relatively high; this is shown in Chapter 18. The costs of preferred stock financing follow interest rate levels more than common stock prices; in other words, when interest rates are low, the cost of preferred stock is also likely to be low. When the costs of fixed-income instruments, such as preferred stock, are low and the costs of variable value securities, such as common stock, are high, the use of preferred stock is favored.

Preferred stock may also be the desired form of financing whenever the use of debt would involve excessive risk but the issuance of common stock would result in problems of control for the dominant ownership group in the company.

RATIONALE FOR DIFFERENT CLASSES OF SECURITIES

At this point the following questions are likely to come to mind: Why are there so many different forms of long-term securities? Why would anybody ever be willing to purchase subordinated bonds or income bonds? The answers to both questions may be made clear by reference to Figure 15–2. The now familiar tradeoff function is drawn to show the risk and the expected returns for the various securities of the Longstreet Company. Longstreet's first mortgage bonds are slightly more risky than U.S. Treasury bonds and sell at a slightly higher expected return. The second mortgage bonds are yet more risky and have a still higher expected return. Subordinated debentures, income bonds, and preferred stocks all are increasingly risky and have increasingly higher expected returns. Longstreet's common stock, the riskiest security the firm issues, has the highest expected return of any of its offerings.

FIGURE 15–2   Risk and Expected Returns on Different Classes of Securities, the Longstreet Company

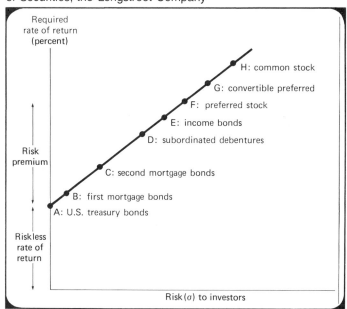

Why does Longstreet issue so many different classes of securities? Why not just offer one type of bond plus common stock? The answer lies in the fact that different investors have different risk-return tradeoff preferences, so if its securities are to appeal to the broadest possible market, Longstreet must offer securities that appeal to as many investors as possible. Used wisely, a policy of selling differentiated securities can lower a firm's overall cost of capital below what it would be if it issued only one class of debt and common stock.

REFUNDING A BOND OR A PREFERRED STOCK ISSUE

Suppose a company sells bonds or preferred stock at a time when interest rates are relatively high. Provided the issue is callable, as many are, the company can sell a new issue of low-yielding securities if and when interest rates drop and use the proceeds to retire the high-rate issue. This is called a *refunding operation.* [9]

The decision to refund a security issue is analyzed in much the same manner as a capital budgeting expenditure. The costs of refunding—the "investment outlay"—include (1) the call premium paid for the privilege of calling the old issue and (2) the flotation costs incurred in selling the new issue. The annual receipts, in the capital budgeting sense, are the interest payments that are saved each year; for example, if interest expense on the old issue is $1 million while that on the new issue is $700,000, the $300,000 saving constitutes the annual benefits.

In analyzing the advantages of refunding, the net present value method is the recommended procedure—discount the future interest savings back to the present and compare the discounted value with the cash outlays associated with the refunding. *In the discounting process, the after-tax cost of the new debt, not the average cost of capital, should be used as the discount factor.* The reason for this is that there is relatively little risk to the savings—their value is known with relative certainty, which is quite unlike most capital budgeting decisions. The following example illustrates the calculations needed in a refunding decision.

The Culver City Company has outstanding a $60 million twenty-five-year bond issue, carrying an 8 percent interest rate. This issue, which was sold five years ago, had flotation costs of $3 million, which the firm is currently amortizing on a straight-line basis over the life of the issue. The bond indenture carries a call provision making it possible for the company to retire the bonds by calling them in at a 6 percent call premium. Investment bankers have assured the company that it could sell an additional $60 to $70 million worth of twenty-year bonds at an interest rate of 6 percent. To insure that funds required to pay off the old debt will be available, the new bonds will be sold one month before the old issue is called, so for one month, interest must be paid on two issues. Predictions are that interest rates are unlikely to fall below 6 percent. [10] Flotation costs on the new issue will amount to $2.65 million. Should the company refund the $60 million worth of bonds? The following steps outline the decision process.

---

[9] For an excellent discussion of refunding, see O. D. Bowlin, "The Refunding Decision," *Journal of Finance,* 21 (March 1966), pp. 55–68.

[10] The firm's management has estimated that interest rates will probably rise to center on 7 percent in the near future, with a standard deviation of ¾ percent. This implies that there is only a 9 percent chance (1.33 standard deviations from the mean) of future rates falling below 6 percent.

Step 1. What is the investment outlay required to refund the issue?

a. Call premium:

Before tax: .06 × $60,000,000 = $3,600,000.
After tax:　　$3,600,000 × .5 = $1,800,000.

Although Culver City Company must expend $3.6 million on the call premium, this is a deductible expense in the year the call is made. Since the company is in a 50 percent tax bracket, it saves $1.80 million in taxes. Therefore, the after-tax cost of the call is only $1,800,000.

b. Flotation costs on new issue:
Total flotation costs are $2.65 million. For tax purposes, flotation costs are amortized over the life of the new bond, or twenty years. Therefore, the annual tax deduction is

$$\frac{\$2,650,000}{20} = \$132,500.$$

Since Culver is in the 50 percent tax bracket, it has a tax saving of $66,250 a year for twenty years. This is an annuity of $66,250 for twenty years. The present value of this annuity, discounted at 3 percent, the after-tax cost of debt, is[11]

$$PV \text{ of tax saving} = PVIF_a \times \$66,250$$
$$= 14.877 \times \$66,250$$
$$= \$985,601.$$

The net after-tax effect of new flotation costs is

New flotation costs　$2,650,000
PV of tax saving　　－ 985,601
　　Net cost　　　　　$1,664,399

c. Flotation costs on old issue:
The old issue has an unamortized flotation cost of $2.4 million (20/25 × $3,000,000). This may be recognized immediately as an expense, thus creating an after-tax savings of $1.2 million. The firm will, however, lose a tax deduction of $120,000 a year for twenty years, or an after-tax benefit of

---

[11] The cost of capital is developed in detail in Chapter 20. There we will see (1) that the cost of capital increases as the riskiness of the firm increases and (2) that there is a cost of debt, a cost of equity, and an "average cost of capital," which is a weighted average of the cost of debt and equity. Also, we will see that the relevant cost of debt is an *after-tax cost,* calculated as follows:

After-tax cost of debt = (interest rate) (1 − tax rate).

This calculation recognizes that interest is tax deductible, so the federal government, in effect, bears a portion of the cost of debt.

$60,000 a year. The present value of this lost benefit, discounted at 3 percent is

$$PV \text{ of } lost \text{ benefit} = PVIF_a \times \$60,000$$
$$= 14.877 \times \$60,000$$
$$= \$892,620.$$

The net after-tax effect of old flotation costs is

Tax savings on old flotation costs	($1,200,000)
PV of lost benefits of old flotation costs	– 892,620
Net after-tax effect of old flotation costs	($ 307,380)

d. Additional interest:[12]

One month "extra" interest on new issue, after taxes:

$$\text{Dollar amount} \times {}^{1}/_{12} \text{ of } 6\% \times (1 - \text{tax rate}) = \text{interest cost}$$
$$\$60,000,000 \times .005 \times .5 = \$150,000.$$

e. Total after-tax investment:

The total investment outlay required to refund the bond issue is thus

Call premium	$1,800,000
Flotation cost, new	1,664,399
Flotation cost, old	(307,380)
Additional interest	150,000
Total investment	$3,307,019

Step 2. What are the annual savings?

a. Old bond interest, after tax:

$$\$60,000,000 \times .08 \times .5 = \$2,400,000.$$

b. New bond interest, after tax:

$$\$60,000,000 \times .06 \times .5 = \$1,800,000.$$

c. Savings $ 600,000.

Step 3. What is the present value of the savings?

a. Twenty-year *PV* of annuity factor at 3 percent:
14.877

---

[12]If the proceeds from the new issue are invested in short-term securities for one month, as they typically will be, this reduces the effect of the "extra" interest.

b. *PV* of $600,000 a year for twenty years:
$$14.877 \times \$600,000 = \$8,926,200.$$

Step 4. Conclusion: Since the present value of the receipts ($8,926,200) exceeds the required investment ($3,307,019), the issue should be refunded.

Two other points should be mentioned. First, since the $600,000 savings is an essentially riskless investment, its present value is found by discounting at the firm's least risky rate—its after-tax cost of debt. Second, since the refunding operation is advantageous to the firm, it must be disadvantageous to bondholders—they must give up their 8 percent bond and reinvest in one yielding 6 percent. This points out the danger of the call provision to bondholders and explains why, at any given time, bonds without a call provision command higher prices than callable bonds.[13]

SUMMARY

Bonds   A *bond* is a long-term promissory note. A *mortgage bond* is secured by real property. An *indenture* is an agreement between the firm issuing a bond and the numerous bondholders, represented by a *trustee.*

Secured long-term debt differs with respect to (1) the priority of claims, (2) the right to issue additional securities, and (3) the scope of the lien provided. These characteristics determine the amount of protection provided to the bondholder by the terms of the security. Giving the investor more security will induce him to accept a lower yield but will restrict the future freedom of action of the issuing firm.

The main classes of unsecured bonds are (1) *debentures,* (2) *subordinated debentures,* and (3) *income bonds.* Holders of debentures are unsecured general creditors. Subordinated debentures are junior in claim to bank loans. Income bonds are similar to preferred stock in that interest is paid only when earned.

The characteristics of long-term debt determine the circumstances under which it will be used when alternative forms of financing are under analysis. The cost of debt is limited, but it is a fixed obligation. Bond interest is an expense deductible for tax purposes. Debt carries a maturity date and may require sinking fund payments to prepare for extinguishing the obligation. Indenture provisions are likely to include restrictions on the freedom of action of the management of the firm.

The nature of long-term debt encourages its use under the following circumstances:

1. Sales and earnings are relatively stable.
2. Profit margins are adequate to make leverage advantageous.

---

[13]See F. C. Jen and J. E. Wert, "The Effects of Call Risk on Corporate Bond Yields," *Journal of Finance,* 22 (December 1967), pp. 637–652.

3. A rise in profits or the general price level is expected.
4. The existing debt ratio is relatively low.
5. Common stock price/earnings ratios are low in relation to the levels of interest rates.
6. Control considerations are important.
7. Cash flow requirements under the bond agreement are not burdensome.
8. Restrictions of the bond indenture are not onerous.

Although seven of the eight factors may favor debt, the eighth can swing the decision to the use of equity capital. The list of factors is, thus, simply a check list of things to be considered when deciding on bonds versus stocks; the actual decision is based on a judgment about the relative importance of the several factors.

Preferred Stocks   The *characteristics of preferred stock* vary with the requirements of the situation under which it is issued. However, certain patterns tend to remain. Preferred stocks usually have priority over common stocks with respect to earnings and claims on assets in liquidation. Preferred stocks are usually cumulative; they have no maturity but are sometimes callable. They are typically nonparticipating and have only contingent voting rights.

The advantages to the issuer are limited dividends and no maturity. These advantages may outweigh the disadvantages of higher cost and the nondeductibility of the dividends as an expense for tax purposes. But their acceptance by investors is the final test of whether they can be sold on favorable terms.

Companies sell preferred stock when they seek the advantages of financial leverage but fear the dangers of the fixed charges on debt in the face of potential fluctuations in income. If debt ratios are already high or if the costs of common stock financing are relatively high, the advantages of preferred stock will be reinforced.

The use of preferred stock has declined significantly since the advent of the corporate income tax, because preferred dividends are not deductible for income tax purposes while bond interest payments are deductible. In recent years, however, there has been a strong shift back to a new kind of preferred stock—convertible preferred, used primarily in connection with mergers. If the stockholders of the acquired company receive cash or bonds, they are required to pay capital gains taxes on any gains that might have been realized. If convertible preferred stock is given to the selling stockholders, this constitutes a tax-free exchange of securities. The selling stockholders can obtain a fixed income security and at the same time postpone the payment of capital gains taxes.

Refunding   If a bond or a preferred stock issue was sold when interest rates were higher than they are at present, and if the issue is callable, it may be profitable to call the old issue and refund it with a new, lower cost issue. An analysis similar to capital budgeting is required to determine whether a refunding operation should be undertaken.

QUESTIONS

15-1. A sinking fund is set up in one of two ways:
a. The corporation makes annual payments to the trustee, who invests the proceeds in securities (frequently government bonds) and uses the accumulated total to retire the bond issue on maturity.
b. The trustee uses the annual payments to retire a portion of the issue each year, either by calling a given percentage of the issue by a lottery and paying a specified price per bond or buying bonds on the open market, whichever is cheaper. Discuss the advantages and disadvantages of each procedure from the viewpoint of both the firm and the bondholders.

15-2. Since a corporation often has the right to call bonds at will, do you believe individuals should be able to demand repayment at any time they so desire?

15-3. What are the relative advantages and disadvantages of issuing a long-term bond during a recession versus during a period of prosperity?

15-4. Missouri Pacific 3¾ percent income bonds due in 2020 are selling for $770, while the company's 4¼ percent first mortgage bonds due in 2005 are selling for $945. Why would the bonds with the lower coupon sell at a higher price? (Each has a $1,000 par value.)

15-5. When a firm sells bonds, it must offer a package acceptable to potential buyers. Included in this package of terms are such features as the issue price, the coupon interest rate, the term to maturity, any sinking fund provisions, and other features. The package itself is determined through a bargaining process between the firm and the investment bankers who will handle the issue. What particular features would you, as a corporate treasurer, be especially interested in having, and which would you be most willing to give ground on, under each of the following conditions:
a. You believe that the economy is near the peak of a business cycle.
b. Long-run forecasts indicate that your firm may have heavy cash inflows in relation to cash needs during the next five to ten years.
c. Your current liabilities are presently low, but you anticipate raising a considerable amount of funds through short-term borrowing in the near future.

15-6. Bonds are less attractive to investors during periods of inflation because a rise in the price level will reduce the purchasing power of the fixed-interest payments and also of the principal. Discuss the advantages and disadvantages to a corporation of using a bond whose interest payments and principal would increase in direct proportion to increases in the price level (an inflation-proof bond).

15-7. If preferred stock dividends are passed for several years, the preferred stockholders are frequently given the right to elect several members of the board of directors. In the case of bonds that are in default on interest payments, this procedure is not followed. Why does this difference exist?

15-8. Preferred stocks are found in almost all industries, but one industry is the really dominant issuer of preferred shares. What is this industry, and why are firms in it so disposed to using preferred stock?

15-9. If the corporate income tax was abolished, would this raise or lower the amount of new preferred stock issued?

15-10. Investors buying securities have some expected or required rate of return in mind. Which would you expect to be higher, the required rate of return (before taxes) on preferred stocks or that on common stocks (a) for individual investors and (b) for corporate investors (for example, insurance companies)?

15-11. Do you think the before-tax required rate of return is higher or lower on very high grade preferred stocks or on bonds (a) for individual investors and (b) for corporate investors?

15-12. For purposes of measuring a firm's leverage, should preferred stock be classified as debt or as equity? Does it matter if the classification is being made (a) by the firm itself, (b) by creditors, or (c) by equity investors?

PROBLEMS

15-1. Several years ago your father purchased a farm adjacent to his existing farm. The deal was financed partly by a long-term mortgage loan. This loan requires payments of $21,909 per year for 20 more years (this includes interest and principal) and has a contract interest rate of 10 percent. Your father is considering refunding the loan because current rates for similar loans have dropped to 8 percent. He is hesitant to refund the mortgage, however, because there is a prepayment penalty of six-months interest on the unpaid balance. Further, it will require about 4 percent of the loan amount for set-up fees for a new loan. Because of other writeoffs, your father pays no income taxes. Should your father refund the loan? (Hint: Begin by finding the unpaid balance of the existing loan, which is equal to the present value of the remaining payments, discounted at the contract interest rate.)

15-2. Three years ago your firm issued some eighteen-year bonds with 10.5 percent coupon rates and a 10 percent call premium. You have just called these bonds. The bonds originally sold at their face value of $1,000.

    a. Compute the realized rate of return for investors who purchased these bonds when they were issued.

    b. Given the rate of return in (a), did investors welcome the call? Explain.

15-3. The Lemming Corporation has a $300,000 long-term bond issue outstanding. This debt has an additional fifteen years to maturity and bears a coupon interest rate of 9 percent. The firm now has the opportunity to refinance the debt with fifteen-year bonds at a rate of 7 percent. Further declines in the interest rate are not anticipated. The bond redemption premium (call premium) on the old bond would be $15,000; issue costs on the new would be $16,000. If tax effects are ignored, should the firm refund the bonds?

15-4. In late 1975 the Erie Power Company of Pennsylvania sought to raise $6 million to refinance present preferred stock issues at a lower rate. The company is a member of the Northeastern Utilities Associates Holding Company system. The company could sell additional debt at 6 percent, preferred stock at 5.34 percent, or common stock at $90 a share. How should the company raise the money? Relevant financial information is provided below.

    (This question should not be answered in terms of precise cost of capital calculations. Rather, a more qualitative and subjective analysis is appropriate. The only calculations necessary are some simple ratios. Careful interpretation of these ratios is necessary, however, to understand and discuss the often complex, subjective judgment issues involved.)

Public Utilities Financial Ratios

Current ratio (times)	1.0
Interest earned (before taxes) (times)	4.0
Sales to total assets (times)	0.3
Average collection period (days)	28.0
Current debt/total assets (percent)	5–10
Long-term debt/total assets (percent)	45–50
Preferred/total assets (percent)	10–15
Common equity/total assets (percent)	30–35
Earnings before interest and taxes to total assets (percent)	5.9
Profits to common equity (percent)	10.1
Expected growth in earnings and dividends (percent)	4.6

Erie Power Company
Balance sheet, July 31, 1975
(in millions of dollars)

Cash	$ 0.75	Current liabilities	$ 3.00
Receivables	1.50	Long-term debt, 3.5%	27.00
Material and supplies	1.20	Preferred stock, 5.60%	6.00
Total current assets	$ 3.45	Common stock, $25 par value	11.25
		Capital surplus	6.60
Net property	56.55	Retained earnings	6.15
Total assets	$60.00	Total claims	$60.00

Erie Power Company
Income statement for year ended July 31, 1975
(in millions of dollars)

Operating revenues	$18.9000
Operating expenses	12.5000
Earnings before interest and taxes	$ 6.4000
Interest deduction	.9450
Earnings before taxes	$ 5.4550
Income taxes at 50%	2.7275
Earnings after taxes	$ 2.7275
Preferred dividends	.3360
Net income available to common	$ 2.3915
Earnings per share	$ 5.31
Dividends per share	$ 4.25

15-5. Shepard Electronics is planning a capital improvement program to provide greater efficiency and versatility in its operations. It is estimated that by mid-1976 the company will need to raise $200 million. Shepard is a leading electronics producer with an excellent credit rating.

You are asked to set up a program for obtaining the necessary funds. Using the following information, indicate the best form of financing. Some items you should include in your analysis are profit margins, relative costs, control of the voting stock, cash flows, ratio analysis, and *pro forma* analysis.

Shepard's common stock is selling at $64 a share. The company could sell debt (twenty-five years) at 8.0 percent or preferred stock at 8.5 percent.

Electronics Industry Financial Ratios

Current ratio (times)	2.1
Sales to total assets (times)	1.8
Coverage of fixed charges (times)	7.0
Average collection period (days)	42.0
Current debt/total assets (percent)	20–25
Long-term debt/total assets (percent)	10.0
Preferred/total assets (percent)	0–5
Net worth/total assets (percent)	65–70
Profits to sales (percent)	3.3
Profits to total assets (percent)	6.0
Profits to net worth (percent)	9.5
Expected growth rate in earnings and dividends	5.3

Shepard Electronics Company
Consolidated balance sheet, December 31, 1975
(in millions of dollars)

Assets		
Current	$ 760	
Other investments	140	
Properties (net)	1,140	
Prepaid expenses	40	
Total assets		$2,080
Liabilities		
Current	$ 320	
Long-term debt, 5.5%	180	
Total liabilities		$ 500
Common stock, $10 par	$ 320	
Capital surplus	300	
Retained earnings	880	
Reserves	80	
Total net worth		1,580
Total liabilities and net worth		$2,080

Shepard Electronics Company
Consolidated income statement
For years ended December 31, 1973, 1974, and 1975
(in millions of dollars)

	1973	1974	1975
Sales	$2,440	$1,820	$2,160
Other income	20	20	20
Total	$2,460	$1,840	$2,180
Cost and expenses	2,120	1,600	1,920
Income before taxes	$ 340	$ 240	$ 260
Federal income tax	172	120	128
Net income	$ 168	$ 120	$ 132
Cash dividends	92	92	92
Interest on long-term debt	$ 7	$ 8.8	$ 10
Depreciation	$ 80.0	$ 64.0	$ 68.0
Shares outstanding (widely held)		40,000,000	

Term Loans
and Leases

Intermediate-term financing is defined as *debt originally scheduled for repayment in more than one year but in less than ten years.* Anything shorter is a current liability and falls in the class of short-term credit, while obligations due in ten or more years are thought of as long-term debt. This distinction is arbitrary, of course—we might just as well define intermediate-term credit as loans with maturities of one to five years. However, the one-to-ten year distinction is commonly used, so we shall follow it here.

The major forms of intermediate-term financing include (1) *term loans* and (2) *lease financing.*[1]

TERM LOANS

A term loan is a business loan with a maturity of more than one year. Ordinarily, term loans are retired by systematic repayments (often called *amortization payments*) over the life of the loan, although there are exceptions to the rule. Security, generally in the form of a chattel mortgage on equipment, is often employed, but the larger, stronger companies are able to borrow on an unsecured basis.

The primary lenders of term credit are commercial banks, life insurance companies, and, to a lesser extent, pension funds. Bank loans are generally

[1]During the 1970s another type of intermediate-term credit—publicly issued notes with five- to eight-year maturities—has come into vogue. These notes are commonly sold together with long-term bonds. For example, in March 1976 Midstates Electric sold $50 million of thirty-year bonds and simultaneously sold $50 million of eight-year notes. The notes were, in effect, short-term bonds.

restricted to maturities of between one and five years, while insurance companies and pension funds make the bulk of their term loans for between five and fifteen years. Therefore, many insurance company term loans are long-term, not intermediate-term, financing. Sometimes, when relatively large loans ($10 million and up) are involved, banks and insurance companies combine to make a loan, with the bank taking the short maturities and the insurance company the long maturities. Some specific features of term loans are discussed in the following sections.

Repayment Schedule

Because the repayment, or amortization, schedule is a particularly important feature of almost all term loans, it is useful to describe how it is determined. The purpose of amortization, of course, is to have the loan repaid gradually over its life rather than fall due all at once. Amortization forces the borrower to retire the loan slowly, thus protecting both the lender and the borrower against the possibility that the borrower will not make adequate provisions for retirement during the life of the loan. This is especially important where the loan is for the purpose of purchasing a specific item of equipment; here the amortization schedule will be geared to the productive life of the equipment and payments will be made from cash flows resulting from use of the equipment.

To illustrate how the amortization schedule is determined, let us assume that a firm borrows $1,000 on a ten-year loan, that interest is computed at 5 percent on the declining balance, and that the principal and interest are to be paid in ten equal installments. What is the amount of each of the ten annual payments? To find this value we must use the present value concepts developed in Chapter 10.

First, notice that the lender advances $1,000 and receives in turn a ten-year annuity of R dollars each year. In the section headed Annual Receipts from an Annuity in Chapter 10, we saw that these receipts could be calculated as

$$R = \frac{A_n}{PVIF_a},$$

where R is the annual receipt, A_n is the present value of the annuity, and $PVIF_a$ is the appropriate interest factor found either in Table 10–5 or in Appendix Table A–4. Substituting the $1,000 for A_n and the interest factor for a ten-year 5 percent annuity, or 7.722, for $PVIF_a$, we find

$$R = \frac{\$1,000}{7.722} = \$130.$$

Therefore, if our firm makes ten annual installments of $130 each, it will have retired the $1,000 loan and provided the lender a 5 percent return on his investment.

Table 16–1 breaks down the annual payments into interest and repayment components and, in the process, proves that level payments of $130 will, in fact, retire the $1,000 loan and give the lender his 5 percent return. This breakdown is important for tax purposes, because the interest payments are deductible expenses to the borrower and taxable income to the lender.

TABLE 16–1 Term-loan Repayment Schedule

Year	Total Payment	Interest[a]	Amortization Repayment	Remaining Balance
1	$ 130	$ 50	$ 80	$920
2	130	46	84	836
3	130	42	88	748
4	130	38	92	656
5	130	34	96	560
6	130	28	102	458
7	130	23	107	351
8	130	18	112	239
9	130	13	117	122
10	130	8	122	0
	$1,300	$300	$1,000	

[a]Interest for the first year is 0.05 × $1,000 = $50; for the second year, 0.05 × $920 = $46; and so on.

Characteristics of Term Loans

Maturity For commercial banks, the term loan runs five years or less, typically three years. For insurance companies, the most typical maturities have been five to fifteen years. This difference reflects the fact that liabilities of commercial banks are shorter term than are those of insurance companies. As we pointed out above, banks and insurance companies occasionally cooperate in their term lending. For example, if a firm (usually a large one) seeks a fifteen-year term loan, a bank may take the loan for the first five years and an insurance company for the last ten years.

Collateral Commercial banks require security on about 60 percent of the volume and 90 percent of the number of term loans made. They take as security mainly stocks, bonds, machinery, and equipment. Insurance companies also require security on nearly one-third of their loans, frequently using real estate as collateral on the longer ones.

Options In recent years institutional investors have increasingly taken compensation in addition to fixed interest payments on directly negotiated loans. The most popular form of additional compensation is an option to buy common stock, the option being in the form of detachable warrants permitting the purchase of the shares at stated prices over a designated period.[2]

Repayment Provisions Most term loans are repayable in equal installments. Only a small percentage of the loans have any balloon segment, or unamortized balance, at the end. It is possible to prepay term loans ahead of schedule, but a prepayment penalty equal to 8 to 10 percent of the outstanding balance is usually assessed in such cases.

Terms of Loan Agreements

A major advantage of a term loan is that it assures the borrower of the use of the funds for an extended period. On a ninety-day loan, since the commercial bank has the option to renew or not renew, the bank has frequent opportunities to reexamine the situation of the borrower. If it has deteriorated unduly, the loan officer simply does not renew the loan. On a term loan, however, the bank or the insurance company has committed itself for a period of years. Because of this long-term commitment, restrictive provisions are incorporated into the loan agreement to protect the lender for the duration of the loan. The most important of the typical restrictive provisions are listed below.

Current Ratio The current ratio must be maintained at some specified level —2½ to 1; 3 to 1; 3½ to 1, depending upon the borrower's line of business. Net working capital must also be maintained at some minimum level.

Additional Long-Term Debt Typically, there are prohibitions against incurring additional long-term indebtedness except with the permission of the lender. Furthermore, the lender does not ordinarily permit the pledging of assets. The loan agreement may also prohibit the borrower from assuming any contingent liabilities, such as guaranteeing the indebtedness of a subsidiary. Finally, the loan agreement probably restricts the borrower from circumventing these provisions by signing long-term leases beyond specified amounts.

Management The loan agreement may require that any major changes in management personnel, or in its composition, must be approved by the lender. The loan agreement may require life insurance on the principals or key people in the business. In addition, the loan agreement may provide for the creation of a voting trust or a granting of proxies for a specified period to ensure that the management of the company will be under the control of the group on which the lender has relied in making the loan.

---

[2]See Chapter 17 for more details on warrants.

Financial Statements   The lender will require the borrower to submit periodic financial statements for his review.

This list does not exhaust all terms found in loan agreements, but it is illustrative. It serves to indicate the kind of protective provisions the bank or the insurance company seeks to embody in the loan agreement.

Cost of Term Loans

Another major aspect of term lending is its cost. As with other forms of lending, the interest rate on term loans varies with the size of the loan and the quality of the borrower. Surveys show that on smaller term loans the interest rate may run up to 15 percent. On loans of $1 million and above, term loan rates have been close to the prime rate. The size of the loan reflects the quality of the borrower as well as the fixed cost involved in making small loans.

The interest rate could be fixed for the life of the loan, or it could vary. Often the loan agreement specifies that the interest rate will be based on the average of the rediscount rate[3] in the borrower's Federal Reserve district during the previous three months, generally 1 or 2 percent above the rediscount rate. In other words, the loan rate can fluctuate during the life of the loan and is often tied to the rediscount rate. It may also be geared to the published prime rate charged by New York City banks.

LEASE FINANCING

Firms are generally interested in *using* buildings and equipment, not in owning them per se. One way for obtaining the use of facilities and equipment is to buy them, but an alternative is to lease them. Prior to the 1950s, leasing was generally associated with real estate—land and buildings—but today it is possible to lease virtually any kind of fixed asset. The following quotation from a recent issue of *Fortune* will give an idea of the importance of equipment leasing; leases for real estate increase the significance of this financing technique:

> Capital equipment with an original cost of somewhat more than $60 billion is now on lease in the U.S. to corporations, institutions, and governments. New equipment worth over $11 billion was leased last year, and it accounted for about 14 percent of all business investment in capital equipment. Overall, the volume of leasing is expanding by around 20 percent a year. If leasing continues to grow at its recent rate, by 1977 about one-fifth of all new capital equipment put in use by business will be leased.[4]

Conceptually, as we show below, leasing is quite similar to borrowing, so leasing provides financial leverage. In effect, a lease is a form of debt. Leasing takes several different forms, the most important of which are sale and

---

[3]The rediscount rate is the rate of interest at which a bank may borrow from a Federal Reserve bank.
[4]Peter Vanderwicken, "The Powerful Logic of the Leasing Boom," *Fortune* (November 1973), 136.

leaseback, service leases, and straight financial leases. These three major types of leases are described below.

Sale and Leaseback

Under a sale and leaseback arrangement, a firm owning land, buildings, or equipment sells the property to a financial institution and simultaneously executes an agreement to lease the property back for a specified period under specific terms. If real estate is involved, the financial institution is generally a life insurance company; if the property consists of equipment and machinery, the financial institution could be an insurance company, a commercial bank, or a specialized leasing company.

Note that the seller, or *lessee,* immediately receives the purchase price put up by the buyer, or *lessor.* At the same time, the seller-lessee retains the use of the property. This parallel is carried over to the lease payment schedule. Under a mortgage loan arrangement, the financial institution would receive a series of equal payments just sufficient to amortize the loan and to provide the lender with a specified rate of return on his investment. The nature of the calculations was described above in the section on term loans. Under a sale and leaseback arrangement, the lease payments are set up in exactly the same manner—the payments are sufficient to return the full purchase price to the financial institution, in addition to providing it with a stated return on its investment.

Service Leases

Service, or operating, leases include both financing and maintenance services. IBM is one of the pioneers of the service lease contract; computers and office copying machines, together with automobiles and trucks, are the primary types of equipment involved in service leases. These leases ordinarily call for the lessor to maintain and service the leased equipment, and the costs of this maintenance are built into the lease payments.

Another important characteristic of the service lease is the fact that it is frequently not fully amortized. In other words, the payments required under the lease contract are *not* sufficient to recover the full cost of the equipment. Obviously, however, the lease contract is written for considerably less than the expected life of the leased equipment, and the lessor expects to recover his cost either in subsequent renewal payments or on disposal of the leased equipment.

A final feature of the service lease is that it frequently contains a cancellation clause giving the lessee the right to cancel the lease and return the equipment before the expiration of the basic lease agreement. This is an important consideration for the lessee, for it means that he can return the equipment if technological developments render it obsolete, or if he simply no longer needs it.

Financial Leases

A strict financial lease is one that does *not* provide for maintenance services, is *not* cancellable, and *is* fully amortized (that is, the lessor receives rental payments equal to the full price of the leased equipment). The typical arrangement involves the following steps:

1. The firm that will use the equipment selects the specific items it requires and negotiates the price and delivery terms with the manufacturer or the distributor.
2. Next, the user firm arranges with a bank or a leasing company to buy the equipment from the manufacturer or the distributor, and the user firm simultaneously executes an agreement to lease the equipment from the financial institution. The terms call for full amortization of the financial institution's cost, plus a return of from 6 to 12 percent a year on the unamortized balance. The lessee is generally given an option to renew the lease at a reduced rental on expiration of the basic lease, but he does not have the right to cancel the basic lease without completely paying off the financial institution.

Financial leases are almost the same as sale and leaseback arrangements, the only difference being that the leased equipment is new and the lessor buys it from a manufacturer or a distributor instead of from the user-lessee. A sale and leaseback may, then, be thought of as a special type of financial lease.

Internal Revenue Service Requirements for a Lease

The full amount of the annual lease payments is deductible for income tax purposes *provided the Internal Revenue Service agrees that a particular contract is a genuine lease and not simply an installment loan called a lease.* This makes it important that a lease contract be written in a form acceptable to the Internal Revenue Service. The following are the major requirements for bona fide lease transactions from the standpoint of the IRS:

1. The term must be less than thirty years; otherwise the lease is regarded as a form of sale.
2. The rent must represent a reasonable return to the lessor, "reasonable" being in the range of 6 to 12 percent on the investment.
3. The renewal option must be bona fide, and this requirement can best be met by giving the lessee the first option to meet an equal bona fide outside offer.
4. There shall be no repurchase option; if there is, the lessee should merely be given parity with an equal outside offer.

Cost Comparison

For an understanding of the possible advantages and disadvantages of lease financing, the cost of leasing must be compared with the cost of owning the equipment. In the typical case a firm that contemplates the acquisition of new equipment must also think about how to finance the equipment—no well-managed firm will ever have idle cash just sitting around. When financing is necessary, the two major alternatives are (1) a term loan secured by the equipment or (2) a lease arrangement. To judge the cost of leasing, we must make a comparison of leasing versus the borrow-to-buy alternative.

This comparison is best carried out in the manner presented in Table 16–2. Here it is assumed that the firm is acquiring a piece of equipment costing $1,000 and that it has the choice of borrowing the $1,000 at 5 percent, to be repaid in ten annual installments of $130 each, or of leasing the machine for $150 a year. (Under the lease arrangement the firm is paying a 5 percent implicit interest rate; this is the rate the lessor is earning.) The machine will be used for ten years, at the end of which time its estimated salvage value will be $100. If the firm leases the equipment, maintenance cost is included in the lease payment; but if it purchases the machine, it must spend an estimated $20 a year on maintenance.

Note that the decision to acquire the machine is not at issue here—this decision was made previously as part of the capital budgeting process. Here we are concerned simply with whether to obtain the use of the machine by a lease or by a purchase. However, if the effective cost of the lease is substantially lower than the cost of debt—and, as explained later in this chapter, this could occur for a number of reasons, including the ability to obtain more debt financing if leasing is employed—then the cost of capital used in capital budgeting would have to be recalculated and, perhaps, projects formerly deemed unacceptable might become acceptable.[5]

Columns 2 through 5 of Table 16–2 show the payment schedule for the loan—note that this section is identical with the schedule shown in Table 16–1 for a term loan. Column 7 gives the annual depreciation charges, assuming the firm owns the equipment and depreciates it on a straight-line basis (the depreciable cost is $900, $1,000 less $100 salvage). Column 8 gives the total tax-deductible expense: interest plus depreciation plus maintenance costs. Assuming a 40 percent tax rate, these tax deductions reduce the tax bill by 40 percent of the amount of the deductions, resulting in the tax savings recorded in column 9.

The total cash outlay associated with the borrow-purchase arrangement is the total annual loan payment recorded in column 2 plus the maintenance costs shown in column 6; this is the gross cash outflow. Deducting the tax

---

[5] An alternative approach to the lease-versus-purchase decision calls for analyzing the NPV of a project if the asset is leased versus the NPV if it is purchased. Johnson and Lewellen assert that some projects may be accepted if the lease plan is sufficiently favorable, but rejected if financed by debt. However, it has been argued that their analysis confuses the investment and financing aspects of leasing. If leasing costs were lower than alternative forms of financing, it would lower the firm's overall cost of capital. The new hurdle rate would then be applicable to all investments, not just those that might be acquired by a leasing arrangement. See R. W. Johnson and W. G. Lewellen, "Analysis of the Lease-or-Buy Decision," *Journal of Finance,* September 1972, 815–823, and comments on the article by Clark, Jantomi, and Gann; Lusztig; Bierman; and Lev and Orgler in the September 1973 issue.

TABLE 16–2 Comparison of Cost of Leasing versus Buying

Year (1)	Applicable to Loan				Applicable to Net Cost of Owning					Applicable to Lease	Comparative Costs		
	Total Payment (2)	Interest (3)	Amortization Payment (4)	Remaining Balance (5)	Maintenance Cost (6)	Depreciation (7)	$(3)+(6)$ $+(7) =$ Tax-deductible Expense (8)	$(0.40)(8) =$ Tax Savings (9)a	$(2)+(6)$ $-(9) =$ Cash Outflow if Owned (10)	$(1-0.4)(Lease$ $Cost) =$ Lease Cost after Tax (11)	PVIF's for 10% (12)	$(10)\times(12)$ Present Value of the Cost of Owning (13)a	$(11)\times(12)$ Present Value of the Cost of Leasing (14)a,b
1	$130	$50	$80	$920	$20	$90	$160	$64	$86	$90	0.909	$78	$82
2	130	46	84	836	20	90	156	62	88	90	0.826	73	74
3	130	42	88	748	20	90	152	61	89	90	0.751	67	68
4	130	38	92	656	20	90	148	59	91	90	0.683	62	61
5	130	34	96	560	20	90	144	58	92	90	0.621	57	56
6	130	28	102	458	20	90	138	55	95	90	0.564	54	51
7	130	23	107	351	20	90	133	53	97	90	0.513	50	46
8	130	18	112	239	20	90	128	51	99	90	0.467	46	42
9	130	13	117	122	20	90	123	49	101	90	0.424	43	38
10	130	8	122	0	20	90	118	47	103	90	0.386	40	35
10									(100)		0.386	(39)	
Totals	$1,300	$300	$1,000	—	$200	$900	$1,400	—	—	—		$531	$553

Assumptions:

1. The firm can borrow $1,000 at 5% to be repaid in ten equal annual installments. The annual payments are computed as
   a. Interest factor for 10 years, 5% annuity = 7.722
   b. Required annual payment = $1,000 ÷ 7.722 = $130
2. The firm can arrange to finance its $1,000 equipment purchase under a 10-year lease plan calling for an annual rental of $150.
3. The equipment is worth $100 at the end of 10 years. This $100 is added to column 10 as a cash inflow for the owning option.
4. The firm uses straight-line depreciation.
6. The investment tax credit does not apply.

aFigures in columns 9, 13, and 14 are rounded to the nearest dollar.
bSince the after-tax cost of leasing is a 10-year annuity of $90, the present value of column 14 could have been found as follows: $90 × (PV of $1 annuity at PVIF for 10%) = $90 × 6.145 = $553.05.

savings shown in column 9 from the total payments in columns 2 and 6 gives the net cash cost of owning shown in column 10.

Assuming that the leasing company—which could even be the same bank that is willing to make the term loan—is willing to accept a 5 percent return on its investment, the annual lease payments must be $150, the same as the loan repayment plus maintenance cost under the loan arrangement. However, the lease charge is a deductible expense, so the after-tax cost is $(1 - t)$ times the lease payment. Thus, the after-tax cost of the lease is $90 a year for ten years; this figure is shown in column 11.

Column 10 shows the firm's net cash outlay each year if it chooses to borrow the money and purchase the machine, while column 11 shows the net cash outflow if it elects the lease alternative. But we can no more add dollars payable in one year to those payable in another than we can add apples to oranges. We must, therefore, put the annual cash flows of leasing and borrowing on a common basis, and this requires converting them to present values.

To convert to present values, we multiply the cash outflows in columns 10 and 11 by the *PVIF* factors in column 12, these are the *PVIF*'s for 10 percent, the firm's assumed cost of capital.[6] The resulting present values are shown in columns 13 and 14; when these columns are summed, we have the net present values of the costs of owning and leasing. The financial method that produces the smaller *PV* of cost is the one that should be selected. The example shown in Table 16–2 indicates that buying has the advantage over leasing: The *PV* of the cost of buying is $22 less than that of leasing ($553 − $531 = $22). Therefore, it is to the firm's advantage to buy in this instance.

Modifications to Account for Other Factors

How would the relative cost of leasing versus owning be affected if the example is modified to allow for accelerated depreciation? Accelerated depreciation would produce a higher tax deduction, hence lower taxes, in the early years. This would reduce the net cost of owning (column 10) in the early years

---

[6]As noted in Chapter 12, and as we discuss in still greater detail in Chapter 20, the appropriate discount rate to apply to an expected future cash flow depends upon the riskiness of the cash flow: cash flows known with relative certainty should be discounted at comparatively low rates, and conversely for risky cash flows. Applying this logic to lease analysis leads to the conclusion that each cash flow stream involved in a lease-versus-purchase decision (for example, the loan payment, maintenance cost, and so on) should be analyzed to determine its degree of risk, then discounted at an appropriate rate. The loan payment and lease payment schedules, which are contractual obligations and must be paid to avoid bankruptcy, are relatively certain streams and should be discounted at low rates. The maintenance expense (unless set by contract) is more uncertain and should be discounted at a higher rate, while the tax savings are somewhat uncertain because maintenance is uncertain and both depreciation schedules and tax rates may change. The salvage value is probably the least certain cash flow, so it should be discounted at a still higher rate.

We do not extend our example to show variable discount rates, but to do so would involve the following steps: (1) assign a risk-adjusted discount rate to each cash flow stream, (2) find the present value of each stream, (3) add up the present value cash flows associated with leasing and with buying, and (4) determine the *NPV* advantage to leasing or borrowing. For an excellent discussion of all this, see R. S. Bower, "Issues in Lease Financing," *Financial Management*, Winter 1973, 25–34.

and raise it later on. Since the lease cost after tax (column 11) is unaffected, the result would be to increase the advantage to owning (column 13) in the early years and to lower it in the later years. When the analysis is carried through to the "Present Value" columns, the final result of accelerated depreciation would be to make owning relatively more attractive than it already is.

It may be useful to summarize a number of variations and their implications for the evaluation of owning versus leasing, and this is done in Table 16–3. The material in the table summarizes frequently encountered arguments about advantages and disadvantages of leasing. Each assumed condition is subject to substantial qualification, so each is considered in turn.

TABLE 16–3 Variations in Assumed Conditions and Their Implications for Costs of Owning versus Leasing

Assumed conditions	Consequences
Use of accelerated depreciation	Costs of owning lower
Implicit interest rates higher in leasing	Costs of owning lower
Large residual values	Costs of owning lower
Rapid obsolescence	Costs of leasing lower
Rapid write-off	Costs of leasing lower
Increased credit availability	Costs of leasing lower
Investment tax credit	Costs of leasing lower

Use of Accelerated Depreciation It is often argued that because of the ability to use accelerated depreciation methods, owning must be less expensive than leasing. Such an argument does not take into account the competitive aspects of the money and capital markets. Lessors benefit from accelerated depreciation, and competition will force tax advantages such as this to be shared between lessor and lessee. The payments pattern under leasing can be quite flexible. Thus, any opportunities available to equipment owners must be reflected in the competitive system of rates charged by leasing companies.

Implicit Interest Rates Higher in Leasing The statement is frequently made that leasing always involves higher interest rates. This argument is probably not true. First, when the nature of the lessee as a credit risk is considered, there may be no difference. Second, it is difficult to separate the money costs of leasing from the other services that may be embodied in a leasing contract. If, because of its specialized operations, the leasing company can perform nonfinancial services such as maintenance of the equipment at a lower cost than the lessee or some other institution can perform them, then the effective cost of leasing may be lower than for funds obtained from borrowing or other sources. The efficiencies of performing specialized services may thus enable the leasing company to operate by charging a lower total cost than the lessee would have to pay for the package of money plus services on any other basis.

Large Residual Values One important point that must be mentioned in connection with leasing is that the lessor owns the property at the expiration of the lease. The value of the property at the end of the lease is called the *residual value.* Superficially, it would appear that where residual values are large, owning will be less expensive than leasing. However, even this obvious advantage of owning is subject to substantial qualification. On leased equipment, the obsolescence factor may be so large that it is doubtful whether residual values will be of a great order of magnitude. If residual values appear favorable, competition between leasing companies and other financial sources, as well as competition among leasing companies themselves, will force leasing rates down to the point where the potentials of residual values are fully recognized in the leasing contract rates. Thus, the existence of residual values of equipment is not likely to result in materially lower costs of owning. However, in connection with decisions whether to lease or to own land, the obsolescence factor is not involved except to the extent of deterioration in areas with changing population or use patterns. In a period of optimistic expectations about land values, there may be a tendency to overestimate rates of increase in land values. As a consequence, the current purchase of land may involve a price so high that the probable rate of return on owned land may be relatively small. Under this condition, leasing may well represent a more economical way of obtaining the use of land than does owning. Conversely, if the probable increase in land values is not fully reflected in current prices, it will be advantageous to own the land.

Thus it is difficult to generalize about whether residual value considerations are likely to make the effective cost of leasing higher or lower than the cost of owning. The results depend on whether the individual firm has opportunities to take advantage of overoptimistic or overpessimistic evaluations of future value changes by the market as a whole.

Rapid Obsolescence Another popular notion is that leasing costs will be lower because of the rapid obsolescence of some kinds of equipment. If the obsolescence rate on equipment is high, leasing costs must reflect such a rate. Thus, in general terms, it might be argued that neither residual values nor obsolescence rates can basically affect the cost of owning versus leasing.

In connection with leasing, however, it is possible that certain leasing companies may be well equipped to handle the obsolescence problem. For example, the Clark Equipment Company is a manufacturer, reconditioner, and specialist in materials handling equipment, with its own sales organization and system of distributors. This may enable Clark to write favorable leases for equipment. If the equipment becomes obsolete to one user, it may still be satisfactory for other users with different materials handling requirements, and Clark is well situated to locate these other users. The position is similar in computer leasing.

This illustration indicates how a leasing company, by combining lending with other specialized services, may reduce the social costs of obsolescence and increase effective residual values. By such operations the total cost of obtaining the use of such equipment is reduced. Possibly other institutions that do not combine financing and other specialist functions, such as manufacturing, reconditioning, servicing, and sales, may, in conjunction with financing institutions, perform the overall functions as efficiently and at as low cost as do integrated leasing companies. However, this is a factual matter depending upon the relative efficiency of the competing firms in different lines of business and different kinds of equipment. To determine which combination of methods results in the lower costs, an analysis along the lines of the pattern outlined in Table 16–2 is required.

Rapid Write-off   If the lease is written for a period that is much shorter than the depreciable life of the asset, with renewals at low rentals after the lessor has recovered his costs during the basic lease period, then deductible depreciation (column 7, Table 16–2) is small in relation to the deductible lease payment in the early years. In a sense, this amounts to a very rapid write-off, which is advantageous to the lessee. However, the Internal Revenue Service correctly disallows as deductions lease payments under leases (1) that call for a rapid amortization of the lessor's costs and (2) that have a relatively low renewal or purchase option.

Increased Credit Availability   Two possible situations may exist to give leasing an advantage to firms seeking the maximum degree of financial leverage. First, it is frequently stated that firms can obtain more money for longer terms under a lease arrangement than under a secured loan agreement for the purchase of a specific piece of equipment. Second, leasing may not have as much of an impact on future borrowing capacity as does borrowing to buy the equipment. This point is illustrated by the balance sheets of two hypothetical firms, A and B, in Table 16–4.

TABLE 16–4 Balance Sheet Effects of Leasing

Before Asset Increase			After Asset Increase							
Firms A and B				Firm A				Firm B		
Total assets	$100	Debt $ 50 Equity 50 $100	Total assets	$200		Debt $150 Equity 50 $200	Total assets	$100		Debt $ 50 Equity 50 $100

Initially, the balance sheets of both firms are identical, and they both have debt ratios of 50 percent. Next, they each decide to acquire assets costing $100. Firm A borrows $100 to make the purchase, so an asset and a liability go on its balance sheet, and its debt ratio is increased to 75 percent. Firm B leases the equipment. The lease may call for fixed charges as high or even higher than the loan, and the obligations assumed under the lease can be equally or more dangerous to other creditors, but the fact that its reported debt ratio is lower may enable firm B to obtain additional credit from other lenders. The amount of the annual rentals is shown as a note to B's financial statements, so credit analysts are aware of it, but evidence suggests that many of them still give less weight to firm B's lease than to firm A's loan.

This illustration indicates quite clearly a weakness of the debt ratio—if two companies are being compared and if one leases a substantial amount of equipment, then the debt ratio as we calculate it does not accurately show their relative leverage positions.[7]

Investment Tax Credit   The investment tax credit, discussed in Chapter 2 of this book, can be taken only if the firm's profits and taxes exceed a certain level. If a firm is unprofitable, or if it is expanding so rapidly and generating such large tax credits that it cannot use them all, then it may be profitable for it to enter a lease arrangement. Here the lessor (a bank or leasing company) will take the credit and give the lessee a corresponding reduction in lease charges. Railroads and airlines have been larger users of leasing for this reason in recent years, as have industrial companies faced with particular situations. Anaconda, for example, financed most of the cost of a $138 million aluminum plant built in 1973 through a lease arrangement.[8] Anaconda had suffered a $356 million tax loss when Chile expropriated its copper mining properties, and the carry-forward of this loss would hold taxes down for years. Thus, Anaconda could not use the tax credit associated with the new plant. By entering a lease arrangement, Anaconda was able to pass the tax credit on to the lessees, who in turn gave Anaconda lower lease payments than would have existed under a loan arrangement. Anaconda's financial staff estimated that financial charges over the life of the plant would be $74 million less under the lease arrangement than under a borrow-and-buy plan.

Incidentally, the Anaconda lease was set up as a "leveraged lease." A group of banks and Chrysler Corporation provided about $38 million of equity and were the owner-lessors. These owner-lessors borrowed the balance of the required funds from Prudential, Metropolitan, and Aetna—large life insurance companies. The banks and Chrysler received not only the investment tax

[7] Two comments are appropriate here. First, financial analysts sometimes attempt to reconstruct the balance sheets of firms such as B by "capitalizing the lease payments," that is, estimating the value of both the lease obligation and the leased assets and transforming B's balance sheet into one comparable to A's. Second, as we indicated in Chapter 3, lease charges are included in the fixed charge coverage ratio, and this ratio will be approximately equal for firms A and B, thus revealing the true state of affairs.

[8] Vanderwicken, "Powerful Logic of the Leasing Boom," 132–194.

credit but also the tax shelter associated with accelerated depreciation on the plant. Such leveraged leases, often with wealthy individuals seeking tax shelters acting as owner-lessors, are an important part of the financial scene today.

SUMMARY

Intermediate-term financing is defined as any liability originally scheduled for repayment in more than one year but in less than ten years. Anything shorter is a current liability, while obligations due in ten or more years are thought of as long-term debt. The major forms of intermediate-term financing include (1) *term loans* and (2) *lease financing.*

Term Loans   A term loan is a business credit with a maturity of more than one year but of less than fifteen years. There are exceptions to the rule, but ordinarily term loans are retired by systematic repayments (amortization payments) over the life of the loan. Security, generally in the form of a chattel mortgage on equipment, is often employed; the larger, stronger companies are able to borrow on an unsecured basis. Commercial banks and life insurance companies are the principal suppliers of term loan credit. Commercial banks typically make smaller, short term loans; life insurance companies grant larger, longer term credits.

The interest cost of term loans, like rates on other credits, varies with the size of the loan and the strength of the borrower. For small loans to small companies, rates may go up as high as 15 percent; for large loans to large firms, the rate will be close to prime. Since term loans run for long periods, during which interest rates can change radically, many loans have variable interest rates, with the rate set at a certain level above the prime rate or above the Federal Reserve rediscount rate.

Another aspect of term loans is the series of *protective covenants* contained in most loan agreements. The lender's funds are tied up for a long period, and during this time the borrower's situation can change markedly. To protect himself, the lender will include in the loan agreement stipulations that the borrower will maintain his current ratio at a specified level, limit acquisitions of additional fixed assets, keep his debt ratio below a stated amount, and so on. These provisions are necessary from the lender's point of view, but they necessarily restrict the borrower's actions.

Lease Financing   Leasing has long been used in connection with the acquisition of equipment by railroad companies. In recent years, it has been extended to a wide variety of equipment.

Three different forms of lease financing were considered: (1) sale and leaseback, in which a firm owning land, buildings, or equipment sells the property and simultaneously executes an agreement to lease the property for a specified period under specific terms; (2) service leases or operating leases, which include both financing and maintenance services, are often cancellable, and call for payments under the lease contract which may not fully recover the cost of the equipment; and (3) financial leases, which do not provide for maintenance services, are not cancellable, and do fully amortize the cost of the leased asset during the basic lease contract period.

To understand the possible advantages and disadvantages of lease financing, the cost of leasing an asset must be compared with the cost of owning the same asset. In the absence of major tax advantages, whether or not leasing is advantageous turns primarily on the firm's ability to acquire funds by other methods. Leasing may provide an advantage by increasing the overall availability of nonequity financing to the firm. However, a financial lease contract is very similar to a straight-debt arrangement and uses some of the firm's debt-carrying ability.

QUESTIONS

16-1. "The type of equipment best suited for leasing has a long life in relation to the length of the lease, is a removable, standard product that could be used by many different firms, and is easily identifiable. In short, it is the kind of equipment that could be repossessed and sold readily. However, we would be quite happy to write a ten-year lease on paper towels for a firm such as General Motors." Discuss the statement.

16-2. Leasing is often called a hedge against obsolescence. Under what conditions is this actually true?

16-3. Is leasing in any sense a hedge against inflation for the lessee? for the lessor?

16-4. One alleged advantage of leasing is that it keeps liabilities off the balance sheet, thus making it possible for a firm to obtain more leverage than it otherwise could. This raises the question of whether or not both the lease obligation and the asset involved should be capitalized and shown on the balance sheet. Discuss the pros and cons of capitalizing leases and the related assets.

16-5. A firm is seeking a term loan from a bank. Under what conditions would it want a fixed interest rate, and under what condition would it want the rate to fluctuate with the prime rate?

16-6. Under what conditions would a "balloon note," or loan that is not fully amortized, be advantageous to a borrower?

PROBLEMS

16-1. The Lawton Company is faced with the decision whether to purchase or to lease a new fork-lift truck. The truck can be leased on a five-year contract for $2,300 a year, or it can be purchased for $6,990. The lease includes maintenance and service. The salvage value of the truck five years hence is $1,890. The company uses the sum-of-the-years'-digits method of depreciation. If the truck is owned, service and maintenance charges (a deductible cost) would be $500 a year. The company can borrow at 9 percent for amortized term loans. It has a 40 percent marginal tax rate, and the average after-tax cost of capital is 12 percent.

    a. Which method of acquiring the use of equipment should the company choose?

    b. What factors could alter the results indicated by the quantitative analysis based on the above facts?

    c. Explain how you chose your discount rate or rates, emphasizing risk differentials and before-tax versus after-tax costs.

16-2. The Scott Brothers Department Store is considering a sale and leaseback of its major property, consisting of land and a building, because it is thirty days late on 80 percent of its accounts payable. The recent balance sheet of Scott Brothers is shown below. Profit before taxes in 1975 is $36,000; after taxes, $20,000.

Scott Brothers Department Store
Balance sheet
December 31, 1975
(thousands of dollars)

Cash	$ 288	Accounts payable	$1,440
Receivables	1,440	Bank loans, 8%	1,440
Inventories	1,872	Other current liabilities	720
Total current assets	$3,600	Total current debt	$3,600
Land	$1,152	Common stock	1,440
Building	720	Retained earnings	720
Fixtures and equipment	288		
Net fixed assets	2,160		
Total assets	$5,760	Total claims	$5,760

Annual depreciation charges are $57,600 a year on the building and $72,000 a year on the fixtures and equipment. The land and building could be sold for a total of $2.8 million. The annual net rental will be $240,000.

    a. How much capital gains tax will Scott Brothers pay if the land and building are sold? (Assume all capital gains are taxed at the capital gains tax rate: that is, disregard such items as recapture of depreciation, tax preference treatment, and so on.)

    b. Compare the current ratio before and after the sale and leaseback if the after-tax net proceeds are used to "clean up" the bank loans and to reduce accounts payable and other current liabilities.

    c. If the lease had been in effect during 1975, what would Scott Brothers' profit for 1975 have been?

    d. What are the basic financial problems facing Scott Brothers? Will the sale and leaseback operation solve them?

Warrants and Convertibles

17

Thus far in the discussion of long-term financing, we have examined the nature of common stock, preferred stock, various types of debt, and leasing. We have also seen how offering common stock through the use of rights can facilitate low-cost stock flotations. In this chapter, we see how the financial manager, through the use of warrants and convertibles, can make his company's securities attractive to an even broader range of investors, thereby lowering his cost of capital. As we show in Chapter 22, "The Timing of Financial Policy," the use of warrants and convertibles has increased more rapidly than any other forms of long-term financing. Therefore, it is important to understand the characteristics of these two types of securities.

WARRANTS

A *warrant* is an option to buy a stated number of shares of stock at a specified price. For example, Trans Pacific Airlines has warrants outstanding that give the warrant holders the right to buy one share of TPA stock at a price of $22 for each warrant held. The warrants generally expire on a certain date—TPA's warrants expire on December 1, 1979—although some have perpetual lives.

Formula Value of a Warrant

Warrants have a calculated, or formula, value and an actual value, or price,

360

that is determined in the marketplace. The formula value is found by use of the following equation:

$$\begin{pmatrix} \text{Formula} \\ \text{value} \end{pmatrix} = \begin{pmatrix} \text{market price of} \\ \text{common stock} \end{pmatrix} - \begin{pmatrix} \text{exercise} \\ \text{price} \end{pmatrix} \times \begin{pmatrix} \text{number of shares each} \\ \text{warrant entitles owner} \\ \text{to purchase} \end{pmatrix}.$$

For instance, a TPA warrant entitles the holder to purchase one share of common stock at $22 a share. If the market price of the common stock is $64.50, the formula price of the warrant may be obtained as follows:

$$(\$64.50 - \$22) \times 1.0 = \$42.50.$$

The formula gives a negative value when the stock is selling for less than the exercise price. For example, if TPA stock is selling for $20, the formula value of the warrants is minus $2. This makes no sense, so we define the formula value to be zero when the stock is selling for less than the exercise price.

Actual Price of a Warrant

Generally, warrants sell above their formula values. When TPA stock was selling for $64.50, the warrants had a formula value of $42.50 but were selling at a price of $46.87. This represented a premium of $4.37 above the formula value.

A set of TPA stock prices, together with actual and formula warrant values, is given in Table 17–1 and plotted in Figure 17–1. At any stock price below $22, the formula value of the warrant is zero; beyond $22, each $1 increase in the price of the stock brings with it a $1 increase in the formula value of the warrant. The actual market price of the warrants lies above the formula value at each price of the common stock. Notice, however, that the premium of market price over formula value declines as the price of the

TABLE 17–1   Formula and Actual Values of TPA Warrants at Different Market Prices

	Value of Warrant		
Price of Stock	Formula Price	Actual Price	Premium
$ 0.00	$ 0.00	Not available	—
22.00	0.00	$ 9.00	$9.00
23.00	1.00	9.75	8.75
24.00	2.00	10.50	8.50
33.67	11.67	17.37	5.70
52.00	30.00	32.00	2.00
75.00	53.00	54.00	1.00
100.00	78.00	79.00	1.00
150.00	128.00	Not available	—

common stock increases. For example, when the common sold for $22 and the warrants had a zero formula value, their actual price, and the premium, was $9. As the price of the stock rises, the *formula value* of the warrants matches the increase dollar for dollar, but for a while the *market price* of the warrant climbs less rapidly and the premium declines. The premium is $9 when the stock sells for $22 a share, but it declines to $1 by the time the stock price has risen to $75 a share. Beyond this point the premium seems to be constant.

FIGURE 17–1   Formula and Actual Values of TPA Warrants at Different Common Stock Prices

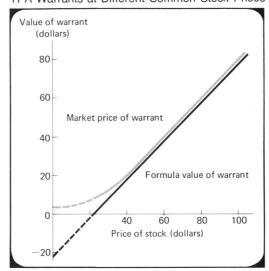

Why do you suppose this pattern exists? Why should the warrant ever sell for more than its formula value, and why does the premium decline as the price of the stock increases? The answer lies in the speculative appeal of warrants—they enable a person to gain a high degree of personal leverage when buying securities. To illustrate, suppose TPA warrants always sold for exactly their formula value. Now suppose you are thinking of investing in the company's common stock at a time when it is selling for $25 a share. If you buy a share and the price rises to $50 in a year, you have made a 100 percent capital gain. However, had you bought the warrants at their formula value ($3 when the stock sells for $25), your capital gain would have been $25 on a $3 investment, or 833 percent. At the same time, your total loss potential with the warrant is only $3, while the potential loss from the purchase of the stock is $25. The huge capital gains potential, combined with the loss limitation, is clearly worth something—the exact amount it is worth to investors is the amount of the premium.[1]

But why does the premium decline as the price of the stock rises? The answer is that both the leverage effect and the loss protection feature decline at high stock prices. For example, if you are thinking of buying the stock at $75 a share, the formula value of the warrants is $53. If the stock price doubles to $150, the formula value of TPA warrants goes from $53 to $128. The percentage capital gain on the stock is still 100 percent, but the percentage gain on the warrant declines from 833 percent to 142 percent. Moreover, notice that the loss potential on the warrant is much greater when the warrant is selling at high prices. These two factors, the declining leverage impact and the increasing danger of losses, explain why the premium diminishes as the price of the common stock rises.

Use of Warrants in Financing

In the past, warrants have generally been used by small, rapidly growing firms as "sweeteners" when selling either debt or preferred stocks. Such firms are frequently regarded by investors as being highly risky. Their bonds could be sold only if the firms were willing to accept extremely high rates of interest and very restrictive indenture provisions, to offer warrants, or to make the bonds convertible. In April 1970, however, AT&T raised $1.57 billion by selling bonds with warrants. This was the largest financing of any type ever undertaken by a business firm, and it marked the first use ever of warrants by a large, strong corporation.[2] It may safely be anticipated that other large firms will follow AT&T's lead, so we can expect to see a more widespread use of warrants in the future than has been true in the past.[3]

Giving warrants along with bonds enables investors to share in the company's growth, if it does, in fact, grow and prosper; therefore, investors are willing to accept a lower bond interest rate and less restrictive indenture provisions. A bond with warrants has some characteristics of debt and some characteristics of equity. It is a hybrid security that provides the financial manager with an opportunity to expand his mix of securities, appealing to a broader group of investors, and, thus, possibly lowering his firm's cost of capital.

Warrants can also bring in additional funds. The option price is generally set 15 to 20 percent above the market price of the stock at the time of the bond

[1] However, a $3 decline in the stock price produces only a 12 percent loss if the stock is purchased, and a 100 percent loss if you buy the warrant and it declines to its formula value.

[2] It is also interesting to note that before the AT&T issue, the New York Stock Exchange had a policy against listing warrants. The NYSE's stated policy was that warrants could not be listed because they were "speculative" instruments rather than "investment" securities. When AT&T issued warrants, however, the Exchange changed its policy and agreed to list warrants that met certain specifications.

[3] In fact, the number of warrants listed on the New York and American stock exchanges increased from eighteen in 1967 to sixty in 1974; although it cannot be documented, the increase is reported to be even larger in the over-the-counter market.

issue. If the firm does grow and prosper, and if its stock price rises above the option price at which shares may be purchased, warrant holders will surrender their warrants and buy stock at the stated price. There are several reasons for this. First, warrant holders will *surely* surrender warrants and buy stock if the warrants are about to expire with the market price of the stock above the option price. Second, warrant holders will *voluntarily* surrender and buy as just mentioned as the company raises the dividend on the common stock. No dividend is earned on the warrant, so it provides no current income. However, if the common stock pays a high dividend, it provides an attractive dividend yield. This induces warrant holders to exercise their option to buy the stock. Third, warrants sometimes have *stepped-up option prices.* For example, the Williamson Scientific Company has warrants outstanding with an option price of $25 until December 31, 1979, at which time the option price rises to $30. If the price of the common stock is over $25 just before December 31, 1979, many warrant holders will exercise their option before the stepped-up price takes effect.

One desirable feature of warrants is that they generally bring in additional funds only if such funds are needed. If the company grows and prospers, causing the price of the stock to rise, the warrants are exercised and bring in needed funds. If the company is not successful and cannot profitably employ additional money, the price of its stock will probably not rise sufficiently to induce exercise of the options.

CONVERTIBLES

Convertible securities are bonds or preferred stocks that are exchangeable into common stock at the option of the holder and under specified terms and conditions. The most important of the special features relates to how many shares of stock a convertible holder receives if he converts. This feature is defined as the *conversion ratio,* which gives the number of shares of common stock the holder of the convertible receives when he surrenders his security on conversion. Related to the conversion ratio is the *conversion price,* or the effective price paid for the common stock when conversion occurs. In effect, a convertible is similar to a bond with an attached warrant.

The relationship between the conversion ratio and the conversion price is illustrated by Adams Electric Company convertible debentures, issued at their $1,000 par value in 1976. At any time prior to maturity on July 1, 1996, a debenture holder can turn in his bond and receive in its place twenty shares of common stock; therefore, the conversion ratio is twenty shares for one bond. The bond has a par value of $1,000, so the holder is giving up this amount when he converts. Dividing the $1,000 by the twenty shares received gives a conversion price of $50 a share:

$$\text{Conversion price} = \frac{\text{par value of bond}}{\text{shares received}} = \frac{\$1,000}{20} = \$50.$$

The conversion price and the conversion ratio are established at the time the convertible bond is sold. Generally, these values are fixed for the life of the bond, although sometimes a stepped-up conversion price is used. Litton Industries' convertible debentures, for example, were convertible into 12.5 shares until 1972, and they may be exchanged into 11.76 shares from 1972 until 1982 and into 11.11 shares from 1982 until they mature in 1987. The conversion price thus started at $80, rose to $85, then to $90. Litton's convertibles, like most, are callable at the option of the company.

Another factor that may cause a change in the conversion price and ratio is a standard feature of almost all convertibles—the clause protecting the convertible against dilution from stock splits, stock dividends, and the sale of common stock at low prices (as in a rights offering). The typical provision states that no common stock can be sold at a price below the conversion price and that the conversion price must be lowered (and the conversion ratio raised) by the percentage amount of any stock dividend or split. For example, if Adams Electric had a two-for-one split, the conversion ratio would automatically be adjusted to 40 and the conversion price lowered to $25. If this protection was not contained in the contract, a company could completely thwart conversion by the use of stock splits and dividends. Warrants are similarly protected against dilution.

Like warrant option prices, the conversion price is characteristically set from 15 to 20 percent above the prevailing market price of the common stock at the time the convertible issue is sold. Exactly how the conversion price is established can best be understood after examining some of the reasons why firms use convertibles.

Advantages of Convertibles

Convertibles offer advantages to corporations as well as to individual investors. The most important of these advantages are discussed below.

As a "sweetener" when selling debt. A company can sell debt with lower interest rates and less restrictive covenants by giving investors a chance to share in potential capital gains. Convertibles, like bonds with warrants, offer this possibility.

To sell common stock at prices higher than those currently prevailing. Many companies actually want to sell common stock, not debt, but feel that the price of the stock is temporarily depressed. Management may know, for example, that earnings are depressed because of a strike but that they will snap back during the next year and pull the price of the stock up with them. To sell stock now would require giving up more shares to raise a given amount of money than management thinks is necessary. However, setting the conversion price 15 to 20 percent above the present market price of the stock will require giving up 15 to 20 percent fewer shares when the bonds are converted than would be required if stock was sold directly.

Notice, however, that management is counting on the stock price's rising above the conversion price to make the bonds actually attractive in conversion. If the stock price does not rise and conversion does not occur, then the company is saddled with debt.

How can the company be sure that conversion will occur when the price of the stock rises above the conversion price? Characteristically, convertibles have a provision that gives the issuing firm the opportunity of calling the convertible at a specified price. Suppose the conversion price is $50, the conversion ratio is 20, the market price of the common stock has risen to $60, and the call price on the convertible bond is $1,050. If the company calls the bond (by giving the usual notification of twenty days), bondholders can either convert into common stock with a market value of $1,200 or allow the company to redeem the bond for $1,050. Naturally, bondholders prefer $1,200 to $1,050, so conversion occurs. The call provision therefore gives the company a means of forcing conversion, provided that the market price of the stock is greater than the conversion price.

To have low-cost capital during a construction period. Another advantage from the standpoint of the issuer is that a convertible issue may be used as a temporary financing device. During the years 1946 through 1957, AT&T sold $10 billion of convertible debentures. By 1959 about 80 percent of these convertible debentures had been converted into common stock. AT&T did not want to sell straight debt in that amount because its financial structure would have been unbalanced. On the other hand, if AT&T had simply issued large amounts of common stock periodically, there would have been price pressure on its stock because the market is slow to digest large blocks of stock.

By using convertible debentures, which provided for a lag of some six to nine months before they were converted into common stock, AT&T received relatively cheap money to finance growth. Transmission lines and telephone exchange buildings must first be built to provide the basis for ultimately installing phones. While AT&T is making such installations, these investments are not earning any money. Therefore, it was important to AT&T to minimize the cost of money during the construction period. After six to nine months had elapsed and the installations were translated into telephones that were bringing in revenues, AT&T was better able to pay the regular common stock dividend.

Disadvantages of Convertibles

From the standpoint of the issuer, convertibles have a possible disadvantage. Although the convertible bond does give the issuer the opportunity to sell common stock at a price 15 to 20 percent higher than it could otherwise be sold, if the common stock greatly increases in price the issuer may find that he would have been better off if he had waited and simply sold the common stock. Further, if the company truly wants to raise equity capital and if the price of the stock declines after the bond is issued, then it is stuck with debt.

DECISIONS ON USE OF WARRANTS AND CONVERTIBLES

The Winchester Company, an electronic circuit and component manufacturer with assets of $12 million, illustrates a typical case where convertibles are useful.

Winchester's profits have been depressed as a result of its heavy expenditures on research and development for a new product. This situation has held down the growth rate of earnings and dividends; the price/earnings ratio is only 18 times, as compared with an industry average of 22. At the current $2 earnings per share and P/E of 18, the stock is selling for $36 a share. The Winchester family owns 70 percent of the 300,000 shares outstanding, or 210,000 shares. It would like to retain majority control but cannot buy more stock.

The heavy R & D expenditures have resulted in the development of a new type of printed circuit that management believes will be highly profitable. Five million dollars is needed to build and equip new production facilities, and profits will not start to flow into the company for some eighteen months after construction on the new plant is started. Winchester's debt amounts to $5.4 million, or 45 percent of assets, well above the 25 percent industry average. Present debt indenture provisions restrict the company from selling additional debt unless the new debt is subordinate to that now outstanding.

Investment bankers inform J. H. Winchester, Jr., the financial vice-president, that subordinated debentures cannot be sold unless they are convertible or have warrants attached. Convertibles or bonds with warrants can be sold with a 5 percent coupon interest rate if the conversion price or warrant option price is set at 15 percent above the present market price of $36, or at $41 a share. Alternatively, the investment bankers are willing to buy convertibles or bonds with warrants at a 5½ percent interest rate and a 20 percent conversion premium, or a conversion (or exercise) price of $43.50. If the company wants to sell common stock directly, it can net $33 a share.

Which of the alternatives should Winchester choose? First, note that if common stock is used, the company must sell 151,000 shares ($5 million divided by $33). Combined with the 90,000 shares held outside the family, this amounts to 241,000 shares versus the Winchester holdings of 210,000, so the family will lose majority control if common stock is sold.

If the 5 percent convertibles or bonds with warrants are used and the bonds are converted or the warrants are exercised, 122,000 new shares will be added. Combined with the old 90,000, the outside interest will then be

212,000, so again the Winchester family will lose majority control. However, if the 5½ percent convertibles or bonds with warrants are used, then after conversion or exercise only 115,000 new shares will be created. In this case the family will have 210,000 shares versus 205,000 for outsiders; absolute control will be maintained.

In addition to assuring control, using the convertibles or warrants also benefits earnings per share in the long run—the total number of shares is less because fewer new shares must be issued to get the $5 million, so earnings per share will be higher. Before conversion or exercise, however, the firm has a considerable amount of debt outstanding. Adding $5 million raises the total debt to $10.4 million against new total assets of $17 million, so the debt ratio will be over 61 percent versus the 25 percent industry average. This could be dangerous. If delays are encountered in bringing the new plant into production, if demand does not meet expectations, if the company should experience a strike, if the economy should go into a recession—if any of these things occur—the company will be extremely vulnerable because of the high debt ratio.

In the present case, the decision was made to sell the 5½ percent convertible debentures. Two years later, earnings climbed to $3 a share, the P/E ratio to 20, and the price of the stock to $60. The bonds were called, but, of course, conversion occurred. After conversion, debt amounted to approximately $5.5 million against total assets of $17.5 million (some earnings had been retained), so the debt ratio was down to a more reasonable 31 percent.

Convertibles were chosen rather than bonds with warrants for the following reason. If a firm has a high debt ratio and its near-term prospects are favorable, it can anticipate a rise in the price of its stock and thus be able to call the bonds and force conversion. Warrants, on the other hand, have a stated life, and even though the price of the firm's stock rises, the warrants may not be exercised until near their expiration date.[4] If, subsequent to the favorable period (during which convertibles could have been called), the firm encounters less favorable developments and the price of its stock falls, the warrants may lose their value and may never be exercised. The heavy debt burden will then become aggravated. Therefore, the use of convertibles gives the firm greater control over the timing of future capital structure changes. This factor is of particular importance to the firm if its debt ratio is already high in relation to the risks of its line of business.

---

[4]To our knowledge, no company has ever issued a "callable" warrant, that is, one that the issuer would call for exercise under specific conditions. We recently recommended to a company that it consider issuing perpetual, but callable, warrants. These could be called to force exercise if the price of the stock exceeded the exercise price by, say, 30 percent; they would otherwise have no expiration date. Such warrants would probably be viewed with favor by investors afraid of warrants that might expire valueless, and they would still give the company control over the warrants similar to that over convertibles.

REPORTING EARNINGS IF CONVERTIBLES OR WARRANTS ARE OUTSTANDING

Before closing the chapter, we should note that firms with convertibles or warrants outstanding are required to report earnings per share in two ways: (1) *primary EPS,* which in essence is earnings available to common stock divided by the number of shares actually outstanding, and (2) *fully diluted EPS,* which shows what EPS would be if all warrants had been exercised or convertibles converted prior to the reporting date. For firms with large amounts of option securities outstanding, there can be a substantial difference between the two EPS figures. The purpose of the provision is, of course, to give investors a more accurate picture of the firm's true profit position.

SUMMARY

Both warrants and convertibles are forms of options used in financing business firms. The use of such long-term options is encouraged by an economic environment combining prospects of both boom or inflation and depression or deflation. The senior position of the securities protects against recessions. The option feature offers the opportunity for participation in rising stock prices.

Both the convertibility privilege and warrants are used as "sweeteners." The option privileges they grant may make it possible for small companies to sell debt or preferred stock that otherwise could not be sold. For large companies, the "sweeteners" result in lower costs of the securities sold. In addition, the options provide for the future sale of the common stock at prices higher than could be obtained at present. The options thereby permit the delayed sale of common stock at more favorable prices.

The conversion of bonds by their holders does not ordinarily bring additional funds to the company. The exercise of warrants will provide such funds. The conversion of securities will result in reduced debt ratios. The exercise of warrants will strengthen the equity position but will still leave the debt or preferred stock on the balance sheet. In comparing the use of convertibles to senior securities carrying warrants, a firm with a high debt ratio should choose convertibles. A firm with a moderate or low debt ratio may employ warrants.

In the past, larger and stronger firms tended to favor convertibles over bonds with warrants, so most warrants have been issued by smaller, weaker concerns. AT&T's use of warrants in its $1.57 billion 1970 financing has caused other large firms to reexamine their positions on warrants, and we anticipate that warrants will come into increasing use in the years ahead.

QUESTIONS

17-1. Why do warrants typically sell at prices greater than their formula values?

17-2. Why do convertibles typically sell at prices greater than their formula values (the higher of the conversion value or straight-debt value)? Would you expect the percentage premium on a convertible bond to be more or less than that on a warrant? (The percentage premium is defined as the market price minus the formula value, divided by the market price.)

17-3. What effect does the trend in stock prices (subsequent to issue) have on a firm's ability to raise funds (a) through convertibles and (b) through warrants?

17-4. If a firm expects to have additional financial requirements in the future, would you recommend that it use convertibles or bonds with warrants? Why?

17-5. If a firm increases its dividend payout ratio (dividends/earnings), how would this affect each of the following?

    a. The value of long-term warrants.

    b. The likelihood that convertible bonds will be converted.

    c. The likelihood that warrants will be exercised.

17-6. Evaluate the following statement: "Issuing convertible securities represents a means by which a firm can sell common stock at a price above the existing market."

17-7. Why do corporations often sell convertibles on a rights basis?

PROBLEMS

17-1. A convertible bond has a face value of $1,000; it has a 10 percent coupon rate and is convertible into stock at $50, i.e., each bond can be exchanged for twenty shares. The current price of the stock is $43 per share.

    a. If the price per share grows at 6 percent per year for five years, what will the approximate conversion value be at that time?

    b. If dividends on the stock are presently $2 per share, and if these also grow at 6 percent per year, would bondholders convert after five years or would they tend to hold onto their bonds?

    c. If the bonds are callable at a 10 percent premium, about how much would you lose per bond if the bonds were called before you converted? (Assume the same conversion value as in part a above, after five years).

17-2. Warrants attached to a bond entitle the bondholder to purchase one share of stock at $10 per share. Compute the approximate value of a warrant if:

    a. The market price of the stock is $9 per share.

    b. Market price of the stock is $12 per share.

    c. Market price of the stock is $15 per share.

    d. Now each warrant entitles you to purchase two shares at $10, and the current price of a share of stock is $15 per share.

17-3. The Garrett Lumber Company's capital consists of 10,000 shares of common stock and 5,000 warrants, each good to buy two shares of common at $55 a share. The warrants are protected against dilution (that is, the subscription price is adjusted downward in the event of a stock dividend or if the firm sells common stock at less than the $55 exercise price). The company issues rights to buy one new share of common at $50 for every two shares held. With the stock selling rights on at $62, compute:

    a. The theoretical value of the rights before the stock sells ex rights.

    b. The new subscription price of the warrant after the rights issue.

17-4. The Williston Manufacturing Company was planning to finance an expansion in the summer of 1975. The principal executives of the company were agreed that an industrial company such as theirs should finance growth by means of common stock rather than by debt. However, they felt that the price of the company's common stock did not reflect its true worth, so they were desirous of selling a convertible security. They considered a convertible debenture but feared the burden of fixed interest charges if the common stock did not rise in price to make conversion attractive. They decided on an issue of convertible preferred stock.

The common stock was currently selling at $28 a share. Management projected earnings for 1975 at $2 a share and expected a future growth rate of 10 percent a year. It was agreed by the investment bankers and the management that the common stock would sell at 18 times earnings, the current price/earnings ratio.

  a. What conversion price should be set by the issuer?

  b. Should the preferred stock include a call-price provision? Why?

17-5. Copy Right Duplicator, Inc., has the following balance sheet:

BALANCE SHEET 1

Current assets	$125,000	Current debt (free)	$ 50,000
Net fixed assets	125,000	Common stock, par value $2	50,000
		Retained earnings	150,000
Total assets	$250,000	Total claims	$250,000

  a. The firm earns 18 percent on total assets before taxes (assume a 50 percent tax rate). What are earnings per share? Twenty-five thousand shares are outstanding.

  b. If the price/earnings ratio for the company's stock is 16 times, what is the market price of the company's stock?

  c. What is the book value of the company's stock?

In the following few years, sales are expected to double and the financing needs of the firm will double. The firm decides to sell debentures to meet these needs. It is undecided, however, whether to sell convertible debentures or debentures with warrants. The new balance sheet would appear as follows:

BALANCE SHEET 2

Current assets	$250,000	Current debt	$100,000
Net fixed assets	250,000	Debentures	150,000
		Common stock, par value $2	50,000
		Retained earnings	200,000
Total assets	$500,000	Total claims	$500,000

The convertible debentures would pay 7 percent interest and would be convertible into forty shares of common stock for each $1,000 debenture. The debentures with warrants would carry an 8 percent coupon and entitle each holder of a $1,000 debenture to buy twenty-five shares of common stock at $50.

  d. Assume that convertible debentures are sold and all are later converted. Show the new balance sheet, disregarding any changes in retained earnings.

BALANCE SHEET 3

		Current debt	_____
		Debentures	_____
		Common stock, par value $2	_____
		Paid-in capital	_____
		Retained earnings	_____
Total assets	=========	Total claims	=========

e. Complete the firm's income statement after the debentures have all been converted:

INCOME STATEMENT 1

Net income after all charges except debenture interest and before taxes (18% of total assets)	_____
Debenture interest	_____
Federal income tax, 50%	_____
Net income after taxes	_____
Earnings per share after taxes	_____

f. Now, instead of convertibles, assume that debentures with warrants were issued. Assume further that the warrants were all exercised. Show the new balance sheet figures.

BALANCE SHEET 4

		Current debt	_____
		Debentures	_____
		Common stock, par value $2	_____
		Paid-in capital	_____
		Retained earnings	_____
Total assets	=========	Total claims	=========

g. Complete the firm's income statement after the debenture warrants have all been exercised.

INCOME STATEMENT 2

Net income after all charges except debenture interest and before taxes	_____
Debenture interest	_____
Taxable income	_____
Federal income tax	_____
Net income after taxes	_____
Earnings per share after taxes	_____

17-6. The Link Printing Company has grown rapidly during the past five years. Recently its commercial bank has urged the company to consider increasing permanent financing. Its bank loan under a line of credit has risen to $175,000, carrying 7 percent interest. Link has been thirty to sixty days late in paying trade creditors.

Discussions with an investment banker have resulted in the suggestion to raise $350,000 at this time. Investment bankers have assured Link that the following alternatives will be feasible (flotation costs will be ignored):

Alternative 1: Sell common stock at $7.
Alternative 2: Sell convertible bonds at a 7 percent coupon, convertible into common stock at $8.
Alternative 3: Sell debentures at a 7 percent coupon, each $1,000 bond carrying 125 warrants to buy common stock at $8.

Additional information is given below.

Link Printing Company balance sheet

		Current liabilities	$315,000
		Common stock, par $1.00	90,000
		Retained earnings	45,000
Total assets	$450,000	Total liabilities and capital	$450,000

Link Printing Company income statement

Sales	$900,000
All costs except interest	810,000
Gross profit	$ 90,000
Interest	10,000
Profit before taxes	$ 80,000
Taxes at 50%	40,000
Profits after taxes	40,000
Shares	90,000
Earnings per share	$0.44
Price/earnings ratio	17 ×
Market price of stock	$7.48

Larry Rinehart, the president, owns 70 percent of the common stock of Link Printing Company and wishes to maintain control of the company. Ninety thousand shares are outstanding.

a. Show the new balance sheet under each alternative. For alternatives 2 and 3, show the balance sheet after conversion of the debentures or exercise of warrants. Assume that one-half the funds raised will be used to pay off the bank loan and one-half to increase total assets.

b. Show Rinehart's control position under each alternative, assuming that he does not purchase additional shares.

c. What is the effect on earnings per share of each alternative, if it is assumed that profits before interest and taxes will be 20 percent of total assets?

d. What will be the debt ratio under each alternative?

e. Which of the three alternatives would you recommend to Rinehart and why?

Financial Structure and the Use of Leverage

Part Five

In Part Four, we examined the major sources and forms of long-term external capital, considering the market for long-term securities and the principal types of securities—common and preferred stocks, bonds, term loans, leases, convertibles, and warrants. We compared the advantages and disadvantages of these different instruments and considered some of the factors that financial managers keep in mind as they decide which form of financing to use at a specific time. Now, in Part Five, we examine the long-term financing decision in a somewhat different manner, searching for the *optimal* financial structure, or the financial structure that simultaneously minimizes the firm's cost of capital and maximizes the market value of its common stock. As we shall see, financing decisions and investment decisions are interdependent—the optimal financing plan and the optimal level of investment must be determined simultaneously— so Part Five also serves the important function of integrating the theory of capital budgeting and the theory of capital structure.

Part Five contains four chapters: First, Chapter 18, Valuation and Rates of Return, examines the way risk and return interact to determine value. Next, Chapter 19, Financial Structure and the Use of Leverage, highlights the manner in which debt not only generally increases expected earnings, but also increases the firm's risk position. Chapter 20, The Cost of Capital, draws on the two preceding chapters to establish the firm's optimal capital structure as well as its cost of capital. Finally, in Chapter 21, Dividend Policy and Internal Financing, we analyze the decision of whether to pay out earnings in the form of dividends or to retain earnings for reinvestment in the business, and we show the interrelationship between capital budgeting and cost of capital.

Valuation and Rates of Return

18

One of the financial manager's principal goals is to maximize the value of his firm's stock; accordingly, an understanding of the way the market values securities is essential to sound financial management. Also, the rate of return concepts developed in this chapter are used extensively in Chapters 19 and 20, where we analyze the optimal capital structure and show how to calculate a marginal cost of capital for use in capital budgeting.

DEFINITIONS OF VALUE

While it may be difficult to ascribe monetary returns to certain kinds of assets —works of art, for instance—the fundamental characteristic of business assets is that they give rise to income flows. Sometimes these flows are easy to determine and measure—the interest return on a bond is an example. At other times, the cash flows attributable to the asset must be estimated, as was done in Chapters 11 and 12 with capital budgeting. Regardless of the difficulties of measuring income flows, it is the prospective income from business assets that gives them value.

Liquidating Value versus Going-Concern Value

Several different definitions of "value" exist in the literature and are used in practice, with different ones being appropriate at different times. The first distinction that must be made is that between liquidating value and going-concern value. *Liquidating value* is defined as the amount that could be realized if an

377

asset or a group of assets (the entire assets of a firm, for example) were sold separately from the organization that had been using them. If the owner of a machine shop decided to retire, he might auction off his inventory and equipment, collect his accounts receivable, then sell his land and buildings to a grocery wholesaler for use as a warehouse. The sum of the proceeds from each category of assets would be the liquidating value of the assets. If his debts are subtracted from this amount, the difference would represent the liquidating value of his ownership in the business.

On the other hand, if the firm is sold as an operating business to a corporation or to another individual, the purchaser would pay an amount equal to the *going-concern value* of the company. If the going-concern value exceeded the liquidating value, the difference would represent the value of the organization as distinct from the value of the assets.[1]

Book Value versus Market Value

We must also distinguish between *book value,* or the accounting value at which an asset is carried, and *market value,* the price at which the asset can be sold. If the asset in question is a firm, it actually has two market values—a liquidating value and a going-concern value. Only the higher of the two is generally referred to as *the* market value.

For stocks, an item of primary concern in this chapter, book value per share is the firm's total common equity—common stock, paid-in capital, and accumulated retained earnings—divided by shares outstanding. For a given firm, book value per share might be $50. The market value, which is what people will actually pay for a share of the stock, could be above or below the book value. Nuclear Research, for example, has a book value per share of $8.27 and a market value of $25.50; West Virginia Railroad, on the other hand, has a book value of $112.80 versus a market value of only $6.75. Nuclear Research's assets produce a high and rapidly growing earnings stream; West Virginia Railroad's assets are far less productive. Since market value is dependent upon earnings, while book value reflects historical cost, it is not surprising to find deviations between book and market values in a dynamic, uncertain world.

Market Value versus "Fair" or "Reasonable" Value

The concept of a fair or reasonable value (sometimes called the "intrinsic" value) is widespread in the literature on stock market investments. Although the market value of a security is known at any given time, the security's fair value as viewed by different investors could differ. Graham, Dodd, and Cottle,

---

[1] Accountants have termed this difference "goodwill," but "organization value" would be a more appropriate description.

in a classic investments text, define fair value as "that value which is justified by the facts, e.g., assets, earnings, dividends . . . The computed [fair] value is likely to change at least from year to year, as the factors governing that value are modified."[2]

Although Graham, Dodd, and Cottle develop this concept for security (that is, stock and bond) valuation, the idea is applicable to all business assets. What it involves, basically, is estimating the future net cash flows attributable to an asset; determining an appropriate capitalization, or discount, rate; and then finding the present value of the cash flows. This, of course, is exactly what was done in Chapters 10, 11, and 12, where the concept of reasonable value was developed for application in finding the present value of investment opportunities.

The procedure for determining an asset's value is known as the *capitalization-of-income method of valuation.* This is simply a fancy name for the present value of a stream of earnings, discussed at length in Chapter 10. *In going through the present chapter, keep in mind that value, or the price of securities, is exactly analogous to the present value of assets as determined in Chapters 11 and 12.* From this point on, whenever the word "value" is used, we mean the *present value* found by capitalizing expected future cash flows.

THE REQUIRED RATE OF RETURN, *k*

The first step in using the capitalization of income procedure is to establish the proper capitalization rate, or discount rate, for the security. *This rate is defined as the required rate of return, and it is the minimum rate of return necessary to induce investors to buy or hold the security.* For any given risky security, the required rate of return, *k,* is equal to the riskless rate of interest, R_F, plus a risk premium, ρ, read "rho":

$$k = R_F + \rho. \tag{18-1}$$

The current yield on U.S. Treasury securities is generally used to measure R_F.

Equation 18–1, in graph form, is commonly known as the *capital market line,* shortened to CML, which specifies the relationship between risk and the required rate of return. Figure 18–1 presents a graph of the CML. The required rate of return is shown on the vertical axis, while risk, measured here as the standard deviation of the expected rate of return (σ), is shown on the horizontal axis.[3]

---

[2]B. Graham, D. L. Dodd, and S. Cottle, *Security Analysis* (New York: McGraw-Hill, Inc., 1961), p. 28.

[3]In this chapter we use the standard deviation of expected returns as an index of risk. An alternative would be to use the "beta coefficient," which takes into account portfolio effects among the securities of different companies. Beta coefficients are discussed in Appendix C to Chapter 19 of *Managerial Finance* (1975). We should also note that we have drawn the CML as a linear function because the rapidly developing theoretical and empirical literature suggests that risk (as measured by beta) and returns are in fact linearly related; that is, the CML is indeed linear.

FIGURE 18–1 The Relationship between Risk and the Required Rate of Return: the Capital Market Line (CML)

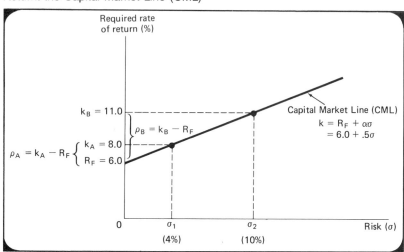

Since a riskless asset, by definition, has no risk, R_F lies on the vertical axis. As risk increases, the required rate of return also increases. A relatively low-risk security, such as that of firm A, might have a risk index of $\sigma_A = 4$ percent and a required rate of return of $k_A = 8$ percent. A more risky security, such as that of firm B, might have a risk index of $\sigma_B = 10$ percent and a required rate of return of $k_B = 11$ percent.

In the illustrative case, the slope of the CML is 0.5, indicating that the required rate of return rises by 0.5 percent for each 1 percent increase in the standard deviation of expected returns. The standard deviation is 4 percent for firm A, so the risk premium on that security is 2 percent ($0.5 \times 4 = 2\%$), while the standard deviation of returns on security B is 10 percent, making its risk premium 5 percent ($0.5 \times 10 = 5\%$). When these two risk premiums are added to the riskless rate, R_F, we obtain the required rates of return:

$$k_A = 6\% + 2\% = 8\%.$$

$$k_B = 6\% + 5\% = 11\%.$$

Notice that the graph can also be used to analyze the securities of a single firm. Since a company's bonds have a smaller standard deviation of expected returns than its common stock, k_A might be the required rate of return on the firm's bonds, while k_B might refer to its common stock. The company's preferred stock would lie on the CML between k_A and k_B.

Shifts in the CML: Changing Interest Rates

We noted in Chapter 7 that interest rates shift markedly over time, and when such shifts occur, the CML also shifts. Figure 18–2 illustrates the effects of an increase in the riskless rate from 6 percent to 8 percent, with the increase perhaps resulting from an increase in the rate of inflation. As we have drawn the graph, the slope of the CML remains constant, but the intercept shifts upward:

Original CML equation: $k = 6.0\% + 0.5\sigma$.

Revised CML equation: $k = 8.0\% + 0.5\sigma$.

This results in increases in the required rates of return for firms A and B, with k_A rising from 8 to 10 percent and k_B from 11 to 13 percent.

FIGURE 18–2   The Effect of Rising Interest Rates on the Required Rate of Return

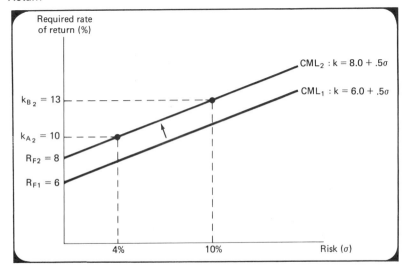

Shifts in the CML: Investor Psychology

The slope of the CML depends upon investors' attitudes toward risk. When investors are gloomy and pessimistic, they are highly averse to risk, and at such times the CML has a relatively steep slope. Conversely, when investors on the whole are optimistic and have a bright outlook, the slope of the CML is not so steep. When investors' attitudes change, the CML shifts. Figure 18–3 illustrates a change in attitudes toward increased pessimism, or an increase in risk aversion. The slope of the CML increases from 0.5 to 0.7:

Original CML equation: $k = 6\% + .5\sigma$.

Revised CML equation: $k = 6\% + .7\sigma$.

This shift increases the required rates of return for firms A and B, with k_A rising from 8 to 8.8 percent and k_B from 11 to 13 percent.

FIGURE 18–3 The Effect of Changing Investor Attitudes on the Required Rate of Return

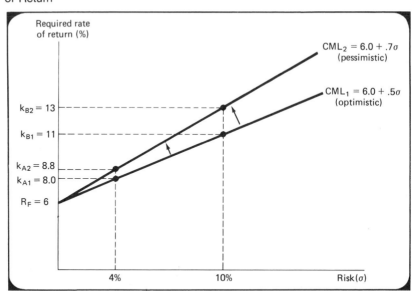

BOND VALUATION

The rate of return concepts developed above may now be used to explain the process of security valuation. In this section we examine bond values; in the two following sections, we go on to study preferred and common stocks.

Bond values are relatively easy to determine. As long as the bond is not expected to go into default, the expected cash flows are the annual interest payments plus the principal amount due when the bond matures. Depending upon differences in the risk of default on interest and principal, the appropriate capitalization (or discount) rate applied to different bonds will vary. A U.S. Treasury security, for example, would have less risk than one issued by the Westbrig Corporation; consequently, a lower discount (or capitalization) rate would be applied to its interest payments. The actual calculating procedures employed in bond valuation are illustrated by the following examples.

Perpetual Bond

After the Napoleonic Wars (1814), England sold a huge bond issue which was used to pay off many smaller issues that had been floated in prior years to pay for the war. Since the purpose of the new issue was to consolidate past debts, the individual bonds were called Consols. Suppose the bonds paid $50 interest annually into perpetuity. (Actually, interest was stated in pounds.) What would the bonds be worth under current market conditions?

First, note that the value (V) of any perpetuity is computed as follows:[4]

$$V = \frac{I}{(1 + k_d)^1} + \frac{I}{(1 + k_d)^2} + \cdots + \frac{I}{(1 + k_d)^\infty}$$

$$= \frac{I}{k_d}. \tag{18–2}$$

Here I is the constant annual interest in dollars and k_d is the appropriate interest rate, or required rate of return, for the bond issue. (In this chapter, we use k_d, k_p, and k_s to designate the required rates of return on debt, preferred stock, and common stock, respectively.) Equation 18–2 is an infinite series of $1 a year, and the value of the bond is the discounted sum of the infinite series.

We know that the Consol's annual interest payment is $50; therefore, the only other thing we need in order to find its value is the appropriate interest rate. This is commonly taken as the going interest rate, or yield, on bonds of similar risk. Suppose we find such bonds to be paying 4 percent under current market conditions. Then the Consol's value is determined as follows:

$$V = \frac{I}{k_d} = \frac{\$50}{0.04} = \$1,250.$$

If the going rate of interest rises to 5 percent, the value of the bond falls to $1,000 ($50/0.05 = $1,000). If interest rates continue rising, when the rate goes as high as 6 percent the value of the Consol will be only $833.33. Values

---

[4] A perpetuity is a bond that never matures; it pays interest indefinitely. Equation 18–2 is simply the present value of an infinite series; its proof is demonstrated below:
Rewrite Equation 18–2 as follows:

$$V = I\left[\frac{1}{(1 + k_d)^1} + \frac{1}{(1 + k_d)^2} + \cdots + \frac{1}{(1 + k_d)^N}\right]. \tag{1}$$

Multiply both sides of Equation (1) by $(1 + k_d)$:

$$V(1 + k_d) = I\left[1 + \frac{1}{(1 + k_d)^1} + \frac{1}{(1 + k_d)^2} + \cdots + \frac{1}{(1 + k_d)^{N-1}}\right]. \tag{2}$$

Subtract Equation (1) from Equation (2), obtaining:

$$V(1 + k_d - 1) = I\left[1 - \frac{1}{(1 + k_d)^N}\right]. \tag{3}$$

As $N \rightarrow \infty$, $\frac{1}{(1 + k_d)^N} \rightarrow 0$, so Equation (3) approaches

$$V(k_d) = I,$$

and

$$V = \frac{I}{k_d}. \tag{18–2}$$

of this perpetual bond for a range of interest rates are given in the following tabulation:

Current Market Interest Rate	Current Market Value
0.02%	$2,500.00
0.03	1,666.67
0.04	1,250.00
0.05	1,000.00
0.06	833.33
0.07	714.29
0.08	625.00

Short-term Bond

Now suppose the British government issues bonds with the same risk of default as the Consols, but with a three-year maturity. The new bonds also pay $50 interest and have a $1,000 maturity value. What will the value of these new bonds be at the time of issue if the going rate of interest is 4 percent? To find this value, we must solve Equation 18–3:

$$V = \frac{I_1}{(1 + k_d)^1} + \frac{I_2}{(1 + k_d)^2} + \frac{I_3 + M}{(1 + k_d)^3} \tag{18–3}$$

Here M is the maturity value of the bond. The solution is given in the following tabulation:[5]

Year	Receipt	4 Percent Discount Factors	Present Value
1	$50	.962	$ 48.10
2	$50	.925	46.25
3	$50 + $1,000	.889	933.45
		Bond value =	$1,027.80

At the various rates of interest used in the perpetuity example, this three-year bond would have the following values:

---

[5] If the bond has a longer maturity, twenty years for example, we would certainly want to calculate its present value by finding the present value of a twenty-year annuity and then adding to that the present value of the $1,000 principal amount received at maturity. Special bond tables have been devised to simplify the calculation procedure. Note also that k_d will frequently differ for the long- and short-term bonds; as we saw in Chapter 7, unless the yield to maturity curve is flat, long- and short-term rates differ.

Current Market Interest Rate	Current Market Value
.02%	$1,086.15
.03	1,056.45
.04	1,027.80
.05	1,000.00
.06	973.65
.07	947.20
.08	922.85

Interest-rate Risk

Figure 18–4 shows how the values of the long-term bond (the Consol) and the short-term bond change in response to changes in the going market rate of interest. Note how much less sensitive the short-term bond is to changes in interest rates. At a 5 percent interest rate, both the perpetuity and the short-term bonds are valued at $1,000. When rates rise to 8 percent, the long-term bond falls to $625, while the short-term security falls only to $923. A similar situation occurs when rates fall below 5 percent. *This differential responsiveness to changes in interest rates always hold true—the longer the maturity of*

FIGURE 18–4 Values of Long-term and Short-term Bonds, 5 Percent Coupon Rate, at Different Market Interest Rates

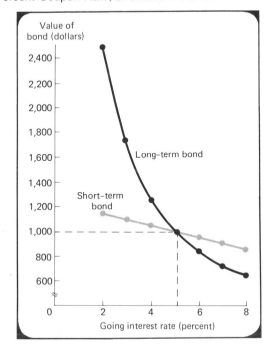

a security, the greater its price change in response to a given change in interest rates. Thus, even if the risk of default on two bonds is exactly the same, the value of the one with the longer maturity is exposed to more risk from a rise in interest rates. This greater *interest rate risk* explains why short-term bonds usually have lower yields, or rates of return, than long-term bonds. It also explains why corporate treasurers are reluctant to hold their near-cash reserves in the form of long-term debt instruments—these near-cash reserves are held for precautionary purposes, and a treasurer would be unwilling to sacrifice safety for a little higher yield on a long-term bond.

Yield to Maturity

The rate of return that is expected if a bond is held to its maturity date is defined as the *yield to maturity.* Suppose a perpetuity has a stated par value of $1,000, has a 5 percent coupon rate (that is, pays 5 percent, or $50 annually, on this stated value), and is currently selling for $625. We can solve Equation 18–2 for k_d to find the yield on the bond:

$$k_d = \frac{I}{V} = \frac{\$50}{\$625} = 8\% = \text{yield on a perpetuity.}$$

If the bond sells for $1,250, the formula will show that the yield is 4 percent.

For the three-year bond paying $50 interest a year, if the price of the bond is $922.85, the yield to maturity is found by solving Equation 18–3; the solution *PVIF* is the one for 8 percent:

$$\$922.85 = \$50(PVIF) + \$50(PVIF) + \$1,050(PVIF)$$

$$= \$50(.926) + \$50(.857) + \$1,050(.794)$$

$$= \$46.30 + \$42.85 + \$833.70 = \$922.85 \text{ when } PVIF = 8\%.$$

The interest factors are taken from the 8 percent column of Table A–2. The solution procedure is exactly like that for finding the internal rate of return in capital budgeting, and the trial-and-error method is required unless special tables are available.[6]

PREFERRED STOCK VALUATION

Most preferred stocks entitle their owners to regular, fixed dividend payments

---

[6] We first tried the *PVIF*'s for 6 percent, found that the equation did not "work," then raised the *PVIF* to 8 percent, where the equation did "work." This indicated that 8 percent was the yield to maturity on the bond. In practice, specialized interest tables called *bond tables,* generated by a computer, are available to facilitate determining the yield to maturity on bonds with different maturities, with different stated interest rates, and selling for various discounts below or premiums above their maturity values.

similar to bond interest. Although some preferred issues are eventually retired, most are perpetuities whose value is found as follows:

$$V = \frac{D}{k_p}. \tag{18-4}$$

In this case, D is the dividend on the preferred stock, and k_p is the appropriate capitalization rate for investments of this degree of risk. For example, General Motors has a preferred stock outstanding that pays a $3.75 annual dividend. The appropriate capitalization rate at the time the stock was issued (1925) was 7.5 percent, so it sold at $50 at the time of issue. Today, however, GM is a much stronger company, and its preferred stock is much less risky. So, in spite of a rise in interest rates and preferred yields generally, the net result is that by 1976 the yield on GM's preferred issue had fallen to 6.8 percent and the value of the stock had climbed to $55 a share:

$$V = \frac{\$3.75}{.068} = \$55.$$

The yield on a preferred stock is similar to that on a perpetual bond, and it is found by solving Equation 18–4 for k_p. For the GM issue, we know that the current price of the stock is $55 and that its annual dividend is $3.75, so the yield is calculated as follows:

$$k_p = \frac{D}{V} = \frac{\$3.75}{\$55} = 6.8\%.$$

COMMON STOCK VALUATION AND RATES OF RETURN

While the same principles apply to the valuation of common stocks as to bonds or preferred stocks, two features make their analysis much more difficult. First is the degree of certainty with which receipts can be forecast. For bonds and preferred stocks, this forecast presents little difficulty, as the interest payments or preferred dividends are known with relative certainty. However, in the case of common stocks, forecasting future earnings, dividends, and stock prices is exceedingly difficult, to say the least. The second complicating feature is that, unlike interest and preferred dividends, common stock earnings and dividends are generally expected to grow, not remain constant. Hence, standard annuity formulas cannot be applied, and more difficult conceptual schemes must be used.

Estimating the Value of a Stock: The Single Period Case

The price today of a share of common stock, P_0, depends upon (1) the cash flows investors expect to receive if they buy the stock and (2) the riskiness of these expected cash flows. The expected cash flows consist of two elements: (1) the dividend expected in each year t, defined as D_t, and (2) the price investors expect to receive when they sell the stock at the end of year n, defined as P_n, which includes the return of the original investment plus a capital gain (or minus a capital loss): If investors expect to hold the stock for one year, and if the stock price is expected to grow at the rate g, the valuation equation is

$$P_0 = \frac{\text{dividend at end of year 1} + \text{price at end of year 1}}{1.0 + \text{required rate of return}}$$

$$= \frac{D_1 + P_1}{(1 + k_s)} = \frac{D_1 + P_0(1 + g)}{(1 + k_s)},$$

(18–5)

which can be simplified to yield Equation 18–6:[7]

$$P_0 = \frac{D_1}{k_s - g}.$$

(18–6)

Equations 18–5 and 18–6 represent the present value of the expected dividends and the year-end stock price, discounted at the required rate of return. Solving Equation 18–6 gives the "fair" or "reasonable" price for the stock. To illustrate, suppose you are thinking of buying a share of American Rubber common stock. If you buy the stock, you will hold it for one year. You note that American Rubber earned $3.43 per share last year, and paid a dividend of $1.90. Earnings and dividends have been rising at about 5 percent a year, on the average, over the last ten to fifteen years, and you expect this growth to continue. Further, if earnings and dividends grow at the expected rate, you think the stock price will likewise grow by 5 percent.

The next step is to determine the required rate of return on American Rubber stock. The current rate of interest on U.S. Treasury securities, R_F, is 8 percent, but American Rubber is clearly more risky than government securities: competitors could erode the company's market; labor problems could disrupt operations; an economic recession could cause sales to fall below the break-even point; auto sales could decline, pulling down American Rubber's own sales and profits; and so on. Further, even if sales, earnings,

---

[7]

$$P_0 = \frac{D_1 + P_0(1 + g)}{(1 + k_s)}$$

(18–5)

$$P_0(1 + k_s) = D_1 + P_0(1 + g)$$

$$P_0(1 + k_s - 1 - g) = D_1$$

$$P_0(k_s - g) = D_1$$

$$P_0 = \frac{D_1}{k_s - g}.$$

(18–6)

Notice that this equation is developed for a one-year holding period. In a later section, we will show that it is also valid for longer periods, provided the expected growth rate is constant.

and dividends meet projections, the stock price could still fall as a result of a generally weak market; this happened in 1974. Given all these risk factors, you conclude that a 4-percent risk premium is justified, so your required rate of return on American Rubber's stock, k_s, is calculated as follows:

$$k_s = R_F + \rho_s = 8\% + 4\% = 12\%.$$

Next, you estimate the dividend for the coming year, D_1, as follows:

$$D_1 = D_0 (1 + g) = \$1.90 \ (1.05) = \$2.$$

Be sure to note that you will not receive the dividend paid last year, $D_0 = \$1.90$; you will receive $D_1 = \$2$.

Now we have the necessary information to estimate the fair value of the stock by the use of Equation 18–6:

$$P_0 = \frac{D_1}{k_s - g}$$

$$= \frac{\$2}{.12 - .05} = \$28.57. \tag{18-6}$$

To you, $28.57 represents a reasonable price for American Rubber's stock. If the actual market price is less, you will buy it; if the actual price is higher, you will not buy it, or you will sell if you own it.[8]

Estimating the Rate of Return on a Stock

In the preceding section we calculated the "fair price" of American Rubber's stock to a given investor. Let us now change the procedure somewhat, and calculate the rate of return the investor can expect if he purchases the stock at the current market price per share. The expected rate of return, which we define as $\hat{k}_s$, is analogous to the internal rate of return on a capital project: $\hat{k}_s$ is the discount rate that equates the present value of the expected dividends (D_1) and final stock price (P_1) to the present stock price (P_0):

$$P_0 = \frac{D_1 + P_1}{(1 + \hat{k}_s)} = \frac{D_1 + P_0 (1 + g)}{(1 + \hat{k}_s)}.$$

---

[8] Notice the similarity between this process and the *NPV* method of capital budgeting described in Chapter 11. In the earlier chapter, we (1) estimated a cost of capital for the firm, which compares with estimating k_s, our required rate of return, (2) discounted expected future cash flows, which are analogous to dividends plus the future stock price, (3) found the present value of future cash flows, which corresponds to the "fair value" of the stock, (4) determined the initial outlay for the project, which compares with finding the actual price of the stock, and (5) accepted the project if the *PV* of future cash flows exceeded the initial cost of the project, which is similar to comparing the "fair value" of the stock to its market price.

Suppose American Rubber is selling for $40 per share. We can calculate $\hat{k}_s$ as follows:

$$\$40 = \frac{\$2 + \$40\,(1.05)}{(1 + \hat{k}_s)} = \frac{\$2 + \$42}{(1 + \hat{k}_s)}$$

$$\$40\,(1 + \hat{k}_s) = \$44$$

$$1 + \hat{k}_s = 1.10$$

$$\hat{k}_s = .10 \text{ or } 10\%.$$

Thus, if you expect to receive a $2 dividend and a year-end price of $42, then your expected rate of return on the investment is 10 percent.

Notice that the expected rate of return, $\hat{k}_s$, consists of two components, an expected dividend yield and an expected capital gains yield:

$$\hat{k}_s = \frac{\text{expected dividend}}{\text{present price}} + \frac{\text{expected increase in price}}{\text{present price}}$$

$$= \frac{D_1}{P_0} + g. \tag{18-6}$$

For American Rubber bought at a price of $40,

$$\hat{k}_s = \frac{\$2}{\$40} + \frac{\$2}{\$40} = 5\% + 5\% = 10\%.$$

Given an expected rate of return of 10 percent, should you make the purchase? This depends upon how the expected return compares with the required return. If $\hat{k}_s$ exceeds k_s, buy; if $\hat{k}_s$ is less than k_s, sell; and if $\hat{k}_s$ equals k_s, the stock price is in equilibrium and you should be indifferent. In our example, your 12 percent required rate of return for American Rubber exceeds the 10 percent expected return, so you should not buy the stock.[9]

Market Equilibrium: Required versus Expected Returns

In the two preceding sections we calculated (1) expected and required rates of return and (2) "fair" or "reasonable" stock prices. Further, we saw that buy/no-buy decisions can be based upon a comparison of either k_s versus $\hat{k}_s$ or "fair" stock value versus actual market price. In this section, we first show that the two decision rules are entirely consistent, then illustrate the process by which stock market equilibrium is maintained.

---

[9] Notice the similarity between this process and the *IRR* method of capital budgeting. The expected rate of return, $\hat{k}_s$, corresponds to the *IRR* on a project, and the required rate of return, k_s, corresponds to the cost-of-capital cutoff rate used in capital budgeting.

Consider again the American Rubber example, when the following data are applicable:

Expected dividend at year end $= D_1 = \$2$.

Expected growth rate in stock price $= g = 5\%$.

Required rate of return $= k_s = 12\%$.

We calculated a "fair" price of $28.57. We next found that the actual market price, as read from a newspaper or obtained from a stockbroker, is $40, and on the basis of that price we calculated a 10 percent expected rate of return.

By either the rate of return or calculated price criteria, American Rubber's stock is overvalued:

Actual price $= \$40 >$ "fair" price $= \$28.57$,

and

Required rate of return $(k_s) = 12\% >$ expected rate of return $(\hat{k}_s) = 10\%$.

You should not buy this stock at the $40 price, and if you own it, you should sell.

Now let us assume that you are a "typical" or "representative" investor, so that your expectations and actions actually determine stock market prices. You and others will start selling American Rubber stock, and this selling pressure will cause the price to decline. The decline will continue until the price reaches $28.57, which you, the typical investor, feel is reasonable. At this price, the expected rate of return will also equal the required rate of return:

$$\hat{k}_s = \frac{D_1}{P_0} + g = \frac{\$2}{\$28.57} + 5\% = 7\% + 5\% = 12\%,$$

and

$$k_s = R_F + \rho = 8\% + 4\% = 12\%.$$

This situation will always hold—*whenever the actual market price is equal to the "fair" price as calculated by a "typical" investor, required and expected returns will also be equal, and the market will be in equilibrium; that is, there will be no tendency for the stock price to go up or down.*

FACTORS LEADING TO CHANGES IN MARKET PRICES

Let us assume that American Rubber's stock is in equilibrium, selling at a price of $28.57 per share. If all expectations are exactly met, over the next year the price will gradually rise to $30, or by 5 percent. However, many different events could occur to cause a change in the equilibrium price of the stock. To illustrate the forces at work, consider again the stock price model, the set of inputs used to develop the price of $28.57, and a new set of assumed input variables:

	Variable Value	
	Original	New
Riskless rate (R_F)	8%	7%
Risk aversion coefficient (α)	.5	.4
Index of stock's risk (σ)	8%	7%
Expected growth rate (g)	5%	6%

The first three variables influence k_s, which declines as a result of the new set of variables from 12 percent to 9.8 percent:

$$\text{Original: } k_s = 8\% + .5(8\%) = 12\%.$$

$$\text{New: } \quad k_s = 7\% + .4(7\%) = 9.8\%.$$

Using these values, together with the new D and g values, we find that P_0 rises from $28.57 to $52.89:

$$\text{Original: } P_0 = \frac{\$1.90(1.05)}{.12 - .05} = \frac{\$2}{.07} = \$28.57.$$

$$\text{New: } \quad P_0 = \frac{\$1.90(1.06)}{.098 - .06} = \frac{\$2.01}{.038} = \$52.89.$$

At the new price, the expected and required rates of return will be equal:

$$\hat{k}_s = \frac{\$2.01}{\$52.89} + 6\% = 9.8\% = k_s$$

as found above.

Evidence suggests that securities adjust quite rapidly to disequilibrium situations. Consequently, equilibrium ordinarily exists for any given stock, and in general the required and expected returns are equal. Stock prices certainly change, sometimes violently and rapidly, but this simply reflects changing conditions and expectations. There are, of course, times when a stock continues to react for several months to a favorable or unfavorable development, but this does not signify a long adjustment period; rather, it merely shows that as more information about the situation becomes available, the market adjusts to these new bits of information. Throughout the remainder of this book, we will assume that security markets are in equilibrium, with $k = \hat{k}$.

MARKETABILITY AND RATES OF RETURN

Throughout the chapter, when we discussed the required rate of return on securities, we concentrated on two factors, the riskless rate of interest and the risk inherent in the security in question. Before closing, however, we should also note that investors value flexibility, or maneuverability. If one becomes disenchanted with a particular investment, or if he needs funds for consumption or other investments, it is highly desirable to be able to liquidate his holdings. Other things the same, the higher the liquidity, or marketability, the lower an investment's required rate of return. Accordingly, one would expect to find listed stocks selling on a lower yield basis than over-the-counter stocks, and widely traded stocks selling at lower yields than stocks with no established market. Since investments in small firms are generally less liquid than those in large companies, we have another reason for expecting to find higher required returns among smaller companies.

SUMMARY

The basic principles underlying valuation theory were discussed in this chapter, and a number of definitions of value were presented: (1) liquidating value versus going-concern value, (2) book value versus market value, and (3) "fair" value versus current market price. Market value is fundamentally dependent upon discounted cash flow concepts and procedures; it involves estimating future cash flows and discounting them back to the present at an appropriate rate of interest.

Rates of return on bonds and preferred stocks are simple to understand and to calculate, but common stock returns are more difficult. First, common stock returns consist (1) of dividends and (2) of capital gains, not a single type of payment, as in the case of bonds and preferred stocks. This fact necessitates the development of a rate of return formula that considers both dividends and capital gains; the rate of return formula for common stock is, therefore, a two-part equation:

Rate of return = dividend yield + capital gains yield.

The second complicating feature of common stock is the degree of uncertainty involved. Bond and preferred stock payments are relatively predictable, but forecasting common stock dividends and, even more, capital gains, is a highly uncertain business.

The expected rate of return for common stocks can be expressed as $\hat{k}_s = D_1/P_0 + g$ if the growth rate is a constant. P_0 is the price, D_1 is the dividend expected this year, and g refers to expected *future growth*.

The required rate of return on any security, k, is the minimum rate of return necessary to induce investors to buy or to hold the security. This rate of return is a function of the riskless rate of interest and the investment's risk characteristics:

$$k = R_F + \rho.$$

This equation, when graphed, is called the *capital market line* (CML), and it shifts over time depending on (1) changes in the riskless rate of interest and (2) investor's psychology, which affects the degree of their risk aversion.

Because investors generally dislike risk, the required rate of return is higher on riskier securities. Bonds, as a class, are less risky than preferred stocks, and preferred stocks, in turn, are less risky than common stocks. As a result, the required rate of return is lowest for bonds, next for preferred stocks, and highest for common stocks. Within each of these security classes, there are variations among the issuing firms' risks; hence, required rates of return vary among firms.

In equilibrium, the expected rate of return $(\hat{k})$ and the required rate of return (k) will be equal. If, however, some disturbance causes them to be different, the market price of the stock (and thus its dividend yield) will quickly change to establish a new equilibrium where k and $\hat{k}$ are again equal.

The required rate of return also depends upon the marketability of a given security issue—the stocks and bonds of larger, better known firms are more marketable, hence the required rates of return on such securities are lower than those on smaller, less well known firms. As we shall see in Chapter 20, the required rate of return is, in essence, a firm's cost of capital, so if small firms have relatively high required rates of return, they also have relatively high costs of capital.

QUESTIONS

18-1. Explain what is meant by the term "yield to maturity" (a) for bonds and (b) for preferred stocks. (c) Is it appropriate to talk of a yield to maturity on a preferred stock that has no specific maturity date?

18-2. Explain why bonds with longer maturities experience wider price movements from a given change in interest rates than do shorter maturity bonds. Preferably give your answer (a) in words (intuitively) and (b) mathematically.

18-3. Explain why a share of no-growth common stock is similar to a share of preferred stock. Use one of the equations developed in the chapter in your explanation.

18-4. Explain the importance in common stock valuation (a) of current dividends, (b) of current market price, (c) of the expected future growth rate, and (d) of the market capitalization rate.

18-5. Suppose a firm's charter explicitly precludes it from ever paying a dividend. Investors *know* that this restriction will never be removed. Earnings last year were $1 a share, and they are expected to grow at a rate of 4 percent forever. If the required rate of return is 10 percent, what is the firm's theoretical P/E ratio?

18-6. Describe the factors that determine the market rate of return on a particular stock at a given point in time.

18-7. Explain how (a) interest rates and (b) investors' aversion to risk influence stock and bond prices.

18-8. Most inheritance tax laws state that for estate tax purposes, property shall be valued on the basis of "fair market value." Describe how an inheritance tax appraiser might use the valuation principles discussed in this chapter to establish the value (a) of shares of a stock listed on the New York Stock Exchange and (b) of shares representing 20 percent of a stock that is not publicly traded.

PROBLEMS

18-1.a. The Criterion Corporation has outstanding a series of *perpetual* bonds that pay $90 interest annually. Bonds of this type currently yield 6 percent. At what price should Criterion's bonds sell?

b. Assume that the required yield for bonds of this type rises to 10 percent. What will be the new price of Criterion's bonds?

c. Assume that the required yield drops to 9 percent. What will be the new price of Criterion's bonds?

d. Now suppose that Criterion has another series of bonds that pay $90 annual interest, mature in ten years, and pay $1,000 on maturity. What will be the value of these bonds when the going rate of interest is (i) 6 percent, (ii) 10 percent, and (iii) 9 percent? (Hint: Use both the *PV* of an annuity and the *PV* of $1 tables.)

e. Why do the longer term bonds (the perpetuities) fluctuate more when interest rates change than do the shorter term bonds (the ten-year bonds)?

18-2. What will be the "yield to maturity" of a perpetual bond with a $1,000 par value, a 5 percent coupon rate, and a current market price of (a) $750, (b) $1,000, and (c) $1,250? Assume interest is paid annually.

18-3. Precision Bearings issues a five-year 8 percent note with a maturity value of $1,000. What will be the value of this note at the time of issue if the going rate of interest is 6 percent?

18-4.a. Assuming that a bond has three years remaining to maturity and that interest is paid annually, what will be the yield to maturity on the bond with a $1,000 maturity value, a 7 percent coupon interest rate, and a current market price (1) of $880 or (2) of $1,083? (Hint: Try 12 percent and 4 percent for the two bonds, but *show your work.*)

b. Would you pay $880 for the bond described in part a if your required rate of return for securities in the same risk class is 10 percent; that is, $k_d = 10$ percent? Explain your answer.

18-5. The current market price of a well-established company is $60 per share. It has paid an annual dividend of $3 per share for the last three years and expects to continue the same dividend for the next three years. An investor whose required rate of return is 10 percent is considering buying 100 shares and holding them for two years. What market price per share does the investor expect in two years?

18-6.a. The bonds of the Johnson Corporation are perpetuities bearing an 8 percent coupon. Bonds of this type yield 7 percent. What is the price of Johnson bonds? Their par value is $1,000.

b. Interest rate levels rise to the point where such bonds now yield 10 percent. What will be the price of the Johnson bonds now?

c. Interest rate levels drop to 8 percent. At what price will the Johnson bonds sell?

d. How would your answers to parts a, b, and c change if the bonds had a definite maturity date of twenty years?

18-7.a. American Aviation is currently earning $6 million a year after taxes. A total of 2,500,000 shares are authorized, and 2,000,000 shares are outstanding. What are the company's earnings per share?

b. Investors require a 15 percent rate of return on stocks in the same risk class as American's ($k_s = 15\%$). At what price will the stock sell if the previous dividend was $1 ($D_0 = \$1$), and investors expect dividends to grow at a constant compound annual rate of (1) *minus* 5 percent, (2) 0 percent, (3) 5 percent, and (4) 14 percent? (Hint: Use $D_1 = D_0(1 + g)$, not D_0, in the formula.)

c. In part b, what is the "formula price" if the required rate of return is 15 percent and the expected growth rate is (1) 15 percent or (2) 20 percent? Are these reasonable results? Explain.

d. At what price/earnings (P/E) ratio will the stock sell, assuming each of the growth expectations given in part b?

18-8. Dan Martin plans to invest in common stocks for a period of fifteen years, after which he will sell out, buy a lifetime room-and-board membership in a retirement home, and retire. He feels that Computech is currently, but temporarily, undervalued by the market. Martin expects Computech's current earnings and dividend to double in the next fifteen years. Computech's last dividend was $3, and its stock currently sells for $35 a share.

a. If Martin requires a 12 percent return on his investment, will Computech be a good buy for him?

b. What is the maximum that Martin could pay for Computech and still earn his required 12 percent?

c. What might be the cause of such a market undervaluation?

d. Given Martin's assumptions, what market capitalization rate for Computech does the current price imply?

18-9. In 1936 the Canadian government raised $55 million by issuing perpetual bonds at a 3 percent annual rate of interest. Unlike most bonds issued today, which have a specific maturity date, these perpetual bonds can remain outstanding forever; they are, in fact, perpetuities.

At the time of issue, the Canadian government stated that cash redemption was *possible* at face value ($100) on or after September 1966; in other words, the bonds were callable at par after September 1966. Believing that the bonds would in fact be called, many investors in the early 1960s purchased these bonds with expectations of receiving $100 in 1966 for each perpetual they held. In 1963 the bonds sold for $55, but a rush of buyers drove the price to just below the $100 par value by 1966. Prices fell dramatically, however, when the Canadian government announced that these perpetual bonds were indeed perpetual and would *not* be paid off. A new thirty-year supply of coupons was sent to each bondholder, and the bond's market price declined to $42 in December 1972.

Because of their severe losses, hundreds of Canadian bondholders have formed the Perpetual Bond Association to lobby for face value redemption of the bonds. Government officials in Ottawa insist that claims for face value payment are nonsense, that the bonds were clearly identified as perpetuals, and that they did not mature in 1966 or at any other time. One Ottawa official states, "Our job is to protect the taxpayer. Why should we pay $55 million for less than $25 million worth of bonds?

a. Would it make sense for a business firm to issue bonds such as the Canadian bonds described above? Would it matter if the firm was a proprietorship or a corporation?

b. If the United States government today offered a five-year bond, a fifty-year bond, a "regular perpetuity," and a Canadian-type perpetuity, what do you think the relative order of interest rates would be; that is, rank the bonds from the one with the lowest to the one with the highest rate of interest. Explain your answer.

c. 1. Suppose that because of pressure by the Perpetual Bond Association, you believe that the Canadian government will redeem this particular perpetual bond issue in five years. Which course of action is more advantageous to you: to sell your bonds today at $42, or to wait five years and have them redeemed? Similar risk bonds earn 8 percent today, and are expected to remain at this level for the next five years.

2. If you have the opportunity to invest your money in bonds of similar risk, at what rate of return are you indifferent between selling your perpetuals today or having them redeemed in five years; that is, what is the expected yield to maturity on the Canadians?

d. Show, mathematically, the perpetuities' value if they yield 7.15 percent, pay $3 interest annually, and are considered as regular perpetuities. Show what would occur to the price of the bonds if the interest rate fell to 2 percent.

e. Are the Canadian bonds more likely to be valued as "regular perpetuities" if the going rate of interest is above or below 3 percent? Why?

f. Do you think the Canadian government would have taken the same action with regard to retiring the bonds if the interest rate had fallen rather than risen between 1936 and 1966?

g. Do you think the Canadian government was "fair" or "unfair" in its actions? Give pros and cons, and justify your reason for thinking that one outweighs the other.

18-10. In a 1972 study prepared for the Federal Recreation Commission, it was determined that the following equation can be used to estimate the required rates of return on various types of long-term capital market securities (stocks and bonds of various companies): $k_i = R_F + 2\sigma_i$. Here k_i is the required rate of return on the ith security; R_F is the riskless rate of interest as measured by the yield on long-term United States Government bonds; and σ_i is the standard deviation of the ith security's rate of return during the past five years.

a. What is the required rate of return, i, if the riskless rate of return is 6 percent and the security in question has a standard deviation of expected return of (1) ½ percent, (2) 1 percent, (3) 2 percent, and (4) 5 percent? Graph your results.

b. What is the required rate of return, k_i, using the standard deviations given in part a but assuming the riskless rate (1) rises to 8 percent or (2) falls to 4 percent? Graph these results.

c. Suppose the required rate of return equation changes from $k_i = 6\% + 2\sigma_i$ to $k_i = 6\% + 3\sigma_i$. What does this imply about investors' risk aversion? Illustrate with a graph.

d. Suppose the equation $k_i = 6\% + 2\sigma_i$ is the appropriate one; that is, this is the equation for the capital market line (CML). Further, suppose a particular stock sells for $20 a share, is expected to pay $1 dividend at the end of the current year, and has a standard deviation of expected return of 3 percent; that is, $\sigma_i = 3$ percent. Information reaches investors that causes them to expect a future growth rate of 3 percent, which is different from the former expected growth rate. σ_i does not change. (1) What was the former growth rate, assuming the stock was in equilibrium before the changed expectations as to growth? (2) What will happen to the price of the stock? that is, calculate the new equilibrium price, and explain the process by which this new equilibrium will be reached. The expected dividend for the current year is still $1.

e. Suppose the Federal Reserve Board tightens credit in the economy and causes the rate of interest on long-term government bonds to rise from 6 percent to 8 percent. (1) Assuming no other changes, what will happen to the CML; that is, what will be the new CML if the old one was $k_i = 6 + 2\sigma_i$? (2) What will be the new required rate of return for a bond with $\sigma_i = 0$ and a stock with $\sigma_i = 3$ percent? (3) Assume that the average stock had $\sigma = 3$ percent, $D_1 = \$2$, $k_s = 12$ percent, and $g = 6$ percent, thus a price of $33.33, before the change in part 2:

$$P_0 = \frac{D_1}{k_s - g} = \frac{\$2}{0.12 - 0.06} = \$33.33.$$

After the change in part 2 and assuming nothing else changes, what will occur to the market averages, such as the Dow-Jones average?

18-11. Because of ill health and old age, Dale Dinkins contemplates the sale of his shoe store. His corporation has the following balance sheet:

Assets		Liabilities and Net Worth	
Cash	$ 6,000	Notes payable—bank	$ 2,000
Receivables, net	2,000	Accounts payable	4,000
Inventories	13,000	Accruals	1,000
Fixtures and equipment less $10,000 reserve for depreciation	14,000	Common stock plus surplus	28,000
Total assets	$35,000	Total liabilities and net worth	$35,000

Annual before-tax earnings (after rent, interest, and salaries) for the preceding three years have averaged $8,000.

Dinkins has set a price of $40,000, which includes all the assets of the business except cash; the buyer assumes all debts. The assets include a five-year lease on the building in which the store is located and the goodwill associated with the name of Dinkins' Shoes. Assume that both Dinkins and the potential purchaser are in the 50 percent tax bracket.

a. Is the price of $40,000 a reasonable one? Explain.

b. What other factors should be taken into account in arriving at a selling price?

c. What is the significance, if any, of the five-year lease?

18-12. The Callaway Company is a small jewelry manufacturer. The company has been successful and has grown. Now, Callaway is planning to sell an issue of common stock to the public for the first time, and it faces the problem of setting an appropriate price on its common stock. The company feels that the proper procedure is to select firms similar to it with publicly traded common stock and to make relevant comparisons.

The company finds several jewelry manufacturers similar to it with respect to product mix, size, asset composition, and debt/equity proportions. Of these, Sonnet and Mailers are most similar.

Relation	Sonnet	Mailers	Callaway (Totals)
Earnings per share, 1975	$ 4.50	$ 7.50	$1,200,000
Average, 1969–1975	3.00	6.00	900,000
Price per share, 1975	36.00	75.00	—
Dividends per share, 1975	2.25	3.75	600,000
Average, 1969–1975	1.80	3.75	480,000
Book value per share	30.00	75.00	9,000,000
Market-book ratio	120%	100%	—

a. How would these relations be used in guiding Callaway in arriving at a market value for its stock?

b. What price would you recommend if Callaway sells 400,000 shares?

18-13. The Data Management Corporation is expected to grow at a rate of about 20 percent for the next four years, then at 10 percent for another three years, and finally settle down to a growth rate of 5 percent for the indefinite future. The company's common stock currently pays a $0.50 dividend, but dividends are expected to increase in proportion to the growth of the firm.

a. What values would you place on the common stock if you require a 10 percent return on your investment?

b. How would your valuation be affected if you intend to hold the stock for only three years?

c. What would you expect the trend (1) of market price, (2) of price/earnings ratio, and (3) of dividend yield to be over the next ten years (up, down, or constant)?

Multi-Period Stock Valuation Models

18A Appendix

Our discussion of stock values and rates of return in Chapter 18 focused on a single-period model, where we expect to hold the stock for one year, receive one dividend, and then sell the stock at the end of the year. In this appendix, we expand the analysis to deal with more realistic, but more complicated, multiperiod models.

Expected Dividends as the Basis for Stock Values

According to generally accepted theory, stock prices are determined as the present value of a stream of cash flows. In other words, the capitalization of income procedure applies to stocks as well as to bonds and other assets. What are the cash flows that corporations provide to their stockholders? For an individual investor, cash flows consist of dividends plus capital gains, but, for investors in total, expected cash flows consist only of future dividends—unless a firm is liquidated or is sold to another concern, the cash flows it provides its stockholders as a whole consist of a stream of dividends. Thus, a share of common stock may be regarded as being similar to a perpetual bond or share of perpetual preferred stock, and its value may be established as the present value of its stream of dividends:

$$\text{Value of stock} = P_0 = PV \text{ of expected future dividends}$$

$$= \frac{D_1}{(1 + k_s)^1} + \frac{D_2}{(1 + k_s)^2} + \cdots \frac{D_\infty}{(1 + k_s)^\infty} = \sum_{t=1}^{\infty} \frac{D_t}{(1 + k_s)^t}. \quad \text{(A18-1)}$$

Unlike bond interest and preferred dividends, common stock dividends are not generally expected to remain constant in the future; hence we cannot work with the convenient annuity formulas. This fact, combined with the much greater uncertainty about common stock dividends than about bond interest or preferred dividends, makes common stock valuation a more complex task than bond or preferred stock valuation.

Equation A18-1 is a quite general stock valuation model in the sense that the time pattern of D_t can be anything; D_t can be rising, falling, constant, or it can even fluctuate randomly, and Equation A18-1 will still hold. For many purposes, however, it is useful to estimate a particular time pattern for D_t and then develop a simplified (that is, easier to evaluate) version of the stock valuation model expressed in Equation A18-1. In the following sections, we consider the special cases of zero growth, constant growth, and "super-normal" growth.

Stock Values with Zero Growth

Suppose the rate of growth is measured by the rate at which dividends are expected to increase. If future growth is expected to be zero, the value of the stock reduces to the same formula as was developed for a perpetual bond:

$$\text{price} = \frac{\text{dividend}}{\text{capitalization rate}}$$

$$P_0 = \frac{D_1}{k_s} .$$

(A18-2)

Solving for k_s, we obtain

$$k_s = \frac{D_1}{P_0} ,$$

(A18-3)

which states that the required rate of return on a share of stock that has no growth prospects is simply the dividend yield.

"Normal," or Constant, Growth

Year after year, the earnings and dividends of most companies have been increasing. In general, this growth is expected to continue in the foreseeable future at about the same rate as GNP. On this basis, it is expected that an average, or "normal," company will grow at a rate of from 3 to 5 percent a year. Thus, if such a company's previous dividend, which has already been paid, was D_0, its dividend in any future year t may be forecast as $D_t = D_0 (1 + g)^t$, where g = the expected rate of growth. For example, if American Rubber just paid a dividend of \$1.90 (that is, $D_0 = \$1.90$), and investors expect a 5 percent growth rate, then the estimated dividend one year hence will be

$D_1 = (\$1.90)(1.05) = \$2$; D_2 will be \$2.10; and the estimated dividend five years hence will be

$$D_t = D_0(1 + g)^t$$
$$= \$1.90(1.05)^5$$
$$= \$2.42.$$

Using this method of estimating future dividends, the current price, P_0, is determined as follows:

$$P_0 = \frac{D_1}{(1 + k_s)^1} + \frac{D_2}{(1 + k_s)^2} + \frac{D_3}{(1 + k_s)^3} + \cdots$$

$$= \frac{D_0(1 + g)^1}{(1 + k_s)^1} + \frac{D_0(1 + g)^2}{(1 + k_s)^2} + \frac{D_0(1 + g)^3}{(1 + k_s)^3} + \cdots \qquad \text{(A18-4)}$$

$$= \sum_{t=1}^{\infty} \frac{D_0(1 + g)^t}{(1 + k_s)^t}.$$

If g is constant, Equation A18-4 may be simplified as follows:[1]

$$P_0 = \frac{D_1}{k_s - g}. \qquad \text{(A18-5)}$$

Notice that the constant growth model expressed in Equation A18-5 is identical to the single-period model, Equation 18-5, developed in Chapter 18.

---

[1] The proof of Equation A18-5 is as follows. Rewrite Equation A18-4 as:

$$P_0 = D_0\left[\frac{(1 + g)}{(1 + k_s)} + \frac{(1 + g)^2}{(1 + k_s)^2} + \frac{(1 + g)^3}{(1 + k_s)^3} + \cdots + \frac{(1 + g)^N}{(1 + k_s)^N}\right]. \qquad (1)$$

Multiply both sides of Equation (1) by $(1 + k_s)/(1 + g)$:

$$\left[\frac{(1 + k_s)}{(1 + g)}\right] P_0 = D_0\left[1 + \frac{(1 + g)}{(1 + k_s)} + \frac{(1 + g)^2}{(1 + k_s)^2} + \cdots + \frac{(1 + g)^{N-1}}{(1 + k_s)^{N-1}}\right]. \qquad (2)$$

Subtract Equation (1) from Equation (2) to obtain

$$\left[\frac{(1 + k_s)}{(1 + g)} - 1\right] P_0 = D_0\left[1 - \frac{(1 - g)^N}{(1 - k_s)^N}\right].$$

$$\left[\frac{(1 + k_s) - (1 + g)}{(1 + g)}\right] P_0 = D_0\left[1 - \frac{(1 + g)^N}{(1 + k_s)^N}\right].$$

Assuming $k_s > g$, as $N \to \infty$ the term in brackets on the right side of the equation $\to 1.0$, leaving

$$\left[\frac{(1 + k_s) - (1 + g)}{(1 + g)}\right] P_0 = D_0,$$

which simplifies to

$$(k_s - g)P_0 = D_0(1 + g) = D_1$$

$$P_0 = \frac{D_1}{k_s - g} \qquad \text{Q.E.D.} \qquad \text{(A18-5)}$$

A necessary condition for the constant growth model is that k_s be greater than g; otherwise, Equation A18-5 gives nonsense answers. If k_s equals g, the equation blows up, yielding an infinite price; if k_s is less than g, a *negative* price results. Since neither infinite nor negative stock prices make sense, it is clear that in equilibrium k_s must be greater than g.

Note that Equation A18-5 is sufficiently general to encompass the no-growth case described above. If growth is zero, this is simply a special case, and Equation A18-5 is identical to Equation A18-2.[2]

"Supernormal" Growth

Firms typically go through "life cycles" during part of which their growth is much faster than that of the economy as a whole. Automobile manufacturers in the 1920s and computer and office equipment manufacturers in the 1960s are examples. Figure A18-1 illustrates such supernormal growth and compares it with normal growth, zero growth, and negative growth.[3]

FIGURE A18–1   Illustrative Dividend Growth Rates

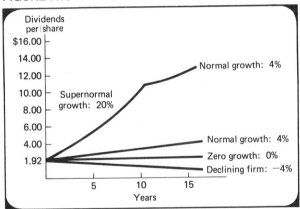

The illustrative supernormal growth firm is expected to grow at a 20 percent rate for ten years, then to have its growth rate fall to 4 percent, the norm for the economy. The value of a firm with such a growth pattern is determined by the following equation:

---

[2] One technical point should at least be mentioned here. The logic underlying the analysis implicitly assumes that investors are indifferent to dividend yield or capital gains. Empirical work has not conclusively established whether this is true or not, but the question is discussed in Chapter 21.

[3] A *negative* growth rate represents a declining company. A mining company whose profits are falling because of a declining ore body is an example.

Present price = *PV* of dividends during supernormal growth period + Value of stock price at end of supernormal growth period discounted back to present

$$= \sum_{t=1}^{N} \frac{D_0 (1 + g_s)^t}{(1 + k_s)^t} + \left(\frac{D_{N+1}}{k_s - g_n} \right) \left(\frac{1}{(1 + k_s)^N} \right). \tag{A18-6}$$

Here g_s is the supernormal growth rate, g_n is the normal growth rate, and N is the period of supernormal growth.

Working through an example will help make this clear. Consider a supernormal growth firm whose previous dividend was $1.92 (that is, $D_0 = \$1.92$), with the dividend expected to increase by 20 percent a year for ten years and thereafter at 4 percent a year indefinitely. If stockholders' required rate of return is 9 percent on an investment with this degree of risk, what is the value of the stock? On the basis of the calculations in Table A18-1, the value is found to be $138.19, the present value of the dividends during the first ten years plus the present value of the stock at the end of the tenth year.

Comparing Companies with Different Expected Growth Rates

It is useful to summarize this section by comparing the four illustrative firms whose dividend trends were graphed in Figure A18-1. Using the valuation equations developed above, the conditions assumed in the preceding examples, and the additional assumptions that each firm had earnings per share during the preceding reporting period of $3.60 (that is, $EPS_0 = \$3.60$) and paid out 53.3 percent of its reported earnings (therefore dividends per share last year, D_0, were $1.92 for each company), we show prices, dividend yields, and price/earnings ratios (hereafter written P/E) in Table A18-2.

Investors require and expect a return of 9 percent on each of the stocks. For the declining firm, this return consists of a relatively high current dividend yield combined with a capital *loss* amounting to 4 percent a year. For the no-growth firm, there is neither a capital gain nor a capital loss expectation, so the 9 percent return must be obtained entirely from the dividend yield. The normal growth firm provides a relatively low current dividend yield, but a 4 percent a year capital gain expectation. Finally, the supernormal growth firm has the lowest current dividend yield but the highest capital gain expectation.

What is expected to happen to the prices of the four illustrative firms' stocks over time? Three of the four cases are straightforward: The zero growth firm's price is expected to be constant (that is, $P_t = P_{t+1}$); the declining firm is expected to have a falling stock price; and the constant growth firm's stock is expected to grow at a constant rate, 4 percent. The supernormal growth case is more complex, but what is expected can be seen from the data in Table A18-1.

First, note that the present price, P_0, is $138.19, and the expected price in year ten, P_{10}, is $247.31. This represents an average growth rate of 6

TABLE A18–1 Method of Calculating the Value of a Stock with Supernormal Growth

Assumptions:

a. Stockholders' capitalization rate is 9 percent, i.e., $k_s = 9\%$.

b. Growth rate is 20 percent for ten years, 4 percent thereafter, i.e., $g_s = 20\%$, $g_n = 4\%$, and $N = 10$.

c. Last year's dividend was $1.92, i.e., $D_0 = \$1.92$.

Step 1. Find present value of dividends during rapid growth period:

End of Year	Dividend $\$1.92(1.20)^t$	$PVIF = 1/(1.09)^t$	Present Value
1	$ 2.30	.917	$ 2.11
2	2.76	.842	2.32
3	3.32	.772	2.56
4	3.98	.708	2.82
5	4.78	.650	3.11
6	5.73	.596	3.42
7	6.88	.547	3.76
8	8.26	.502	4.15
9	9.91	.460	4.56
10	11.89	.442	5.02

$$PV \text{ of first 10 years' dividends} = \sum_{t=1}^{10} \frac{D_0(1+g_s)^t}{(1+k_s)^t} = \underline{\underline{\$33.83}}$$

Step 2. Find present value of year 10 stock price:

a. Find value of stock at end of year 10:

$$P_{10} = \frac{D_{11}}{k_s - g_n} = \frac{\$11.89(1.04)}{.05} = \$247.31.$$

b. Discount P_{10} back to present:

$$PV = P_{10} \left(\frac{1}{1+k_s}\right)^{10} = \$247.31(.422) = \$104.36.$$

Step 3. Sum to find total value of stock today:

$$P_0 = \$33.83 + \$104.36 = \$138.19.$$

percent.[4] We do not show, but we could, that the expected growth rate of the stock's price is higher than 6 percent in the early part of the ten-year supernormal growth period and less than 6 percent toward the end of the period, as investors perceive the approaching end of the supernormal period. From year eleven on, the company's stock price and dividend are expected to grow at the "normal" rate, 4 percent.

[4] Found from Table A18-1; $247.31/$138.19 = 1.79, and this is approximately the CVIF for a 6 percent growth rate.

TABLE A18–2 Prices, Dividend Yields, and Price/Earnings Ratios for 9 Percent Returns under Different Growth Assumptions

		Price	Current Dividend Yield	P/E Ratio[a]
Declining firm:	$P_0 = \dfrac{D_1}{k_s - g} = \dfrac{\$1.84}{0.09 - (-0.04)}$	\$ 14.15	13%	3.9
No-growth firm:	$P_0 = \dfrac{D_1}{k_s} = \dfrac{\$1.92}{0.09}$	\$ 21.33	9%	5.9
Normal growth firm:	$P_0 = \dfrac{D_1}{k_s - g} = \dfrac{\$2.00}{0.09 - 0.04}$	\$ 40.00	5%	11.1
Supernormal growth firm:	$P_0 = $ (See Table 18–1)	\$138.19	1.7%	38.4

[a] It was assumed at the beginning of this example that each company is earning \$3.60 initially. This \$3.60, divided into the various prices, gives the indicated P/E ratios.

We might also note that as the supernormal growth rate declines toward the normal rate (or as the time when this decline will occur becomes more imminent), the high P/E ratio must approach the normal P/E ratio; that is, the P/E of 38.4 will decline year by year and equal 11.1, that of the normal growth company, in the tenth year. See A. A. Robichek and M. C. Bogue, "A Note on the Behavior of Expected Price/Earnings Ratios over Time," *Journal of Finance* (June 1971).

Note also that D_1 differs for each firm, being calculated as follows:

$$D_1 = EPS_0 (1 + g) \text{ (payout)} = \$3.60(1 + g) (0.533).$$

The relationships among the P/E ratios, shown in the last column of Table A18-2, are similar to what one would intuitively expect—the higher the expected growth (all other things the same), the higher the P/E ratio.[5]

[5] Differences in P/E ratios among firms can also arise from differences in the rates of return, k_s, which investors use in capitalizing the future dividend streams. If one company has a higher P/E than another, this could be caused by a higher g, a lower k, or a combination of these two factors.

Financial Structure and the Use of leverage

19

In the last chapter, we saw that each security has a required rate of return, k, and an expected rate of return, $\hat{k}$. The required rate of return is determined in part by the level of interest rates (the risk-free rate) in the economy, and in part by the riskiness of the individual security. The expected rate of return on a bond or a share of preferred stock is determined primarily by the interest or preferred dividend, while the expected rate of return on common stock depends upon dividends (which flow from earnings) and growth. Both risk and expected returns are fundamentally affected by financial leverage, as we see in this chapter.

BASIC DEFINITIONS

To avoid ambiguity in the use of key concepts, the meanings of frequently used expressions are given here. *Financial structure* refers to the way the firm's assets are financed: it is the entire right-hand side of the balance sheet. *Capital structure* is the permanent financing of the firm, represented primarily by long-term debt, preferred stock, and common equity, but excluding all short-term credit. Thus, a firm's capital structure is only a part of its financial structure. *Common equity* includes common stock, capital surplus, and accumulated retained earnings.

Our key concept for this chapter is *financial leverage*, or the *leverage factor*, defined as the ratio of total debt to total assets. For example, a firm having assets of $100 million and a total debt of $50 million would have a leverage factor of 50 percent.[1]

Finally, we should distinguish at the outset between business risk and financial risk. By *business risk* we mean the inherent uncertainty or variability of expected pretax returns on the firm's "portfolio" of assets. This kind of risk was examined in Chapter 12, where it was defined in terms of the probability distribution of returns on the firm's assets. By *financial risk* we mean the additional risk that is induced by the use of financial leverage.

THEORY OF FINANCIAL LEVERAGE

Perhaps the best way to understand the proper use of financial leverage is to analyze its impact on profitability under varying conditions. Suppose there are three firms in a particular industry, and these firms are identical except for their financial policies. Firm A has used no debt and consequently has a leverage factor of zero; firm B, financed half by debt and half by equity, has a leverage factor of 50 percent; firm C has a leverage factor of 75 percent. Their balance sheets are shown in Table 19-1.

TABLE 19–1   Alternative Financial Structures

		Firm A	
		Total debt	$ 0
		Net worth	200
Total assets	$200	Total claims	$200
		Firm B	
		Total debt (6%)	$100
		Net worth	100
Total assets	$200	Total claims	$200
		Firm C	
		Total debt (6%)	$150
		Net worth	50
Total assets	$200	Total claims	$200

How do these different financial patterns affect stockholder returns? As can be seen from the top section of Table 19-2, the answer depends partly on the state of the industry's economy. When the economy is depressed, sales and profit margins are low, and the firms earn only 2 percent on assets. When conditions become somewhat better, the return on assets is 5 percent. Under normal conditions, the return goes to 8 percent. In a moderate boom the figure goes to 11 percent, while under extremely favorable circumstances, the companies have a 14 percent return on assets. These percentages, multiplied

[1] The present discussion will consider variations in financial leverage in the context of a debt-equity tradeoff. No distinction will be made between long- and short-term debt.

by the $200 of assets, give the earnings before interest and taxes *(EBIT)* of the three companies under the various states of the economy.

TABLE 19–2 Stockholder Returns under Various Leverage and Economic Conditions

	Economic Conditions					
	Very Poor	Poor	Indifference Level	Normal	Good	Very Good
Rate of return on assets before interest and taxes	2%	5%	6%	8%	11%	14%
Earnings before interest and taxes *(EBIT)*	$ 4	$10	$12	$16	$22	$28
Firm A: Leverage factor 0%						
EBIT	$ 4	$10	$12	$16	$22	$28
Less: Interest expense	0	0	0	0	0	0
Taxable income	$ 4	$10	$12	$16	$22	$28
Taxes (50%)[a]	2	5	6	8	11	14
Available to common stock	$ 2	$ 5	$ 6	$ 8	$11	$14
Percent after-tax return on net worth	1%	2.5%	3%	4%	5.5%	7%
Firm B: Leverage factor 50%						
EBIT	$ 4	$10	$12	$16	$22	$28
Less: Interest expense	6	6	6	6	6	6
Taxable income	$ (2)	$ 4	$ 6	$10	$16	$22
Taxes (50%)[a]	(1)	2	3	5	8	11
Available to common stock	$ (1)	$ 2	$ 3	$ 5	$ 8	$11
Percent after-tax return on net worth	−1%	2%	3%	5%	8%	11%
Firm C: Leverage factor 75%						
EBIT	$ 4	$10	$12	$16	$22	$28
Less: Interest expense	9	9	9	9	9	9
Taxable income	$ (5)	$ 1	$ 3	$ 7	$13	$19
Taxes (50%)[a]	(2.5)	.5	1.5	3.5	6.5	9.5
Available to common stock	$ (2.5)	$ .5	$ 1.5	$ 3.5	$ 6.5	$ 9.5
Percent after-tax return on net worth	−5%	1%	3%	7%	13%	19%

[a]The tax calculation assumes that losses are carried back and result in tax credits.

The lower portion of Table 19-2 demonstrates how the use of financial leverage magnifies the impact on the stockholders of changes in the rate of return on assets. When economic conditions go from normal to good, for example, returns on assets go from 8 to 11 percent, an increase of 37.5 percent. Firm A uses no leverage, gets no magnification, and consequently experiences the same 37.5 percent jump in the rate of return to stockholders. However, firm B enjoys a 60 percent increase in stockholder returns as a result of the 37.5 percent rise in returns on assets. Firm C, which uses still more leverage, has an 85.7 percent increase. Just the reverse holds in economic downturns, of course: the 37.5 percent drop in returns on assets when the economy goes from normal to poor results in return-on-net-worth declines of 37.5 percent, 60 percent, and 85.7 percent for firms A, B, and C, respectively.

Using the same illustrative numbers, Figure 19-1 gives a graphic presentation of the interaction between the rates of return on assets and net worth, given the three different leverage factors. The interesting point to note here is the intersection of the three lines at the point where assets are returning 6 percent, the interest cost of debt. At this point, the return on net worth is 3 percent. The assumed 50 percent tax rate reduces the 6 percent return on total assets to a return of 3 percent on net worth, regardless of the degree of leverage. When returns on assets are higher than 6 percent, debt-financed assets can pay their interest cost and still leave something over for the stockholders, but the reverse holds if assets earn less than 6 percent. *In general, whenever the return on assets exceeds the cost of debt, leverage is favorable, and the higher the leverage factor, the higher the rate of return on common equity.*

FIGURE 19–1   Relationship between Rates of Return on Assets and Rates of Return on Net Worth under Different Leverage Conditions

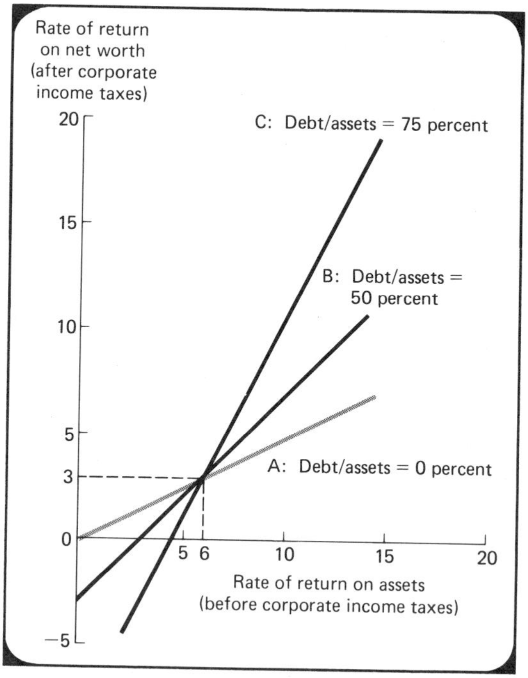

EFFECTS OF FINANCIAL LEVERAGE

The effects of financial leverage can be further clarified by an example. The Universal Machine Company, whose latest balance sheet is shown in Table

19-3, manufactures equipment used by steel producers. The major product is a lathe used to trim the rough edges off hot rolls of steel; the lathes sell for $10,000 each. As is typically the case for producers of durable capital assets, the company's sales fluctuate widely, far more than does the overall economy. For example, during nine of the preceding twenty-five years, sales have been below the breakeven point, so losses have been relatively frequent.

TABLE 19–3   Universal Machine Company Balance Sheet[a]
December 31, 1976

Cash	$ 200,000	Total liabilities having	
Receivables (net)	800,000	an average cost of 5%	$2,000,000
Inventories	1,000,000	Common stock ($10 par;	
Plant (net)	2,200,000	250,000 shares outstanding)	2,500,000
Equipment (net)	2,800,000	Retained earnings	2,500,000
Total assets	$7,000,000	Total claims on assets	$7,000,000

[a] Figures are rounded for convenience.

In addition to the normal fluctuations inherent in the business, Universal faces three additional elements of uncertainty: (1) new methods of processing steel now being discussed in the industry may obsolesce much of Universal's equipment; (2) the long-run demand for steel and steel-processing equipment may decline because of the competitive inroads of plastics, cement, and aluminum; and (3) a tariff conference scheduled for late 1977 may open the door for increased foreign competition by Japanese machinery manufacturers.

Although future sales are uncertain, current demand is high and appears to be headed higher, and if Universal is to continue sharing in this expansion, it will have to increase capacity. For this increase, $3 million of new capital is required. James Walter, the financial vice-president, learns that he can raise $3 million by selling bonds with a 5 percent coupon. Alternatively, he can raise the money by selling 75,000 shares of common stock at $40 a share.

During the preceding five years, Universal's sales have fluctuated between $500,000 and $4,000,000; at the higher volume, the firm is operating at full capacity and has to turn down orders. With the additional plant expansion, sales capacity will increase to $6 million. Fixed costs, after the planned expansion, will be $400,000 a year, and variable costs (excluding interest on the debt) will be 40 percent of sales.[2] The marketing department has analyzed future supply and demand conditions and, on the basis of this analysis, has supplied Walter with a probability distribution for future sales (see Table 19-4).

Although Walter's recommendation will be given much weight, the final decision for the method of financing rests with the company's board of

[2] The assumption that variable costs will be a constant percentage of sales over the entire range of output is not valid, but variable costs are relatively constant over the output range likely to occur.

TABLE 19–4 Universal Machine Company, Profit Calculations at Various Sales Levels

Probability of indicated sales	.025	.10	.20	.35	.20	.10	.025
Sales in units	0	100	200	300	400	500	600
Sales in dollars	$ -0-	$1,000,000	$2,000,000	$3,000,000	$4,000,000	$5,000,000	$6,000,000
Fixed costs	$ 400,000	$ 400,000	$ 400,000	$ 400,000	$ 400,000	$ 400,000	$ 400,000
Variable costs (40% of sales)	-0-	400,000	800,000	1,200,000	1,600,000	2,000,000	2,400,000
Total costs (except interest)	$ 400,000	$ 800,000	$1,200,000	$1,600,000	$2,000,000	$2,400,000	$2,800,000
Earnings before interest and taxes *(EBIT)*	$(400,000)	$ 200,000	$ 800,000	$1,400,000	$2,000,000	$2,600,000	$3,200,000

Financing with bonds

Less: Interest on new debt (5% × $3,000,000)	$ 150,000	$ 150,000	$ 150,000	$ 150,000	$ 150,000	$ 150,000	$ 150,000
Interest on old debt (5% × $2,000,000)	$ 100,000	$ 100,000	$ 100,000	$ 100,000	$ 100,000	$ 100,000	$ 100,000
Earnings before taxes	$(650,000)	$ (50,000)	$ 550,000	$1,150,000	$1,750,000	$2,350,000	$2,950,000
Less: Income taxes (50%)[a]	(325,000)	(25,000)	275,000	575,000	875,000	1,175,000	1,475,000
Net profit after taxes	$(325,000)	$ (25,000)	$ 275,000	$ 575,000	$ 875,000	$1,175,000	$1,475,000
Earnings per share on 250,000 shares of common *(EPS)*[d]	$ -1.30	$-0.10	$1.10	$2.30	$3.50	$4.70	$5.90
Expected *EPS*[b]	$ 2.30						
Coefficient of variation[c]	.67						

Financing with stock

Less: Interest on old debt (5% × $2,000,000)	$ 100,000	$ 100,000	$ 100,000	$ 100,000	$ 100,000	$ 100,000	$ 100,000
Earnings before taxes	$(500,000)	$ 100,000	$ 700,000	$1,300,000	$1,900,000	$2,500,000	$3,100,000
Less: Income taxes (50%)[a]	(250,000)	50,000	350,000	650,000	950,000	1,250,000	1,550,000
Net profit after taxes	$(250,000)	$ 50,000	$ 350,000	$ 650,000	$ 950,000	$1,250,000	$1,550,000
Earnings per share on 325,000 shares of common *(EPS)*[d]	$-0.77	$+0.15	$1.08	$2.00	$2.92	$3.85	$4.77
Expected *EPS*[b]	$ 2.00						
Coefficient of variation[c]	.59						

[a] Assumes tax credit on losses.
[b] Calculated by multiplying the *EPS* at each sales level by the probability of that sales level, then summing these products.
[c] Calculated as follows: Coefficient of variation = (standard deviation of *EPS*)/(expected *EPS*).
[d] The *EPS* figures can also be obtained using the following formula:

$$EPS = \frac{(sales - fixed\ cost - variable\ costs - interest)(1 - tax\ rate)}{shares\ outstanding}.$$

For example, at S = $4 million,

$$EPS_{stock} = \frac{(4 - .4 - 1.6 - .1)(.5)}{.325} = \$2.92.$$

$$EPS_{bonds} = \frac{(4 - .4 - 1.6 - .25)(.5)}{.250} = \$3.50.$$

Since in this case the equation is linear, the break-even or indifference level of S can be found as follows:

$$EPS_s = \frac{(S - .4 - .4S - .1)(.5)}{.325} = \frac{(S - .4 - .4S - .25)(.5)}{.250} = EPS_b.$$

$$S = \$1.92\ million.$$

directors. Procedurally, the financial vice-president will analyze the situation, evaluate all reasonable alternatives, come to a conclusion, and then present the alternatives with his recommendations to the board. For his own analysis, as well as for presentation to the board, Walter prepares the materials shown in Table 19-4.

In the top third of the table, earnings before interest and taxes *(EBIT)* are calculated for different levels of sales ranging from $0 to $6 million. The firm suffers an operating loss until sales are almost $1 million, but beyond that point it enjoys a rapid rise in gross profit.

The middle third of the table shows the financial results that will occur at the various sales levels if additional bonds are sold. First, the $250,000 annual interest charges ($100,000 on existing debt plus $150,000 on the new bonds) are deducted from the earnings before interest and taxes. Next, taxes are taken out; notice that if the sales level is so low that losses are incurred, the firm receives a tax credit. Then, net profits after taxes are divided by the 250,000 shares outstanding to obtain earnings per share *(EPS)* of common stock. The various *EPS* figures are multiplied by the corresponding probability estimates to obtain an expected *EPS* of $2.30. Finally, the coefficient of variation is calculated and used as a measure of the riskiness of the financing plan.

The financial results that will occur with stock financing are calculated in the bottom third of the table. Net profit after interest and taxes is divided by 325,000 shares—the original 250,000 plus the 75,000 new shares—to find earnings per share. Expected *EPS* and the coefficient of variation are computed in the same way as they were for the bond financing.

FIGURE 19–2 Probability Curves for Stock and Bond Financing

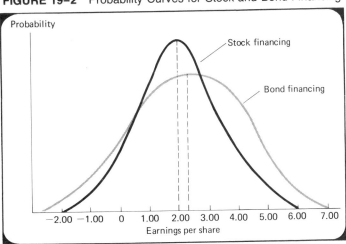

Figure 19–2 shows the probability distributions of earnings per share. Stock financing has the tighter, more peaked distribution, and we saw from Table 19–4 that it also has the smaller coefficient of variation; hence, stock financing is less risky than bond financing. However, the expected *EPS* is lower for stock than for bonds, so we are again faced with the kind of risk-return tradeoff that characterizes most financial decisions.

The nature of the tradeoff can be made somewhat more specific. First, consider Table 19–5, which shows how both expected earnings per share and the coefficient of variation of these earnings vary with leverage, and Figure 19–3, which graphs the points shown in the table. Two of the items in Table 19–5—the data associated with 20 percent and with 50 percent debt—were obtained directly from Table 19–4, while data on the other leverage ratios were obtained from similar tables.[3] It is clear that in order to obtain the higher expected earnings that go with increased leverage, the firm must accept more risk. What choice should Walter recommend to the board? How much leverage should Universal Machine use? These questions cannot be answered at this point—we must defer answers until we have covered some additional concepts and examined the effects of leverage on the cost of both debt and equity capital.

TABLE 19–5 Risk-return Tradeoff for Various Leverage Ratios, Universal Machine Company

Leverage Ratio	Expected EPS	Coefficient of Variation
0%	$1.87	.552
10	1.93	.570
20	2.00[a]	.591
30	2.08	.615
40	2.18	.651
50	2.30[b]	.669
60	2.44	.700

[a] If stock financing is used, Universal will have 20 percent debt, and we saw in Table 19–4 that the Expected *EPS* is $2.00.

[b] This figure was calculated in Table 19–4; it represents bond financing.

[3] In Table 19–5 we assume that additional debt could be sold at a 5 percent rate of interest. As Chapter 20 shows, interest rates increase with leverage, so the figures shown here overstate the effect of leverage on earnings and understate the effect on risk. In other words, if we consider the fact that increased leverage leads to higher interest rates, the curve shown in Figure 19–3(a) would rise *less* steeply, and the curve shown in Figure 19–3(b) would rise *more* steeply.

Also, in both Table 19–5 and Figure 19–3 we are implicitly assuming that Universal Machine can vary its capital structure while holding its assets constant. This could be done by selling debt and using the proceeds to retire stock, or vice versa.

FIGURE 19–3   Relationship between Earnings, Risk, and Leverage

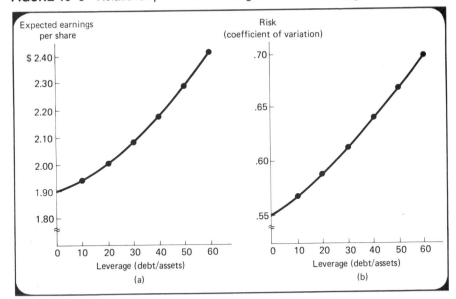

BREAK-EVEN ANALYSIS

Another way of presenting the data on Universal's two financing methods is shown in Figure 19–4, a break-even chart similar to the charts used in Chapter 4. If sales are depressed to zero, the debt financing line would cut the Y axis at $-\$1.30$, well below the $-\$0.77$ intercept of the common stock financing line. The debt line has a steeper slope and rises faster, however, showing that earnings per share will go up faster with increases in sales if debt is used. The two lines cross at sales of $1.92 million. Below that sales volume the firm would be better off issuing common stock; above that level, debt financing would produce higher earnings per share.

If Walter and his board of directors *know with certainty* that sales will never again fall below $1.92 million, bonds would be the preferred method of financing the asset increase. But they cannot know this for certain; in fact, they probably have good reason to expect future business cycles to drive sales down to, and even below, this critical level. They know that during the preceding five years sales have been as low as $500,000. If sales fall to this level again, the company would not be earning enough to cover its interest charges. Such a situation, if it continues for several years, could jeopardize the very existence of the firm. Further, if any of the three detrimental long-run events occur—Universal's products are obsolesced, steel demand declines, or Japanese imports increase—future sales may average less than $2 million.

If sales continue to expand, however, there would be higher earnings per share from using bonds; no officer or director would want to forego these substantial advantages.

FIGURE 19–4 Earnings Per Share for Stock and Debt Financing

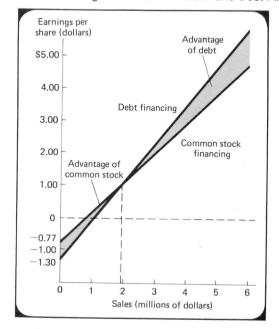

Walter's recommendation, and the decision of each director, will depend upon (1) each person's appraisal of the future and (2) his psychological attitude toward risks.[4] The pessimists, or risk averters, will prefer to employ common stock, while the optimists, or those less sensitive to risk, will favor bonds. This example, which is typical of many real-world situations, suggests that the major disagreements over the choice of forms of financing are likely to reflect uncertainty about the future levels of the firm's sales. Such uncertainty, in turn, reflects the characteristics of the firm's environment—general business conditions, industry trends, and quality and aggressiveness of management.

---

[4] Theory suggests that the decision should be based upon stockholders' utility preferences, or the market risk-return tradeoff function discussed in Chapter 12. In practice, it is difficult to obtain such information as *data*, so decisions such as this one are generally based upon the subjective judgment of the decision-maker. A knowledge of the theory, even if it cannot be applied directly, is extremely useful in making good judgmental decisions. Further, knowing the theory permits us to structure research programs and data-collecting systems that will make direct application of the theory increasingly feasible in future years.

RELATIONSHIP OF FINANCIAL LEVERAGE TO OPERATING LEVERAGE[5]

In Chapter 4 it was shown that a firm has some degree of control over its production processes; it can, within limits, use either a highly automated production process with high fixed costs but low variable costs or a less automated process with lower fixed costs but higher variable costs. If a firm uses a high degree of operating leverage, it was seen that its break-even point is at a relatively high sales level and that changes in the level of sales have a magnified (or "leveraged") impact on profits. Notice that financial leverage has exactly the same kind of effect on profits: the higher the leverage factor, the higher the break-even sales volume and the greater the impact on profits from a given change in sales volume.

The *degree of operating leverage* was defined as the percentage change in operating profits associated with a given percentage change in sales volume, and Equation 4–2 was developed for calculating operating leverage:

$$\text{Degree of operating leverage at point } Q = \frac{Q(P - V)}{Q(P - V) - F} \quad (4\text{--}2)$$

$$= \frac{S - VC}{S - VC - F} \quad (4\text{--}2a)$$

Here Q is units of output, P is the average sales price per unit of output, V is the variable cost per unit, and F is total fixed costs, while S is sales in dollars and VC is total variable costs. Applying the formula to Universal Machine at an output level of 200 units (see Table 19–4 above), we find its operating leverage to be 1.50, so a 100 percent increase in volume produces a 150 percent increase in profit:

$$\text{Degree of operating leverage} = \frac{200(\$10,000 - \$4,000)}{200(\$10,000 - \$4,000) - \$400,000}$$

$$= \frac{\$2,000,000 - \$800,000}{\$2,000,000 - \$800,000 - \$400,000}$$

$$= \frac{\$1,200,000}{\$800,000} = 1.50 \text{ or } 150\%.$$

Operating leverage affects *earnings before interest and taxes (EBIT),* while financial leverage affects *earnings after interest and taxes,* the earnings available to common stockholders. In terms of Table 19–4, operating leverage affects the top section of the table, financial leverage the lower sections. Thus, if Universal Machine had more operating leverage, its fixed costs would be higher than $400,000, its variable cost ratio would be lower than 40 percent

---

[5] This section may be omitted without loss of continuity.

of sales, and earnings before interest and taxes would vary with sales to a greater extent. Financial leverage takes over where operating leverage leaves off, further magnifying the effect on earnings per share of a change in the level of sales. For this reason, operating leverage is sometimes referred to as *first-stage leverage* and financial leverage as *second-stage leverage*.

Degree of Financial Leverage

The *degree of financial leverage* is defined as the percentage change in earnings available to common stockholders that is associated with a given percentage change in earnings before interest and taxes *(EBIT)*. An equation has been developed as an aid in calculating the degree of financial leverage for any given level of *EBIT* and interest charges *(I)*:[6]

$$\text{Degree of financial leverage} = \frac{EBIT}{EBIT - I}. \tag{19-1}$$

For Universal Machine at 200 units of output and an *EBIT* of $800,000, the degree of financial leverage with bond financing is

$$\text{Financial leverage: bonds} = \frac{\$800,000}{\$800,000 - \$250,000} = 1.45.$$

Therefore, a 100 percent increase in *EBIT* would result in a 145 percent increase in earnings per share. If stock financing is used, the degree of financial leverage may be calculated and found to be 1.14, so a 100 percent increase in *EBIT* would produce a 114 percent increase in *EPS*.

---

[6] The equation is developed as follows:

1. Notice that $EBIT = Q(P - V) - F$.
2. Earnings per share $(EPS) = \frac{(EBIT - I)(1 - t)}{N}$, where *EBIT* is earnings before interest and taxes, *I* is interest paid, *t* is the corporate tax rate, and *N* is the number of shares outstanding.
3. *I* is a constant, so ΔEPS, the change in *EPS*, is

$$\Delta EPS = \frac{\Delta EBIT(1 - t)}{N}.$$

4. The percentage increase in *EPS* is the change in *EPS* over the original *EPS*, or

$$\frac{\dfrac{\Delta EBIT(1 - t)}{N}}{\dfrac{(EBIT - I)(1 - t)}{N}} = \frac{\Delta EBIT}{EBIT - I}.$$

5. The degree of financial leverage is the percentage change in *EPS* over the percentage change in *EBIT*, so

$$\text{Financial leverage} = \frac{\dfrac{\Delta EBIT}{EBIT - I}}{\dfrac{\Delta EBIT}{EBIT}} = \frac{EBIT}{EBIT - I}.$$

Combining Operating and Financial Leverage

Operating leverage causes a change in sales volume to have a magnified effect on *EBIT,* and if financial leverage is superimposed on operating leverage, changes in *EBIT* will have a magnified effect on earnings per share. Therefore, if a firm uses a considerable amount of both operating leverage and financial leverage, even small changes in the level of sales will produce wide fluctuations in *EPS.*

Equation 4–2 for the degree of operating leverage can be combined with Equation 19–1 for financial leverage to show the total leveraging effect of a given change in sales on earnings per share.[7]

$$\text{Combined leverage effect} = \frac{Q(P-V)}{Q(P-V)-F-I}. \qquad (19\text{--}2)$$

For Universal Machine at an output of 200 units (or $2 million of sales), the combined leverage effect, using debt financing, is

$$\frac{\text{Combined}}{\text{leverage effect}} = \frac{200(\$10{,}000 - \$4{,}000)}{200(\$10{,}000 - \$4{,}000) - \$400{,}000 - \$250{,}000}$$

$$= \frac{\$1{,}200{,}000}{\$1{,}200{,}000 - \$400{,}000 - \$250{,}000}$$

$$= 218 \text{ percent.}$$

Therefore, a 100 percent increase in sales from 200 units to 400 units would cause *EPS* to increase by 218 percent, so the new *EPS* figure would be 3.18 times the original *EPS:*

$$EPS_{(400 \text{ units})} = EPS_{(200 \text{ units})} + (EPS_{(200 \text{ units})}) \times 2.18$$

$$= EPS_{(200 \text{ units})} \times (1 + 2.18)$$

$$= \$1.10 \times 3.18 = \$3.50.$$

These figures agree, of course, with those worked out in Table 19–4.

---

[7] Equation 19–2 is developed as follows:
1. Recognize that $EBIT = Q(P-V) - F$, then rewrite Equation 19–1 as

$$\frac{EBIT}{EBIT - I} = \frac{Q(P-V) - F}{Q(P-V) - F - I}. \qquad (19\text{--}1a)$$

2. The total leverage effect is equal to the degree of operating leverage times the degree of financial leverage, or Equation 4–2 times Equation 19–1a:

$$\text{Combined leverage effect} = \text{Equation 4--2} \times \text{Equation 19--1a}$$

$$= \frac{Q(P-V)}{Q(P-V) - F} \cdot \frac{Q(P-V) - F}{Q(P-V) - F - I} \qquad (19\text{--}2)$$

$$= \frac{Q(P-V)}{Q(P-V) - F - I}.$$

Financial and operating leverage can be employed in various combinations. In the Universal Machine example, the combined leverage factor of 3.18 was obtained by using operating leverage of degree 1.50 and financial leverage of 1.45, but many other combinations of financial and operating leverage would have produced the same combined leverage factor. Within limits, firms can and do make tradeoffs between financial and operating leverage.

The usefulness of the degree of leverage concept lies in the facts (1) that it enables us to specify the precise effect of a change in sales volume on earnings available to common stock and (2) that it permits us to show the interrelationship between operating and financial leverage. The concept can be used to show a businessman, for example, that a decision to automate and to finance new equipment with bonds will result in a situation wherein a 10 percent decline in sales will produce a 50 percent decline in earnings, whereas a different operating and financial leverage package will be such that a 10 percent sales decline will cause earnings to decline by only 20 percent. In our experience, having the alternatives stated in this manner gives the decision-maker a better idea of the ramifications of his actions.[8]

VARIATIONS IN FINANCIAL STRUCTURE

As might be expected, wide variations in the use of financial leverage may be observed among industries and among the individual firms in each industry. Illustrative of these differences is the range of ratios of debt to total assets shown in Table 19–6. Service industries use the most leverage, reflecting (1) that services include financial institutions, which as a group have high liabilities, and (2) that there are many smaller firms in the service industries, and small firms as a group are heavy users of debt. Public utility use of debt stems from a heavy fixed asset investment, coupled with extremely stable sales. Mining and manufacturing firms use relatively little debt, because of their exposure to fluctuating sales.

TABLE 19–6   Variation in Financial Leverage in Industry Groups, 1976

Type of Industry	Debt and Preferred Stock to Total Assets
Service	68%
Public utilities	66
Wholesale trade	53
Retail trade	51
Mining	47
Manufacturing	46

Sources: Key Business Ratios, 1976, by the Business Economics Division, Dun & Bradstreet, Inc. Reprinted by permission. Also Missouri Public Service Commission.

[8]The concept is also useful for investors. If firms in an industry are classified as to their degrees of total leverage, an investor who is optimistic about prospects for the industry might favor those firms with high leverage, and vice versa if he expects industry sales to decline.

Within the broad category "manufacturing," wide variations are observed for individual industries. Table 19–7 presents an array of total-debt-to-total-assets ratios for selected manufacturing industries. The lowest ratios are found among soft drink companies and petroleum refining companies, in which cost pressures have been severe. Low debt ratios are also found among the durable goods industries. The highest debt ratios are found in consumer nondurable goods, where demand is relatively insensitive to fluctuations and general business activity.

TABLE 19–7   Total-debt-to-total-assets Ratios
(Selected manufacturing industries, 1976)

Soft drinks	33%
Petroleum refining	42
Control instruments	47
Meat packing	49
Agricultural chemicals	60
Women's clothing	65

Source: Key Business Ratios, 1976, by the Business Economics Division, Dun & Bradstreet, Inc. Reprinted by permission.

Even within a given industry, there are wide variations in the use of financial leverage, as illustrated for the electric utility industry in Table 19–8. These variations reflect a number of different considerations, including the volatility of business in the companies' operating areas, the extent to which they use preferred stock, and their managements' willingness to assume risk. Montana Power, for example, sells a large proportion of its electricity to copper producers, whose volume of business, and hence demand for power, is quite cyclical. This largely explains its low debt ratio. American Electric Power, by contrast, has a stable demand pattern, which permits its relatively high leverage factor.

TABLE 19–8   Total-debt-to-total-assets Ratios
(Selected electric utility companies, 1976)

Montana Power	43%
Central Illinois Public Service	47
Detroit Edison	49
Consolidated Edison of New York	52
Dayton Power & Light	53
American Electric Power	58

FACTORS INFLUENCING FINANCIAL STRUCTURE

Thus far the discussion has touched on the factors that are generally considered when a firm formulates basic policies relating to its financial structure. The more important of these financial structure determinants are now listed and briefly discussed.

1. Growth rate of future sales.
2. Stability of future sales.
3. Competitive structure of the industry.
4. Asset structure of the firm.
5. Control position and attitudes toward risk of owners and management.
6. Lenders' attitudes toward the firm and the industry.

Growth Rate of Sales

The future growth rate of sales is a measure of the extent to which the earnings per share of a firm are likely to be magnified by leverage. If sales and earnings grow at a rate of 8 to 10 percent a year, for example, financing by debt with limited fixed charges should magnify the returns to owners of the stock.[9] This can be seen from Figure 19–4, above.

However, the common stock of a firm whose sales and earnings are growing at a favorable rate commands a high price; thus, it sometimes appears that equity financing is desirable. The firm must weigh the benefits of using leverage against the opportunity of broadening its equity base when it chooses between future financing alternatives. Such firms may be expected to have a moderate-to-high level of debt financing.

Sales Stability

Sales stability and debt ratios are directly related. With greater stability in sales and earnings, a firm can incur the fixed charges of debt with less risk than it can when its sales and earnings are subject to periodic declines; in the latter instance it will have difficulty in meeting its obligations. The stability of the utility industry, combined with a large need for new capital and low common stock prices, has resulted in high leverage ratios in that industry.

Competitive Structure

Debt-servicing ability is dependent upon the profitability, as well as the volume, of sales. Hence, the stability of profit margins is as important as the stability of sales. The ease with which new firms may enter the industry and the ability of competing firms to expand capacity will influence profit margins. A growth industry promises higher profit margins, but such margins are likely to narrow if the industry is one in which the number of firms can be easily increased through additional entry. For example, the franchised fast-service food companies were a very profitable industry in the early 1960s, but it was relatively easy for new firms to enter this business and go into competition with the older firms. As the industry matured during the late 1960s and early

---

[9]Such a growth rate is also often associated with a high profit rate.

1970s, the capacity of the old and the new firms grew at an increased rate. As a consequence, profit margins declined.

Other firms in other industries are better able to resist competitive pressures. For example, to duplicate the unique technical, service, and distribution facilities of IBM or Kodak would be very difficult, a fact suggesting that profit margins for these firms are less subject to erosion.

Asset Structure

Asset structure influences the sources of financing in several ways. Firms with long-lived fixed assets, especially when demand for their output is relatively assured (for example, utilities), use long-term mortgage debt extensively. Firms whose assets are mostly receivables and inventory whose value is dependent on the continued profitability of the individual firm—for example, those in wholesale and retail trade—rely less on long-term debt financing and more on short term.

Management Attitudes

The management attitudes that most directly influence the choice of financing are those concerning (1) control of the enterprise and (2) risk. Large corporations whose stock is widely owned may choose additional sales of common stock because they will have little influence on the control of the company. Also, because management represents a stewardship for the owners, it is often less willing to take the risk of heavy fixed charges.[10]

In contrast, the owners of small firms may prefer to avoid issuing common stock in order to be assured of continued control. Because they generally have confidence in the prospects of their companies and because they can see the large potential gains to themselves resulting from leverage, managers of such firms are often willing to incur high debt ratios.

The converse can, of course, also hold—the owner-manager of a small firm may be *more* conservative than the manager of a large company. If the net worth of the small firm is, say, $1 million, and if it all belongs to the owner-manager, he may well decide that he is already prosperous enough, and may elect not to risk using leverage in an effort to become still more wealthy.

---

[10] It would be inappropriate to delve too far into motivational theory in an introductory finance textbook, but it is interesting to note that the managers of many larger, publicly owned corporations have a relatively small ownership position and derive most of their income from salaries. Some writers assert that in such cases managements do not strive for profits, especially if this effort involves using leverage with its inherent risk. Presumably, these managers feel that the risks of leverage for them, the ones who actually decide to use debt or equity, outweigh the potential gains from successful leverage. If sales are low, there is a chance of failure and the loss of their jobs, whereas if sales and profits are high, it is the stockholders, not management, who receive the benefits. Another way of looking at the situation is to say that most stockholders are more diversified than most managers—if the firm fails, a stockholder loses only that percentage of his net worth invested in the firm, but the manager loses 100 percent of his job. While there is undoubtedly some merit to this argument, it should be pointed out that companies are increasingly using profit-based compensation schemes—bonus systems and stock-option plans—to motivate management to seek profitability, and low leverage companies are subject to take-over bids (see Chapter 23).

Lender Attitudes

Regardless of managements' analyses of the proper leverage factors for their firms, there is no question but that lenders' attitudes are frequently important —sometimes the most important—determinants of financial structures. In the majority of cases, the corporation discusses its financial structure with lenders and gives much weight to their advice. But when management is so confident of the future that it seeks to use leverage beyond norms for the industry, lenders may be unwilling to accept such debt increases. They will emphasize that excessive debt reduces the credit standing of the borrower and the credit rating of the securities previously issued. The lenders' point of view has been expressed by a borrower, a financial vice-president, who stated, "Our policy is to determine how much debt we can carry and still maintain an AA bond rating, then use that amount less a small margin for safety."

SUMMARY

Financial leverage, which means using debt to boost rates of return on net worth over the returns available on assets, is the primary topic covered in this chapter. Whenever the return on assets exceeds the cost of debt, leverage is favorable and the return on equity is raised by using it. However, leverage is a two-edged sword, and if the returns on assets are less than the cost of debt, then leverage reduces the returns on equity. This reduction is greater the more leverage a firm employs. As a net result, leverage may be used to boost stockholder returns, but it is used at the risk of increasing losses if the firm's economic fortunes decline.

Probability data, whenever it is available, can be used to make the risk-return tradeoff involved in the use of financial leverage more precise. The expected earnings per share *(EPS)* and coefficient of variation *(v)* of these earnings may be calculated under alternative financial plans, and these *EPS* versus *v* comparisons aid in making choices among plans.

Financial leverage is similar to operating leverage, a concept discussed in Chapter 4. As is true for operating leverage, financial leverage can be defined rigorously and measured in terms of the *degree of financial leverage.* In addition, the effects of financial and operating leverage may be combined, with the *combined leverage factor* showing the percentage changes in earnings per share that will result from a given percentage change in sales.

In the following chapter the concepts developed to this point in the book will be extended to the formal theory of the cost of capital. The way investors appraise the relative desirability of increased returns versus higher risks is seen to be a most important consideration, one that, in general, invalidates the theory that firms should strive for maximum earnings per share regardless of the risks involved.

QUESTIONS

19-1. How will each of the occurrences listed below affect a firm's financial structure, capital structure, and net worth?
   a. The firm retains earnings of $100 during the year.
   b. A preferred stock issue is refinanced with bonds.
   c. Bonds are sold for cash.
   d. The firm repurchases 10 percent of its outstanding common stock with excess cash.
   e. An issue of convertible bonds is converted.

19–2. From an economic and social standpoint, is the use of financial leverage justifiable? Explain by listing some advantages and disadvantages.

19–3. Financial leverage and operating leverage are similar in one very important respect. What is this similarity and why is it important?

19-4. How does the use of financial leverage affect the break-even point?

19-5. Would you expect risk to increase (a) proportionately, (b) more than proportionately, or (c) less than proportionately, with added financial leverage? Give reasons for your answer.

19-6. What are some reasons for variations of debt ratios among the firms in a given industry?

19-7. Why is the following statement true? "Other things being the same, firms with relatively stable sales are able to incur relatively high debt ratios."

19-8. Why do public utility companies usually pursue a different financial policy from that of trade firms?

19-9. The use of financial ratios and industry averages in the financial planning and analysis of a firm should be approached with caution. Why?

19-10. Some economists believe that swings in business cycles will not be as wide in the future as they have been in the past. Assuming that they are correct in their analysis, what effect might this added stability have on the types of financing used by firms in the United States? Would your answer be true for all firms?

PROBLEMS

19-1. John MacMillan is considering forming a new company, and he is presently investigating the alternative capital structures. Investment bankers tell him that debt capital would cost the following under different debt ratios (Debt/Total Assets):

Debt Ratio	up to 20%	21–40%	41–50%	51–65%
Before-tax cost of debt	8%	9%	11%	14%

Common stock can be issued to net $5 per share. The tax rate is 50 percent. MacMillan plans to raise $5 million. The following alternative capital structures are under consideration:

	(1)	(2)	(3)	(4)	(5)	(6)	(7)	(8)
Debt	0%	20%	21%	40%	41%	50%	51%	65%
Equity	100%	80%	79%	60%	59%	50%	49%	35%

a. Compute the EPS for each alternative assuming an EBIT of $1 million. Which alternative would maximize EPS?

b. Discuss the advantages and disadvantages of employing this capital structure.

19-2. Associated Bearings is considering an expansion program that would require $10 million in external financing. The alternatives are (1) issue common stock that would net $50 per share (2) issue debt at 8 percent or (3) a combination of 50 percent common stock and 50 percent debt. Assume that the $50 per share and 8 percent rate would exist for the latter alternative.

The expected earnings before interest and taxes (EBIT) for recessionary, normal, and booming economies are $2 million, $4 million, and $6 million respectively.

The company has 800,000 shares of common stock outstanding and has a tax rate of 50 percent.

a. Calculate EPS for each alternative given each economic condition.

b. If the probabilities of recession, normal and boom economies are 0.2, 0.3 and 0.5 respectively, which financing alternative should be selected? Comment.

c. Determine the degree of financial leverage for normal economic conditions for each of the three financing alternatives.

19-3. In early 1976, the Davis Supply Company planned to raise an additional $100 million for financing plant additions and for working capital. Davis manufactures educational equipment and aids.

Investment bankers state that the company could sell common stock at a market price of $21 a share to net $20, or it could sell sinking fund debentures to yield 8 percent. Costs of flotation would be slightly higher for common stock but not enough to influence the decision.

The balance sheet and the income statement of Davis Supply prior to the financing are given below.

David Supply Company
Balance sheet, March 31, 1976
(in millions of dollars)

Current assets	$350	Accounts payable	$ 28
Investments	35	Notes payable to banks	112
Net fixed assets	175	Taxes payable	56
		Other current liabilities	49
		Total current liabilities	$245
		Long-term debt	140
		Common stock, $2 par	40
		Retained earnings	135
Total assets	$560	Total claims	$560

Davis Supply Company
Income statement
For year ended March 31, 1976
(in millions of dollars)

Sales	$980
Net income before taxes, 10%	98
Interest on debt	8
Net income subject to tax	90
Tax, 50%	45
Net income after tax	$ 45

    a. Assuming that net income before interest and taxes remains at 10 percent of sales, calculate earnings per share under both the stock-financing and debt-financing alternatives at sales levels of $600, $900, $1,200, $1,500, and $1,800 million.

    b. Assuming that the probability distribution of sales is: (1) 10 percent chance of $600; (2) 25 percent chance of $900; (3) 30 percent chance of $1,200; (4) 25 percent chance of $1,500; and (5) 10 percent chance of $1,800, calculate the expected *EPS* for both debt and stock financing. (The standard deviations for these *EPS* figures are given to be $\sigma_{debt} = \$.86$ and $\sigma_{stock} = \$.68$.)

    c. If the market value of the stock has been based on a *P/E* ratio of 11, but it is believed that the use of debt financing will drop the *P/E* ratio to 9, compute expected price per share under each financing alternative. (The standard deviations for these price figures are given to be $\sigma_{debt} = \$7.70$ and $\sigma_{stock} = \$7.53$.)

    d. Using the data and assumptions given above, which form of financing should Davis adopt? (Answer in terms of both the quantitative factors listed above and the qualitative factors discussed in the chapter.) In your answer, consider the facts that the industry average debt ratio is 30 percent, the current ratio is 2×, and the times interest earned ratio is 7×.

19-4. United Battery Corporation produces one product, a long-life rechargeable battery for use in small calculators. Last year 50,000 batteries were sold at $20 each. United Battery's income statement is shown below:

United Battery Corporation
Income statement
For year ended December 31, 1975

Sales		$1,000,000
Less: Variable cost	$400,000	
Fixed cost	200,000	600,000
EBIT		$ 400,000
Less: Interest		125,000
Net income before tax		$ 275,000
Less: Income tax ($t = 0.40$)		110,000
Net income		$ 165,000
EPS (100,000 shares)		$1.65

a. Calculate (1) the degree of operating leverage, (2) the degree of financial leverage, and (3) the combined leverage effect for United Battery for the 1975 level of sales.

b. United Battery is considering changing to a new production process for manufacturing the batteries. Highly automated and capital intensive, the new process will double fixed costs to $400,000 but will decrease variable costs to $4 a unit. If the new equipment is financed with bonds, interest will increase by $70,000; if the equipment is financed by common stock, total stock outstanding will increase by 20,000 shares. Assuming that sales remain constant, calculate for each financing method (1) earnings per share and (2) the combined leverage if the new process is employed.

c. Under what conditions would you expect United Battery to want to change its operations to the more automated plant?

d. If sales are expected to increase, which alternative will have the greatest impact on *EPS*? Illustrate with an example.

19-5. The Wilder Corporation plans to expand assets by 50 percent; to finance the expansion, it is choosing between a straight 7 percent debt issue and common stock. Its current balance sheet and income statement are shown below.

Wilder Corporation
Balance sheet
December 31, 1975

		Debt, 6%	$140,000
		Common stock, $10 par	350,000
		Retained earnings	210,000
Total assets	$700,000	Total claims	$700,000

Wilder Corporation
Income statement
For year ended December 31, 1975

Sales	$2,100,000	
Total costs (excluding interest)	1,881,600	Earnings per share: $\frac{\$105,000}{35,000} = \$3$
Net income before taxes	$ 218,400	Price/earnings ratio = 10 × *
Debt interest	8,400	
Income before taxes	$ 210,000	Market price: 10 × 3 = $30
Taxes at 50%	105,000	
Net income	$ 105,000	

*The price/earnings ratio is the market price per share divided by earnings per share. It represents the amount of money an investor is willing to pay for $1 of current earnings. The higher the riskiness of a stock, the lower its *P/E* ratio, other things held constant. The concept of price/earnings ratios was discussed at some length in Chapter 18.

If Wilder Corporation finances the $350,000 expansion with debt, the rate on the incremental debt will be 7 percent and the price/earnings ratio of the common stock will

be 8 times. If the expansion is financed by equity, the new stock can be sold at $25, the rate on debt will be 6 percent, and the price/earnings ratio of all the outstanding common stock will remain at 10 times earnings.

a. Assuming that net income before interest and taxes (*EBIT*) is 10 percent of sales, calculate earnings per share at sales levels of $0, $700,000, $1,400,000, $2,100,000, $2,800,000, $3,500,000, and $4,200,000, when financing is with (1) debt and (2) common stock. Assume no fixed costs of production.

b. Make a break-even chart for *EPS* and indicate the break-even point in sales (that is, where *EPS* using bonds = *EPS* using stock).

c. Using the price/earnings ratio, calculate the market value per share of common stock for each sales level for both the debt and the equity financing.

d. Make a break-even chart of market value per share for the company using data from part c, and indicate the break-even point.

e. If the firm follows the policy of seeking to maximize (1) *EPS* or (2) market price per share, which form of financing should be used?

f. Now assume that the following probability estimates of future sales have been made: 5 percent chance of $0; 7.5 percent chance of $700,000; 20 percent chance of $1,400,000; 35 percent chance of $2,100,000; 20 percent chance of $2,800,000; 7.5 percent chance of $3,500,000; and 5 percent chance of $4,200,000. Calculate expected values for *EPS* and market price per share under each financing alternative.

g. What other factors should be taken into account in choosing between the two forms of financing?

h. Would it matter if the presently outstanding stock was all owned by the final decision-maker, the president, and that this represented his entire net worth? Would it matter if he was compensated entirely by a fixed salary? that he had a substantial number of stock options?

The Cost
of Capital

20 The cost of capital is a critically important topic.[1] First, as we saw in Chapter 11, capital budgeting decisions have a major impact on the firm, and proper capital budgeting requires an estimate of the cost of capital. Second, in Chapter 19 we saw that financial structure can affect both the size and riskiness of the firm's earnings stream, hence the value of the firm. A knowledge of the cost of capital, and how it is influenced by financial leverage, is useful in making capital structure decisions. Finally, a number of other decisions, including those related to leasing, to bond refunding, and to working capital policy, require estimates of the cost of capital.[2]

In this chapter, we first point out the necessity of using a weighted average cost of capital. Second, the costs of the individual components of the capital structure—debt, preferred stock, and equity—are considered: because investors perceive different classes of securities to have different degrees of risk, there are variations in the costs of different types of securities. Third, the individual component costs are brought together to form a weighted cost of capital. Fourth, the concepts developed in the earlier sections are illustrated with an example of the cost of capital calculation for an actual company. Finally, the interrelationship between the cost of capital and the investment opportunity schedule is developed, and the simultaneous deter-

---

[1] This chapter is relatively long and difficult; students should allow for this in their preparation schedules.

[2] The cost of capital is also vitally important in regulated industries, including electric, gas, telephone, and transportation. In essence, regulatory commissions seek to measure a utility's cost of capital, then set prices so that the company will just earn this rate of return. If the estimate is too low, then the company will not be able to attract sufficient capital to meet long-run demands for service, and the public will suffer. If the estimate of capital costs is too high, customers will pay too much for service. We might also note that, if price controls for industrial companies are reinstituted, there is a strong likelihood that utility-type controls will be used.

mination of the marginal cost of capital and the marginal return on investment is discussed.

COMPOSITE, OR OVERALL, COST OF CAPITAL

Suppose a particular firm's cost of debt is estimated to be 8 percent, its cost of equity is estimated to be 12 percent, and the decision has been made to finance next year's projects by selling debt. The argument is sometimes advanced that the cost of these projects is 8 percent, because debt will be used to finance them. However, this position contains a basic fallacy. To finance a particular set of projects with debt implies that the firm is also using up some of its potential for obtaining new low-cost debt. As expansion occurs in subsequent years, at some point the firm will find it necessary to use additional equity financing or else the debt ratio will become too large.

To illustrate, suppose the firm has an 8 percent cost of debt and a 12 percent cost of equity. In the first year it borrows heavily, using up its debt capacity in the process, to finance projects yielding 9 percent. In the second year it has projects available that yield 11 percent, well above the return on first-year projects, but it cannot accept them because they would have to be financed with 12 percent equity money. To avoid this problem, the firm should be viewed as an on-going concern, and its cost of capital should be calculated as a weighted average, or composite, of the various types of funds it uses: debt, preferred, and equity.

BASIC DEFINITIONS

Both students and practitioners are often confused about how to calculate and use the cost of capital. To a large extent, this confusion results from imprecise, ambiguous definitions, but a careful study of the following definitions will eliminate such unnecessary difficulties.

Capital, or Financial, Components

Capital (or financial) components are the items on the right-hand side of the balance sheet: various types of debt, preferred stock, and common equity. Any net increase in assets must be financed by an increase in one or more capital components.

Component Costs

Capital is a necessary factor of production, and like any other factor, it has a cost. The cost of each component is defined as the *component cost* of that particular component. For example, if the firm can borrow money at 8 percent, the before-tax component cost of debt is defined as 8 percent. Throughout most of this chapter, we concentrate on debt, preferred stock, retained earnings, and new issues of common stock. These are the capital structure components, and their component costs are identified by the following symbols:

k_d = interest rate on firm's new debt = component cost of debt, before-tax.

$k_d(1 - t)$ = component cost of debt, after-tax, where t = marginal corporate tax rate; $k_d(1 - t)$ is the debt cost used to calculate the marginal cost of capital.

k_p = component cost of preferred stock.

k_r = component cost of retained earnings (or internal equity). k_r is identical to k_s, the required rate of return on common equity as developed in Chapter 18. Here we distinguish between equity obtained from retained earnings versus selling new stock, hence the distinction between k_r and k_s.

k_e = component cost of new issues of common stock (or external equity).

k_a = an average, or "composite," cost of capital. If a firm raises $1 of new capital to finance asset expansion, and if it is to keep its capital structure in balance (that is, if it is to keep the same percentage of debt, preferred, and equity), then it will raise part of the dollar as debt, part as preferred, and part as common equity (with equity coming either as retained earnings or from the sale of new common stock).[3] k_a is also a *marginal cost*: there is a value of k_a for each dollar the firm raises during the year. k_a is, in effect, the marginal cost of capital used in Chapter 11, and the relationship between k_a and the amount of funds raised during the year is expressed as the *MCC* schedule in Figure 11–1.[4]

These definitions and concepts are explained in detail in the remainder of this chapter, where we seek to accomplish two goals: (1) to develop a marginal cost of capital schedule ($k_a = MCC$) which can be used in capital budgeting, and (2) to determine the mix of types of capital that will minimize the MCC schedule. If the firm finances so as to minimize its *MCC,* uses this MCC to calculate *NPV*'s, and makes capital budgeting decisions on the basis of the *NPV* method, this will lead to a maximization of stock prices.

---

[3] Firms do try to keep their debt, preferred stock, and common equity in balance, but they *do not* try to maintain any proportional relationship between the common stock and retained earnings accounts as shown on the balance sheet.

[4] k_a also reflects the riskiness of the firm's various assets as discussed in Chapter 12, Investment Decisions Under Uncertainty. If a firm uses risk-adjusted discount rates for different capital projects, the average of these rates, weighted by the sizes of the various investments, should equal k_a.

BEFORE-TAX COMPONENT COST OF DEBT (k_d)

If a firm borrows $100,000 for one year at 6 percent interest, the investors who purchase the debt receive, and the firm must pay them, a total of $6,000 interest on their investment:

$$k_d = \text{before-tax cost of debt} = \frac{\text{interest}}{\text{principal}}$$

(20–1)

$$= \frac{\$6,000}{\$100,000} = 6\%.$$

For now, assume that there is no corporate income tax on the firm; the effect of income taxes on the analysis of cost of capital is treated in a later section of the chapter. Under this assumption, the firm's dollar interest cost is $6,000, and its percentage cost of debt is 6 percent. As a first approximation, *the component cost of debt is equal to the rate of return earned by investors, or the interest rate on debt.* If the firm borrows and invests the borrowed funds to earn a return just equal to the interest rate, then the earnings available to common stock remain unchanged.[5] This is demonstrated below.

The ABC Company has sales of $1 million, operating costs of $900,000, and no debt. Its income statement is shown in the Before column of Table 20–1. Then it borrows $100,000 at 6 percent and invests the funds in assets whose use causes sales to rise by $7,000 and operating costs to rise by $1,000. Hence, profits before interest rise by $6,000. The new situation is shown in the After column. Earnings are unchanged, as the investment just earns its component cost of capital.

Note that the cost of debt is applicable to *new* debt, not to the interest on any old, previously outstanding debt. In other words, we are interested in the cost of new debt, or the *marginal* cost of debt. Our primary concern with the cost of capital is to use it in a decision-making process—the decision whether

---

[5] Note that this definition is a *first approximation;* it is modified later to take account of the deductibility of interest payments for income tax purposes. Note also that here the cost of debt is considered in isolation. The impact of debt on the cost of equity, as well as on future increments of debt, is treated when the weighted cost of a combination of debt and equity is derived. Finally, flotation costs, or the costs of selling the debt, are ignored. Flotation costs for debt issues are generally quite low; in fact, most debt is placed directly with banks, insurance companies, pension funds, and the like, and involves no flotation costs. If flotation costs are involved, the cost of debt can be approximated by the following equation:

$$k_d = \frac{I_t + \frac{M - P}{n}}{\frac{M + P}{2}}$$

Here I_t is the periodic interest payment in dollars, M is the par or maturity value of the bond, P is the bond's issue price (hence $M - P$ is the premium or discount), and n is the life of the bond. The equation is an approximation, as it does not consider compounding effects. However, the approximation is quite close; for example, with a 5 percent, twenty-five year, $1,000 par value bond sold at $980, the formula gives $k_d = 5.13$ versus 5.15 as found from a bond table.

to obtain capital to make new investments; whether the firm borrowed at high or low rates in the past is irrelevant.[6]

TABLE 20-1 Income Statement for the ABC Company

	Before	After
Sales	$1,000,000	$1,007,000
Operating costs	900,000	901,000
Earnings before interest	$ 100,000	$ 106,000
Interest (I)	—	6,000
Earnings	$ 100,000	$ 100,000

PREFERRED STOCK

Preferred stock, described in detail in Chapter 15, is a hybrid between debt and common stock. Like debt, preferred stock carries a fixed commitment on the part of the corporation to make periodic payments, and, in liquidation, the claims of the preferred stockholders take precedence over those of the common stockholders. Failure to make the preferred dividend payments does not result in bankruptcy, as does nonpayment of interest on bonds. Preferred stock is thus somewhat more risky *to the firm* than common stock, but it is less risky than bonds. Just the reverse holds for investors. To the investor, preferred is less risky than common but more risky than debt. Thus, if an investor is willing to buy the firm's bonds on the basis of a 6 percent interest return, he might, because of risk aversion, be unwilling to purchase the firm's preferred stock at a yield of less than 8 percent. Assuming the preferred issue is a perpetuity that sells for $100 a share and pays an $8 annual dividend, its yield is calculated as follows:

$$\text{Preferred yield} = \frac{\text{preferred dividend}}{\text{price of preferred stock}} = \frac{D_p}{P_p} = \frac{\$8}{\$100} = 8\%. \qquad (20\text{-}2)$$

Because of flotation costs, a firm will receive *less than* the current market price of preferred stock when it sells new preferred. Thus, P_p in the denominator of Equation 20-2 should be the net price received by the firm. Suppose, for example, the firm must incur a selling or flotation cost of $4 a share. In other words, buyers of the preferred issue pay $100 a share, but brokers

---

[6] The fact that the firm borrowed at high or low rates in the past is, of course, important in terms of the effect of the interest charges on current profits, but this past decision is not relevant for *current* decisions. For current financial decisions, only current interest rates are relevant.

charge a selling commission of $4 a share, so the firm nets $96 a share. *The cost of new preferred to the firm is calculated as shown in Equation 20–2a:*

$$k_p = \text{cost of preferred} = \frac{D_p}{P_{pn}} = \frac{\$8}{\$96} = 8.33\%. \qquad (20\text{–}2a)$$

TAX ADJUSTMENT

As they stand, the definitions of the component costs of debt and preferred stock are incompatible when we introduce taxes into the analysis, because interest payments are a deductible expense whereas preferred dividends are not. The following example illustrates the point.

The ABC Company can borrow $100,000 at 6 percent, or it can sell 1,000 shares of $6 preferred stock to net $100 a share. Assuming a 48 percent tax rate, its before-investment situation is given in the Before column of Table 20–2. At what rate of return must the company invest the proceeds from the new financing to keep the earnings available to common shareholders from changing?

TABLE 20–2. Tax Adjustment for Cost of Debt

| | | Invest in Assets Yielding | | |
| | | 6% | | 11.538% |
	Before	*Debt*	*Preferred*	*Preferred*
Earnings before interest and taxes (*EBIT*)	$100,000	$106,000	$106,000	$111,538
Interest (*I*)	—	6,000	—	—
Earnings before taxes (*EBT*)	$100,000	$100,000	$106,000	$111,538
Taxes 48% (*T*)	(48,000)	(48,000)	(50,880)	(53,538)
Preferred dividends	—	—	(6,000)	(6,000)
Available for common dividends	$ 52,000	$ 52,000	$ 49,120	$ 52,000

As can be seen from the tabulations in Table 20–2, if the funds are invested to yield 6 percent before taxes, earnings available to common stockholders are constant if debt is used, but they decline if the financing is with preferred stock. To maintain the $52,000 net earnings requires that funds generated from the sale of preferred stock be invested to yield 11.538 percent before taxes or 6 percent after taxes.[7]

---

[7] The 11.538 percent is found as follows: 6%/(1 − tax rate) = 6%/0.52.

Since stockholders are concerned with after-tax rather than before-tax earnings, only the cost of capital *after* corporate taxes should be used. The cost of preferred stock is already on an after-tax basis as defined, but a simple adjustment is needed to arrive at the after-tax cost of debt. It is recognized that interest payments are tax deductible—the higher the firm's interest payments, the lower its tax bill. In effect, the federal government pays part of a firm's interest charges. Therefore, the cost of debt capital is calculated as follows:

$$k_d (1 - t) = \text{after-tax cost of debt}$$
$$= (\text{before-tax cost}) \times (1.0 - \text{tax rate}). \qquad (20\text{-}3)$$

Whenever the composite, or average cost of capital (k_a) *is calculated,* $k_d(1 - t)$ *and not* k_d *is used.*

Example

Before-tax cost of debt = 6 percent; tax rate = 48 percent.
$$k_d (1 - t) = \text{after-tax cost} = (0.06)(1 - 0.48) = (0.06)(0.52) = 3.12 \text{ percent.}$$

If the tax rate had been 50 percent, the after-tax cost of debt would have been one-half the interest rate. We should also note that the tax rate is zero for a firm with no profits. Therefore, for a corporation without taxable income, the cost of debt is not reduced; that is, in Equation 20-3 the tax rate equals zero, so the after-tax cost of debt is equal to the interest rate.

COST OF RETAINED EARNINGS (k_r)[8]

The cost of preferred stock is based on the return investors require if they are to purchase the preferred stock; the cost of debt is based on the interest rate investors require on debt issues, adjusted for taxes. The cost of equity obtained by retaining earnings can be defined similarly: *it is* k_r, *the rate of return stockholders require on the firm's common stock.* (k_r is identical to k_s as developed in Chapter 18.)

As we saw in Chapter 18, the value of a share of common stock with a constant expected growth rate is calculated by use of the following equation:

$$P_0 = \frac{D_1}{k_r - g}. \qquad (20\text{-}4)$$

[8] The term "retained earnings" can be interpreted to mean the balance sheet item "retained earnings," consisting of all the earnings retained in the business throughout its history, or it can mean the income statement item "additions to retained earnings." This latter definition is used in the present chapter: *"Retained earnings" for our purpose here refers to that part of current earnings which is not paid out in dividends but, rather, is retained and reinvested in the business.*

"Equity" is defined in this chapter to *exclude* preferred stock. Equity is the sum of capital stock, capital surplus, and accumulated retained earnings.

Here P^0 is the current price of the stock; D is the dividend expected to be paid at the end of the year; k_r is the required rate of return, and g is the expected growth rate. We can solve for k_r to obtain the required rate of return on common equity:

$$k_r = \frac{D_1}{P_0} + \text{expected } g. \qquad (20\text{–}5)$$

Example

To illustrate this calculation, consider Aubey Rents, a firm expected to earn $2 a share and to pay a $1 dividend during the coming year. The company's earnings, dividends, and stock price have all been growing at about 5 percent a year, and this growth rate is expected to continue indefinitely. The stock is in equilibrium and currently sells for $20 a share. Using this information, we compute the required rate of return on the stock in equilibrium, using Equation 20–5, as follows:

$$k_r = \frac{\$1}{\$20} + 5\% = 10\%.$$

The expected growth rate for the price of the shares is 5 percent, which, on the $20 initial price, should lead to a $1 increase in the value of the stock, to $21. This price increase will be attained (barring changes in the general level of stock prices) if Aubey invests the $1 of retained earnings to yield 10 percent. However, if the $1 is invested to yield only 5 percent, then earnings will grow by only 5 cents during the year, not by the expected 10 cents a share. The new earnings will be $2.05, a growth of only 2½ percent, rather than the expected $2.10, or 5 percent increase. If investors believe that the firm will earn only 5 percent on retained earnings in the future and attain only a 2½ percent growth rate, they will reappraise the value of the stock downward according to Equation 20–4 as follows:

$$P_0 = \frac{D_1}{k_r - g} = \frac{\$1}{.10 - .025} = \frac{\$1}{.075} = \$13.33.$$

Note, however, that Aubey Rents will suffer this price decline *only if it invests equity funds—retained earnings—at less than its component cost of capital.*

If Aubey refrains from making new investments and pays all its earnings in dividends, it will cut its growth rate to zero. However, the price of the stock will not fall, because investors will still get the required 10 percent rate of return on their shares:

$$k_r = \frac{D_1}{P_0} + g = \frac{\$2}{\$20} + 0 = 10\%, \text{ or}$$

$$P_0 = \frac{\$2}{.10 - 0} = \$20.$$

All the return would come in the form of dividends, but the actual rate of return would match the required 10 percent.

The preceding example demonstrates a fundamentally important fact: *If a firm earns its required rate of return,* k_r, *then when it retains earnings and invests them in its operations, its current stock price will not change as a result of this financing and investment. However, if it earns less than* k_r, *the stock price will fall; if it earns more, the stock price will rise.*

COST OF NEWLY ISSUED COMMON STOCK, OR EXTERNAL EQUITY (k_e)

The cost of new common stock, or *external* equity capital, k_e, is higher than the cost of retained earnings, k_r, because of flotation costs involved in selling new common stock. What rate of return must be earned on funds raised by selling stock to make the action worthwhile? To put it another way, what is the cost of new common stock? The answer is found by applying the following formula:[9]

$$k_e = \frac{D_1}{P_0(1 - F)} + g = \frac{D_1}{P_n} + g$$

$$= \frac{\text{dividend yield}}{(1 - \text{flotation percentage})} + \text{growth,}$$

(20–6)

or

$$k_e = \frac{\text{dividend yield}}{(1 - \text{flotation percentage})} + \text{growth}$$

$$= \frac{D_1/P_0}{(1 - F)} + g.$$

(20–7)

[9] The equation is derived as follows:

Step 1. The old stockholders expect the firm to pay a stream of dividends, D_t; this income stream will be derived from existing assets. New investors will likewise expect to receive the same stream of dividends, D_t. For new investors to obtain this stream *without impairing the* D_t *stream of the old investors,* the new funds obtained from the sale of stock must be invested at a return high enough to provide a dividend stream whose present value is equal to the price the firm receives:

$$P_n = \sum_{t=1}^{\infty} \frac{D_t}{(1 + k_e)^t}.$$

(20–8)

Here P_n is the net price to the firm; D_t is the dividend stream to new stockholders; and k_e is the cost of new outside equity.

Step 2. If flotation costs are expressed as a percentage, F, of the gross price of the stock, P_0, we may express P_n as follows:

$$P_n = P_0(1 - F).$$

Step 3. When growth is a constant, Equation 20–8 reduces to

$$P_n = P_0(1 - F) = \frac{D_1}{k_e - g}.$$

(20–8a)

Step 4. Equation 20–8a may be solved for k_e:

$$k_e = \frac{D_1}{P_0(1 - F)} + g.$$

(20–7)

Here F is the percentage cost of selling the issue, so $P_0(1 - F) = P_n$ is the net price received by the firm. For example, if $P_0 = \$10$ and $F = 10$ percent, then the firm receives $9 for each new share sold; hence $P_n = \$9$. Notice that Equations 20–6 and 20–7 are strictly applicable only if future growth is expected to be constant.

For Aubey Rents, the cost of new outside equity is computed as follows:

$$k_e = \frac{\$1}{\$20(1 - .10)} + 5\% = 10.55\%,$$

or

$$k_e = \frac{5\%}{.9} + 5\% = 10.55\%.$$

Investors require a return of $k_r = 10$ percent on Aubey's stock. However, because of flotation costs, Aubey must earn *more* than 10 percent on stock-financed investments to provide this 10 percent. Specifically, if Aubey Rents earns 10.55 percent on investments financed by new common stock issues, then earnings per share will not fall below previously expected earnings; its expected dividend can be maintained; the growth rate for earnings and dividends will be maintained; and as a result of all this, the price per share will not decline. If Aubey earns less than 10.55 percent, then earnings, dividends, and growth will fall below expectations, causing the price of the stock to decline. Since the cost of capital is *defined* as the rate of return that must be earned to prevent the price of the stock from falling, we see that the company's cost of external equity, k_e, is 10.55 percent.[10]

FINDING THE BASIC REQUIRED RATE OF RETURN ON COMMON EQUITY

It is obvious by now that the basic rate of return investors require on a firm's common equity, k_s as developed in Chapter 18, is a most important quantity. This required rate of return is the cost of retained earnings, and it forms the basis for the cost of capital obtained from new stock issues. How is this all-important quantity estimated?

Although one *can* use very involved, highly complicated procedures for making this estimation, satisfactory estimates may be obtained in one of three ways:

  1. Estimate the capital market line (CML) as described in Chapter 18;

---

[10] The cost of external equity is sometimes defined as follows:

$$k_e = \frac{k_r}{1 - F}.$$

This equation is correct if the firm's expected growth rate is zero; see Equation 20–7. In other cases it tends to overstate k_e.

estimate the relative riskiness of the firm in question; and then use these estimates to obtain the required rate of return on the firm's stock:

$$k_s = k_r = R_F + \rho.$$

Under this procedure, the estimated cost of equity (k_r) will move up or down with changes in interest rates and with changes in "investor psychology."

2. An alternative procedure, the use of which is recommended in conjunction with the one described above, is to estimate the basic required rate of return as follows:

a. Assume that investors expect the past-realized rate of return on the stock, $\overline{k}_r$, to be earned in the future, so the expected rate of return, $\hat{k}_r$, is equal to $\overline{k}_r$.

b. Assume that the stock is in equilibrium, with $k_r = \hat{k}_r$.

c. Under these assumptions, the required rate of return may be estimated as equal to the past realized rate of return:

$$k_r = \hat{k}_r = \overline{k}_r = \frac{D_1}{P_0} + \text{past growth rate.}$$

Stockholder returns are derived from dividends and capital gains, and the total of the dividend yield plus the average growth rate over the past five to ten years may give an estimate of the total returns that stockholders expect in the future from a particular share of stock.

3. For "normal" companies in "normal" times, past growth rates may be projected into the future, and the second method will give satisfactory results. *However, if the company's growth has been abnormally high or low, either because of its own unique situation or because of general economic conditions, then investors will not project the past growth rate into the future, so method 2 will not yield a good estimate of* k_r. In this case, g must be estimated in some other manner. Security analysts regularly make earnings growth forecasts, looking at such factors as projected sales, profit margins, competitive factors, and the like. Someone making a cost of capital estimate can obtain such analysts' forecasts and use them as a proxy for the growth expectations of investors in general, combine g with the current dividend yield, and estimate k_r as

$$k_r = \frac{D_1}{P_0} + \text{growth rate as projected by security analysts.}$$

Again, note that this estimate of k_r is based upon the assumption that g is expected to remain constant in the future.

In our own work, we typically use only methods 1 and 3. The "normal conditions" needed for method 2 have not generally existed in recent years, so that method has been invalid. Based on our own experience in estimating equity capital costs, we recognize that both careful analysis and some very fine judgments are required in this process. It would be nice to pretend that these judgments are unnecessary and to specify an easy, precise way of determining the exact cost of equity capital. Unfortunately, this is not possible. Finance is in large part a matter of judgment, and we simply must face this fact.

EFFECT OF LEVERAGE ON THE COST OF EQUITY

We have seen in earlier chapters that investors in general are averse to risk, and that risk aversion leads investors to require higher yields on riskier investments. In Chapter 19, we used the Universal Machine Company case to demonstrate that for any given degree of business risk, the higher the debt ratio, the larger the coefficient of variation (v) in earnings per share.[11] Combining these results leads us to conclude that the more debt a given company employs, other things held constant, the higher its required rate of return on equity capital will be.

To illustrate this relationship, consider Table 20–3, which extends the example of the Universal Machine Company to incorporate the risk-return tradeoff, and Figure 20–1, where the tradeoff function between leverage and rate of return is plotted.[12] The required rate of return on equity is 12 percent if the company uses no debt, but k_r increases with debt and is 19.5 percent if the leverage ratio is as high as 60 percent.[13]

TABLE 20–3 Universal Machine Company: Leverage, Risk, and Required Rates of Return on Equity

Leverage (Debt/Assets)	Risk (v)	Required Rate of Return (k_r)
0%	.552	12.0%
10	.570	12.2
20	.591	12.5
30	.615	13.0
40	.641	14.0
50	.669	16.0
60	.700	19.5

[11] This relationship was worked out for Universal Machine in Table 19–5.

[12] In this example we assume that the risk-return tradeoff function has been estimated, perhaps in a subjective manner, by the financial manager. The precise specification of such risk-return functions is one of the more controversial areas of finance, and having attempted to measure them empirically ourselves, we can attest to the difficulties involved. However, even though the precise shape of the function is open to question, it is generally agreed (1) that the curve is upward sloping and (2) that some estimate, be it better or worse, is necessary if we are to obtain a cost of capital for use in capital budgeting. In this chapter our main concern is that the broad concepts be grasped.

[13] Keep in mind that throughout this analysis we are holding constant the firm's assets and the *EBIT* on these assets. We wish to consider the effect of leverage on the cost of capital *holding other things constant*.

FIGURE 20-1 Relationship between Cost of Equity and Financial Leverage

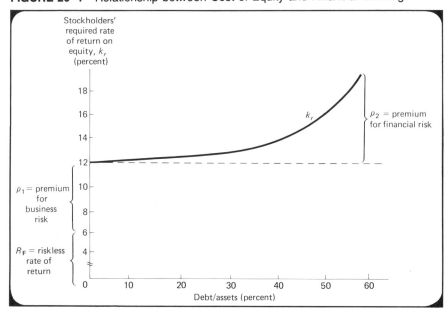

In Chapter 18 we indicated that the required rate of return consisted of the riskless rate plus a risk premium: $k_r = R_F + \rho$. Here we divide ρ into two components, ρ_1 (read "rho one"), a premium for business risk; and ρ_2, a premium required to compensate equity investors for the additional risk brought on by financial leverage. Expressed as an equation,

$$k_r = R_F + \rho_1 + \rho_2. \qquad (20\text{-}9)$$

The riskless rate of return, R_F, is a function of general economic conditions, Federal Reserve policy, and the like. The premium for business risk, ρ_1, is a function of the nature of the firm's industry, its degree of operating leverage, its diversification, and so on. Financial risk, ρ_2, depends upon the degree of financial leverage employed.[14]

EFFECT OF LEVERAGE ON THE COMPONENT COST OF DEBT

The component cost of debt is also affected by leverage: the higher the leverage ratio, the higher the cost of debt. Further, the cost of debt can be expected to rise at an increasing rate with leverage. To see why this is so, we can again

---

[14] ρ_2 increases at an increasing rate with leverage because bankruptcy, as opposed to simply lower earnings, becomes an increasing threat as the debt ratio rises, and bankruptcy has some high costs of its own (see Chapter 24). As we saw in Chapter 15, the specific terms of the firm's debt also affect its financial risk. Especially important here is the maturity structure of the debt.

consider the Universal Machine Company example. For simplicity, let us assume the following: (1) the company has $10 million of assets, and this level of assets will be maintained regardless of any financing decisions; (2) the company can adjust its capital structure any way it chooses, selling stock and using the proceeds to retire bonds if it elects to reduce its leverage, or selling bonds and using the funds to buy and retire its stock if it elects to increase leverage; (3) the probability distribution of earnings before interest and taxes (*EBIT*) is represented by Figure 20–2; (4) the company could realize $2 million from the sale of its land, plant, equipment, and inventories if it is forced to liquidate;[15] and (5) risk-free debt yields 6 percent.[16]

FIGURE 20–2   Probability Distribution of *EBIT* for Universal Machine Company

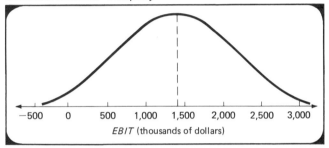

EBIT (thousands of dollars)

Suppose Universal raises $1 million of its total funds as debt; how risky would this debt be, and what interest rate would creditors require? First, if the debt is riskless, it should yield the riskless rate, or 6 percent. Since Universal could net $2 million from sale of assets if it is forced into bankruptcy, and since these funds would be available to pay off the bondholders, the first $2 million of debt may be considered riskless.[17]

Next, consider the fact that the more debt the firm has, the higher the interest requirements; and the higher the interest charges, the greater the probability that earnings (*EBIT*) will not be sufficient to meet these charges.[18] Creditors will perceive this increasing risk as the debt ratio rises, and they will begin charging a risk premium above the riskless rate, causing the firm's interest rate to rise: Since creditors are risk averters and are assumed to have a

[15] The liquidation value should be considered as a probability distribution, but we shall abstract from this and assume that the $2 million is a certain sum.

[16] To simplify the example, we disregard the existing 5 percent debt and assume that all debt bears interest at the new debt cost, K_d.

[17] Actually, for liquidity (marketability) and for other reasons, corporate debt never sells at yields as low as Treasury securities' rates. So even if Universal Machine's debt is riskless, it would have a marketability premium that would cause its yield to exceed the government bond rate. Also, we abstract here from the many problems that arise in bankruptcy. As we show in Chapter 24, these problems are sufficient to keep corporate debt from ever being truly riskless.

[18] The area under the curve in Figure 20–2 to the left of any level of fixed charges represents the probability of not covering these charges.

diminishing marginal utility for money, they will demand that interest rates be increased to compensate for the increased risk.

One other effect that may operate to raise interest rates at an increasing rate is the fact that a firm may need to use a variety of sources in order to borrow large amounts of funds in relation to its equity base. For example, a firm may be able to borrow from banks only up to some limit set by bank policy or bank examiner regulations. In order to increase its borrowings, the firm would have to seek other institutions, such as insurance companies, finance companies, and so on, that may demand higher interest rates than those charged by banks. Such an effect might tend to cause interest rates to jump whenever the firm was forced to find new lenders.

Table 20–4 shows the estimated relationships between leverage, the interest rate, and the after-tax cost of debt for Universal Machine. Assuming a 50 percent tax rate, the after-tax cost of debt is one-half the interest rate; these figures are also shown in Figure 20–3, where they are plotted against the debt ratio. In the example, Universal's cost of debt is constant until the debt ratio passes 20 percent or $2 million; then it begins to climb.

TABLE 20–4 Universal Machine Company
Effect of Leverage on the Cost of Debt

Leverage (Debt/Assets)	Interest Rate (k_d)	After-tax Cost of Debt $k_d(1-t)$
0%	6%	3.0%
10	6	3.0
20	6	3.0
30	7	3.5
40	9	4.5
50	12	6.0
60	17	8.5

FIGURE 20–3 Universal Machine Company:
Leverage and the After-tax Cost of Debt

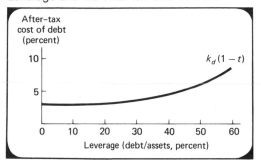

COMBINING DEBT AND EQUITY: WEIGHTED AVERAGE, OR COMPOSITE, COST OF CAPITAL

Debt and equity may now be combined to determine Universal Machine's average, or composite, cost of capital, and Table 20–5 shows the calculations used to determine the weighted average cost.[19] The average cost, together with the component cost of debt and equity, is plotted against the debt ratio in

TABLE 20–5   Calculation of Points on Average Cost of Capital Curve (percent), or the Composite Cost of Capital for Different Capital Structures

	Percent of Total (1)	Component Costs (2)	Weighted, or Composite, Cost: $K_a = (1) \times (2) \div 100$ (3)[a]
Debt	0	3.0	0
Equity	100	12.0	12.00
	100		12.00
Debt	10	3.0	.30
Equity	90	12.2	11.00
	100		11.30
Debt	20	3.0	.60
Equity	80	12.5	10.00
	100		10.60
Debt	30	3.5	1.05
Equity	70	13.0	9.10
	100		10.15
Debt	40	4.5	1.80
Equity	60	14.0	8.40
	100		10.20
Debt	50	6.0	3.00
Equity	50	16.0	8.00
	100		11.00
Debt	60	8.5	5.10
Equity	40	19.5	7.80
	100		12.90

[a] We divide by 100 to obtain percentages; figures rounded to nearest hundredth.

[19] A generalized equation can be used to calculate the weighted cost of capital:

$$k_a = \sum_{i=1}^{n} w_i k_i$$

where w_i is the weight of the ith type of capital and k_i is the cost of the ith component. If the firm had one class of debt, preferred stock, and equity, k_a would be found as

$$k_a = w_d k_d + w_p k_p + w_{equity} [k_r \text{ or } k_e].$$

It would, of course, be possible to expand this equation to encompass long- and short-term debt, convertibles, trade credit, and the like.

Figure 20–4. Here we see that the composite cost of capital is minimized when its debt ratio is approximately 35 percent, so Universal's optimal capital structure calls for about 35 percent debt, 65 percent equity.

FIGURE 20–4   Universal Machine Company: Average, or Composite, Cost of Capital

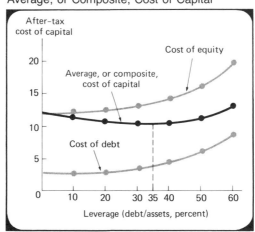

It is important to note that the average cost of capital curve is relatively flat over a fairly broad range: if Universal Machine's debt ratio is in the range of 25 to 45 percent, the average cost of capital cannot be lowered very much by moving to the optimal point. This appears to be a fairly typical situation, as almost any "reasonable" schedule for the component costs of debt and equity will produce a saucer-shaped average cost of capital schedule similar to that shown in Figure 20–4. This gives financial managers quite a degree of flexibility in planning their financing programs, permitting them to sell debt one year, equity the next, in order to take advantage of capital market conditions and to avoid high flotation costs associated with small security issues.

Table 20–5 and Figure 20–4 are based on the assumption that the firm is planning to raise a given amount of new capital during the year. For a larger or smaller amount of new capital, some other cost figures might be applicable; the optimal capital structure might call for a different debt ratio, and the minimum average cost of capital (k_a) might be higher or lower. This point is discussed in detail later in the chapter.

HIGH-RISK AND LOW-RISK FIRMS

Shown in Figure 20–5 are the cost of capital schedules for a firm in a risky industry (R) and for one in a stable industry (S). Firm R, the one on which Figure

20–4 was based, is Universal Machine; firm S is a relatively stable, safe company. We have already examined the interrelationships of the curves of Universal Machine—after declining for a while as additional low-cost debt is averaged in with equity, the average cost of capital for firm R begins to rise after debt has reached 35 percent of total capital. Beyond this point, the fact that both debt and equity are becoming more expensive offsets the fact that the component cost of debt is less than that of common equity.

FIGURE 20–5 Hypothetical Cost of Capital Schedules for High-risk (R) and Low-risk (S) Firms

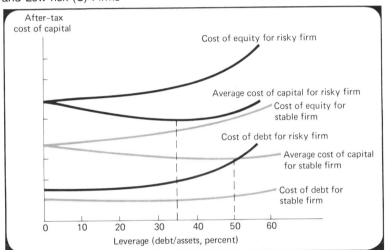

While the same principles apply to the less risky firm, its cost functions are quite different from those of Universal Machine. In the first place, S's overall business risk is lower, giving rise to lower debt and equity costs at all debt levels. Further, its relative stability means that less risk is attached to any given percentage of debt; therefore, its costs of both debt and equity—and, consequently, its average cost of capital—turn up further to the right than do the corresponding curves for Universal Machine. The optimum debt ratio for the firm in the stable industry is 50 percent as compared to only 35 percent for Universal.

Determining the actual optimal capital structure for a specific firm requires both analysis and judgment, and it is up to a firm's financial manager to decide on the best capital structure for his company. Once this decision has been reached, the weighting system for the average cost of capital calculation is also determined. Unless otherwise noted, we will assume that management deems its present book value capital structure to be optimal, and we shall use this set of weights in our calculations.[20]

CALCULATING THE MARGINAL COST OF CAPITAL FOR AN ACTUAL COMPANY

The procedures discussed above are now applied to an actual company, the Continental Container Company, to illustrate the cost of capital calculation. Continental Container is a large firm, with assets of over $950 million and sales of over $1 billion. Sales and earnings are relatively stable, as food and beverage companies make up the bulk of the firm's customers. Dividends have been paid since 1923, even during the depression of the 1930s. On the basis of an indicated dividend rate of $2 and a current price of $33.50 a share, the dividend yield is 6 percent. Over the past ten years, earnings, dividends, and the price of the stock have grown at a rate of about 5 percent; all indications suggest that this same rate of growth will be maintained in the foreseeable future.[21] Since internally generated funds provide sufficient equity, only the costs of internal equity, found in this case to be the 6 percent dividend yield plus the 5 percent growth rate, or a total of 11 percent, need be considered.

---

[20] The weights used to calculate the marginal cost of capital, k_a, should be based on the *market value of the capital raised,* not the book value of the existing capital structure. However, if a firm seeks to maintain a constant book value capital structure—as most firms do—*then the market value of the capital raised will be proportional to the book value capital structure.* Consider a firm with assets and capital of $100, whose stock sells at a premium of 40 percent over its book value, and whose debt sells at its book value:

	Book Value Capital Structure		Market Value Capital Structure	
Debt	$ 50	50%	$ 50	42%
Common equity	50	50	70	58
	$100	100%	$120	100%

Suppose this firm plans to raise $50 of new capital. If it raises $25 of debt and $25 of equity, its book value capital structure will remain constant, but its market value percentages will change to 44% debt and 56% equity. Conversely, if it raises new capital as $21 debt and $29 equity, its market value capital structure will remain constant, but its book value structure will change to 47% debt, 53% equity. Thus, we see that a firm whose securities sell at prices different from their book values can maintain a book value capital structure or a market value structure, but not both.

Most firms do, in fact, target on book value capital structures, and there seem to be three reasons for this choice: (1) market values fluctuate widely, and financial planning would be unstable if a market value target was used; (2) it is difficult if not impossible to specify a precise optimal capital structure anyway, whether it is measured in book or market terms; and (3) regardless of which choice is made with regard to the target capital structure, the book and market values of *marginal* capital are approximately equal. Of course, if the *wrong* target capital structure is used as the target, the MCC will be higher than it needs to be, but with the present state of the art, it is almost impossible to *prove* that one capital structure is better than another, at least for capital structures in the broad range of 25–60 percent debt, whether measured at book or market.

[21] Earnings per share for 1966 were $2.25, while *EPS* for 1976 were $3.65. Dividing $3.65 by $2.25 gives 1.62, which is the *CVIF* for 10 years at 5 percent from Table A-1. Thus, *EPS* grew at a 5 percent rate over the ten-year period from 1966 through 1976. Dividends grew similarly, and security analysts are projecting a continuation of these rates.

The average interest rate on Continental Container's outstanding debt is 4.5 percent, but much of this debt was issued in earlier years when interest rates were much lower than they are now. Current market yields on both long-term and short-term debt are about 8 percent, and approximately this cost will be associated with new debt issues. After a 48 percent income tax, the cost of debt is estimated to be 4.2 percent. The preferred stock is stated to be 3.75 percent preferred, but it was also issued when rates were low. On the basis of current market yields, the estimated cost of new preferred stock is 7.5 percent.

The right-hand side of Continental Container's balance sheet is given in Table 20–6. A large portion (24 percent) of the firm's funds are "free" in the sense that no interest is charged for them—accounts payable and accruals are in this class. Some would argue that in the calculation of the overall cost of capital, this "free" capital should be included. Under certain circumstances this procedure is valid; usually, however, only "non-free" capital need be considered.[22] Of the target, or chosen long-term capital structure, 22 percent is debt, 1 percent is preferred stock, and 77 percent is common equity. This means, in effect, that each $1.00 of new capital is raised as $0.22 of debt, $0.01 of preferred stock, and $0.77 as common equity (retained earnings or new stock).

TABLE 20–6 Continental Container Company
Right-hand Side of Balance Sheet
(millions of dollars)

			Non-free funds only	
Payables and accruals	$186	19.4%		
Tax accruals	44	4.6		
Total "free" current funds	$230	24.0%		
Interest-bearing debt	$160	16.7%	$160	22%
Preferred stock	7	0.8	7	1
Common equity	560	58.5	560	77
Non-free funds	727	76.0%	$727	100%
Total financing	$957	100.0%		

[22]The primary justification for ignoring "free" capital is that, in the capital budgeting process, these spontaneously generated funds are netted out against the required investment outlay, then ignored in the cost of capital calculation. To illustrate, consider a retail firm thinking of opening a new store. According to customary practices, the firm should (1) estimate the required outlay, (2) estimate the net receipts (additions to profits) from the new store, (3) discount the estimated receipts at the cost of capital, and (4) accept the decision to open the new store only if the net present value of the expected revenue stream exceeds the investment outlay. The estimated accruals, trade payables, and other costless forms of credit are deducted from the investment to determine the "required outlay" before making the calculation. Alternatively, "free" capital could be costed in, and working capital associated with specific projects added in when determining the investment outlay. The two procedures will result in similar decisions.

If management believes that some other capital structure is optimal, then other weights would be used; for purposes of illustration it is assumed that the existing structure has been determined to be the optimum. Further, let us assume that Continental Container plans to raise $20 million during the current year. To maintain the target capital structure, this $20 million must be raised as follows: $4.4 million as debt, $0.2 million as preferred stock, and $15.4 million as equity. Also, note that all equity is obtained in the form of retained earnings. On the basis of these weights and the previously determined costs of debt, equity, and preferred stock, the calculations shown in Table 20–7 indicate that Continental Container's composite cost of new capital is 9.5 percent. As long as Continental Container finances in the indicated manner and uses only retained earnings for equity, each dollar of new funds should cost this amount.

TABLE 20–7 Continental Container
Illustrative Calculation of Average Cost of Capital: $20 Million New Capital

	Amount of Capital (1)	Proportions (2)	Component Costs (3)	Product (2) × (3) = (4)
Debt	$ 4.4	22.0%	4.2%	.0092
Preferred stock	2	1.0	7.5	.0008
Common equity	15.4	77.0	11.0	.0847
	$20.0	100.0%		$k_a = .0947 = 9.5\%$

Marginal Cost of Capital When New Common Stock Is Used

In the preceding example of Continental Container, we assumed that the company would finance only with debt, preferred stock, and *internally generated equity.* On this basis we found the weighted average cost of new capital, or the marginal cost of capital, to be 9.5 percent. What would have occurred, however, if the firm's need for funds had been so great that it was forced to sell new common stock? The answer is that its marginal cost of new capital would have increased. To show why this is so, we shall extend the Continental Container example.

First, suppose that during 1977 Continental Container had total earnings of $59 million available for common stockholders, paid $27 million in dividends, and retained $32 million. We know that to keep the capital structure in balance, the retained earnings should equal 77 percent of the net addition to capital, the other 23 percent being debt and preferred stock. Therefore, the total amount of new capital that can be obtained on the basis of the retained earnings is

$$\text{Retained earnings} = (\text{percent equity})(\text{new capital})$$

$$\text{New capital} = \frac{\text{retained earnings}}{\text{percent equity}}$$

$$= \frac{\$32 \text{ million}}{0.77} = \$41.6 \text{ million}.$$

Next, we note that 1 percent of the new capital, or about $400,000, should be preferred stock and that 22 percent, or $9.2 million, should be debt. In other words, Continental Container can raise a total of $41.6 million—$32 million from retained earnings, $9.2 million in the form of debt, and $400,000 in the form of preferred stock—and still maintain its target capital structure in exact balance.

If all financing up to $41.6 million is in the prescribed proportions, the composite cost of each dollar of new capital *up to $41.6 million* is still 9.5 percent, the previously computed weighted average cost of capital. In Table 20–7, we showed the calculation of the weighted average cost of raising $20 million; had we made the calculation for any other amount *up to $41.6 million,* the weighted average cost would have also been 9.5 percent. Thus, each dollar of new capital costs 9.5 percent, so this is the marginal cost of capital.

As soon as the total of the required funds exceeds $41.6 million, however, Continental must begin relying on more expensive new common stock. Therefore, beyond $41.6 million we must compute a new marginal cost of capital. Assuming Continental Container would incur a flotation cost on new equity issues equal to 10 percent, we could compute the cost of capital for funds over $41.6 million as shown in Table 20–8.

TABLE 20–8 Calculation of Continental Container's Marginal Cost of Capital Using New Common Stock

1. Find the cost of new equity:

$$\text{Cost of new common stock} = \frac{\text{dividend yield}}{(1 - \text{flotation percentage})} + \text{growth}$$

$$k_e = \frac{.06}{.90} + 5\% = 11.7\%.$$

2. Find a new weighted or composite cost of each dollar of new capital in excess of $41.6 million, using only new common stock for the equity component:

	Proportion ×	component cost =	product
Debt	22%	4.2	.0092
Preferred stock	1	7.5	.0008
Equity (new)	77	11.7	.0901
	100%		$k_a = .1001 \approx 10\%$

According to Table 20–7, as long as Continental Container raises no more than $41.6 million, its weighted average and marginal cost of new or incremental capital is 9.5 percent, but as we have shown in Table 20–8, every dollar over $41.6 million has a cost of 10 percent, so the marginal cost beyond $41.6 million is 10 percent.

Other Breaks in the MCC Schedule

The *marginal cost of capital schedule* shows the relationship between the average cost of each dollar raised (k_a) and the total amount of capital raised during the year, other things, such as the riskiness of the assets acquired, held constant. In the preceding section, we saw that Continental Container's MCC schedule increases at the point where its retained earnings are exhausted and it begins to use more expensive new common stock.

Actually, any time any component cost rises, a similar break will occur. For example, if Continental could obtain only $10 million of debt at 8 percent, with additional debt costing 9 percent, then this rise in k_d would produce a higher $k_d(1 - t)$ which in turn would lead to a higher k_a. Where would this break occur? Under the assumptions made thus far for Continental Container, it would occur at $45.5 million, found as

$$\begin{array}{c} \text{break in } MCC \\ \text{schedule caused by} \\ \text{rising debt cost} \end{array} = \dfrac{\begin{array}{c}\text{amount of lower-cost}\\ \text{debt}\end{array}}{\begin{array}{c}\text{debt as percentage}\\ \text{of capital raised}\end{array}}$$

$$= \frac{\$10}{0.22} = \$45.5 \text{ million.}$$

Now suppose only an additional $5 million, over and above the first $10 million, can be borrowed at 9 percent, after which the component cost of new debt rises to 10 percent. A new break will occur, this one at $68.2 million:

$$\frac{\begin{array}{c}\text{amount of lower-cost}\\ \text{debt}\end{array}}{\text{debt/total capital}} = \frac{\$10 + \$5}{0.22} = \$68.2 \text{ million.}$$

Similar breaks could be caused by increases in the cost of preferred stock, higher common stock flotation costs as more stock is sold, and perhaps even a change in k_r, the basic required rate of return on the firm's common equity as discussed in Chapter 18.[23]

---

[23] It has been argued that, as a company sells more and more stock or other types of securities, it must attract investors who are less and less familiar with and impressed by the company, hence that the securities must be sold at lower prices and higher yields. This pressure could affect all securities, new and old. If the sale of additional stock (permanently) lowers the price of old stock, then this reduction in value must be assessed as a marginal cost of the new stock. This situation is said to exist for the utilities, whose huge, recurrent issues of securities in recent years have been depressing the prices of their outstanding securities.

In general, breaks in the *MCC* schedule will occur whenever any component cost increases as a result of the volume of capital raised, and the breaking points can be calculated by use of Equation 20–10:

$$\text{Break in } MCC = \frac{\begin{array}{c}\text{total amount of lower-cost capital}\\\text{for a given component}\end{array}}{\begin{array}{c}\text{percentage of total capital}\\\text{represented by the component}\end{array}}. \quad (20\text{--}10)$$

If we determined that Continental Container would experience higher component costs for debt at $10 million and at $15 million, for preferred at $5 million, and for common equity at $32 million (when retained earnings are exhausted) and at $50 million, then Equation 20–10 could be used to compute a number of breaks in the company's *MCC* schedule.

Cause of Break	Point Where Break Occurs
(shift from k_r to k_e)	$ 41.6 million
(rising k_d)	45.5
(rising k_e)	64.9
(rising k_d)	68.2
(rising k_p)	500.0

It is necessary to calculate a different $MCC = k_a$ for the interval between each of the breaks in the *MCC* schedule. For example, we have already calculated the *MCC* from zero to $41.6 million as 9.5 percent, and that from $41.6 to $45.5 million as 10 percent. The values of k_a for the other intervals were calculated (but not shown here), and they are plotted as the step-function *MCC* schedule shown in Figure 20–6, panel a.

FIGURE 20–6   Relationship between Marginal Cost and Amount of Funds Raised

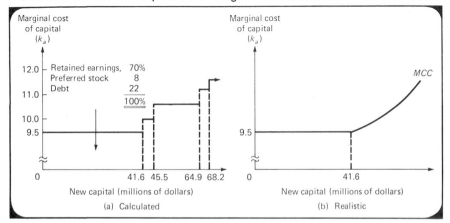

(a) Calculated

(b) Realistic

This graph is highly idealized; in fact, the actual *MCC* curve looks much more like that shown in Figure 20–6(b). Here we see that the curve is flat until it reaches the vicinity of $41.6 million; it then turns up gradually and continues rising. It will go up gradually rather than suddenly because the firm will probably make small adjustments to its target debt ratio, its dividend payout ratio, the actual types of securities it uses, and so on. And the curve will continue to rise, because, as more and more of its securities are put on the market during a fairly short period, it will experience more and more difficulty in getting the market to absorb the new securities.

Ordinarily, a firm will calculate its *MCC* schedule as a step-function similar to the one shown in Figure 20–6(a), then "smooth it out" by connecting the values of k_a shown in the middle of each interval. When one recognizes the types of estimates and approximations that go into the step-function curve, the smoothing process is less arbitrary than it might first appear to be.

COMBINING THE *MCC* AND THE INVESTMENT OPPORTUNITY SCHEDULES

Having developed his firm's *MCC* schedule, and planned its financing mix so as to minimize the schedule, the financial manager's next task is to utilize the *MCC* in the capital budgeting process. How is this done? First, suppose that the k_a value in the flat part of the *MCC* schedule is used as the discount rate for calculating the *NPV* and the total cost of all projects with *NPV* > 0 is less than the dollar amount at which the *MCC* schedule turns up. In this case, the value of k_a that was used is the correct one. For example, if Continental Container used 9.5 percent as its cost of capital and found that the acceptable projects totalled $41.6 million or less, then 9.5 percent is the appropriate cost of capital for capital budgeting.[24]

But suppose the acceptable projects totalled *more than* $41.6 million with a 9.5 percent discount rate. What do we do now? The most efficient procedure is given below:

Step 1 Calculate and plot the *MCC* schedule as shown in Figure 20–6.

Step 2 Ask the operating personnel to estimate the dollar volume of acceptable projects at a range of discount rates, say 14, 13, 12, 11, 10, and 9 percent.

---

[24]We are, of course, abstracting from project risk; here we assume that the average riskiness of all projects undertaken is equal to the average riskiness of the firm's existing plant. Some projects may be more risky than average, hence call for a risk-adjusted cost of capital > 9.5 percent, while others are less risky than average and call for a cost of capital < 9.5 percent. For a discussion of the use of different discount rates for projects and divisions with risk different from the corporate average, see "Union Chemical" case in Brigham, Nantell, Aubey, & Pettway, *Decisions in Financial Management: Cases.*

There will, thus, be an estimate of the capital budget at a series of k_a values. For Continental Container, these values were estimated as follows:

k_a	Capital Budget
14%	$20 million
13	30
12	40
11	50
10	60
9	70

Step 3 Plot the k_a, capital budget points as determined in Step 2 on the same graph as the *MCC;* this plot is labeled *IRR* in Figure 20–7.[25]

FIGURE 20–7 Interfacing the *MCC* and *IRR* Curves to Determine the Capital Budget

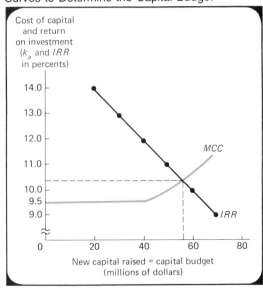

---

[25]To see why the k_a, capital budget line is a type of *IRR* curve, consider the following:

1. The *NPV* of a project is zero if the project's *IRR* is equal to k_a. This point was demonstrated in Chapter 11, footnote 11.
2. Now suppose we determine that no projects have *NPV* $\geq$ 0 at k_a = 15%. This means that no projects have *IRR* $\geq$ 15%.
3. Next, suppose we determine that $20 million of projects have *NPV* $\geq$ 0 at k_a = 14%. This means that these projects all have 14% $\leq$ *IRR* $\leq$ 15%.
4. If the projects were completely divisible, and if we examined very small changes in k_a, then we would have a continuous *IRR* curve. As it is, the curve labeled *IRR* in Figure 20–7 is an approximation. In any event, the example does illustrate how an *IRR* curve can be developed even though a company uses the *NPV* capital budgeting method.

Step 4 The correct *MCC* for use in capital budgeting—assuming both the *MCC* and *IRR* curves are developed correctly—is the value at the intersection of the two curves, 10.4 percent. If this value of k_a is used to calculate *NPV*'s, then projects totalling $56 million will have *NPV*'s greater than zero. This is the capital budget that will maximize the value of the firm.

In practice, both the *IRR* and *MCC* schedules are developed on an *ex ante* basis; that is, the schedules are estimated during the planning or budgeting process, when the firm is planning its operations for the coming year. We cannot delve into all the details of this part of the planning process, but the reader is referred to the references at the end of this chapter and to the Union Chemical Case.[26]

DYNAMIC CONSIDERATIONS

Conditions change over time; when they do, the firm must make adjustments. First, the firm's own individual situation may change. For example, as it grows and matures, its business risk may decline; this may, in turn, lead to an optimal capital structure that includes more debt. Second, capital market conditions could undergo a pronounced, long-run change, making either debt or equity relatively favorable. This too could lead to a new optimal capital structure. Third, even though the long-run optimal structure remains unchanged, temporary shifts in the capital markets could suggest that the firm use either debt or equity, departing somewhat from the optimal capital structure, then adjust back to the long-run optimum in subsequent years. Fourth, the supply and demand for funds varies from time to time, causing shifts in the cost of both debt and equity, and, of course, in the marginal cost of capital. Finally, the firm may experience an almost unconscious change in capital structure because of retained earnings unless its growth rate is sufficient to call for the employment of more debt on a continual basis.

For all these reasons, it is important that the firm reexamine its cost of capital periodically, especially before determining the annual capital budget or engaging in new long-term financing.[27]

LARGE FIRMS VERSUS SMALL FIRMS

Before closing this chapter, we should note that significant differences in capital costs exist between large and small firms; these differences are espe-

---

[26]Brigham, Nantell, Aubey, and Pettway, *Ibid*.

[27]Note that an exact calculation of a firm's need for funds cannot be made until the marginal cost of capital to be used in the capital budgeting process has been calculated. Thus, the marginal cost of capital and the amount of financing required for new projects should be simultaneously determined. This simultaneous determination is considered in Chapter 21, where dividend policy and internal financing decisions are discussed.

cially pronounced in the case of small, privately owned firms. The same concepts are involved, and the methods of calculating the average and marginal costs of capital are similar, but several points of difference arise:

1. It is especially difficult to obtain reasonable estimates of equity capital costs for small, privately owned firms.
2. Tax considerations are generally quite important for privately owned companies, as owner-managers may be in the top personal tax brackets. This factor can cause the effective after-tax cost of retained earnings to be considerably lower than the after-tax cost of new outside equity.
3. Flotation costs for new security issues, especially new stock issues, are much higher for small than for large firms (see Chapter 13).

Points 2 and 3 both cause the marginal cost curves for small firms to rise rapidly once retained earnings are exhausted. These relationships have implications for the growth and development of large versus small firms; recognizing the plight of smaller companies, the federal government has set up programs to help small businesses obtain capital.

SUMMARY

In Chapter 18, the nature of the valuation process and the concept of expected rates of return were considered in some detail. The present chapter used these valuation concepts to develop an average cost of capital for the firm. First, the cost of the individual components of the capital structure—debt, preferred stock, and equity—were analyzed. Next, these individual component costs were brought together to form an average, or composite, cost of capital. Finally, the conceptual ideas developed in the first two sections were illustrated with an example of the cost of capital for an actual company —Continental Container Company.

Cost of Individual Capital Components The *cost of debt*, $k_d(1 - t)$, is defined as the interest rate that must be paid on new increments of debt capital multiplied by (1 − tax rate). The *preferred stock cost* to the company is the effective yield and is found as the annual preferred dividend divided by the net price the company receives when it sells new preferred stock. In equation form, the cost of preferred stock is

$$\text{cost of preferred stock} = k_p = \frac{\text{preferred dividend}}{\text{net price of preferred}}.$$

The *cost of common equity* is defined as the minimum rate of return that must be earned on equity-financed investments to keep the value of the existing common equity unchanged. This required rate of return is the rate of return that investors expect to receive on the company's common stock—the dividend yield plus the capital gains yield. Sometimes, we assume that the investors expect to receive about the same rates of return in the future that they have received in the past; in this case, we can estimate the required rate of return on the basis of actual historical returns.

Equity capital comes from two sources, retained earnings and sale of new issues of common stock. The basic required rate of return (k_r) is used for the cost of retained earnings. However, new stock has a higher cost because of the presence of flotation costs associated with the sale of stock. The cost of new common stock issues is computed as follows:

$$\text{Cost of new stock} = k_e = \frac{\text{dividend yield}}{(1 - \text{flotation percentage})} + \text{growth}.$$

New common stock is therefore more expensive than retained earnings.

Weighted Average, or Composite, Cost of Capital The first step in calculating the weighted average cost of capital, k_a, is to determine the cost of the individual capital components as described above. The next step is to establish the proper set of weights to be used in the averaging process. Unless we have reason to think otherwise, we generally assume that the present capital structure of the firm is at an optimum, where optimum is defined as the capital structure that will produce the minimum average cost of capital for raising a given amount of funds, or a minimum cost of incremental capital. The optimal capital structure varies from industry to industry, with more stable industries having optimal capital structures that call for the use of more debt than in the case of unstable industries.

Marginal cost The marginal cost of capital schedule, defined as the cost of each additional dollar raised during the current year, is of interest for two reasons. First, the firm should finance in a manner that minimizes the *MCC* schedule, and therefore it must measure the *MCC*. Second, the *MCC* is the rate that should be used in the capital budgeting process—the firm should take on new capital projects only if their net present values are positive when evaluated at the marginal cost of capital.

The marginal cost of capital is constant over a range, then begins to rise. The rise is probably gradual, not abrupt, because firms make small adjustments in their target debt ratios, begin to use an assortment of securities, retain more of their earnings, and so on, as they reach the limit of internally generated equity funds.

QUESTIONS

20-1. Suppose that basic business risks to all firms in any given industry are similar.
  a. Would you expect all firms in each industry to have approximately the same cost of capital?
  b. How would the averages differ among industries?

20-2. Why are internally generated retained earnings less expensive than equity raised by selling stock?

20-3. Prior to the 1930s the corporate income tax was not very important, as rates were fairly low. Also prior to the 1930s preferred stock was much more important than it has been since that period. Is there a relation between the rise of corporate income taxes and the decline in importance of preferred stock?

20-4. Describe how each of the following situations would affect the cost of capital to corporations in general.

    a. The federal government solves the problem of business cycles (that is, cyclical stability is increased).

    b. The Federal Reserve Board takes action to lower interest rates.

    c. The cost of floating new stock issues rises.

20-5. The formula $k_r = (D_1/P_0) + g$, where D_1 = expected current dividend, P_0 = the current price of a stock, and g = the past rate of growth in dividends, is sometimes used to estimate k_r, the cost of equity capital. Explain the reasoning behind the formula and this use of it.

20-6. What factors operate to cause the cost of debt to increase with financial leverage?

20-7. Explain the relationship between the required rate of return on common equity (k_r) and the debt ratio.

20-8. How would the various component costs of capital, and the average cost of capital, be likely to change if a firm expands its operations into a new, more risky industry?

20-9. The stock of XYZ Company is currently selling at its low for the year, but management feels that the stock price is only temporarily depressed because of investor pessimism. The firm's capital budget this year is so large that the use of new outside equity is contemplated. However, management does not want to sell new stock at the current low price and is therefore considering a departure from its "optimal" capital structure by borrowing the funds it would otherwise have raised in the equity markets. Does this seem to be a wise move?

20-10. Explain the following statement: "The marginal cost of capital is actually an average cost."

PROBLEMS

20-1. You are planning to form a new company, and several alternative capital structures might be employed. Investment bankers indicate that debt and equity capital would cost the following under different debt ratios (debt/total assets).

Debt Ratio	20% and below	21 to 40%	41 to 50%	51 to 65%
Before-tax cost of debt	8%	9%	11%	14%
Cost of equity capital	12%	13%	18%	25%

    a. Assuming a 40% tax rate, what is the after-tax weighted cost of capital for the following capital structures?

	(1)	(2)	(3)	(4)	(5)	(6)	(7)	(8)
Debt	0	20%	21%	40%	41%	50%	51%	65%
Equity	100%	80%	79%	60%	59%	50%	49%	35%

b. Which capital structure minimizes the weighted average cost of capital?

20-2. On January 1, 1975, the total assets of the Gould Company were $60 million. By the end of the year total assets are expected to be $90 million. The firm's capital structure, shown below, is considered to be optimal. Assume there is no short-term debt.

Debt (6% coupon bonds)	$24,000,000
Preferred stock (7%)	6,000,000
Common equity	30,000,000
	$60,000,000

New bonds will have an 8 percent coupon rate and will be sold at par. Preferred will have a 9 percent rate and will also be sold at par. Common stock, currently selling at $30 a share, can be sold to net the company $27 a share. Stockholders' required rate of return is estimated to be 12 percent, consisting of a dividend yield of 4 percent and an expected growth of 8 percent. Retained earnings are estimated to be $3 million (ignore depreciation). The marginal corporate tax rate is 50 percent.

a. Assuming all asset expansion (gross expenditures for fixed assets plus related working capital) is included in the capital budget, what is the dollar amount of the capital budget? (Ignore depreciation.)

b. To maintain the present capital structure, how much of the capital budget must be financed by equity?

c. How much of the new equity funds needed must be generated internally? externally?

d. Calculate the cost of each of the equity components.

e. At what level of capital expenditures will there be a break in the *MCC* schedule?

f. Calculate the *MCC* (1) below and (2) above the break in the schedule.

g. Plot the *MCC* schedule. Also, draw in an *IRR* schedule that is consistent with the *MCC* schedule and the projected capital budget.

20-3. The Collins Glass Company has the following capital structure as of December 31, 1975:

Debt (6½%)		$12,000,000
Preferred (7½%)		4,000,000
Common stock	$ 4,000,000	
Retained earnings	12,000,000	
Common equity		16,000,000
Total capitalization		$32,000,000

Earnings per share have grown steadily from $0.93 in 1967 to $2 estimated for 1975. The investment community, expecting this growth to continue, applies a price/earnings ratio of 18 to yield a current market price of $36. Collins' last annual dividend was $1.25, and it expects the dividend to grow at the same rate as earnings. The addition to retained earnings for 1975 is projected at $4 million; these funds will be available during the next budget year. The corporate tax rate is 50 percent.

Assuming that the capital structure relations set out above are maintained, new securities can be sold at the following costs:

Bonds: Up to and including $3 million of new bonds, 8 percent yield to investor on all new bonds.

From $3.01 to $6 million of new bonds, 8½ percent yield to investor on this increment of bonds.

Over $6 million of new bonds, 10 percent yield to investor on this increment of bonds.

Preferred: Up to and including $1 million of preferred stock, 8½ percent yield to investor on all new preferred stock.

From $1.01 to $2 million of preferred stock, 9 percent yield to investor on this increment of preferred stock.

Over $2 million of preferred stock, 10 percent yield to investor on this increment of preferred stock.

Common: Up to $4 million of new outside common stock, $36 a share less $2.50 a share flotation cost.

Over $4 million of new outside common stock, $36 a share less $5 a share flotation cost on this increment of new common.

a. At what dollar amounts of new capital will breaks occur in the *MCC?*

b. Calculate the *MCC* in the interval between each of these breaks, then plot the *MCC* schedule.

c. Discuss the breaking points in the marginal cost curve. What factors in the real world would tend to make the marginal cost curve smooth?

d. Assume now that Collins has the following investment opportunities:

1. It can invest any amount up to $4 million at an 11 percent rate of return.
2. It can invest an additional $8 million at a 10.2 percent rate of return.
3. It can invest still another $12 million at a 9.3 percent rate of return.

Thus, Collins' total potential capital budget is $24 million. Determine the size of the company's optimal capital budget for the year.

20-4. The following tabulation gives earnings-per-share figures for Template Manufacturing during the preceding ten years. The firm's common stock, 140,000 shares outstanding, is now selling for $50 a share, and the expected dividend for the current year is 50 percent of the 1975 *EPS.* Investors expect past trends to continue.

Year	EPS
1966	$2.00
1967	2.16
1968	2.33
1969	2.52
1970	2.72
1971	2.94
1972	3.18
1973	3.43
1974	3.70
1975	4.00

New preferred stock paying a $5 dividend could be sold to the public at a price of $52.50, which includes a $2.50 flotation cost (that is, the net price to Template is $50).

The current interest rate on new debt is 8 percent. The firm's marginal tax rate is 40 percent. The firm's capital structure, considered to be optimal, is as follows:

Debt (6%)	$ 2,500,000
Preferred stock (7%)	500,000
Common equity	7,000,000
	$10,000,000

a. Calculate the after-tax cost (1) of new debt, (2) of new preferred stock, and (3) of common equity, assuming new equity comes only from retained earnings. Calculate the cost of equity as $k_r = D_1/P_0 + g$.

b. Find the marginal cost of capital, again assuming no new common stock is sold.

c. How much can be spent for capital investments before external equity must be sold? (Assume that retained earnings available for 1976 investment is 50 percent of 1975 earnings.)

d. What is the marginal cost of capital (cost of funds raised in excess of the amount calculated in part c) if the firm can sell new common stock at $50 a share to net $45 a share? The cost of debt and of preferred stock is constant.

e. In the problem, we assume that the capital structure is optimal. What would happen if the firm deviated from this capital structure? Use a graph to illustrate your answer.

Dividend Policy and Internal Financing

21 Dividend policy determines the division of earnings between payments to stockholders and reinvestment in the firm. Retained earnings are one of the most significant sources of funds for financing corporate growth, but dividends constitute the cash flows that accrue to stockholders. Although both growth and dividends are desirable, these two goals are in conflict—a higher dividend rate means less retained earnings and, consequently, a slower rate of growth in earnings and stock prices. One of the financial manager's most important functions is to determine the allocation of profits between dividends and retained earnings, as this decision can have a critical influence on the value of the firm. The factors that influence the allocation of earnings to dividends or retained earnings are the subject of this chapter.

FACTORS INFLUENCING DIVIDEND POLICY

What factors determine the extent to which a firm will pay out dividends instead of retain earnings? As a first step toward answering this question, we shall consider some of the factors that influence dividend policy.

Legal Rules

Although state statutes and court decisions governing dividend policy are complicated, their essential nature may be stated briefly. The legal rules provide that dividends must be paid from earnings, either from the current year's earnings or from past years' earnings as reflected in the balance sheet account "retained earnings."

463

State laws emphasize three rules: (1) the net profits rule, (2) the capital impairment rule, and (3) the insolvency rule. The *net profits* rule provides that dividends may be paid from past and present earnings. The *capital impairment* rule protects creditors by forbidding the payment of dividends from capital. Paying dividends from capital would be distributing the investment in a company rather than its earnings.[1] The *insolvency* rule provides that corporations may not pay dividends while insolvent. Insolvency is here defined in the bankruptcy sense that liabilities exceed assets, and to pay dividends under such conditions would mean giving stockholders funds that rightfully belong to the creditors.

Legal aspects are significant. They provide the framework within which dividend policies can be formulated. Within these boundaries, however, financial and economic factors have a major influence on policy.

Liquidity Position

Profits held as retained earnings (which show up in the right-hand side of the balance sheet in the account labeled "retained earnings") are generally invested in assets required for the conduct of the business. Retained earnings from preceding years are already invested in plant and equipment, inventories, and other assets; they are not held as cash. Thus, although a firm has had a record of earnings, it may not be able to pay cash dividends because of its liquidity position. Indeed, a growing firm, even a very profitable one, typically has a pressing need for funds. In such a situation the firm may elect not to pay cash dividends.

If this point is not clear, refer back to Table 3–1, the Walker-Wilson Company's balance sheet. The retained earnings account shows $400,000, but the cash account shows only $50,000. Since some cash must be retained to pay bills, it is clear that Walker-Wilson's cash position precludes a dividend of even $50,000.

Need to Repay Debt

When a firm has sold debt to finance expansion or to substitute for other forms of financing, it is faced with two alternatives: it can refund the debt at maturity by replacing it with another form of security, or it can make provision for paying off the debt. If the decision is to retire the debt, this will generally require the retention of earnings.

---

[1] It is possible, of course, to return stockholders' capital; when this is done, however, it must be clearly stated as such. A dividend paid out of capital is called a *liquidating* dividend.

Restrictions in Debt Contracts

Debt contracts, particularly when long-term debt is involved, frequently restrict a firm's ability to pay cash dividends. Such restrictions, which are designed to protect the position of the lender, usually state (1) that future dividends can be paid only out of earnings generated *after* the signing of the loan agreement (that is, future dividends cannot be paid out of past retained earnings), and (2) that dividends cannot be paid when net working capital (current assets minus current liabilities) is below a specified amount. Similarly, preferred stock agreements generally state that no cash dividends can be paid on the common stock until all accrued preferred dividends have been paid.

Rate of Asset Expansion

The more rapid the rate at which the firm is growing, the greater will be its needs for financing asset expansion. The greater the future need for funds, the more likely the firm is to retain earnings rather than pay them out.

Profit Rate

The rate of return on assets determines the relative attractiveness of paying out earnings in the form of dividends to stockholders who will use them elsewhere, compared with the productivity of their use in the present enterprise.

Stability of Earnings

If earnings are relatively stable, a firm is better able to predict what its future earnings will be. A stable firm is therefore more likely to pay out a higher percentage of its earnings than is a firm with fluctuating earnings. The unstable firm is not certain that in subsequent years the hoped-for earnings will be realized, so it is more likely to retain a high proportion of earnings in order to maintain dividends if earnings should fall off in the future.

Access to the Capital Markets

A large, well-established firm with a record of profitability and some stability of earnings will have easy access to capital markets and other forms of external financing. The small, new, or venturesome firm, however, is riskier for potential investors. Its ability to raise equity or debt funds from capital markets is restricted, and it must retain more earnings to finance its operations. A well-established firm is thus likely to have a higher dividend payout rate than is a new or small firm.

Control

Another important variable is the effect of alternative sources of financing on the control situation in the firm. Some corporations, as a matter of policy, will expand only to the extent of their internal earnings. This policy is defended on the grounds that raising funds by selling additional common stock dilutes the control of the dominant group in the company. At the same time, selling debt increases the risks of fluctuating earnings to the present owners of the company. Reliance on internal financing in order to maintain control reduces the dividend payout.

Tax Position of Stockholders

The tax position of the owners of the corporation greatly influences the desire for dividends. For example, a corporation closely held by a few taxpayers in high income tax brackets is likely to pay a relatively low dividend. The owners of the corporation are interested in taking their income in the form of capital gains rather than as dividends, which are subject to higher personal income tax rates. However, the stockholders of a large, widely held corporation may be interested in a high dividend payout.

At times there is a conflict of interest in large corporations between stockholders in high income tax brackets and those in low tax brackets. The former may prefer to see a low dividend payout and a high rate of earnings retention in the hope of an appreciation in the capital stock of the company. The lower income stockholders may prefer a relatively high dividend payout rate. The dividend policy of such a firm may be a compromise between a low and a high payout—an intermediate payout ratio. If, however, one group dominates and sets, let us say, a low payout policy, those stockholders who seek income are likely to sell their shares over time and shift into higher yielding stocks. *Thus, to at least some extent, a firm's payout policy determines its stockholder types, as well as vice versa.*

Tax on Improperly Accumulated Earnings

In order to prevent wealthy stockholders from using the corporation as an "incorporated pocketbook" by which they can avoid the high rates of personal income tax, tax regulations applicable to corporations provide for a special surtax on improperly accumulated income. However, Section 531 of the Revenue Act of 1954 places the burden of proof on the Internal Revenue Service to justify penalty rates for accumulation of earnings. That is, earnings retention is justified unless the Internal Revenue Service can prove otherwise.

DIVIDEND POLICY DECISIONS

A fundamental relation observed in dividend policy is the widespread tendency of corporations to pursue a relatively stable dividend policy. Profits of firms fluctuate considerably with changes in the level of business activity, but Figure 21–1 shows that dividends are more stable than earnings.

FIGURE 21–1   Corporate Earnings after Taxes and Dividends

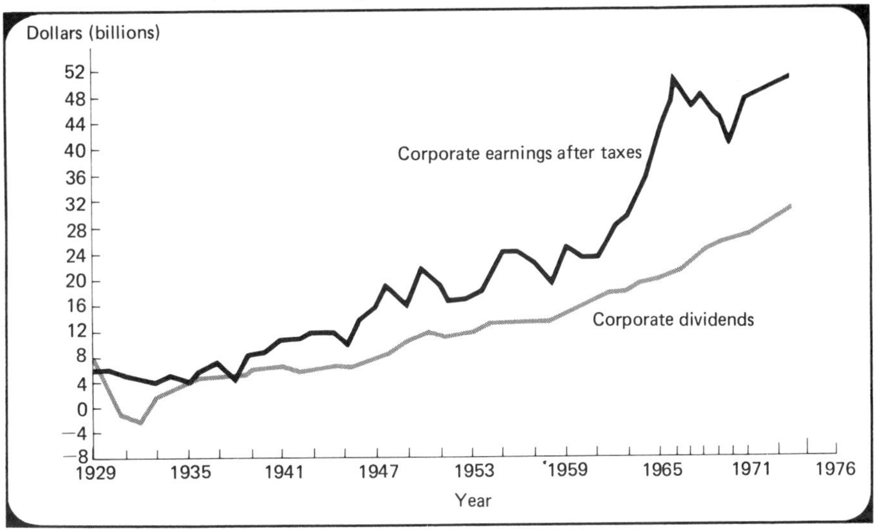

Source: Economic Report of the President, 1976

Most corporations seek to maintain a target dividend per share. However, dividends increase with a lag after earnings rise. Dividends are increased only after an increase in earnings appears clearly sustainable and relatively permanent. When dividends have been increased, strenuous efforts are made to maintain them at the new level. If earnings decline, the existing dividend will generally be maintained until it is clear that an earnings recovery will not take place.

Figure 21–2 illustrates these ideas by showing the earnings and dividends patterns for the Walter Watch Company over a thirty-year period. Initially, earnings are $2 and dividends $1 a share, providing a 50 percent payout ratio. Earnings rise for four years, while dividends remain constant; thus, the payout ratio falls during this period. During 1955 and 1956, earnings fall substantially; however, the dividend is maintained and the payout rises above the 50 percent target. During the period between 1956 and 1960, earnings experience a sustained rise. Dividends are held constant for a time, while management seeks to determine whether the earnings increase is permanent. By 1961, the earnings gain seems permanent, and dividends are raised in three steps to reestablish the 50 percent target payout. During 1965 a strike causes earnings to fall below the regular dividend; expecting the earnings decline to be temporary, management maintains the dividend. Earnings fluctuate on a fairly high plateau from 1966 through 1972, during which time dividends remain constant. A new increase in earnings induces management to raise the dividend in 1973 to reestablish the 50 percent payout ratio.

FIGURE 21–2 Dividends and Earnings Patterns, Walter Watch Company

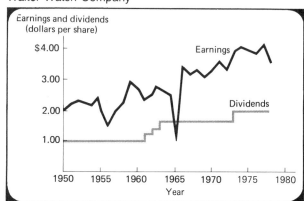

RATIONALE FOR STABLE DIVIDENDS

Walter Watch, like the great majority of firms, kept its dividend at a relatively steady dollar amount but allowed its payout ratio to fluctuate. Why would it follow such a policy?

Consider the stable dividend policy from the standpoint of the stockholders as owners of a company. Their acquiescence with the general practice must imply that stable dividend policies lead to higher stock prices on the average than do alternative dividend policies. Is this a fact? Does a stable dividend policy maximize equity values for a corporation? There has been no truly conclusive empirical study of dividend policy, so any answer to the question must be regarded as tentative. On logical grounds, however, there is reason to believe that a stable dividend policy will lead to higher stock prices. First, investors might be expected to value more highly dividends they are more sure of receiving, since fluctuating dividends are riskier than stable dividends. Accordingly, the same average amount of dividends received under a fluctuating dividend policy is likely to have a higher discount factor applied to it than is applied to dividends under a stable dividend policy. In the terms used in Chapter 20, this means that a firm with a stable dividend would have a lower required rate of return—or cost of equity capital—than one whose dividends fluctuate.

Second, many stockholders live on income received in the form of dividends. Such stockholders would be greatly inconvenienced by fluctuating dividends, and they would likely pay a premium for a stock with a relatively assured minimum dollar dividend.

A third advantage of a stable dividend from the standpoint of a corporation and its stockowners is the requirement of *legal listing.* Legal lists are lists of securities in which mutual savings banks, pension funds, insurance companies, and other fiduciary institutions are permitted to invest. One of the criteria for placing a stock on the legal list is that dividend payments be maintained. Thus, legal listing encourages pursuance of a stable dividend policy.

On the other hand, if a firm's investment opportunities fluctuate from year to year, should it not retain more earnings during some years in order to take advantage of these opportunities when they appear, then increase dividends when good internal investment opportunities are scarce? This line of reasoning would lead to the recommendation of a fluctuating payout for companies whose investment opportunities are unstable. However, the logic of the argument is diminished by recognizing that it is possible to maintain a reasonably stable dividend by using outside financing, especially debt, to smooth out the differences between the funds needed for investment and the amount of money provided by retained earnings.

ALTERNATIVE DIVIDEND POLICIES

Before going on to consider dividend policy at a theoretical level, it is useful to summarize the three major types of dividend policies.

Stable Dollar Amount per Share   The policy of a stable dollar amount per share, followed by most firms, is the policy that is implied when we say "stable dividend policy."

Constant Payout Ratio   A very few firms follow a policy of paying out a constant percentage of earnings. Earnings will surely fluctuate, so following this policy necessarily means that the dollar amount of dividends will fluctuate. For reasons discussed in the preceding section, this policy is not likely to maximize the value of a firm's stock. Before its bankruptcy, Penn-Central Railroad followed the policy of paying out one-half its earnings: "A dollar for the stockholders and a dollar for the company," as one director put it.

Low Regular Dividend plus Extras   The low-regular-dividend-plus-extras policy is a compromise between the first two. It gives the firm flexibility, but it leaves investors somewhat uncertain about what their dividend income will be. However, if a firm's earnings are quite volatile, this policy may well be its best choice.

The relative merits of these three policies can be evaluated better after a discussion of the residual theory of dividends, the topic covered in the next section.

RESIDUAL THEORY OF DIVIDENDS[2]

In the preceding chapters on capital budgeting and the cost of capital, we indicated that, generally, the cost of capital schedule and the investment opportunity schedule must be combined before the cost of capital can be established. In other words, the optimum capital budget, the marginal cost of capital, and the marginal rate of return on investment are determined *simultaneously*. In this section we examine this simultaneous solution in the framework of what is called *the residual theory of dividends*. The theory draws on materials developed earlier in the book—capital budgeting and the cost of capital—and serves to provide a bridge between these key concepts.

The starting point in the theory is that investors prefer to have the firm retain and reinvest earnings rather than pay them out in dividends *if the return on reinvested earnings exceeds the rate of return the investor could, himself, obtain on other investments of comparable risk.* If the corporation can reinvest retained earnings at a 20 percent rate of return, while the best rate the stockholder can obtain if the earnings are passed on to him in the form of dividends is 10 percent, then the stockholder would prefer to have the firm retain the profits.

We saw in Chapter 20 that the cost of equity capital obtained from retained earnings is an *opportunity cost* that reflects rates of return open to equity investors. If a firm's stockholders could buy other stocks of equal risk and obtain a 10 percent dividends-plus-capital-gains yield, then 10 percent is the firm's cost of retained earnings. The cost of new outside equity raised by selling common stock is higher because of the costs of floating the issue.

Most firms have an optimum debt ratio that calls for at least some debt, so new financing is done partly with debt and partly with equity. Debt has a different, and generally lower, cost than equity, so the two forms of capital must be combined to find the *weighted average cost of capital*. As long as the firm finances at the optimum point, using an optimum amount of debt and equity, and provided it uses only internally generated equity (retained earnings), its marginal cost of each new dollar of capital will be minimized.

Internally generated equity is available for financing a certain amount of new investment; beyond this amount, the firm must turn to more expensive new common stock. At the point where new stock must be sold, the cost of equity and, consequently, the marginal cost of capital, rises.

These concepts, which were developed in Chapter 20, are illustrated in Figure 21–3. The firm has a marginal cost of capital of 10 percent so long as retained earnings are available; the marginal cost of capital begins to rise when new stock must be sold.

---

[2]"Residual" implies *left over*. The residual theory of dividend policy implies that dividends are paid after internal investment opportunities have been exhausted.

FIGURE 21–3 The Marginal Cost of Capital

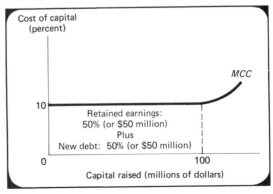

Our hypothetical firm has $50 million of earnings and a 50 percent optimum debt ratio. It can make net investments (investments in addition to asset replacements financed from depreciation) up to $100 million: $50 million from retained earnings plus $50 million new debt supported by the retained earnings if it does not pay dividends. Therefore, its marginal cost of capital is constant at 10 percent for up to $100 million of capital. Beyond $100 million, the marginal cost of capital begins rising as the firm begins to use more expensive new common stock.

Next, suppose the firm's capital budgeting department draws up a list of investment opportunities, ranked in the order of each project's *IRR*, and plots them on a graph. The investment opportunity curves of three different years—one for a good year (IRR_1), one for a normal year (IRR_2), and one for a bad year (IRR_3)—are shown in Figure 21–4. IRR_1 shows that the firm can invest more money, and at higher rates of return, than it can when the investment opportunities are those given in IRR_2 and IRR_3.

FIGURE 21–4 Investment Opportunities

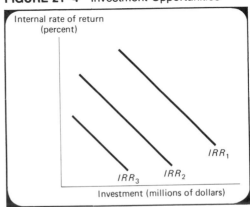

Now we combine the investment opportunity schedule with the cost of capital schedule; this is done in Figure 21–5. The point where the investment opportunity curve cuts the cost of capital curve defines the proper level of new investment. When investment opportunities are relatively poor, the optimum level of investment is $25 million; when opportunities are about normal, $75 million should be invested; and when opportunities are relatively good, the firm should make new investments in the amount of $125 million.

FIGURE 21–5   Interrelation among Cost of Capital, Investment Opportunities, and New Investment

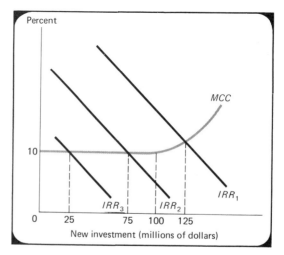

Consider the situation where IRR_1 is the appropriate schedule. Suppose the firm has $50 million in earnings and a 50 percent target debt ratio, so it can finance $100 million, $50 million earnings plus $50 million debt, from retained earnings plus new debt *if it retains all its earnings.* If it pays part of the earnings in dividends, then it will have to begin using expensive new common stock sooner, so the cost of capital curve will rise sooner. This suggests that under the conditions of IRR_1 the firm should retain all its earnings and actually sell some new common stock in order to take advantage of its investment opportunities. Its payout ratio would thus be zero percent.

Under the conditions of IRR_2, however, the firm should invest only $75 million. How should this investment be financed? First, notice that if it retains the full amount of its earnings, $50 million, it will need to sell only $25 million of new debt. However, by retaining $50 million and selling only $25 million of new debt, the firm will move away from its target capital structure. To stay on target, the firm must finance the required $75 million half by equity (retained earnings) and half by debt, or $37.5 million by retained earnings and $37.5 million by debt. Now if the firm has $50 million in total earnings and decides to retain and reinvest $37.5 million, it must distribute the $12.5 million residual to its stockholders. In this case, the payout ratio is 25 percent ($12.5 million divided by $50 million).

Finally, under the bad conditions of IRR_3, the firm should invest only $25 million. Because it has $50 million in earnings, it could finance the entire $25 million out of retained earnings and still have $25 million available for dividends. Should this be done? Under the assumptions, this would not be a good decision, because it would move the firm away from its target debt ratio. To stay in the 50-50 debt/equity position, the firm must retain $12.5 million and sell $12.5 million of debt. When the $12.5 million of retained earnings is subtracted from the $50 million of earnings, the firm is left with a residual of $37.5, the amount that should be paid out in dividends. In this case the payout ratio is 75 percent.

LONG-RUN VIEWPOINT

There seems to be a conflict between the residual theory and the statement made in an earlier section that firms should and do maintain reasonably stable cash dividends. How can this conflict be reconciled?

Actually, the reconciliation is quite simple if we recognize that the theory is not meant to be applied *exactly*. In other words, we would not recommend that a firm adjust its dividend each and every year—indeed, this is not necessary. Firms do have target debt ratios, but they also have a certain amount of flexibility—they can be moderately above or below the target debt position in any one year with no serious adverse consequences. This means that if an unusually large number of good investments are available in a particular year, the firm does not necessarily have to cut its dividend to take advantage of them—it can borrow somewhat more heavily than usual in that particular year without getting its debt ratio too far out of line. Obviously, however, this excessive reliance on debt could not continue for too many years without seriously affecting the debt ratio, necessitating either a sale of new stock or a cut in dividends and an attendant increase in the level of retained earnings.

HIGH AND LOW DIVIDEND PAYOUT INDUSTRIES

Some industries are experiencing rapid growth in the demand for their products, affording firms in these industries with many good investment opportunities. Electronics, office equipment, and entertainment are examples of such industries in recent years. Other industries have experienced much slower growth, or perhaps even declines. Examples of such slow-growth industries are cigarette manufacturing and textiles. Still other industries are growing at about the same rate as the general economy—oil, steel, and banking are representative.

The theory suggests that firms in rapidly growing industries should generally have *IRR* curves that are relatively far out to the right on graphs such as Figure 21–5; for example, Xerox, Polaroid, and IBM might have investment opportunities similar to IRR_1. The tobacco companies, on the other hand, could be expected to have investment schedules similar to IRR_3, while IRR_2 might be appropriate for Union Carbide and U.S. Steel.

Each of these firms would, of course, experience shifts in investment opportunities from year to year, but the curves would *tend* to be in about the same part of the graph. In other words, firms such as Xerox would *tend* to have more investment opportunities than money, so they would *tend* to have zero (or very low) payout ratios. Reynolds Tobacco, on the other hand, would *tend* to have more money than good investments, so we would expect to find Reynolds paying out a relatively high percentage of earnings in dividends. These companies do, in fact, conform with our expectations.

CONFLICTING THEORIES ON DIVIDENDS

Two basic schools of thought on dividend policy have been expressed in the theoretical literature of finance. One school, associated with Myron Gordon and John Lintner, among others, holds that the capital gains expected to result from earnings retention are more risky than are dividend expectations. Accordingly, this school suggests that the earnings of a firm with a low-payout ratio will typically be capitalized at higher rates than the earnings of a high-payout firm, other things held constant.

The other school, associated with Merton Miller and Franco Modigliani, holds that investors are basically indifferent to returns in the form of dividends or of capital gains. Empirically, when firms raise or lower their dividends, their stock prices tend to rise or fall in like manner; does this not prove that investors prefer dividends? Miller and Modigliani argue that it does not, that any effect a change in dividends has on the price of a firm's stock is related primarily to *information about expected future earnings conveyed by a change in dividends.* Recalling that corporate managements dislike cutting dividends, Miller and Modigliani argue that increases in cash dividends raise expectations about the level of future earnings—dividend increases have favorable *information content.* In terms of Figure 21–2, Miller and Modigliani would say that Walter Watch's dividend increases in 1961, 1962, 1963, and 1973 had information content about future earnings—these dividend increases signaled to stockholders that management expected the recent earnings increases to be permanent.

Dividends are probably subject to less uncertainty than capital gains, but dividends are taxed at a higher rate than capital gains. How do these two forces balance out? Some argue that the uncertainty factor dominates; others feel that the differential tax rate is the stronger force and causes investors to favor corporate retention of earnings; still others—and we put ourselves in this group—argue that it is difficult to generalize. Depending on the tax status and the current income needs of its set of stockholders (both brokerage costs and capital gains taxes make it difficult for individual stockholders to shift companies), as well as the firm's internal investment opportunities, the optimum dividend policy will vary from firm to firm.

DIVIDEND PAYMENTS

Dividends are normally paid quarterly. For example, AT&T paid dividends of $3.80 during 1975, 95 cents each quarter. In common financial language, we say that AT&T's *regular quarterly dividend* is 95 cents, or that its *regular annual dividend* is $3.80. The management of a company such as AT&T, sometimes by an explicit statement in the annual report and sometimes by implication, conveys to stockholders an expectation that the regular dividend will be maintained if at all possible. Further, management conveys its belief that earnings will be sufficient to maintain the dividend.

Under other conditions, a firm's cash flows and investment needs may be too volatile for it to set a very high regular dividend; on the average, however, it needs a high dividend payout to dispose of funds not necessary for reinvestment. In such a case, the directors can set a relatively low regular dividend—low enough that it can be maintained even in low profit years or in years when a considerable amount of reinvestment is needed—and supplement it with an extra dividend in years when excess funds are available. General Motors, whose earnings fluctuate widely from year to year, has long followed the practice of supplementing its regular dividend with an *extra dividend* paid at the end of the year, when its profits and investment requirements are known.

PAYMENT PROCEDURE

The actual payment procedure is of some importance, and the following is an outline of the payment sequence.

1. *Declaration Date.* The directors meet, say on November 15, and declare the regular dividend. On this date, the directors issue a statement similar to the following: "On November 15, 1977, the directors of the XYZ Company met and declared the regular quarterly dividend of 50 cents a share, plus an extra dividend of 75 cents a share, to holders of record on December 15, payment to be made on January 2, 1978."

2. *Holder-of-Record Date.* On December 15, the *holder-of-record date,* the company closes its stock transfer books and makes up a list of the shareholders as of that date. If XYZ Company is notified of the sale and transfer

of some stock on or before December 15, the new owner receives the dividend. If notification is received on or after December 16, the old stockholder gets the dividend.

3. *Ex Dividend Date.* Suppose Edward Johns buys 100 shares of stock from Robert Noble on December 13; will the company be notified of the transfer in time to list Johns as the new owner and, thus, pay the dividend to him? To avoid conflict, the stock brokerage business has set up a convention of declaring that the right to the dividend remains with the stock until four days prior to the holder-of-record date; on the fourth day before the record date, the right to the dividend no longer goes with the shares. The date when the right to the dividend leaves the stock is called the *ex dividend date.*

In this case, the ex dividend date is four days prior to December 15, or December 11. Therefore, if Johns is to receive the dividend, he must buy the stock by December 10. If he buys it on December 11 or later, Noble will receive the dividend.

The total dividend, regular plus extra, amounts to $1.25, so the ex dividend date is important. Barring fluctuations in the stock market, we would normally expect the price of a stock to drop by approximately the amount of the dividend on the ex dividend date.

4. *Payment Date.* The company actually mails the checks to the holders of record on January 2, the payment date.

STOCK DIVIDENDS AND STOCK SPLITS

One of the significant aspects of dividend policy is that of *stock dividends* and *stock splits.* A *stock dividend* is paid in additional shares of stock instead of in cash and simply involves a bookkeeping transfer from retained earnings to the capital stock account.[3] In a *stock split* there is no change in the capital accounts. A larger number of shares of common stock is issued. In a two-for-one split, each stockholder would receive two shares for each one previously held. Book value per share would be cut in half. The par, or stated, value per share of common stock is similarly changed. From a practical standpoint there is little difference between a stock dividend and a stock split. Since the two are similar, the issues outlined below are discussed in connection with both stock dividends and stock splits.

---

[3]One point that should be made in connection with stock dividends is that the transfer from retained earnings to the capital stock account must be based on market value. In other words, if a firm's shares are selling for $100 and it has 1,000,000 shares outstanding, a 10 percent stock dividend requires the transfer of $10 million (100,000 × $100) from retained earnings to capital stock. Quite obviously, stock dividends are thus limited by the size of retained earnings. The rule was put into effect to prevent the declaration of stock dividends unless the firm has had earnings. This is another in a long series of rulings designed to prevent investors from being fooled by the practices of unscrupulous firms.

Price Effects

The results of a careful empirical study of the effects of stock dividends are available and can be used as a basis for observations on the price effects of stock dividends.[4] The findings of the study are presented in Table 21–1. When stock dividends were associated with a cash dividend increase, the value of the company's stock six months after the ex dividend date had risen by 8 percent. On the other hand, where stock dividends were not accompanied by cash dividend increases, stock values fell by 12 percent during the subsequent six-month period.

TABLE 21–1   Price Effects of Stock Dividends

	Price at Selected Dates (in Percentages)		
	Six Months Prior to ex Dividend Date	At ex Dividend Date	Six Months after ex Dividend Date
Cash dividend increase	100	109	108
No cash dividend increase	100	99	88

These data seem to suggest that stock dividends are seen for what they are—simply additional pieces of paper—and that they do not represent true income. When they are accompanied by higher earnings and cash dividends, investors bid up the value of the stock. However, when stock dividends are not accompanied by increases in earnings and cash dividends, the dilution of earnings and dividends per share causes the price of the stock to drop. The fundamental determinant is underlying earnings and dividend trends.

Effects on Extent of Ownership

Table 21–2 shows the effect of stock dividends on common stock ownership. Large stock dividends resulted in the largest percentage increases in stock ownership. The use of stock dividends increased shareholders by 25 percent on the average. For companies and industries that did not offer stock splits or stock dividends, the increase in ownership was only 5 percent. Furthermore, the degree of increase in ownership increased with the size of the stock dividend.

---

[4]C. A. Barker, "Evaluation of Stock Dividends," *Harvard Business Review,* 36 (July–August 1958), 99–114. Reprinted by permission. Barker's study has been replicated several times in recent years, but his results are still valid—they have withstood the test of time.

TABLE 21–2 Effect of Stock Dividends on Stock Ownership

	Percentage Increase in Stockholders, 1950–1953
Stock dividend, 25% and over	30
Stock dividend, 5–25%	17
All stock dividends	25
No stock dividends or splits	5

Source: C. Austin Barker, "Evaluation of Stock Dividends," *Harvard Business Review,* 36 (July–August 1958), 99–114. Reprinted by permission.

This evidence suggests that stock dividends increase share ownership. Regardless of the effect on the total market value of the firm, the use of stock dividends and stock splits effectively increases stock ownership by lowering the price at which shares are traded to a more popular range.

STOCK REPURCHASES AS AN ALTERNATIVE TO DIVIDENDS[5]

Treasury stock is the name given to common stock that has been repurchased by the issuing firm, and the acquisition of treasury stock represents an alternative to the payment of dividends. If some of the outstanding stock is repurchased, fewer shares will remain outstanding; and assuming the repurchase does not adversely affect the firm's earnings, the earnings per share of the remaining shares will increase. This increase in earnings per share should result in a higher market price per share, so capital gains will have been substituted for dividends. These effects can be seen from the following example.

Example

American Development Corporation (ADC) earned $4.4 million in 1977; of this amount, 50 percent, or $2.2 million, has been allocated for distribution to common shareholders. There are currently 1,100,000 shares outstanding, and the market value is $20 a share. ADC can use the $2.2 million to repurchase 100,000 of its shares through a tender offer for $22 a share, or it can pay a cash dividend of $2 a share.[6]

---

[5] This section is relatively technical and may be omitted without loss of continuity.

[6] Stock repurchases are commonly made in three ways. First, a publicly owned firm can simply buy its own stock through a broker on the open market. Second, it can issue a *tender* under which it permits stockholders to send in (that is, "tender") their shares to the firm in exchange for a specified price per share. When tender offers are made, the firm generally indicates that it will buy up to a specified number of shares within a specified time period (usually about two weeks); if more shares are tendered than the company wishes to purchase, then purchases are made on a pro rata basis. Finally, the firm can purchase a block of shares from one large holder on a negotiated basis. If the latter procedure is employed, care must be taken to insure that this one stockholder does not receive preferential treatment not available to other stockholders.

The effect of the repurchase on the *EPS* and market price per share of the remaining stock can be determined in the following way:

1. Current *EPS* $= \dfrac{\text{total earnings}}{\text{number of shares}} = \dfrac{\$4.4 \text{ million}}{1.1 \text{ million}}$

$= \$4$ per share.

2. Current *P/E* ratio $= \dfrac{\$20}{\$4} = 5\text{X}.$

3. *EPS* after repurchase of 100,000 shares $= \dfrac{\$4.4 \text{ million}}{1 \text{ million}} = \$4.40$ per share.

4. Expected market price after repurchase $= (P/E)(EPS) = (5)(\$4.40) = \$22$ per share.

It should be noticed from this example that investors would receive benefits of $2 a share in any case, either in the form of a $2 cash dividend or a $2 increase in stock price. This result occurs because we assumed (1) that shares could be repurchased at exactly $22 a share and (2) that the *P/E* ratio would remain constant. If shares could be bought for less than $22, the operation would be even better for *remaining* stockholders, but the reverse would hold if ADC paid more than $22 a share. Furthermore, the *P/E* ratio might change as a result of the repurchase operation, rising if investors view it favorably, falling if they view it unfavorably. Some factors that might affect *P/E* ratios are considered next.

Advantages of Repurchases from the Stockholder's Viewpoint

1. Profits earned on repurchases are taxed at the capital gains rate, whereas a dividend distribution would be taxed at the stockholder's marginal tax rate. This is significant. For example, it has been estimated that, on the average, stockholders pay a tax of about 45 percent on marginal income. Since the capital gains tax rate is generally only one-half the ordinary tax rate, the typical shareholder would clearly benefit, other things the same, if the distribution is in the form of a stock repurchase rather than a dividend.
2. The stockholder has a choice: He can either sell or not sell. On the other hand, with a dividend, he has to accept the payment and pay the tax.
3. A qualitative advantage advanced by market practitioners is that repurchase can often remove a large block of stock overhanging the market.

Advantages of Repurchases from Management's Viewpoint

1. Studies have shown that dividends are *sticky* in the short run because managements are reluctant to raise dividends if the new dividend cannot be maintained in the future. Managements dislike cutting cash dividends, so they are reluctant to raise dividends if they are not confident that the

dividend can be maintained in the future. Hence, if the excess cash flow is thought to be only *temporary*, management may prefer to "conceal" the distribution in the form of share repurchases rather than to declare a cash dividend they believe cannot be maintained.

2. Repurchased stock can be used for acquisitions or released when stock options are exercised. Discussions with financial managers indicate that it is frequently more convenient and less expensive to use repurchased stock than newly issued stock for these purposes, and also when convertibles are converted or warrants exercised.

3. If directors have large holdings themselves, they may have especially strong preferences for repurchases rather than dividend payments because of the tax factor.

4. One interesting use of stock repurchases was Standard Products' strategy of repurchasing its own stock to thwart an attempted takeover. Defiance Industries, Inc., attempted to acquire a controlling interest in Standard Products through a tender offer of $15 a share. Standard's management countered with a tender offer of its own at $17.25 a share, financed by $1.725 million in internal funds and by $3.525 million in long-term debt. This kept stockholders from accepting the outside tender offer and enabled Standard Products' management to retain control.

5. Repurchases can be used to effect large-scale changes in capital structure. For example, at one time American Standard had virtually no long-term debt outstanding. The company decided that its optimal capital structure called for the use of considerably more debt, but even if it financed *only* with debt it would have taken years to get the debt ratio up to the newly defined optimal level. What could the company do? It sold an issue of long-term debt and used the proceeds to repurchase its common stock, thus producing an instantaneous change in its capital structure.

6. Treasury stock can be resold in the open market if the firm needs additional funds.

Disadvantages of Repurchases from the Stockholder's Viewpoint

1. Stockholders may not be indifferent between dividends and capital gains, and the price of the stock might benefit more from cash dividends than from repurchases. Cash dividends are generally thought of as being relatively dependable, but repurchases are not. Further, if a firm announces a regular, dependable repurchase program, the improper accumulation tax discussed below would probably become more of a threat.

2. The *selling* stockholders may not be fully aware of all the implications of a repurchase or may not have all pertinent information about the corporation's present and future activities. For this reason, firms generally announce a repurchase program before embarking on it.

3. The corporation may pay too high a price for the repurchased stock, to the disadvantage of remaining stockholders. If the shares are inactive and if the firm seeks to acquire a relatively large amount of its stock, the price may be bid above a maintainable price and then fall after the firm ceases its repurchase operations.

Disadvantages of Repurchases from Management's Viewpoint

1. Studies have shown that firms which repurchase substantial amounts of stock have poorer growth rates and investment opportunities than ones that do not. Thus, some people feel that announcing a repurchase program is like announcing that management cannot locate good investment projects. One could argue that instituting a repurchase program should be regarded in the same manner as announcing a higher dividend payout, but if repurchases are regarded as indicating especially unfavorable growth opportunities, then repurchases can have an adverse impact on the firm's image, and also on the price of its stock.
2. Repurchases might involve some risk from a legal standpoint. If the Internal Revenue Service can establish that the repurchases are primarily for the avoidance of taxes on dividends, then penalties may be imposed on the firm under the improper accumulation of earnings provision of the tax code. Actions have been brought against privately held companies under Section 531, but we know of no case where such an action has been brought against a publicly owned firm, even though some firms have retired over one-half their outstanding stock. Also, the SEC may raise serious questions if it appears that the firm may be manipulating the price of its shares.

Conclusion on Stock Repurchases

When all the pros and the cons on stock repurchases are totaled, where do we stand? Our own conclusions may be summarized as follows:

1. Repurchases on a regular, systematic, dependable basis, like quarterly dividends, are not feasible because of uncertainties about the tax treatment of such a program and uncertainties about such things as the market price of the shares, how many shares would be tendered, and so forth.
2. However, repurchases do offer some significant advantages over dividends, so this procedure should be given careful consideration on the basis of the firm's own unique situation.
3. Repurchases can be especially valuable to effect a significant shift in capital structure within a short period.

SUMMARY

Dividend policy determines the extent of internal financing by a firm. The financial manager decides whether to release corporate earnings from the control of the enterprise. Because dividend policy affects the financial structure, the flow of funds, corporate liquidity, stock prices, and investor satisfaction—to list a few ramifications—it is clearly an important aspect of financial management.

In theory, once the firm's debt policy and cost of capital have been determined, dividend policy should automatically follow. Under our theoretical model, dividends are simply a residual after investment needs have been met; if this policy is followed and if investors are indifferent to receiving their investment returns in the form of dividends or of capital gains, stockholders are better off than they are under any other possible dividend policy. However, the financial manager simply does not have all the information assumed in the theory, and rule-of-thumb guidelines are needed.

As a guide to financial managers responsible for dividend policy, the following check list summarizes the major economic and financial factors influencing dividend policy:

1. Rate of growth and profit level.
2. Stability of earnings.
3. Age and size of firm.
4. Cash position.
5. Need to repay debt.
6. Control.
7. Maintenance of a target dividend.
8. Tax position of stockholders.
9. Tax position of the corporation: improper accumulation.

Of the factors listed, some lead to higher dividend payouts, some to lower payouts. It is not possible to provide a formula that can be used to establish the proper dividend payout for a given situation; this is a task requiring the exercise of judgment. The considerations summarized above provide a check list for guiding dividend decisions.

Empirical studies indicate a wide diversity of dividend payout ratios not only among industries but also among firms in the same industry. Studies also show that dividends are more stable than earnings. Firms are reluctant to raise dividends in years of good earnings, and they resist dividend cuts as earnings decline. In view of investors' observed preference for stable dividends and of the probability that a cut in dividends is likely to be interpreted as forecasting a decline in earnings, stable dividends make good sense.

Stock Dividends and Splits   Neither stock dividends nor stock splits alone exert a fundamental influence on prices. The fundamental determinant of the price of the company's stock is the company's earning power compared with the earning power of other companies. However, both stock splits and stock dividends can be used as an effective instrument of financial policy. They are useful devices for reducing the price at which stocks are traded, and studies indicate that stock dividends and stock splits tend to broaden the ownership of a firm's shares.

Stock Repurchases   Stock repurchases have been used as an alternative to cash dividends. Although repurchases have significant advantages over dividends, they also have disadvantages, in particular the fact that stock repurchases necessarily involve greater uncertainty than cash dividends. As with so much in finance, generalizations about stock repurchases are difficult—each firm has its own unique problems and conditions, and repurchase policy must be formulated within the context of the firm as a whole.

QUESTIONS

21-1. As an investor, would you rather invest in a firm with a policy of maintaining (a) a constant payout ratio, (b) a constant dollar dividend per share, or (c) a constant regular quarterly dividend plus a year-end extra when earnings are sufficiently high or corporate investment needs are sufficiently low? Explain your answer.

21-2. How would each of the following changes probably affect aggregate payout *ratios?* Explain your answer.
   a. An increase in the personal income tax rate.
   b. A liberalization in depreciation policies for federal income tax purposes.
   c. A rise in interest rates.
   d. An increase in corporate profits.
   e. A decline in investment opportunities.

21-3. Discuss the pros and cons of having the directors formally announce what a firm's dividend policy will be in the future.

21-4. Most firms would like to have their stock selling at a high P/E ratio and also have an extensive public ownership (many different shareholders). Explain how stock dividends or stock splits may be compatible with these aims.

21-5. What is the difference between a stock dividend and a stock split? As a stockholder, would you prefer to see your company declare a 100 percent stock dividend or a two-for-one split?

21-6. In theory, if we had perfect capital markets, we would expect investors to be indifferent between cash dividends and an equivalent repurchase of stock outstanding. What factors might in practice cause investors to value one over the other?

21-7. "The cost of retained earnings is less than the cost of new outside equity capital. Consequently, it is totally irrational for a firm to sell a new issue of stock and to pay dividends during the same year." Discuss this statement.

21-8. Would it ever be rational for a firm to borrow money in order to pay dividends? Explain.

21-9. Union spokesmen have presented arguments similar to the following: "Corporations such as General Foods retain about one-half their profits for financing needs. If they financed by selling stock instead of by retained earnings, they could cut prices substantially and still earn enough to pay the same dividend to their shareholders. Therefore, their profits are too high." Evaluate this statement.

21-10. "Executive salaries have been shown to be more closely correlated to size of firm than to profitability. If a firm's board of directors is controlled by management instead of by outside directors, this might result in the firm's retaining more earnings than can be justified from the stockholders' point of view." Discuss the statement, being sure (a) to use Figure 21–5 in your answer and (b) to explain the implied relationship between dividend policy and stock prices.

PROBLEMS

21-1. Precision Instruments is currently earning $4 per share. The rate of return required by its shareholders, k_s, is 10 percent and the current market price is $40 per share. The company has experienced approximately a 3 percent growth in earnings, dividends, and market value over the past several years, and it is expected that this growth rate will continue. Using the constant growth stock valuation model, calculate the dividend anticipated next year. What is the anticipated dividend payout ratio?

21-2. The directors of Lancing Lumber Supply have been comparing the growth of their market price with the growth of one of their competitors, Davidson Panels, Inc. Their findings are summarized below.

Lancing Lumber Supply

Year	Earnings	Dividend	Payout	Price	P/E
1975	$4.30	$2.58	60%	$68	15.8
1974	3.85	2.31	60	60	15.6
1973	3.29	1.97	60	50	15.2
1972	3.09	1.85	60	42	13.6
1971	3.05	1.83	60	38	12.5
1970	2.64	1.58	60	31	11.7
1969	1.98	1.19	60	26	13.1
1968	2.93	1.76	60	31	10.6
1967	3.48	2.09	60	35	10.1
1966	2.95	1.77	60	30	10.2

Davidson Panels, Inc.

Year	Earnings	Dividend	Payout	Price	P/E
1975	$3.24	$1.94	60%	$70	21.6
1974	2.75	1.79	65	56	20.4
1973	2.94	1.79	61	53	18.0
1972	2.93	1.73	59	48	16.4
1971	2.90	1.65	57	44	15.2
1970	2.86	1.57	55	41	14.3
1969	2.61	1.49	57	35	13.4
1968	1.55	1.50	97	20	12.9
1967	2.24	1.50	67	34	15.2
1966	2.19	1.49	68	30	13.7

Both companies are in the same markets, and both are similarly organized (approximately the same degrees of operating and financial leverage). Lancing has been consistently earning more per share yet, for some reason, has not been valued at as high a *P/E* ratio as Davidson. What factors would you point out as possible causes for this lower market valuation of Lancing's stock?

21-3. The Airpac Corporation was organized approximately ten years ago. It has experienced good growth until recently, when a high inflation rate coupled with increased environmental protection concerns caused a serious decline in sales. For the past several years, annual EPS have averaged $6. Throughout that period, the dividend payout was approximately 50 percent or $3 per share, payable 75 cents per quarter.

The fiscal year ending December 31, 1977 showed an earnings decline to $2.50 per share. Because it was felt that the earnings decline was temporary, the annual dividend of $3 was maintained for that fiscal year, as well as the first six months of the current year. However, recent projections have caused management to revise downward the expected EPS. For this current fiscal year, the forecast of EPS has been reduced to approximately $2 per share, and to approximately $2.20 for next year. The stock is currently selling for $15 per share, and Airpac's latest balance sheet is given below.

Management is considering maintaining the $3 cash dividend for the next two years. (a) Is this feasible? (b) Could the company eliminate the cash dividend and substitute for it a 25 percent stock dividend? (c) What action do you think management should take?

Airpac Corporation
Balance Sheet
December 31, 1977

Cash	$ 1,000,000		
Inventory	3,500,000		
Accounts receivable	3,000,000	Accts. Payable	$ 2,000,000
Prepaid expenses	500,000	Notes Payable	4,000,000
Total current assets	$8,000,000	Total current liabilities	$ 6,000,000
Net property, plant and		Long term debt	1,800,000
equipment	6,000,000	Common Stock ($10 par)	$ 6,000,000
Other assets	800,000	Retained Earnings	1,000,000
Total assets	$14,800,000	Total liabilities and equity	$14,800,000

21-4. Hazard Tobacco Company has for many years enjoyed a moderate but stable growth in sales and earnings. However, cigarette consumption and, consequently, Hazard's sales have been falling off recently, partly because of a national awareness of the dangers of smoking to health. Anticipating further declines in tobacco sales for the future, Hazard's management hopes eventually to move almost entirely out of the tobacco business and, instead, develop a new diversified product line in growth-oriented industries.

Hazard has been especially interested in the prospects for pollution-control devices—its research department having already done much work on problems of filtering smoke. Right now, the company estimates that an investment of $24 million is necessary to purchase new facilities and begin operations on these products, but the investment could return about 18 percent within a short time. Other investment opportunities total $9.6 million and are expected to return about 12 percent.

The company has been paying a $2.40 dividend on its 6,000,000 shares outstanding. The announced dividend policy has been to maintain a stable dollar dividend, raising it only when it appears that earnings have reached a new, permanently higher level. The directors might, however, change this policy if reasons for doing so are compelling. Total earnings for the year are $22.8 million, common stock is currently selling for $45, and the firm's current leverage ratio (D/A) is 45 percent. Current costs of various forms of financing are:

New bonds	7%
New common stock sold at $45 to yield the firm	$41
Investors required rate of return on equity	9%
Tax rate	50%

a. Calculate the marginal cost of capital above and below the point of exhaustion of retained earnings for Hazard.

b. How large should Hazard's capital budget be for the year?

c. What is an appropriate dividend policy for Hazard? How should the capital budget be financed?

d. How might risk factors influence Hazard's cost of capital, capital structure, and dividend policy?

e. What assumptions, if any, do your answers to the above make about investors' preference for dividends versus capital gains, that is, investors' preference regarding different D/P and g components of k?

21-5. Gemstone, Inc., has earnings this year of $16.5 million, 50 percent of which is required to take advantage of excellent investment opportunities of the firm. The firm has 206,250 shares outstanding, selling currently at $320 a share. Greg Beaumont, a major stockholder (18,750 shares), has expressed displeasure with a great deal of managerial policy. Management has approached him with the prospect of selling his holdings back to the firm, and he has expressed a willingness to do this at a price of $320 a share. Assuming that the market uses a constant P/E ratio of 4 in valuing the stock, answer the following questions:

a. Should the firm buy Beaumont's shares? Assume that dividends will not be paid on Beaumont's shares if repurchased.

b. How large a cash dividend should be declared?

c. What is the final value of Gemstone's stock after all cash payments to shareholders?

Integrated Topics in Financial Management

Part Six

In the final four chapters we take up important but somewhat specialized topics which draw on the concepts developed in earlier sections.

Chapter 22, "Timing of Financial Policy," introduces dynamics into the decision process, showing how financial managers react to changing conditions in the capital markets. Chapter 23 deals with the growth of firms through mergers and holding companies, and the reasoning behind this development. Throughout the text, we have dealt with growing and successful firms; however, many firms face financial difficulties, and the causes and possible remedies to these difficulties are discussed in Chapter 24. Finally, in Chapter 25, we summarize and integrate the various topics covered in the book.

Timing of Financial Policy

22 This chapter deals with the timing of financial policy. Although the topic has always been important, the recent inflationary environment has caused timing to take on greater significance than ever before. Since the mid-1960s, the U.S. economy has experienced a series of "credit crunches," during which the costs of financing have risen substantially. Minimizing the need to raise capital during these crunches is important. Also, a key question facing financial managers is whether financing costs will return to lower levels in the reasonably near future, or whether the continued upward trends in recent years will continue. How this question is resolved will greatly influence the costs, amounts, and types of capital raised by business firms.

In an inflationary environment, changes in asset requirements are magnified by rising price levels; financial managers must consider this when planning their requirements. Also, when analyzing prospective returns from capital assets, the financial manager must realize that the prices of similar capital assets will increase substantially in future years because of inflation. Finally, it is exceedingly difficult to raise long-term funds in an inflationary environment, and, as a consequence, the problem of planning to meet future maturing obligations is crucial.

SIGNIFICANCE TO FINANCIAL MANAGEMENT

The significance of financial timing is suggested by the following quotation from *Business Week:*

Even a modest increase in monetary restraint will be hard for most companies to handle. Ever since the end of last year's credit drought, companies have worked hard to rebuild liquidity.

However, there's a "difference between actual and desired liquidity," says an economist for a major New York City bank, "and companies haven't succeeded in loosening up balance sheets."

In contrasting money market conditions that lie ahead with 1966, economists stress the expected impact of inflation itself. During late 1966, the wholesale price index remained relatively stable. But if price increases get larger in coming months, interest rates are almost sure to climb.

"People who borrow under conditions of sharp inflation are willing to pay any amount for money," says Milton Friedman of the University of Chicago, "and people who lend ask high rates to protect themselves from loss of purchasing power." If the Fed doesn't tighten, Friedman expects prices to rise by at least 5 percent and possibly 7 percent during 1968 and predicts that interest rates will be in the 9 percent to 10 percent range.[1]

Milton Friedman's forecast was subsequently borne out. But financial managers have also had to face another problem—fluctuating rates. This increased volatility is highlighted by a study of interest rate patterns in recent years. Interest rates have fluctuated very sharply over the past decade, although the trend in yields has generally been upward. In 1969 and early 1970, when inflationary expectations were strong and bank credit expansion was curtailed, market rates reached the highest level in U.S. history. Then during 1970 and early 1971, as economic activity slowed and monetary policy eased, interest rates dropped more sharply than in most earlier periods of decline. In 1974, under the stimulus of "double-digit inflation," new records were set; major corporations and the U.S. government paid record amounts for long-term debt, and the prime rate hit a new high of 12 percent. Rates declined again in 1975 and 1976, but even so, most money managers expect interest rate increases in the future.

Financial managers generally agree that major fluctuations in money costs will continue to occur in the future, but they are divided about whether interest rates will continue their upward trend. Experience suggests that both possibilities should be taken into account in financial planning. Accordingly, in this chapter we first analyze cyclical patterns in the costs of financing and then review the nature of monetary and fiscal policies, focusing particular attention on the implications of these policies for future patterns in the cost of external financing.

HISTORICAL PATTERNS IN THE COSTS OF FINANCING

Table 22–1 highlights changes in recent years, while Figure 22–1 presents the broad pattern of long- and short-term interest rates since the turn of the cen-

---

[1] "Is a Money Crunch on Its Way?" *Business Week* (September 29, 1967), p. 36.

tury. One outstanding characteristic of interest rate behavior is the wide magnitude of the changes in the price of money over the years. For example, the borrowing rate on four-to-six months' commercial paper, which is the best indication of the cost of short-term money to large corporations, reached a low of 0.53 percent in 1941. By 1953, this rate stood at 2.52 percent, but it declined to 1.58 percent during the business recession of the following year. In the early 1960s prime commercial paper rates rose to over 3 percent; during the credit stringency of the late 1960s, they rose to almost 9 percent. Between December 1969 and February 1972, commercial paper rates declined from 8.84 percent to a low of 3.93 percent. Rates fluctuated slightly between 4.5 percent and 5.2 percent for the remainder of 1972, but during 1973 and 1974, under inflationary pressures after price controls were lifted, rates rose again and hit new highs in July 1974. Rates fell again during the recession of 1975–76, hitting a low of 5½ percent in May 1976.

TABLE 22–1 Selected Interest Rates (Percent)

Rates	1971 Lows[a]	July 1974	May 1976
Short-term			
Treasury bills, 3 months	3.38 (March)	7.75	5.18
Commercial paper, 4–6 months	4.19 (March)	11.72	5.50
Long-term			
10–year U.S. government[b]	5.70 (March)	8.10	8.16
Corporate AAA, new issues	7.00 (February)	10.10	8.65

[a] Monthly averages.
[b] Estimated from yield curve.
Source: Federal Reserve Bulletin, various issues.

Yields on high-grade, long-term corporate bonds have fluctuated similarly, but not to the same degree. For example, the corporate AAA bond rate reached a low of 2.53 percent in 1946. It rose to over 3 percent in 1953 and, after declining to 2.90 percent during the business downturn of 1954, it climbed to 4.41 percent by 1960. During August 1966, yields on AAA corporates rose above 5½ percent, and the rise continued to over 10 percent in 1974. Long-term rates receded somewhat in 1975 and 1976, but the decline was less than that on short rates. Long-term rates are geared to expectations about long-term inflation, and in 1975–76 investors still expected substantial future inflation.

FIGURE 22–1 Long- and Short-term Interest Rates

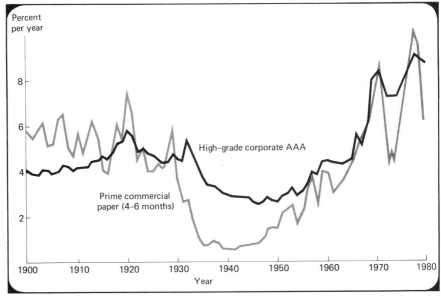

Sources: *Federal Reserve Historical Chart Book, Financial and Business Statistics*, 1976; and *Federal Reserve Bulletin*, May 1976.

The cost of equity capital is more difficult to measure than is the cost of debt, and time series data on equity costs are not available. However, as the cost of equity is dependent upon the cost of debt ($k = R_F$ + risk premium), fluctuations in the cost of debt certainly reflect corresponding fluctuations in the cost of equity.

This brief review of fluctuations in short- and long-term interest rates is sufficient to demonstrate that the cost of capital is one of the most volatile inputs purchased by firms. Within relatively short time periods, money costs have fluctuated by over 100 percent.

The significance of fluctuations in interest rates is especially important when one considers the large amounts of financing that may be involved. In August 1974, AT&T's Northwestern Bell unit sold $150 million of debentures at a cost of 10.14 percent. Earlier in 1974, AT&T subsidiaries sold bonds with a cost of only 8.11 percent. Had the company anticipated this rise and borrowed earlier in the year, its interest cost would have been reduced by over $3 million per year.

INTEREST RATES AS AN INDEX OF AVAILABILITY OF FUNDS

While the cost variations associated with interest rate fluctuations are substantial, the greatest significance of interest rates is their role as an index of the availability of funds. A period of high interest rates reflects tight money, which is in turn associated with tight reserve positions at commercial banks. At such times interest rates rise, but there are conventional limits on interest rates. Consequently, a larger quantity of funds is demanded by borrowers than banks are able to make available. Banks therefore begin to ration funds among prospective borrowers by continuing lines of credit to traditional customers but restricting loans to new borrowers.

Small firms characteristically have greater difficulty obtaining financing during periods of tight money, and even among large borrowers, the bargaining position of financial institutions is stronger. It is a lender's rather than a borrower's market. Consequently, the conditions in all loan agreements are more restrictive when demand for funds is high.

Interest rates are therefore of very great significance to financial managers as an index of the availability of funds. For small- and medium-size firms, a period of rising interest rates may indicate increasing difficulty in obtaining any financing at all. Or, if financing is obtained, it will be at a higher cost and under less favorable conditions.

A period of tight money will have a particularly strong impact on the utilities and other heavy industries, state and local governments, and the housing and construction sectors. The heavy, long-term investments in these areas cause the impact of interest rates on profitability to be especially significant. Thus, during the credit crunch of 1974, the sectors listed above have seen funds become virtually unavailable. Utility companies are being forced to reduce planned expansions; state and local financing has become onerous; and the housing and construction sectors have declined substantially.

COSTS OF DIFFERENT KINDS OF FINANCING OVER TIME

The preceding section showed that interest rates vary widely over time. In addition, the relative costs of debt, preferred stock, and equity fluctuate. Data on these relative costs are presented in Fig. 22–2, which shows that earnings/price ratios have fluctuated from 16 percent to 1 percent.[2] During the 1960s, E/P ratios averaged about 6 percent, ranging from 4.7 to 6.7 percent. However, the rising costs of capital associated with inflation in the 1970s drove stock prices down and E/P ratios up to about 14 percent by 1974. Rising stock prices reduced E/P ratios to about 10 percent by 1976. Yields on bonds and preferred stocks have fluctuated to a much lesser extent. Furthermore, since bonds and preferred stocks both provide a stable, fixed income to investors,

---

[2] An earnings/price ratio, the reciprocal of a P/E ratio, does not measure exactly the cost of equity capital, but it does indicate *trends* in this cost. In other words, when earnings/price ratios are high, the cost of equity capital tends to be high, and vice versa.

they are close substitutes for each other, and their yields parallel each other closely.[3]

FIGURE 22–2   Long-term Security Yields

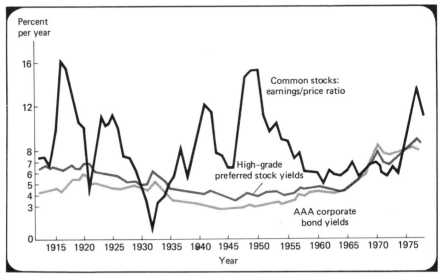

Sources: *Historical Supplement to Federal Reserve Chart Book on Financial and Business Statistics*, 1976; and *Federal Reserve Bulletin*, May 1976.

The pronounced decline in earnings/price ratios that began in the early 1950s resulted largely from investors' increasing awareness of the growth potential in common stock earnings, dividends, and stock prices. The economy was strong during this period, and security analysts and investors became aware of the importance of the *g* component in the expected rate of return equation $k = D/P + g$. A recognition of the dangers of inflation and of its effect on fixed income securities was driving bond and preferred stock yields up, further closing the gap between interest rates and earnings/price ratios. In terms of the capital market line *(CML)* discussed in Chapter 18, the slope of the line was declining, indicating a narrowing of the spread between required rates of return on equity and interest rates. In 1974, however, fears

---

[3] Note also that bond yields tended to lie below those on preferred stocks during most of the period covered; this relationship resulted from the fact that bonds have priority over preferred stocks and, hence, are less risky. However, preferred stock dividends are largely tax exempt to corporate owners, so after-tax yields (to corporations) are considerably higher than those on bonds. Recall that 85 percent of the dividends received by a corporate stockholder are tax exempt to the receiver, whereas interest income is fully taxable to the recipient. During the 1960s, certain corporations (insurance companies, savings and loans, mutual savings banks) which had previously paid very low taxes became subject to higher taxes; these firms bought preferred stocks, pushing preferred stock before-tax yields below those of bonds in the late 1960s and early 1970s.

of a recession induced by attempts to curb inflation increased the slope of the *CML* and drove equity costs up relative to debt costs.[4]

RELATION BETWEEN LONG-TERM AND SHORT-TERM INTEREST RATES

One of the important elements in the financial manager's timing decisions is an understanding of the relationship between long-term and short-term interest rates.[5] Long-term interest rates are rates on securities with maturities in excess of ten years. Short-term interest rates are those on securities with maturities of under one year.

Figure 22–3 is an enlarged version of Figure 22–1; it shows the relationship between long- and short-term interest rates from 1962 to 1976. In some periods, short-term interest rates were higher than long-term interest rates; this was true in 1966 and again in 1969, 1973, and 1974–75, when the money market was extremely tight. Under certain conditions there is greater risk to holding long-term securities than short-term securities. The longer the maturity of the security, the greater the danger that the issuer may not make an effective adaptation to its environment and therefore may not be able to meet its obligations in ten, fifteen, or twenty years. Furthermore, the *prices* of long-term bonds are much more volatile than those of short-term bonds when interest rates change; the reason for this is largely arithmetic and was described in Chapter 18.

The *expectations theory* states that long-term interest rates may in general be regarded as an average of expected future short-term interest rates. Thus the relation between long and short rates will depend on what is expected to happen in the future to short-term interest rates, as illustrated in Table 22–2. In section A it is assumed that short-term interest rates will rise 1 percent each year, beginning at 2 percent in year one. The corresponding long-term interest rate in year one for a five-year period is approximately 4 percent; that is, the average of the five short-term rates. Thus, in year one, the long-term rate is double the short-term rate.

Consider, however, the situation under section B—in a tight-money situation in year one, short-term rates are 6 percent, but they are expected to decline by 1 percent each year. The average of these rates is the same as in section A, because the numbers are identical—their order is simply reversed. Now, however, the long-term rate of 4 percent lies below the initial short-term rate of 6 percent.

---

[4] These statements about the *CML* are probably correct, but they cannot be extended too far. In Chapter 18 we saw that stock prices are dependent upon both k and g, so a changing spread between E/P and interest rates could be caused either by changes in the slope of the *CML* or by changes in expected growth rates.

[5] The relationship between long-term and short-term interest rates—generally referred to as the "term structure of interest rates"—was discussed in Chapter 7.

FIGURE 22–3   Long-term and Short-term Interest Rates (Detail of Figure 22–1)

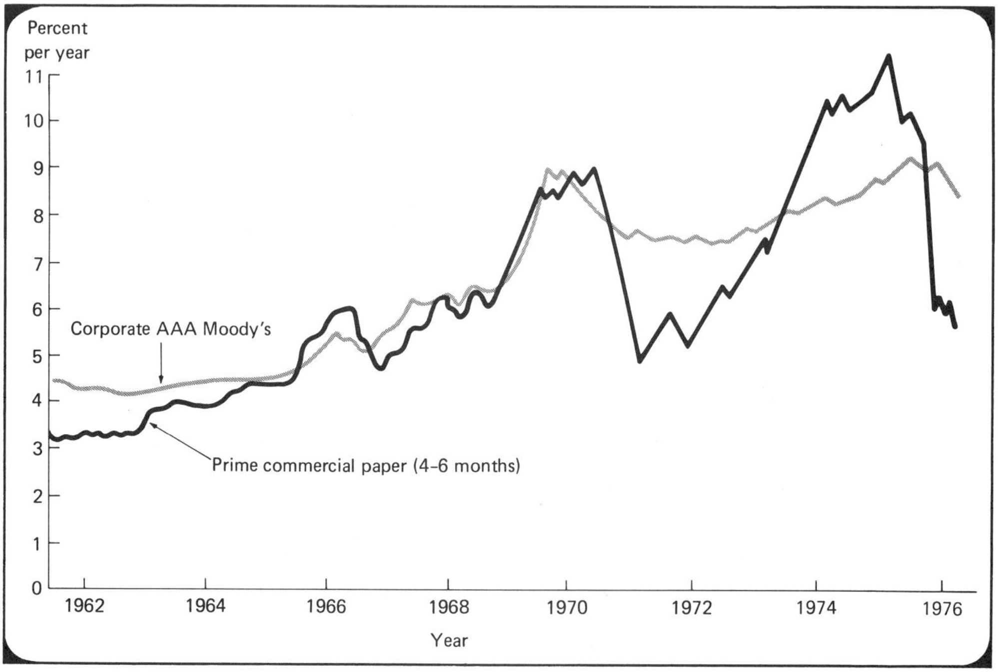

Source: Federal Reserve Bulletin, various issues.

TABLE 22–2   Relation between Short-Term and Long-Term Interest Rates

	A		B	
Year	5-Year Note	Short-Term Rates	5-Year Note	Short-Term Rates
1	4	2	4	6
2		3		5
3		4		4
4		5		3
5		6		2

These examples do not prove the relation between short- and long-term rates. They do, however, illustrate the pattern that would exist if the only factor operating was expected changes in interest rate movements, which themselves reflect a broad group of supply and demand factors. However, many other factors operate in the market. Some of these include differences in the risks of loss and failure among individual business firms, in the economic outlook for different industries, in the degree to which price-level changes affect different products and industries, and in the impact that changes in government legislation will have on different firms in an industry.

CHARACTERISTIC PATTERNS IN COST OF MONEY

Summary data on long-term and short-term interest rates, on changes in rates, on gross national product (GNP), on price level changes, and on the money supply are given in Table 22–3. Then, in Figure 22–4, we depict in a general way the pattern between GNP and interest rates. Short-term interest rates show the widest amplitude of swings. Since long-term interest rates are *averages* of short-term rates, they are not as volatile as short-term rates—short-term rates move more quickly and fluctuate more than long-term rates. The cost of debt money tends to coincide with movements in general business conditions, both at the peak and at the trough. Thus, as we see in Table 22–3, the economy slowed significantly in 1967 and 1971, and interest rates declined during those periods, while the booming economy in 1965–1966 precipitated an increase in rates; in all three periods short rates changed more than long rates. More recent data reveal the same basic patterns—rates rose during the booming 1973–74 period, then fell in the recession of 1975–76.

TABLE 22–3 Summary Data for Six Periods of Interest Rate Changes (Percent) End 1963 to early 1976[a]

Item	First Quarter, 1964– Second Quarter, 1965	Third Quarter, 1965– Fourth Quarter, 1966	First Half, 1967	First Quarter, 1967– Second Quarter, 1968	First Quarter, 1970– First Quarter, 1971	Fourth Quarter, 1975– Second Quarter, 1976
Interest rate levels, end of period						
Commercial paper	4.38	6.00	4.72	6.08	4.59	6.00
Corporate AAA, new issues	4.48	5.76	5.58	6.56	7.05	8.62
Interest rate changes						
Commercial paper	0.47	1.62	−1.28	1.36	−4.03	−0.86
Corporate bonds	0.14	1.28	−0.18	0.98	−1.36	−0.33
Annual rates of increase						
Real GNP	5.6	6.2	1.1	5.0	0.4	6.3
GNP deflator	1.8	2.8	2.4	4.2	5.4	5.2
Current dollar GNP	7.4	9.2	3.6	9.4	5.8	11.5
Money stock (M_1)	4.1	3.5	6.8	7.2	6.2	3.7

[a]Based on quarterly data for terminal quarters in each period, except growth rate of M_1—which is calculated from averages for terminal months in the periods—and high-employment budget surplus—which shows average levels for the entire span of each period. Data for yields on AAA newly issued corporate bonds are First National City Bank estimates and data for high-employment budget surplus (NIA basis) are unpublished estimates by the Division of Research and Statistics of the Federal Reserve. (M_1) is the narrowly defined money stock—currency and demand deposits (other than U.S. government and interbank).
Source: "Interest Rates, Credit Flows, and Monetary Aggregates Since 1964," *Federal Reserve Bulletin*, June 1971, p. 426, and *Federal Reserve* Bank of St. Louis, *U.S. Financial Data*, June 1976.

FIGURE 22–4 Relation between Movements of Gross National Product and Interest Rates

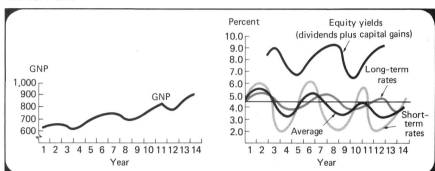

The cost of equity funds may best be approximated by expected equity yields—dividends plus capital gains. To understand the behavior of equity yields, one must analyze the behavior of earnings, dividends, and stock prices. Corporate earnings are highly volatile—they lead the business cycle both on the upturn and on the downturn, and dividends follow earnings. Prices of common stocks anticipate changes in corporate earnings. Prices of equities are also influenced by money market conditions. Owing to the gradual tightening in money market conditions as expansion continues, bond yields rise and attract money out of stocks and into bonds, causing the prices of equities to turn down before corporate profits reach their peak. Hence, the cost of equity financing turns up because firms receive lower prices for the stocks they sell.[6] In other words, the cost of equity capital begins to rise in the later stages of the business cycle.

The relationships between the costs of financing over time illustrated in Figure 22–4 represent generalizations that provide a frame of reference for the financial manager; the patterns are not intended as precise guidelines. A basic requirement for sound financial management is the ability to make judgments about future economic and financial conditions that will affect financial timing and the forms and sources of financing that are used. The next section seeks to provide a foundation for evaluating trends in financial markets.

---

[6] Recall that in Chapter 18 we showed that, at least conceptually, stock prices may be determined by the equation

$$P = \frac{D}{k - g}$$

where p = the price of a share of stock, D = the dividend on the stock, k = the required rate of return on the stock (or the cost of equity capital), and g = the expected growth rate. Since stocks and bonds compete with each other for investors' funds, if monetary policy drives interest rates up, k will likewise rise and P must decline.

MONEY AND CAPITAL MARKET BEHAVIOR

Federal Reserve Policy

Fundamental to an understanding of the behavior of the money and capital markets is an analysis of the role of the central bank, which in the United States is the Federal Reserve System. The Fed, as it is called, has a set of instruments with which to influence the operations of commercial banks, whose loan and investment activities in turn have an important influence on the cost and availability of money. The most powerful of the Fed's instruments, hence the one used most sparingly, is changing *reserve requirements* (the percentage of deposits that must be kept in reserve with the Fed). The one most often used is changing the pattern of *open-market operations* (the Fed's buying and selling of securities, which expands and contracts the amount of funds in the public's hands).

Changes in the *discount rate* (the interest rate charged to commercial banks when they borrow from Federal Reserve Banks) are likely to have more of a psychological influence than direct quantitative effects. These changes represent an implicit announcement by Federal Reserve authorities that a change in economic conditions has occurred and that these new conditions call for a tightening or easing of monetary conditions. The data demonstrate that increases in the Federal Reserve bank discount rate have been followed by rising interest rate levels, and conversely.

When the Federal Reserve System purchases or sells securities in the open market, makes changes in the discount rate, or varies the reserve requirement, this procedure changes interest rates on most securities.

FISCAL POLICY

The fiscal policy of the federal government has great impact on movements in interest rates. A cash budget deficit represents a stimulating influence by the federal government, and a cash surplus exerts a restraining influence from the government-spending sector of the economy. However, this generalization must be modified to reflect the way a deficit is financed and the way a surplus is used. To have the most stimulating effect, the deficit should be financed by sale of securities through the banking system, particularly the central bank—this provides a maximum amount of bank reserves and permits a multiple expansion in the money supply. To have the most restrictive effect, the surplus should be used to retire bonds held by the banking system, particularly the central bank, thus reducing bank reserves and causing a multiple contraction in the supply of money.

The impact of Treasury financing programs varies. Ordinarily, when the Treasury needs to draw funds from the money market, it competes with other potential users of funds; the result may be a rise in interest rate levels. However, the desire to hold down interest rates also influences Treasury and Federal Reserve policy. To ensure the success of a large new offering, Federal Reserve authorities may temporarily ease money conditions, a procedure that will tend to soften interest rates. If the Treasury encounters resistance in selling securities in the nonbanking sector, they may be sold in large volume to the commercial banking system, which expands its reserves and thereby increases the monetary base. This change in turn tends to lower the level of interest rates.

INTEREST RATE FORECASTS

Within this framework of general economic and financial patterns, short-term interest rate patterns and forecasts may be analyzed through the use of flow of funds accounts. The flow of funds accounts are summarized in Table 22–4 to depict the behavior of the major categories of suppliers and demanders of funds. By projecting the sources and uses of funds in different categories, we can estimate the direction of the pressure on interest rates.[7]

The table can be used in the following way: Historical patterns can be established to show uses and sources of funds in relation to the growth of the economy as a whole as measured by GNP. When in any particular year the demand for funds grows faster than the supply in relation to historical patterns, interest rates are likely to rise. These extra funds are supplied by drawing on the commercial banking system, which is the pivot in the financial mechanism. Whenever the demand for funds must be met by drawing on the commercial banking system to a greater-than-normal degree, interest rates rise.

Another significant statistic in the table is the rise in the supply of funds from "individuals and miscellaneous"; funds from this source increased tremendously in 1973 and 1974. Because of restrictive Federal Reserve policies, the ability of the commercial banks and other financial institutions to supply funds was held back in relation to demand. This produced high interest rates (see Figure 22–1), and these high rates induced individuals, businesses, and others to make their surplus funds available to borrowers. Thus, the supply of funds was augmented from nonbanking sources, but only at substantially higher interest rates.

Most longer term predictions for the financial market call for continued high interest rates with only moderate declines of short duration from time to time. The causes are diverse, but a major factor reflects efforts of govern-

---

[7]Compilations of studies of this kind are facilitated by the flow of funds data developed by the Federal Reserve System and published monthly in the *Federal Reserve Bulletin*.

TABLE 22–4. Summary of Supply and Demand for Credit
Annual Net Increases (Billions of dollars)

	1970	1971	1972	1973	1974	1975e	1976p	Amounts Outstanding 12/31/75e
	Annual Net Increases in Amounts Outstanding							
Net Demand								
Privately held mortgages	20.2	41.7	58.7	60.2	37.0	34.8	39.9	651.1
Corporate bonds	22.8	23.7	19.1	12.7	25.7	31.3	19.5	300.4
State and local securities	14.7	21.7	12.8	14.1	14.5	13.4	9.7	226.4
Domestically held foreign bonds	0.9	0.9	1.0	1.0	2.2	5.5	7.2	24.1
Subtotal long-term nonfederal	58.6	88.0	91.6	88.0	79.4	85.0	76.3	1,202.0
Business loans	2.5	7.7	24.8	38.4	34.3	−14.8	10.1	231.4
Consumer loans	6.0	11.2	19.2	22.9	9.6	6.0	14.0	196.1
All other bank loans	2.0	7.3	10.1	7.8	4.4	−0.4	3.5	74.1
Open market paper	2.1	−0.1	1.6	8.3	16.6	−0.5	4.1	67.1
Subtotal short-term private	12.6	26.1	55.7	77.4	64.9	−9.7	31.7	568.7
Privately held treasury debt	5.8	19.0	15.2	−2.0	10.2	72.0	61.2	340.4
Privately held federal agency debt	9.0	2.8	9.2	21.5	18.4	5.1	11.9	105.0
Subtotal federal	14.8	21.8	24.4	19.5	28.6	77.1	73.1	445.4
Total net demand for credit	86.0	135.9	171.7	184.9	172.9	152.4	181.1	2,216.1
Net Supply[1]								
Mutual savings banks	3.8	9.0	8.8	5.3	2.8	9.2	13.1	107.9
Savings and loan associations	11.9	30.5	37.3	28.0	21.7	41.1	46.8	323.2
Credit unions	1.5	2.6	3.1	2.9	2.7	4.8	6.0	30.8
Life insurance companies	4.7	7.2	8.8	10.0	11.0	12.7	16.0	208.4
Fire and casualty companies	3.8	3.7	3.8	3.5	4.6	6.0	5.8	51.8
Private noninsured pension funds	2.5	−1.8	−0.5	2.0	5.8	6.2	5.2	49.7
State and local retirement funds	3.8	3.7	3.7	4.6	8.6	10.3	9.8	79.4
Open-end mutual funds	0.5	0.0	0.0	−0.2	1.4	1.7	1.6	10.1
Real estate investment trusts	2.1	2.5	4.9	4.5	0.9	−2.7	−3.8	13.2
Total nonbank investing institutions	34.6	57.4	69.9	60.6	59.5	89.3	100.5	874.5
Commercial banks[2]	33.7	51.0	73.3	77.6	59.8	29.5	56.0	739.9
Finance companies	0.7	4.2	10.7	10.2	3.9	0.2	5.0	85.5
Business corporations	0.8	4.1	2.9	5.1	10.5	12.9	14.1	90.9
State and local governments	−0.5	−1.5	5.5	4.8	1.2	−2.0	−0.8	28.1
Foreigners	10.4	26.4	8.4	0.6	10.8	9.0	5.0	81.9
Subtotal	79.7	141.6	170.7	158.9	145.7	138.9	179.8	1,900.8
Residual: Individuals and misc.	6.3	−5.7	1.0	26.0	27.2	13.5	1.3	315.3
Total net supply of credit	86.0	135.9	171.7	184.9	172.9	152.4	181.1	2,216.1

[1]Excludes funds for equities, cash, and miscellaneous demands not tabulated above.
[2]Includes nonoperating holding and other bank-related companies.
e = Estimated; p = Preliminary.
Source: Adapted from Henry Kaufman and James McKeon, *Supply and Demand for Credit in 1976,* (Salomon Brothers, 1976).
Reprinted by permission.

ments throughout the world to achieve full employment and high growth rates.[8] A worldwide capital shortage has resulted.

The outlook for continued price-level increases and high interest rates has already had a number of effects on corporate financial policy. Table 22–5 presents the sources and uses of corporate funds for the period 1963–1976, expressed as a percentage of the annual net increases. Dramatic shifts have taken place in the role of internal financing. Total internal financing declined from 79 percent of total sources in 1963 to 53 percent in 1974. Most of the decline has been in retained earnings, reflecting larger capital outlays in relation to profits. However, internal sources increased again in 1975 and 1976.

Another significant change has been an increase in dependence on external long-term financing from loans, stocks, and bonds. New common

TABLE 22–5 Selected Elements of Corporate Sources and Uses of Corporate Funds Expressed as Percentages of Annual Net Increases in Total Sources or Uses, 1963 and 1967–1976

	Percentages of Annual Net Increases in Sources or Uses										
	1963	*1967*	*1968*	*1969*	*1970*	*1971*	*1972*	*1973*	*1974*	*1975*	*1976*
Uses											
Plant and equipment	66	72	70	76	81	68	65	63	68	85	72
Total physical investment (includes inventory)	81	86	80	88	93	76	77	80	89	88	86
Accounts receivable	6	1	5	4	5	6	3	5	2	2	3
Other	13	13	15	8	2	18	20	15	9	10	11
Total uses	100	100	100	100	100	100	100	100	100	100	100
Sources											
Retained earnings	22	23	17	11	7	8	11	10	9	13	19
Depreciation	53	48	47	51	56	49	47	48	44	60	51
Total internal sources	79	65	67	59	60	61	59	58	53	73	70
Loans from banks and other institutions	6	8	10	12	2	3	12	22	31	−3	11
Net new stock issues	a	3	−1	4	6	10	9	6	3	7	8
Net new bond issues	7	17	13	12	21	16	10	14	13	23	11
Total external sources	21	35	33	41	40	39	41	42	47	27	30
Total sources	100	100	100	100	100	100	100	100	100	100	100

[a] Less than 1 percent.

Source: Based on material in Henry Kaufman and James McKeon, *Supply and Demand for Credit in 1976* (Salomon Brothers, 1976), table IIIB. Reprinted by permission.

[8] The reasons for this forecast are set forth in the papers by R. Solomon, O. Eckstein, R. E. Moor, J. W. Knowles, R. A. Kavesh, W. C. Freund, and J. J. O'Leary in *Business Economics,* 5 (January 1970), pp. 12–49.

stock financing rose from negligible amounts in 1963 to 10 percent of total sources of funds in 1971, and this percentage was of course much higher in certain industries and for some individual firms. Long-term bond financing likewise grew from 7 percent to 21 percent by 1970, and to 23 percent in 1975.

These relations are further emphasized in Table 22–6. Part I of the table presents data on gross proceeds (total funds raised before using part of the

TABLE 22–6   Long-Term Corporate Capital by Type, 1963–1976

I. Gross Proceeds of Bond and Stock Financing (Percentages of Annual Net Increases in Amounts Outstanding), 1963 and 1967–1976

	1963	1967	1968	1969	1970	1971	1972	1973	1974	1975e	1976p
Straight debt, public offerings	42	50	42	49	78	67	57	58	78	77	63
Straight debt, privately placed	53	28	29	20	12	22	35	34	20	20	29
Convertible debt for cash	3	21	17	21	9	11	8	8	1	3	7
Convertible debt in mergers	2	1	12	10	1	a	a	a	1	a	1
Total bonds	100	100	100	100	100	100	100	100	100	100	100
Total bonds	91	85	79	71	78	70	66	67	84	78	65
Total stocks	9	15	21	29	22	30	34	33	16	22	35
Total bonds and stocks	100	100	100	100	100	100	100	100	100	100	100

II. Net Proceeds of Bond and Stock Financing (Percentages of Annual Net Increases in Amounts Outstanding)

	1963	1967	1968	1969	1970	1971	1972	1973	1974	1975e	1976p
Straight debt, public offerings	41	59	48	59	92	80	67	68	90	87	73
Straight debt, privately placed	55	19	19	6	a	13	30	28	8	12	22
Convertible debt	4	22	33	35	8	7	3	4	2	1	5
Total bonds	100	100	100	100	100	100	100	100	100	100	100
Total bonds	104	87	107	77	77	64	58	61	86	75	57
Total stocks	(4)	13	(7)	23	23	36	42	39	14	25	43
Total bonds and stocks	100	100	100	100	100	100	100	100	100	100	100

III. Analysis of Convertible Bond Offerings (Annual Net Increases in Amounts Outstanding in Billions of Dollars)

	1963	1967	1968	1969	1970	1971	1972	1973	1974	1975e	1976p
Total convertibles offered	0.5	4.6	5.6	6.0	2.9	3.7	2.4	2.4	1.1	1.3	2.2
Less convertibles called, retired, or converted	0.3	1.1	1.0	1.2	1.1	2.0	1.8	1.7	0.6	1.0	1.2
Called, retired, or converted as a percent of total offered	60.0	23.9	17.8	20.0	37.9	54.0	75.0	70.8	54.5	76.9	54.5
Yearly net convertible debt	0.2	3.5	4.6	4.8	1.8	1.7	0.6	0.7	0.5	0.3	1.0
Cumulative net convertible debt outstanding[b]	0.2	6.9	11.5	16.3	18.1	19.8	20.4	21.1	21.6	21.9	22.9

[a] Less than 1 percent.
[b] Cumulative 1963 through 1974.
[e] Estimated.
[p] Preliminary.
Source: Based on material in Henry Kaufman and James McKeon, *Supply and Demand for Credit in 1976* (Salomon Brothers, 1976), tables IIIA and IIIC. Reprinted by permission.

cash proceeds to retire obligations previously outstanding). Part II presents data on net proceeds after refundings and other adjustments. Part III analyzes some patterns in convertible debt financing. These data indicate, as one would expect, a changing pattern of financing as interest rates rose during the 1960s and 1970s.

1. Stock financing as a percent of long-term external financing almost tripled on a gross basis and rose from -4 percent to over 40 percent on a net basis.

2. Bond financing dropped from 91 percent to 65 percent of the total.

3. In 1970, private placement of debt dropped from over one-half of total long-term debt financing to 12 percent on a gross basis and less than 1 percent on a net basis. This dramatic change reflects the impact of tight money on the financing demands of insurance companies, a major source of direct placement financing. As the table shows, private placement of debt increased again in the seventies.

4. With rising price levels, buyers of debt increasingly sought potential equity participation through the convertibility feature, and convertible debt rose from less than 5 percent to almost one-half of total bond financing in 1969; it has since decreased to 2 percent, primarily because a weak stock market has made convertibles less attractive.

5. Convertible debt issued in mergers rose from less than 2 percent before 1967 to over 10 percent in 1968 and 1969, but more recently declined to the 1 percent level.

6. The percentage of convertible debt reduced by conversion into stock was relatively high in 1963, but it declined substantially from 1967 through 1969 because of the increased use of convertible debt. As new offerings declined in 1970, the reduction of convertible debt by conversion once again increased significantly, peaking in 1975.

7. The cumulative total of net convertible debt outstanding rose from $6.9 billion in 1967 to $22.9 billion for 1976. It is clear that the increased uncertainties about the rate of inflation and the increased difficulties of forecasting interest rate patterns during this period have led to the greater use of hybrid forms of financing—debt with equity participation such as convertibles or warrants. The percentage of direct loans with such equity sweeteners, or interest adjustment provisions, is reported to be even higher than was true in the public flotations on which data are available.

8. The credit stringency that reached a climax in May 1970 with the Penn Central bankruptcy led to a massive effort to restructure corporate balance sheets. Long-term financing accounted for about 84 percent of total external financing in 1970 versus an average of 62 percent for the five years prior to 1969.[9] The use of net short-term external financing sources,

[9] Richard L. Gady, "Recent Patterns in Corporate Financing," *Economic Commentary* (Federal Reserve Bank of Cleveland, June 14, 1971).

including bank loans and commercial paper, actually declined during the first quarter of 1971 and during 1975. Thus short-term debt was repaid as longer term debt and equity were used to improve corporate liquidity. Interestingly, this movement to longer term financing occurred at a time when short-term rates were almost three full percentage points below long-term rates, as contrasted with a spread of only three-tenths of 1 percent previously. But while long-term rates were much higher than short-term rates, they were still low in relation to long-term rates during the previous credit stringency and low in relation to longer term expectations of interest rate levels.

9. The broad package of economic controls introduced in August 1971, then modified in the several phases of Presidents Nixon and Ford's economic policies, could radically alter future interest rate patterns. If the new economic policies succeed in checking inflation, interest rates will probably decline significantly. If not, rates may rise further, and they will certainly stay on a high plateau.

10. If interest rates remain high, and if the huge fluctuations experienced in recent years continue, then the use of floating-rate long-term securities can be anticipated, and long-term debt redeemable at par at the option of the lender can be anticipated.

TABLE 22–7 Calculation of Real and Nominal Interest Rates

	Interest Rate on Prime Commercial Paper Plus 1.0	$\dfrac{CPI_{t-1}}{CPI_t}$	Col. 1 Times Col. 2	Real Rate of Interest: Col. 3 Minus 1.0 Times 100	Nominal Rate of Interest: Col. 1 Minus 1.0 Times 100
	(1)	(2)	(3)	(4)	(5)
1962	1.03				
1963	1.03	.988	1.02	2%	3%
1964	1.04	.987	1.03	3	4
1965	1.04	.983	1.02	2	4
1966	1.06	.972	1.03	3	6
1967	1.05	.972	1.02	2	5
1968	1.06	.962	1.02	2	6
1969	1.07	.947	1.01	1	7
1970	1.09	.944	1.03	3	9
1971	1.07	.959	1.03	3	7
1972	1.05	.968	1.02	2	5
1973	1.07	.941	1.01	1	7
1974	1.11	.914	1.01	1	11
1975	1.11	.937	1.01	1	8

Note: Interest rates are rounded to nearest whole number to eliminate unwarranted appearance of accuracy.
Source: Figure 22–3 and *Economic Indicators,* June 1974.

EFFECTS OF PRICE LEVEL CHANGES ON INTEREST RATES

Price level trends affect interest rates in two important ways. First, the "nominal" interest rate—the contract, or stated, interest rate—reflects expectations about future price level behavior. If prices are rising, and are expected to rise further, the expected rate of inflation is added to the interest rate that would have prevailed in the absence of inflation to adjust for the decline in purchasing power represented by price increases.

This concept is illustrated in Table 22–7 and Figure 22–5. In Table 22–7, column 1 gives the interest rate on prime commercial paper plus 1.0; column 2 indicates the reduction in purchasing power during the year; column 3 gives the interest-minus-inflation value of the original principal amount; column 4 gives the real or inflation-adjusted rate of interest; and column 5 shows the nominal rate of interest prevailing during the year. The real and nominal interest rates obtained from Table 22–7 are graphed in

FIGURE 22–5 Nominal and Real Interest Rates on Prime Commercial Paper, 1963–1974

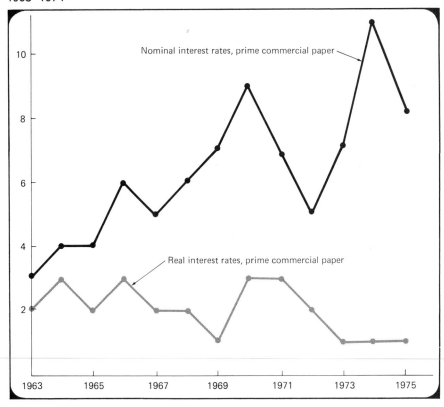

Source: Table 22–7.

Figure 22–5. It is interesting to note that real rates of interest have generally been in the 2 to 3 percent range, while nominal interest rates increase sharply when inflation increases rapidly, as it did in 1974 and 1975.

IMPLICATIONS OF INTEREST RATE PATTERNS FOR FINANCIAL TIMING

Variations in the cost of money and its availability are likely to be of great significance to financial managers. The importance of sound financial timing is further underscored by the mistakes observed in the past and the uncertainties of the future.

A question that is currently challenging financial managers is whether interest rates, which are now down from their historic peaks, will go back up to the 1974 levels or even higher once the 1976 recession ends. Should firms finance now with long-term debt in anticipation of even higher rates in the future? Or would it be a mistake to lock the company into high-cost, long-term capital?

Easy answers to these questions are not available, and the uncertainties have given rise to new forms and patterns of financing as documented throughout this book. No one can give definitive answers to the questions raised above, but financial executives must make decisions, and they must, therefore, make judgments about these issues.

SUMMARY

Financial managers have at least some flexibility in their operations. Even though a firm may have a target debt/assets ratio, it can deviate from this target to some extent in a given year to take advantage of favorable conditions in either the bond market or the stock market. Similarly, although it may have a target relationship between its long-term and short-term debt, it can vary from this target if market conditions suggest that such action is appropriate.

As a basis for making sound decisions with respect to financial timing, we have analyzed data covering both cyclical and long-term trends. Uncertainties about the future have increased in recent years, with a resultant increase in the importance of sound financial timing. Moreover, attempts to deal with an increasing level of uncertainty in the economy have given rise to new innovations in financing techniques and patterns. Some important changes in financing that have developed in response to changes in the economy, especially in the money and capital markets, are listed below.

1. Long-term financing has increased in comparison to the use of short-term commercial bank financing. Bond flotations in the capital markets have risen to record levels.

2. Public flotations of equity issues have increased substantially.
3. A large increase in debt ratios has occurred in response to the inflationary environment. From 1966 to 1975 the ratio of debt to assets for all manufacturing companies rose from 33 to 46 percent.
4. An increase has occurred in the use of equity participations in the form of convertibility or warrants.
5. Insurance companies and other institutional lenders have virtually ceased to provide credit to small- and medium-size borrowers on a straight debt basis. For business loans, warrants are usually required, while on mortgages supplementary payments based on a percentage of gross or net income are stipulated in loan contracts.
6. New equity securities have been issued in spite of the decline in equity prices beginning in early 1969. As the debt ratios of large corporations rose and as their liquidity positions declined, larger corporations began selling equity issues in substantial amounts.
7. Since larger firms have greater access to the financial markets, an increase in the volume of trade credit has occurred, with larger firms increasing their extension of credit to smaller ones.

These developments indicate that trends in the money and capital markets are increasing in importance to financial managers. The changes have been so massive that not only has financial timing been involved but also innovations in forms of financing used have been stimulated. Thus, financial policies have been broadened and have taken on greater importance in the overall management of business firms.

QUESTIONS

22-1. "It makes good sense for a firm to fund its floating debt, because this relieves the possibility that it will be called upon to pay off debt at an awkward time. From the standpoint of cost, however, it is always cheaper to use short-term debt than long-term debt." Discuss the statement.

22-2. Historical data indicate that more than twice as much capital is raised yearly by selling bonds than by selling common stocks. Does this indicate that corporate capital structures are becoming overburdened with debt?

22-3. Is the Federal Reserve's tight money policy restraining the country's economic growth? Discuss the pros and cons from the corporation's viewpoint.

22-4. Why do interest rates on different types of securities vary widely?

22-5. What does GNP represent? Why are its levels and growth significant to the financial manager?

22-6. Figure 22–1 indicates that short-term interest rates were higher than long-term interest rates for most of the period 1900–1930. Is there any reason to believe that this relationship may again prevail during the period 1975–1985?

22-7. Are short-term rates of any value in forecasting future rates in the long-term market?

PROBLEMS

22-1. In mid-1958 the Westcal Company made a reappraisal of its sales forecasts for the next one, two, and five years. It was clear that the product development program that had been under way for the previous five years was then coming to fruition. The officers of Westcal were confident that a sales growth of 12 to 15 percent a year (on a compound basis) for the next five years was strongly indicated unless general business declined.

The Westcal Company had total assets of $10 million. It had a debt-to-total assets ratio of 29 percent. Since it had been spending heavily on research and development during the past five years, its profits had been depressed and the stock had not been favorably regarded by investors.

The Westcal Company learned that it could borrow on a short-term basis at 2.5 percent (the rate for prime commercial paper at mid-1958 was 1.6 percent) and sell some common stock or float some nonconvertible long-term bonds at 4 percent. Westcal financed by selling $2 million of common stock (the maximum to avoid control problems) and by short-term loans at the lower rates until early 1960, when it found that its growing financial requirements could not be met by short-term borrowing. Its need for financing was so great that Westcal sold $10 million of convertible debentures at 5.5 percent (the rate on prime commercial paper at this time was almost 5 percent) and with terms requiring a strong current ratio and limitations on fixed asset purchases. The price of its common stock had quadrupled by mid-1959 but had dropped by 10 percent in early 1960.

Evaluate the timing and the selection of forms of financing by the Westcal Company.

22-2. In July 1975, as the economy in general was emerging from the 1973–1974 downturn and the Recyclable Container Corporation's business was resuming its strong growth in sales, Sam Lincoln, the treasurer, concluded that the firm would require more working capital financing during the year ending June 30, 1976. Below are the historical and the *pro forma* income statements and balance sheets of the Recyclable Container Corporation.

Recyclable Container Corporation, Income statements
For years ended June 30, 1975 and 1976 (In thousands of dollars)

	1975	Pro Forma 1976
Sales, net	$20,000	$28,000
Cost of sales	16,000	20,000
Gross profit	4,000	8,000
Operating expenses	2,000	3,000
Operating profit	2,000	5,000
Other income, net	400	200
Profits before taxes	2,400	5,200
Taxes	1,200	2,600
Net profit after taxes	1,200	2,600
Dividends	200	400
To retained earnings	$ 1,000	$ 2,200

Recyclable Container Corporation
Balance sheets, June 30, 1975 and 1976
(In thousands of dollars)

Assets	1975	Pro Forma 1976
Cash	$ 400	$ 1,200
Receivables	1,600	2,400
Inventories	2,000	3,200
Total current assets	$4,000 ·	$ 6,800
Fixed assets, net	2,000	4,000
Total assets	$6,000	$10,800

Liabilities and Capital	1975	Pro Forma 1976
Accounts payable	600	$ 1,000
Accruals	200	400
Reserves for taxes	1,200	1,600
Total current liabilities	$2,000	$ 3,000
Additional financing needed	0	1,600
Common stock, $10 par	2,000	2,000
Retained earnings	2,000	4,200
Total liabilities and capital	$6,000	$10,800

How should the financing needs be met? Why? (Although the $1,600,000 *pro forma* financial requirements are shown in the long-term section of the balance sheet, they can be met with either long- or short-term funds.)

22-3. Drake Manufacturing Company has decided to undertake a two-part capital expansion program, from which no benefits will accrue until both phases are com-

Drake Manufacturing Company
Balance Sheet
December 31, 1976
(Dollars in millions)

Current Assets:		Current liabilities:	
Cash	$ 2.0	Accounts payable	$ 5.0
Accounts receivable (net)	10.0	Accruals	2.4
Inventory	20.0	Current portion of LTD	2.0
Total current assets	$32.0	Total current liabilities	$ 9.4
		Long-term debt (7%)	16.0
Net property plant and equipment	50.0	Common stock ($10 par)	21.5
Total assets	$82.0	Paid in capital	13.0
		Retained earnings	22.1
		Total	$82.0

pleted. As treasurer of Drake it is your responsibility to examine the various sources of funds available to the company to finance each phase. The first phase will cost $5 million and will be undertaken immediately. It is anticipated that the company will begin the second phase, which also has an estimated cost of $5 million, approximately one year from now. The estimate for the second phase includes an adjustment for the rate of inflation, which is expected to increase from the current rate of 6 percent to approximately 9 percent at the end of the coming year. Drake's common stock is widely held and is traded on the over-the-counter market. Drake's balance sheet, income statement and market information for the last fiscal year are given here:

Drake Manufacturing Company
Income statement
For year ending December 31, 1976
(Dollars in millions)

Sales	$150.00	
Gross margin	60.00	
Operating expenses	39.00	
Operating income	21.00	EPS = $4.59
Interest	1.26	DPS = 1.60
Pretax earnings	$ 19.74	P/E = 10×
Taxes (50 percent)	9.87	Market price = $45.90
Net income	$ 9.87	

After a thorough review of the situation, and discussions with several banks and underwriters, you conclude that the following options are open to Drake. (Note: in any given year, assume that only one source of funds may be used.)

1. Use short-term debt to cover phases 1 and 2 of the construction program, then refund this debt with any of the long-term methods noted in 2 below at the end of the construction period.

2. Obtain long-term financing now for phase 1 of the construction program, then obtain additional financing next year for phase 2. The long-term financing methods available are bank term loans, debentures, and common stock.

3. Obtain long-term financing now to cover both phases of the expansion program, using one of the methods outlined in 2 above, to raise $10 million.

A review of the latest issue of the *Wall Street Journal* indicated that the following interest rates are now prevailing:

Bank Loans

Prime bank rate	6.75%
Revolving loan	8.75
Long-term	9.25

Commercial Paper

90–119 days	5.93%
4–6 months	6.27

U.S. Treasury Securities

3 months	4.93%
6 months	5.33
1 year	5.78

Corporate Bonds (20 years)

Aa	8.8%

Your analysis of the economy shows that economic activity began showing strong signs of improvement about two months ago, following a long period of sluggishness. You also notice that, according to today's *Wall Street Journal,* the average *P/E* ratio for Dow Jones Industrials is 13.1 compared to 8.6 less than one year ago.

You are concerned about the effect the additional financing will have on Drake's EPS and market price, as the benefits from the expansion will not begin to be realized for about three years. You also wish to maintain a strong, liquid balance sheet. The maximum acceptable ratio of long-term debt to total long-term capital is 33 percent. Discussions with underwriters have indicated that a stock issue could be sold at the current market price. However, the discussion of public or private debt issue, or the rating for a public issue of bonds, was not conclusive. Management believed that a public bond issue would probably be rated A.

As treasurer, you are requested to analyze the situation completely, and to support what you feel is the optimum financing plan and timing.

22-4. The objective of this assignment is to evaluate the timing decision associated with a recent issue of corporate bonds.

a. From an issue of the *Wall Street Journal* published within the most recent thirty-day period, in the pages that describe new issues of stock and bonds sold to the public, identify a public issue of corporate bonds that came to market (were issued) the preceding day. Record information identifying the issuer, the date of issue, the amount of the issue, its maturity, coupon rate, issue price, yield to maturity, rating, any other stated terms of the issue, and the degree of success of the first day sales. Much of this information can be found in the "tombstone" advertisement for the issue. Somewhere on the immediate surrounding pages will be a paragraph or a very short statement about the issue, its rating, and the way the issue was received by the market.

b. In the most recent monthly issue of the *Federal Reserve Bulletin (FRB),* locate in the index the item "Interest Rates: Bond and Stock Yields," and in that table under "Corporate Bonds" locate the column headed "Total." Record the yields under "Total" for each of the last fifteen months reported, and also the yield reported for each of the five years preceding the monthly data. Plot these data. Also, indicate the yield for your new issue as determined in part a above on this graph.

c. Briefly explain what has happened to long-term corporate interest rates in general in the interim between the most recent *FRB* data and the date of your new issue in part a. Given the current state of the economy, what is the outlook for interest rates over the next six months to one year?

d. Discuss the percentage interest cost incurred by the issuer of your bonds, and the timing of the new issue.

External Growth: Mergers and Holding Companies

23

Growth is vital to the well-being of a firm; without it, a business cannot attract able management because it cannot give recognition in promotions or offer challenging, creative activity. Without able executives, the firm is likely to decline and die. Much of the material in the previous chapters dealing with analysis, planning, and financing has a direct bearing on the financial manager's potential contribution to the growth of a firm. Because of the central importance of the growth requirement, the present chapter focusses on strategies for promoting growth.

Merger activity has played an important part in the growth of firms in the United States, and financial managers are required both to appraise the desirability of a prospective purchase and to participate directly in evaluating the respective companies involved in a merger.[1] Consequently, it is essential that the study of financial management provide the background necessary for effective participation in merger negotiations and decisions.

Financial managers—and intelligent laymen—also need to be aware of the broader significance of mergers. Despite the heightened merger activities in the 1920s, again after World War II, and during the 1960s, recent merger movements have neither approached the magnitude nor had the social consequences of those that took place from 1890 to 1905. During this period, more than two hundred major combinations were effected, resulting in the concentration that has characterized the steel, tobacco, and other important

---

[1]As we use the term, "merger" means any combination that forms one economic unit from two or more previous ones. For legal purposes there are distinctions between the various ways these combinations can occur, but our emphasis is on fundamental business and financial aspects of mergers or acquisitions.

513

industries. Regardless of the business objectives and motives of merger activity, its social and economic consequences must also be taken into account.

MERGERS VERSUS INTERNAL GROWTH

Many of the objectives of size and diversification may be achieved either through internal growth or by external growth through acquisitions and mergers. In the post-World War II period, considerable diversification was achieved by many firms through external acquisition. Some financial reasons for utilizing external acquisition instead of internal growth to achieve diversification are discussed below.

Financing

Sometimes it is possible to finance an acquisition when it is not possible to finance internal growth. A large steel plant, for example, involves a large investment. Steel capacity may be acquired in a merger through an exchange of stock more cheaply than it can be obtained by buying the facilities themselves. Sellers may be more willing to accept the stock of the purchaser in payment for the facilities sold than would investors in a public offering. The use of stock reduces cash requirements for the acquisition of assets.

Market Capitalization Rates

While it is not strictly an operating factor, the fact that the earnings of larger economic units are frequently capitalized at lower rates and hence produce higher market values has stimulated many mergers. The securities of larger firms have better marketability; these firms are more able to diversify and thus reduce risks, and they are generally better known. All these factors lead to lower required rates of return and higher price/earnings ratios. As a result, it may be possible to consolidate firms and have the resulting market value greater than the sum of their individual values, even if there is no increase in aggregate earnings. To illustrate, three companies may each be earning $1 million and selling at 10 times earnings, for a total market value of ($1 million) (10)(3) equals $30 million. When these companies combine, the new company may obtain a stock exchange listing or may take other actions to improve the price of its stock. If so, the price/earnings ratio may rise to 15, in which case the market value of the consolidated firm would be $45 million.[2]

---

[2]The market capitalization rate is related to the cost of equity, as we discussed in Chapter 20. A lower capitalization rate results in a lower cost of capital. Therefore, the same actions that raise the market value of the equity also lower the firm's cost of new capital.

Taxes

Without question, the high level of taxation was a factor stimulating merger activity in the postwar period. Studies have indicated that taxes appear to have been a major reason for the sale of about one-third of the firms acquired by merger. Inheritance taxes precipitated these sales in some cases; in others, the advantage of buying a company with a tax loss provided the motivation.

TERMS OF MERGERS

For every merger actually consummated, a number of other potentially attractive combinations fail during the negotiating stage. In some of these cases, negotiations are broken off when it is revealed that the companies' operations are not compatible. In others, tangible benefits would result, but the parties are unable to agree on the merger terms. Of these terms, the most important is the price to be paid by the acquiring firm for the firm acquired. Factors that influence this important aspect of a merger are now considered.

Effects on Price and Earnings

A merger carries potentialities for either favorable or adverse effects on earnings, on market prices of shares, or on both. Previous chapters have shown that investment decisions should be guided by the effects on market values, and these effects should in turn be determined by the effects on future earnings and dividends. These future events are difficult to forecast, however, so stockholders, as well as managers, attribute great importance to the immediate effects of a contemplated merger on earnings per share. Directors of companies will often state, "I do not know how the merger will affect the market price of the shares of my company because so many forces influencing market prices are at work. But the effect on earnings per share can be seen directly."

An example will illustrate the effects of a proposed merger on earnings per share and thus suggest the kinds of problems that are likely to arise. Assume the following facts for two companies:

	Company A	Company B
Total earnings	$20,000	$50,000
Number of shares of common stock	5,000	10,000
Earnings per share of stock	$ 4.00	$ 5.00
Price/earnings ratio per share	15×	12×
Market price per share	$ 60.00	$ 60.00

Suppose the firms agree to merge, with B, the surviving firm, acquiring the shares of A by a one-for-one exchange of stock. The exchange ratio is determined by the respective market prices of the two companies. Assuming no increase in earnings, the effects on earnings per share are shown in the following tabulation:

	Shares of Company B Owned after Merger	Earnings per Share	
		Before merger	After merger
A's stockholders	5,000	$4	$4.67
B's stockholders	10,000	5	4.67
Total	15,000		

Since total earnings are $70,000 and a total of 15,000 shares will be outstanding after the merger has been completed, the new earnings per share will be $4.67. Earnings will increase by 67 cents for A's stockholders, but they will decline by 33 cents for B's.

The effects on market values are less certain. If the combined company sells at company A's price/earnings ratio of 15, the new market value per share of the new company will be $70. In this case, shareholders of both companies will have benefited. This result comes about because the combined earnings are now valued at a multiplier of 15, whereas prior to the merger one portion of the earnings was valued at a multiplier of 15 and another portion was valued at a multiplier of 12.

If, on the other hand, the earnings of the new company are valued at B's multiplier of 12, the indicated market value of the shares will be $56. The shareholders of each company will have suffered a $4 dilution in market value.

Because the effects on market value per share are less certain than those on earnings per share, the impact of earnings per share tends to be given great weight in merger negotiations. Because of this, the following analysis also emphasizes effects on earnings per share, while recognizing that maximizing market value is the valid rule of investment decisions.

If the merger takes place on the basis of earnings, neither earnings dilution nor earnings appreciation will take place, as indicated below.

It is clear that the equivalent earnings per share after the merger are the same as before the merger. The effects on market values will depend upon whether the 15-times multiplier of A or the 12-times multiplier of B prevails.

Of the numerous factors affecting the valuation of the constituent companies in a merger, all must ultimately be reflected in the earnings per share, or market price, of the companies. Hence, all the effects on the earnings posi-

	Shares of Company B Owned after Merger	Earnings per Old Share	
		Before merger	*After merger*
A's stockholders[a]	4,000	$4	$4
B's stockholders	10,000	5	5
Total	14,000		

[a]On the basis of earnings, the exchange ratio is 4:5; that is, company A's shareholders receive four shares of B stock for each five shares of A stock they own. Earnings per share of the merged company is $5. But, since A's shareholders now own only 80 percent of the number of their old shares, their equivalent earnings per *old* share is the same $4. For example, suppose one of A's stockholders formerly held 100 shares. He will own only 80 shares of B after the merger, and his total earnings will be 80 × $5 = $400. Dividing his $400 total earnings by the number of shares he formerly owned, 100, gives the $4 per *old* share.

tion or wealth position of stockholders are encompassed by the foregoing example. We will now consider both quantitative and qualitative factors that will influence the terms on which a merger is likely to take place.

Quantitative Factors Affecting Terms of Mergers

Five factors have received the greatest emphasis in arriving at merger terms:

1. Earnings and the growth rate of earnings.
2. Dividends.
3. Market values.
4. Book values.
5. Net current assets.

Analysis is typically based on the per share values of the foregoing factors. The relative importance of each factor and the circumstances under which each is likely to be the most influential determinant in arriving at terms will vary. The nature of these influences is described below.

Earnings and Growth Rates   Both expected earnings and capitalization rates as reflected in P/E ratios are important in determining the values that will be established in a merger. The analysis necessarily begins with historical data on the firms' earnings, whose past growth rates, future trends, and variability are important determinants of the earnings multiplier, or P/E ratio, that will prevail after the merger.

How future earnings growth rates affect the multiplier can be illustrated by extending the preceding example. First, we know that high P/E ratios are commonly associated with rapidly growing companies. Since company A has the higher P/E ratio, it is reasonable to assume that its earnings are expected to grow more rapidly than those of company B. Suppose A's expected growth rate is 10 percent and B's 5 percent. Looking at the proposed merger from the point of view of company B and its stockholders, and assuming that the exchange ratio is based on present market prices, it can be seen that B will suffer a dilution in earnings when the merger occurs. However, B will be acquiring a firm with more favorable growth prospects; hence, its earnings after the merger should increase more rapidly than before. In this case, the new growth rate is assumed to be a weighted average of the growth rates of the individual firms, weighted by their respective total earnings before the merger. In the example, the new expected growth rate is $(^4/_{14})(10\%) + (^{10}/_{14})(5\%) = 6.43$ percent.

With the new growth rate it is possible to determine just how long it will take company B's stockholders to regain the earnings dilution, that is, how long it will take earnings per share to revert back to their previous position before the merger. This can be determined graphically from Figure 23–1.[3] Without the merger, B would have initial earnings of $5 a share, and these earnings would have grown at a rate of 5 percent a year. With the merger, earnings drop to $4.67 a share, but the rate of growth increases to 6.43 percent. Under these conditions, the earnings dilution is overcome after five years; from the fifth year on, B's earnings will be higher, assuming the merger is consummated.

FIGURE 23–1 Effect of Merger on Future Earnings

---

[3]The calculation could also be made algebraically by solving for N in the following equation: $E_1(1 + g_1)^N = E_2(1 + g_2)^N$, where E_1 = earnings before the merger, E_2 = earnings after the merger, g_1 and g_2 are the growth rates before and after the merger, and N is the break-even number of years.

This same relationship could be developed from the point of view of the faster growing firm. Here there would be an immediate earnings increase but a reduced rate of growth. Working through the analysis would show the number of years before the earnings accretion would be eroded.

It is apparent that the critical variables are (1) the respective rates of growth of the two firms; (2) their relative sizes, which determine the actual amount of the initial earnings per share dilution or accretion, as well as the new weighted average growth rate; (3) the firms' P/E ratios; and (4) the exchange ratio. These factors interact to produce the resulting pattern of earnings per share for the surviving company. It is possible to generalize the relationships somewhat; for our purposes, it is necessary simply to note that in the bargaining process the exchange ratio is the variable that must be manipulated in an effort to reach a mutually satisfactory earnings pattern.[4]

Dividends Because they represent the actual income received by stockholders, dividends may influence the terms of merger. As the material in Chapter 21 suggests, however, dividends are likely to have little influence on the market price of companies with a record of high growth and high profitability. For example, some companies, such as Laser Industries, have not yet paid cash dividends but command market prices representing a high multiple of current earnings. At the end of 1976, Laser was selling at a multiplier of approximately 40 times. However, for utility companies and for companies in industries where growth rates and profitability have declined, the dollar amount of dividends paid may have a relatively important influence on the market price of the stock. Dividends may therefore influence the terms on which these companies would be likely to trade in a merger.[5]

Market Values The price of a firm's stock reflects expectations about its future earnings and dividends, so current market values are expected to have a strong influence on the terms of a merger. However, the value placed on a firm in an acquisition is likely to exceed its current market price for a number

---

[4]We should also mention at this point that certain companies, especially the "conglomerates," are reported to have used mergers to produce a "growth illusion" designed to increase the prices of their stocks. When a high P/E ratio company buys a low P/E ratio company, the earnings per share of the acquiring firm rise *because* of the merger. Thus, mergers can produce growth in reported earnings for the acquiring firm. This growth by merger, in turn, can cause the acquiring firm to keep its high P/E ratio. With this ratio, the conglomerates can seek new low P/E merger candidates and thus continue to obtain growth through mergers. The chain is broken (1) if the rate of merger activity slows, or (2) if the P/E ratio of the acquiring firm falls. In 1968 and 1969 several large conglomerates reported profit declines caused by losses in certain of their divisions. This reduced the growth rate in *EPS*, which in turn led to a decline in the P/E ratio. A change in tax laws and antitrust suits against some conglomerate mergers also made it more difficult to consummate favorable mergers. All these factors, along with tight money and depressed conditions in some industries, caused a further reduction in the P/E ratio and compounded these firms' problems. The net result was a drastic revaluation of conglomerate share prices, with such former favorites as LTV falling from a high of $169 to $7½ and Litton Industries, from $115 to $6¾.

[5]If a company that does not pay dividends on its stock is seeking to acquire a firm whose stockholders are accustomed to receiving dividends, the exchange can be on a convertibles-for-common-stock basis. This will enable the acquired firm's stockholders to continue receiving income.

of reasons. (1) If the company is in a depressed industry, its stockholders are likely to overdiscount the dismal outlook for the company; this will result in a very low current market price. (2) The prospective purchaser may be interested in acquiring the company for the contribution that it may make to the acquiring company. Thus, the acquired company is worth more to an informed purchaser than it is in the general market. (3) Stockholders are offered more than current market prices for their stock as an inducement to sell. For these reasons, the offering price is usually in the range of 10 to 20 percent above the market price before the merger announcement.

Book Value per Share   Book values are generally considered to be relatively unimportant in determining the value of a company, as they merely represent the historical investments that have been made in the company. These investments may have little relation to current values or prices. At times, however, especially when book values substantially exceed market values, they may well have an impact on merger terms. The book value is an index of the amount of physical facilities made available in the merger. Despite a past record of low earning power, it is always possible that, under effective management, a firm's assets may once again achieve normal earning power, in which case the market value of the company will rise. Because of the potential contribution of physical properties to improved future earnings, book values may have an influence on actual merger terms.

Net Current Assets per Share   Net current assets (current assets minus current liabilities) per share are likely to have an influence on merger terms because they represent the amount of liquidity that may be obtained from a company in a merger. In the postwar textile mergers, net current assets were very high, and this was one of the characteristics making textile companies attractive to the acquiring firms. By buying a textile company, often with securities, an acquiring company was in a position to look for still other merger candidates, paying for the new acquisition with the just-acquired liquidity. Similarly, if an acquired company is debt-free, the acquiring firm may be able to borrow funds required for the purchase, using the acquired firm's assets and earning power as security for the loan.[6]

Relative Importance of Quantitative Factors

Attempts have been made to determine statistically the relative weights assigned to each of the above factors in actual merger cases. These attempts have been singularly unsuccessful. In one case, one factor seems to dominate; in another, some other determinant appears to be most important. This

---

[6]By the same token, a firm seeking to *avoid* being acquired will reduce its liquid position and use up its borrowing potential.

absence of consistent patterns among the quantitative factors suggests that qualitative forces are also at work, and we now turn our attention to these more nebulous variables.

Qualitative Influences: Synergy

Sometimes the most important influence on the terms of a merger is a business consideration not reflected at all in historical quantitative data. A soundly conceived merger is one in which the combination produces what may be called a *synergistic,* or "two-plus-two-equals-five," effect. By the combination, more profits are generated than could be achieved by the individual firms operating separately.

To illustrate, in the merger between Merck and Company and Sharp and Dohme, it was said that each company complemented the other in an important way. Merck had a strong reputation for its research organization. Sharp and Dohme had a most effective sales force. The combination of these two pharmaceutical companies added strength to both. Another example is the merger between Carrier Corporation and Affiliated Gas Equipment, Inc. The merger enabled the combined company to provide a complete line of air-conditioning and heating equipment. The merger between Hilton Hotels and Statler Hotels led to economies in the purchase of supplies and materials. One Hilton executive estimated that the savings accruing simply from the combined management of the Statler Hotel in New York and Hilton's New York Hotel amounted to $700,000 a year. The bulk of the savings were in laundry, food, advertising, and administrative costs.

The qualitative factors may also reflect other influences. The merger or acquisition may enable one company which lacks general management ability to obtain it from the other company. Another factor may be the acquisition of a technically competent scientific or engineering staff if one of the companies has fallen behind in the technological race. In such a situation, the company needing the technical competence possessed by the other firm may be willing to pay a substantial premium over previous levels of earnings, dividends, market values, or book values.

The purpose of the merger may be to develop a production capability a firm does not possess. Some firms are strong in producing custom-made items with high performance characteristics, yet these firms, on entering new markets, must make use of mass-production techniques. If the firm has had no such experience, this skill may have to be obtained by means of a merger. The firm may perhaps need to develop an effective sales organization. For example, some of the companies previously oriented to the defense market, such as those in aerospace, found that they had only a limited industrial sales organization; merger was the solution to the problem.

The foregoing are the kinds of qualitative considerations that may have an overriding influence on the actual terms of merger, and the values of these contributions are never easy to quantify. The all-encompassing question, of course, is how these factors will affect the contribution of each company to future earnings per share in the combined operation. The historical data and the qualitative considerations described, in addition to judgment and bargaining, combine to determine merger terms.

HOLDING COMPANIES

In 1889, New Jersey became the first state to pass a general incorporation law permitting corporations to be formed for the sole purpose of owning the stocks of other companies. This law was the origin of the holding company. The Sherman Act of 1890, which prohibits combinations or collusion in restraint of trade, gave an impetus to holding company operations as well as to outright mergers, because companies could do as one company what they were forbidden to do, by the terms of the act, as separate companies.

Many of the advantages and disadvantages of holding companies are no more than the advantages and disadvantages of large-scale operations already discussed in connection with mergers and consolidations. Whether a company is organized on a divisional basis or with the divisions kept as separate companies does not affect the basic reasons for conducting a large-scale, multiproduct, multiplant operation. However, the holding company form of large-scale operations has different advantages and disadvantages from those of completely integrated divisionalized operations.

Advantages of Holding Companies

Control with Fractional Ownership   Through a holding company operation, a firm may buy 5, 10, or 50 percent of the stock of another corporation. Such fractional ownership may be sufficient to give the acquiring company effective working control or substantial influence over the operations of the company in which it has acquired stock ownership. An article in the *New York Times* states this point clearly.

> Working control is often considered to entail more than 25 percent of the common stock, but it can be as low as 10 percent if the stock is widely distributed. One financier says that the attitude of management is more important than the number of shares owned, adding that "if they think you can control the company, then you do." In addition, control on a very slim margin can be held through friendship with large stockholders outside the holding company group.

Sometimes holding company operations represent the initial stages of the transformation of an operating company into an investment company, particularly when the operating company is in a declining industry. When the sales of an industry begin to decline permanently and the firm begins to liquidate its operating assets, it may use these liquid funds to invest in industries having a more favorable growth potential.

Isolation of Risks Because the various operating companies in a holding company system are separate legal entities, the obligations of any one unit are separate from those of the other units. Catastrophic losses incurred by one unit of the holding company system are therefore not transmitted as claims on the assets of the other units.

Although this is the customary generalization of the nature of a holding company system, it is not completely valid. In extending credit to one of the units of a holding company system, an astute financial manager or loan officer will require a guarantee or a claim on the assets of all the elements in a complete holding company system. To some degree, therefore, the assets in the various elements of a holding company are joined. The advantage remains to the extent that unanticipated catastrophes that may occur to one unit in a holding company system will not be transmitted to the other units.

Approval Not Required If a holding company group is seeking to obtain effective working control of a number of companies, it may quietly purchase a portion of their stock. This is a completely informal operation, and the permission or approval of the stockholders of the acquired company or companies is not required. Thus the guiding personalities in a holding company operation are not dependent upon negotiations and approval of the other interest groups in order to obtain their objectives. This feature of holding company operations has, however, been limited somewhat by the recent SEC actions described later in the chapter.

Disadvantages of Holding Companies

Partial Multiple Taxation Provided the holding company owns at least 80 percent of a subsidiary's voting stock, the Internal Revenue regulations permit the filing of consolidated returns, in which case dividends received by the parent are not taxed. However, if less than 80 percent of the stock is owned, returns may not be consolidated, but 85 percent of the dividends received by the holding company may be deducted. With a tax rate of 48 percent, this means that the effective tax on intercorporate dividends is 7.2 percent. This partial double taxation somewhat offsets the benefits of holding company control with limited ownership, but whether the penalty of 7.2 percent of dividends received is sufficient to offset other possible advantages is a matter that must be decided in individual situations.[7]

Ease of Enforced Dissolution In the case of a holding company operation that falls into disfavor with the U.S. Department of Justice, it is relatively easy

---

[7]The 1969 Tax Reform Law also empowers the Internal Revenue Service to prohibit the deductibility of debt issued to acquire another firm where the following conditions hold: (1) the debt is subordinated to a "significant portion" of the firm's other creditors; (2) the debt is convertible or has warrants attached; (3) the debt/assets ratio exceeds 67 percent; and (4) on a *pro forma* basis, the times-interest-earned ratio is less than 3. The IRS can use discretion in invoking this power.

to require dissolution of the relationship by disposal of stock ownership; for instance, du Pont was required to dispose of its 23 percent stock interest in General Motors Corporation, acquired in the early 1920s. Because there was no fusion between the corporations, there were no difficulties, from an operating standpoint, in requiring the separation of the two companies. However, if complete amalgamation had taken place, it would have been much more difficult to break up the company after so many years, and the likelihood of forced divestiture would have been reduced.

Risks of Excessive Pyramiding While pyramiding magnifies profits if operations are successful, as we shall see in the financial leverage analysis, it also magnifies losses. The greater the degree of pyramiding, the greater the degree of risk involved for any fluctuations in sales or earnings of the company. This potential disadvantage of pyramiding operations through holding companies is discussed in the next section.

Leverage in Holding Companies

The problem of excessive leverage is worthy of further note, for the degree of leverage in certain past instances has been truly staggering. For example, in the 1920s, Samuel Insull and his group controlled electric utility operating companies at the bottom of a holding company pyramid by a one-twentieth of 1 percent investment. As a ratio, this represents 1/2,000. In other words, $1 of capital at the top holding company level controlled $2,000 of assets at the operating level. A similar situation existed in the railroad field. It has been stated that Robert R. Young, with an investment of $254,000, obtained control of the Allegheny system, consisting of total operating assets of $3 billion.

The nature of leverage in a holding company system and its advantages and disadvantages are illustrated by the hypothetical example developed in Table 23–1. Although this is a hypothetical example, not an actual case, it illustrates actual situations. One-half of the operating company's class B common stock is owned by holding company 1; in fact, it is the only asset of holding company 1. Holding company 2 holds as its total assets one-half of the class B common stock of holding company 1. Consequently, $1,000 of class B common stock of holding company 2 controls $2 million of assets at the operating company level. Further leverage could, of course, have been postulated in this situation by setting up a third company to own common stock B of holding company 2.

Table 23–2 shows the results of holding company leverage on gains and losses at the top level. In the first column, it is assumed that the operating company earns 12 percent before taxes on its $2 million of assets; in the second column it is assumed that the return on assets is 8 percent. The operating and holding companies are the same ones described in Table 23–1.

TABLE 23–1   Leverage in a Holding Company System

		Holding Company 2	
Common stock B of holding company 1	$5,000	Debt Preferred stock Common stock: class A[a] Common stock: class B	$2,000 1,000 1,000 1,000
	$5,000		$5,000
		Holding Company 1	
Common stock B of operating company	$100,000	Debt Preferred stock Common stock: class A[a] Common stock: class B	$ 50,000 10,000 30,000 10,000
	$100,000		$100,000
		Operating Company	
Total assets	$2,000,000	Debt Preferred stock Common stock: class A[a] Common stock: class B	$1,000,000 150,000 650,000 200,000
	$2,000,000		$2,000,000

[a]Common stock A is nonvoting.

A return of 12 percent on the operating assets of $2 million represents a total profit of $240,000. The debt interest of $40,000 is deducted from this amount, and the 50 percent tax rate applies to the remainder. The amount available to common stock after payment of debt interest, preferred stock dividends, and an 8 percent return to the nonvoting common stock A is $40,500. Assuming a $40,000 dividend payout, holding company 1, on the basis of its 50 percent ownership of the operating company, earns $20,000. If the same kind of analysis is followed through, the amount available to common stock B in holding company 2 would be $4,421. This return is on an investment of $1,000, representing a return on the investment in common stock B of holding company 2 of about 440 percent. The power of leverage in a holding company system can indeed be great.

On the other hand, if a decline in revenues caused the pretax earnings to drop to 8 percent of the total assets of the operating company, the results would be disastrous. The amount earned under these circumstances is $160,000. After deducting the bond interest, the amount subject to tax is $120,000, resulting in a tax of $60,000. The after-tax-but-before-interest earnings are $100,000. The total prior charges are

$99,500, leaving $500 available to common stock B. If all earnings are paid out in dividends to common stock B, the earnings of holding company 1 are $250. This is not enough to meet the debt interest. The holding company system would be forced to default on the debt interest of holding company 1 and, of course, holding company 2.

TABLE 23-2 Results of Holding Company Leverage on Gains and Losses

Assume that each company pays:	4% on debt	
	5% on preferred stock	
	8% on common stock A	

	Earnings before Taxes	
Operating Company	12%	8%
Amount earned	$240,000	$160,000
Less tax[a]	100,000	60,000
Available to meet fixed charges	$140,000	$100,000
Debt interest	$ 40,000	$ 40,000
Preferred stock	7,500	7,500
Common stock A	52,000	52,000
Total charges	$ 99,500	$ 99,500
Available to common B	40,500	500
Dividends to common B	40,000	500
Holding Company 1		
Amount earned	$ 20,000	$ 250
Less tax (0.5 × 0.15 × $18,000)[a]	1,350	0
Available to meet fixed charges	$ 18,650	$ 250
Debt interest	$ 2,000	$ 2,000
Preferred stock	500	500
Common stock A	2,400	2,400
Total charges	$ 4,900	$ 4,900
Available to common B	$ 13,750	loss
Dividends to common B	10,000	
Holding Company 2		
Amount earned	$ 5,000	
Less taxes (0.5 × 0.15 × $4,920)[a]	369	
Available to meet fixed charges	$ 4,631	
Debt interest	$ 80	
Preferred stock	50	
Common stock A	80	
Total charges	$ 210	
Available to common B	$ 4,421	
Percent return on common B	442%	

[a]Tax computed on earnings less interest charges at a 50 percent tax rate. Since earnings are entirely in the form of intercorporate dividends, only 15 percent of the holding company's earnings are taxable.

This example illustrates the potential for tremendous gains in a holding company system. It also illustrates that a small decline in earnings on the assets of the operating companies would be disastrous.

TENDER OFFERS

In a tender offer, one party, generally a corporation seeking a controlling interest in another corporation, asks the stockholders of the firm it is seeking to control to submit, or "tender," their shares in exchange for a specified price. The price is generally stated as so many dollars per share of acquired stock, although it can be stated in terms of shares of stock in the acquiring firm. The tender offer is a direct appeal to stockholders, so it need not be approved by the management of the target firm. Tender offers have been used for a number of years, but the pace greatly accelerated after 1965.

If one firm wishes to gain control over another, it typically approaches the other firm's management and seeks its approval of the merger. If approval cannot be obtained, the acquiring company can appeal directly to stockholders by means of the tender offer, unless the management of the target firm holds enough stock to retain control.

During 1967, Congressional investigations were conducted to obtain information that could be used to legislate controls over tender offers. The reasons for the investigations were (1) the frequency of tender offers, (2) the thought that the recent merger trend was leading to "too much concentration" in the economy, and (3) the feeling that tender offers were somehow "unfair" to the managements of the firms acquired through this vehicle. A new law became effective on July 29, 1968, placing tender offers under full SEC jurisdiction. Disclosure requirements written into the statute include the following: (1) The acquiring firm must give both to the management of the target firm and the SEC thirty days' notice of its intentions to make the acquisition. (2) When substantial blocks are purchased through tender offers (or through open market purchases—that is, on the stock exchange), the beneficial owner of the stock must be disclosed, together with the name of the party putting up the money for the transaction.

The example of Tenneco's acquisition of Kern County Land Company illustrates many of these points. First, Kern was a relatively old, conservatively managed company whose assets consisted largely of oil properties and agricultural land, together with some manufacturing subsidiaries. Many informed investors believed that Kern's assets had a potential long-run value in excess of its current market price. Occidental Petroleum, a relatively aggressive company, made an investigation of Kern's assets and decided to make a tender offer for the company. At that time, Kern's market price on the New York Stock Exchange was about $60 a share, while the price Occidental decided to offer Kern's stockholders was $83.50 a share. According to Kern's management, Occidental's management got in touch with the former over a weekend and informed Kern that the tender offer would be made the following Monday.

Kern's management resisted the offer. Because the published statements of Occidental indicated that it felt Kern's undervalued position was partly the result of unimaginative management, Kern's management could anticipate being replaced in the event that Occidental effected the takeover. Naturally, Kern's management resisted the takeover. Kern's president wrote a letter to stockholders condemning the merger and published the letter as an advertisement in the *Wall Street Journal.* His position was that Kern's stock was certainly valuable and that it was worth more than had been offered by Occidental Petroleum.

How would Kern County's stockholders react to this exchange? In the first place, the stock had been selling at about $60 a share, and now they were offered $83.50 a share. With this differential, stockholders would certainly accept the tender unless Kern's management could do something to keep the price above $83.50. What Kern did was to obtain "marriage proposals" from a number of other companies. Kern's management reported to the newspapers—while Occidental's tender offer was still outstanding—that it had received a substantial number of proposals calling for the purchase of Kern's stock at a price substantially in excess of $83.50.

The offer Kern's management finally accepted—and presumably the one giving Kern's stockholders the highest price—was from Tenneco Corporation. Tenneco offered one share of a new $5.50 convertible preferred stock for each share of Kern's stock. At the time of Tenneco's offer, the market value of this convertible preferred was estimated to be worth about $105 a share. Further, Kern's stockholders would not have to pay capital gains tax on this stock at the time of the exchange. (Had they accepted Occidental's offer, the difference between $83.50 and the cost of their stock would have been taxable income to Kern's stockholders.) According to newspaper reports, Tenneco planned to keep Kern's existing management after the merger was completed.

When the Kern-Tenneco merger was finalized, Tenneco owned the Kern stock and thus became a holding company, with Kern being one of its operating subsidiaries.

SUMMARY

Growth is vital to the well-being of a firm, for without it a business cannot attract able management because it cannot give men recognition in promotions and challenging, creative activity. Mergers have played an important part in the growth of firms, and since financial managers are required both to appraise the desirability of a prospective merger and to participate in evaluating the respective companies involved in the merger, the present chapter has been devoted to background materials on merger decisions.

Terms of Mergers   The most important term that must be negotiated in a merger arrangement is the price the acquiring firm will pay for the acquired business. The most important *quantitative* factors influencing the terms of a merger are (1) current earnings, (2) current market prices, (3) book values, and (4) net working capital. *Qualitative* considerations may suggest that *synergistic,* or "two-plus-two-equals-five," effects may be present to a sufficient extent to warrant paying more for the acquired firm than the quantitative factors would suggest.

Holding Companies   In mergers, one firm disappears. However, an alternative is for one firm to buy all or a majority of the common stock of another and to run the acquired firm as an operating subsidiary. When this occurs, the acquiring firm is said to be a *holding company.* A number of advantages arise when a holding company is formed.

1. It may be possible to control the acquired firm with a smaller investment than would be necessary in a merger.
2. Each firm in a holding company is a separate legal entity, and the obligations of any one unit are separate from the obligations of the other units.
3. Stockholder approval is required before a merger can take place. This is not necessary in a holding company situation.

There are also some disadvantages to holding companies, some of which are listed below:

1. If the holding company does not own 80 percent of the subsidiary's stock and does not file consolidated tax returns, it is subject to taxes on 15 percent of the dividends received from the subsidiary.
2. The leverage effects possible in holding companies can subject the holding company to a great deal of risk.
3. The Antitrust Division of the U.S. Department of Justice can much more easily force the breakup of a holding company situation than it can the dissolution of two completely merged firms.

QUESTIONS

23-1. The number of mergers tends to fluctuate with business activity, rising when GNP rises and falling when GNP falls. Why does this relationship exist?

23-2. A large firm has certain advantages over a smaller one. What are some of the *financial* advantages of large size?

23-3. What are some of the potential benefits that can be expected by a firm that merges with a company in a different industry?

23-4. Distinguish between a holding company and an operating company. Give an example of each.

23-5. Which appears to be more risky, the use of debt in the holding company's capital structure or the use of debt in the operating company's? Why?

23-6. Is the public interest served by an increase in merger activity? Give arguments both pro and con.

23-7. Would the book value of a company's assets be considered the absolute minimum price to be paid for a firm? Why? Is there any value that would qualify as an absolute minimum?

23-8. Discuss the situation where one firm, Midwest Motors, for example, calls off merger negotiations with another, American Data Labs, because the latter's stock price is overvalued. What assumption concerning dilution is implicit in the above situation?

23-9. There are many methods by which a company can raise additional capital. Can a merger be considered a means of raising additional equity capital? Explain.

23-10. Are the negotiations for merger agreements more difficult if the firms are in different industries or in the same industry? if they are about the same size or quite different in size? if the ages of the firms are about the same or if they are very different? Why?

23-11. How would the existence of long-term debt in a company's financial structure affect its valuation for merger purposes? Could the same be said for any debt account regardless of its maturity?

23-12. During 1964–1965, the Pure Oil Company was involved in merger negotiations with at least three other firms. The terms of these arrangements varied from a transfer of stock to a direct cash purchase of Pure Oil. Discuss the relative advantages to a corporation of paying for an acquisition in cash or in stock.

23-13. In late 1968 the SEC and the New York Stock Exchange each issued sets of rulings on disclosure of information which, in effect, required that firms disclose that they have entered into merger discussions as soon as they start such discussions. Since the previous procedure had been to delay disclosure until it was evident that there was a reasonably good expectation the merger under discussion would actually go through (and not to bring the matter up at all if the merger died in the early stages), it can safely be predicted that, in a statistical sense, a larger percentage of prospective mergers will be "abandoned" in the future than in the past.

    a. Why do you suppose the new rulings were put into effect?

    b. Will the new rulings have any adverse effects? Why?

PROBLEMS

23-1. You are given the following balance sheets:

Southern Holding Company
Consolidated balance sheet

Cash	$1,500	Borrowings	$1,125
Other current assets	1,125	Common stock	1,875
Net property	1,875	Retained earnings	1,500
Total assets	$4,500	Total claims on assets	$4,500

Gordon Engineering Company
Balance sheet

Cash	$375	Net worth	$750
Net property	375		
Total assets	$750	Total net worth	$750

a. The holding company, Southern, buys the operating company, Gordon, with "free" cash of $750. Show the new consolidated balance sheet for Southern after the acquisition.

b. Instead of buying Gordon, Southern buys LaBelle Company with free cash of $1,125. The balance sheet of LaBelle follows:

LaBelle Company
Balance sheet

Cash	$ 750	Borrowings	$ 750
Net property	1,125	Net worth	1,125
Total assets	$1,875	Total claims on assets	$1,875

Show the new consolidated balance sheet for Southern after acquisition of LaBelle.

c. What are the implications of your consolidated balance sheets for measuring the growth of firms resulting from acquisitions?

23-2. Texas Mining Company is a holding company owning the entire common stock of Metco Company and Jenkins Company. The balance sheet as of December 31, 1975, for each subsidiary is identical with the following one.

Balance sheet, December 31, 1975

Current assets	$ 7,500,000	Current liabilities	$ 1,250,000
Fixed assets, net	5,000,000	First mortgage bonds (9%)	2,500,000
		Preferred stock (7%)	2,500,000
		Common stock	5,000,000
		Retained earnings	1,250,000
Total assets	$12,500,000	Total claims on assets	$12,500,000

Each operating company earns $1,375,000 annually before taxes and before interest and preferred dividends. A 50 percent tax rate is assumed.

a. What is the annual rate of return on each company's net worth (common stock plus retained earnings)?

b. Construct a balance sheet for Texas Mining Company based on the following assumptions: (1) The only asset of the holding company is the common stock of the two subsidiaries; this stock is carried at par (not book) value. (2) The holding company has $1.2 million of 8 percent coupon debt and $2.8 million of 6 percent preferred stock.

c. What is the rate of return on the book value of the holding company's common stock if (1) Texas Mining files a consolidated income tax return, and (2) subsidiary earnings available to common are taken as dividends by the holding company?

d. With regard to part c, which method of income taxation should Texas Mining employ?

e. How can the rate of return in part c be increased?

f. What investment is necessary to control the three companies under the assumptions specified in part b?

g. If ownership of 25 percent of the holding company's common stock ($6 million of common) could control all three firms, what percentage would this be of the total operating assets?

23-3. Every merger agreement is subject to negotiation between the companies involved. One significant indicator of the compensation received by the acquired company is the respective market prices of the companies' stocks in relation to the merger terms. Some actual merger data are given below.

Calculate the percent premium, or discount, received by the acquired company, using market prices as the criteria. Compare the results of your calculations on the basis of the stock prices of the two previous quarters with that of your results on the basis of the prices immediately preceding the merger. Which is the proper measure of the actual discount or premium received: the one indicated by the earlier stock prices or the one indicated by the stock prices immediately preceding the merger? Explain.

	Company	Terms	Market Price Two Quarters before Merger A	B	Market Price Immediately Preceding Merger A	B
1	A Celanese Corporation B Champlain Oil	2 shares of Celanese for every 3 shares of Champlain	62	34	67	42
2	A Cities Service Company B Tennessee Corporation	0.9 shares (2.25 pref.) for each Tenn. Corp. share (common)	65	48	61	55
3	A Ford Motor Company B Philco Corporation	1 share of Ford for every 4½ shares of Philco	81	22	113	25
4	A General Telephone B Sylvania Electric	Share-for-share basis	52	46	69	69

23-4. To meet its growth objectives, Proxmire Manufacturing is planning to expand via acquisition. It has two potential acquisition candidates, Apex Corporation and Allied Engineering. The latest balance sheet for Proxmire is given below, along with certain statistical data for all three companies. Assume that the pre-tax cost of new debt to Proxmire is 9 percent, that its cost of equity is 10 percent, and that Proxmire has an effective tax rate of 50 percent.

Proxmire Manufacturing
Balance sheet
December 31, 1976
($ in thousands)

Current Assets	$120,000	Current liabilities	$ 50,000
Net fixed assets	150,000	Long-term debt (9%)	70,000
		Common equity	150,000
Total	$270,000	Total	$270,000

Statistical Data

	EPS	DPS	Growth Rate	Market Price	Shares Outstanding
Proxmire	$3.00	$1.80	6%	$45.00	5,000,000
Apex	$2.00	$0.50	7.5%	$50.00	2,000,000
Allied	$4.00	$3.00	2%	$42.00	3,000,000

a. Based on the above information, determine an appropriate price for Proxmire to pay for each acquisition candidate. Proxmire computes the value of an acquisition candidate's stock using the constant growth model, based on the target company's growth rate and projected dividends. Proxmire uses its own marginal cost of capital as the minimum required rate of return.

b. If Proxmire is forced to make a tender offer for each of the two candidates at 20 percent above their current market value, compute the following items.

1. The exchange ratio based on a stock offering.

2. Proxmire's new earnings growth rate for next year after the acquisition of each company—Apex and Allied.

3. Calculate Proxmire's new EPS following each acquisition.

c. Chart Proxmire's growth in EPS for the next ten years with and without each acquisition to illustrate the dilutive effect of the purchase price computed in part 2-b above.

Accounting Policies in Mergers

23A Appendix

After merger terms have been agreed upon, the financial manager must be familiar with the accounting principles for recording the financial results of the merger and for reflecting the initial effect on the earnings of the surviving firm. This appendix deals with these matters.

The financial statements of the survivor in a merger must follow the regulations and supervision of the Securities and Exchange Commission. The SEC's requirements follow the recommendations of professional accounting societies on combinations, but interpretations of actual situations require much financial and economic analysis.

On August 2, 1970, the eighteen-member Accounting Principles Board (APB) of The American Institute of Certified Public Accountants issued Opinion 16, dealing with guidelines for corporate mergers, and Opinion 17, dealing with goodwill arising from mergers. The recommendations, which became effective October 31, 1970, modify and elaborate previous pronouncements on the "pooling of interests" and "purchase" methods of accounting for business combinations. For reasons that will become clear later in this appendix, corporate managements generally prefer pooling. Six broad tests are used to determine whether the conditions for the pooling of interests treatment are met. If all of these are met, then the combination is, in a sense, a "merger among equals," and the *pooling of interests* method may be employed.

1. The acquired firm's stockholders maintain an ownership position in the surviving firm.

2. The basis for accounting for the assets of the acquired entity is unchanged.
3. Independent interests are combined; each entity had autonomy for two years prior to the initiation of the plan to combine; no more than 10 percent ownership of voting common stock is held as intercorporate investments.
4. The combination is effected in a single transaction; contingent payouts are not permitted in poolings but may be used in purchases.
5. The acquiring corporation issues only common stock with rights identical to its outstanding voting common stock in exchange for substantially all the voting common stock of the other company; "substantially" is defined as 90 percent.
6. The combined entity does not intend to dispose of a significant portion of the assets of the combining companies within two years after the merger.

In contrast, a *purchase* involves (1) new owners, (2) an appraisal of the acquired firm's physical assets and a restatement of the balance sheet to reflect these new values, and (3) the possibility of an excess or deficiency of consideration given up vis-a-vis the book value of equity. Point (3) refers to the creation of goodwill. In a purchase, the excess of the purchase price paid over the book value (restated to reflect the appraisal value of physical assets) is set up as goodwill, and capital surplus is increased (or decreased) accordingly. In a pooling of interests, the combined total assets after the merger represent a simple sum of the asset contributions of the constituent companies.

In a *purchase,* if the acquiring firm pays more than the acquired net worth, the excess is associated either with tangible depreciable assets or with goodwill. Asset write-offs are deductible, but goodwill written off is not deductible, for tax purposes, even though the new recommendations require that goodwill be written off over some reasonable period but no longer than forty years. This requires a write-off of at least 2.5 percent a year of the amount of goodwill arising from a purchase. Therefore, if a merger is treated as a purchase, reported profits will be lower than if it is handled as a pooling of interests. This is one of the reasons that pooling is popular among acquiring firms.

Previous to issuance of APB Opinion 16, another stimulus to pooling was the opportunity to dispose of assets acquired at depreciated book values, selling them at their current values, and recording subsequent profits on sales of assets. Opinion 16 attempted to deal with this practice by the requirement that sales of major portions of assets are not to be contemplated for at least two years after the merger has taken place. For example, suppose firm A buys firm B, exchanging stock worth $100 million for assets worth $100 million but carried at $25 million. After the merger, A could, before the change in rules, sell the acquired assets and report the difference between book value and the purchase price, or $75 million, as earned income. Thus, mergers could be used in still another way to create an illusion of profits and growth.

These general statements may be made more meaningful by concrete illustrations of first a purchase and then a pooling of interests.

Financial Treatment of a Purchase

The financial treatment of a purchase may best be explained by use of a hypothetical example. The Mammoth Company has just purchased the Petty Company under an arrangement known as a *purchase.* The facts are as given in Table A23–1, which also shows the financial treatment. The illustration conforms to the general nature of a purchase. Measured by total assets, the Mammoth Company is 20 times as large as Petty, while its total earnings are 15 times as large. Assume that the terms of the purchase will be one share of Mammoth for two shares of Petty, based on the prevailing market value of their shares of common stock. Thus, in terms of Mammoth's stock, Mammoth is giving to Petty's stockholders $30 of market value and $7 of book value for each share of Petty stock. Petty's market value is $30 a share, its book value is $3 a share, and the book value of the equity is $6,000.[1] The total market value of Mammoth paid for Petty is $60,000. The goodwill involved may be calculated as follows:

Value given by Mammoth	$60,000
Book value of net worth of Petty purchased	6,000
Goodwill	$54,000

The $54,000 goodwill represents a debit in the "Adjustments" column and is carried to the pro forma balance sheet. The pro forma balance sheet is obtained by simply adding the adjustments to Mammoth's balance sheet.

A total value of $60,000 has been given by Mammoth, and it has assumed $4,000 of debt. This amount represents, in addition to the debt, a payment of $1,000 for the common stock of Petty, $5,000 for the retained earnings, and $54,000 goodwill. The corresponding credit is the 1,000 shares of Mammoth given in the transaction at their par value of $4 a share, resulting in a credit of $4,000, and the capital surplus of Mammoth is increased by $56,000 (equals $60,000 paid minus $4,000 increase in common stock). When these adjustments are carried through to the *pro forma* balance sheet, total assets are increased from the uncombined total of $210,000 to a new total of $264,000. Total tangible assets, however, still remain $210,000.

---

[1] Under purchase accounting, the acquiring company "should allocate the cost of an acquired company to the assets acquired and liabilities assumed." (*APB Opinion No. 16,* p. 318, par. 87.) A specific procedure is set forth. First, all identifiable assets acquired should be assigned a portion of the cost of the acquired company, normally equal to their fair (market or appraised) values at date of acquisition. Second, the excess of the cost of the acquired company over the sum of the amounts assigned to net assets should be recorded as goodwill. The sum of fair market values assigned may exceed the cost of the acquired company. If so, values otherwise assignable to noncurrent assets should be reduced by a proportionate part of the excess. If noncurrent assets are reduced to zero and some excess still remains, it should be set up as a deferred credit.

TABLE A23–1   Financial Treatment of a Purchase

	Mammoth Company	Petty Company	Adjustments		Pro Forma Balance Sheet
			Debit	Credit	
Assets					
Current	$ 80,000	$ 4,000	$ 4,000		$ 84,000
Other assets	20,000	2,000	2,000		22,000
Net fixed assets	100,000	4,000	4,000		104,000
Goodwill			54,000		54,000
Total assets	$200,000	$10,000			$264,000
Liabilities and net worth					
Current liabilities	$ 40,000	$ 4,000		$ 4,000	$ 44,000
Long-term debt	20,000				20,000
Common stock	40,000	1,000		4,000	44,000
Capital surplus	20,000			56,000	76,000
Retained earnings	80,000	5,000			80,000
Total liab. and net worth	$200,000	$10,000			$264,000
Explanation					
Par value per share, common stock	$4	$0.50			
Number of shares outstanding	10,000	2,000			
Book value per share	$14	$3			
Total earnings	$30,000	$2,000			
Earnings per share	$3	$1			
Price/earnings ratio	20×	30×			
Market value per share	$60	$30			

The effects on earnings per share for stockholders in each company are shown below:

Total earnings (before write-off of goodwill)	$32,000
Amortization of goodwill	1,350
Total net earnings	$30,650
Total shares	11,000
Earnings per share	$2.79
For Petty shareholders	
New earnings per share[a]	$1.40
Before-purchase earnings per share	$1.00
Accretion per share	$0.40
For Mammoth shareholders	
Before-purchase earnings per share	$3.00
New earnings per share	$2.79
Dilution per share	$0.21

[a]Petty shareholders, after the one-for-two exchange, have only one-half as many shares as before the merger.

Total earnings represent the combined earnings of Mammoth and Petty. Mammoth believes that the value reflected in goodwill will be permanent, but under *APB Opinion 17,* it is required to write off the goodwill account over a minimum of 40 years. The annual charge of $1,350 is the goodwill of $54,000 divided by 40. The total amount of net earnings is, therefore, $30,650.

The total shares are 11,000, because Mammoth has given one share of stock for every two shares of Petty previously outstanding. The new earnings per share are therefore $2.79. The calculation of earnings accretion or dilution proceeds on the same principles as the calculations set forth earlier in the chapter. The results require two important comments, however.

It will be noted that although the earnings accretion per share for Petty is 40 cents, the earnings dilution per share for Mammoth is relatively small, only 21 cents a share. The explanation is that the size of Mammoth is large in relation to that of Petty. This example also illustrates a general principle—when a large company acquires a small one, it can afford to pay a high multiple of earnings per share of the smaller company. In the present example, the price/earnings ratio of Petty is 30, whereas that of Mammoth is 20. If the acquiring company is large in relation to the acquired firm, it can pay a substantial premium and yet suffer only small dilution in its earnings per share.

It is, however, unrealistic to assume that the same earnings on total assets will result after the merger. After all, the purpose of the merger is to achieve something that the two companies could not have achieved alone. When Philip Morris & Company purchased Benson & Hedges maker of Parliament, a leading filter-tip brand, it was buying the ability and experience of Benson & Hedges. By means of this merger, Philip Morris & Company was able to make an entry into the rapidly growing filter-cigarette business more quickly than it could otherwise have done. The combined earnings per share were expected to rise.

In the Mammoth-Petty illustration, the earnings rate on the tangible assets of Mammoth is 15 percent and on the total assets of Petty is 20 percent. Let us now assume that the return on total tangible assets of the combined companies rises to 20 percent. The 20 percent of tangible assets of $210,000 equals $42,000; less the amortization of goodwill over forty years of $1,350 per year, equals $40,650 net earnings. With the same total shares of 11,000 outstanding, the new earnings per share will be $3.70. Thus there will be accretion of $2.70 for the Petty shareholders and an accretion of 70 cents for the Mammoth shareholders as well.

This illustrates another general principle—if the purchase of a small company adds to the earnings of the consolidated enterprise, earnings per share may increase for both participants in the merger. Even if the merger results in an initial dilution in earnings per share of the larger company, it may still be advantageous. The initial dilution in the earnings per share may be regarded as an investment that will have a payoff at some future date in terms of increased growth in earnings per share of the consolidated company.

Treatment of Goodwill

In a purchase, goodwill is likely to arise; since goodwill represents an intangible asset, its treatment is subject to the exercise of judgment. It will therefore be useful to set out a few generalizations on good practice in the treatment of goodwill.

1. When goodwill is purchased, it should not be charged to surplus immediately on acquisition. Preferably, goodwill should be written off against income and should go through the income statement. Since goodwill is to be written off against income, it is not appropriate to write it off entirely on acquisition, because this would be of such magnitude that distortion of earnings for that year would result.

2. The general view is not to write off purchased goodwill by charges to capital surplus. Purchased goodwill is supposed to represent, and to be reflected in, a future rise of income. It should be written off against income rather than against capital surplus.

3. When goodwill is purchased, an estimate should be made of its life. Annual charges, based on the estimated life of the goodwill, should then be made against income to amortize the goodwill over the estimated period of the usefulness of the goodwill purchased.

4. Intangibles must be written off over a maximum of forty years by *APB Opinion 17.*

When goodwill is purchased, it should be treated like any other asset. It should be written off to the extent that the value represented by any part of goodwill has a limited life, as is likely to be the situation. In a free enterprise economy, the existence of high profits represented by superior earning power attracts additional resources into that line of business. The growth of capacity and the increase in competition are likely to erode the superior earning power over time.

Financial Treatment of Pooling of Intersts

When a business combination is a *pooling of interests* rather than a purchase, the accounting treatment is simply to combine the balance sheets of the two companies. Goodwill will not ordinarily arise in the consolidation.

The financial treatment may be indicated by another example, which reflects the facts as they are set forth in Table A23–2. In order to focus on the critical issues, the balance sheets are identical in every respect. However, a difference in the amount and rate of profit (after interest) of the two companies is indicated.

Book value per share is $10. The amount of profit after interest and taxes is $42,000 for company A and $21,000 for company B. Earnings per share are therefore $3.50 and $1.75, respectively. The price/earnings ratio is 18 for A and 12 for B, so the market price of stock for A is $63 and for B $27. The net working capital per share is $4.17 in each instance. The dividends per share are $1.75 for A and $0.875 for B.

TABLE A23–2 Financial Treatment of Pooling of Interest

	A	B	Net Adjustments on A's Books — Debit	Net Adjustments on A's Books — Credit	Acquiring Firms A's New Balance Sheets and Earnings if the Exchange Basis is 2/1	Acquiring Firms A's New Balance Sheets and Earnings if the Exchange Basis is 3/1
Current assets	$100,000	$100,000			$200,000	$200,000
Fixed assets	100,000	100,000			200,000	200,000
Total assets	$200,000	$200,000			$400,000	$400,000
Current liabilities	$ 50,000	$ 50,000			$100,000	$100,000
Long-term debt	30,000	30,000			60,000	60,000
Total debt	80,000	80,000			160,000	160,000
Common stock, par value $5	60,000	60,000	$30,000[a] $40,000[b]		90,000	80,000
Capital surplus	50,000	50,000		$30,000[a] $40,000[b]	130,000	140,000
Retained earnings	10,000	10,000			20,000	20,000
Total claims on assets	$200,000	$200,000			$400,000	$400,000
			Ratios A/B			
Number of shares of stock	12,000	12,000			18,000	16,000
Book value	$ 10	$ 10	1.0			
Amount of profit after interest and taxes	$ 42,000	$ 21,000			$ 63,000	$ 63,000
Earnings per share	$ 3.50	$ 1.75	2.0		$ 3.50	$ 3.94
Price/earnings ratio	18	12				
Market price of stock	$ 63.00	$ 21.00	3.0			
Net working capital per share	$ 4.17	$ 4.17	1.0			
Dividends per share	$ 1.75	$ 0.875	2.0			

					Shareholders' New EPS — A	Shareholders' New EPS — B
Exchange ratio No. 1: earnings basis	2/1					
Equivalent earnings per share (new basis)					$3.50	$1.75
Exchange ratio No. 2: price basis	3/1					
Equivalent earnings per share (new basis)					$3.94	$1.31

[a] = 2/1 ratio basis.
[b] = 3/1 ratio basis.

Now assume that the terms of the merger would reflect either (1) earnings or (2) market price per share. In both cases it is assumed that A is the acquiring and surviving firm. If A buys B on the basis of earnings, it exchanges 0.5 shares of A's common stock for 1 share of B common stock. The total number of shares of A's common stock that will be outstanding after the acquisition is 18,000, of which 6,000 shares will be held by the old stockholders of B. The new earnings per share in the now larger A company will be the total earnings of $63,000 divided by 18,000, which equals $3.50 per share. Thus, the earnings per share for A remain unchanged. The old shareholders of B now hold 0.5 shares of A for each share of B held before the acquisition. Hence, their equivalent earnings per share from their present holdings of A shares are $1.75, the same as before the acquisition. We see that the stockholders of neither A nor B have experienced earnings dilution or earnings accretion.

When the terms of exchange are based on market price per share, the terms of acquisition would be the exchange of ⅓ share of A stock for 1 share of B stock. The number of A shares is increased by the 4,000 exchanged for the 12,000 shares of B. The combined earnings of $63,000 are divided by 16,000 shares to obtain an increase in A's earnings per share to $3.94, which represents earnings accretion of $0.44 per share for the A shareholders. The old B shareholders now hold ⅓ share of A for each 1 share of B held before the acquisition. Their equivalent earnings are now $3.94 divided by 3, or $1.31, representing earnings dilution of $0.44 per share.

The adjustment to the common stock account in surviving company A's balance sheet reflects the fact that only 6,000 shares of A were used to buy 12,000 shares of B when the acquisition is made on the basis of earnings. The decrease of 6,000 shares times the par value of $5 requires a net debit of $30,000 to the common stock account of A ($60,000 + $60,000 − $30,000 = $90,000) with an offsetting increase of $30,000 in the capital surplus account of company A ($50,000 + $50,000 + $30,000 = $130,000). When the exchange is made on the basis of market values, only 4,000 shares of A are needed to acquire the 12,000 shares of B. Hence, the net decrease in the common stock account of A is $40,000, with an offsetting increase of the same amount in A's capital surplus.

The general principle is that when terms of merger are based on the market price per share and the price/earnings ratios of the two companies are different, earnings accretion and dilution will occur. The company with a higher price/earnings ratio will attain earnings accretion; the company with the lower price/earnings ratio will suffer earnings dilution. If the sizes of the companies are greatly different, the effect on the larger company will be relatively small, whether in earnings dilution or in earnings accretion. The effect on the smaller company will be large.

Failure, Reorganization, and Liquidation

24 Thus far the text has dealt with issues associated mainly with the growing, successful enterprise. Not all businesses are so fortunate, however, so we must examine financial difficulties, their causes, and their possible remedies. This material is significant for the financial managers of successful, as well as of potentially unsuccessful, firms. The successful firm's financial manager must know his firm's rights and remedies as a creditor and must participate effectively in efforts to collect from financially distressed debtors. Conversely, the financial manager of a less successful firm must know how to handle his own firm's affairs if financial difficulties arise. Such understanding may often mean the difference between loss of ownership of the firm and rehabilitation of the operation as a going enterprise.

THE FIRM'S LIFE CYCLE

The life cycle of an industry or firm is often depicted as an S-shaped curve, as shown in Figure 24–1. The figure represents a hypothetical life cycle of a firm, and although it is an oversimplification, it does provide a useful framework for analysis. The hypothesis represented by the four-stage life-cycle concept is based on a key assumption—competent management in the growth periods and insufficient management foresight prior to the decline phase. Obviously, one of management's primary goals is to prolong phase B and to forestall completely phase D; many firms are apparently successful in these endeavors.

542

FIGURE 24–1 Hypothetical Life Cycle of a Firm

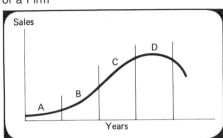

If an industry experiences the period of decline, financial readjustment problems will arise, affecting most firms in the industry. Furthermore, specific events may result in business failure—for example, a prolonged strike, a fire not adequately covered by insurance, or a bad decision on a new product.

FAILURE

Although failure can be defined in several ways according to various applications of the term, it does not necessarily result in the collapse and dissolution of a firm.

Economic Failure

Failure in an economic sense usually signifies that a firm's revenues do not cover costs. Another definition of economic failure states that a firm has failed if the rate of earnings on the historical cost of investment is less than the firm's cost of capital. According to still another definition, a firm can be considered a failure if its actual returns have fallen below expected returns. There is no consensus on the definition of failure in an economic sense.[1]

Financial Failure

Although financial failure is a less ambiguous term than the concept of economic failure, even here, two aspects are generally recognized:

Technical Insolvency A firm can be considered a failure if it is insolvent in the sense that it cannot meet its current obligations as they fall due, even though its total assets may exceed its total liabilities. This is defined as *technical insolvency.*

---

[1]In still another economic sense, a firm that goes bankrupt may not be a failure at all. To illustrate, suppose someone starts a business to *attempt* to develop a product that, if successful, will produce very large returns and, if unsuccessful, will result in a total loss of invested funds. The entrepreneur *knows* that he is taking a risk but thinks the potential gains are worth the chance of loss. If a loss in fact results, then the outcome simply occurred in the left tail of the distribution of returns.

Bankruptcy   A firm is a failure, or is *bankrupt,* if its total liabilities exceed a fair valuation of its total assets. The "real" net worth of the firm is negative.

When we use the word "failure" hereafter, we include both technical insolvency and bankruptcy.

CAUSES OF FAILURES

Different studies assign the causes of failure to different factors. The Dun & Bradstreet compilations assign these causes as follows:[2]

Cause of Failure	Percentage of Total
Neglect	2.0
Fraud	1.5
Disaster	.9
Management incompetence	93.1
Unknown	2.5

A number of other studies of failures may be generalized into the following groups:[3]

Cause of Failure	Percentage of Total
Unfavorable industry trends (secular)	20
Management incompetence	60
Catastrophes	10
Miscellaneous	10

Both classifications include the effects of recessions and place the resulting failures in the category of managerial incompetence. This method is logical—managements should be prepared to operate in environments in which recessions occur and should frame their policies to cope with downturns as well as to benefit from business upswings. Also, managements must anticipate unfavorable industry trends.

A number of financial remedies are available to management when it becomes aware of the imminence or occurrence of insolvency. These remedies are described in the remainder of this chapter.

[2]*The Failure Record,* 1972 (New York: Dun & Bradstreet, Inc., 1975).
[3]See studies referred to in A. S. Dewing, *The Financial Policy of Corporations* (New York: Ronald, 1953), Vol. II, Chap. 28.

THE FAILURE RECORD[4]

How widespread is business failure? Is it a rare phenomenon, or do failures occur fairly often? In Table 24–1, we see that a fairly large number of businesses do fail, although the failures in any one year are not a large percentage of the business population. In 1974, for example, there were 10,158 failures, but these represented only 0.39 percent of all business firms. The average failed firm owed $306,600 when it "went under." It is interesting to note that the failure rate rose significantly in 1970–71, and again in 1975; in both periods, high interest rates, a shortage of credit, and a weakened economy combined to cause weaker firms to declare bankruptcy.

TABLE 24–1 Historical Failure Rate Experience of United States Businesses

Years	Number of Failures	Average Failure Rate [a]	Average Liability per Failure [b]
1857–1968	1,258,141	87	$ 28,292
(average per year)	(11,233)		
1900–1968	942,447	70	32,889
(average per year)	(13,659)		
1946–1968	255,041	42	61,101
(average per year)	(11,089)		
1959–1968	138,805	54	84,724
(average per year)	(13,881)		
1961	17,075	64	63,843
1965	13,514	53	97,800
1966	13,061	52	106,091
1967	12,364	49	102,332
1968	9,636	39	97,654
1969	9,154	37	124,767
1970	10,748	44	175,638
1971	10,326	42	185,641
1972	9,566	38	209,099
1973	9,345	36	245,912
1974E	10,158	39	306,600

[a]Per 10,000 concerns.
[b]"Average" here means the median, that is, one-half the failed firms had more liabilities while one-half had less. The arithmetic average is much larger.
Source: Reprinted by permission of the publisher from *Corporate Bankruptcy in America* by Edward I. Altman (Lexington, Mass.: Lexington Books, D. C. Heath & Company, 1971); Dun & Bradstreet, *The Failure Record, 1972,* and August 1974 *Monthly Failure Report.* © 1972, 1974 by the Business Economics Division, Dun & Bradstreet, Inc. Reprinted by permission.

[4]This section draws heavily from Edward I. Altman, *Corporate Bankruptcy in America* (Lexington, Mass.: Heath Lexington Books, 1972).

Large firms are not immune to bankruptcy; this is clear from Table 24–2, which lists the major corporate bankruptcies during 1970 and 1971. In a sense, Table 24–2 understates financial problems among larger firms, because, as Altman notes, except in cases of fraud or where the failing company is too large to be absorbed by another firm, mergers or governmental intervention are generally arranged as an alternative to outright bankruptcy. Thus, in recent years the Federal Home Loan Bank System arranged the mergers of several very large "problem" savings and loan associations into sound institutions, and the Federal Reserve System has done the same thing for banks. Several United States government agencies, principally the Defense Department, arranged to "bail out" Lockheed when it would have otherwise failed in 1970; the "shotgun marriage" of Douglas Aircraft and McDonnell was designed to prevent Douglas' failure in the late 1960s. Similar instances could be cited in the securities brokerage industry in the late 1960s and early 1970s.

TABLE 24–2 Large Corporate Bankruptcies in America, by Asset Size, 1970 and 1971

1970 Bankruptcies	*1969 Assets* [a]
Penn Central Transportation Company	4,700.0
Boston & Maine Railroad	224.1
Lehigh Valley Railroad	173.8
Beck Industries	156.9
Dolly Madison Industries	92.4
Four Seasons Nursing Centers	37.7
Roberts Company	36.8
Visual Electronics	24.3
Bishop Industries	16.3
Milo Electronics	13.0
National Radio Company	10.2
RIC International Industries, Inc.	10.2
GF Industries, Inc.	9.6
Century Geophysical Corp.	8.9
1971 Bankruptcies [b]	*1970 Assets* [a]
King Resources Company	176.7
Bermac Corporation	102.3
Farrington Manufacturing Company	37.6
Computer Applications	28.9
Remco Industries	25.1
Transogram Inc.	21.5
Cle-ware Industries	20.0
Executive House Inc.	13.6

[a] In millions of dollars
[b] Through July, 1971
Source: Reprinted by permission of the publisher from *Corporate Bankruptcy in America* by Edward I. Altman (Lexington, Mass.: Lexington Books, D. C. Heath & Company, 1974).

Why do government and industry seek to avoid bankruptcy among larger firms? There are many reasons—to prevent an erosion of confidence in the case of financial institutions, to maintain a viable supplier in the cases of Lockheed and Douglas, and to avoid disrupting a local community. Also, bankruptcy is a very expensive process, so even when "the public interest" is not at stake, private industry has strong incentives to avoid out-and-out bankruptcy. The costs of bankruptcy, as well as some further alternatives to it, are discussed in subsequent sections.

EXTENSION AND COMPOSITION

Extension and *composition* are discussed together because they both represent voluntary concessions by creditors. Extension postpones the date of required payment of past-due obligations. Composition voluntarily *reduces* the creditors' claims on the debtor. Both have the purpose of keeping the debtor in business and avoiding court costs. Although creditors absorb a temporary loss, the recovery is often greater than if one of the formal procedures had been followed, and the hope is that a stable customer will emerge.

Procedure

A meeting of the debtor and his creditors is held. The creditors appoint a committee consisting of four or five of the largest creditors and one or two of the smaller ones. These meetings are typically arranged and conducted by *adjustment bureaus* associated with local credit managers' associations or by trade associations.

After a meeting is held at the adjustment bureau and it is judged that the case can be worked out, the bureau assigns investigators to make an exhaustive report. The bureau and the creditors' committee use the facts of the report to formulate a plan for adjustment of claims. Another meeting between the debtor and his creditors is then held in an attempt to work out an extension or a composition, or a combination of the two. Subsequent meetings may be required to reach final agreements.

Necessary Conditions

At least three conditions are usually necessary to make an extension or a composition feasible:

1. The debtor is a good moral risk.
2. The debtor shows ability to make a recovery.
3. General business conditions are favorable to recovery.

Extension

An extension is preferred by creditors because it provides for payment in full. The debtor buys current purchases on a cash basis and pays off his past balance over an extended time. In some cases, creditors may agree not only to extend time of payment but also to subordinate existing claims to new debts incurred in favor of vendors extending credit during the period of the extension. The creditors must have faith that the debtor will solve his problems. Because of the uncertainties involved, however, creditors will want to exercise controls over the debtor while waiting for their claims to be paid.

As examples of controls, the committee may insist that an assignment (turnover of assets to the creditors' committee) be executed, to be held in escrow in case of default. Or, if the debtor is a corporation, the committee may require that stockholders transfer their stock certificates into an escrow until repayment as called for under the extension has been completed. The committee may also designate a representative to countersign all checks. Furthermore, the committee may obtain security in the form of notes, mortgages, or assignment of accounts receivable.

Composition

In a composition, a pro rata cash settlement is made. Creditors receive in cash from the debtor a uniform percentage of the obligations. The cash received is taken as full settlement of the debt. The ratio may be as low as 10 percent. Bargaining will take place between the debtor and the creditors over the savings that result from avoiding certain costs associated with the bankruptcy: costs of administration, legal fees, investigators, and so on. In addition to avoiding such costs, the debtor gains in that he avoids the stigma of bankruptcy, and thus he may be induced to part with most of the savings that result from avoiding bankruptcy.

Combination Settlement

Often the bargaining process will result in a compromise involving both an extension and a composition. For example, the settlement may provide for a cash payment of 25 percent of the debt and six future installments of 10 percent each. Total payment would thereby aggregate 85 percent. Installment payments are usually evidenced by notes. Creditors will also seek protective controls.

Appraisal of Voluntary Settlements

The advantages of voluntary settlements are informality and simplicity. Investigating, legal, and administrative expenses are held to a minimum. The procedure is the most economical and results in the largest return to creditors.

One possible disadvantage is that the debtor is left in control of his business. This situation may involve legal complications or erosion of assets still operated by the debtor. However, numerous controls are available to give the creditors protection.

A second disadvantage is that small creditors may take a nuisance role in that they may insist on payment in full. As a consequence, settlements typically provide for payment in full for claims under $50 or $100. If a composition is involved and all claims under $50 are paid, all creditors will receive a base of $50 plus the agreed-on percentage of the balance of their claims.

REORGANIZATION

Reorganization is a form of extension or composition of the firm's obligations. However, the legal formalities are much more involved than the procedures thus far described. Regardless of the legal procedure followed, the reorganization processes have several features in common.

1. The firm is insolvent either because it is unable to meet cash obligations as they come due or because claims on the firm exceed its assets. Hence, some modifications in the nature or amount of the firm's obligations must be made. A scaling down of terms or amounts must be formulated. This procedure may represent scaling down fixed charges or converting short-term debt into long-term debt.
2. New funds must be raised for working capital and for property rehabilitation.
3. The operating and managerial causes of difficulty must be discovered and eliminated.

The procedures involved in effecting a reorganization are highly legalistic and are, in fact, thoroughly understood only by attorneys who specialize in bankruptcy and reorganization. We shall therefore confine our remarks to the general principles involved.

A reorganization is, in essence, a composition, a scaling down of claims. In any composition, two conditions must be met: (1) the scaling down must be fair to all parties and (2) in return for the sacrifices, the likelihood of successful rehabilitation and profitable future operation of the firm must be feasible. These are the standards of *fairness* and *feasibility,* which are analyzed further in the next section.

FINANCIAL DECISIONS IN REORGANIZATION

When a business becomes insolvent, a decision must be made whether to dissolve the firm through liquidation or to keep it alive through reorganization. Fundamentally, this decision depends upon a determination of the value of the firm if it is rehabilitated versus the value of the sum of the parts if it is dismembered.

Liquidation values depend upon the degree of specialization of the capital assets used in the firm and hence their resale value. In addition, liquidation itself involves costs of dismantling, including legal costs. Successful reorganization also involves costs. Typically, better equipment must be installed, obsolete inventories must be disposed of, and improvements in management must be made.

Net liquidation values are compared with the value of the firm after reorganization, net of the costs of rehabilitation. The procedure that promises the higher returns to the creditors and owners will be the course of action favored. Often the greater indicated value of the firm in reorganization, compared with its value in liquidation, is used to force a compromise agreement among the claimants in a reorganization, even when they feel that their relative position has not been treated fairly in the reorganization plan.

In reorganizations, both the SEC and the courts are called upon to determine the *fairness* and the *feasibility* of proposed plans of reorganization.[5] In developing standards of fairness in connection with such reorganizations, both the courts and the SEC have adhered to two court decisions that established precedent on these matters.[6]

Standards of Fairness

The basic doctrine of fairness states that claims must be recognized in the order of their legal and contractual priority. Junior claimants may participate only to the extent that they have made an additional cash contribution to the reorganization of the firm.

Carrying out this concept of fairness involves the following steps:

1. An estimate of future sales must be made.
2. An analysis of operating conditions must be made so that the future earnings on sales can be estimated.
3. A determination of the capitalization rate to be applied to these future earnings must be made.
4. The capitalization rate must be applied to the estimated future earnings to obtain an indicated value of the properties of the company.
5. Provision for distribution to the claimants must then be made.

Example of Reorganization and Standards of Fairness

The meaning and content of these procedures may best be set out by the use of an actual example of reorganization involving the Simmons Manufacturing

---

[5] The federal bankruptcy laws specify that reorganization plans be worked out by court-appointed officials and be reviewed by the SEC.

[6] *Case v. Los Angeles Lumber Products Co.*, 308 U.S. 106 (1939) and *Consolidated Rock Products Co. v. duBoise,* 213 U.S. 510 (1940). Securities and Exchange Commission, Seventeenth Annual Report, 1951 (Washington, D.C.: U.S. Government Printing Office), p. 130.

Company. Table 24–3 gives the balance sheet of Simmons as of March 31, 1975. The company had been suffering losses running to $2.5 million a year, and, as will be made clear below, the asset values in the March 31, 1975, balance sheet are overstated. Accordingly, the company filed a petition for reorganization under Chapter 11 of the Bankruptcy Act with a federal court.[7] The court, in accordance with the law, appointed a disinterested trustee. On June 13, 1975, the trustee filed with the court a plan of reorganization, which was subsequently analyzed by the SEC.

TABLE 24–3 Simmons Manufacturing Company
Balance sheet
March 31, 1975
(millions of dollars)

Assets	
Current assets	$ 3.50
Net property	12.50
Miscellaneous assets	0.70
Total assets	$16.70
Liabilities and capital	
Accounts payable	$ 1.00
Taxes	0.25
Notes payable	0.25
Other current liabilities	1.75
4½% First-mortgage bonds, due 1990	6.00
6% Subordinated debentures, due 1985	7.00
Common stock ($1)	1.00
Paid-in capital	3.45
Retained earnings	(4.00)
Total liabilities and capital	$16.70

The trustee found that the company could not be internally reorganized, and he concluded that the only feasible program would be to combine Simmons with another firm. Accordingly, the trustee solicited the interest of a number of large companies. Late in March 1975, Reliance Corporation showed an interest in Simmons. On June 3, 1975, Reliance made a formal proposal to take over the $6 million of 4½ percent first-mortgage bonds of Simmons, to pay $250,000 taxes owed by Simmons, and to pay 40,000 shares of Reliance common stock to the company. Since the stock had a market price of $75 a share, the value of the stock was equivalent to $3 million. Thus, Reliance was offering $3 million, plus the $6 million loan take over and the $250,000 taxes, a total of $9.2 million on assets that had a net book value of $16.7 million.

[7]Chapter 10 of the Bankruptcy Act deals with situations where a firm's creditors force it into bankruptcy; generally, liquidation follows. Chapter 11 of the Act deals with situations where a firm requests permission to reorganize. Chapter 10 involves action taken by creditors and is *involuntary* from the bankrupt firm's viewpoint. Chapter 11 involves *voluntary reorganization*.

Trustee's Plan The trustee's plan, based on 40,000 shares at $75 equaling $3 million, is shown in Table 24–4. The total claims of the unsecured creditors equals $10 million. However, the amounts available total only $3 million. Thus, each claimant would be entitled to receive 30 percent before the adjustment for subordination. Before this adjustment, holders of notes payable would receive 30 percent of their $250,000 claim, or $75,000. However, the debentures are subordinated to the *notes payable,* so an additional $175,000 would be transferred to notes payable from the subordinated debentures. In the last column of Table 24–4, the dollar claims of each class of debt are restated in terms of the number of shares of Reliance common stock received by each class of unsecured creditors.

TABLE 24–4 Simmons Manufacturing Company
Trustee's plan

Prior claims	Amount	Receives
Taxes	$ 250,000	Cash paid by Relaince
Mortgage bonds, 4½%, 1990	6,000,000	Same assumed by Reliance

Trustee's plans for remainder of claims

Valuation based on 40,000 shares at $75 equals $3 million, or 30% of $10 million liabilities.

Claims	Amount	30 Percent × Amount of Claim	Claim after Subordination	Number of Shares of Common Stock
Notes payable	$ 250,000	$ 75,000	$ 250,000	3,333
General unsecured creditors	2,750,000	825,000	825,000	11,000
Subordinated debentures	7,000,000	2,100,000	1,925,000	25,667
	$10,000,000	$3,000,000	$3,000,000	40,000

SEC Evaluation The Securities and Exchange Commission, in evaluating the proposal from the standpoint of fairness, made the following analysis. The SEC began with an evaluation of the prospective value of Simmons (Table 24–5.) After a survey and discussion with various experts, it arrived at estimated sales of Simmons of $25 million a year. It was further estimated that the profit margin on sales would equal 6 percent, thus giving an indicated future earnings of $1.5 million a year.

The SEC analyzed price/earnings ratios for comparable steel companies and arrived at 8 times future earnings for a capitalization factor. Multiplying 8 by $1.5 million gave an indicated total value of the company of $12 million.

Since the mortgage bonds assumed by Reliance totalled $6 million, a net value of $6 million was left for the other claims. This value is double that of the 40,000 shares of Reliance stock offered for the remainder of the company. Because the SEC felt that the value of these claims was $6 million rather than $3 million, it concluded that the trustee's plan for reorganization did not meet the test of fairness. Note that under both the trustee's plan and the SEC plan, the holders of common stock were to receive nothing, while the holders of the first-mortgage bonds were to be paid in full.

TABLE 24–5 Simmons Manufacturing Company
SEC evaluation of fairness

Valuation	
Estimated sales of Simmons	$25,000,000 per year
Earnings at 6% of sales	1,500,000
Price/earnings ratio of 8 times earnings	12,000,000
Mortgage bonds assumed, $6,000,000	6,000,000
Net value	$ 6,000,000

Claims	Amount	Claim	Claim after Subordination
Notes payable	$ 250,000	$ 150,000	$ 250,000[a]
General unsecured creditors	2,750,000	1,650,000	1,650,000
Subordinated debentures (subordinate to notes payable)	7,000,000	4,200,000	4,100,000[a]
Totals	$10,000,000	$6,000,000	$6,000,000
Total available	$ 6,000,000		
Percentage of claims	60%		

[a]Notes payable must be satisfied before subordinated debentures receive anything.

Because no better alternative offer could be obtained, the proposal of Reliance was accepted despite the SEC disagreement with the valuation.

Standard of Feasibility

The primary test of feasibility is that the fixed charges on the income of the corporation after reorganization are amply covered by earnings or, if a value for a firm that is to be sold is established, that a buyer can be found at that price. Adequate coverage of fixed charges for a company that is to continue in operation generally requires an improvement in earnings or a reduction of fixed charges, or both.

Policies Required Among the actions that will have to be taken to improve the earning power of the company are the following:

1. Where the quality of management has been inefficient and inadequate for the task, new talents and abilities must be brought into the company if it is to operate successfully subsequent to the reorganization.
2. If inventories have become obsolete they should be disposed of and the operations of the company streamlined.
3. Sometimes the plant and the equipment of the firm need to be modernized before it can operate and compete successfully on a cost basis.
4. Reorganization may also require an improvement in production, marketing, advertising, and other functions, to enable the firm to compete successfully and earn satisfactory profits.
5. It is sometimes necessary to develop new products so that the firm can move from areas where economic trends have become undesirable into areas where the growth and stability potential is greater.

Application of Feasibility Tests Let us refer again to the Simmons Manufacturing example. The SEC observed that the reorganization involved taking over the properties of Simmons by Reliance. It judged that the direction and aid of Reliance would remedy the production deficiencies that had troubled Simmons. Whereas the debt-to-assets ratio of Simmons had become unbalanced, Reliance went into the purchase with only a moderate amount of debt. After consolidation, the total debt of Reliance was approximately $17.5 million compared with total assets of more than $63 million. Therefore, the debt ratio of 27 percent after the reorganization was not unreasonable.

The net income after taxes of Reliance had been running at a level of approximately $6 million. The interest on the long-term debt of Reliance would be $270,000 and, taking short-term borrowings into account, would total a maximum of $600,000 a year. The $6 million profit after taxes would therefore provide a 10-times coverage of fixed charges; this exceeds the standard of 5 times for the industry.

Notice that the question of feasibility would have been irrelevant (from the standpoint of the SEC) if Reliance had offered $3 million in cash rather than in stock. It is the SEC's function to protect the interests of Simmons' creditors. Since they are being forced to take common stock in another firm, the SEC must look into the feasibility of the transaction. If Reliance had made a cash offer, however, the feasibility of Reliance's own operation after the transaction was completed would have been none of the SEC's concern. Notice also that the SEC feasibility study is much more important if a small, weak firm buys the assets of a reorganized firm for stock than if the purchase is made by a stronger firm. Thus, the SEC would be more concerned with the feasibility of a takeover of Simmons by Wesbrig Corporation than it would be if General Motors made the takeover.

LIQUIDATION PROCEDURES

Liquidation of a business occurs when the estimated value of the firm is greater "dead than alive."

Assignment is a liquidation procedure that does not go through the courts, although it can be used to achieve full settlement of claims on the debtor. *Bankruptcy* is a legal procedure carried out under the jurisdiction of special courts in which a business firm is formally liquidated and claims of creditors are completely discharged.

Assignment

Assignment (as well as bankruptcy) takes place when the debtor is insolvent and the possibilities of restoring profitability are so remote that the enterprise should be dissolved—that is, when the firm is "worth more dead than alive." Assignment is a technique for liquidating a debt and yielding a larger amount to the creditors than is likely to be achieved in formal bankruptcy.

Technically, there are three classes of assignments: (1) common law assignment, (2) statutory assignment, and (3) assignment plus settlement.

Common Law Assignment The common law provides for an assignment whereby a debtor transfers his title to assets to a third person, known as an assignee or a trustee. The trustee is instructed to liquidate the assets and to distribute the proceeds among the creditors on a pro rata basis.

Typically, an assignment is conducted through the adjustment bureau of the local credit managers' association. The assignee may liquidate the assets through what is known as a bulk sale, which is a public sale through an auctioneer. The auction is preceded by sufficient advertising so that there will be a number of bids. Liquidation may also be by a piecemeal auction sale conducted on the premises of the assignor by a competent licensed auctioneer, rather than by a bulk sale. On-premises sales are particularly advantageous in the liquidation of large machine shops of manufacturing plants.

The common law assignment, as such, does not discharge the debtor from his obligations. If a corporation goes out of business and does not satisfy all its claims, there will still be claims against it, but in effect the corporation has ceased to exist. The people who have been associated with the company can then proceed to organize another corporation free of the debts and obligations of the previous corporation. There is always the danger, however, that the court may hold the individuals responsible: therefore, it is usually important to obtain a statement from creditors that claims have been completely settled. Such a statement is, of course, even more important for an unincorporated business.

Although a common law assignment has taken place, the assignee, in drawing up checks paying the creditors, may write on each check the requisite legal language to make the payment a complete discharge of the obligation. There are technical legal requirements for this process, which are best carried out with the aid of a lawyer, but essential is a statement that endorsement of this check represents acknowledgment of full payment for the obligation.

Statutory Assignment   Statutory assignment is similar in concept to common law assignment. Legally, it is carried out under state statutes regulating assignment; technically, it requires more formality. The debtor executes an instrument of assignment, which is recorded. This recordation provides notice to all third parties. The proceedings are handled under court order: the court appoints an assignee and supervises the proceedings, including the sale of the assets and distribution of the proceeds. As in the common law assignment, the debtor is not automatically discharged from the balance of his obligations. He can discharge himself, however, by printing the requisite statement on the settlement checks.

Assignment Plus Settlement   Both the common law assignment and the statutory assignment may take place with recognition and agreement beforehand by the creditors that the assignment will represent a complete discharge of obligation. Normally, the debtor communicates with the local credit managers' association. The adjustment bureau of the association arranges a meeting of all the creditors, and a trust instrument of assignment is drawn up. The adjustment bureau is designated to dispose of the assets, which are sold through regular trade channels, by bulk sales, by auction, or by private sales. The creditors will, typically, leave all responsibility for the liquidation procedure with the assignee, the adjustment bureau of the local credit managers' association.

Having disposed of the assets and obtained funds, the adjustment bureau will then distribute the proceeds pro rata among the creditors, with the designation on the check that this is in full settlement of the claims on the debtor. Ordinarily, a release is not agreed upon before the execution of the assignment. After full examination of the facts, the creditors' committee will usually make a recommendation for the granting of a release following the execution of the assignment. If releases are not forthcoming, the assignor may, within four months of the date of the assignment, file a voluntary petition in bankruptcy. In this event the assignment is terminated and the assignee must account and report to the trustee and the referee in bankruptcy, and deliver to the trustee all assets in the estate (usually by that time assets have been reduced to cash).

Assignment has substantial advantages over bankruptcy. Bankruptcy through the courts involves much time, legal formalities, and accounting and legal expenses. An assignment saves the costs of bankruptcy proceedings, and it may save time as well.

Furthermore, an assignee usually has much more flexibility in disposing of property than does a bankruptcy trustee. He may be more familiar with the normal channels of trade. Since he takes action much sooner, before the inventories become more obsolete, he may achieve better results.

BANKRUPTCY

Although the bankruptcy procedures leave room for improvement, the Federal Bankruptcy Act itself represents two main achievements: (1) It provides safeguards against fraud by the debtor during liquidation, and, simultaneously, it provides for an equitable distribution of the debtor's assets among his creditors. (2) Insolvent debtors may discharge all their obligations and start new businesses unhampered by a burden of prior debt.

Prerequisites for Bankruptcy

A *voluntary petition of bankruptcy* may be filed by the debtor, but if an *involuntary petition* is to be filed by his creditors under Chapter 10 of the Act, three conditions must be met.

1. The total debts of the insolvent must be $1,000 or more.
2. If the debtor has fewer than twelve creditors, any one of the creditors may file the petition if the amount owed him is $500 or more. If there are twelve or more creditors, the petition must be signed by three or more creditors, each having provable total claims of $500 or more.
3. Within the four preceding months, the debtor must have committed one or more of the following six acts of bankruptcy.

Acts of Bankruptcy

The six acts of bankruptcy can be summarized briefly.

1. Concealment or Fraudulent Conveyance Concealment constitutes hiding of assets with intent to defraud creditors. Fraudulent conveyance is transfer of property to a third party without adequate consideration and with intent to defraud creditors.

2. Preferential Transfer A preferential transfer is the transfer of money or assets by an insolvent debtor to a creditor, giving the creditor a greater portion of his claim that other creditors would receive on liquidation.

3. Legal Lien or Distraint If an insolvent debtor permits any creditor to obtain a lien on his property and fails to discharge the lien within thirty days, or if the debtor permits a landlord to distrain (to seize property that has been pledged as security for a loan) for nonpayment of rent, he has committed an act of bankruptcy. In this way creditors, by obtaining a lien, may force an insolvent but obdurate debtor into bankruptcy.

4. Assignment If a debtor makes a general assignment for the benefit of his creditors, an act of bankruptcy likewise exists. Again, this enables creditors who have become distrustful of the debtor in the process of assignment to transfer the proceedings to a bankruptcy court. As a matter of practice, typically in common law assignments, creditors will require that a debtor execute a formal assignment document to be held in escrow, to become effective if informal and voluntary settlement negotiations fail. If they do fail, the assignment becomes effective and the creditors have the right to throw the case into the bankruptcy court.

5. Appointment of Receiver or Trustee If an insolvent debtor permits the appointment of a receiver or a trustee to take charge of his property, he has committed an act of bankruptcy. In this event, the creditors may transfer a receivership or an adjustment proceeding to a bankruptcy court.

6. Admission in Writing If the debtor admits in writing his inability to pay his debts and his willingness to be judged bankrupt, he has committed an act of bankruptcy. The reason for this sixth act of bankruptcy is that debtors are often unwilling to engage in voluntary bankruptcy because it carries some stigma of avoidance of obligations. Sometimes, therefore, negotiations with a debtor reach an impasse. Admission in writing is one of the methods of forcing the debtor to commit an act of bankruptcy and of moving the proceedings into a bankruptcy court, where the debtor will no longer be able to reject all plans for settlement.

Adjudication and the Referee

On the filing of the petition of involuntary bankruptcy, a subpoena is served on the debtor. There is usually no contest by the debtor, and the court adjudges him bankrupt. On adjudication, the case is transferred by the court to a referee in bankruptcy. A referee in bankruptcy is generally a lawyer appointed for a specified term by the judge of the bankruptcy court to act in his place after adjudication.

In addition, on petition of the creditors, the referee in voluntary proceedings or the judge in involuntary proceedings may appoint a receiver, who serves as the custodian of the property of the debtor until the appointment of a trustee. This arrangement was developed because a long period elapses between the date of the filing of a petition in bankruptcy and the election of a trustee at the first creditors' meeting. To safeguard the creditors' interest during this period, the court, through either the referee or the judge, may appoint a receiver in bankruptcy. The receiver in bankruptcy has full control until the trustee is appointed.

First Creditors' Meeting: Election of Trustee

At the first meeting of the creditors, a trustee is elected. If different blocks of creditors have a different candidate for trustee, the election may become drawn out. Frequently, the trustee will be the adjustment bureau of the local credit managers' association. At this first meeting the debtor may also be examined for the purpose of obtaining necessary information.

Subsequent Procedure

The trustee and the creditors' committee act to convert all assets into cash. The trustee sends a letter to people owing the debtor money, warning that all past-due accounts will result in instant suit if immediate payment is not made, and that, if necessary, he will institute such suit. Appraisers are appointed by the courts to set a value on the property. With the advice of the creditors' committee and by authorization of the referee, the merchandise is sold by approved methods. As in an assignment, auctions may be held.

Property may not be sold without consent of the court at less than 75 percent of the appraised value that has been set by the appraisers appointed by the court. Cash received from the disposition of the property is used first to pay all expenses associated with the proceedings of the bankruptcy and then to pay any remaining funds to the claimants.

Final Meeting and Discharge

When the trustee has completed his liquidation and has sent out all the claimants' checks, he makes an accounting, which is reviewed by the creditors and the referee. The bankruptcy is then discharged and the debtor is released from all debts. If the hearings before the referee indicate the probability of fraud, the FBI is required to undertake an investigation. If the fraud was not committed and the bankruptcy is discharged, the debtor is again free to engage in business. Since business is highly competitive in many fields, the debtor will probably not have great difficulty in obtaining credit again. Under the National Bankruptcy Act, however, a debtor may not be granted a discharge more often than at six-year intervals.

Priority of Claims on Distribution of Proceeds of a Bankruptcy

The order of priority of claims in bankruptcy is as follows:

1. Costs of administering and operating the bankrupt estate.
2. Wages due workers if earned within three months prior to the filing of the petition in bankruptcy. The amount of wages is not to exceed $600 per person.
3. Taxes due the United States, state, county, or any other government agency.

4. Secured creditors, with the proceeds of the sale of specific property pledged for a mortgage.
5. General or unsecured creditors. This claim consists of the remaining balances after payment to secured creditors from the sale of specific property, and includes trade credit, bank loans, and debenture bonds. Holders of subordinated debt fall into this category, but they must turn over required amounts to the holders of senior debt.
6. Preferred stock.
7. Common stock.

To illustrate how this priority of claims works out, let us take a specific example. The balance sheet of a bankrupt firm is shown in Table 24–6. Assets total $90 million. The claims are those indicated on the right-hand side of the balance sheet. It will be noted that the subordinated debentures are subordinated to the notes payable to commercial banks.

Table 24–6 Bankrupt Firm
                 Balance sheet

Current assets	$80,000,000	Accounts payable	$20,000,000
Net property	$10,000,000	Notes payable (due bank)	10,000,000
		Accrued wages,	
		1,400 @ $500	700,000
		U.S. taxes	1,000,000
		State and local taxes	300,000
		Current debt	$32,000,000
		First mortgage	$ 6,000,000
		Second mortgage	1,000,000
		Subordinated debentures[a]	8,000,000
		Long-term debt	$15,000,000
		Preferred stock	2,000,000
		Common stock	26,000,000
		Capital surplus	4,000,000
		Retained earnings	11,000,000
		Net worth	$43,000,000
Total assets	$90,000,000	Total claims	$90,000,000

[a] Subordinated to $10 million notes payable to the First National Bank

Now assume that the assets of the firm are sold. These assets as shown in the balance sheet in Table 24–6 are greatly overstated—they are, in fact, worth much less than the $90 million at which they are carried. The following amounts are realized on liquidation:

Current assets	$28,000,000
Net property	5,000,000
Total assets	$33,000,000

The order of priority of payment of claims is shown by Table 24–7. Fees and expenses of administration are typically about 20 percent of gross proceeds, and in this example they are assumed to be $6 million. Next in priority are wages due workers, which total $700,000. The total amount of taxes to be paid is $1.3 million. Thus far, the total of claims paid for the $33 million is $8 million. The first mortgage is then paid from the net proceeds of $5 million from the sale of fixed property, leaving $20 million available to the general creditors.

TABLE 24–7 Bankrupt Firm
Order of priority of claims

Distribution of Proceeds on Liquidation	
1. Proceeds of sale of assets	$33,000,000
2. Fees and expenses of administration of bankruptcy	$ 6,000,000
3. Wages due workers earned three months prior to filing of bankruptcy petition	700,000
4. Taxes	1,300,000
	$25,000,000
5. First mortgage, paid from sale of net property	5,000,000
6. Available to general creditors	$20,000,000

Claims of General Creditors	Claim (1)	Application of 50 Percent (2)	After Subordination Adjustment (3)	Percentage of Original Claims Received (4)
Unsatisfied portion of first mortgage	$ 1,000,000	$ 500,000	$ 500,000	92
Unsatisfied portion of second mortgage	1,000,000	500,000	500,000	50
Notes payable	10,000,000	5,000,000	9,000,000	90
Accounts payable	20,000,000	10,000,000	10,000,000	50
Subordinated debentures	8,000,000	4,000,000	0	0
	$40,000,000	$20,000,000	$20,000,000	56

Notes: 1. Column 1 is the claim of each class of creditor. Total claims equal $40 million.
2. From line 6 in the upper section of the table we see that $20 million is available. This sum, divided by the $40 million of claims, indicates that general creditors will receive 50 percent of their claims. This is shown in column 2.
3. The debentures are subordinated to the notes payable. Four million dollars is transferred from debentures to notes payable in column 3.
4. Column 4 shows the results of dividing the column 3 figure by the original amount given in Table 24–6, except for first mortgage, where $5 million paid on sale of property is included. The 56 percent total figure includes the first mortgage transactions, that is, ($20,000,000 + $5,000,000) ÷ ($40,000,000 + $5,000,000) = 56%.

The claims of the general creditors total $40 million. Since $20 million is available, each claimant would receive 50 percent of his claim before the subordination adjustment. This adjustment requires that the subordinated debentures turn over to the notes to which they are subordinated all amounts received until the notes are satisfied. In this situation, the claim of the notes payable is $10 million, but only $5 million is available; the deficiency is therefore $5 million. After transfer by the subordinated debentures of $4 million, there remains a deficiency of $1 million, which will be unsatisfied. It will be noted that 90 percent of the bank claim is satisfied, whereas only 50 percent of other unsecured claims will be satisfied. These figures illustrate the usefulness of the subordination provision to the security to which the subordination is made. Since no other funds remain, the claims of the holders of preferred and common stock are completely wiped out.

Studies of the proceeds in bankruptcy liquidations reveal that unsecured creditors receive, on the average, about 15 cents on the dollar. Consequently, where assignment to creditors is likely to yield more, assignment is to be preferred to bankruptcy.

SUMMARY

Problems associated with the decline and failure of a firm, and methods of rehabilitating or liquidating one that has failed, were the subjects treated in this chapter. The major cause of failure is incompetent management. Bad managers should, of course, be removed as promptly as possible; if failure has occurred, a number of remedies are open to the interested parties.

The first question to be answered is whether the firm is better off "dead or alive"—whether it should be liquidated and sold off piecemeal or be rehabilitated. Assuming the decision is made that the firm should survive, it must be put through what is called a *reorganization.* Legal procedures are always costly, especially in the case of a business failure. Therefore, if it is at all possible, both the debtor and the creditors are better off if matters can be handled on an informal basis rather than through the courts. The informal procedures used in reorganization are (1) *extension,* which postpones the date of settlement, and (2) *composition,* which reduces the amount owed.

If voluntary settlement through extension or composition is not possible, the matter is thrown into the courts. If the court decides on reorganization rather than liquidation, it will appoint a trustee (1) to control the firm going through reorganization and (2) to prepare a formal plan of reorganization. The plan, which must be reviewed by the SEC, must meet the standards of *fairness* to all parties and *feasibility* in the sense that the reorganized enterprise will stand a good chance of surviving instead of being thrown back into the bankruptcy courts.

The application of standards of fairness and feasibility developed in this chapter can help to determine the probable success of a particular plan for reorganization. The concept of *fairness* involves the estimation of sales and earnings and the application of a capitalization rate to the latter to determine the appropriate distribution to each claimant.

The *feasibility* test examines the ability of the new enterprise to carry the fixed charges resulting from the reorganization plan. The quality of management and the company's assets must be assured. Production and marketing may also require improvement.

Finally, where liquidation is treated as the only solution to the debtor's insolvency, the creditors should attempt procedures that will net them the largest recovery. *Assignment* of the debtor's property is the cheaper and the faster procedure. Furthermore, there is more flexibility in disposing of the debtor's property and thus providing larger returns. *Bankruptcy* provides formal procedures in liquidation to safeguard the debtor's property from fraud and provides equitable distribution to the creditors. The procedure is long and cumbersome. Moreover, the debtor's property is generally poorly managed during bankruptcy proceedings unless the trustee is closely supervised by the creditors.

QUESTIONS

24-1. "A certain number of business failures is a healthy sign. If there are no failures, this is an indication (a) that entrepreneurs are overly cautious, hence not as inventive and as willing to take risks as a healthy, growing economy requires, (b) that competition is not functioning to weed out inefficient producers, or (c) that both situations exist." Discuss, giving pros and cons.

24-2. How can financial analysis be used to forecast the probability of a given firm's failure? Assuming that such analysis is properly applied, can it always predict failure?

24-3. Why do creditors usually accept a plan for financial rehabilitation rather than demand liquidation of the business?

24-4. Would it be possible to form a profitable company by merging two companies, both of which are business failures? Explain.

24-5. Distinguish between a reorganization and a bankruptcy.

24-6. Would it be a sound rule to liquidate whenever the liquidation value is above the value of the corporation as a going concern? Discuss.

24-7. Why do all liquidations usually result in losses for the creditors or the owners, or both? Would partial liquidation or liquidation over a period limit their losses? Explain.

24-8. Are liquidations likely to be more common for public utility, railroad, or industrial corporations? Why?

PROBLEMS

24-1. The financial statements of the Johnston Publishing Company for 1975 are shown below.

A recapitalization plan is proposed in which each share of the $6 preferred will be exchanged for one share of $2.40 preferred (stated value, $37.50) plus one 8 percent subordinated income debenture (stated principal, $75). The $10.50 preferred would be retired from cash.

a. Show the *pro forma* balance sheet (in millions of dollars) giving effect to the recapitalization and showing the new preferred at its stated value and the common stock at its par value.

b. Present the *pro forma* income statement (in millions of dollars carried to two decimal places).

c. How much does the firm increase income available to common stock by the recapitalization?

d. How much less is the required pretax earnings after the recapitalization compared to those before the change? Required earnings is the amount that is just enough to meet fixed charges, debenture interest, and/or preferred dividends.

e. How is the debt-to-net-worth position of the company affected by the recapitalization?

f. Would you vote for the recapitalization if you were a holder of the $6 prior preferred stock?

Johnston Publishing Company
Balance sheet
December 31, 1975
(in millions of dollars)

Current assets	$120	Current liabilities	$ 42
Investments	48	Advance payments for subscriptions	78
Net fixed assets	153	Reserves	6
Goodwill	15	$6 preferred stock, $112.50 par	
		($1,200,000 shares)	135
		$10.50 preferred stock, no par	
		(60,000 shares, callable at $150)	9
		Common stock, par value	
		of $1.50 (6,000,000 shares outstanding)	9
		Retained earnings	57
Total assets	$336	Total claims	$336

Johnston Publishing Company
Consolidated statement of income and expense for year ended
December 31, 1975
(in millions of dollars)

Operating income		$540.0
Operating expense		516.0
Net operating income		$ 24.0
Other income		3.0
Other expense		0.0
Earnings before income tax		$ 27.0
Income tax at 50 percent		13.5
Income after taxes		$ 13.5
Dividends on $6 prior preferred stock	$7.2	
Dividends on $10.50 preferred stock	0.6	7.8
Income available for common stock		$ 5.7

24-3. The Sun Instrument Company produces precision instruments. The company's products are designed and manufactured according to specifications set out by its customers and are highly specialized.

Declines in sales and increases in development expenses in recent years resulted in a large deficit at the end of 1975.

Sun Instrument Company
Balance sheet
December 31, 1975
(in thousands of dollars)

Current assets	$375	Current liabilities	$450
Fixed assets	375	Long-term debt (unsecured)	225
		Capital stock	150
		Retained earnings (deficit)	(75)
Total assets	$750	Total claims	$750

Sun Instrument Company
Sales and profits, 1972–1975
(in thousands of dollars)

Year	Sales	Net Profit after Tax before Fixed Charges
1972	$2,625	$ 262.5
1973	$2,400	$ 225.0
1974	$1,425	$(75.0)
1975	$1,350	$(112.5)

Independent assessment led to the conclusion that the company would have a liquidation value of about $600,000. As an alternative to liquidation, the management concluded that a reorganization was possible with additional investment of $300,000. The management was confident of eventual success of the company and stated that the additional investment would restore earnings to $125,000 a year after taxes and before fixed charges. The appropriate multiplier to apply is 8 times. The management is negotiating with a local investment group to obtain the additional investment of $300,000. If the funds are obtained, the holders of the long-term debt would be given one-half the common stock in the reorganized firm in place of their present claims.

Should the creditors agree to the reorganization or should they force liquidation of the firm?

24-3. During the past several months, the American Industrial Products Company has had difficulty meeting its current obligations. Attempts to raise additional working capital have failed. To add to AIP's problems, its principal lenders, The 1st National Bank and the General Insurance Company, have been placing increased pressure on AIP because of its continued delinquent loan payments and apparent lack of fiscal responsibility.

The 1st National Bank is first mortgage holder on AIP's production facility and, in addition, the bank has a $1 million, unsecured, revolving loan with AIP that is past due and on which certain restrictive clauses have been violated. The General Insurance Company is holding $5 million of AIP's subordinated debentures. These debentures are subordinate to the notes payable.

Because of the bank's increasing concern for the long-term future of AIP, it exercised its right of offset and attached $750,000 of AIP's deposits. Because of this action, the bank has forced the company into reorganization or bankruptcy.

General Insurance has located a large manufacturing company that is interested in taking over AIP's operations. This company has offered to assume the $8 million mortgage, pay all back taxes, and in addition pay $4.3 million in cash for the company.

    a. Given the data in Exhibit I and the fact that AIP cannot be reorganized internally, show the effect of the above reorganization plan on claims of AIP's creditors.

    b. Based on the information in Exhibit II, test for the standard of fairness.

    c. Comment on the actions of the bank in offsetting AIP's deposits.

    d. Do you feel the bank and the insurance company were right in not advancing AIP additional money?

EXHIBIT I
($000's)

Current assets	$ 3,000
Net property, plant, and equipment	12,000
Other assets	2,800
Total assets	$17,800
Accounts payable	2,000
Taxes	200
Notes payable to bank	250
Other current liabilities	1,350
Total current liabilities	3,800
Mortgage	8,000
Subordinated debentures	5,000
Common stock	1,000
Paid-in capital	2,000
Retained earnings	(2,000)
Total liabilities and stockholders, equity	$17,800

EXHIBIT II
(000's)

Estimated Sales	$20,000
Estimated Earnings	1,294
Capitalization factor	10×

Managerial Finance: A Summary

25 Perhaps the biggest single failing of both finance texts and finance courses is that they often leave the student with the impression that managerial finance consists of a series of discrete, unconnected parts. *This is decidedly not true.* Because the nature of each element must be understood before the interrelationships among elements can be made meaningful, we have considered the various topics in semi-isolation. But to truly understand finance, one simply must recognize the interdependencies and see how the pieces fit together. Our purpose in this chapter is to draw together the various components in order to present a unified, integrated view of managerial finance.

ROLE OF MANAGERIAL FINANCE WITHIN THE ECONOMY

Because business firms produce the vast majority of the economy's goods and services, if the economy is to function efficiently so must the firms within it. By efficient operations we mean that firms must accurately determine what goods and services consumers desire, then produce and distribute these products at the lowest possible cost.[1]

---

[1] Cost must include all social costs, such as air and water pollution. One procedure for forcing the inclusion of such costs in operating decisions of firms is for a governmental agency to assess charges to polluters, with the charges being an increasing function of the level of pollution and the estimated social cost of the particular pollution. This is a thorny problem, but it is perfectly obvious that business firms can and will reduce pollution, just as they reduce labor usage or raw materials wastage, if their pollution costs are assessed against them. Charges based on the extent to which a firm creates pollution would provide this incentive. We might also note that it is unrealistic to expect voluntary controls to work in a competitive industry, as even one noncooperative firm can gain an advantage over other firms and literally force them to abandon voluntary controls. Thus, mandatory industry-wide controls are necessary.

The financial manager plays a key role in the operations of his firm. Through his exercise of internal controls he helps insure that the resources available to the firm are used as efficiently as possible. Included here are both cost control and cost analysis designed to achieve the most efficient use of assets. The financial manager also plays a key role with regard to the use of external resources or to the decision to acquire resources not presently under the control of the firm. In the first place, the capital budgeting decision is designed to insure that the firm makes desirable investments but forgoes undesirable ones. If all costs, social as well as private, are taken into account, and if the cost of capital is estimated appropriately, then the capital budgeting process will ensure that the firm's capital expenditures are optimal from the points of view of both stockholders and society as a whole. The cost of capital, if it is determined in the correct manner, will reflect the opportunity cost of employing resources in the particular firm versus using them elsewhere in the economy. Further, if the firm is to produce funds in the least-cost manner, it must provide the package of investment securities that investors (that is, savers) consider to be the most desirable.

Finance, then, plays an important role both in increasing operating efficiency within individual business units and in allocating productive resources among firms.

FINANCIAL ANALYSIS, PLANNING, AND CONTROL

Managerial finance consists, in essence, of a set of decision rules designed to help management maximize the value of existing stockholders' equity. We define *value* as the present value of the firm's expected future cash flows, discounted at a rate that reflects the uncertainty inherent in the projected cash flows. In theory, we can set up a simultaneous equation model, then solve the model for the set of controllable variables that maximizes the firm's value. In practice, such a mathematical approach is out of the question. We recognize that everything is related to everything else, but we cannot specify the full set of relationships well enough to optimize in the mathematical sense.

We wish to optimize, but we cannot. What can we do? The best alternative, and the one followed by both academicians and financial managers, is to suboptimize, or examine one aspect of a given decision and explicitly assume that the decision at hand has only a minimal effect on other dimensions of the firm's operations. The EOQ inventory model is an example of a suboptimizing model.

Suboptimization is dangerous, however—there is always the possibility that a series of suboptimal decisions will work at cross-purposes and produce very bad overall results. Because of this, we must constantly keep "the big picture" in mind, altering individual decisions if it becomes clear that they are inconsistent. In Part II of this book, An Overview of Finance: Analysis, Planning, and Control, we examined certain tools and techniques that are useful in developing an overall framework into which suboptimizing models can be fitted.

Ratio Analysis

First, we examined a number of financial ratios and saw how ratio analysis could be used to appraise key aspects of a firm's operating position. *Liquidity ratios*—especially the current and the quick ratios—were seen to provide information on the firm's ability to meet its short-run obligations. *Leverage ratios*—particularly the debt ratio, the times interest earned, and the fixed charge coverage—were used to make judgments about the firm's risk of financial leverage. *Activity ratios*—relating to the turnover of such asset categories as inventories, accounts receivable, and fixed assets, as well as total assets—were studied to see how intensively the firm is employing its assets. Finally, *profitability ratios*—the profit margin on sales, and the rate of return on net worth and total assets—were examined. The firm's primary operating objective is to earn a good return on its invested capital, and the rate-of-return ratios show how successfully the firm is meeting this objective.

The ratios are interrelated, and the set of relationships can be studied through the so-called du Pont system. Basically the du Pont system makes use of the fact that the profit margin on sales times the turnover of total assets equals the rate of return on investment.

$$\text{Return on assets} = \frac{\text{profit}}{\text{sales}} \times \frac{\text{sales}}{\text{assets}} = \frac{\text{profit}}{\text{assets}}.$$

This equation can be expanded to include financial leverage, in which case the final product is the rate of return on net worth.

$$\text{Return on net worth} = \frac{\text{percentage return on assets}}{1.0 - \text{debt ratio}}.$$

The significant advantage of the du Pont approach is that it helps the financial manager focus on problem areas. If his rate of return on net worth is lower than that of other firms in the same industry, he can trace back through the du Pont system to see where the trouble lies—for example, is some category of assets (such as inventories) too high, or are labor costs excessive? Note that in addition to comparing a firm with others in its industry, the financial manager can use the du Pont system of ratio analysis to study the trend in his firm's performance over time, thus helping to forestall developing problems.

By categorizing the ratios into four groups, we stressed the uses of the ratios rather than their definitions. Our emphasis was on the generality of ratio analysis, and we sought to show that the purpose of a ratio determines how it is defined. The financial manager faces a myriad of situations calling for analysis—for example, appraising the credit-worthiness of his firm's customers and analyzing the performance of his own firm's various operating divisions. Ratios facilitate this analysis, and because of their simplicity and flexibility they are one of the most widely used tools in the financial manager's kit.

Profit Planning

Ratio analysis is used to examine the firm's current operating posture. Such constant surveillance is a critical part of the control process, but even if no current weaknesses are detected, the firm must still plan for future growth. One important element of such planning relates to decisions about expansion of existing operations, as well as movements into new product lines. Also, whatever type of expansion occurs, the firm must choose between using more or less highly automated productive processes. If a greater degree of automation is to be employed, then relatively heavy investments in fixed assets must be made, and this will increase fixed costs. Variable costs will, however, be relatively low in such cases. The extent to which fixed costs are incurred in the production process is defined as *operating leverage,* while the relationship between changing levels of sales and profits is known as *break-even analysis.*

Financial Forecasting

Although each specific asset expansion decision must be evaluated in detail in reaching the capital budgeting decision, the financial manager should also make broad-brush, aggregate forecasts of future asset requirements to assure that funds will be available to finance new investment programs. These forecasts are, in effect, made because of the explicit recognition that the capital budgeting procedures used in practice are suboptimizing models.

The first step in the aggregate forecast is to obtain an estimate of sales during each year of the planning period. This estimate is worked out jointly by the marketing, production, and finance departments—the marketing manager estimates demand, the production manager estimates capacity, and the financial manager estimates the availability of funds to finance new accounts receivable, inventories, and fixed assets.

Given the approximate level of sales, the financial manager must determine, as accurately as possible, the amount and timing of financial requirements over the planning horizon. On the basis of past relationships between sales and individual balance sheet items, the funds requirements can be forecast by using either (1) the *percent-of-sales method,* or (2) *regression analysis* (simple or multivariate, linear or curvilinear). Asset requirements by balance sheet category are forecast, spontaneously generated funds (increases in accounts payable plus retained earnings) are estimated, and the difference is determined. If the growth rate is quite rapid, asset requirements will exceed internal sources of funds, so plans must be made to obtain new debt or external equity money. If growth is slow, then more funds will be generated than are required to support the estimated growth in sales. In this case the financial manager will consider a number of alternatives, including increasing the dividend payout ratio, retiring debt, using excess funds to acquire other firms, or, perhaps, going back to the operating departments to encourage more R&D expenditures and a further search for profitable investment opportunities.

Control through Budgeting

Once the firm's broad goals for the planning period have been established, the next step is to set up a detailed plan of operation—the *budget.* A complete budget system encompasses all aspects of the firm's operations over the planning horizon; modifications in plans as required by variations in factors outside the firm's control, especially the level of economic activity, are accounted for by use of *flexible budgets.*

A good budgeting system is a most important management tool. It starts with a sales forecast, then works through various intermediate schedules to the *cash budget, budgeted income statement,* and *budgeted,* or *projected* (pro forma), *balance sheet.* The cash budget provides a relatively precise estimate of when funds will be needed and the extent of the firm's short-run financing requirements. The budgeted income statement gives an indication of projected profits, and the budgeted balance sheet indicates the firm's financial picture at the end of the period. If projected profits are too low, or if the *pro forma* balance sheet suggests that the financial ratios are getting out of line, actions can be taken to correct these imbalances.

Interrelationships among Ratio Analysis, Profit Planning, Forecasting, and Budgeting

Ratio analysis is used to highlight certain key features of a firm's operations. Such an analysis can be conducted relatively quickly, and it can be updated frequently to permit early detection of developing problems. Further, ratio analysis is useful in that it facilitates a comparison between the firm in question and other firms in the industry. Once ratio analysis has been used to take stock of the firm's present condition, actions must be taken to exploit its strong points and to strengthen its weak ones. Here, the planning techniques come into play. Break-even analysis can be used both to appraise the prospects of new product decisions and to analyze the effects of expansion or plant modernization decisions on earnings variability.

Sales forecasts are made and used to determine asset requirements and the funds needed to finance these assets. Specific, detailed plans for the current year are drawn up to implement the firm's long-run goals and objectives—this is the annual budget. A key part of the total budget—the cash budget—pinpoints when and how much money will be required during the budget period.

Finally, the financial manager continually compares actual operating results with budgeted figures: Are sales running at the forecast level? Are costs being kept within the estimated limits? Are cash flows running on schedule? Are all divisions meeting their own individual budgeting objectives? This process, called *budgetary control,* is an important key to successful operations.

WORKING CAPITAL MANAGEMENT

In theory, investments in current assets should be analyzed in the same way as investments in capital assets. In practice, however, important differences in the two classes of assets lead to variations in the way the financial manager controls current and fixed asset investments. The most important difference is the fact that investments in capital assets commit the firm to a certain course of action over an extended period, while current asset investments can be modified relatively quickly. This means that capital budgeting must emphasize long-run projections, discounting procedures, and the like. Current asset management, in contrast, is more short-run oriented; the primary objective is to use current assets efficiently. There is an opportunity cost of tying funds up in inventories, cash, and accounts receivable. If the investment in these assets can be reduced without increasing costs or reducing sales, then such a reduction increases the firm's profitability. However, operating with low levels of current assets involves risks, so in working capital policy we encounter the familiar risk-return tradeoff.

LONG-TERM INVESTMENT DECISIONS

In addition to his role in the analysis-planning-control process described above, the financial manager must make decisions on specific individual investments. These capital budgeting decisions involve the whole process of evaluating projects whose returns are expected to extend beyond one year.

Compound Interest

Since long-term returns are involved, the effects of compound interest must be considered. Chapter 10 was devoted to a discussion of compound interest and the ways of taking it into account in financial analysis. Perhaps the most fundamental idea developed in Chapter 10 was that of *present value:* The present value of any asset is equal to the sum of future cash flows from the asset, discounted at an "appropriate" interest rate, later defined as the firm's cost of capital.

Capital Budgeting

Capital budgeting, as it is practiced by sophisticated firms, involves (1) estimating the cost of each prospective project, (2) estimating annual net cash flows from each project, (3) determining the appropriate risk-adjusted discount rate (cost of capital) for the project, and (4) using the present value equation to see if the project's net present value (NPV) is positive. If the NPV is positive or, alternatively, if the internal rate of return (the IRR) exceeds the cost of capital, the project should be accepted.

This sketch of capital budgeting is, of course, highly simplified. At times it is difficult to estimate either the cost of a project or the cash flows that will come from it. Ordinarily, the NPV and the IRR give identical answers to these questions: Which of two mutually exclusive projects should be selected? How large should the total capital budget be? However, under certain circumstances conflicts may arise. In general, the NPV is preferred.

Uncertainty, or Risk Analysis

Both logic and empirical evidence suggest that investors prefer investments with relatively certain returns, other things the same. This being the case, investment decisions should encompass more than just the *expected return* from a project—the decision maker should also take into account any *risk differentials* that may exist among projects.

The first task in risk analysis is to measure the riskiness of various projects. The measure of risk that we employ, and the one used most frequently in practice, is the *coefficient of variation* of the probability distribution of expected returns from a project. The larger the coefficient of variation, the greater the probability that the actual return will deviate significantly from the expected return, and the greater the riskiness of the project.

The risk to the firm embodied in a single project is dependent upon the correlation between returns on the project at hand and the remainder of the firm's assets. If this correlation is positive, returns on the project are high when other assets are also providing high returns, and vice versa. However, if the correlation is negative, returns on the project will be high when those on other assets are low, so taking on the project in question will reduce earnings fluctuations for the firm as a whole. In this case, favorable *portfolio effects* are said to be present, because the overall risk to the firm is less than the apparent risk of the project considered alone. Portfolio effects are taken into account when the firm considers diversification measures in its capital budget.

The typical method for dealing with risk in capital budgeting is to employ a lower cost of capital for less risky projects and a higher cost for more risky ones—this is called the *risk-adjusted discount rate method.* For example, a firm may determine that its average cost of capital is 10 percent and may use this discount rate to find the NPV of "average risk" projects. It will use rates less than 10 percent for low-risk projects and more than 10 percent for high-risk investments.

LONG-TERM FINANCING

In our discussion of capital structure and the cost of capital, we emphasized the risk differences between debt and equity. We did not consider other differences, nor did we attempt to show the alternative ways "debt" and "equity" securities can be packaged. These points, which are essential to a thorough understanding of managerial finance, were covered in Chapters 13, 14, 15, 16, and 17.

One critical distinction between debt and equity is the fact that equity— the common stock—has control of a firm's operations. In theory, management should operate in strict accordance with "what is best for stockholders" —subject to external constraints imposed by labor, government, and so on. In practice, however, if a firm's managers are not also its major stockholders, management will also be concerned about maintaining its control position. This factor can influence the stock-versus-bonds decision and thus perhaps affect the firm's capital structure.

Long-term debt can be issued with a number of alternative features. Depending on the firm's own position and investor's preferences, it will be advantageous for the financial manager to use different ones of these features at different times. For example, if the financial manager feels that interest rates are presently high and are likely to decline in the near future, he will probably insist on making new long-term debt callable. Similarly, if investors think that a sinking fund will reduce the riskiness of the firm's bonds, they will accept a lower interest rate if the bonds have a sinking fund. However, a sinking fund will increase the cash flow requirements for servicing the debt, and this may be unattractive from the firm's standpoint. The financial manager must balance all these alternatives and decide upon the specific set of features that will be in the best interests of his firm.

Two particularly important financial instruments are *term loans* and *leases.* A term loan is generally of intermediate maturity—over one year but less than five, although some term loans run for fifteen years. Leases have maturities similar to those for term loans, and these two forms of financing are frequently alternatives to each other. The recommended procedure for comparing the cost of a loan versus a lease calls for determining the present value cost differential between the two instruments and choosing the one with the lower present value cost.

Convertible debt and preferred stock, or bonds with warrants, can be issued to raise new money. When either convertibles or bonds with warrants are used, the purchaser receives a package consisting of both a fixed income component and the possibility of a capital gain. Thus, the investor is able to hedge his position somewhat—he is more protected against losses than if he owned only common stock, yet he can still share the benefits if the firm is highly successful or if inflation dilutes the value of fixed return securities. Because of this protection, investors may be willing to accept lower overall expected rates of return on convertibles or bonds with warrants than on straight debt plus common stock. The usefulness of convertibles and warrants varies over time. They are most attractive in times of uncertainty such as the early 1970s, and at such times the financial manager can use them to lower his firm's cost of capital.

Why do firms issue so many different types and forms of securities? The primary reason has to do with the risk-return tradeoff function. Different classes of investors, as well as different individual investors within a given class, exhibit differing degrees of willingness to assume risks. Recognizing these investor preferences, an astute financial manager can create a whole array of different securities with differential risk characteristics, thereby appealing to many kinds of investors and broadening the market for his firm's issues. Also, having an array of instruments permits the financial manager to issue the types of securities that are most popular at any given point in time; this is an important advantage because, as we saw in Chapter 22, costs of different types of securities vary markedly over time.

FINANCIAL STRUCTURE AND THE COST OF CAPITAL

In Chapter 12 we saw that risk aversion leads investors to seek higher returns on more risky investments—the riskier the investment, the greater the *risk premium* (the amount by which the expected return on a risky investment exceeds the riskless rate of return). These concepts were extended in Chapters 18, 19, and 20, where we showed the effect of capital structure on risk and thus on the firm's cost of capital.

Financial Leverage

Whenever a firm uses debt capital, it is employing *financial leverage.* Since debt typically involves a fixed interest charge, any fluctuation in operating income will produce a magnified fluctuation in earnings available to common stock. The greater the extent of financial leverage, the greater the earnings variability of the common stock.

The impact of financial leverage can be examined graphically, but it can also be studied more rigorously and can be measured in terms of its effect on the coefficient of variation. Typically, the higher the leverage factor, the larger the variability in earnings per share. Finally, the effects of leverage can be examined in terms of the *degree of financial leverage.* In addition, the effects of financial and operating leverage may be combined, with the *combined leverage factor* showing the percentage change in earnings per share that results from a given percentage change in sales.

Valuation and Rates of Return

When the present value concepts developed in Chapter 10 were used in Chapter 11 to determine the desirability of investing in specific assets, we determined the value of the asset *to the firm* by discounting the expected cash flows by the appropriate cost of capital. This same valuation technique may be applied to the firm as a whole by investors—common and preferred stock-holders, and bondholders. In this latter case, the cash flows are the expected returns on the firm's securities—interest plus maturity value on bonds, dividends on preferred stocks, and dividends plus capital gains on common stocks. The appropriate discount rate is dependent primarily on the riskiness of the particular security and supply and demand conditions in the capital market—the riskier the security, the higher the appropriate discount rate, and the greater the demand for funds vis-à-vis the supply of funds, the higher the rate.

Notice particularly that the firm can influence its cost of capital. If it uses a high degree of operating leverage and invests in assets which produce highly uncertain returns, then it will be subject to a high degree of *basic business risk,* which will cause its cost of capital to be relatively high. If it super-imposes financial leverage on top of its basic business risk, it further increases the risk borne by investors.

Cost of Capital

Each component of the capital structure has what we have called a *component cost,* and each individual component cost is a function (1) of the riskiness of the income stream expected by owners of the particular component security (for example, bondholders or stockholders), and (2) of the opportunity cost of the security holders (for example, the interest rate on other bonds or the expected rate of return on comparable stocks of other companies). The firm can do little to influence opportunity costs, but its decisions with regard to both asset purchases and the use of financial leverage affect the riskiness of its securities.

Both theory and empirical evidence suggest that for each firm there is an *optimum capital structure,* that is, a mix of debt and equity securities that minimizes the cost of raising any given amount of capital.[2] Shifts in this opti-mum structure as capital market conditions vary is the issue discussed in Chapter 20. However, at any point in time there is an optimum structure.[3]

Recall that we have two primary reasons for wishing to know the cost of capital: (1) we need it for capital budgeting purposes, and (2) we want to minimize it. The cost of capital we need is the *marginal cost,* which is deter-mined as follows:

---

[2]Theories have been advanced by Modigliani and Miller, among others, that no optimum capital struc-ture would exist if there were no corporate taxes and if capital markets were perfect. Since neither condition holds, even advocates of these theories agree that in the real world there is an optimum capital structure.

[3]Empirical evidence suggests that the average cost of capital curve is u-shaped, not v-shaped, so there is generally a *range* of capital structures within which the average cost of capital is *approximately* minimized. This greatly facilitates the financial manager's task, as it is much easier to locate a range than a unique point.

1. Decide on a tentative optimum capital structure.
2. Determine the cost of the various capital components under this capital structure:
   a. Debt cost = (interest rate)(1 − tax rate).
   b. Preferred cost=(preferred dividend)/(price of preferred net of flotation costs).
   c. Retained earnings cost = $k = (D_1/P_0) + g$. Alternatively, k may be thought of as consisting of a riskless return plus a premium for business and financial risk: $k = R_F + \rho$.
   d. Newly issued common stock = $k_e = [D_1/P_0(1 − F)] + g$, where F is a flotation cost and g is the expected (and constant) growth rate.
3. Use the capital structure percentages and the estimated component costs to calculate a weighted average cost.
4. The marginal cost is constant until retained earnings have been used up. At this point, newly issued common stock must be sold, raising the component cost of equity. Here, the marginal cost begins to rise.

Dividend Policy

Our study of the cost of capital makes it clear that because of flotation costs, if for no other reason, retained earnings have a lower cost than new outside equity. However, dividends, which constitute an important part of the return to common stockholders, must be lowered if a firm increases its retained earnings. Thus, dividend policy—or the determination of how net income will be split between dividends and reinvestment—is an important component of overall financial policy.

We found in Chapter 21 that because of capital budgeting and cost of capital considerations, a firm with many good investment opportunities will tend to have a low dividend payout ratio, while a firm with few good investments will have a high payout. We also found that the firm's own individual situation—its cash or liquidity position, its access to capital markets, the tax position of its stockholders, and so on—has an important bearing on its dividend policy.

REVIEW OF FINANCIAL THEORY

It is useful to review developments to this point. First, the operating goal of the firm is to maximize the market value of stockholders' equity. To achieve this maximization, the firm must satisfy a number of conditions.

Operating Efficiency

The firm must operate efficiently in the sense of recognizing customer demands, both actual and potential, and of producing to meet this demand at a minimum cost.[4] The planning and control techniques introduced earlier are designed to enhance operating efficiency.

Rate of Expansion

Expansion decisions (capital budgeting) should be made if, and only if, the expected present value of a specific project exceeds the cost of undertaking the project. In this connection, note that since more efficient firms have higher expected cash flows than inefficient ones, resources shift over time to efficient businesses.

Risk Characteristics

The degree of business risk inherent in a firm's assets combines with any additional risk resulting from financial leverage to determine its overall risk characteristics. These, in turn, affect the firm's cost of capital.

Average Cost of Capital

To maximize its value the firm must minimize the cost of capital for financing its chosen set of assets. This means selecting the set of securities—long-term and short-term debt, preferred and common stock, retained earnings and new outside equity, convertibles or bonds with warrants, and the specific provisions attached to each of these instruments—that minimizes capital costs.

Marginal Cost of Capital

The marginal cost of capital is dependent upon basic business risk and financial leverage. It is also a function of the amount of capital the firm raises during a given period. If the rate of expansion is quite rapid, the firm must bring in new outside equity capital, which causes the marginal cost of capital to rise.

Simultaneous Determination

The cost of capital is a necessary ingredient in asset expansion decisions, because we must know the marginal cost of capital to determine if each particular project should be accepted or rejected. We must also know the size of the capital budget before we can determine the marginal cost of capital. Therefore, the cost of capital and the capital budget must be determined simultaneously. If we knew the cost of capital schedule and the investment opportunity schedule *precisely,* then we could use mathematical techniques

[4]We emphasized that for the firm to be efficient in a *social* sense, cost must include social costs as well as private costs. Government agencies must assess the level of these costs and force firms either to eliminate them or be taxed to cover them.

to obtain the simultaneous solution to a system of equations and thus determine a precise value-maximizing set of investments. As a practical matter, we do not have sufficient information to warrant using this approach.

Although we cannot obtain the simultaneous solution, the pragmatic usefulness of the theoretical concepts that have been developed should not be ruled out. The financial manager can obtain an estimate of his cost of capital which, if not exact, is sufficiently accurate to use in the capital budgeting process. Further, under normal conditions the rate of expansion, or even changes in the firm's mix of assets that would cause significant changes in its basic business risk, is not large enough to alter its cost of capital seriously. If the cost of capital is relatively constant, the simultaneity conditions are not important, and straightforward capital budgeting techniques, such as the risk-adjusted NPV method, are appropriate. Further, even if the firm is contemplating a significant change in operations—such as a shift in product lines, entry into a new industry, or an important change in dividend or capital structure policy—the wisdom of such a move can certainly be better ascertained if it is considered within the framework of our theory of financial policy.

TIMING OF FINANCIAL POLICY

Financial managers ordinarily have a great deal of flexibility in their operations. Even though a firm may have a target debt/total-assets ratio, it can deviate from this target to some extent in a given year to take advantage of favorable conditions in either the bond market or the stock market. Similarly, although it may have a target relationship between its long-term and short-term debt, it can vary from this target if market conditions suggest that such action is appropriate.

As a basis for making sound decisions with respect to financial timing, we analyzed data covering both cyclical and long-term trends. Uncertainties about the future have increased in recent years, and this has increased the importance of sound financial timing. Also, attempts to deal with the greater uncertainties have given rise to innovations in financing techniques and patterns. Some important changes in financing that have developed in response to changes in the economy and in the money and capital markets include the following.

1. Long-term financing has increased in comparison to the use of short-term commercial bank financing. Bond flotations in the capital markets have risen to record levels as firms seek to lengthen the maturity of their debt structures.
2. Public flotations of equity issues have increased substantially.
3. A large increase in debt ratios has occurred in response to the inflationary environment. From 1966 to 1969 the ratio of debt to assets for all manufacturing companies rose from 33 percent to 41 percent. After the May

1970 bankruptcy of Penn Central and the ensuing money crunch, many firms sold equity in an effort to return to lower debt ratios. However, once the "Penn-Central panic" abated, manufacturing firms turned again to debt, and by 1976 the average firm's debt ratio was almost 50 percent.

4. An increase has occurred in the use of convertibles and warrants.

5. Insurance companies and other nonbank lenders have virtually ceased providing credit to small- and medium-sized borrowers on a straight-debt basis. For business loans, warrants are usually required, while on mortgages supplementary payments based on a percentage of gross or net income are stipulated in loan contracts.

6. New equity securities have been issued in spite of the decline in equity prices beginning in early 1969. As the debt ratios of large corporations rose and as their liquidity positions declined, larger corporations began (in 1970) to sell equity issues in substantial amounts.

7. Since larger firms have greater access to the financial markets, an increase in the volume of trade credit has occurred, with larger firms increasing their extension of credit to smaller ones.

The developments outlined above indicate that trends in the money and capital markets have become of increased importance to financial managers. The changes have been so massive that not only has financial timing been involved but also innovations in the forms of financing used have been stimulated.

MERGER POLICY

Because of his strategic position, the financial manager has a key role in corporate mergers and acquisitions. In a sense, a merger is like any other long-term investment decision—one firm acquires another in much the same way that it would acquire a new plant or office building. From this point of view, the merger decision should be analyzed in the capital budgeting framework, and the acquisition should be made if it increases the acquiring firm's net present value as reflected in the price of its stock. However, mergers are frequently quite significant in terms of their impact both on the acquiring firm and on the economy. Not only can a bad merger decision literally wreck a firm, but mergers among competing firms can turn a competitive market into an oligopolistic one. Accordingly, both managements and the federal government are generally more concerned over merger decisions than over most other decisions made by corporations.

CONCLUSION

Finance is a complex subject, blending abstract theory, practical decision models, and a description of the institutional setting in which financial decisions are made. Further, it is a dynamic area, ever changing in response to new technology and developments within the economy. These characteristics make finance a difficult subject, but one which is exciting and challenging. Finance is also important to the economy, for we must have efficient firms if the economy is to cope with the problems it faces. We can only hope that this book has, by helping the reader to understand the theory and methodology of finance, assisted in preparing him to meet the challenges of the future.

QUESTIONS

25-1. Assume that a holding company is analyzing a potential acquisition candidate. The target firm, if acquired, will operate completely independently of the holding company, and the only cash flows from the subsidiary to the holding company will be dividends. There will be no synergistic effects.

    a. How would you determine a "fair" price to pay for the target firm? Be explicit, giving (1) a valuation model, (2) an idea of the cash flows that should be used, and (3) the appropriate discount rate. Justify your answers.

    b. Now assume that the holding company would truly merge the target company into the operations of its other holdings and that synergistic effects would occur. How would this affect your answers to part a?

25-2. In what sense is an inventory model an example of suboptimization? Could the same thing be said about the NPV capital budgeting model? Explain.

25-3. Why do firms use different types of securities? In your discussion of this question, use a graph and be sure to include considerations that would apply over time as well as those that would apply at any one instant of time.

25-4. Assume that a firm uses, in addition to long-term debt and equity, the following types of financing:

    1. convertible bonds
    2. bonds with warrants
    3. accounts payable
    4. long-term financial leases

    a. Explain how to calculate the component cost of each type of capital.

    b. How would you calculate the average cost of capital for a firm with a large amount of long-term leases outstanding?

PROBLEMS

25-1[5] To obtain a position in the underwriting department of a major investment banking house is difficult, but it is especially hard to land a job that calls for contact with the top partners so that one may really learn the inside of the business. Through family connections, however, Gordon Hammrick was fortunate enough to get the job of assistant to William Murray, senior partner and managing officer of Murray, Finch,

[5]This case study is taken from E. F. Brigham, Timothy J. Nantell, Robert T. Aubey, and Richard H. Pettway, *Cases in Managerial Finance, Third Edition* (New York: Holt, Rinehart and Winston, Inc., 1977).

Price, Farmer & Smith. Hammrick received his bachelor's degree in history only two weeks before getting his job, and this was his first day on the job. After a rather pleasant morning spent meeting various people around the office, including some attractive secretaries, Hammrick was given his first task.

Murray had not only been forced to miss his regular Thursday afternoon golf match, but he also had to stay up long after midnight finishing some recommendations on the types of financing that a group of clients should use. The next morning, having completed the analyses and made his recommendations, Murray turned over to Hammrick the folder on each client and, attached to each of the folders, his recommendation on the type of financing that each should use. He then told Hammrick, first, to have the analyses and financing recommendations typed and sent immediately to each of the client companies and, second, that he was taking his secretary away for a weekend of uninterrupted dictation. Murray particularly stressed that he should be consulted during the weekend only in the event of an emergency.

The first thing Hammrick did was to detach the analyses and recommendations from the folders and give them to a secretary to type. When the secretary returned the typed reports, Hammrick discovered that he did not know which recommendation belonged to which company! He had folders on nine different companies and financing recommendations for nine companies, but he could not match them up. Hammrick's major was history, so he could not be expected to be able to match the financing recommendations with the appropriate companies. You, as a finance student, should be able to help Hammrick by telling him which companies (listed on the following pages) should use which financing methods.

Financing Methods

1. Common stock: nonrights
2. Debt with warrants
3. Factoring
4. Friends or relatives
5. Preferred stock (nonconvertible)
6. Common stock: rights offering
7. Long-term bonds
8. Leasing arrangement
9. Convertible debentures

Companies

a. **Arizona Mining Company**   Arizona Mining needs $10 million to finance the acquisition of mineral rights to some land in south-central Arizona, as well as to pay for some extensive surveys, core borings, magnetic aerial surveys, and other types of analyses designed to determine whether the mineral deposits on this land warrant development. If the tests are favorable, the company will need an additional $10 million. Arizona Mining's common stock is currently selling at $12, while the company is earning approximately $1 a share. Other firms in the industry sell at from 10 to 15 times earnings. Arizona Mining's debt ratio is 25 percent, which compares with an industry average of 30 percent. Total assets at the last balance sheet date were $105 million.

b. **New York Power Company**   Since New York Power, a major electric utility, is organized as a holding company, the Securities and Exchange Commission must approve all security issues; such approval is automatic if the company stays within conventional norms for the electric utility industry. Reasonable norms call for long-term debt in the range of 55 to 65 percent, preferred stock in the range of 0 to 15 percent, and common equity in the range of 25 to 35 percent. New York Power Company currently has total assets of $1 billion, financed as follows: $600 million debt, $50 million preferred stock, and $350 million common equity. The company plans to raise an additional $25 million at this time.

c. **Wilson Brothers, Inc.**   Wilson Brothers, Inc., a wholesale grocery business in Cincinnati, Ohio, is owned by the three Wilson brothers; each owns one-third of the outstanding stock. The company is profitable, but rapid growth has put it under a severe financial strain. The real estate is all under mortgage to an insurance company, the inventory is being used under a blanket chattel mortgage to secure a bank line of credit, and the accounts receivable are being factored. With total assets of $5 million, the company now needs an additional $100,000 to purchase twenty forklift trucks and related equipment to facilitate handling in the shipping and receiving department.

d. **Alabama Milling Company**   Alabama Milling manufactures unbleached cotton cloth, then bleaches the cloth and dyes it in various colors and patterns. The finished cloth is packaged in bulk and is sold on sixty-day credit terms, largely to relatively small clothing companies operating in the New York City area. The company's plant and equipment have been financed in part by a mortgage loan, and this is the only long-term debt. Raw materials—cotton and dyes—are purchased on terms calling for payment within thirty days of receipt of goods, but no discounts are offered. Because the national economy is currently so prosperous, apparel sales have experienced a sharp increase, which, in turn, has produced a marked increase in the demand for Alabama Milling's products. To finance a higher level of output, Alabama Milling needs approximately $500,000.

e. **Florida-Pacific Corporation**   Florida-Pacific is a major producer of plywood, paper, and other forest products. The company's stock is widely held, actively traded, and listed on the New York Stock Exchange; recently it has been trading in the range of $30 to $35 a share. The latest twelve-months earnings were $2.12; the current dividend rate is 80 cents a year, and earnings, dividends, and the price of the company's stock have been growing at a rate of about 7 percent over the preceding few years. Florida-Pacific's debt ratio is currently 42 percent versus 25 percent for other large forest product firms. Other firms in the industry, on the average, have been growing at a rate of about 5 percent a year, and their stocks have been selling at a price/earnings ratio of about 13. Florida-Pacific has an opportunity to acquire a substantial stand of forest in Northern California. The current owners of the property are asking $20 million in cash for the land and timber.

f. **Toy World**   Joseph Marino, an employee of the state of Pennsylvania and an avid model airplane and model automobile builder, has just learned that some of the stores in a new neighborhood shopping center are still available for lease. Marino knows that no good toy and hobby store exists in the southwest section of the city of Harrisburg, and he believes that if he can obtain approximately $20,000 for fixtures and stock, he can open a successful store in the new shopping center. His liquid savings total $5,000, so Marino needs an additional $15,000 to open the proposed store.

g. **Knight Electronics Corporation**   Knight Electronics is a medium-size electronics company whose sales distribution is approximately 30 percent for defense contracts and 70 percent for nonmilitary uses. The company has been growing rapidly in recent years, and projections based on current research and development prospects call for continued growth at a rate of 10 to 12 percent a year. Although recent reports of several brokerage firms suggest that the firm's rate of growth might be slowing down, Knight's management believes, on the basis of internal information, that no decline is in sight. The company's stock, which is traded on the Pacific Stock Exchange, is selling at 20 times earnings; this is slightly below the 23 times ratio of Standard & Poor's electronics industry average. The firm's debt ratio is 40 percent, just above the 38 percent average for the industry. The company has assets of $28 million and needs an additional $4 million, over and above retained earnings, to support the projected level of growth during the next twelve months.

h. **Utah Chemical Company**   Utah Chemical is a closely held company that was founded in 1952 to extract from the Great Salt Lake minerals used in agricultural fertilizers. The company's debt ratio is 48 percent versus an average ratio of 36 percent for agricultural fertilizer producers in general. The stock is owned in equal parts by ten individuals, none of whom is in a position to put additional funds into the business. Sales for the most recent year totaled $10 million, and earnings after taxes amounted to $600,000. Total assets, as of the latest balance sheet, amounted to $8 million. Utah Chemical needs an additional $3 million to finance expansion during the current fiscal year; given the worldwide growth in demand for agricultural chemicals, the firm can anticipate additional outside capital needs in the years ahead.

i. **Universal Container Corporation**   Universal Container is engaged in the manufacture of cans, glass bottles, paper boxes of various sorts, a variety of plastic tubes, and other packaging materials. Since the firm sells to a great many producers of nondurable consumer goods, sales are relatively stable. The current price of the company's stock, which is listed on the New York Stock Exchange, is $42, and the most recent earnings and dividends per share are $4 and $2, respectively. The rate of growth in sales, earnings, and dividends in the last few years has averaged 5 percent. Universal Container has total assets of $360 million. Current liabilities, which consist primarily of accounts payable and accruals, are $25 million; long-term debt is $75 million; and common equity totals $260 million. An additional $30 million of external funds is required to build and equip a new can manufacturing complex in central California and to supply the new facility with working capital.

25-2. a. A firm with $60 million of assets judges that it is at the beginning of a three-year growth cycle. It is a manufacturing firm with a total-debt-to-assets ratio of 16 percent. It expects sales and net earnings to grow at a rate of 10 percent a year.

Stock prices are expected to rise 30 percent a year over the three-year period. The firm will need $6 million at the beginning of the three-year period and another $3 million by the middle of the third year. It is at the beginning of a general business upswing, when money and capital costs are what they generally are after about a year of recession and at the beginning of an upswing. By the middle of the third year, money and capital costs will have their characteristic pattern near the peak of an upswing.

How should the firm raise the $6 million and the $3 million?

b. An aerospace company with sales of $25 million a year needs $5 million to finance expansion. It has a debt-to-total-assets ratio of 65 percent. Its common stock, which is widely held, is selling at a price/earnings ratio of 25 times. It is comparing the sale of common stock and convertible debentures.

Which do you recommend? Why?

c. A chemical company has been growing steadily. To finance a growth of sales from $40 million a year to $50 million over a two-year period, it needs $2 million in additional equipment. When additional working capital needs are taken into account, the total additional financing required during the first year is $5 million. Profits will rise by 50 percent after the first ten months. The stock is currently selling at 20 times earnings. It can borrow on straight debt at 7½ percent or with a convertibility or warrant "sweetener" for ¾ percent less. The present debt-to-total-assets ratio is 25 percent.

Which form of financing should it employ?

25-3. Allied Chemists, Inc., has experienced the following sales, profit, and balance sheet patterns. Identify the financial problem that has developed and recommend a solution for it.

Allied Chemists, Inc.
Financial data, 1968–1977
(in millions of dollars)

Income Statements	1968	1969	1970	1971	1972	1973	1974	1975	1976	1977
Sales	$100	$140	$180	$200	$240	$400	$360	$440	$480	$680
Profits after tax	10	14	18	20	24	40	36	44	48	68
Dividends	8	10	12	12	14	20	20	28	36	48
Retained earnings	$ 2	$ 4	$ 6	$ 8	$ 10	$ 20	$ 16	$ 16	$ 12	$ 20
Cumulative retained earnings	$ 2	$ 6	$ 12	$ 20	$ 30	$ 50	$ 66	$ 82	$ 94	$114

Balance Sheets	1968	1969	1970	1971	1972	1973	1974	1975	1976	1977
Current assets	$ 20	$ 30	$ 40	$ 50	$ 60	$100	$ 80	$110	$120	$160
Net fixed assets	30	40	50	50	60	100	100	110	120	180
Total assets	$ 50	$ 70	$ 90	$100	$120	$200	$180	$220	$240	$340
Trade credit	$ 8	$ 12	$ 16	$ 18	$ 20	$ 36	$ 30	$ 40	$ 40	$120
Bank credit	8	12	20	20	26	58	28	40	40	40
Other	2	10	12	12	14	16	16	18	16	16
Total current liabilities	$ 18	$ 34	$ 48	$ 50	$ 60	$110	$ 74	$ 98	$ 96	$176
Long-term debt	0	0	0	0	0	10	10	10	20	20
Total debt	$ 18	$ 34	$ 48	$ 50	$ 60	$120	$ 84	$108	$116	$196
Common stock	$ 30	$ 30	$ 30	$ 30	$ 30	$ 30	$ 30	$ 30	$ 30	$ 30
Retained earnings	2	6	12	20	30	50	66	82	94	114
Net worth	$ 32	$ 36	$ 42	$ 50	$ 60	$ 80	$ 96	$112	$124	$144
Total claims on assets	$ 50	$ 70	$ 90	$100	$120	$200	$180	$220	$240	$340

Appendix A
Mathematical Tables

TABLE A–1 Compound Sum of $1: $CVIF = (1 + k)^t$

Period	1%	2%	3%	4%	5%	6%	7%
1	1.010	1.020	1.030	1.040	1.050	1.060	1.070
2	1.020	1.040	1.061	1.082	1.102	1.124	1.145
3	1.030	1.061	1.093	1.125	1.158	1.191	1.225
4	1.041	1.082	1.126	1.170	1.216	1.262	1.311
5	1.051	1.104	1.159	1.217	1.276	1.338	1.403
6	1.062	1.126	1.194	1.265	1.340	1.419	1.501
7	1.072	1.149	1.230	1.316	1.407	1.504	1.606
8	1.083	1.172	1.267	1.369	1.477	1.594	1.718
9	1.094	1.195	1.305	1.423	1.551	1.689	1.838
10	1.105	1.219	1.344	1.480	1.629	1.791	1.967
11	1.116	1.243	1.384	1.539	1.710	1.898	2.105
12	1.127	1.268	1.426	1.601	1.796	2.012	2.252
13	1.138	1.294	1.469	1.665	1.886	2.133	2.410
14	1.149	1.319	1.513	1.732	1.980	2.261	2.579
15	1.161	1.346	1.558	1.801	2.079	2.397	2.759
16	1.173	1.373	1.605	1.873	2.183	2.540	2.952
17	1.184	1.400	1.653	1.948	2.292	2.693	3.159
18	1.196	1.428	1.702	2.026	2.407	2.854	3.380
19	1.208	1.457	1.754	2.107	2.527	3.026	3.617
20	1.220	1.486	1.806	2.191	2.653	3.207	3.870
25	1.282	1.641	2.094	2.666	3.386	4.292	5.427
30	1.348	1.811	2.427	3.243	4.322	5.743	7.612

Period	8%	9%	10%	12%	14%	15%	16%
1	1.080	1.090	1.100	1.120	1.140	1.150	1.160
2	1.166	1.186	1.210	1.254	1.300	1.322	1.346
3	1.260	1.295	1.331	1.405	1.482	1.521	1.561
4	1.360	1.412	1.464	1.574	1.689	1.749	1.811
5	1.469	1.539	1.611	1.762	1.925	2.011	2.100
6	1.587	1.677	1.772	1.974	2.195	2.313	2.436
7	1.714	1.828	1.949	2.211	2.502	2.660	2.826
8	1.851	1.993	2.144	2.476	2.853	3.059	3.278
9	1.999	2.172	2.358	2.773	3.252	3.518	3.803
10	2.159	2.367	2.594	3.106	3.707	4.046	4.411
11	2.332	2.580	2.853	3.479	4.226	4.652	5.117
12	2.518	2.813	3.138	3.896	4.818	5.350	5.926
13	2.720	3.066	3.452	4.363	5.492	6.153	6.886
14	2.937	3.342	3.797	4.887	6.261	7.076	7.988
15	3.172	3.642	4.177	5.474	7.138	8.137	9.266
16	3.426	3.970	4.595	6.130	8.137	9.358	10.748
17	3.700	4.328	5.054	6.866	9.276	10.761	12.468
18	3.996	4.717	5.560	7.690	10.575	12.375	14.463
19	4.316	5.142	6.116	8.613	12.056	14.232	16.777
20	4.661	5.604	6.728	9.646	13.743	16.367	19.461
25	6.848	8.623	10.835	17.000	26.462	32.919	40.874
30	10.063	13.268	17.449	29.960	50.950	66.212	85.850

Period	18%	20%	24%	28%	32%	36%
1	1.180	1.200	1.240	1.280	1.320	1.360
2	1.392	1.440	1.538	1.638	1.742	1.850
3	1.643	1.728	1.907	2.067	2.300	2.515
4	1.939	2.074	2.364	2.684	3.036	3.421
5	2.288	2.488	2.932	3.436	4.007	4.653
6	2.700	2.986	3.635	4.398	5.290	6.328
7	3.185	3.583	4.508	5.629	6.983	8.605
8	3.759	4.300	5.590	7.206	9.217	11.703
9	4.435	5.160	6.931	9.223	12.166	15.917
10	5.234	6.192	8.594	11.806	16.060	21.647
11	6.176	7.430	10.657	15.112	21.199	29.439
12	7.288	8.916	13.215	19.343	27.983	40.037
13	8.599	10.699	16.386	24.759	36.937	54.451
14	10.147	12.839	20.319	31.961	48.757	74.053
15	11.974	15.407	25.196	40.565	64.359	100.712
16	14.129	18.488	31.243	51.923	84.954	136.97
17	16.672	22.186	38.741	66.461	112.14	186.28
18	19.673	26.623	48.039	85.071	148.02	253.34
19	23.214	31.948	59.568	108.89	195.39	344.54
20	27.393	38.338	73.864	139.38	257.92	468.57
25	62.669	95.396	216.542	478.90	1033.6	2180.1
30	143.371	237.376	634.820	1645.5	4142.1	10143.

Period	40%	50%	60%	70%	80%	90%
1	1.400	1.500	1.600	1.700	1.800	1.900
2	1.960	2.250	2.560	2.890	3.240	3.610
3	2.744	3.375	4.096	4.913	5.832	6.859
4	3.842	5.062	6.544	8.352	10.498	13.032
5	5.378	7.594	10.486	14.199	18.896	24.761
6	7.530	11.391	16.777	24.138	34.012	47.046
7	10.541	17.086	26.844	41.034	61.222	89.387
8	14.758	25.629	42.950	69.758	110.200	169.836
9	20.661	38.443	68.720	118.588	198.359	322.688
10	28.925	57.665	109.951	201.599	357.047	613.107
11	40.496	86.498	175.922	342.719	642.684	1164.902
12	56.694	129.746	281.475	582.622	1156.831	2213.314
13	79.372	194.619	450.360	990.457	2082.295	4205.297
14	111.120	291.929	720.576	1683.777	3748.131	7990.065
15	155.568	437.894	1152.921	2862.421	6746.636	15181.122
16	217.795	656.84	1844.7	4866.1	12144.	28844.0
17	304.914	985.26	2951.5	8272.4	21859.	54804.0
18	426.879	1477.9	4722.4	14063.0	39346.	104130.0
19	597.630	2216.8	7555.8	23907.0	70824.	197840.0
20	836.683	3325.3	12089.0	40642.0	127480.	375900.0
25	4499.880	25251.	126760.0	577060.0	2408900.	9307600.0
30	24201.432	191750.	1329200.	8193500.0	45517000.	230470000.0

TABLE A-2 Present Value of $1: $PVIF = \dfrac{1}{(1+k)^t} = \dfrac{1}{CVIF}$

Period	1%	2%	3%	4%	5%	6%	7%	8%	9%	10%	12%	14%	15%
1	.990	.980	.971	.962	.952	.943	.935	.926	.917	.909	.893	.877	.870
2	.980	.961	.943	.925	.907	.890	.873	.857	.842	.826	.797	.769	.756
3	.971	.942	.915	.889	.864	.840	.816	.794	.772	.751	.712	.675	.658
4	.961	.924	.889	.855	.823	.792	.763	.735	.708	.683	.636	.592	.572
5	.951	.906	.863	.822	.784	.747	.713	.681	.650	.621	.567	.519	.497
6	.942	.888	.838	.790	.746	.705	.666	.630	.596	.564	.507	.456	.432
7	.933	.871	.813	.760	.711	.665	.623	.583	.547	.513	.452	.400	.376
8	.923	.853	.789	.731	.677	.627	.582	.540	.502	.467	.404	.351	.327
9	.914	.837	.766	.703	.645	.592	.544	.500	.460	.424	.361	.308	.284
10	.905	.820	.744	.676	.614	.558	.508	.463	.422	.386	.322	.270	.247
11	.896	.804	.722	.650	.585	.527	.475	.429	.388	.350	.287	.237	.215
12	.887	.788	.701	.625	.557	.497	.444	.397	.356	.319	.257	.208	.187
13	.879	.773	.681	.601	.530	.469	.445	.368	.326	.290	.229	.182	.163
14	.870	.758	.661	.577	.505	.442	.388	.340	.299	.263	.205	.160	.141
15	.861	.743	.642	.555	.481	.417	.362	.315	.275	.239	.183	.140	.123
16	.853	.728	.623	.534	.458	.394	.339	.292	.252	.218	.163	.123	.107
17	.844	.714	.605	.513	.436	.371	.317	.270	.231	.198	.146	.108	.093
18	.836	.700	.587	.494	.416	.350	.296	.250	.212	.180	.130	.095	.081
19	.828	.686	.570	.475	.396	.331	.276	.232	.194	.164	.116	.083	.070
20	.820	.673	.554	.456	.377	.312	.258	.215	.178	.149	.104	.073	.061
25	.780	.610	.478	.375	.295	.233	.184	.146	.116	.092	.059	.038	.030
30	.742	.552	.412	.308	.231	.174	.131	.099	.075	.057	.033	.020	.015

Period	16%	18%	20%	24%	28%	32%	36%	40%	50%	60%	70%	80%	90%
1	.862	.847	.833	.806	.781	.758	.735	.714	.667	.625	.588	.556	.526
2	.743	.718	.694	.650	.610	.574	.541	.510	.444	.391	.346	.309	.277
3	.641	.609	.579	.524	.477	.435	.398	.364	.296	.244	.204	.171	.146
4	.552	.516	.482	.423	.373	.329	.292	.260	.198	.153	.120	.095	.077
5	.476	.437	.402	.341	.291	.250	.215	.186	.132	.095	.070	.053	.040
6	.410	.370	.335	.275	.227	.189	.158	.133	.088	.060	.041	.029	.021
7	.354	.314	.279	.222	.178	.143	.116	.095	.059	.037	.024	.016	.011
8	.305	.266	.233	.179	.139	.108	.085	.068	.039	.023	.014	.009	.006
9	.263	.226	.194	.144	.108	.082	.063	.048	.026	.015	.008	.005	.003
10	.227	.191	.162	.116	.085	.062	.046	.035	.017	.009	.005	.003	.002
11	.195	.162	.135	.094	.066	.047	.034	.025	.012	.006	.003	.002	.001
12	.168	.137	.112	.076	.052	.036	.025	.018	.008	.004	.002	.001	.001
13	.145	.116	.093	.061	.040	.027	.018	.013	.005	.002	.001	.001	.000
14	.125	.099	.078	.049	.032	.021	.014	.009	.003	.001	.001	.000	.000
15	.108	.084	.065	.040	.025	.016	.010	.006	.002	.001	.000	.000	.000
16	.093	.071	.054	.032	.019	.012	.007	.005	.002	.001	.000	.000	
17	.080	.060	.045	.026	.015	.009	.005	.003	.001	.000	.000		
18	.069	.051	.038	.021	.012	.007	.004	.002	.001	.000	.000		
19	.060	.043	.031	.017	.009	.005	.003	.002	.000	.000			
20	.051	.037	.026	.014	.007	.004	.002	.001	.000	.000			
25	.024	.016	.010	.005	.002	.001	.000	.000					
30	.012	.007	.004	.002	.001	.000	.000						

TABLE A-3 Sum of an Annuity of $1 for N Periods: $CVIF_a = \sum_{t=0}^{n-1} (1 + k)^t = \dfrac{(1 + k)^n = 1}{k}$

Period	1%	2%	3%	4%	5%	6%
1	1.000	1.000	1.000	1.000	1.000	1.000
2	2.010	2.020	2.030	2.040	2.050	2.060
3	3.030	3.060	3.091	3.122	3.152	3.184
4	4.060	4.122	4.184	4.246	4.310	4.375
5	5.101	5.204	5.309	5.416	5.526	5.637
6	6.152	6.308	6.468	6.633	6.802	6.975
7	7.214	7.434	7.662	7.898	8.142	8.394
8	8.286	8.583	8.892	9.214	9.549	9.897
9	9.369	9.755	10.159	10.583	11.027	11.491
10	10.462	10.950	11.464	12.006	12.578	13.181
11	11.567	12.169	12.808	13.486	14.207	14.972
12	12.683	13.412	14.192	15.026	15.917	16.870
13	13.809	14.680	15.618	16.627	17.713	18.882
14	14.947	15.974	17.086	18.292	19.599	21.051
15	16.097	17.293	18.599	20.024	21.579	23.276
16	17.258	18.639	20.157	21.825	23.657	25.673
17	18.430	20.012	21.762	23.698	25.840	28.213
18	19.615	21.412	23.414	25.645	28.132	30.906
19	20.811	22.841	25.117	27.671	30.539	33.760
20	22.019	24.297	26.870	29.778	33.066	36.786
25	28.243	32.030	36.459	41.646	47.727	54.865
30	34.785	40.568	47.575	56.805	66.439	79.058

Period	7%	8%	9%	10%	12%	14%
1	1.000	1.000	1.000	1.000	1.000	1.000
2	2.070	2.080	2.090	2.100	2.120	2.140
3	3.215	3.246	3.278	3.310	3.374	3.440
4	4.440	4.506	4.573	4.641	4.770	4.921
5	5.751	5.867	5.985	6.105	6.353	6.610
6	7.153	7.336	7.523	7.716	8.115	8.536
7	8.654	8.923	9.200	9.487	10.089	10.730
8	10.260	10.637	11.028	11.436	12.300	13.233
9	11.978	12.488	13.021	13.579	14.776	16.085
10	13.816	14.487	15.193	15.937	17.549	19.337
11	15.784	16.645	17.560	18.531	20.655	23.044
12	17.888	18.977	20.141	21.384	24.133	27.271
13	20.141	21.495	22.953	24.523	28.029	32.089
14	22.550	24.215	26.019	27.975	32.393	37.581
15	25.129	27.152	29.361	31.772	37.280	43.842
16	27.888	30.324	33.003	35.950	42.753	50.980
17	30.840	33.750	36.974	40.545	48.884	59.118
18	33.999	37.450	41.301	45.599	55.750	68.394
19	37.379	41.446	46.018	51.159	63.440	78.969
20	40.995	45.762	51.160	57.275	72.052	91.025
25	63.249	73.106	84.701	98.347	133.334	181.871
30	94.461	113.283	136.308	164.494	241.333	356.787

TABLE A–3 *(continued)*

Period	16%	18%	20%	24%	28%	32%
1	1.000	1.000	1.000	1.000	1.000	1.000
2	2.160	2.180	2.200	2.240	2.280	2.320
3	3.506	3.572	3.640	3.778	3.918	4.062
4	5.066	5.215	5.368	5.684	6.016	6.362
5	6.877	7.154	7.442	8.048	8.700	9.398
6	8.977	9.442	9.930	10.980	12.136	13.406
7	11.414	12.142	12.916	14.615	16.534	18.696
8	14.240	15.327	16.499	19.123	22.163	25.678
9	17.518	19.086	20.799	24.712	29.369	34.895
10	21.321	23.521	25.959	31.643	38.592	47.062
11	25.733	28.755	32.150	40.238	50.399	63.122
12	30.850	34.931	39.580	50.985	65.510	84.320
13	36.786	42.219	48.497	64.110	84.853	112.303
14	43.672	50.818	59.196	80.496	109.612	149.240
15	51.660	60.965	72.035	100.815	141.303	197.997
16	60.925	72.939	87.442	126.011	181.87	262.36
17	71.673	87.068	105.931	157.253	233.79	347.31
18	84.141	103.740	128.117	195.994	300.25	459.45
19	98.603	123.414	154.740	244.033	385.32	607.47
20	115.380	146.628	186.688	303.601	494.21	802.86
25	249.214	342.603	471.981	898.092	1706.8	3226.8
30	530.312	790.948	1181.882	2640.916	5873.2	12941.0

Period	36%	40%	50%	60%	70%	80%
1	1.000	1.000	1.000	1.000	1.000	1.000
2	2.360	2.400	2.500	2.600	2.700	2.800
3	4.210	4.360	4.750	5.160	5.590	6.040
4	6.725	7.104	8.125	9.256	10.503	11.872
5	10.146	10.846	13.188	15.810	18.855	22.370
6	14.799	16.324	20.781	26.295	33.054	41.265
7	21.126	23.853	32.172	43.073	57.191	75.278
8	29.732	34.395	49.258	69.916	98.225	136.500
9	41.435	49.153	74.887	112.866	167.983	246.699
10	57.352	69.814	113.330	181.585	286.570	445.058
11	78.998	98.739	170.995	291.536	488.170	802.105
12	108.437	139.235	257.493	467.458	830.888	1444.788
13	148.475	195.929	387.239	748.933	1413.510	2601.619
14	202.926	275.300	581.859	1199.293	2403.968	4683.914
15	276.979	386.420	873.788	1919.869	4087.745	8432.045
16	377.69	541.99	1311.7	3072.8	6950.2	15179.0
17	514.66	759.78	1968.5	4917.5	11816.0	27323.0
18	700.94	1064.7	2953.8	7868.9	20089.0	49182.0
19	954.28	1491.6	4431.7	12591.0	34152.0	88528.0
20	1298.8	2089.2	6648.5	20147.0	58059.0	159350.0
25	6053.0	11247.0	50500.0	211270.0	824370.0	3011100.0
30	28172.0	60501.0	383500.0	2215400.0	11705000.0	56896000.0

TABLE A–4 Present Value of an Annuity of $1: $PVIF_a = \sum_{t=1}^{n} \dfrac{1}{(1+k)^t} = \dfrac{1 - \dfrac{1}{(1+k)^n}}{k}$

Period	1%	2%	3%	4%	5%	6%	7%	8%	9%	10%
1	0.990	0.980	0.971	0.962	0.952	0.943	0.935	0.926	0.917	0.909
2	1.970	1.942	1.913	1.886	1.859	1.833	1.808	1.783	1.759	1.736
3	2.941	2.884	2.829	2.775	2.723	2.673	2.624	2.577	2.531	2.487
4	3.902	3.808	3.717	3.630	3.546	3.465	3.387	3.312	3.240	3.170
5	4.853	4.713	4.580	4.452	4.329	4.212	4.100	3.993	3.890	3.791
6	5.795	5.601	5.417	5.242	5.076	4.917	4.766	4.623	4.486	4.355
7	6.728	6.472	6.230	6.002	5.786	5.582	5.389	5.206	5.033	4.868
8	7.652	7.325	7.020	6.733	6.463	6.210	5.971	5.747	5.535	5.335
9	8.566	8.162	7.786	7.435	7.108	6.802	6.515	6.247	5.995	5.759
10	9.471	8.983	8.530	8.111	7.722	7.360	7.024	6.710	6.418	6.145
11	10.368	9.787	9.253	8.760	8.306	7.887	7.499	7.139	6.805	6.495
12	11.255	10.575	9.954	9.385	8.863	8.384	7.943	7.536	7.161	6.814
13	12.134	11.348	10.635	9.986	9.394	8.853	8.358	7.904	7.487	7.103
14	13.004	12.106	11.296	10.563	9.899	9.295	8.745	8.244	7.786	7.367
15	13.865	12.849	11.938	11.118	10.380	9.712	9.108	8.559	8.060	7.606
16	14.718	13.578	12.561	11.652	10.838	10.106	9.447	8.851	8.312	7.824
17	15.562	14.292	13.166	12.166	11.274	10.477	9.763	9.122	8.544	8.022
18	16.398	14.992	13.754	12.659	11.690	10.828	10.059	9.372	8.756	8.201
19	17.226	15.678	14.324	13.134	12.085	11.158	10.336	9.604	8.950	8.365
20	18.046	16.351	14.877	13.590	12.462	11.470	10.594	9.818	9.128	8.514
25	22.023	19.523	17.413	15.622	14.094	12.783	11.654	10.675	9.823	9.077
30	25.808	22.397	19.600	17.292	15.373	13.765	12.409	11.258	10.274	9.427

Period	12%	14%	16%	18%	20%	24%	28%	32%	36%
1	0.893	0.877	0.862	0.847	0.833	0.806	0.781	0.758	0.735
2	1.690	1.647	1.605	1.566	1.528	1.457	1.392	1.332	1.276
3	2.402	2.322	2.246	2.174	2.106	1.981	1.868	1.766	1.674
4	3.037	2.914	2.798	2.690	2.589	2.404	2.241	2.096	1.966
5	3.605	3.433	3.274	3.127	2.991	2.745	2.532	2.345	2.181
6	4.111	3.889	3.685	3.498	3.326	3.020	2.759	2.534	2.339
7	4.564	4.288	4.039	3.812	3.605	3.242	2.937	2.678	2.455
8	4.968	4.639	4.344	4.078	3.837	3.421	3.076	2.786	2.540
9	5.328	4.946	4.607	4.303	4.031	3.566	3.184	2.868	2.603
10	5.650	5.216	4.833	4.494	4.193	3.682	3.269	2.930	2.650
11	5.938	5.453	5.029	4.656	4.327	3.776	3.335	2.978	2.683
12	6.194	5.660	5.197	4.793	4.439	3.851	3.387	3.013	2.708
13	6.424	5.842	5.342	4.910	4.533	3.912	3.427	3.040	2.727
14	6.628	6.002	5.468	5.008	4.611	3.962	3.459	3.061	2.740
15	6.811	6.142	5.575	5.092	4.675	4.001	3.483	3.076	2.750
16	6.974	6.265	5.669	5.162	4.730	4.033	3.503	3.088	2.758
17	7.120	5.373	5.749	4.222	4.775	4.059	3.518	3.097	2.763
18	7.250	6.467	5.818	5.273	4.812	4.080	3.529	3.104	2.767
19	7.366	6.550	5.877	5.316	4.844	4.097	3.539	3.109	2.770
20	7.469	6.623	5.929	5.353	4.870	4.110	3.546	3.113	2.772
25	7.843	6.873	6.097	5.467	4.948	4.147	3.564	3.122	2.776
30	8.055	7.003	6.177	5.517	4.979	4.160	3.569	3.124	2.778

Appendix B
Answers to Selected
End-of-Chapter
Problems

We present here some partial answers to selected end-of-chapter problems. For the most part, the answers given are only the final answers (or answers at intermediate steps) to the more complex problems. Within limits, these answers will be useful to see if the student is "on the right track" toward solving the problem. The primary limitation, which must be kept in mind, is that some questions may have more than one solution, depending upon which of several equally plausible assumptions are made in working the problem. Also, many of the problems involve some verbal discussion as well as numerical calculations. We have not presented any of this verbal material here.

2-1. (a) $13,044; (b) 48%.
2-2. $2,715.
2-3. 1977 refund: $46,500.
2-5. (a) $255,300
2-6. years 1–6 DDB, 7–10 SL.
2-7. 1974–1977: 0, 0, $4,490, $17,502.

3-1. (a) TIE = 5.8, ACP = 37, ROE = 4.8%.
3-2. $100,000.

4-1. (a) ($40,000); (b) 6,000 units; (c) 8,000 units: 4.0; (d) 4,800 units.
4-2. (a) FC = $50,000, VC = $600,000; (c) 1.5.
4-4. BEP = 500 and 1,000 units.
4-5. (a) (ii) BEP = 64,286 units; (b) (iii) OL = 9.71; (c) (i) $382,500; (f) $631.3, $620.6, $570.4.

5-1. (a) Total assets, $2,800,000, 5-year addition to R/E, $360,000.
5-2. (a) Total assets, $1,440,000.

5-3. (a) Total assets, $8,760,000; (b) $229,200; (c) Total assets, $9,198,000; (d) (2) (i) $304,800.

6-1. (a) $85,250, $233,000, ($151,750), ($26,500), $91,250, $160,250.

7-2. (a) 12.79%, 12.00%, 10.64%.
7-3. (a) $65,600, $66,800, $66,200; (b) Worst: ($28,000), ($6,400), ($17,200), Best: $142,800, $136,800, $139,800.

8-1. 20.99%
8-2. (b) $196,000.
8-3. $8,125, ($18,750).
8-4. (c) $750,000, ($3,250,000)
8-5. (a) $9,000; (b) $4,163; (c) $458; (d) $4,379.
8-6. (a) 4,000 units; (b) 75; (c) 22,000 units.

9-1. (b) 14.69%; (e) 12.12%.
9-2. (c) 11.8%.
9-4. $59,728, $49,375.
9-5. (a) $125,000, $112,360.
9-6. $2,583.34, $4,000, $2,000.

10-2. Nine years.
10-3. (c) $1,086.14.
10-4. $5,990.13
10-5. $29,464.
10-6. (c) $1,044.58.
10-7. (b) $24,927.25.
10-10. 6%.
10-12. $1,150,000, $1,322,000, $1,521,000, $1,749,000, $2,011,000.
10-14. (a) $1.15, $1.32, $1.52, $1.75, $2.01; (b) $5.00; (c) $10.00, (d) $15.00.
10-15. (a) $140,350.

11-1. Red: NPV = $2,027.50, IRR = 20%.
11-2. HQ: NPV = $5,147, IRR = 20%.
11-3. (a) $720,000; (b) $160,000; (d) NPV = ($51,340).
11-4. (a) NPV = $36,407.50; (b) NPV = $44,815.
11-5. (a) NPV = ($3,226.45); (b) NPV = ($1,588.65); (c) NPV = $411.35; (d) NPV = $3,519.60.
11-6. Project S
(a) (i) $8,000, (ii) $7,332, (iii) $6,944, (iv) $6,112; (b) 21.5%.

12-1. (a) E(CF) = $19,500, E(NPV) = $10,175, E(IRR) = 14%.
12-3. 5 years: NPV = ($207.60), 8 years: NPV = $8,546, 10 years: NPV = $13,406.
12-4. (b) E(CF) = $16,200, E(NPV) = ($8,470); (e) 41%.

13-1. 11.5%.
13-2. 13.6%.
13-3. (1) 5.02%; (2) 12.0%, 10.7%.

14-1. 224,517 shares.
14-2. $5.00.
14-4. (a) $3.00.
14-5. (a) $25 $50 $80

       (iii) $3.10 $4.65 $5.72

       (v) $1.74 $2.60 $3.20

15-1. NPV = $11,782.
15-3. (c) $23,648, $23,662.

16-1. PV of owning = $4,290, PV of leasing = $4,975.

17-1. (a) $1,150.60; (b) $53.52.
17-2. (b) $2.00, (d) $10.00.
17-3. (b) subscription price = $51.00.
17-5. (a) $.90; (b) $14.40; (d) Total assets = $500,000; (f) Total assets = $687,500.
17-6. (b) 45%, 47%, 47%; (c) $.45, $.47, $.61; (d) 22%, 22%, 50%.

18-1. (a) $1,500; (d) (ii) $939.
18-3. $1,084.
18-4. (a) (i) 12%, (ii) 4%.
18-5. $66.30.
18-6. (b) $800.
18-7. (a) $3.00; (b) (ii) $6.67; (d) (ii) 2.22.
18-9. (c) (i) (a) $42.00, (b) $80.08; (d) $41.96, $150.
18-10. (a) (i) 7%, (iii) 10%; (b) (i) (1) 9%, (ii) (1) 5%; (d) (i) 7%; (e) (ii) 14%.
18-11. (a) Net assets = $22,000.
18-13. (a) PV of price at end of year 7 = $14.88.

19-1. (a) EPS = $.50, $.58, $.57, $.68, $.66, $.73, $.66, $.78.
19-2. (a)

	Stock	Debt	Both
EPS	$1.00, $2.00, $3.00	$.75, $2.00, $3.25	$.89, $2.00, $3.11
(b)	$2.30	$2.38	$2.33
(c)	1.0	1.25	1.11

19-3. (a) Debt EPS: $1.10, $1.85, $2.60, $3.35, $4.10; Stock: $1.04, $1.64, $2.24, $2.84, $3.44; (b) debt: E(EPS) = $2.60, σ = $.86; (c) debt: E(Price) = $23.40, σ = $7.70.
19-4. (a) (i) 1.5, (ii) 1.45, (iii) 2.18.
19-5. (a) Bond: EPS = ($.47), $.53, $1.53, $2.53, $3.53, $4.53, $5.53; (f) Bond: E(EPS) = $2.53, E(Price) = $20.24.

20-1. (b) 40%.
20-2. (b) $15,000,000; (c) $12,000,000; (e) $6,000,000; (f) MCC below = 8.5%, MCC above = 8.7%.
20-3. (a) $8,000,000 $16,000,000; (b) MCC_1 = 9.47%, MCC_2 = 9.76%, MCC_3 = 10.33%.
20-4. (a) (i) 4.8%, (ii) 10%, (iii) 12%; (b) 10.10%; (d) (i) 12.44%, (ii) 10.41%.

21-1. $2.80.

21-4. (a) with dividend: total financing = $15,270,000, MCC_1 = 6.53%, MCC_2 = 6.82%.

21-5. (b) $12; (c) $352.

23-1. (a) Total assets = $4,500; (b) Total assets = $5,250.

23-2. (a) 6.4%; (c) (i) 9.73%, (ii) 8.73%.

23-3. (1) 20%; (2) 22%; (4) 13%.

23-4. (a) Apex: $45,000, Allied: $45.67; (b) (2) growth with Apex = 6.3%, growth with Allied = 4.2%.

24-1. (a) Total assets = $327,000,000; (c) $1,320,000.

24-3. (b) Percent of claims = 57.4%.

25-1. (1) h; (2) a; (3) d; (4) f; (5) b; (5) b; (6) e; (7) i; (8) c; (9) g.

Glossary

Accelerated Depreciation Depreciation methods that write off the cost of an asset at a faster rate than the write-off under the straight line method. The three principal methods of accelerated depreciation are: (1) sum of years' digits, (2) double declining balance, and (3) units of production.

Accruals Continually recurring short-term liabilities. Examples are accrued wages, accrued taxes, and accrued interest.

Aging Schedule A report showing how long accounts receivable have been outstanding. It gives the percent of receivables not past due and the percent past due by, for example, one month, two months, or other periods.

Amortize To liquidate on an installment basis; an amortized loan is one in which the principal amount of the loan is repaid in installments during the life of the loan.

Annuity A series of payments of a fixed amount for a specified number of years.

Arbitrage The process of selling overvalued and buying undervalued assets so as to bring about an equilibrium where all assets are properly valued. One who engages in arbitrage is called an arbitrager.

Arrearage Overdue payment; frequently, omitted dividends on preferred stocks.

Assignment A relatively inexpensive way of liquidating a failing firm that does not involve going through the courts.

Balloon Payment When a debt is not fully amortized, the final payment is larger than the preceding payments and is called a "balloon" payment.

Bankruptcy A legal procedure for formally liquidating a business, carried out under the jurisdiction of courts of law.

Beta Coefficient Measures the extent to which the returns on a given stock move with "the stock market."

Bond A long-term debt instrument.

Book Value The accounting value of an asset. The book value of a share of common stock is equal to the net worth (common stock plus retained earnings) of the corporation divided by the number of shares of stock outstanding.

599

Break-even Analysis An analytical technique for studying the relation between fixed cost, variable cost, and profits. A break-even *chart* graphically depicts the nature of break-even analysis. The break-even *point* represents the volume of sales at which total costs equal total revenues (that is, profits equal zero).

Business Risk The basic risk inherent in a firm's operations. Business risk plus financial risk resulting from the use of debt equals total corporate risk.

Call (1) An option to buy (or "call") a share of stock at a specified price within a specified period. (2) The process of redeeming a bond or preferred stock issue before its normal maturity.

Call Premium The amount in excess of par value that a company must pay when it calls a security.

Call Price The price that must be paid when a security is called. The call price is equal to the par value plus the call premium.

Call Privilege A provision incorporated into a bond or a share of preferred stock that gives the issuer the right to redeem (call) the security at a specified price.

Capital Asset An asset with a life of more than one year that is not bought and sold in the ordinary course of business.

Capital Budgeting The process of planning expenditures on assets whose returns are expected to extend beyond one year.

Capital Gains Profits on the sale of capital assets held for six months or more.

Capital Losses Losses on the sale of capital assets.

Capital Market Line A graphical representation of the relationship between risk and the required rate of return.

Capital Rationing A situation where a constraint is placed on the total size of the capital investment during a particular period.

Capital Structure The permanent long-term financing of the firm represented by long-term debt, preferred stock, and net worth (net worth consists of capital, capital surplus, and retained earnings). Capital structure is distinguished from *financial structure,* which includes short-term debt plus all reserve accounts.

Capitalization Rate A discount rate used to find the present value of a series of future cash receipts; sometimes called *discount rate.*

Carry-back; Carry-forward For income tax purposes, losses that can be carried backward or forward to reduce federal income taxes.

Cash Budget A schedule showing cash flows (receipts, disbursements, and net cash) for a firm over a specified period.

Cash Cycle The length of time between the purchase of raw materials and the collection of accounts receivable generated in the sale of the final product.

Certainty Equivalents The amount of cash (or rate of return) that someone would require *with certainty* to make him indifferent between this certain sum (or *rate of return*) and a particular uncertain, risky sum (or rate of return).

Chattel Mortgage A mortgage on personal property (not real estate). A mortgage on equipment would be a chattel mortgage.

Coefficient of Variation Standard deviation divided by the mean.

Collateral Assets that are used to secure a loan.

Commercial Paper Unsecured, short-term promissory notes of large firms, usually issued in denominations of $1 million or more. The rate of interest on commercial paper is typically somewhat below the prime rate of interest.

Commitment Fee   The fee paid to a lender for a formal line of credit.

Compensating Balance   A required minimum checking account balance that a firm must maintain with a commercial bank. The required balance is generally equal to 15 to 20 percent of the amount of loans outstanding. Compensating balances can raise the effective rate of interest on bank loans.

Composite Cost of Capital   A weighted average of the component costs of debt, preferred stock, and common equity. Also called the "weighted average cost of capital," but it reflects the cost of each additional dollar raised, not the average cost of all capital the firm has raised throughout its history.

Composition   An informal method of reorganization that voluntarily reduces creditors' claims on the debtor firm.

Compound Interest   An interest rate that is applicable when interest in succeeding periods is earned not only on the initial principal but also on the accumulated interest of prior periods. Compound interest is contrasted to *simple interest,* in which returns are not earned on interest received.

Compounding   The arithmetic process of determining the final value of a payment or series of payments when compound interest is applied.

Conditional Sales Contract   A method of financing new equipment by paying it off in installments over a one-to-five-year period. The seller retains title to the equipment until payment has been completed.

Consolidated Tax Return   An income tax return that combines the income statement of several affiliated firms.

Continuous Compounding (Discounting)   As opposed to discrete compounding, interest is added continuously rather than at discrete points in time.

Conversion Price   The effective price paid for common stock when the stock is obtained by converting either convertible preferred stocks or convertible bonds. For example, if a $1,000 bond is convertible into twenty shares of stock, the conversion price is $50 (= $1,000/20).

Conversion Ratio or Conversion Rate   The number of shares of common stock that may be obtained by converting a convertible bond or share of convertible preferred stock.

Convertibles   Securities (generally bonds or preferred stocks) that are exchangeable at the option of the holder for common stock of the issuing firm.

Correlation Coefficient   Measures the degree of relationship between two variables.

Cost of Capital   The discount rate that should be used in the capital budgeting process.

Coupon Rate   The stated rate of interest on a bond.

Covenant   Detailed clauses contained in loan agreements. Covenants are designed to protect the lender and include such items as limits on total indebtedness, restrictions on dividends, minimum current ratio, and similar provisions.

Cumulative Dividends   A protective feature on preferred stock that requires all past preferred dividends to be paid before any common dividends are paid.

Cut-off Point   In the capital budgeting process, the minimum rate of return on acceptable investment opportunities.

Debenture   A long-term debt instrument that is not secured by a mortgage on specific property.

Debt Ratio   Total debt divided by total assets.

Decision Tree A device for setting forth graphically the pattern of relationship between decisions and chance events.

Default The failure to fulfill a contract. Generally, default refers to the failure to pay interest or principal on debt obligations.

Degree of Leverage The percentage increase in profits resulting from a given percentage increase in sales. The degree of leverage may be calculated for financial leverage, operating leverage, or both combined.

Devaluation The process of reducing the value of a country's currency stated in terms of other currencies; e.g., the British pound might be devalued from $2.30 for one pound to $2.00 for one pound.

Discount Rate The interest rate used in the discounting process; sometimes called *capitalization rate.*

Discounted Cash Flow Techniques Methods of ranking investment proposals. Included are (1) internal rate of return method, (2) net present value method, and (3) profitability index or benefit/cost ratio.

Discounting The process of finding the present value of a series of future cash flows. Discounting is the reverse of compounding.

Discounting of Accounts Receivable Short-term financing where accounts receivable are used to secure the loan. The lender does not *buy* the accounts receivable but simply uses them as collateral for the loan. Also called *pledging of accounts receivable.*

Dividend Yield The ratio of the current dividend to the current price of a share of stock.

Du Pont System A system of analysis designed to show the relationship between return on investment, asset turnover, and the profit margin.

EBIT Abbreviation for "earnings before interest and taxes."

Economical Ordering Quantity (EOQ) The optimum (least cost) quantity of merchandise which should be ordered.

EPS Abbreviation for "earnings per share."

Equity The net worth of a business, consisting of capital stock, capital (or paid-in) surplus, earned surplus (or retained earnings), and, occasionally, certain net worth reserves. *Common equity* is that part of the total net worth belonging to the common stockholders. *Total equity* would include preferred stockholders. The terms "common stock," "net worth," and "common equity" are frequently used interchangeably.

Excise Tax A tax on the manufacture, sale, or consumption of specified commodities.

Ex Dividend Date The date on which the right to the current dividend no longer accompanies a stock. (For listed stock, the ex dividend date is four working days prior to the date of record.)

Exercise Price The price that must be paid for a share of common stock when it is bought by exercising a warrant.

Expected Return The rate of return a firm expects to realize from an investment. The expected return is the mean value of the probability distribution of possible returns.

Ex Rights The date on which stock purchase rights are no longer transferred to the purchaser of the stock.

Extension An informal method of reorganization in which the creditors voluntarily postpone the date of required payment on past-due obligations.

External Funds Funds acquired through borrowing or by selling new common or preferred stock.

Factoring A method of financing accounts receivable under which a firm sells its accounts receivable (generally without recourse) to a financial institution (the "factor").

Field Warehousing A method of financing inventories in which a "warehouse" is established at the place of business of the borrowing firm.

Financial Lease A lease that does not provide for maintenance services, is not cancellable, and is fully amortized over the life of the lease.

Financial Leverage The ratio of total debt to total assets. There are other measures of financial leverage, especially ones that relate cash inflows to required cash outflows. In this book, the debt/total asset ratio is generally used to measure leverage.

Financial Risk That portion of total corporate risk, over and above basic business risk, that results from using debt.

Financial Structure The entire right-hand side of the balance sheet—the way in which a firm is financed.

Fixed Charges Costs that do not vary with the level of output, especially fixed financial costs such as interest, lease payments, and sinking fund payments.

Float The amount of funds tied up in checks that have been written but are still in process and have not yet been collected.

Floating Exchange Rates Exchange rates may be fixed by government policy ("pegged") or allowed to "float" up or down in accordance with supply and demand. When market forces are allowed to function, exchange rates are said to be floating.

Flotation Cost The cost of issuing new stocks or bonds.

Funded Debt Long-term debt.

Funding The process of replacing short-term debt with long-term securities (stocks or bonds).

Goodwill Intangible assets of a firm established by the excess of the price paid for the going concern over its book value.

Holding Company A corporation operated for the purpose of owning the common stock of other corporations.

Hurdle Rate In capital budgeting, the minimum acceptable rate of return on a project; if the expected rate of return is below the hurdle rate, the project is not accepted. The hurdle rate should be the marginal cost of capital.

Improper Accumulation Earnings retained by a business for the purpose of enabling stockholders to avoid personal income taxes.

Income Bond A bond that pays interest only if the current interest is earned.

Incremental Cash Flow Net cash flow attributable to an investment project.

Incremental Cost of Capital The average cost of the increment of capital raised during a given year.

Indenture A formal agreement between the issuer of a bond and the bondholders.

Insolvency The inability to meet maturing debt obligations.

Interest Factor (IF) Numbers found in compound interest and annuity tables.

Internal Financing Funds made available for capital budgeting and working capital expansion through the normal operations of the firm; internal financing is approximately equal to retained earnings plus depreciation.

Internal Rate of Return (IRR) The rate of return on an asset investment. The internal rate of return is calculated by finding the discount rate that equates the present value of future cash flows to the cost of the investment.

Intrinsic Value That value which, in the mind of the analyst, is justified by the facts. It is often used to distinguish between the "true value" of an asset (the intrinsic value) and the asset's current market price.

Investment Banker One who underwrites and distributes new investment securities; more broadly, one who helps business firms to obtain financing.

Investment Tax Credit Business firms can deduct as a credit against their income taxes a specified percentage of the dollar amount of new investments in each of certain categories of assets.

Legal List A list of securities in which mutual savings banks, pension funds, insurance companies, and other fiduciary institutions are permitted to invest.

Leverage Factor The ratio of debt to total assets.

Lien A lender's claim on assets that are pledged for a loan.

Line of Credit An arrangement whereby a financial institution (bank or insurance company) commits itself to lend up to a specified maximum amount of funds during a specified period. Sometimes the interest rate on the loan is specified; at other times, it is not. Sometimes a commitment fee is imposed for obtaining the line of credit.

Liquidity Refers to a firm's cash position and its ability to meet maturing obligations.

Listed Securities Securities traded on an organized security exchange.

Lock-box Plan A procedure used to speed up collections and to reduce float.

Margin—Profit on Sales The *profit margin* is the percentage of profit after tax to sales.

Margin—Securities Business The buying of stocks or bonds on credit, known as *buying on margin.*

Marginal Cost The cost of an additional unit. The marginal cost of capital is the cost of an additional dollar of new funds.

Marginal Efficiency of Capital A schedule showing the internal rate of return on investment opportunities.

Marginal Revenue The additional gross revenue produced by selling one additional unit of output.

Merger Any combination that forms one company from two or more previously existing companies.

Money Market Financial markets in which funds are borrowed or lent for short periods. (The money market is distinguished from the capital market, which is the market for long-term funds.)

Mortgage A pledge of designated property as security for a loan.

Net Present Value (NPV) Method   A method of ranking investment proposals. The NPV is equal to the present value of future returns, discounted at the marginal cost of capital, minus the present value of the cost of the investment.

Net Worth   The capital and surplus of a firm—capital stock, capital surplus (paid-in capital), earned surplus (retained earnings), and, occasionally, certain reserves. For some purposes, preferred stock is included; generally, net worth refers only to the common stockholders' position.

Nominal Interest Rate   The contracted or stated interest rate, undeflated for price level changes.

Normal Probability Distribution   A symmetrical, bell-shaped probability function.

Objective Probability Distributions   Probability distributions determined by statistical procedures.

Operating Leverage   The extent to which fixed costs are used in a firm's operation. Break-even analysis is used to measure the extent to which operating leverage is employed.

Opportunity Cost   The rate of return on the best *alternative* investment that is available. It is the highest return that will *not* be earned if the funds are invested in a particular project. For example, the opportunity cost of *not* investing in bond A yielding 8 percent might be 7.99 percent, which could be earned on bond B.

Ordinary Income   Income from the normal operations of a firm. Operating income specifically excludes income from the sale of capital assets.

Organized Security Exchanges   Formal organizations having tangible, physical locations. Organized exchanges conduct an auction market in designated ("listed") investment securities. For example, the New York Stock Exchange is an organized exchange.

Overdraft System   A system where a depositor may write checks in excess of his balance, with his bank automatically extending a loan to cover the shortage.

Over-the-counter Market   All facilities that provide for trading in unlisted securities, that is, those not listed on organized exchanges. The over-the-counter market is typically a "telephone market," as most business is conducted over the telephone.

Par Value   The nominal or face value of a stock or bond.

Payback Period   The length of time required for the net revenues of an investment to return the cost of the investment.

Payout Ratio   The percentage of earnings paid out in the form of dividends.

Pegging   A market stabilization action taken by the manager of an underwriting group during the offering of new securities. He does this by continually placing orders to buy at a specified price in the market.

Perpetuity   A stream of equal future payments expected to continue forever.

Pledging of Accounts Receivable   Short-term borrowing from financial institutions where the loan is secured by accounts receivable. The lender may physically take the accounts receivable but typically has recourse to the borrower; also called *discounting of accounts receivable.*

Pooling of Interest   An accounting method for combining the financial statements of two firms that merge. Under the pooling-of-interest procedure, the assets of the merged firms are simply added to form the balance sheet of the surviving corporation. This method is different from the "purchase" method, where goodwill is put on the balance sheet to reflect a premium (or discount) paid in excess of book value.

Portfolio Effect   The extent to which the variation in returns on a combination of assets (a "portfolio") is less than the sum of the variations of the individual assets.

Portfolio Theory   Deals with the selection of optimal portfolios, i.e., portfolios that provide the highest possible return for any specified degree of risk.

Preemptive Right   A provision contained in the corporate charter and bylaws that gives holders of common stock the right to purchase on a pro rata basis new issues of common stock (or securities convertible into common stock).

Present Value (PV)   The value today of a future payment, or stream of payments, discounted at the appropriate discount rate.

Price/Earnings Ratio *(P/E)*   The ratio of price to earnings. Faster growing or less risky firms typically have higher *P/E* ratios than either slower growing or riskier firms.

Prime Rate   The lowest rate of interest commercial banks charge very large, strong corporations.

Pro Forma   A projection. A *pro forma* financial statement is one that shows how the actual statement will look if certain specified assumptions are realized. *Pro forma* statements may be either future or past projections. An example of a backward *pro forma* statement occurs when two firms are planning to merge and show what their consolidated financial statements would have looked like if they had been merged in preceding years.

Profit Center   A unit of a large, decentralized firm that has its own investments and for which a rate of return on investment can be calculated.

Profit Margin   The ratio of profits after taxes to sales.

Profitability Index (PI)   The present value of future returns divided by the present value of the investment outlay.

Progressive Tax   A tax that requires a higher percentage payment on higher incomes. The personal income tax in the United States, which is at a rate of 14 percent on the lowest increments of income to 70 percent on the highest increments, is progressive.

Prospectus   A document issued for the purpose of describing a new security issue. The Securities and Exchange Commission (SEC) examines prospectuses to insure that statements contained therein are not "false and misleading."

Proxy   A document giving one person the authority or power to act for another. Typically, the authority in question is the power to vote shares of common stock.

Put   An option to sell a specific security at a specified price within a designated period.

Rate of Return   The internal rate of return on an investment.

Recourse Arrangement   A term used in connection with accounts receivable financing. If a firm sells its accounts receivable to a financial institution under a recourse agreement, then, if the account receivable cannot be collected, the selling firm must repurchase the account from the financial institution.

Rediscount Rate   The rate of interest at which a bank may borrow from a Federal Reserve Bank.

Refunding   Sale of new debt securities to replace an old debt issue.

Regression Analysis   A statistical procedure for predicting the value of one variable (dependent variable) on the basis of knowledge about one or more other variables (independent variables).

Reinvestment Rate   The rate of return at which cash flows from an investment are reinvested. The reinvestment rate may or may not be constant from year to year.

Reorganization   When a financially troubled firm goes through reorganization, its assets are restated to reflect their current market value, and its financial structure is restated to reflect any changes on the asset side of the statement. Under a reorganization the firm continues in existence; this is contrasted to bankruptcy, where the firm is liquidated and ceases to exist.

Required Rate of Return   The rate of return that stockholders expect to receive on common stock investments.

Residual Value   The value of leased property at the end of the lease term.

Retained Earnings   That portion of earnings not paid out in dividends. The figure that appears on the balance sheet is the sum of the retained earnings for each year throughout the company's history.

Right   A short-term option to buy a specified number of shares of a new issue of securities at a designated "subscription" price.

Rights Offering   A securities flotation offered to existing stockholders.

Risk   The probability that actual future returns will be below expected returns. Measured by standard deviation or coefficient of variation of expected returns.

Risk-adjusted Discount Rates   The discount rate applicable for a particular risky (uncertain) stream of income: the riskless rate of interest plus a risk premium appropriate to the level of risk attached to the particular income stream.

Risk Premium   The difference between the required rate of return on a particular risky asset and the rate of return on a riskless asset with the same expected life.

Risk-Return Tradeoff Function   (See *Capital Market Line.*)

Sale and Leaseback   An operation whereby a firm sells land, buildings, or equipment to a financial institution and simultaneously executes an agreement to lease the property back for a specified period under specific terms.

Salvage Value   The value of a capital asset at the end of a specified period. It is the current market price of an asset being considered for replacement in a capital budgeting problem.

Securities, Junior   Securities that have lower priority in claims on assets and income than other securities *(senior securities)*. For example, preferred stock is junior to debentures, but debentures are junior to mortgage bonds. Common stock is the most junior of all corporate securities.

Securities, Senior   Securities having claims on income and assets that rank higher than certain other securities *(junior securities)*. For example, mortgage bonds are senior to debentures, but debentures are senior to common stock.

Selling Group   A group of stock brokerage firms formed for the purpose of distributing a new issue of securities; part of the investment banking process.

Sensitivity Analysis   Simulation analysis in which key variables are changed and the resulting change in the rate of return is observed. Typically, the rate of return will be more sensitive to changes in some variables than it will in others.

Service Lease   A lease under which the lessor maintains and services the asset.

Short Selling   Selling a security that is not owned by the seller at the time of the sale. The seller borrows the security from a brokerage firm and must at some point repay the brokerage firm by buying the security on the open market.

Simulation   A technique whereby probable future events are simulated on a computer. Estimated rates of return and risk indexes can be generated.

Sinking Fund   A required annual payment designed to amortize a bond or a preferred stock issue. The sinking fund may be held in the form of cash or marketable securities, but more generally the money put into the sinking fund is used to retire each year some of the securities in question.

Small Business Administration (SBA)   A government agency organized to aid small firms with their financing and other problems.

Standard Deviation   A statistical term that measures the variability of a set of observations from the mean of the distribution.

Stock Dividend   A dividend paid in additional shares of stock rather than in cash. It involves a transfer from retained earnings to the capital stock account; therefore, stock dividends are limited by the amount of retained earnings.

Stock Split   An accounting action to increase the number of shares outstanding; for example, in a 3-for-1 split, shares outstanding would be tripled and each stockholder would receive three new shares for each one formerly held. Stock splits involve no transfer from surplus to the capital account.

Subjective Probability Distributions   Probability distributions determined through subjective procedures without the use of statistics.

Subordinated Debenture   A bond having a claim on assets only after the senior debt has been paid off in the event of liquidation.

Subscription Price   The price at which a security may be purchased in a rights offering.

Surtax   A tax levied in addition to the normal tax. For example, the normal corporate tax rate is 22 percent, but a surtax of 26 percent is added to the normal tax on all corporate income exceeding $25,000.

Synergy   A situation where "the whole is greater than the sum of its parts"; in a synergistic merger, the postmerger earnings exceed the sum of the separate companies' premerger earnings.

Systematic Risk   That part of a security's risk which cannot be eliminated by diversification.

Tangible Assets   Physical assets as opposed to intangible assets such as goodwill and the stated value of patents.

Tender Offers   A situation wherein one firm offers to buy the stock of another, going directly to the stockholders, frequently over the opposition of the management of the firm whose stock is being sought.

Term Loan   A loan generally obtained from a bank or an insurance company with a maturity greater than one year. Term loans are generally amortized.

Trade Credit   Interfirm debt arising through credit sales and recorded as an account receivable by the seller and as an account payable by the buyer.

Treasury Stock Common stock that has been repurchased by the issuing firm.

Trust Receipt An instrument acknowledging that the borrower holds certain goods in trust for the lender. Trust receipt financing is used in connection with the financing of inventories for automobile dealers, construction equipment dealers, appliance dealers, and other dealers in expensive durable goods.

Trustee The representative of bondholders who acts in their interest and facilitates communication between them and the issuer. Typically these duties are handled by a department of a commercial bank.

Underwriting (1) The entire process of issuing new corporate securities. (2) The insurance function of bearing the risk of adverse price fluctuations during the period in which a new issue of stock or bonds is being distributed.

Underwriting Syndicate A syndicate of investment firms formed to spread the risk associated with the purchase and distribution of a new issue of securities. The larger the issue, the more firms typically are involved in the syndicate.

Unlisted Securities Securities that are traded in the over-the-counter market.

Unsystematic Risk That part of a security's risk associated with random events; unsystematic risk can be eliminated by proper diversification.

Utility Theory A body of theory dealing with the relationships among money income, utility (or "happiness"), and the willingness to accept risks.

Warrant A long-term option to buy a stated number of shares of common stock at a specified price. The specified price is generally called the "exercise price."

Weighted Cost of Capital A weighted average of the component costs of debt, preferred stock, and common equity. Also called the "composite cost of capital."

Working Capital Refers to a firm's investment in short-term assets—cash, short-term securities, accounts receivable, and inventories. *Gross working capital* is defined as a firm's total current assets. *Net working capital* is defined as current assets minus current liabilities. If the term "working capital" is used without further qualification, it generally refers to gross working capital.

Yield The rate of return on an investment; the internal rate of return.

Index